The Managerial Cybernetics
of Organization

THE HEART
OF ENTERPRISE

Stafford Beer

Companion volume to
BRAIN OF THE FIRM

JOHN WILEY & SONS
Chichester · New York · Brisbane · Toronto

Copyright © 1979 by John Wiley & Sons Ltd.

British Library Cataloging in Publication Data:

Main entry under title:

Beer, Stafford
  The heart of enterprise — (The managerial
cybernetics of organization; 2).
  1. Cybernetics 2. Management
  I. Title II. Series
  658.4'03   HD38   79-40532

  ISBN 0 471 27599 9

Photoset by Photo-Graphics of Yarcombe, Honiton,
Devon.
Printed in Great Britain by
The Pitman Press, Bath

THE HEART
OF ENTERPRISE

TO SALLIE

Many waters cannot quench love.

The Song of Solomon

CONTENTS

PART THREE: VENTURES IN VIABILITY

PART FOUR: THE LONG AND THE SHORT OF IT
Notes on Implementation

APPENDICES

Preface

In 1972 *Brain of the Firm* was published. It proposed a neurocybernetic model of any enterprise, conceived of as a viable system. It suggested that the human nervous system stipulates the rules whereby an organization is survival-worthy: is regulated, learns, adapts, evolves. Certainly there are other control systems in the body, such as the endocrine system; but these can be regarded as facilitators of effects which are dominated by the brain.

Some people have referred to this model as an analogy, and have therefore been led to question whether that analogy fittingly applies to a firm or to any other type of organization. If the model *were* an analogy, I should myself doubt its perfectly general relevance; but as the book itself argued (pages 110 to 112) a model is *not* an analogy. Once we have understood how the brain obtains reliable decisions from its network of unreliable components, for example, we have grasped principles of redundancy that can be expressed mathematically, and which hold for *all* informational networks. The argument is expanded in the second edition of *Brain*. Meanwhile, anyone puzzled by this contention may wish to read Chapter 6, 'About Models', in my book *Decision and Control* (John Wiley, 1966).

The issue is raised here because it explains the genesis of the present book. The neurocybernetic model took over twenty years to develop. During that time, but even more intensively since *Brain* was published, it has been used in every kind of organization in many different countries; it gained my total confidence. Now if it is not an analogy, then regardless of where the cybernetic insights were obtained (and in this case from neurophysiology) it ought to be possible to argue out the nature of a viable system, and to create that model, from first principles. That is exactly what this book does. There is almost no overlap with *Brain of the Firm* — except that, in the end, the model of the viable system is the same. In the place of the neurocybernetic insights that *Brain* put forth, a whole set of managerial principles emerges.

Then this is why the two books are described as 'companion volumes'. Each stands on its own, but they are mutually supportive. The second edition of *Brain* pays special attention to that role; and I record a great debt of gratitude to my publisher, James Cameron of John Wiley, for making both books available in this sense.

I now come to the meaning of this present title. These cybernetics relate not only to firms, but to every kind of organization; I have chosen the word *enterprise* to refer to them all. The choice of the word *heart* is deliberately ambiguous. The heart of enterprise is its effective organization as a viable system. But management that is based on however profoundly scientific principles, and lacks 'heart', in the sense of human concern, will not succeed.

In prefaces to all my books, I have remarked that the world is in a terrible mess, and that managerial cybernetics has something important to contribute to the amelioration of that mess. The mess gets worse: the capacities of managerial cybernetics improve; they are increasingly used, but certainly not on any adequate scale. Therefore this work constitutes my latest challenge to managers, and my best help to them.

It operates at several levels. In my last book, *Platform for Change,* those levels were marked out by the use of differently coloured pages. The device was costly, and technically difficult for the printers. Then please be alert to my new devices, which I hope will be clear by the end. In the course of their development, a number of characters appear — nominated by their first (so-called Christian) names. The choice of these names was by no means coincidental; but I would remind my friends that their names are not unique to them. There are many Bills and Dicks and Pauls and Davids around ...

Well, from my standpoint at least, we are talking here about the future of the world. It is a complex subject. But: 'out of the mouths of babes and sucklings ...' I have learned to be cautious of six-year-old children in particular, because their sensibility has not yet been 'educated' out of them. When my youngest daughter, Polly Persephone, at the age of six, asked this neurocybernetician to explain how the brain works, I knew that I was going to learn something. I did my best for her. Then came my lesson:

> 'Did you know that hedgehogs have *very good* brains?
> Hedgehogs can curl up into a ball and roll away.
> Hedgehogs can escape.
> *We* can't escape.'

The question before us really is: was Polly Persephone right?

Messages of thanks

to my dear wife Sallie, who made various suggestions that are used in this book, which she also typed, its dedication;

to four very special friends, with each of whom (in diverse contexts) I have flogged through the actual doing of these managerial cybernetics:

PAUL RUBINYI, who has contrived so many cybernetic assignments in Canada for our collaboration, and whose friendship matters beyond all confusing circumstances;

RAÚL ESPEJO, whose brilliantly incisive mind produced much true if abrasive criticism of this text. If some of that criticism remains unanswered, it is not his fault;

GEORGE GOULD, whose second best talent is calm persistence, for the gift of his best talent *au fond du temple saint;*

ROBERT ABBOTT, who understands the human values, and also (that much rarer gift) can do something about them;

to all those others who have made potent use of this very work: notably Roberto Cañete (unwinding his snake), Robert Bittlestone (ignorant of snakes, but not much else), and Barry Clemson (who knows about teaching);

to my dear friends Professors Russell L. Ackoff, Gordon Pask, Humberto Maturana, and Heinz von Foerster, who are mentioned all too briefly in the text: I have not taken your names in vain;

to my fellow faculty members of the Business School within the University of Manchester, especially Professors John Morris and Roger Collcutt, Dr Sidney Howell and Mr. Normal Powell; and to ten beloved generations of my doctoral students (*Lamentations,* 3, 27);

finally to Compañero Enrique Farné and all our mutual friends, who remember the inspiration of Professor Venceremos Condorito, of the Universidad de Pelotillehue at Las Huevas — *avis quondam atque avis futurus.*

PART ONE

CONCEPTS, PERCEPTS, PRECEPTS

Summary of Part One

Here we are first of all concerned to understand the conceptual tools that will be needed to fashion the model of the enterprise that the book constructs and deploys.

The concept of **system** *is central to any discussion of organization; few managers, perhaps, would think of that concept exactly as a tool. It is, they might consider, a term to be defined, and then to be properly used. In Chapter One, however, we begin to probe the connotation of the word 'system'. The target definition turns out to be elusive. It seems more important to recognize that we are handling a conceptual tool, because a tool has to be understood in terms of its capability to facilitate the work undertaken, and also in terms of the limitations that its own shortcomings (in this case of reliable definition) impose on that work. In an effort to elucidate all this, the chapter engages in some mental exercises intended to loosen-up rigid attitudes to whatever is systemic about enterprises, and to promote an enquiry rather than a didactic ethos for the whole book. The examples are exclusively managerial, and deal with both economic and human affairs.*

In Chapter Two, the issue of how to measure the complexity of the system that the manager must needs regulate is addressed. Complexity, it is argued, is the stuff of management. The basic unit of complexity is any one possible state of the system. For, as the number of possible states increases, the complexity rises — to very alarming proportions, because that rise is exponential. Management is shown to be the task of manipulating that complexity. The measure of the number of possible states is called VARIETY. Then it is the manager's job to be a Variety Engineer. This is a new vision of that job; but it by no means excludes the familiar tasks of regulating performance: in material, economic and human terms. Thus this concept of measurement is also a conceptual tool, and learning how to measure variety throws further light on the nature of system itself. Even so, there are objects of perception, or percepts, and variety measurement begins the necessary managerial process of objectifying the concepts of system. The exercises used here are a little more demanding than before, because they use numerical instances, couched in abstract terms. However, the mathematics involved does not go beyond what we learned in school, and the effort of abstraction is alleviated by concomitant reflections on the relevance of the examples to real life: here are percepts again.

Having come to (some preliminary) terms with the nature of system, and with the flux of variety that determines its dynamic complexity, the cybernetic question arises: how can all this be regulated? The answer, which is the topic of the whole book, is by organization. *In Chapter Three, we begin the exploration of the notion of organization: not through the conventional schemata of functions, responsibilities, territories, and so on, but through an investigation of the basic requirements for a regulated system. The discoveries made by control engineers are of course used: they have understood the scientific rules of regulation. Nonetheless, this is a management book; no attempt is made to teach engineering. Why not? Because, although the* principles *are inescapable, the whole world of the manager is different from that of the engineer. This is because variety proliferates for the manager, and cannot be tamed by reducing the structure of the system to agreed parameters. Therefore the management cybernetician must deploy the principles in a different way, to address a different problem. Chapter Three begins this process. It sets out to show how management systems employ feedback, why this feedback has to be adjusted to deal with time lags (all of which is standard to control engineering); why adjuster organizers are required and what is the role of hierarchy (neither of which notions is standard to engineering in practice). Although the obvious examples of this kind of regulation are concerned with physical things, the opportunity is not lost to point to psychological correlates. We arrive at a conceptual tool called the 'management unit'. This is developed through a series of diagrams to determine what are its invariant characteristics. Attention is drawn to the circumstance that the detailed content of this box will not be reproduced later in the book. The management unit will reappear later under the symbol of a simple empty square.*

The book is concerned with management cybernetics: *the science of effective organization. And what this can possibly mean is gradually brought out in the first three chapters. Concepts may be clarified, percepts may be identified. But a science is expected to deliver precepts as well: the rules that apply to the exercise of any art. Chapter Three contains two precepts, which it chooses to call 'aphorisms'; but Chapter Four is devoted to something dignified as a law of nature. That might be defined as a rule that cannot be flouted, within a given framework of concepts and percepts. This basic precept is called Ashby's Law. It states the key relationship governing all variety engineering. In exploring it for managerial insights, we find once again both physical and psychological manifestations of the law in action. Out of this exploration, three principles of organization are educed. These are not management slogans, but statements as to the design of managerial systems that take account of the necessity to encompass Ashby's Law in ways that are both humane and economic.*

Finally, Chapter Five considers the meaning of the viability *of any enterprise. This is not meant in the purely economic sense; it refers to the ability of the enterprise to maintain a separate existence — to survive. What are the criteria of viability? The answer will not be complete until the book is finished, but Chapter Five begins the investigation. In particular, it takes a collection of management units (as defined in Chapter Three), a collection which exhausts the operational elements of the enterprise, and examines their interconnectedness. This examination results in a completed description of System One, the term that shall be used to name the operational component of the viable system. The emerging model conceives of System One as related to a metasystem, an organizational construct of logically higher order, which (in orthodox terminology) would probably be called 'corporate management'. However: this metasystem turns out to constitute the System One of the next larger enterprise that contains the enterprise that we happen to be considering. Thus the concept of* recursion *is explained. Every viable system contains, and is contained in, a viable system. This concept of an organizational* nest *is crucial to this account of how enterprises really work, and is contrasted with the orthodox concept of hierarchy.*

At the end of Part One, the tool-kit of concepts, percepts, and precepts that is needed to construct a total model of the enterprise in general is complete. When that model in turn becomes available, the means will be to hand to model any enterprise in particular.

CHAPTER ONE

An entry

and first of all —

What IS a System?

> We have to be extremely cautious
> about any definition.
>
> If you try out a few possibilities,
> you may well find that almost
> anything you say begs a host of questions.

Here is a start:

> 'A System consists of a group of elements
> dynamically related in time
> according to some coherent pattern.'

That much seems to be essential. And it is not clear that we can say much more.

The point that I find that I am most anxious to add is that this System has a PURPOSE.

The trouble is:

> WHO SAYS SO?

Some Systems themselves declare that they have a purpose, a political party for instance, or an insurance company, or a hospital. On analysis, however, not everyone — even of those most involved — might agree what the purpose actually is.

Then there are a great many Systems that do not say anything at all about their purposes. But all sorts of people are willing to assert what these purposes are. Unfortunately, again, they do not all agree.

So where does the idea that Systems in general have a purpose come from?

IT COMES FROM YOU!

It is you
the observer of the System
who recognizes its purpose.

Come to think of it, then, is it not just YOU — the observer — who recognizes that there is a System in the first place?

Well, you may say, perhaps so. But there is quite a lot of agreement about that. We could all agree that there is a System called 'government' — even if we do not all agree about its purpose.

The trouble is this: if we do not agree about the purpose of 'government' as a System, we shall not agree about its *boundaries*. I bet that we DON'T agree.

If there is no agreement about the boundaries of a System, and there usually is not (when we get down to it), then how can we be sure that we have actually RECOGNIZED the thing?

Consider the System called a tiger. We recognize *that,* by agreement, or else the science of zoology is impossible.

But suppose that you were travelling in the Arctic, and met a tiger. Would it really BE a tiger?

Suppose that you caught a tiger 10 centimetres long in a mousetrap. Would that really BE a tiger?

Rubbish! Tigers belong in a tropical sort of climate, and tigers are bigger than mice. That is that.

That may well be that to any sane person.

But what does it tell us about the boundaries of the System that we label 'tiger'?

The trouble is that we are accustomed to looking at tigers in the zoo. In that context we are fairly sure about the boundaries of the Tiger System. Those boundaries were imposed on the Tiger System by the curator of the zoo, and we accepted his say-so on the matter.

Can tigers climb trees?

How do you know? Are you *sure*? In any case, is your view of the question a judgment about the Tiger System or a judgment about the Zoo System?

If none of this gives you any sense of uneasiness, then congratulations — and perhaps you would write and tell me the purpose of the System we call Tiger...

The purpose of a tiger is:

- to be itself
- to be its own part of the Jungle System
- to be a link in animal evolution
- to eat whatever it eats, for Ecology's sake
- to provide tiger-skins
- to perpetuate the genes of which it is the host
- ...
- ...

For the moment, I am prepared to say that the purpose of a tiger is to demonstrate that the recognition of a System and of its purpose is a highly subjective affair.

All of this turns out to mean that we simply cannot attribute purposes, or even boundaries, to systems *as if* these were objective facts of nature.

The facts about the system are in the eye of the beholder.

This sounds like an unproductive conclusion, but we can make something of it. It means that both the nature and the purpose of a System are recognized by an observer within his perception of WHAT THE SYSTEM DOES.

The definition of the purpose of a System as being *what it does* lays the onus not on 'nature' but on the particular observer concerned. It immediately accounts for UNRESOLVABLE disagreements about systems too. For two people may well disagree about anything at all, and never become reconciled. They *say* that they will be convinced, and give way, if the FACTS show that they were mistaken. But the facts about the nature and purpose of a System are not objective realities. Once you have declared, as an observer, what the facts are, the nature and purpose of the System observed are ENTAILED. The other side of this coin is even more disconcerting. Once you have declared that you know the nature and the purpose of the System, the facts that are relevant to your conceptualizations are the ONLY facts that you can recognize.

Does this mean that we can never communicate about systems, and still less essay scientific statements about systems — since we all see them differently?

No. What it means is that we have to agree on the CONVENTION about the nature, the boundaries, and the purposes of any System before we can agree on what is to count as a fact.

For instance, we can agree to call a given dead carcass a tiger, and then we may scientifically establish how many ribs this tiger has. The answer will now have some objective reality — provided that we have also agreed the convention as to what is to count as a rib.

Well, enough of tigers: let us turn to motor cars. That sounds more realistic. Everyone would agree that the motor car is a system for getting people from A to B more quickly than they can walk. *Most* people would agree on that, anyway. Well, *some* people think that the motor car is a System for poisoning the atmosphere. Personally, I think that the motor car is a System for covering cities completely in asphalt and concrete.

Hold it: this was going to be realistic. Let us agree on the A to B convention, for the sake of the argument. At the very least, we can expect agreement about this A to B nature and purpose of the Motor Car System between the manufacturer and the customer. They both accepted the convention before the money changed hands.

I was myself in just this situation once, and I had this brand new car. Unfortunately, a door handle came off before I could get the car home. Next day, on the way to the garage a windscreen-wiper flew off at speed, and I could not retrieve it. I think that the next thing to go was the mileometer. For many months, and for one reason or another, this motor car was always less than the System that the purchasing convention has agreed that it was. I shrugged: no doubt I had the unlucky production number.

But the motor car was a prestige motor car. At the time, I lived in the London area. It turned out that all the servicing stations for this motor car had a mutual agreement to supply each other with spares. Then surely it followed that if I could not catch up with my car's defects before something else failed, then neither could anyone else. It was not just a matter of having an unlucky production number: the whole provisioning system for spare parts must be faulty.

I wrote to the managing director of the manufacturing company to point out that the System for spare-part provisioning did not work. He disagreed. He said that there was nothing the matter with the System. He was sorry, of course, that I had had so much difficulty in obtaining spares. But, he firmly said, in the exact words that I have quoted before: 'I am of the opinion that our system is efficient and that it only fails to maintain availability, due to manufacturing conditions or outside deficiencies'. And this leading industrialist took special pride in the fact that he was not a mere businessman, but a fully-qualified engineer.

What is the nature, and what is the purpose, of a spare parts provisioning System — and what are its boundaries? And if we may know the purpose of a System by WHAT IT DOES, then what did *this* System actually do? From my point of view it was a System for not supplying spare parts. From the managing director's point of view, it must have had a different purpose: minimizing the capital tied up in spare parts, perhaps. In any case, the nature of the System was certainly a subjective affair.

Returning to the point at issue: 'the System' is not presented to us on a plate — it is what we declare it to be. And, moreover, there are a great many things that can be scientifically said about systems, that will avail us nothing in *managing* systems whose nature and purpose are not already agreed in advance.

The outstanding examples are the social services and the nationalized industries. Who knows what their nature, boundaries, and purposes are? Oh yes: we have a general idea. But the critical management problems continually defy proper definitions (and therefore any solutions that would be agreed to COUNT as solutions) because the nature of these systems is not at all agreed, their boundaries are extremely fuzzy, and they have as many (conflicting) purposes as there are (conflicting) observers.

Should the Railways make a profit? Should they, at any rate, not make a loss? And how are these concepts of profit and loss to be defined for a national industry owned by the nation? These questions have totally defeated successive chairmen of British Rail, as they have all vociferously complained. They thought that the responsible Ministers should give the answers; but, on the basis of this exposition, how COULD they? There are no privileged observers of systems, not even those who in some sense (what sense?) own them.

Anyone who now expects *me* to answer these questions has not understood the argument at all. I am not a privileged observer of the railway System. Perhaps I am more privileged than either the chairman or the responsible Minister; because I use the System, and therefore see what it does — without the intervention of theoretical explications of its doing, and without any responsibility to agglomerate the observations of *all* railway users into a 'railway policy'. Please note: if systems are subjective, the last remark identifies the problem facing the Chairman. Evidently it is insoluble; and hence this whole book. For the moment, however, consider this one observer's account of railway purposes — as deduced from what the railway does to me.

Typically, I need to go to Manchester, to London, and back to my cottage in West Wales. I live forty miles south of the railhead at Aberystwyth, which leads to Manchester, and forty miles north of the railhead at Carmarthen, which leads back from London. From the absence of links between my home and the two railheads, I conclude that the purpose of the railway system is to dissuade me from travelling by rail. It would be more sensible to travel by car. Unknown to the railways, however, I do not have a suitable car.

To move from Aberystwyth to Manchester, I must travel right across Wales as far as Crewe in a small diesel train. This has two coaches, each with two classes. The popular class (depending on the time of year) is full of holiday-makers, shoppers, students, drunken rugby-players, and schoolchildren. I cannot work in this ambience. The first-class compartments in the two coaches are supposed to offer one smoking and one non-smoking compartment. Normaly, *both* are heavily labelled NON-SMOKING. I judge the system by what it does. It is determined either to stop me from working or from smoking: if it succeeds in the latter, it succeeds in the former also. I conclude that its purpose is strong, since it is doubly effective. The obvious solution, whereby the coaches are not permanently labelled for non-smokers, in first class, but can be temporarily allocated one for smokers and one for non-smokers by the train's guard, is inadmissible — or so I am firmly told. I conclude that the system's purpose to stop me both working and smoking is being carefully reinforced: surely it *must* be deliberate...

The legs of the journey from Manchester to London, and from London to Swansea, are superb in terms of fast and effective movement from A to B, and the seating is comfortable. (I am back in a diesel from Swansea to Carmarthen.) But this voyager finds himself in need of sustenance. I have spent up to an hour in queues in the rattling corridors of these fast moving trains, and on the last two trips the food ran out before I got any. What is the purpose of the commissariat system?

You will notice that I am deliberately reducing my argument to absurdity: but that does not mean to say that it is absurd. Only a paranoid would contend, even on this evidence, that the *purpose* of the railway system is to discountenance this particular traveller. Nonetheless, *all* travellers *are* discountenanced, each in his or her own way. Presumably this means that the railway system, from its own standpoint, embraces purposes that include discountenancing its clients. To that the railway would surely reply that this is accidental, and that it is 'doing its best' to please everyone. 'Everyone' includes its own staff, the ministry that appoints its board, and parliament — as well as the travelling public. None of these intends an identical purpose for the system; and there is no one privileged observer whose own purposes can properly be reflected as embodying the truth of the matter.

It is for these sorts of reason that care is required in seizing the term 'purposeful system' from the literature and applying it without due discrimination. If we do not define such a system in terms of its environment and especially of its observer(s), we are likely to become involved in a teleological fallacy.

Purpose is imputed to a system by its observer, and there is no concensus (why should there be?) between observers — each of whom has his own individual view of what the system is supposed to do. Of course, that means: 'do for him', despite his willingness to try to comprehend the needs of others. That degree of comprehension is no more than an extension of his personal awareness of needs in general. Any railway user may honestly try to conceive of the problems facing other users, and of the Railway Chairman himself. But can he encompass in his thinking the needs of a motor-transport bloc whose aim is to abolish the railways? There are limits.

Systems are nested within other systems; the observer who imputes purpose to a system belongs to several of them, and is excluded from others. Thus his perception of purpose in any one system is not only subjective, not only conditioned by his acceptance or rejection of boundaries, but is also a function of the *relationships* that he maintains across the complicated webs of interactive systems, one with another. Returning to our example: the purposes attributed to the railway system will vary with the observer's geographical network of significant locations, with the availability to him of other transport, and with all manner of personal-preference systems concerning smoking, working, gregariousness and so on.

This book will attempt to supply a model of organization conceived as a system. It is first necessary to loosen-up our thinking about what a system *is*. In doing so thus far, we have already created a good deal of confusion (although it is better to face up to that than to be saddled with a naive notion that the answers are obvious). The question immediately arises: if a little loosening-up of our thinking about systems results in so much confusion, in which it certainly looks risky to make any kind of formal assertion, how is it that management normally proceeds *as if* we all knew perfectly well what the system to be managed really is? The answer lies in those conventions already mentioned. They are established in the managerial language to make it impossible to formulate propositions that lead to confusion. But obviously, by the arguments of this chapter, this is a dangerous device. The conventions do not fully account for the systemic realities. The attempt to question the 'fit' is impossible within the conventions; and if the conventions are breached, then the suggestions cannot be heard. This kind of deafness on the part of established managements is a major factor in the lethal resistance to institutional change that is eroding the viability of our society.

To examine this point in more detail, we might as well remain with the railways, because they are familiar systems to everyone, and their history in Britain is in the public domain. This particular story starts, many years ago, with the appointment of Dr Richard Beeching as Chairman of British Railways. He was a management expert. He took it as a convention that the Railways were intended to make a profit — or, at any rate, not intended to make a loss. He also implicitly accepted the inherited convention that a substantial part of the Railway System was the 'iron road': that network of steel rails connecting one geographical place to another, and carrying various kinds of traffic from A to B. (A and B are major characters in transportation systems. But need they be?)

Well, it follows from all these conventions that if there are sections of the iron road that earn less than the cost of their upkeep, the efficient management strategy is to close down those sections. And that is what Dr Beeching proceeded to do.

Now I have gradually begun to insist that there *are* things that can be said about systems, once the conventions about their nature, boundaries, and purposes have been established. Let us forget about railways (along with motor cars and tigers) for a moment, and consider one such thing.

Given accepted conventions, any system has an effort applied to make it work. This effort produces a pay-off from the system (otherwise the system would soon be abolished). Except in exceptionally simple systems, the pay-off is NON-LINEAR in relation to the effort put into the operation. This means that we do not reap 10 percent of the rewards for 10 percent of the effort put in, and 50 percent reward for 50 percent of effort. On the contrary, experience shows that it is relatively easy to get results out of the system at the start, or so long as we are using our most appropriate efforts, and relatively difficult to get the last bit of pay-off from the system at the finish, or when our efforts are least appropriate.

Economists know this, and they can be heard talking about 'diminishing returns'. Psychologists know this, and they may exhibit 'learning curves' which are equally convex. Engineers, too, know all too well that it becomes increasingly difficult to get an extra percent of efficiency out of any system that converts energy, as it approaches the limits of its performance. There are various names for relationships of this kind, of which the Pareto curve is rather well known. The non-linear curve typically looks like this:

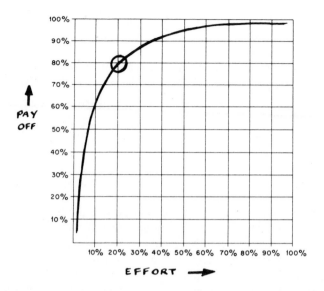

Figure 1. A typical convex curve relating effort to pay-off

Lots of 'rule of thumb' people know about this curve too, and especially recognize the point on it that is marked with a circle — where 20 percent of the effort achieves 80 percent of the result. They speak of an 80-20 Law.

In round terms, this so-called law usually works — which is why people have noticed it. Twenty percent of fighter pilots shoot down eighty percent of the shot-down bombers. Eighty percent of the shares are held by twenty percent of the shareholders. Twenty percent of the sizes (coats, trousers, shoes) fit eighty percent of the customers. Eighty percent of production goes to twenty percent of the orders.

The relationship works for most large, complex, probabilistic systems. (If large numbers are not involved, then we may not observe this essentially 'mass' effect.) Just why this happens is a highly technical issue; it is enough to say for now that, on the basis of much experience of the behaviour of large, complex, probabilistic systems, we would expect some such relationship to arise.

So let us go back to the railways. It was quite likely, given the system conventions used by Dr Beeching, that eighty percent of the traffic would be carried on twenty percent of the 'iron road'.

I do not know whether Dr Beeching expected this or not. But it is a matter of record that he discovered a convex curve relating the 'effort' (miles of maintained railway) to the 'pay-off' (earnings), and also that it ran straight through the 80-20 point.

Given the rest of the set of conventions that I mentioned, then the obvious management strategy is to CHOP OFF the uneconomic tail of the curve. Too much effort — in the final eighty percent — is expended in trying to raise the pay-off through *its* final twenty percent. So the strategy says in effect: save eighty percent of the cost, accept a twenty percent cut in earnings, and BECOME PROFITABLE.

But now we come to the snags, from the standpoint of systems theory. People who use the doomed twenty percent of the railways also use the remaining eighty percent. If they are compelled to change their mode of transport locally (say by buying a car) they may abandon the railways altogether. Various systemic consequences of this kind can be proposed; but there is a more fundamental problem to consider. If the relationship between effort and pay-off tends to stabilize itself on a highly convex curve, typically running through an 80-20 point, then it will do so again — AFTER we have chopped off the original tail. And if we are consistent in our managerial strategy, we shall chop off the new tail as uneconomic. And so on.

The next diagram shows how the process looks. This time I have interfered with the scales, or the process would be very difficult to see — since the system is collapsing to 16 percent of its total area on each 'economy' cut. Thus the picture is of the upper left-hand corner alone, and is still distorted. But we can now readily see how the original system (A) is cut to create system B. Two more cuts (the shaded areas) reduce the system to become consecutively systems C and D.

We have defined a Machine for Eating the Railways. (see Figure 2).

The whole process, like the component convex curve of any one system, is never as clear cut as I have shown it. If it were, managements would not do such destructive things as they do. The point is that we so often fail to contemplate the systemic consequences of policies which are considered, through the accepted conventions, as discrete decisions. It sounds like an absurd oversight, and certainly the outcomes are often quite farcical or even tragic. The reason is, of course, that there is not enough agreement as to the real nature of the system concerned: if there were, sets of possible consequences could be discussed, and followed through the ramifications of the agreed system.

In this we discover a major objective of this book. If we can agree on the nature of a system for viable organization, then it will be possible to elucidate

17

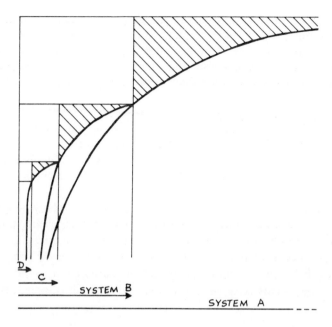

D
C
SYSTEM B
SYSTEM A

Figure 2. Continuous adaptation of the non-linear system to
economy cuts

the systemic relationships that uphold it. To do this we shall have to find ways
of avoiding the traps of thought that this chapter is concerned to point out.

But that is reserved for later; and it would be rather unconstructive to restrict
the present loosening-up exercises to the dangers associated with the traps. Let
us take a look at a case history concerning systems that generate uneconomic
tails, in which their recognition and handling was turned to profitable
outcomes. The story goes back nearly thirty years: before computers
therefore.

Scientifically, I was the head of a small operational research group in a steel
company. Managerially, I was the production controller. This activity may
well be described as the balancing factor on a see-saw. At one end sits
manufacturing, with the task of maximizing the utility of given machinery,
labour, and work-in-progress investment. At the other end sits selling, with the
task of maximizing the satisfaction of the customer. In many ways, I used to
think, it would be a most glorious accident if the see-saw ever came into
balance.

Naturally, Sales were trying to serve all comers. Naturally, Production wanted
large orders, long runs, and straightforward scheduling. So it was sensible to
examine the relationship between the production *effort* and the sales *pay-off*.

The limits of the process were easy to recognize. The Company made so much money on the production-convenient staples that there could well be a government enquiry. That Company lost so much money on production-inconvenient, ad-hoc, small items that the sales value of the order (forget all about the profit) was less than the cost of the office system required to process that order.

The curve relating effort to pay-off, which is to say the monetary measure of disbalance on the see-saw, was drawn for hundreds of products in several locations. The curves were nearly identical. They were all highly convex. They all ran through a point extremely close to the 80-20 'saddlepoint'.

When all this became clear, there was much discussion. Many people thought that the mass of unprofitable small orders, having been clearly identified by this work, should be abandoned. But if the curve characterizes interactions in a large, complex, probabilistic system, then this policy could result in 'eating the steelworks'. The question was, would the curve go on restabilizing itself until the departments concerned were reduced to small, simple, deterministic systems?

I collected a vast amount of empirical evidence (some of it referred to earlier) that this curve is quite general. The evidence collapses at some point for a system that is either smaller, or simpler, or more deterministic. The recognition of these degrees is unfortunately subjective; but then, so is the recognition of the system itself — as we saw.

Next, I devised a series of precisely defined 'games' between such systems, played with dice and counters; and also a version of the game of chess played entirely at random (each side moving according to the throw of dice). By ranking the value of the chess pieces according to a scoring system used by the master Tartakower, it was possible to verify that about twenty percent of the white pieces annihilated about eighty percent of the black pieces, and vice versa, until the game began to disintegrate as a very complex system. (It is clearly not possible to play an end-game to checkmate by random moves.) After several years of playing these games, I found that they generated a family of convex curves — and moreover that these tended to have a point of inflection at the 80-20 mark.

From the definitions of the games, I tried to formalize a mathematical theory. This would show how the convexity of the curve is inevitable, and how it tends to stabilize around an 80-20 'saddlepoint'. It would also show the limiting conditions for size, complexity and probabilism of a system in which this behaviour could be expected. The attempt failed. To this day I believe that such a theory could be constructed; but meanwhile decisions had to be taken, and I was convinced, as the experiments continued, that these 'uneconomic tails' functioned more like the tails of kites, or keels on ships, to keep the whole system steady.

The plans developed were these. Something certainly *happens* at or around the 80-20 point. To its left on the diagram, we are vastly profitable; to its right we rapidly tend to disaster. We cannot risk Eating Ourselves by axing the notorious tail. Then the answer is to put the *effort* of production control, keeper of the see-saw, into the profitable left-hand side: we can spend real money there, and it will have a *pay-off*. And instead of annihilating the unprofitable right-hand-side, we will find a cheap way of handling it.

Sometimes this meant making for stock, and doing a warehousing job for the small customer. That may sound an extremely obvious solution. In fact, it was a conclusion hostile to the basic production philosophy of the firm, and it took two or three years of argument and simulation (still no computers) to gain acceptance. Sometimes it meant treating the uneconomic customer as 'second class', and using his orders, like graphite between the major wheels to 'lubricate' the major production system. This was not a popular notion either, once it was overtly stated. The convention is, after all, that every customer is equally highly valued. Within the language of such old-fashioned conventions the statement: 'demonstrable nonsense' cannot be heard. Overridingly the systemic answer is to use the uneconomic tail to SERVICE the economic zone. But, to this day, that answer is not generally understood, because the nature of system is not generally understood, and because slogans such as 'cut the costs' sound better in the managerial ear than admonitions to study systems theory.

It is tempting, but would be unprofessional, to hazard guesses as to how such thinking would have affected the railway problem earlier discussed. (Of course, it was offered; but 'deafness' was specially defined earlier on.) Nonetheless, we can at least note that private groups have succeeded in reopening defunct local lines, and that clearly they must have adopted wholly different criteria of service and success from those used by British Rail itself. The problem of the tails involves drawing a distinction in those terms, and that is something that monolithic organizations seem unable to do. They are systematic about being unsystemic. In particular, they set priorities; and this means that low-priority issues (such as uneconomic lines) receive no attention, sink still further in priority, and eventually are lost.

This question of priority is the final issue to be raised in this loosening-up. We are unsure what constitutes the system, what is its nature, where are its boundaries, which are its purposes; and we have noted that attempts to be systematic are sometimes unsystemic. A suspicion of slogans has already been voiced. In the light of all these matters, what is to be made of that most over-used slogan of them all: *let us get our priorities right*?

If we truly believe that we treat the systems we manage as if they really are systems, we have to be extremely careful about the notion of priorities. Developing countries, for example, need to build houses, roads, schools, and hospitals. What are their priorities? Do they build houses, and find that there is nowhere for the children to go to school; or do they build schools that are unattended because no-one lives anywhere near? Do they build hospitals that no-one can reach as soon as it rains; or do they build roads that stop suddenly in the middle of nowhere? Any reader who thinks that these questions are fatuous cannot have been to a developing country. Setting priorities is a very dangerous game indeed. The process partitions the total system, and gives power on a relative scale to its parts. It is notorious in the history of World War II that Lord Beaverbrook's single-minded success as Minister for Aircraft Production, when planes were desperately needed, nearly lost Britain the tank war in North Africa.... .

Priorities *can* be set: very often people become disoriented if they are not. The point is that there is a price to pay; and it always has to do with a failure to understand the system, and a subsequent loss of systemic synergy. Synergy has to do with physiology; that is to say with the *body* that happens to consist of all the parts. One can imagine the concept mechanically too. Think of a piece of machinery in which a dozen subsystems are all working away to do something useful. On top of each is a revolving cogwheel, not connected to anything. Then suddenly a lever is thrown. The twelve floating cogwheels come together. The dozen subsystems continue to play their separate roles; but now the entire machine rises up on caterpillar tracks, and moves off. We could have set priorities between the subsystems, considering each on its own merits, and in so doing we could have failed to understand the first thing about the nature of the system as a whole. But this is not going to concern those whose psychological paradigm demands that priorities necessarily exist, because they think that they understand the purposes of the system. We come full circle: if the purposes are known, then the priorities are clear. It is all very convenient — and all very damaging.

Pray consider this issue in an entirely human context. We are all members of a board which is due to reconsider its fundamental *raison d'être*. What is this 'thing' of which we are board members; what are we really trying to do; and how? Now this scenario is very familiar. Boards of companies and of national services are implicitly faced with this problem all the time. They usually pretend that they are not, by carrying forward the minutes of one meeting into the agenda of the next, and simply slipping in — unobtrusively — any new item which has raised its head. And if this device fails to work, then they have that ultimately incompetent item 'Any Other Business', in which to catch the residue. But sometimes a meeting really will convene with the explicit purpose of reviewing *purpose*. Or a whole conference may be set up to consider, *ab initio,* how to handle an entirely new issue in human affairs.

Pray consider, then, how the convenors of this meeting set about their task. They identify key issues (— and yet if we actually knew what are the key issues, maybe there would be no problems: all of this hinges upon the acknowledgement of purpose). Next, they identify alternative strategies within the key issues (— and yet if we actually knew all the strategies available, the answers would probably be obvious: all of this hinges upon the acknowledgement of systemic boundaries). Finally, they put the agenda in a particular order (— and yet if this order were actually known, a computer could track through to the proper conclusions: all of this hinges upon the attribution of priorities).

Again, it is surely clear that this systematic structuring of the meeting is unsystemic. We are meeting to try to understand the nature of the system with whose management we are charged. We do not understand it; but all of these preliminaries are based upon the implicit contention that we do. The situation is like that of a man on his hands and knees in the middle of the night, grovelling in the ground under a lamp-post. A policeman asks him what he thinks he is doing. 'I am looking for a lost ring.' 'Where did you lose it?' 'Over there', says the man, pointing ten yards away into the dark bushes. 'Then why are you hunting for it here?' 'Because this is where the light is.'

The board has a number of lighted lamp-posts. They are labelled 'cost effectiveness', 'locations', 'staff availability', 'liquidity', and so on. They illuminate very familiar patches of terrain. But the answers the board seeks are in the dark bushes. There is no light over there; there is no guide into that unknown. Thus even when the board recognizes that it does not understand its priorities, it has no hesitation in setting up specialist committees to consider 'obvious areas of concern'. It will set up the priorities when it receives the committees' reports. That is an advance: it shows some care for the priority trap. However, all the committees are sitting around lamp-posts. Well, fair enough — they have to be able to read the minutes of the last meeting, surely. . . .

Let us now demolish the whole of this apparatus, on the grounds that it is systemically incompetent. Then we have to ask what that leaves. It leaves a collection of individuals each of whom (we may certainly hope, because of his or her membership of the board) understands *something* about the issues. Of course Mr A is well-known to be a world expert on *x*. Of course Dr B is well-known to ride a hobby-horse about *y*. They have respectively bored us to death already on their respective topics. Ms C, on the other hand is wise and learned, and does not seem to represent a vested interest: etcetera.

Pray consider now a large room. There are (say) ten tables in this room, surrounded by easy chairs and supportive refreshment. Beside each table is a vertical pole; on each table is a stack of large white cards. The protocol of the meeting is that anyone who reckons that he or she has a point to make, one that is relevant to the policy that we are met to create, should proceed to one of these tables, write the name of a topic on a white card, and fix it to the top of the pole. Obviously Mr A and Dr B will install themselves without delay; it is to be hoped that Ms C will do so as well — although the topic that she announces may well occasion surprise, because no-one else had thought of *that*.

The protocol continues thus. Members of the board may sit down at any table, and join in the discussion. Meanwhile, they may observe the apathy or frenzy of other groups, and watch the emergence of new tables, set up under new banners. It should be remembered that these people know each other, and can 'read the signs'. Anyone is entitled to move, without apology. Anyone is entitled to initiate a new table.

It should be obvious already that boredom cannot set into this situation. Much experience of meetings has convinced me that boredom is the dominating factor in decision-taking. Any conclusion, however obnoxious, is better than sitting through one further minute of this absurd drivel. And yet we sacrifice to the graces: it is simply not permitted that one should scream 'enough! I'm leaving'. Under the new protocol, this is possible without offence; one simply wanders away.

As soon as the group sitting round a table recognizes that nothing will come of its deliberations, it may either disperse, or change the topic inscribed on its masthead. Others will notice those changes, taking note of topics, and taking note of those involved. If, on the other hand, those at the table consider that they have agreed on something worth saying, they write it down, and each person present signs the note. There are no rules whatever about the format of any such declaration. It could be a sentence asserting a belief, a declaration about a boundary, a draft paragraph towards a policy: it could be anything considered worth saying. Outstandingly, it could formulate a crucial *question*. A signal is then attached to the masthead, while the group continues, or not, as it wishes.

Staff assistants, observing the signals, collect the notes, and deliver them to the Chairperson. The Chairperson (as always) has a most important role. This is, however, no longer to bully and cajole the board into observing the rules set by the agenda — for there are none. It is to *sort* the notes coming in; it is to be an intelligent computer for the meeting (and to keep quiet).

Gradually, the issues that the board considers worth considering will emerge. They may not be at all in line with the 'lamp-posted' areas of established light. The Chair must of course recognize that likelihood from the start. The Chair's job is instead to recognize what the areas of concern actually *are*. Thus the

Chairperson cautiously sorts the incoming notes into foci of concern, and tries to create an appropriate taxonomy. The staff assistants are at hand to undertake typing and duplicating.

By the first agreed break, let us say luncheon, all members of the board are issued with a first review of their deliberations. Anyone is entitled at this point to add his or her name to any declaration that has been made, via the secretariat. All right: he or she missed the whole discussion (which is a relief), but had thought something like that all along. People are also entitled to start a 'denial' list, or to propose amendments, and these will also gain signatures or not as the process continues.

For, indeed yes, the process is intended to be iterative. It may go on for two or three days, if so arranged, and given that the issues are weighty. The role of the Chair is crucial, and remains so: some issues will be declared closed, as having no general interest, while others will be amalgamated, as entailing similar outcomes. The Chair was always important, but its role now is wholly subvient to the meeting's needs: that may call for a different chairperson. These duties call for considerable mental dexterity, since the first attempts to derive a suitable taxonomy for the system may have to be radically changed as the meeting iteratively shifts its foci of concern. Moreover, there is no scope, under this protocol, for writing the minutes of the meeting before it has taken place...

Quite apart from the flexibility and sense of ease that an enquiry conducted in this way exhibits, the protocol is explicitly designed to avoid the traps that we have been considering. The purposes of this board are gradually emerging as an amalgam of the purposes of each member, considered as a participant observer in the process. This amalgam is not the same thing as a consensus, which may be generated by the traditional meeting. The search for consensus is made within artificial limits, artificial codifications of topic, and artificial orders of priority. That is why the consensus tends to state a lowest common denominator of purposes which often ends up to everyone's chagrin as a 'motherhood' statement. But the amalgam on purpose generated by the new protocol may be expected to include elements that are perceived as important by subsets of board members, while earning no more than aimiable acceptance by others. People are inclined to say of such a purpose: 'well, if all those good people think that this aspect of the matter ought to be made explicit and pursued, I daresay they are right. It doesn't really turn me on'. In the orthodox meeting this is an unlikely outcome, because the issue is an agenda item to which all present are forced to address themselves; thus those who are indifferent, finding it embarrassing to say just that, become hostile. In short, the orthodox meeting tends to polarize the board — and this is not only unnecessary, but damaging to a constructive outcome.

Secondly, the new protocol enables board members to probe the boundaries of the system. In the orthodox meeting, someone says: 'why should we not consider what would happen if. . .?' Someone else says: 'I think that's outside our terms of reference', and appeals to the Chair. The Chair is prudent: nothing happens. Under the new protocol, a small group of members is enabled to develop the *what if* question to the point where it can be considered as a serious prospect. After all: if something is regarded as important to our purposes, as we observe those to be emerging, how can it be that their consideration takes us outside the boundaries of the system? Surely, those boundaries have been wrongly defined. Even if the definition is merely a matter of internal convention, it will be difficult to change. I have seen the situation in which the definition was determined by the legal interpretation of an Act of Parliament. The agreement remained at this level; no-one on this board (a nationalized industry) would even consider the possibility of moving to amend the Act. It is not surprising. People *do* accept 'the system' as if it were given in nature, or handed to them on an institutional plate.

What truly is given in nature is a collection of principles that systems cannot violate if they are to maintain their identity. These principles are the content of the science of cybernetics, which may conveniently be defined as the science of effective organization. This book is about the cybernetics of a particular kind of system, that I call *the viable system*. We shall discover what that means as we proceed. But this ENTRY into the whole discussion (which is the loosening-up exercise) is pointing to an unassailable fact. We cannot successfully handle any system that we are disposed to manage unless we obtain an insight into its nature. That nature, as we have seen, has to do with purposes, with boundaries, and with other matters which are not customarily investigated within our institutions — because their *mores* effectively forbid it.

The story about 'tails' took us back thirty years. The story about 'meetings' is quite recent. I devised the new protocol in 1970, and have had four opportunities to use it since — although only once in its full setting. (The other occasions did not offer sufficient preparation time, and were reduced in the 'technology' of the meeting.) But in the examples that I have quoted, spanning a quarter of a century in time, and spanning the range of essentially mechanical to essentially human affairs, the questioning of the nature of the involved system itself was paramount.

Ought we not to question that more often?

LATER IN THE BAR...

'Has Concorde knocked down the travel time by half, or has it not? There's nothing 'subjective' about that.'

'You're talking like the airline executive you are. I'm just your passenger. The system you're talking about has no reality to me. The journey starts at home in England and ends in São Paulo, Brazil. To take the Concorde leg, I have to go to Paris, and I get dumped in Rio de Janeiro.'

'Well, it's early days yet... unfair!'

'I'm not criticizing your progress. I'm saying that your perception of the air travel system is necessarily different from mine. Subjective, like the man says.'

'Obviously. But what Bill's saying is that he's trying to run an airline — and he knows fine what his boundaries are. He can't be responsible for where you choose to live.'

'I'm not moving to Heathrow. Shouldn't Bill take account of where his customers start and finish their journeys?'

'Then he'd need to run a travel agency, not an airline.'

'Presumably God laid down the difference.'

'Conversation stopper. The purpose of a system is what it does. I take it that the purpose of this system is to stop me from having another drink.'

'Sorree: my round. After that motor car story, I think I'll leave the industry.'

'Well, I must say I thought that story was quite unfair. What on earth could that managing director have done about his suppliers and distributors?'

'It's because you motor guys talk like that we're losing out to foreign cars. They must have broken the problem of spares.'

'No — it's not that. Foreign cars have a special cachet: they're different. People like that.'

'Dangerous area. People were supposed to like the Edsel, and they didn't.'

'Someone misdefined the system. Wrong subjectivity.'

25

'*Dangerous area, as I said. Keep off it.*'

'*Oh, that's just great. Stick to classic definitions of your system, and what happens? That's how we lost the cotton industry, the shipbuilding industry —*'

'*— Wait a* minute. *I was in on that. The Japanese did it all on cheap rice.*'

'*What utter nonsense! I suppose that they build electronic systems out of rice... The Japanese are better entrepreneurs, that's all.*'

'*Well, its true that* we *virtually invented computers, and so on. We did have the lead, back in the early 1950's, and we lost it. We could easily have outdistanced the United States at that time.*'

'*The problem is that managers aren't risk-takers.*'

'*I can't AFFORD to take risks. If things go wrong, I've had it. Stick to proven methods, proven technology — work on the strengths we have.*'

'*The strengths become weaknesses while you're not looking. Then when things get rough you HAVE to Eat your own Tail, like the railways.*'

'*What else could Beeching have done? Even the packed commuter services around London aren't profitable.*'

'*We're back to where people live.*'

'*They can't all live in the City, that's for sure.*'

'*Then make the bill a charge on the rates in the stockbroker belt.*'

'*That wasn't within Beeching's say-so.*'

'*You see? It's a question of defining the system's boundaries.*'

'*Well,* someone *must be responsible. Where's the Government?*'

'*Telling Beeching to make a profit.*'

'*On* what*? A railway system relevant to a bygone age?*'

'*Exactly. The whole thing needs rethinking.*'

'*Well, only the Government can do that. It's no good their handing out briefs to the Beechings of this world that God himself could do nothing with.*'

'*Come on in, David: you're the government.*'

'*Thanks very much. We do our best, you know.*'

'*Oh, come off it. You simply grind on with the old system, and the number of bureaucrats is the only national statistic that keeps on going up. Why don't you reform the Civil Service?*'

'*We have. Haven't you noticed? We reformed the centre after Fulton. We reformed local government after Radcliffe-Maud. We've reformed the Health Service. Now we're in to Devolution. Scotland, Wales, all that?*'

'*What about England, then?*'

'*England?*'

'*David: did you know that the author of this very text we're now reading said of each of those reforms in turn that they 'betrayed every cybernetic canon in the book?*'

'*Did he, indeed. Any idea why?*'

'*Well, I for one know nothing about this assertion. But if you apply the arguments of this chapter, its perfectly obvious why.*'

'*I don't get it.*'

'*Look: you inherit a system that goes back hundreds of years. It has small units: too many of them, given modern technology and administrative convenience. But at least there were geographical reasons for their existence. So you can't quite bring yourself to kill them off. You keep them; but you deny their automony. You create larger units anyway, and end up with a new tier of government which simply bolsters the bureaucracy.*'

'*That's right. Meanwhile you're tinkering with the central government function, to try and make everything fit.*'

'*Yes: I'm getting the idea now. When the political aspirations of the Scottish and Welsh nationalists become threatening, the solution has to be to instal yet* another *tier of government.*'

'*Oh that's because England is running the whole show from Whitehall in any case, pretending to be Britain. Isn't that so, David?*'

'I don't know what you fellows think you're talking about. The whole development is... quite orderly.'

'Systematically unsystemic, that's what.'

'You've caught the jargon, Rhys, like the measles.'

'Not so, I've taken the point — which I knew in advance, in any case. It is redolent of oriental philosophy. You can't redesign a total system by redesigning all the bits in turn — especially if the bits really belong to a total system long vanished. As in the case of governing Britain.'

'That certainly seems to be the point made in this chapter. What are the purposes of government — and who says so? And where are the boundaries at each level? You have to admit, David, that all your 'quite orderly' procedures flatly assume that you Whitehall people know all that in advance.'

'All very well. I suppose that you'd like to have seen the Prime Minister and his cabinet take off to the hills to hold one of these farcical meetings with flag-poles and so on.'

'Better than Eating Britain by its Uneconomic Tails — so called — like my favourite county, poor little Rutland.'

'Don't you realize that meetings to review 'the nature, boundaries, and purposes' of the system are being held all the time?'

'The heavy sarcasm is noted, David; but the answer, in terms of this chapter, is NO. You're all kidding yourselves.'

'Correct. Systematically unsystemic. *That phrase pleases me.'*

'All right, Rhys: are we to have another dose of oriental philosophy? I thought that your subject was French.'

'David — poor David, cast in the role of defender of the established faith — is typifying the problem. A system is an integral whole, otherwise we would not be sitting here talking about the nature of system itself. For anyone who cannot see that this is a physiological *notion, has dismembered the systemic body in advance...'*

'But taking the system apart is the basis of scientific enquiry, isn't it Rhys?'

'Well, Bill, we have suffered for the advances that this reductionism has imposed. As to oriental philosophy, which takes another route, the Zen master for instance waits for years to show his pupil his enlightenment.'

'Rhys: what on earth has that got to do with understanding systems?'

'Understanding has to be at the physiological level — the level at which the whole system is a whole — or not at all.'

'That could take a long time. I suppose this stuff we are reading is supposed to shorten it. But I'm far from sure that an outlook which you say is deep in the oriental tradition, has much relevance to my work in the occidental automotive industry.'

'Oh, but it has. Westerners have understood it you know. Take Paul Valéry. Roughly translating, he says: 'it takes so long for the truths we've created to become our own flesh'.'

'The embodiment of system, we could say... hmm. What is it in French, Rhys, as a matter of interest?'

'Il faut tant d'années pour que les vérités que l'on s'est faites deviennent notre chair même.'

'Merci.'

CHAPTER TWO

Double entry

and second of all —

What MEASURES are appropriate?

We used to say that management dealt
with the FOUR Ms:

- Men
- Materials
- Machinery
- Money

There are obvious measures of these.

Today, the stuff of management includes the Four Ms, but is best denoted as:

- COMPLEXITY.

Why should this be true?

It is the net result of social and technological change. Small things have become larger, simple things more elaborate, slow things faster... Typically, all these changes are increasing their *rate* of change. Then on top of everything, the *nature* of the changes is such that separate things increasingly become connected together. Individuals move about the world more; and the world comes to them through instant television. Firms amalgamate, and grow foreign branches. Government agencies proliferate, and connect up with other governments. International activities are spawned. All of these developments impinge on each other. Thus the individual is again affected: as his employer and his city changes, as regional policies are devised, as international deals are struck (oil, common markets), as *global* intentions materialize between super-powers.

Management at every level, from our management of ourselves through every sort and size of aggregation to the management of the Earth is itself 'complexifying' — and it receives complexifying interference from every other level too. Thus complexity proliferates; and it has become virtually unmanageable with existing managerial tools.

Once upon a time, in order to check on the correct BALANCE of what came into the system with what went out, Double Entry book-keeping was devised. What equivalent method have we now to keep a check on the balance of complexity?

First of all, we need a *measure*. The book-keepers managed to quantify the Four M's in terms of money, and we still try to manage all our systems through the accounts. But no-one has found a way of bringing complexification as such into the fiscal picture. That is why — although complexification is literally proving the death of us — it is actually ignored in the equations of management. The nearest we come to recognizing it is indeed as a cost: the cost of ever-increasing installations for data processing. People are resigned to that. 'The world is getting more complex', they say, 'we need all this expensive machinery to handle it'. But is *that* true? If we cannot measure complexity except as the cost of a data-processing activity which is itself a major cause of complexification, we are in a circular trap.

Then let us investigate the measurement of complexity itself. We need to bear in mind that complexity is the result of the way that systems behave and interact. And if systems are subjective phenomena, then we are going to have trouble in determining a measure. The whole idea of measures is to be objective. . . . Yet the problem we face is not unique. In fact, the measures that we are accustomed to call objective work only because we accept a set of conventions about how they are to be employed. For example, if we quote the height of Mount Everest, we do not mean that this is the distance you would travel from the base camp to climb it; nor do we mean that if we look at Mount Everest while holding a ruler at arm's length we can read off its height. We *might* have agreed on either of these conventions: they would both work, given certain other stateable conditions. It seems that objective measures, like objective systems, exist only as conventional crystallizations of one out of a virtually infinite number of subjective possibilities. We shall find the same is true of our measure of complexity.

The measure of complexity is called VARIETY.

VARIETY is defined as the number of possible states of whatever it is whose complexity we want to measure.

Now the number of possible states is something to be **counted**, so the measure will be a pure number. This means that we can in principle compare the complexity of one company with another (for example), even though everything else about the two companies is different. Thus variety has the same virtue as money, when considered as a measure: it makes unlike things commensurable.

How tempting at this point (was it not?) to object instantly about the phrase 'in principle'. Who could possibly count all the possible states of a company? In practice, that is. But we do, in practice, compare the *profitability* of two companies. And if all we knew about how to do that was to say that there is a measure called money, and that everything has a cost and a value, then the comparison of profitabilities would look grossly impracticable too. It has taken hundreds of years' experience in commerce for the rules of the money game to be drawn up. They become more elaborate every year, as complexification poses new situations to describe and to regulate. And still subjectivity intervenes: thousands of accountants and lawyers devote their professional lives to the resolution of the ambiguities thereby induced. We need not only the measure, but the conventions that go with it. We shall come to them.

Then let us proceed, but circumspectly.

I shall suppose that you are sitting in a room that has an ordinary central light fitting. There is a bulb hanging there, governed by a switch at the door: it is standard equipment.

How complex is this lighting system? Please measure its variety: count the number of possible states of the system.

Did you say TWO? On or off, after all.

As a matter of fact, the bulb in this room is defunct. That is a different possible state from 'off', which would be corrected by flicking the switch, whereas this state cannot. That puts the variety up to THREE, presumably.

Having replaced the bulb, we find we still have no light. The system is turned off at the mains. Having turned on the master switch, we find that there is still no available light. It turns out that we neglected to pay the electricity bill. The variety is now FIVE: there is the ON state, and FOUR different OFF states of the system.

Well, **what** system are we talking about? With a little ingenuity, we could probably invent distinguishable OFF states that would raise the total variety to TEN — or some other number.

This 'measure' seems to be slopping about in a thoroughly unscientific way. It is not, of course: all that is happening is that we keep on changing our perception of the system. Once we agree what the system is, we shall have agreement on the variety measure. And what the system is will depend on its PURPOSE. If the purpose of the lighting system is to illuminate the home, we shall recognize all possible OFF states of the light — back to a failure at the electricity generating station. We do not want to waste time inspecting fuses if there is no supply; therefore we look out-of-doors to see if the lights in other houses are also off. But if the purpose of the lighting system is to illuminate a conversation in a borrowed office, we could well settle for a variety of TWO. If the light does not come on, move to another office. (Note that an observer of these two situations could deduce something about the purpose of the system from the way we behave.)

Now let us intervene in the single ON state that we have so far acknowledged. I am going to replace the standard on-off switch with a stepping-switch having six positions. This allows us to have average illumination, softer or brighter illumination, very bright light, or a mere glow. The sixth position is of course OFF. So now we have a variety of FIVE for ON conditions, plus as many OFF conditions as our recognition of the system itself demands.

Is this the end of the story? Then suppose that you switch to the GLOW position — and the light goes out. There are certainly TEN possible ON states, and not five — since any of the contacts may be broken. What is more, that was true of the two-way switch as well: its ON state always had a variety of two, and not one as I allowed: no doubt you noticed that... .

If all of this appears to be mere teasing, a monstrous practical joke, that is not at all how it is intended. As we shall see later, we have — we absolutely MUST have — built-in mechanisms in our own nervous system that reduce variety. If we did not have them (it must be obvious by now), we should as human beings be PARALYSED by the complexity of our environment. There would be so many stimuli to which we were attending, and therefore so many possible states of our own reactions (many of which would contradict each other), that we should be in a permanently catatonic state. The human being may well take comfort in this, since evolution has found a highly functional way of reducing overwhelming variety: it is to delimit the system that the brain takes into account at the conscious level. Therefore most people are not often troubled by visitations of angels or demons. You can change this, of course. If you take psychedelic drugs, you denature the variety-blocking mechanisms. There are other less dangerous and more profitable ways of achieving heightened awareness. The point to take is that our 'normal' state is heavily attenuated in its perception of variety, which may be restored under certain conditions to a level that is actually present all the time; it is not that variety is pumped into us from some extraneous source such as a drug. So it is for the 'normal' managerial state too. If we consider the amount of variety that a manager is in principle responsible for regulating, we can see at once that most of it is blocked off in practice. But could it be that what is functional for you, the human being, is highly dysfunctional for you, the manager? I honestly cannot conceive of a manager who could honestly say that he never in his career took an action that did not result in an outcome he had not considered as a 'possible state of the system'.

Too much honesty; too many negatives: then let us return to the elegant simplicities of the electric light. For during the questioning of the state of your soul, I altered the state of your light-switch. It has been replaced by a 'dimmer' — a rheostat that continuously varies the illumination from GLOW to BRIGHT. *Now* what is the variety of the system?

I had you saying TWO to my very first question. This time I have you saying INFINITE. You can interpose a position between any two positions, after all.

Somehow I doubt that any practical manager was caught out by that question. Infinities hardly come into practical management. One can soon see why, in this case. Setting the switch calls for coordination of the hand with the inertia of the switch's drum (and that probably has dust in it). Well, let's think. The switch goes round full circle. That is $360°$. Probably we can set the switch accurately (especially if we calibrate it) for every two degrees of arc. Then the variety is 180 — plus all the OFF states of course. And could ONE of the 180 states be a broken state, without all the others being broken too? We really have to study the system to understand it.

Finally, then, having gone through all the possible states of the fixtures and fittings, we should check on our final understanding of variety as a measure of complexity of this room's light.

You are now sitting in your room, which has a central light bulb, and you are equipped not only with a measure of the complexity of the lighting system. You are equipped with a dimmer switch, whereby you can regulate the light intensity to 180 different levels. Or so the technology of lighting *says*. How, otherwise, would you *know?*

Neither of us could possibly differentiate between each of 180 levels of light intensity. So why did we go along with a variety measure of this order? It is meaningless. I cannot invent a scenario that makes this much variety plausible — unless we are both experimenters with luminosity.

Another practical joke, you might think. Not at all. I used to work for a company that quoted its stock value — which even in those days ran into twenties of millions of pounds — down to *shillings and pence*. Not even the National Physical Laboratory could measure anything at all to this degree of accuracy. But the point is not so much that the company should have been sued for misrepresentation, though such it was, as that a measure of this kind is IRRELEVANT to any conceivable response. The addition of one penny to the stock value, the removal of one penny — it is impossible to define a system in which either shift could possibly have any operational significance. Never mind the shift of a penny, in fact. Knowing those dispersed, inaccurately recorded, rusting stocks, I doubt if a meaning could be ascribed to a shift of less than half a million pounds.

So back he or she comes into the action: the OBSERVER, who defines the system, *and* its purposes, *and* (it turns out) its variety.

As you sit in that room, I doubt if you can distinguish more than seven levels of light intensity — or possibly nine. The neurophysiological equipment is thus limited in its perceptual acuity. So it is MEANINGLESS to talk about a variety of 180 'possible states' of illumination: it is a fiction. The best that we can do is to declare a scale between the points of which there is a Just Noticeable Difference (JND). Who determines what is Just Noticeable? Only you yourself — *because you are an intrinsic part of the system.* The observer is always part of the system: he determines its nature, its purpose, its variety.

This whole issue is far from academic, of course. The relationship between management and union, manufacturer and client, government and company, parent and child, husband and wife, depends on a variety measure that registers a JND. Now it is *normal,* and not at all pathological, that each member of the foregoing pairs should be using a different variety scale, and a different JND, from the other member. The idea is familiar enough: 'you are not sufficiently *sensitive* to my changes of mood — or reaction — or strategy — or policy'. (Namely: 'I have a higher variety than you have', which is a common and usually false assumption.) But it is a long way from this familiar notion, with which we consciously try to cope, to the CONSEQUENCE. Our variety measures, with their inbuilt JNDs, are at the root of our perception of the nature and the purpose of the systems with which we deal. The contending pairs just listed tend to fall out, because they perceive the relationship that links them quite differently. One can read as much in a popular magazine. But there is little hope of doing anything about it without the variety measure that enables us to probe the mis-match of relevant complexity. That is a tool of management.

Let us now take a little time to exercise understanding of the variety measure at a more abstract level. Because the problem of complexity is bound into the world of interacting systems, the theory that we need to handle it is combinatorial mathematics. In this exercise we shall see what this *means,* without going beyond school algebra. Once again, the object is to observe the flexibility of our measure, and the astonishing range of variety that a system can exhibit — depending on the definition that we decide to use.

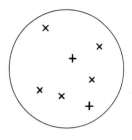

Figure 3. This exhibit depicts something-or-other: we are treating it as an abstraction. The question is: what is the variety of this exhibit?

First Answer:

The exhibit's purpose is to exemplify the appearance of a cross. Several examples of a cross are provided, so that there will be no misunderstanding. A cross is one distinctive mark selected from a huge range of distinctive marks. A cross has no other possible state than to be itself.

$V = 1$

Second Answer:

The purpose of this exhibit is to exemplify what is meant by 'number'. It is a kind of diagrammatic abacus on which we may count from one through to seven, and we may fix its state according to the population that we are counting. The abacus permits us to illustrate the advanced notion of 'nought', corresponding to a zero population.

$V = 8$

Third Answer:

The purpose is to mark seven locations, at each of which — as the system develops in time, something may either happen or not. For instance, these may be seven lights any combination of which may be lighted at any one time.

$V = 2^7 = 128$

Fourth Answer:

The purpose is to exemplify an interacting system consisting of seven elements. The number of possible states of this system is given by the number of possible connexions that can subsist between the elements.

$$V = \frac{n(n-1)}{2} = \frac{7 \times 6}{2} = 21$$

Fifth Answer:

The fourth answer does not admit that a relationship between any two elements may be directional. To connect A to B is not necessarily to mark the same relation as would be marked by connecting B to A. (That is, for example, to say that an uncle is different from a nephew.)

$$V = n(n - 1) = 7 \times 6 = 42$$

Sixth Answer:

The purpose of the exhibit is to exemplify a dynamic system in which, at any one time, any one of the directional relationships between elements may or may not be active.

$$V = 2^{42} = 4,398,046,511,104$$

or, to take note of the realities of accurate measurement that were discussed earlier, we should say:

$$4.0 < V < 4.5 \text{ million million.}$$

Certainly these six answers do not exhaust all possible systems which the original exhibit might be taken to exemplify; but they do illustrate the subjectivity with which we are forced to understand the systems that confront us, and the range of complexity which those systems may encompass. In particular, the exercise demonstrates — through the sixth answer — the well-nigh incredible explosion of variety that occurs once the system concerned is perceived to be (a) richly interconnected, and (b) dynamic — that is, unfolding its richness through time. Unfortunately for managers, ALL the systems with which they deal are both (a) and (b) systems in this sense. . . .

Having taken a large number of managers through this exercise, I know that it often terrifies them. After all, no-one was ever appointed to manage so simple a system as the one we have been studying — and already the variety generated is far beyond the human compass. Then this naturally evokes the question: how is management even possible?

Not surprisingly, managers have learned how to cope with the variety proliferation that the exercise reveals as inevitable. Here is the answer: MANAGERS DESTROY VARIETY. They *stop* variety from proliferating, basically by *preventing* interaction — which (the exercise shows) is the main cause of the trouble. Do we not 'divisionalize', do we not 'functionalize', do we not 'manage by exception' do we not 'set objectives'? All of these management devices (and many more) should be correctly seen as variety destroyers. We can easily provide all the rationalizations that explain why we do these things in terms of good accounting practice, good behavioural science, good planning, or even consideration for others. But VARIETY DESTRUCTION is what they are all FOR. It is critically important to understand this; because every move we make that constrains complexity also blocks off opportunity. As we said earlier, these quite necessary devices may turn out to be dysfunctional. The divisions that we have preclude the possible divisions that we do not have. The figures we do not see, because they were not exceptional under the existing protocol, may contain the vital information for future development. The perfect opportunity that is offered us may remain out of all consideration because it cannot be classified under the objectives that we have set. And so on.

These are hard words: but these are hard problems. And before too many hackles rise too disastrously, let me add that this dangerous destruction of variety is only half of the manager's role. The other half consists in the promotion of variety proliferation, which is dangerous too (because of those enormous numbers that are generated). So this is our DOUBLE ENTRY of variety book-keeping: it aims at *balance*, just like the accounting version. It is modelled, to quote an earlier example, by the production control see-saw. The manager is a VARIETY ENGINEER. He has not seen himself like this before, although he perfectly well knows that he cuts down on information that it is his prerogative to claim, that he puts out more information in some situations than in others, and that he manipulates the complexity of his managerial environment. He also perfectly well knows that he balances his personal inputs and outputs so as to preserve his own sanity and to make the best of his time. Then you may ask what is to be gained by viewing the whole problem in terms of variety engineering. It is because that formulation makes the whole set of processes deliberate, rather than haphazard; and because it opens up the prospect that such a set of processes, answerable to the criterion of a balance that lies within the human variety-compass of the manager, might be scientifically designed.

There will be much, much more to say about this in the rest of the book. Meanwhile, there is one more theoretical concept to introduce that will help to demonstrate how we actually deal with the management of complexity.

A manager has a number of activities under his control, and these are usually depicted on an organization chart as a series of boxes bearing labels — which are dependent from his box, bearing his label. Each of the subordinate boxes is, of course, busily generating variety. In fact, as has by now been made abundantly clear, each box is generating far more variety than the manager can possibly cope with in detail. We have already seen how management techniques have been developed to destroy whole areas of this variety. At a deeper level, however, there is a fundamental operation that has to do with the perception of system. It would be grandiose to dignify this operation as a 'management technique', although it is the strongest of all variety reducers. It is called SHEER IGNORANCE. The manager cannot possibly be aware of all the states of his subordinate boxes.

In cybernetic terminology, the nomenclature is more polite than this. We note that a box within which all possible states are observable, and therefore accountable, is *transparent*. If this is not the case, the box is *opaque*. Most of the boxes with which managers deal are not completely transparent and not completely opaque either. Let us call them MUDDY BOXES. This distinguishes them from the truly opaque boxes that are known to cybernetic theory as *black* boxes. Now managers, especially as they rise in seniority, find their muddy boxes becoming more opaque: obviously this is because they are more distant, and there are more boxes to be considered. Indeed, it is possible that any may become a truly black box. For instance, I have met directors of forty or fifty companies each, who did not know what many of those companies actually manufactured. (There ought to be legislation against this, but that is not my province.)

For the sake of exposition, then, let us talk about black boxes — considered as the limiting state of the manager's typically muddy boxes. Is it possible that we can do anything about the management, or regulation, of the performance of a truly *black* box? Well, if you have ever had a nice new baby you will know what it is like to be in charge of a black box. The first phenomena that you notice are the baby's outputs. But you are aware that you have control of the baby's inputs. So the solution is to manipulate the inputs in order to regulate the outputs. This can be done without much knowledge of what is happening inside the baby. At once it makes sense to assert (what I shall proceed to call):

The First Regulatory Aphorism

> *It is not necessary to enter the black box*
> *to understand the nature*
> *of the function it performs.*

The nature of the function can be deduced from those relationships between input and output schemata that turn out to be *invariant*.

For example, let us imagine an encounter with a black box. We watch it operate four times, and our observations are recorded in Figure 4.

There is no difficulty in inserting '26' as the missing output, because the black box is demonstrating an *invariant transformation*. The name of this transformation is 'times two'; the point is that so long as we can identify this

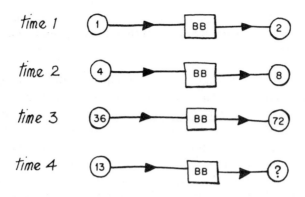

Figure 4. Four observations made on a black box.
Question: determine what the box is doing without
entering it to find out

invariance we do not need to ask how the trick is done. Technologically, there are all manner of devices that will multiply by two. Who cares which is in use? Philosophically, we are confronting a dilemma about causality; because it lies in our heritage to consider that 'every event has a cause' which we ought to be able to explain. No explanations can be offered about the internal operation of black boxes, by definition. But, in the philosophy of science, there are other treatments of invariant relationships than the postulation of causes, and this is one of them. It is in fact a pity that the customary notion of causation is buried so deeply in our culture, and it ought to have been expunged as long as two hundred years ago (when died the philosopher David Hume, who demonstrated all its weakness). Had this happened, we should not now be entrapped in so many medical dilemmas about causal hypotheses — of which tobacco as the 'cause' of carcinoma of the lung is the outstanding example. Nor, so far as management is concerned, should I have experienced difficulty in the last chapter in talking about the '80—20 law', just because I do not know what 'causes' it.

Managers in general, given a little reflection, know that they have almost no causal theory at all to underwrite their actions. But they do have experience. And the cybernetic explanation is that they treat systems as black boxes, for which they have reliable notions of the relationships between input and output schemata. It would be splended if these relationships turned out to be literally invariant, as in Figure 4, but 'reliable' is in practical terms enough.

Moreover, in real life the boxes are not wholly black, but muddy. Then this fact admits of *partial* explanations that go some way to satisfying the cultural demand to explicate the cause. Perhaps it is a pity that this is so, because it distracts attention from methodologies that do not rely on causal explanation, and because it encourages managers to disregard — in action — the First Regulatory Aphorism. They are prone to enter the box, hunting down 'causes' with the jawbone of an ass.

The point is especially relevant to the management of those *grown-up* babies, the men and women who staff the enterprise. Many managers are given to constructing theories about the 'causes' of their problems in industrial relations, which theories blind them to the input-output invariances that they might otherwise discover. Witness: 'All that interests them is the pay packet'. Witness: 'I can rely on the loyalty of my staff'. However much evidence the manager has who says such things, there is one thing he should note. His theory has reduced the variety of the human being to two (because the theory is either true or not, and does not admit of other possible states). Now human beings have very high variety. It takes a great deal of pressure to reduce that variety to two, as for example in the declarations: 'it's either you or me', or 'better dead than red'. And one of the main sources of such pressure in our society is, in my opinion, the existence of these managerial theories. The theories themselves, and especially their constant iteration, are the major factor in the polarizations that the theories are trying to explain. If, noting this, we try to become more scientific, and use behavioural science to examine our theories, that is a commendable course. It is a safe prediction that such scientific work will put back much of the variety that the theory annihilated. If, on the other hand, managers embrace the dogmas of particular scientists who pander to their own desire for such simplifications, their theories will be reinforced. Witness: 'Theory X and Theory Y'.

The *heart of enterprise* is the human being. It is the enterprise itself that reduces his and her variety. It does so by its 'rules and regulations', which may be necessary or not (and much more on this later). It does so also by projecting theories about how one of 'our people' is supposed to behave. This projection can be highly beneficial, both to the enterprise and to the individual. It can also be devastatingly destructive, when it solemnly informs people (because of a theory) that they are actually expected by the management to behave inimically to the enterprise. A useful example of the contentions of this paragraph is that enterprise called the family. It may maintain its cohesion and its values; it cannot do so by constantly *teaching* the daughter that she is a slut and the son that he is a very bad boy, through daily repetitions of these flat statements, which are made from the need to reinforce a parental theory. There are better ways of reducing proliferating variety; and they come only from self-learning.

In any case, the manager of the enterprise must try to understand what is going on. Two basic mistakes are commonly made, which are illustrated by the following example. In this case, the system is accepting its own output as its next input. This is a very usual arrangement: the previous output state of the system is a major fresh input — and this is surely *always* true of people as their lives unfold.

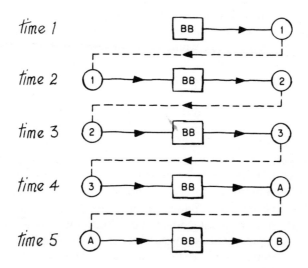

Figure 5. Five observations on a black box. Question: determine the valves of *A* and *B*

Here we begin our observations just as the black box is producing its first output — which is the value '1'. So the task is to identify the invariant transformation, and thereby to predict the values of *A* and *B*.

Now it would not be surprising if you identified the invariance by the name 'plus one', and therefore predicted $A = 4$, $B = 5$. If so, you have the wrong answer. In fact $A = 5$ and $B = 8$. What this system is actually doing (something known to me only because I designed it) is to add together its current input and its *previous* input (that is, it is exhibiting memory). There is no way that anyone 'ought' to be able to spot this because, although the evidence is there, there is not enough of it.

So the first of the common mistakes is to conclude that we understand invariance in a system without studying it for a sufficient length of time. In systems work, this says rather more than an ordinary 'don't jump to conclusions' admonition. We have to bear constantly in mind that a system is a variety generator. Therefore the sample of behaviour that we need in order to make a statistically sound judgment is very much larger than it may at first appear from the schematic lay-out of that system. Remember the exercise on seven crosses.

The second mistake is a more subtle one. I have repeatedly said that we are compelled to cut down the variety presented to us, and so far that has meant simply that information is ignored (in one way or another). Anyone who produced the wrong answer to this problem did something more ingenious than that — by ignoring information that was not there! That missing information is the input to the system at time 1. Of course this input has to be a one; if I had shown it, no-one would have made the error of thinking that this system was 'plus one' invariant. The mistake then was to assume that the first input was a nought.

It is worth reflecting on the nature of this assumption, since you may well say that you did not make it — whereas I am saying that you *did*. The impertinence vanishes when I add: you may not have made it consciously. The point is twofold. In declaring 'plus one' invariance there is a logical assumption that the first input is a nought, *whether we are aware of making it or not*. Secondly and this is especially important, we have not simply cut down variety in this case — we have added variety in the form of that missing input. We have projected our muddy understanding onto the system. In short, if the problem had been presented as it was, and the answer had been given as 'plus one' invariance, that would have been acceptable. Then suppose that you were asked tomorrow to reproduce the diagram. Remember that no attention would have been drawn to the missing input. Is there not a fair chance that you would show that missing input in the drawing, and mark it 'nought'?

The case is that we constantly take a high-variety system, slash down its variety in order to penetrate its invariance, get the wrong answer — and then project that wrong answer onto the system, which we subsequently insist is as it is not — and never was. There are two realms of life in which this process appears with bizarre frequency. The first is in politics. Before joining in a laugh against politicians, we should recall that each of us is a citizen, and has a political standpoint of some kind. . . . The second realm is inter-personal relationship. Most people seem to be extremely incautious about falling into this trap. Speaking personally, and given that hardly anything that happens any longer occasions me much surprise, I am nonetheless repeatedly astonished to hear my behaviour described and my motives ascribed by others — even close friends. In politics and in human relationships alike, we have no choice but to hold in our heads low-variety models of high-variety realities. We also have no choice but to attenuate the variety of new states of the system, since this is proliferating too fast for anyone to accommodate. Then obviously we shall make terrible mistakes in our judgments. Witness: 'How *could* a socialist government in Britain allow its economic policy to be dictated by the International Monetary Fund?' The answer is: with no trouble at all. Witness: 'All I can say is that what he has done is completely out of character'. The answer is: it isn't.

There yet remains one choice, however, that we **can** make, once we are alert to these risks. Given that incoming information has too much variety to be assimilated, and that we have no choice but to cut that variety down, we can *either* casually select aspects of the new variety generated that reinforce the low-variety model in our heads, *or* we can actively search for manifested states of the system that clash with that model, and constantly adjust it. Of course, it is far more 'comfortable' to do the former. Then the variety of the model shrinks, because the selection of inputs to it focusses more and more on its own most salient features; and this in turn leads to more astringent selection of inputs in the future, since the model in our heads tells us that many manifested new states are simply irrelevant. After this process has well and truly set in, it is only a matter of time before the unthinkable happens. It was unthinkable because the shrivelled model in our heads became incompetent to encompass it. To understand this (and perhaps variety analysis is an aid to that understanding) might be to change a vote, to preserve a marriage, to save a friendship, to cross a generation gap, or to avert a strike.

Before leaving this general consideration of variety, the measure of complexity, which we shall be using throughout the book, there is one further complication to add. In the first exercise, we experienced the proliferation of variety in a simple system (the seven crosses). The second exercise demonstrated some features of a black box treatment of variety in terms of input-output manipulation. This leaves the question of the variety *measures* that are generated by black boxes. For, if we do not enter the black box (which is the whole point), we do not understand its internal structure — and therefore its number of possible states is provisionally a function of the total variety manifested by the interaction of its input and output schemata. That is to say: a black box may relate *any* input configuration to *any* output configuration.

The mathematical rule for computing the variety of a black box is:

raise the output variety to the power of the input variety.

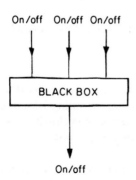

Figure 6. A black box with three inputs, and one output. Each of these has two possible states. Question: what is the total variety (the number of possible states) that the *entire system* can generate?

Now consider the question raised in Figure 6. Well, the input configuration has a variety of $2^3 = 8$. The output variety is simply 2. It looks very simple. But, by applying the rule of powers given above, we get the answer: $2^8 = 256$. If this seems amazing, it would nonetheless just be possible to write down all those possibilities. An easier trial would be to eliminate an input, yielding an input variety of $2^2 = 4$, and a total variety of $2^4 = 16$. Testing the theory is not however advisable in the second example — which treats the performance of *this* black box as an input to a *second* black box, although this too has only one input.... .

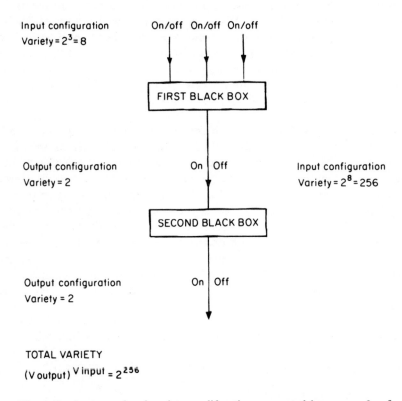

Figure 7. An example of variety proliferation generated by a **cascade** of black boxes

It is very difficult to 'make anything' of the variety value generated by this simple little cascade, as anyone accustomed to the handling of exponentials will realize. It is simply gigantic; and a lot of the space in this book would be used up in trying to write it out. Remember how far 2^{42} took us.

I chose this number more than twenty years ago to illustrate the quantification of black boxes for a particular reason, which pleases me still. A physicist might (but perhaps will not) recognize the following number — which is, thanks to the problems of accurate measurement, virtually indistinguishable from the total just calculated:

$$\frac{3}{2} \cdot 136 \cdot 2^{256}$$

This is the measure of the 'cosmical number' worked out by that great physicist Sir Arthur Eddington as the total number of fundamental particles in the entire universe. Another physicist might (but perhaps will not) take this number seriously. None the less, the number is incredibly large: the machinery schematized above is capable of giving a separate name to every particle in the universe on Eddington's showing. (Our physicist might (but perhaps will not) be as clever as Eddington was.)

At any rate, it is being demonstrated that we can measure the intrinsic variety of a black box, or even of a cascade of black boxes, by studying the mathematical implications of the interactions of their input and output schemata. Thus it makes sense to assert:

The Second Regulatory Aphorism

> *It is not necessary to enter the black box*
> *to calculate the variety*
> *that it potentially may generate.*

There are now two things to say about the gigantic numbers that have arisen in these quite simple studies. They are almost unbelievably large — yet nonetheless are advanced here as proper measures of complexity, the stuff of management. (No wonder that managing turns out to be quite difficult.)

Firstly, a reminder that the discussion concerns *dynamic* systems that 'unfold their richness through time'. When we are counting 'the number of possible states' in order to measure variety, we are not simply pointing to connectivities that might subsist between elements at a given moment. As every manager well knows, time-dependent data are generated in 'runs'. Thus the two series: 7,4,1,8,2,3,9,5,6 and 1,2,3,4,5,6,7,8,9, betoken something very different if they me⁻sure (for instance) output on consecutive days. Then the way in which systems generate their variety through time makes those systems distinguishable, one from another. This is why huge variety numbers so quickly become gigantic; but the fact of this *temporal* variety proliferation is a managerial reality, and the cybernetician defers to that.

Secondly, and although it is surely best to recognize the size of the problem that managers face, it will be remembered that there are variety reducers as well as variety generators. Some of the management techniques involved have already been mentioned. As we shall soon see, the gigantic variety totals can be slashed just as quickly as they can be generated in the first place.

For example, the cascading diagram that we have just been considering (Figure 7) might have started out as this diagram:

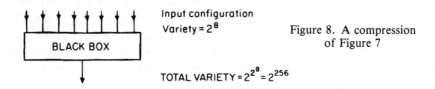

Input configuration
Variety = 2^8

Figure 8. A compression of Figure 7

TOTAL VARIETY = $2^{2^8} = 2^{256}$

Here we have the same enormous variety-generating capacity as before: since the input variety is 2^8, the total variety is 2^{256}. But Figure 7 illustrates a schema that looks more amenable to management than that shown in Figure 8. Of course it does; and that is Lesson One in the matter of the evolution of managerial hierarchies. Levels of management are introduced precisely in order to contain proliferating variety by the cascading trick.

By the same token, a manager might instinctively think of reorganizing Figure 8 in the following way.

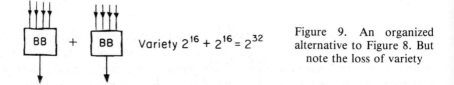

Variety $2^{16} + 2^{16} = 2^{32}$

Figure 9. An organized alternative to Figure 8. But note the loss of variety

This arrangement is also much more amenable to management, and illustrates the process of divisionalization. But we have to ask the question: how are these two chunks of the system to be combined? And we have to face the problem: where did the lost variety go — and does it matter? It was remarked before that every variety attenuating device carries with it all the dangers of misapprehension that a shrunken model of the system may project.

Surely, these are the sorts of issue that determine the nature of organization. Organization is the manager's way of engineering with variety to produce a system that is IN BALANCE. It is his Double Entry technique.

LATER IN THE BAR...

'It was just a neat pun on the title of Chapter One. Double Entry book-keeping is totally irrelevant.'

'No it isn't. He's talking about striking a balance, after all.'

'A balance between what?'

'The variety of the systems we have to manage, and... well, I suppose the disposable variety that the manager has.'

'If his numbers are right, that's a lost battle.'

'Not necessarily. He keeps on saying that management techniques slash variety as fast as nature builds it up.'

'In that case, why bother? — Why make the problem infinitely more difficult, only to say that in practice it becomes easy again?'

'It's not what you do, it's the way that you do it.'

'Joe; singing — especially yours — makes my head ache. It's supposed to be important, is it, how the variety balance is struck?'

'Evidently it is — if every blasted technique in the book plays havoc with the variety equations, which selections are we supposed to use?'

'Call in consultants.'

'You have to know the answer before you do that. Otherwise what can they tell you?'

'Drown your cynicism in this, Frank.'

'No, seriously — have you ever met a consultant who talked about measuring variety?'

'Just as well. I have enough problems with monitoring cash flow. Anyway, he hasn't told us how to strike this variety balance. The numbers mount on one side, get slashed on the other — he talks about see-saws, and this one makes me sea-sick.'

50

'*Who was complaining about puns? Good grief. There must be a way of looking at this balance. What IS it?'*

'*Damned if I know. If you haven't resigned, you're in balance.'*

'*Perhaps it's coming up in Chapter Three.'*

'*Optimist. Ah — Bill. I've had this on ice for you. Where've you been?'*

'*Thanks. Look here: I've been looking at all that phoney maths. It's* wrong!'

'*Oh God. We weren't supposed to check on the stuff were we? Can't believe anything one hears these days.'*

'*No, look. It won't take long. Fellow says 'check it with a simple example — two inputs, one output. I've done it, and it doesn't work.'*

'*As you're waving that envelope around, Bill, we can probably take it. It doesn't* look *like a thesis. Tell us all'.*

'*Well, Bob's the mathematician. I'm just your humble physicist in action.'*

'*I'm listening, Bill — even if you're* not *as clever as Eddington.'*

'*Poor old chap was ga-ga at the time.'*

'*That's what they all say.'*

'*Oh, shut up Derek. You're only a manager.'*

'*Variety Engineer. Do you* mind?'

'*Well, congratulations. That, I think, makes it your round. Bill?'*

'*Here it is, then. Two inputs, one output. Everything has two possible states. Look:*

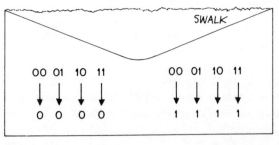

Figure 10. Marks on an envelope. The eight states of a static system having two binary inputs and one binary output

'For heavens sake, there are no more 'possible states' than that. What have I left out?'

'Pure genius, swalk. It's all there.'

'THANK you George. And lay off my love-life. Now you're the one who's supposed to understand this stuff. Then start counting.'

'Eight distinguishable states. So what?'

'So what, he says! Chapter Two says that the input variety is $2^2 = 4$. That I agree. There it IS. Then it says: 'a total variety of $2^4 = 16$'. Well, 2^4 is 16 all right — but where's the other eight? Non-est.'

'Latin, David. Your throw.'

'I don't understand a word of it.'

'There's government for you. Well, come on George, what's the answer?'

'It's my round.'

'Oh, brilliant. Don't go back to Toronto for it.'

'Well, that seems to have been conceded. Good for Bill. What say, Derek?'

'It's sixteen. I can't articulate it though. What's bothering me is why directors shouldn't direct companies just because they don't know what they manufacture. If the black box theory is right, we don't need to know — we just manipulate inputs against outputs. 'It is not necessary to enter the black box to understand the nature of the function it performs'.'

'Well learned, Derek.'

'I heard it before. What's the answer?'

'It's immoral, that's what. There are living human beings in that black box.'

'Yes; I wouldn't want to talk about manipulation.'

'Oh come now. He didn't mean it that way. He's talking about the cybernetics of input-output interaction.'

'Well, he should be more careful.'

'Now then, Tom, you're the first one to complain when he introduces technical jargon.'

'In that case, I've enough to complain about already.'

'Fact remains: he said that there should be legislation against those multiple directorships. Obviously he means they're immoral, regardless of the possible cybernetic contradiction. We have to put two and two together.'

'Does that mean $2+2$, 2×2, or 2^2?'

'A scintillating point. So happens that all of them make four.'

'You're a great help, Bob.'

'Thanks.'

'I wish to make a managerial forecast. One of those damned electric light bulbs is shortly going out. Mine. I'm tired. And so are all of you.'

'Hark at Joe. Projecting his misconception of the system on to the lot of us. Are you tired Paul?'

'Yes. I went to bed half an hour ago. And I just want to make the point that I have never projected anything on anybody.'

'If the argument was right, you can hardly have avoided it.'

'Well, I deny it.'

'That tells me that you haven't understood the argument. You're always telling me what I'm like, and I get to the point where I think I never even met myself.'

'You have little self-knowledge, Tony.'

'Dammit, Paul, there you go again — projecting your models. . . '

'Don't get paranoid about it, Tony.'

'Just because you're paranoid, doesn't mean that they're not after you.'

'That wouldn't surprise me, Bob. Nothing surprises me.'

'Now we're back to the book. He says that.'

'Pythagoras said it first: μηδὲν θαυμάζω.'

'Thank god for David's scholarship.'

'Why does nobody talk ENGLISH around here? If it isn't cybernetics, it's Greek.'

'Cybernetics is Greek, you oaf. It means 'steersmanship'.'

'Looks like you're in the wrong camp, David.'

'Steersmanship? Is that what management is supposed to be about?'

'That's precisely the allegation, you chauvinist bully. You don't think you're managing until someone has a black eye. You're a rightist.'

'Now who's projecting his simplistic model?'

'Let's not get back to those old politics, fellows, please. *Why should we barter our 'shrivelled models' of political verities here? Apparently we don't know what we're talking about.'*

'Well, I was thinking about that. Maybe the leading articles in newspapers are too consistent. *They reinforce their own models.'*

'They pander to their readers' models, more likely.'

'Either way, I begin to see the circularity in the dynamics of opinion-forming systems.'

'Phew, Bob. Actually I was thinking more about the media's influence on economics than politics.'

'Same thing. We are all monetarist middle-roaders today.'

'Is Friedman more high-variety than Keynes? The Robinson Crusoe economy is a variety attenuator with a vengeance; and no-one has got beyond that, when you get down to it. Not even Marx.'

'Especially him. *Did you see Hazel Henderson quoted as calling conventional economics 'a kind of brain damage'? Wow.'*

'What is the estimable George scribbling — when he could be drinking?'

'I have here a new back-of-an-envelope. It's marked SIXTEEN instead of EIGHT.'

'*Are you* serious*? We settled that hash ages ago.*'

'*George is always serious. Never fails. He's an* .... '

'*... We know what he is. Found something 'unfolding its richness through time', unquote, have you George?*'

'*Sarcasm noted, but that's exactly the point. Bill's envelope represents all the states of the system in a static world. The real world isn't static, and we need the time dimension to explore the behaviour of a black box or even murky box.*'

'*Well, that's true. But how will that turn Bill's eight states into sixteen?*'

'*Once time is admitted to our thinking, we can see that Bill never got as far as eight states. He only got* two. *He defined one machine that produced a zero output for all four input states, and then defined another machine that always produces a one. To say that the output is* always *zero or* always *one does not admit a time dimension at all.*'

'*You mean because* 'always'*?*'

'*Sure. You have to see this thing as cycling through time. Have a look at my envelope. There are the same four input states that Bill used — 00, 10, 10, 11 — agreed, there aren't any more. But the outputs?*'

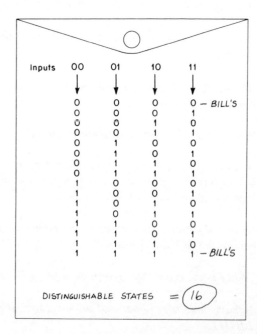

Figure 11. Different marks on a different envelope. The sixteen states of a dynamic system having two binary inputs and one binary output.

'*Bill defined two possible black boxes. All I've done is added the other fourteen. Total: sixteen.*'

'*And you had to fish out a mighty large official-looking envelope to do it.*'

'*That's just what this variety proliferation business is all about. I think George has got it. Do you accept that, Bill?*'

'*I'll need to sleep on it. I thought we were talking about output states, not whatever it is that George calls 'machines' — where did that notion come from?*'

'*Surely a black box is a machine of some sort. It transforms inputs into outputs. It needs time to run through all its possible states.*'

'*Fair enough. Must say that in my managing I get very interested in the pattern of sequential events, because my business is seasonal...*'

'*... then your black box is different in the summer and the winter.*'

'*No it isn't. It's the same black box taking time to exhibit its total variety. But you'd be crazy not to mark some of its behaviour 'summertime' if you knew that.*'

'*Sure; that would chuck away valuable information. But that wasn't the issue. All we set out to do was to measure the variety.*'

'*Yes. Good for you, George, you did it. The mathematics seems to work.*'

'*Thank you, gentlemen. And now I have news for you. I don't agree with the book's mathematics either.*'

'*But you just proved the point, George!*'

'*I showed what the book meant by its numbers. The fact is that I could easily stipulate all sorts of frameworks for the interpretation of Figures 6, 7 and 8 which would lead to different outcomes. The book chooses to consider a very special case.*'

'*Well, George, doesn't that just demonstrate that systems are indeed subjective?*'

'*I'm uncomfortable with it.*'

'*But if a black box is carefully defined as it was defined, then surely there is no ambiguity left?*'

'Sorry, Tony: I'm still uncomfortable with it.'

'Come on Bob, you mathematician: where do you stand?'

'Mathematics was called 'the queen and servant of the sciences'. It's servant for Tony, and queen for George.'

'Obviously George has more respect.'

'So where's the manager, I'd like to know? I just happen to be running a company. . . '

'Relax Derek: I'm running my airline, too. I don't think that squabbles about such large numbers will turn out to matter to either of us.'

'You're right. We are being misled by all these fun and games. The point is to get to grips with variety proliferation — wherever that takes the mathematician — and to look to the variety engineering involved.'

'Wise remark, Derek. How do we reckon to do it?'

'This stuff doesn't threaten me. I shall just read on.'

'Listen to these two! They have time to 'finish their game of bowls'. Well, I am threatened by these gigantic numbers, and I don't mind admitting it.'

'Hush-a-bye-a-baby: that's because you are a junior *manager, and not accustomed to the big league yet.'*

'That does it. I'm buying my last round. And I'll leave George to find a big enough envelope to do the 2 to the 256 display.'

'Every particle in the universe, eh? It's mind-boggling.'

'Yes. Suppose that the universe really is a black box with eight inputs and one output, and nothing more — cycling through time.'

'Well, at least that would define time.*'*

'Do you know, I've had enough. Through. Kaput.'

'I'm only sorry about George's official envelope. No SWALK, George?'

'That's all you know.'

CHAPTER THREE

Emergency exit

Variety

the measure of complexity,
itself the STUFF of modern management —
proliferates.

This is the natural law of interactive systems; and the task of the manager is to handle the proliferating variety of his muddy box. That proposition applies to the entire contents of the box, including those lovable, irritating, and all-important variety proliferators — people.

It is quite certain that managerial variety is lower than the variety of the muddy box, since the operation managed contains more activities of every kind, and certainly more people generating variety, than the management unit itself. That is why we were able to point to many management techniques directed towards reducing operational variety. We have already noted some of these methods, including the limiting case of Sheer Ignorance about what is actually happening. And we have also observed that, by manipulating the inputs of the muddy box, one may influence the outputs. This is a clever approach; because it uses all the unknown variety generators inside the box to proliferate managerial variety *alongside* the proliferation of variety-to-be-managed.

However, to do this in practice proposes a subtle problem. If the box is by definition MUDDY, meaning that its internal mechanisms are nearly opaque to our understanding, how can the management *know* which strings to pull, and how hard? In other words, there is by definition no way of establishing the appropriate input pattern — even if one is observing the output pattern. It is agreed that the box is muddy, and not black. So some things can successfully be done with insight by the management, as we all concede. The point is that such actions presuppose a transparency of the box where these transformations of variety occur. We know what those transformations are. It is again agreed that muddy areas of the box can be made transparent, by

58

undertaking special enquiries into the variety transformations concerned — *if,* in the general muddiness, we can identify which they are. (In the context of this cybernetic language, I should offer the last sentence as a very good definition of Operational Research: just because of the conditional clause.) What is *not* agreed is the very possibility of undertaking sufficiently numerous studies to clear the muddiness altogether. In managerial reality, variety proliferates too far and too fast. Then we must return to the 'subtle problem': that for those parts of the muddy system that in fact remain muddy, there is no way of deciding on an input pattern by the analysis that these definitions preclude — much as we would like to believe that there is, and often though we may behave as if we knew what it was.

Then the answer to the problem, which cannot be an analytic answer, is to operate *outside* the confines of the muddy box. To illustrate how this works, let us take the simplest muddy box system possible: it has one input and one output, although each may take on a whole range of values. The management wishes to reduce the variety of the output: it SELECTS from the set of possible output states ONE state that it seeks to hold constant, whatever the variations in the input state. This procedure is realistic, after all: a management may well decide to allow freedom to a subsidiary on condition that it maintains a specified percentage return on investment, for example. Then this diagram depicts (the beginning of) a regulatory system:

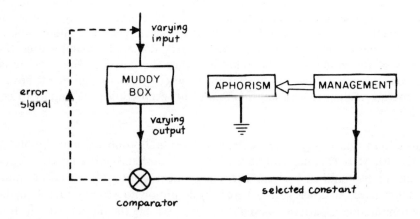

Figure 12. First draft of a muddy box regulator, intended to operate against a *standard* output — and without entering the box

The management is shown as moving off (double line) in the general direction of the muddy box that it is due to manage. It runs into the First Regulatory Aphorism:

> It is not necessary to enter the black (or in this case, muddy) box to understand the nature of the function it performs.

And so the diagram shows that approach as running to Earth. Instead, manangement selects the constant state (of all the possible output states) that it requires, and sets that up in the device $\otimes$, which is a comparator. The function of this device, not surprisingly, is to compare the actual output — from moment to moment — with the constant. Thus the comparator measures the deviation between the two, and continuously returns an error signal to modify the input.

It all looks very straightforward. I think I can hear a shout of 'it's feedback!' Yes, it is feedback. And for the rather superior person who shouted: 'it's error-controlled negative feedback', yes again. Yet I detest the odious word. Not only does it suggest vomiting; it has been adopted by all and sundry to mean simply 'a response'. Please beware. If we use the term in that colloquial sense, we shall never understand what is going on. That dotted line on the diagram appears to be capable of accounting for everything that needs to be done. If an error is detected by the comparator, then something can be done to change the input to the box... certainly it can: but only *after* the event. Once again, the static diagram suggests a static system; whereas the real system is dynamic. It takes time for the box to operate; and by the time the comparator has measured the error, a different set of input states will obtain from that which generated the error. In a sense, therefore, the error signal would appear to be irrelevant. In fact it is not, and it is worthy of a detailed illustration to understand exactly why.

Let us suppose first of all that the variation generated in the output is completely regular. In fact (although we do not have foreknowledge of this) the muddy box is generating a sine wave. Outputs are not usually this regular in management, of course; on the other hand, they usually do manifest some sort of periodicity, of which the sine wave is the simplest example. Then the regulatory system that we designed will emit an error signal that regularly alternates between the peaks and troughs. This assumes that the error is measured at consecutive time epochs (because that is the normal rule in management). It also assumes that our regulatory system will work. Then the output signal will look like this, compared against the mean level set into the comparator; and the error signals (the corrections to be made) are calculated on the diagram for each epoch.

60

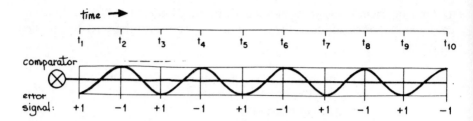

Figure 13. An output varying regularly about a mean value that is its target, showing the corrections that appear necessary at each time epoch when a measurement is taken

On the face of it, this scheme must be successful. But the system that we designed will not behave like this. That is because of the time lag. The correction is correctly measured; but by the time that it has been signalled, and become effective, the operation of the muddy box has *reversed* its output. What will actually happen, according to our rules, is this:

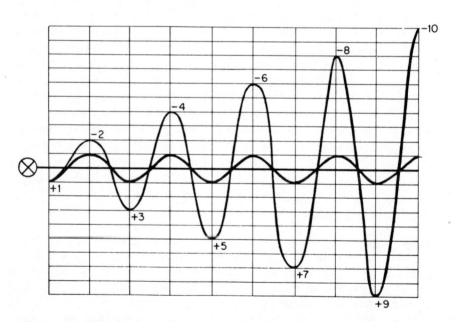

Figure 14. Explosive behaviour induced by the direct application of error corrections to a system that has meantime reversed its input states

It is a simple matter to follow this diagram through. The first correction is made as we anticipated: +1. However, by the time that the 'correction' is applied (in the second epoch), the muddy box — of whose behaviour we have no foreknowledge — has already over-corrected itself. Therefore our 'correction' is precisely *in*correct. We should be deducting, and not adding, one unit. What is worse, the system *adds* our incorrect correction to the error that it was generating in the first place. So the time series continues; and so our 'regulation' becomes worse and worse. This whole system is *exploding*.

Anyone with a knowledge of control engineering is likely to dismiss this exposition as both obvious and inadequate. Lags have to be 'smoothed', and oscillations have to be 'damped'. The techniques are understood. They *are* understood (which is what I am getting at); but only engineers understand them, and they are applied in practice only to engineering systems. The Chancellor of the Exchequer, the Treasury, and the Bank of England intervene in economic affairs without appearing to understand anything about these 'obvious' facts. As to the average manager: he often copes with this kind of thinking in transparent areas of his muddy box, such as sales forecasting. When he gets to the opaque areas, however, he usually forgets what he perfectly well knows. It is because of the mudiness; nothing any longer seems relevant. Yet it *is* relevant — the more so.

The submission here is that it was worth the manager's time to think through that alarming example, not in order to become a control engineer *manqué*, but to obtain a feel for the effect of time lags in any regulatory system. When he is dealing with routine techniques such as inventory control, he is likely to call on the design expertise required. But in so many other contexts, the formal problem exposed here may never occur to him. I suppose that this is especially true in human affairs. It takes time to devise and to promulgate 'people' policies; and the time lag involved might easily generate explosions of the sort described. This is especially true if (remember last chapter) the model-in-the-head expects aberrant behaviour that could not possibly be self-correcting (as in the sine wave); yet human responses quite typically incorporate *learning*. Think of a two-person argument. Person A, with very good reason, admonishes person B. Person B bites his lip. ('Ah, says A, no reaction, 'he is incorrigible'.) But B has gone away, and decides that A is right. Next day, B has the difficult task of trying to admit his mistake. Before he can say a word, A says: 'you again! And here's another thing... ' It is all to familiar. This system, too is exploding. Surely we can now see why — in formal, unemotive terms.

What is required is a Feedback Adjuster, as we might call it. Then our regulatory diagram will look like Figure 15.

The role of the Feedback Adjuster is, in our example, to make adjustments for the time-lag in the measurement system. If it fails to do so, the output will 'explode'; and we shall call the entire system unstable — as indeed most of our societary regulative systems *are* unstable, I fear. Why should this be so, if all that is necessary is to design the Adjuster properly to deal with time-lags? Well, apart from high-level ignorance of managerial cybernetics, it turns out that there are other destabilizing elements in the total system — and some of them are disturbances from outside. These cause enormous further variety proliferation in the muddy box and further obscure its basic problem; recognition of the existence of these perturbations is also introduced into Figure 15.

From the standpoint of orthodox control theory, these disturbances can also be handled. We list them; and we use their range of effects on the variety characteristics of the muddy box. Then the Feedback Adjuster can be designed to make all the necessary adjustments to all the expected disturbances. It simply gets bigger, and more complicated, and more expensive. The arrangement again works — if you are designing a given machine, to operate in a given environment, with a given set of purposes. This is a privilege handed to professional engineers along with their certificates of qualification; and they are lucky people. For them, our 'adjuster' is the calculable feedback function given by the characteristic equation of the system (which incorporates the time constants involved). No disparagement is intended to engineers by this remark. They are simply not asked to design control devices to stabilize systems that are not properly specified. Managers are not so fortunate: that condition is firmly stated in their contracts, albeit among the 'small print'. The tragedy is that, as a result, managers do not know how relevant the discoveries of control engineering are to their own task. It is part of the role of management cybernetics to bridge this gap.

In management, as we argued early on, the system is *not* given, and *nor* is its environment; its nature and its boundaries are uncertain. Like its purposes also, they are subjective. All this being so, it is impossible to draw up proper categories of disturbance — especially as some disturbances may come along that are utterly without precedent. We may never have heard of them before. No-one can stop the government, for example, from devising an entirely new tax. Just as we call a system STABLE once its Adjuster can handle predicted and classified input fluctuations and predicted and categorized external disturbances, so we call a system that can damp its own explosiveness in the face of unlisted uncertainties ULTRASTABLE. An ultrastable system, that is, will operate in the face of perturbations that have not been envisaged in advance — at the design stage.

The very idea of ultrastability thus defined may well seem incomprehensible at first. Once again, our culture blocks off our own creative variety. How could a computer, for example, *designed* to undertake some prosaic accounting work, possibly respond to the fact that the building is on fire? We sigh sadly. We say that its designers were not asked to take this into account. And we watch the computer, churning out payrolls to the bitter end, *melt*. If the designers had

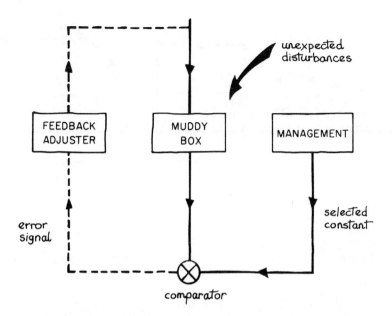

Figure 15. A new version of Figure 12, showing the damping mechanism (feedback and adjuster) needed to deal with time lags in the system — and also the existence of new perturbations from outside

been alerted to the fire risk, they could have equipped the computer with warning thermostats. But they did not know, and they did not do it. An *ultra*stable computer, on the other hand, would turn on its automotive engine when the fire came, and trundle out of the building — even though it had no thermostats. Herein lies the clue to the way that ultrastable systems work. We return to the managerial situation now, and will worry about our soggy computer later on.

It is inevitable that the Adjuster we need to achieve ultrastability cannot be specified analytically; because we do not know what are the nature, boundaries, purposes and disturbances of the system. Then we have the original 'subtle problem' that faced management in the muddy box issue all over again. Consideration of that problem led to the Earthing Aphorism in the management case, and certainly it applies here too: the Adjuster cannot enter the muddy box — it does not have the variety to make it transparent. The solution previously was to move outside the system, and to re-enter it, by feedback, in order to induce SELF-REGULATION. The solution *now* is to do the same thing, a second time. But this time we shall have to move outside the system that we designed to move outside the *original* system. . . . By doing so, we shall induce SELF-ORGANIZATION.

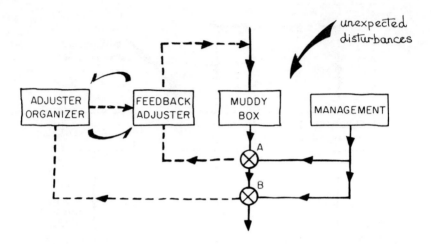

Figure 16. The regulatory system, growing from Figure 12 through Figure 15, acquires a *learning* facility

The object of the Adjuster Organizer is to *modify the design* of the Feedback Adjuster. This is assumed to be doing something to damp the oscillations of the muddy box output by the use of comparator A. For example, suppose that we are dealing with the management of a production department. The muddy box is the representation of the state of affairs that the management confronts. This representation includes accounts of the operational reality on the shop floor, of the raw material flow arriving as part of the input pattern, of the sales requirement that forms part of the output pattern. One of the management problems implicit in this representation is the control of stocks.

Now the claim might be made that we know exactly what items are in stock, what items are on order, and what items are currently on demand. By continuously updating the paperwork system, the muddy box of stockholding is rendered completely transparent. The reality is otherwise. My own first encounter with such a stockholding system, which on paper was foolproof, was concerned with stocking parts for a transportation system. Bin checks revealed many absentee items: sparking plugs, for example. Such components are easy to carry away, of course; but a deficiency of two *million* took some explaining. Moreover, the twenty-odd five-ton trucks that were 'missing' would not have been easy to carry away, past armed guards. Similarly, it is hard to account for a visible stock of ten thousand outlet manifolds to fit a vehicle that was nowhere in use, and which in consequence had neither been ordered nor received. This stockholding representation was a muddy box indeed. But it actually existed, at the end of World War 2, in India; I was the president of the Court of Inquiry. And if we ask how *could* a system designed for total transparency have become so opaque, the answer is that the variety of reality had a capacity for the proliferation of states that was totally unrecognized by the designers of the regulatory system.

Gradually, it comes to be understood that such high-variety boxes *cannot* be made transparent, and must be accepted as muddy. The development of techniques whereby reordering decisions are taken according to the level of stock present in the stock bin, constitutes a perfect example of managing a high-variety box by manipulations of the input pattern in terms of the reading taken from the output pattern. Such a device is a Feedback Adjuster. Moreover, the success of elaborate uses of mathematical statistics in these developments shows how the Adjuster can be designed with increasingly effective results — as the input-to-output relationship is increasingly revealed.

However: all that supposes that we can adequately define the inputs and the outputs themselves. We think that we can; meanwhile (remember?) the computer has *melted*. It has melted just as the cast-iron stock control system in India melted — and that was nothing to do with computers. Then how do I mean: 'melted'? Well, for instance, all but one of the signatures on the bin cards (in that example) were applied by rubber stamp. The only signature that appeared in ink, and it appeared on all the bin cards, was on the part of a single Officer Commanding. Naturally, I tried to trace *him*. It turned out that he had indeed been appointed to command the depot, but had fallen ill on the way, and had never arrived.

Now it is no use saying: what is all this about computers that melt, and about officers who sign bin cards when they were never on site — as if that were at all unusual. It is *normal* to management that the system, including its feedback adjuster, does not work, although we have shown that it should work. The reason is perfectly clear. The proliferating variety of the system swamps the variety of the regulatory devices. If this were not so, vice of every kind would not be the major contributor to the Gross National Product — which it probably is, although it is not adequately measured.

If a regulatory device works (and we have both seen some work), and if it gradually converges on a smooth performance (which we have both seen happen), we can infer that the Feedback Adjuster is steadily acquiring an adequate representation inside itself of the input-output relationship. The fact points to a most important insight. It is that regulation presupposes a representation of equivalent variety in the regulator as is exhibited in practice by the muddy box configuration. But this will not be the total variety that the box is capable of generating. If it were so, the box would be transparent to the regulator — and we already know that it is not. So *that* is why the Feedback Adjuster needs behind itself an Adjuster Organizer. 'Something-or-other' has to oversee the process whereby the Adjuster is coping with the time lags. And that something-or-other is modelling the whole system with which the Feedback Adjuster is trying to cope.

All right. What then happened to the melting computer that trundled out? It had in itself a Feedback Organizer. Nothing in the melting computer was competently designed to recognize fire. The physical equipment had no thermostats. What it did have was an *internal* organizer program, intended to recognize that something is wrong. When the fire began, various Organizer subroutines did not perform properly. The machine recognized the fact. It had no concept of 'fire', no sensors for 'temperature', and no explanations. But it did have a higher-order program that said: *get out of here*. That is why it 'trundled off'. That machine was ultrastable.

If management were not ultrastable in this exact sense, no enterprise would last a thousand days. The managerial consequences are familiar to managers in the fact that they know what it is like to circumvent the advanced techniques of control for which they have expensively paid. They are functioning as Adjuster Organizers themselves.

When disturbances arise from sources external to the feedback circuit (as our last diagram envisioned), a higher variety is released in the muddy box than the regulator can accommodate. Therefore the regulator breaks down. All too often, the manager's reaction is to complain that the people who installed the regulator (that is, designed the Feedback Adjuster) did a faulty job, and to remove the offending arrangements. But our enquiry reveals that it is the *management* system that is at fault. It is obvious, from the variety equations involved, that the Adjuster needs continuous monitoring as to its own design. That is the role of the Adjuster Organizer. We need an arrangement that will create the learning machine depicted in the last diagram. And now it is clear what the role of this machine has to be: it is to modify the design of the Feedback Adjuster (as was noted earlier) so as to accommodate a higher variety representation of the muddy box. How much higher? Just that much higher as will permit the incorporation of whatever extra variety is induced in the muddy box by disturbances that are external to it. . . .

There are two approaches to this problem in cybernetics, and both are reflections of the equivalent problem that arises in the evolution of biological systems. The first says that there should be a mechanism (which we are calling the Adjuster Organizer) which *continuously experiments* with the design of the Adjuster. It reinforces design features which tend to have beneficial effects at the output stage, and quenches design developments which tend to have deleterious effects. In this the proposed mechanism operates like biological 'natural selection' conceived in its elementary form. We simply have a 'mutant gene' in our design; we reinforce success, and punish failure. This approach has indeed been used in the management context (it began with the Box-

Jenkins techniques for evolutionary development of a regulator, and there are now many control engineering designs for *adaptive* regulators).

However, there is a big problem implicit in this approach when it is considered as a general answer to the management issue that we address. It is that *random* experimentation takes too long to achieve convergence between the representation of the muddy box in the regulator, and the performance of the muddy box under disturbance. The varieties do not match. I have made calculations that indicate this fact in the processes of biological evolution (see *Decision and Control,* John Wiley, 1966, pp.363-5), and I have demonstrated the fact on a number of experimental cybernetic machines. Therefore I have not even attempted to apply random experimentation with Adjuster design in an actual management situation. The cybernetics of the enquiry indicate that it would not work; so to try it would be irresponsible.

Meanwhile, however, the biologists were confronting the same difficulty in giving an account of evolution, and produced the second approach. This was due to C. H. Waddington (see *The Strategy of the Genes,* George Allen and Unwin, 1957), and he spoke of an 'epigenetic landscape' in which the experimentation is supposedly set. A flat genetic landscape (as it were) would have to rely on totally random mutations in genetic design; but an epigenetic landscape would *predispose* the Adjuster Organizer (as we are calling it) to particular, rather than random, experiments. They would still have unpredictable outcomes, but the variety of those outcomes would be very much constrained. This landscape is to be imagined as a set of hills and valleys laid out (like a sand model) on a large table. If we drop a ball onto this model, it might roll to the edge of the table at almost any point on its perimeter. But its path, and therefore its destination, is now biased by the landscape of hills and valleys. Thus 'random' experiments with the ball-throwing have a much reduced variety — and a much better chance of succeeding in evolutionary terms.

Epigenesis stands for the *accretion* of design beyond the merley developmental process. Waddington's 'landscape' provides an image (with its hills and valleys) of this prior build-up of an evolutionary terrain — before the random experiment is made, and onto which the experimental die is cast. How could this landscape have come into existence? It demands a *different order* of response to the muddy box than the one we have been considering: an order of perception that takes account of the disturbances that are external to the muddy box, and hence are beyond the capacity of its management to formulate. In biology, this is readily regarded as the development by accretion of the genetic characteristics of the *species*. The 'experiment' of making a new individual, which involves a random pairing of chromosoes from the parent individuals (and may or may not involve a mutant gene), is preconditioned by the epigenetic landscape. It cannot be accounted for solely on the level of the experimental coupling itself.

This approach makes sense of the variety computations with which we are dealing — in biology *and* in management. It is a matter of observation that the experiments made by the manager of the muddy box with the design of his Feedback Adjusters are preconditioned by a different level of organization. We should ordinarily say that there are higher-level ordinances to be observed, or that 'the company has made certain provisions', or at the least that there exists an institutional ethos, which provide the 'epigenetic landscape' of managerial experimentation in the organization of itself. And we should ordinarily say that this is what the notion of managerial hierarchy actually *means*. But our enquiry suggests that what we ordinarily say to account for hierarchy ('the boss is the boss') is extremely naive. The species does not 'tell' the individual what to do. And in real management, we do not observe the ordering-about that the naive view of the organization chart projects. When this is realized, people often say: 'well, we are civilized; matters have to be settled by consent; but in the limiting case, 'the boss is the boss'; therefore the meaning of hierarchy is fundamentally the exercise of command — even though commands are rarely issued in the event'.

I believe that this is completely false in Western society today. Furthermore, on the occasions when I have observed commands to be issued in circumstances where those commanded did not want to accept those commands, they were *never* obeyed. (Notice that this formulation excludes, for example, the operation of the armed forces in action. Then there is agreement that commands should be obeyed. This agreement does not necessarily extend to peacetime, especially in the higher eschelons of military management.) On the contrary, our enquiry suggests that the role of the 'higher' level is to express a perception of the scene observed by the 'lower' level, that is actually inaccessible to this 'lower' level. That is why the 'higher' level is able to formulate the epigenetic landscape. Moreover: the 'higher' level has a language to talk which is of a different *logical* order from the language of the 'lower' level. This is partly because it has a way of observing the impact of external disturbances on the 'lower' muddy box, and accounting for what is happening in its own language — whereas the only words for these shocks that are available in the 'lower' language are such as 'OUCH' and 'HELP'. And it is partly because it is the recipient of a landscape from *its* 'higher' order, which (naturally) cannot be transmitted to its 'lower' order — because it would have no meaning there.

Well, we cannot go on denying that the higher level in a managerial hierarchy is actually *higher* by writing 'higher', or denying that the lower level is actually lower by writing 'lower'. The 'higher' level is characterized not by its capacity to command, but by its order of perception and its order of language in logic. (It is because of this reliance on these perceptions and this logic that it sometime exercises its 'right' to command. But there go the quotation marks again. . . and that is why the commands are often disobeyed.) A better account of the 'higher' level is to call it METASYSTEMIC to the 'lower' level. 'Meta' means 'over and beyond', referring to the perception and the logic, and not to Seniority. As the book proceeds, a way of dealing with systems embraced by metasystems will be developed. The reader will have to judge at the end whether this approach disposes of the notion of hierarchy in the accepted sense. I think that it does; but it is a vexed point, and it is well to be alert to it from the start. In the meantime, with whatever feelings of discomfort, I shall often have recourse to the concept of hierarchy — because it is endemic to management's own thinking, and it will take time to develop the promised alternative.

At the end of the last chapter we saw how a black box could readily be designed to generate variety roughly equivalent to Eddington's cosmical number. This can be done by feeding eight binary inputs into a box with a single binary output. Then the task that faces the management of that box is immense. It was better, therefore, to approach the matter as we did, using *two levels* of black box. The box higher up the page was not conceived, nor was it presented, as Senior in the ordinary managerial sense. It was conceived and presented as a function (which we may now call metasystemic) whereby the task of managing the muddy box would be reduced to manageable proportions. The demonstration was then called: Lesson One in the matter of management hierachies.

We have just been considering Lesson Two. It says that the managerial task of creating an Adjuster Organizer cannot be accomplished as a developmental activity at its own perceptual and logical level, without a metasystemic input. This input operates, not as a set of commands, but as the derivation of an organizational landscape. This will precondition, though not determine, the work of the Adjuster Organizer in continuously monitoring the design of the Feedback Adjuster.

Here is a further point, couched in terms of variety engineering. The input channel from the metasystemic landscape to the Organizer provides the extra variety (having to do with external disturbances to the muddy box) that the Organizer needs in order to enrich the variety of the Feedback Adjuster. Only thus can the representation of the total behaviour of the box inside the Adjuster provide sufficient variety to meet the regulatory demands of the box itself. (Please recall this point when we shortly come to consider the status of the Adjsuter's model of the muddy box.)

So: the Feedback Adjuster *reduces operational variety* in the representation of reality that constitutes the muddy box. The Adjuster Organizer *induces organizational variety* in that regulatory process. It is a learning device.

To set up a metasystem that will elucidate all of this in our developing diagram is to take an hierarchical step. This is exhibited in part by the vertical separation of muddy boxes at two levels (as we did before, breaking up the eightfold input of the cosmical number system), and in part by providing a regulatory device on the horizontal plane that takes the feedback system (already provided) *outside* the existing management arrangements and into the metasystem through the organizational landscape that it provides.

Thus the diagram which follows at Figure 17 is simply an amalgam of the two-level cosmical number organization structure, and the last of our muddy box management structures, to which is added the landscaping facility provided by the metasystem in the light of its view of the impact of external disturbances on the muddy box itself. The connexions are marked by a dotted line. Finally, a direct connexion is shown (it surely exists) between the actual managers at each level. This is the interpersonal relationship between the 'boss' and his subordinate; here then will be found such 'commands' as may exist.

This final diagram depicts, inside the heavily marked box, something that shall in future be referred to as a MANAGEMENT UNIT. Its fundamental characteristic is that it treats the proliferating variety of its representation of the world it manages as a muddy box, and regulates it by manipulating the inputs in relation to the outputs. This it does by means of a special class of feedback system — which we studied in the example of stock control. In fact, *whatever* outputs of the muddy box require regulation (the delimitation of acceptable variety) will use this method. Therefore the task of management, which is not to dive into the opaqueness of the muddy box, is to design these Feedback Adjusters, and to determine the performance characteristics to which indeed they adjust. These (the 'constants' of our earlier discussion) may be at least partly prescribed, as the diagram shows, by the metasystem. For instance, it is a metasystemic remark to say to the management unit: 'a minimal return on investment of x per cent is expected', or to say: 'people retire at the age of 65 at the latest'. But we shall have more to say about these restraining policies later. The meaning of the dot that breaks the line between management units where the selection of constants is concerned, is that *some* of the criteria for selection may be received from the metasystem.

The other feature of this exposition is the arrangement whereby the Feedback Adjusters are made adaptive. This involves Adjuster Organizers: and we have observed that these require input from an organizational landscape formulated at the metasystemic level. It is easy to see that current management practice conforms, in some vague way, to this expectation. Surely any manager would agree that he has a major responsibility to check that his methods of regulation remain relevant. Surely he would agree that they can be continually improved in an evolutionary way. Surely too, he would agree that the principles (or the *mores,* or the acceptable bases, or even the precise models) prescribing how this organizational task should be approached are available to him from the 'boss' — who may in turn receive them from some other management unit of

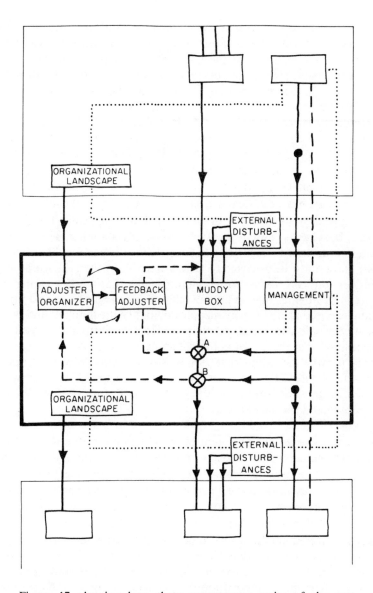

Figure 17. showing how three management units of the sort described, are arranged in an hierarchical cascade in which all mechanisms and all vertical connexions are invariant. The diagram exhibits organizational recursiveness

the institution. But this manager will surely *not* use the nomenclature developed here, and he will surely *not* perceive these responsibilities as variety engineering. Yet such it is. Obviously, both the nomenclature and the variety engineering concept are proposed as helping to formalize what the organizational task really is, and as offering an approach to its satisfaction.

The fact is that however strongly the hierarchical structure operates, which is to say however much the individual manager at his own level reads out his organizational landscape from the boss's handed-down world-view, *nothing* can save that manager from his personal obligation to regulate his own muddy box — which is the model-in-his-head of the operations for which he is responsible. Some pages ago, something then called 'a most important insight' was offered, appertaining to this task. It said that 'regulation presupposes a representation of equivalent variety in the regulator as is exhibited in practice by the muddy box configuration'. There the point was let go, but it needs reiteration. Here is a second way of stating the point. No regulator is competent to regulate anything beyond the real-world projection of the model it contains. This has been demonstrated cybernetically. Like all truths, once stated, it appeals to the intellect; but it does not much appeal to the managerial emotions, because its consequences are thoroughly alarming. The controls we institute are devised to regulate what we *think* the world is like. Since that representation must be expected to have lower variety than the world actually proliferates, the controls are often circumvented. (As we saw earlier, this is nowhere more obvious than in human relationships.) So why should the whole question be raised again? Firstly, people do not like the thought, and therefore forget it. Secondly, to point out that Feedback Adjusters are based on the presupposition that the model in the regulator is of adequate variety, which is probably not the case, and that *this* is why we need Adjuster Organizers. Thirdly, to fertilize the ground for the next chapter, wherein we shall encounter the most important law of cybernetics — of which this present issue is no more than a special case.

Our entry to the question of organization, not to mention our double entry, propounded equations of variety generation and variety reduction of frightening magnitude and fiendish quantification. Our emergency exit from this scene is the organization of a management unit which can cope with both. It is moreover a *general* solution to the problem of managing black (or muddy) boxes, without diving into them — and, as a result, vanishing from sight (or emerging covered in mud). A very important conlcusion indeed is enshrined in this generality; and it is exhibited in Figure 17, in that each of the three boxes is structurally identical. It is central to the total thesis of this book; and we shall meet this concluding demonstration again later in an ever more powerful context.

Consider the familiar appearance of any organization chart. It looks something like Figure 18.

The contention of generality for the arguments of this chapter is firstly that every one of the twelve boxes illustrated here shares *the same* organization. Clearly this is completely untrue in the terms usually adopted to describe an institution. We are working towards a description of the enterprise in which it is true. And that will be a cybernetic truth, elicited from fundamental considerations about the nature and the quantification of systems. Secondly and this is the less obvious fact, the vertical connexions between A, B, and C above (or of any hierarchal subset) are also identical. They may be studied on the preceding diagram. That is to say that B is C's metasystem, and A is B's metasystem. The same would be true, however far down the page we projected the chart: box X would be the metasystem of box Y, which would in turn be the metasystem of box Z. This assertion can be checked by examining the set of connexions that *link* the three boxes depicted on the full-page diagram. They are identical.

Now if, as has been repeatedly averred, the stuff of management is complexity, and the task of management is to handle proliferating variety, this generality of box-organization and interconnectedness is a massive variety reducer. It means that whatever variety-handling learning-machines we can devise to ensure the adaptability of management regulation are universally applicable in their structure — regardless of their context. It means that whatever variety-handling computer programs we can write to filter the variety passing between systems and their metasystems are universally applicable to the interactive channels — regardless of the nature of the information that needs to be passed.

Hence: if anyone feels a need to justify the expenditure of his or her effort to pursue this cybernetic exposition of organization, s/he is likely to find it in massive economy.

The principle of organizational and interactional invariance is called RECURSIVENESS. Each level of organization is a RECURSION of its metasystem. Let us establish the word now, because it will be a part of our vocabulary by the time the book is finished.

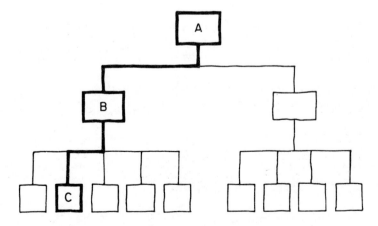

Figure 18. Typifying the orthodox 'organization chart'

LATER IN THE BAR...

'Is all this supposed to be about Management Information Systems?'

'He hasn't mentioned 'information' once. Only 'variety'. Is that supposed to be the same thing?'

'Can't be. If variety measures the number of possible states of the system, that doesn't tell me whether our subsidiary in Croynge has made a profit.'

'But its all about numbers — numbers that we have never even measured. Information isn't like that in my book.'

'Oh well; my guru is Russell Ackoff, and his key paper on the topic of MIS is called 'Management Misinformation Systems'. He's right. I provided myself with just one of those, at vast expense.'

'I sympathize. Surely, if variety measures the number of possible states of the system, management information tells us which of the possible states currently obtains.'

'I agree. The system managed continuously selects a particular, measurable configuration out of its variety, and we — managers — want to know what it is.'

'I should have thought it was our job to make the selection. You're abdicating, Tony.'

'Oh no. Our model-in-the-head doesn't have the regulatory variety to make the selection. The system will adopt a posture from moment to moment as a result of many muddy factors — of which managerial action is one.'

'Fair enough: then when we don't like the selection that the system has made, we use all these feedback loops to try and change it. That's not abdication.'

'Well, management information is a very... antiseptic thing, in that case. It just tells you which state the system has selected. What happened to the idea that management information had to be designed to supply the manager with the knowledge he needs to take a decision?'

'That's how we got to misinformation systems. It supposes that some pixie in the machinery understands all about purposes —'

74

'And about all the variety transformations that are actually muddy. I like Sid's notion of 'antiseptic' information that doesn't claim to do more than indicate the selection made from available variety. A sound, cybernetic notion.'

'Will you be any better off with measures of variety, Frank?'

'Don't know yet. There's something in it, but why does this godforsaken word 'cybernetics' keep coming in?'

'It's in the title of the book, that's why.'

'There's got to be a better reason.'

'Cybernetics. κυβερνῆτης. It's Greek...'

'Not AGAIN, David — for heaven's sake.'

'Well, you asked. It means 'steersman'. Presumably we're reading an organized knock against the idea of command.'

'The steersman needs a commander — or where the hell are we going?'

'The steersman won't take us there if he doesn't agree with the destination.'

'Then beat him to death.'

'— Theory X or Theory Y?'

'Theory Z. I'm fed up with this pussyfooting. Let's damn well MANAGE.'

'The steersman manages very well. We get there.'

'He points the boat to the desination. If the wind and sea move the prow off beam, the steersman moves the rudder until the prow is on beam again.'

'GOT it: that's why all this stuff is non-analytic.'

'Rhubarb. These days you put it all into a computer. That's analytic enough for me.'

'But it just isn't analytic. Analysis would mean computing the effects of the moon and the wind and so on, and calculating the effect on the ship. That's just not possible.'

'But it is possible to compute the position of the ship, and to calculate a course that offsets the effects of wind and sea.'

'Sure. That's a computerized steersman. Not an analyst.'

'Back to square one.'

'No, I don't think so. The steersman treats the boat as a black box, and manipulates the input-output relationship by adjusting the rudder. He doesn't dive into the sea, and try to understand it analytically.'

'Oh well: this is where the famous BALANCE comes in. The steersman is a balancer.'

'We are assured that all this is only an Emergency Exit.'

'I'm off towards it. Goo'night.'

'Night Bill. Seriously, David, is this steersman — the cybernetic bit — actually part of the language?'

'Guess so, by now, David. It's in the dictionaries. Coined by the mathematician Norbert Wiener in the early forties'.'

'Homework, Jim!'

'You're telling me. It's well written-up you know.'

'Well, I don't know about that. I do not know that the Greek $\kappa\upsilon\beta\epsilon\rho\nu\hat{\eta}\tau\eta\varsigma$ got transposed into the English governor, through the Latin gubernator.'

'That's the steersman again, David, isn't it? I'm an engineer after all; and the governor on an engine modifies its speed by feeding back excessive revs to cut off the fuel supply. It's a classic case of the input-output relationship. The engine governor doesn't ask why the engine is racing. That's a black box.'

'As a manager, I damn well insist on knowing why.'

'You're fooling yourself, Frank. What you get is a post-hoc rationalization — which it costs money to devise for you.'

'Thank's very much. If David has finished explaining the philiological, or is it etymological, origins of the word cybernetics —'

'I haven't. Ampère, him of the Amps, used 'la cybernétique' in his classification of all knowledge, to stand for the Science of Government.'

'That's more than the French mean by it now, I can tell you. La cybernétique is their passport to technocracy. It's all about engineering: control, you know.'

'*Same goes for the Russians. The Americans too, I suspect, even though they may have* started *the subject — with quite other insights, and quite other intentions.*'

'*Have you ever read the original papers on cybernetics — by Norbert Wiener and the others? Or even the other writings by our present author? To a man, they are ANTI-technocracy.*'

'*Well, it doesn't sound like it. These boys want to computerize us all out of existence.*'

'*Coming from a banker, Charles, I find that extremely funny. And since you're* my *bank, I'll withdraw the jocularity.*'

'*Banks are no worse than anyone else. We certainly avoid techocracy. We remain concerned for the individual.*'

'*Charles: which bank do you patronize, for God's sake, if it's not a rude answer?*'

'*I'll ignore that. Richard has been sunk in his beer for twenty minutes. Are you all right?*'

'*I'm thinking over the philosophy of science angle on all this stuff. You can falsify an hypothesis by a single counter instance. Right?*'

'*Right. Counter instance of what?*'

'*If this bold, bad, and doubtless unjustifiable claim to generality in the organization of the management unit and its above-and-below connexions were valid, it would mean that no enterprise could ever be taken-over by another institution and maintain its identity.*'

'*Then the claim is absurd.*'

'*I sure* hope *it is. As you know, my little firm is in the process of being taken over. I have been* guaranteed *the preservation of my show's identity. Why did Richard say it won't work?*'

'*I didn't. I said that it wouldn't work if the claim were valid. The point is that if a taken-over show is sucked into a homogeneous organization as described, it will acquire a metasystem, and become a metasystem in its turn. Then it couldn't act individualistically.*'

'*Huh! In that case the claim probably* is *valid. I've been through this FOUR times. Guarantees! In each case, even the* name *of the taken-over company had been lost in six months. Despite the calculated 'goodwill' that the take-over economics ascribed to the value of those names.'*

'No doubt the consultant among us has seen it all...'

'I've seen what I've seen. Has anyone wider experience?'

'In a way I have. You know I'm an historian by origin.'

'And you run a mail order operation. Where does that get us?'

'Well, as an historian, I remind you of the Act of Union.'

'Selling pornography by mail order, are we?'

'I am thinking, he said with deliberation, of the debates in the last parliament of Scotland, when union with England was approved. Speeches were made to say that in all of history, the nation that acquiesced in a Federation lost out, and that Scotland would do the same. It would be swamped; centralized.'

'Hell, that happened — or we wouldn't have the devolution issue now. When was this?'

'1707. But I did say that the speeches at the time called the whole of history in evidence.'

'Has no—one *Richard's famous counter-example?'*

'What about Europe — the EEC?'

'We don't know yet do we? But I'm sure it will prove to be a counter-example. Otherwise I wouldn't have voted for it.'

'Didn't you vote for the European Community?'

'Of course not. I had *read the speeches. And I observe the outcome for the Scots. The speeches were spot-on.'*

'As an Englishman, I'm worried.'

'As a Welshman, I'm laughing.'

'You can't beat the metasystem, so long as its there.'

'But it's not supposed to command.'

'*Much more subtle. I'm waiting to see what the mechanism is. Must be one.*'

'*Meaning that you accept this outrageous claim to generality?*'

'*You wanted a counter-example, Richard. No-one's got one. In all history it seems. Certainly not in my own experience.*'

'*Maybe Quebec. It's playing hell. Right, George?*'

'*Right. Seems to me that supports the cybernetic case.*'

'*Why? They — the Quebecois — may well separate from the Canadian Federation.*'

'*If so, they won't be part of it any longer, will they?*'

'*What's your comment, David?*'

'*My lips are sealed.*'

'*They always are, aren't they, when it comes to any practicality of government. You're the one who can instruct us all about the origins and nature of cybernetics, but you're never willing to draw the consequences.*'

'*Have to keep an eye on my masters, old chap.*'

'*Look, I'm lost. And I must say that all this idea of generality worries me no end. My business is unique. No-one is going to convince me otherwise.*'

'*Meaning you can disobey universal laws? It's like saying that your uniqueness means that if you drop a glass it won't shatter on the floor.*'

'*We haven't had anything like the law of gravity yet.*'

'*Well, wait and see. The arguments so far certainly seem equally applicable to all the institutions I know, and that's quite a lot.*'

'*Occupationally unstable, Tony?*'

'Recursive, *that's what.*'

'*You play the same role wherever you are? And disaster supervenes.*'

'*That's no accident. He steers them to disaster.*'

'*I'm tired. What are you thinking now, Richard?*'

'*About the variety of the representation being necessarily reproduced in the regulator.*'

'*Is that actually right?*'

'Every Good Regulator of a System must be a Model of that System.'

'*You don't make it right by sounding pontifical, Sid.*'

'*Don't be an idiot. I'm quoting the title of the relevant paper. Its by Roger C. Conant and W. Ross Ashby — in the* International Journal of Systems Science, *1970.*'

'*How impressive. You've been checking up.*'

'*Well, I wanted to know. The thing's a mathematical proof all right. Bourbakian set theory: very difficult.*'

'*So we have to buy it. Does it say anything else than the title says?*'

'*It ends: 'There can no longer be question about* whether *the brain models its environment: it must'.*'

'*We're all very subdued. But it makes sense, doesn't it?*'

'*I'm not subdued. So what, is what I say.*'

'*Don't you see Peter, that it means we can only control a system to the extent that we understand it. We think we're in control; but all we're controlling is the projection of the model-in-our-heads. If that isn't a good fit to whatever is out there, we're useless.*'

'*Maybe whatever is out there is too high variety . . .*'

'*It's a shattering thought for any manager who expects to have simple, cheap regulators.*'

'*Yes. I'm remembering all the simple, cheap control systems that I've set up in my time. All of them grew and grew, and ended up on computers. Simple and cheap? You're joking.*'

'*At least that suggests that the argument's correct. You have an Adjuster Organizer working for you.*'

'Hey, that's right...'

'Well, if it all gets out of hand, you can always use the COMMAND channel — which doesn't actually exist...'

'Oh, BLAST it. They've closed the bar.'

'So the command channel does exist.'

'And, as usual, it's misapplied.'

CHAPTER FOUR

The exit

It is given in the nature of things that interactive systems proliferate variety at a thoroughly alarming rate.

- And we have seen that the black box treatment offers a managerial approach to controlling these explosions of variety.

- We have also noted that a great many standard management techniques are basically dedicated to the reduction of variety.

Even so: if it is *nature* that is so organized as to proliferate variety at a thoroughly alarming rate, is there no *natural* answer to the problems so generated? Nature, as far as we know, does not appoint managers. And yet, in the words of the tombstone inscription called *Desiderata,* three hundred years old: 'No doubt the Universe is unfolding as it should.' How so? Why is the Universe not instead totally chaotic in our eyes?

We entered, and double-entered, the problem. The managerial exits we have uncovered, devised on the part of the managers who were not appointed by Nature, are clearly therefore no more than Emergency Exits. Where is *the* Exit, that Nature indicates?

Yes, indeed, there is one. Like everything else that matters in the Universe, the answer is wholly apparent. It is in front of our eyes and under our nose: just like the Holy Grail. It is lying around on every highway and under our feet: just like the Philosopher's Stone. We do not see and smell it, we do not touch it and fall over it, because we do not understand what we are seeking.

If humankind had known that it sought a *law of gravity,* it would have known it in the fall of a leaf, the weight of a load. It would not have waited for Newton.

If humankind had known that it sought a *law of relativity,* it would have known it in the relative perceptions of reality that have been manifest between Eastern and Western philosophy for two thousand years. It would not have waited for Einstein.

And if humankind had known that it sought (or if you, the management man, had known that you seek) the *law of requisite variety,* it would have known it in every transaction of complexity since before the pyramids were built — and you, my reader now, would have elicited it already from this very book. It would not have waited for Ashby.

It did wait for Ashby; and after thirty years the Law of Requisite Variety is still not understood, while Ross Ashby is dead. Never mind: a cosmic joke lies behind all this. It took a long time (two hundred years) for Newton's gravity to be properly understood; only then could Einstein amend it. It is taking a long time (sixty years so far) for Einstein's relativity to become part of civilized currency; and the signs are already written into contemporary physics as to *its* imminent amendment. Well, Ashby's Law is certainly within the currency of cyberneticians, who profess the science of effective organization. But what of the managers, steersman all, who practice cybernetics as their *profession.* They have mostly not heard of it yet.

Then WHAT IS IT?

Please, please be patient. If the physicist, offering to expound gravity, declared: 'Look what happens when you leave go of this glass!' then the listener who had never heard of gravity (such as an aboriginal) would surely reply: 'It is smashed. So what?' He knows, but does not know. If you have read these pages so far, you know the Law of Requisite Variety. The question is. . . .

Let us approach the whole matter freshly. It is as if I were holding up the glass and asking what would happen if I dropped it. Be cautious; be sophisticated; we are not aboriginals. Nor, unhappily, are we any longer childlike. Here then is the glass that I am holding up:

> We are building a whole community project — shops, houses, libraries and the rest — of bricks.

> Many, many bricks are involved. The variety of the project, as measured by the number of possible states of the possible number of bricks, is overwhelming.

> Even so, we could count the number of bricks. The number, though vast, is finite — and, indeed, definite. Each of these

bricks has to be *laid:* it must be individually plastered with mortar, individually set in place. Then the counting of the bricks is perfectly feasible. We could easily set up an auditing requirement to check on the number of bricks.

But we do not actually count the number of bricks at all. When the project is finished, even, no-one has the faintest idea of the countable but uncounted number of bricks that are in place.

In that case, how is it possible that the *correct* number of bricks has been laid, and that *each one* has individually been plastered with mortar and *correctly* positioned?

Given the absence of any management information system to regulate this, and the absence of any auditing, is it not *unbelievable* that the number of bricks used will be exactly right?

I repeat that not before the start of the project, not during the operation of building, and not after the project's completion, does a living soul know the number of bricks. He never will.

Then an innocent child might suspect that there will surely be a brick-sized hole in a wall somewhere; or that there is an extra brick sticking out somewhere. How could anyone *guess* such a large number as this number of bricks, and not make a mistake, even of *one* brick? A scientist, in his own childlike fashion, might point out that the error of one brick out of many millions could not even be measured. Both he and the child conclude that it is inevitable that at least one brick too few or too many has been laid.

You and I know that this is not true. All the bricks are there: not one more, not one less.

It is an astonishing fact of nature that the glass falls to the floor when I drop it. We know, of course, that the apple when dropped from the tree falls onto Newton's head. It is also an astonishing fact of nature that not even one more or one less brick than is needed happens to be laid in the building project. We know, of course, that to lay a brick the bricklayer covers it with mortar.

To comprehend either situation involves the perception of an attribute of nature: something that infallibly occurs in circumstances that can be *generally* defined within the limits of a stated knowledge and experience. The gravity example is familiar; the bricklaying example is not. Let us try to penetrate to the natural attribute involved by thinking carefully through these propositions:

- each brick laid has a bricklayer;

- the bricklayer contains the variety of each brick, which could in principle be laid in many postures, be put in a wrong place, or left out;

- the variety of the brick-built structure (the possible number of relationships between the possible number of bricks) is in turn assimilated by the variety generated by the bricklaying team and the protocol under which it operates;

- on the other hand, the bricklaying team might have gone for a walk instead, or played cards, or built a tower covered with pinacles and other merry designs. They have so much variety...

Then it is INHERENT in this situation, that one lot of variety absorbs the other lot of variety.

We can soon think of other examples whereby antithetical sets of variety generators absorb each other's variety — or at least tend to do so within some statistical variation. In nature itself, exploding populations of insects have their variety absorbed by predators, which (by becoming prey in their turn) have their explosive vartiety absorbed. Very complicated food webs are embedded in total ecological systems and operate so that (give or take the occasional plague of locusts) enormously potent variety generators have outputs regulated to criteria which relate to the STABILITY of the system. We see exactly the same phenomenon in team games, where pairs of players contain variety by 'marking' each other.

Thus the first stage of our perception about variety regulation says that

VARIETY ABSORBS VARIETY.

Let us allow for a moment that this statement may turn out to be important, and note its managerial consequence. When those earlier calculations of variety proliferation were undertaken, not only did the results look thoroughly alarming, they invited the reaction: who could possibly USE this variety measure in a real-life situation? Could we ever say: *this* is the variety of the chemical industry, say? Of course we could not; therefore the measure that was developed might look valueless. But now we begin to see that the potential use of the variety measure is not the naive use of *counting* states, but of *matching* state generators. We do not count out the variety of the player in a game; but we do rely on his generating as much variety as his opposite number. On the average this reliance is justified — and we are not surprised, because both generators are human beings built to roughly the same blueprint and selected to play according to roughly the same criteria under the same rules. Therefore it is unusual that a game results in an overwhelming victory for one side or the other. We typically say that the two sides were 'evenly matched'.

So the statement *variety absorbs variety* begins to have meaning as a perception; the question is why it should have special relevance to management. If it has none, it is trivial. Then let us move on to the second stage of perception.

Although we can think of countless examples of systems, natural or contrived, in which variety absorbs variety as an inherent attribute of the system, we can *also* think of many systems for which, unlike formal games, this is not true. This fact rescues our thinking from triviality; but it also means that something has to be added to the statement to make it a useful perception. First, some examples.

If a citizen begins to proliferate his social variety in a criminal fashion, we say that he is 'breaking the law'. There is nothing in the promulgation of the law to contain this variety generation. Therefore society has a countervailing variety generator known as law enforcement. Hence, if a policeman apprehends the criminal, the felonious variety is contained — otherwise not. OTHERWISE NOT. And there are many criminals who 'get away with it'. What has gone wrong? By way of investigation:

> Consider Jim. He is the best insurance salesman in the business. Less than half a mile away from Jim's own house, a family is buying an insurance package from Jim's rival company — at a cost that is indisputably higher than Jim could have offered.

> Then there is Helen, machine-minder in a textile factory. She looks after six looms. A thread breaks on machine 5, so the dropper drops and stops the machine. While Helen is repairing the warp, machine 2 runs out of thread: the cost of down-time is incurred.

> Sir John, managing director of a chemical corporation, is on the way to lunch with senior representatives of a computer company. In his car, he reads a two-hundred page report

from his technical advisors on the best computer for the job. After lunch, he returns to his office and signs the contract. As a result, the director of his computer division resigns.

The school-teacher says to her class: '7 sixes are 42, 7 sevens are 49, 7 eights are 56, 7 nines are 63. Polly, what are 7 eights?' Polly says: '49'. The teacher says: 'Harry?' Harry says: 'I don't know'.

The senior economic ministers of the government and the head of the central bank agree that inflation is getting out of hand, and so they increase the minimal lending rate. Money is too cheap. So money becomes dearer; people cannot afford their rents and mortgages, and there is a net increase in the charge on social security. This releases more money, and the rate of inflation rises.

What has gone wrong?

The question can be answered in all manner of ways — especially as the examples quote all manner of situations. A weaver might feel happy to elucidate the example of the looms, whereas Sir John (although he is a manager) might not want to try. A child (no less) might elucidate the multiplication problem, whereas the school-teacher (although she too is a manager) might not care to comment on the escape of the bank robbers from the police.

But all the examples concern regulation, and all are the province of managers. Using the analysis so far made, and using the measure called variety, can we not determine — not why all the examples are quite different, which is easy to do, but — why all the examples are the same?

In every case, something is supposed to be regulated. In every case, an attempt is made (according to the very structure of the system) to make *variety absorb variety*. In every case, the attempt fails, regulation is lost, and the management is looking foolish. What is more, we can take a small bet that in every case the manager is convinced that the trouble is not his fault.

Nevertheless: the fault IS managerial — in every case. And each of the managers is making the same mistake. He or she is relying on the natural law that variety absorbs variety, without pursuing that notion to the second stage of perception. That second stage is still there, lying dormant, with the bricklayers.

There has to be a bricklayer for every brick.

There does not have to be a policeman for every potential criminal — and there is not. That is exactly why *most* felons are not apprehended. The criminal variety of society is *greater* than the law enforcement variety. Every football player has a marker, and every prey has its predator. But every citizen does not have his own personal policeman. If he did, the law would never be broken. As was said earlier, it is not a matter of COUNTING possible states, but of MATCHING them.

In short, the regulator has to be capable of generating a variety *equivalent* to the variety that has to be regulated — or the regulator will fail. It really is no use to hope for the best. To maintain regulation — equilibrium between antithetical sub-systems, or stability in the whole — there is a certain variety REQUIRED in the regulator; and this cannot be less than the variety the black box of our concern itself proliferates. We saw it all happening in the last chapter.

This was the discovery of the British cybernetician Ross Ashby. It leads straight to the amendment of the realization that *variety absorbs variety,* with a simple but effective second stage:

ONLY variety absorbs variety.

There is nothing else that can do the job. Equivalent variety in the regulator with respect to the variety of the black or muddy box regulated is *required.* It is not required by ukase, by democratic decision, by the manager, or by me: it is required by nature — in the sense that this is how things are. Hence it is appropriate to call the natural attribute of systems that guarantees their self-regulatory powers the LAW OF REQUISITE VARIETY — Ashby's Law.

I consider that this law stands in the same relation to management as the law of gravity stands to Newtonian physics. It is equally central to an understanding of why things are as they are. And it is just as impossible to 'repeal' the one law as the other. Thus both laws inevitably assert themselves, and may not be 'disobeyed'. It is true that by aeronautical engineering an aeroplane appears to resist gravity in the short run. But we know that this is done at a price — in the expenditure of energy. So, by variety engineering, requisite variety can be pumped into a management system that does not (like the bricklaying) have it inherently. Again this is done at a price — in the expenditure of *information.*

Before attending further to the details of this engineering with variety, we should look for the lessons revealed in the simple examples. Regulation is lost in each case, we were saying; and now it is evident that it is lost because

Ashby's Law has asserted itself. Normally we regard the systems quoted in the examples as utterly different, and the managerial facts as incommensurable. The commonality lies precisely in the proliferation of variety by the system for which its regulatory component's variety is not requisite.

It was seen that the police cannot generate sufficient variety to monitor continuously the behaviour of every citizen. There is a shortcoming in requisite variety that we have already learned is not to be measured by counting all possible states of citizens and subtracting all possible states of policemen. If we instead match one set of variety generators against the other, the lack of requisite variety can be found by dividing the number of citizens by the number of policemen. Suppose that this number is 500 (which is roughly correct in Britain). Then it follows that the cost of meeting requisite variety will be that of providing a five-hundred fold increase in the capacity of the police system to generate variety. This is done by collecting records and finger prints and photographs; by spending money on storage, comparison and retrieval; by making information sources cover a wider front, through the provision of cars, radios and informers; and so on. All of these facilities, normally viewed through their respecitve technologies as evidently different, may instead be viewed equivalently as VARIETY AMPLIFIERS. The total collection of these facilities, whose individual varieties can at least be added together, must constitute an amplifier of variety that is 'times five hundred', if there is to be a fair chance of making a 'fair cop'. And once this approach is taken, it becomes clear that the set of facilities should be designed as a *total system,* so that the varieties of the component facilities tend to be multiplicative rather than just additive.

Anyone would imagine that this is what happens. For instance, surely no authority would provide a fleet of police cars, and fail to equip them with radios. Very well: then the mobility and the communication varieties will indeed interact. But because the general perception of the variety amplifier is missing, and because the criterion of requisite variety is not acknowledged, the net result is necessarily inefficient. The implications of Ashby's Law have not been worked out. Besides, the police activity is no more than a subsystem of some larger system that includes punishment and correction. In the total criminological scene, the attempts to disobey Ashby's Law fail to the extent that the penal subsystem becomes a training machine for felons. This is well-known, because of the measured rate of recidivism; but no-one examines the cybernetics of the total system, looking for the entailments of the law of requisite variety.

In simpler cases, such as the machine-minder Helen's, the issue is self-evident. The industrial engineer has to determine, on the basis of probability theory, how much variety is generated by a loom's non-automatic features, how much variety Helen disposes, and then to calculate how many looms she can mind.

In the scene depicted, Helen did not have requisite variety, and a loss resulted. This does not necessarily mean that her looms should be reduced from six to five: that would incur another cost as measured by the price of labour. But it does show how difficult it is for a human being to generate requisite variety in the face of variety proliferation from a muddy box, and draws attention to the important difficulty that the box is operating continuously, without remit; whereas human beings become tired or distracted. At those moments, requisite variety is lost. So what is the industrial engineer to do? In the past, he has broken down tasks and presented them to the worker in such a way as to hold off the consequences of Ashby's Law. It is by now fairly widely conceded that this process has resulted in a dehumanization of factory labour that is intolerable. Now for 'the exit' in this example: we certainly can use automation to provide guaranteed requisite variety by the variety matching process. The solution is (as it is found on an engine governor) so to design the machine that *in the very process* of going out of control, it is brought back onto control. This regulatory process of INTRINSIC CONTROL sees to it that Ashby's Law is automatically obeyed; therefore there is no loss possible in balancing the variety equations.

But once again, the issues raised here are not perceived through cybernetic eyes. Thus although the dehumanization of factory labour may be conceded, it is certainly not conceded that bad variety engineering (as distinguished from good production engineering) is the root of the problem. In consequence, the cost of automation has been directly compared with the cost of mechanization-plus-labour, and is very often regarded as too expensive. But this leaves out of account the costs that the reassertion of Ashby's Law will incur in the labour-intensive case, and also the social cost of the ensuing dehumanization of factory labour.

Next we come to Sir John. It is not generally realized that Sir John has been largely automated. His ego is huge, and his personality is stamped on everyone's television screen. He looks like the last word in free-ranging variety. But all this is illusory. Much of the variety that he handles as input has been processed by machines, in the cause of reducing its variety. He himself, as we met him, has been processed by machines: his secretarial machine, his transportation machine, the restaurant machine. . . . It is proper to refer to these processors as machines, for they very much constrain his personal variety. Moreover, all this partial automation has been very badly done, since no competent engineers were involved in its design. It is not yet generally conceded that all of this has led to the dehumanization of board-room labour, but it certainly has.

In any event, Sir John does not have requisite variety for the task in which he is engaged. His technical advisors have suppressed a large amount of relevant variety from his report for 'political' reasons. His education and preledictions have reduced his intellectual variety, so that he cannot understand the report he has got. His secretarial machine that launched him on this journey has allowed him twenty-two minutes to read and digest the two-hundred pages, whereas his variety generators cannot work that fast. The restaurant machine reduces his variety further, and the manufacturer's representatives (who know about computers, whereas Sir John does not) see to the rest.

This is not a caricature, but a slice of history; that is why I am sure that it is no use blaming Sir John, human nature, or ineffective management. This man has fallen victim to Ashby's Law, as all top managers are destined to do under the current patterns of institutional organization — which are of course reflected in national and international affairs. It is my deeply considered view that the consequences for humanity will probably be cataclysmic.

THE exit from so grave a problem arena is the design of organizations that take account of the law of requisite variety, using the generation of variety in the regulators to absorb proliferating variety in the muddy boxes we create to represent the world. The world *itself,* which is the province of nature, will go on exhibiting the continuous application of Ashby's Law as it has always done. And just as nature would continue with its affairs, and continue to exemplify the law of gravity, even if the entire human race denied the existence of that law and agreed that every person would jump off the nearest cliff next Tuesday, so nature will continue with its affairs, and continue to exemplify the law of requisite variety, even if humanity insists on organizing affairs in its despite.

To design organizations that do not flout the canons of nature means designing appropriate attenuators of variety, as we saw in the last chapter, but it also means designing appropriate amplifiers of variety too. The law of REQUISITE variety entails an EQUATION, in which both attenuators and amplifiers are inevitably involved. There are two important aspects to that remark, which appears to be innocuous:

- the attenuators and the amplifiers do have to be DESIGNED. When they are not designed, they simply occur (because Ashby's Law asserts itself). When that happens, human beings suffer. At the best, for example, insurance salesman Jim will lose income and business for his company. At the worst, for example, an unsupportably large human population might be cut by two-thirds in an atomic holocaust. DESIGN is the clue. Humankind soon saw that it could not hope for the best in acquiring shelter, clothing, and food. It had to *design* tools and weapons. From that stage, humankind was led by its technological nose to the moon — and to every other kind of dysfunctional habitat: the big city, the supersonic aircraft, and the collapsing institution. En route we gave up designing for humankind, and designed for aggrandisement instead.

● the attenuators and the amplifiers have to be inserted on the appropriate side of the equation. The school-teacher reciting the seven-times table does not have requisite variety to reach her class of forty children. Polly and Harry do not have requisite variety to understand her utterance. But they will all battle together towards success in a set of highly formalized examinations. Ashby's Law will then assert itself by turning the educational process, which everyone thinks is a variety amplifier (as is indeed needed by a collapsing civilization), into a variety attenuator. Polly and Harry will end up knowing that the response to '7 eights' is *not* 49, *not* 63, *not* 'don't know'. They will also know that God is on our side, and that to practice medicine you either drug or cut, and that *this* is how to run a brewery or a nation.

Finally, as far as the examples go, and over-ridingly:

● if handling a requisite variety calls for an equation, and if it calls for inserting attenuators and amplifiers on the proper sides of the equation, then there has to be some agreement about the nature, function and purposes of the system that proposes variety equations on every side. But these are subjective judgments. The reason why the senior economic ministers fail to control the economy is that the minimal lending rate (together with the other regulators they use) does not have requisite variety to intervene in a system that no-one has defined or understood. What is far worse, everyone is acting as if such a problem as inflation could be accounted for in terms of economics at all. But inflation is a phenomenon of the total societary system. Economics itself does not have requisite variety to handle the proliferation of variety involved in that. This is surely the reason why economists who have anything relevant to say are forced to create or to presuppose a politics, and why in turn politicans themselves cannot derive any help from economists except as apologists for their own political stance.

Having made a discursive approach to requisite variety, and having attempted to tease out its meaning and significance from numerous examples, the time comes to present some more formal statements that shall underlie the theory of organization presented in this book. The last chapter gave a preliminary description (which will later be enriched) on the so-called Management Unit, which was formally shown to be recursive. This Unit (including whatever enrichments shall later be added) will henceforth be depicted by a square box. Then here is a drawing intended to define this and two other symbols:

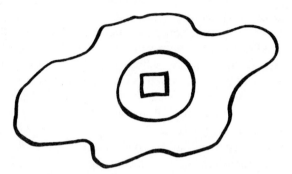

Figure 19. A management unit (square) embedded in the operation it regulates (circle) embedded in a loosely-defined environment

The management unit (the box) is seen to be embedded in a circle. This symbol stands for the operations that the management unit is supposed to regulate: they are 'under its control'. Those operations are in turn embedded in the amoeba-like symbol, which stands for the relevant environment of the operations concerned. This environment is multi-dimensional; it consists of a market, of a supply-situation, of customers or users, of the general public, and so on. Its boundaries are hazy. . . .

These three detectable activities are illustrated as embedded in each other, partly because that is the organizational fact, and partly because the representation gives a clear indication of their relative varieties. Any given operation (the circle) has a particular variety. Since any given state of that operation will surely prove to relate to more than one state of its multiple environment, the environmental variety will be greater than the operational variety. But the management unit has a lower variety than the operational variety: we just do not have a manager (or his representative) available to invigilate every action that contributes to the operation. Thus the diagram correctly reflects a progression of varieties, when we observe the symbolic containment of one symbol by another. And again it is noteworthy that statements can be made about *relative* varieties without actually counting the number of possible states. It is the same trick as to say that we can tell that A is taller than B, without measuring the height of either A or B.

Next: the notion of embedding is used to indicate another fact of organizational life. The interaction of one system with another system in which it is embedded is *by diffusion* across the boundaries between them. When we draw diagrams that connect organizational boxes by thin arrows (and we shall be forced to do this soon), we detract from our understanding of multi-faceted diffusions: the new diagrams suggest simple 'channels of communication'; but this is not what the arrows represent. They represent variety exchangers — on the model of heat exchangers. Thus, when we 'tease apart' the last diagram to reveal Figure 20, the arrows pose a question about variety diffusion as governed by Ashby's Law.

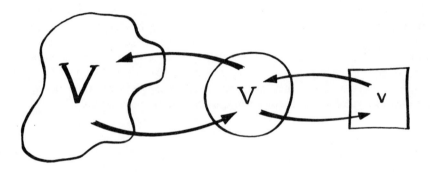

Figure 20. The embedment of Figure 19 is teased apart, and the diffusion processes that tend towards the establishment of requisite variety between the components are simplified into arrows

The three Vs-for-variety in the three boxes are of different sizes, in accordance with an earlier argument. Ashby's Law determines that, whatever we do about it, these varieties will tend to equate. Thus, as we look at the variety diffusion subsisting between either the environment and the operation, or the operation and the management unit, we can see that

either	● the variety on the right-hand side will be amplified in the diffusion process,
or	● the variety on the left-hand side will be attenuated in the diffusion process,
although	● these strategies are not mutually exclusive, and both may be operating.

A typographical fuss has been made of these alternatives for a very good reason. There is *no other way* that Ashby's Law can operate, within this framework. If so, then it is important to be very clear about it. These three varieties are necessarily going to equate; in the limiting case it will happen by the automatic imposition of that attenuating filter called Sheer Ignorance on the lower two loops. The operation will take cognizance only of those environmental factors that it necessarily models because it is the operation that it is. The management unit will restrict the variety perceived in the operation it is supposed to control according to its regulatory model-in-the-head — which will be determined by some theory about the world. Ashby's Law will be satisfied. And management will be a farce. It often is.

To deal with this situation competently, professionally, and responsibly, it is necessary to raise the performance level of each system to cope with the greater variety exhibited by the system lying to its left in the diagram. That means improving its muddy-box models through an array of adjuster organizers. But, as we have just seen, that in turn entails a combination of amplification and attenuation of variety vis-à-vis the adjacent box in terms of the variety diffusion process. Then the last diagram may be redrawn thus (using the standard electrical symbols for an amplifier and an attenuator):

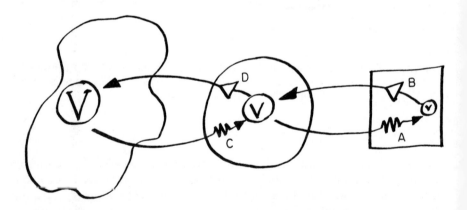

Figure 21. Figure 20 redrawn to show how amplifiers and attenuators are introduced into the variety diffusion process to accommodate Ashby's Law

Just as the square box on the right, which was studied in the last chapter, was called a Management Unit, so the mechanism of Figure 21 will be called an ELEMENTAL ORGANIZATIONAL UNIT. It is an embedment of the Management Unit in its operation, and an embedment of all that in an environment. The diagram teases the three pieces apart, in order to show how Ashby's Law necessarily operates to procure an equilibrium of variety: once the arrangement of Figure 21 has operated for a time, the three Vs will be the same size. But if this is not to occur by happenstance, because a natural law is operating, then it is management's job to DESIGN the necessary amplifiers and attenuators.

Out of this analysis is enunciated:

The First Principle of Organization

> Managerial, operational and environmental varieties, diffusing through an institutional system, tend to equate; they should be *designed* to do so with minimal damage to people and to cost.

This question of design is crucial. Now that computers are standard adjuncts of management, it has become normal to realize that the filtration systems they embody have necessarily to be designed. But by whom, and in response to what criteria? We shall be lucky indeed merely to inherit an automated version of the system that we used before anyone realized the need for design. In that case, we lose on the absence of design, and we lose a second time because the enormous powers that the computer disposes are not harnessed. We lose a third time because we do not even retain the flexibility that the manual system had. And we lose a fourth time because the human being is now a victim of the machinery.

Since the computerized system had to be designed in some sense, in what other sense is design absent? The answer lies in the belief of managers and their data processing staffs that the *purpose* of the system is to 'tell the manager what he needs to know'. Nobody knows what the manager needs to know; since that is hidden and unnamed in the proliferating variety of the muddy box. Certainly the manager reckons that he knows some information that he wants. Some of this, on cybernetic analysis, he does not actually need. But more importantly, most of what he needs he cannot possibly find out: it has been lost in the muddiness.

The cybernetic advice of the First Principle of Organization is to avoid futile debates about wants and needs, as of purposes, and to attend to the higher-order problem of regulating the force of requisite variety. In our own bodies, we have little choice as to the mode of variety attenuation that presents us with the low-variety world that our little brains can handle. That model has been largely settled by evolution and by upbringing. We *can* contest it (in the pursuit of esoteric studies and a massive programme of self-regulation), but most people do not. The question does not arise for them. Equally, the question does not arise for most managers. Once it does, it is easier to contest the inherited system than it is in ourselves, because there is marginally less egoistic commitment. However, institutions also become wise in their own conceits.

This much is said about attenuation between the operation and its management unit simply as an introduction to much more that will follow. We have just been looking at the variety reducer marked A in Figure 21. Let us now reflect, equally briefly, on the amplifier between them, marked B.

The manager has many means of amplifying his relatively low variety towards his operation — simply because he is 'the boss'. He may call a meeting, he may start a newsletter, he may appoint staff to develop his policies by location and by function. And so on. But again, his amplifiers ought to be properly designed to solve the equation of requisite variety. In the present state of the managerial art, this scientific proposition is represented, in cavalier fashion, as a matter of style. And style is certainly relevant: one manager will create a very different state of morale from another because of his style, although each may (but probably will not) generate an equivalent amount of variety.

Behavioural scientists have attempted various means of introducing measurement into this stylistic situation. However, their management grids do not seem to take account of the underlying facts that style is a determinant of variety amplification, and that the degree of amplification required depends upon the requisite variety generated in the situation to be handled. This, in any given organization, is not a constant. In terms of variety analysis, therefore, it is hard to accept that any one style should be regarded as uniformly applicable. Rather should the manager adapt his stylistic approach to the variety needs of the moment. Agreed that he may find this difficult; but it is not at all plausible that he should be asked to choose a uniform stance on quasi-ideological grounds, as some would have him do. Then let us make a note to return to this issue when we are ready (it will take us to Chapter Fourteen).

The variety adjusters between the operation and the environment also call for detailed design, and once again the relevance of requisite variety is obscured by historical managerial practice. For example, to fix a planning horizon is to attenuate environmental variety (C) and so is the compilation of an opinion poll. But the second is regarded as if it were an amplifier; and no-one regards these two techniques as in any way related. They are. They are parts of the total package of techniques that constitutes attenuator C, and they ought to be regarded in that way. For the law of requisite variety refers to the *total* balance of two sub-systems: we can tolerate an over-severe variety reducer if its stringent effect is offset by a more liberal one.

Similarly with the amplifier D. The advertising policy and appropriation are not normally seen as related in any way to the cost of quality control in the factory. Yet both techniques amplify operational variety to the environment, and once again quality control might be thought of naively as an attenuator. It is, of course, as far as the production manager is concerned. But we are not discussing him, any more than we were discussing the market research manager in relation to his opinion poll. We are instead discussing requisite variety in the operation-environment dynamics of variety diffusion. Perhaps the point will be clearer if we note that we could spend less on quality control and more on advertising, and just possibly bully the public into buying the same volume of shoddier goods.

But these are preliminary exercises only in thinking about the first principle of organization, and we return to our last diagram to discover:

The Second Principle of Organization

> The four directional channels carrying information between
> the management unit, the operation and the environment
> must each have a higher capacity to transmit a given
> amount of information relevant to variety selection in a
> given time than the originating sub-system has to generate
> it in that time.

Having taken pains to understand the nature of the variety measure, it would be sad if at this point anyone were to forget that it counts the number of possible states of the system. Clearly, in a dynamic system, there is a minimal time in which all possible states could be exhibited, and therefore there is a *rate* of variety generation possible per unit time. It would be a pity to forget this, because the consideration of communication channels automatically leads people to think of the information *content* transmitted. This is not what we are talking about.

A channel carrying a message in the morse code has to distinguish a variety of five states: the dot and the dash; and the pause that separates them within a letter, from the pause between letters, from the pause between words. It makes no difference whether the information conveyed is a declaration of war or a grocery order.

Equally, in a management system, the point of the Second Principle is simply to ask whether the channel itself has sufficient variety to register the number of states it is supposed to transmit at a given rate. All too often, we find on examination that it has not.

We begin by forgetting about the time factor. Suppose that you are managing a production unit, and a critical situation develops in No 4 furnace. You have requisite variety to distinguish between furnaces, and to distinguish between various degrees of crisis — of which 'critical' is the penultimately bad. Your boss, a mile away, also has this requisite variety. Thus the first principle is satisfied (it is because you are both trained men). Now the crisis has put your telephone out of action, and you therefore send a message by word of mouth. The messenger is oafish, sad to say. What he tells the boss is: 'things are in a hell of a state down there'. Well, he *might* have forgotten the real message. But I take the case where lack of knowledge means that he was incapable of registering it. 'No 4' and 'critical' were just not states of the system that he could recognize as distinguishable.

As soon as we admit time to the illustration, the point becomes more familiar. If we witness an accident, we are perfectly capable in principle of distinguishing each successive state of the system. But we end up by saying: 'Sorry. It all happened so quickly'.

In management it has become a cliché to talk about 'informational overload', meaning that we are getting more papers and figures than we have the time to read. Therefore we attend the meeting without important facts that are buried on our desks. But this is not so profound a problem as that indicated in the Second Principle. After all, we might be lucky next time, and pick up the relevant paper first. The principle questions whether the fact is there at all; it questions whether the channel has the capacity to distinguish between two states that matter to you.

There are two kinds of filter in universal mangerial use that worry me very much in this regard. One deals with the mass of quantitative information that the institution generates by adding it up. We often find that, without appreciating the fact, managers are studying figures that are averages of averages of averages. This is a statistically heinous arrangement. But even if it is made statistically respectable by some kind of weighting system, it may well mean that the channel is incapable of registering requisite variety. There are other ways of cutting down the mass of data without betraying Ashby's Law (which will reassert itself). The other filter deals with the plethora of human intervention, advice, lobbying, and so forth, by cocooning the manager in a 'management team'. The idea of the team is most attractive: it detracts from the image of authoritarian rule. Nonetheless, it operates a variety filter that I have often observed to destroy requisite variety.

There is need to check the variety carrying capacity of all four channels. One of the most suspect (in my experience) is that carrying amplifier D. The assumptions made in advertising, for example, with its talk of readership, seem to ignore the variety matching that has to occur between the readers and the journal. Consider a limiting case: many professional people subscribe to journals that they feel they 'should' take, and do not even open a copy from one year's end to another. The operation for them of the law of requisite variety has attenuated the advertisers' variety to zero.

You will note that by treating the three component sub-systems of the management unit as black boxes, and by examining their interrelationship through their capacity to handle variety and obey its laws, we have already uncovered two principles which ought to count as criteria of systemic effectiveness. Although this already seems a lot to have deduced from so simple a model, there is yet a third principle implicit in the last diagram. You may find it interesting to search the diagram again for something that is happening there that has not so far been mentioned. After all, we have only three boxes and four lines of connexion, and those have already been discussed. . . .

The answer is that all the interconnections entail the crossing of boundaries. Because the 'language' of each subsystem is unique to it, messages have to be 'translated' when a boundary is crossed. to be more precise: there has to be a mechanism at the boundary capable of coding or decoding these messages as they pass. This mechanism is called a *transducer,* because it 'leads across'.

The Third Principle of Organization

> Wherever the information carried on a channel capable
> of distinguishing a given variety crosses a boundary, it
> undergoes transduction; and the variety of the
> transducer must be at least equivalent to the variety of
> the channel.

We saw that each sub-system of the management unit has to *generate* requisite variety, and that the channels it uses to pass information must themselves exceed that variety recognition capacity (over a suitable time interval) in order to *convey* requisite variety. Now we see that all of this is unavailing if the transducer cannot itself cope with the variety it is called upon to handle. Again, this is not simply a question of a capacity to process information. It refers to the more profound necessity to take on as many states as are required to accept the distinguishable states presented to it. Thus a morse code receiver capable of accepting information at the rate of fifty words a minute would have plenty of information handling capacity to receive a message transmitted at thirty words a minute. But if he could not discriminate the pause between dots and dashes from the pause between letters, he would not have requisite variety to do the job.

How often do we find in management systems that the transducers, which ought neither to amplify nor to attenuate variety, are almost annihilating it.

For example, I have often been amazed to hear senior managers reporting on different situations to the board in terms which attenuate the variety of that situation by an order of magnitude. Now it is true that the senior manager has a duty to condense the *information* he is transducing, although he often fails to discharge this duty by talking interminably. But he has a contrary duty to preserve transduction variety: that is, he should not be portraying the complicated situation in a black-and-white fashion when it is capable of accommodating many shades of grey.

Here is an actual though bizarre example that once occurred on channel D. The company realized that it had many salesmen in the field who did nothing more than handle enquiries and transmit orders, whereas they could be trained to collect more information than this — about client stocks, credit-worthiness, market prospects, and so on. A new scheme was therefore negotiated, whereby sales forces would be slightly increased and also trained to make these new investigations. Six months later it turned out that the salesmen were using the extra time thus made available in personal pursuits, and were filling in the new record cards in the bar — with more or less random figures. The reason for this was that the management had not worked out any arrangements to 'operationalize' the results of this data gathering back in the operational circle (they were too busy, and simply reckoned that the new information would 'come in useful' when they got round to it), and the salesmen had discovered this fact. Thus the transducer simply did not work.

Let us further take note that once a transducer has been denatured in this way, it is extremely difficult to make it operational again in any context. People must believe in the effectiveness of the tools that they are supposed to use. One advantage of making the sort of analysis that our three criteria of effectiveness can be used to make, is that it examines in turn the specific mechanisms of amplifiers and attenuators, of channels, and of transducers, with the intention of establishing not only their cybernetic validity but their human credibility. It is because this approach is not in normal use that no-one knows who or what is to blame for systemic failure in management, with the result that it is not (say) a particular and maybe purely mechanical transducer that loses credibility, but the entire human administration.

The tendency to talk in such blanket terms is in itself an example of a failure to preserve requisite variety, and I fear that we often make the same mistake in issuing judgments about other people. This has been called the 'halo' effect. We have a list of human qualities, and a very strong impression that a particular person rates very high (or low) on *one* of them. Then there is a risk that this impression will be transferred, without any evidence, to the other qualities on the list. Confidence tricksters use their 'halos' with effect: someone so well educated, so well dressed, so well mannered, having so much wit and charm *must* be also honest. Equally, when someone has delivered a personal affront (albeit unknowingly), we tend to go around saying that he is somehow 'unreliable'. These points are familiar to the psychologist. But the psychologist is not pointing to the underlying cybernetics of such cases. They involve the loss of requisite variety. As we saw in the last chapter, regulatory models-in-our-heads of other people annihilate many, and perhaps most, of their possible states. Consciously to preserve requisite variety in our relationships with other people is helpful to those relationships; to attenuate variety in our perception of another is to degrade his or her humanity. When this point is writ large, we observe a root cause of ethnic, religious, and political persecution that has nothing to do with 'prejudice', unless that is simply a label for refusing to recognize variety. And that, come to think of it, would not be a bad definition at all. 'Them and us' has a variety of precisely two.

Here, finally, is a little exercise in handling the concept of requisite variety in the context of human affairs:

> I have observed that people with truly creative minds
> tend to throw out an endless stream of ideas in a
> half-baked state; to embark on many projects that
> they do not see through to completion; to detail
> their latest experiences to friends at great length and
> with histrionic effects; and to use large amounts of
> time conversing with people who appear from the
> wings and distract the course of play.
>
> I have heard these characteristics severely criticised
> as (in turn) lack of rigour and professionalism;
> instability and unreliability; ego-boosting; and
> profligacy of talent.
>
> Could you develop plausible cybernetic replies to
> those four criticisms?

Of course, this exercise does not ask for psychiatric conclusions: one would need to know the instances. It so happens that the cybernetician Ashby *was* a psychiatrist, and also that he liked to end his chapters by setting exercises. This chapter is devoted to a managerial exploration of Ashby's Law. Unless answers to the exercise are forthcoming, my exposition has sadly failed.

LATER IN THE BAR...

'*Say a prayer for me while you're on your knees down there Joe.*'

'*It's all right: my lighter rolled under the table — got it. Anyway we can't say prayers any more, I suppose.*'

'*How do you mean?*'

'*Requisite variety, that's what. We haven't got it. God has too many possible states.*'

'*In the channel, or in the transducer?*'

'*Hmmm... overall.*'

'*Hey — I wonder if that explains the prayer wheels in Tibet?*'

'*Well, I can certainly see variety amplifiers and attenuators in our churches: sacraments, the ritual... .*'

'*Sounds blasphemous to me.*'

'*Don't see why. Anyway, to get away from anything too dangerous, what about auricular confession — to a priest. That's a direct exercise in providing requisite variety.*'

'*Can't we get away from this idea at all? It's like reading Freud, and seeing phallic symbols in everything you meet.*'

'*This is supposed to be a natural law. If it isn't everywhere, it's a fallacy.*'

'*There you go: a phallusy.*'

'*Kill him, somebody. But, really, this business about bricklayers and bricks — does it make sense? I mean, of course the number of bricks would work out right. What's so odd about that?*'

'*Why should there by anything odd about a natural law? It's a question of recognizing it.*'

'*If I may come in here, I feel about this like someone looking at one of those optical illusions: one minute it's a corridor, and the next you're looking down on a pyramid. I think I've seen the point, and then it's gone.*'

'Well, it's a different way of thinking. We're not used to it. I'm certainly not used to thinking of my Chairman as automated — *probably because his name is not Sir John.'*

'Ah — now that example really grabbed me. There's a lot in it, you know. It cuts us down to size somehow.'

'If I tried that on my chief I'd be fired. Besides, I believe in human values — and already I'm feeling distinctly cramped inside this book. All this cybernetics denigrates the spirit of man.'

'Look, David, seriously: you can't hurt the spirit of man by acknowledging basic facts of life. Any spirit we've got is somehow mediated through our bodies — and our institutions.'

'Like wearing trousers.'

'Pardon?'

'Well, we're all wearing trousers. Not much choice. Doesn't mean a gross betrayal of individual freedom.'

'I'm not so sure. We are forced into patterns, given labels. If we do something that isn't on the label, we're freaks. So no-one does it — guess that's the point about being automated.'

'Go outside the pattern, and the Establishment critics scream with rage. Isn't that a bigger loss of human freedom than having to use computers?'

'What do you make of the critics who appeared in that final exercise? Were they justified?'

'Justified or not, they're for real.'

'I think they're right.'

'But you *are always on about freedom.... .'*

'We don't have the freedom to behave irresponsibly. All these so-called 'creative' people should get down to a solid job of work.'

'How are you going to answer the exercise then?'

'I'm not.'

'He can't.'

'Can you?'

'I haven't thought about it yet.'

'None of us will think about it, I don't suppose.'

'Well, I don't see how you can apply this stuff to people.'

'Organizations are all about people. Just now you were complaining that the approach degrades humanity. When you're asked to use it in defence of humanity, you don't want to play.'

'Look, I don't take that. The world is full of degradation — of tyranny, of torture. I hold the people who want to turn us into automata responsible. Cybernetics is right in the thick of all that.'

'Rubbish. The torturers are psychopaths.'

'How many psychopaths does it take?'

'Not so many. They staff the elite groups in every tyrannical regime. Nobody knows the members of the elite group — it might be your boss, or your father, or the greengrocer. So you keep quiet, and the psychopaths are allowed to get on with it.'

'John: you just defined the variety amplifier of all time.'

'Hell, yes — that's exactly what it is. Are the Three Principles of Organization being used by these devils?'

'Probably. See what I mean? — it's all very dangerous.'

'You mean it, don't you? I think you're crazy. The argument is that those three principles exist because they follow from natural laws that will assert themselves. How can KNOWING what the facts are make anything worse? And if you're right in thinking that fascist regimes know all this and are using it — which I doubt — that would be the strongest argument of all that we should be using it too.'

'Why should the devil have all the best tunes?'

'Precisely.'

'Well, I've actually read *Ashby*. He doesn't propose principles of organization — nor does he talk about the human predicament in terms of requisite variety.'

'What about it? Newton didn't discuss the problems of landing a lunar module.'

'Fair enough. I don't think this man is trying to lay anything on Ashby; give him due credit, more likely.'

'Even so, I've never seen Principles of Organization that look anything like these. I mean, it's usually 'one man, one boss' or 'the span of control' — things like that.'

'They're just slogans.'

'Well, these aren't slogans, agreed; but have they anything to do with practical management?'

'We'll have to find out.'

'It sounds theoretical.'

'Why are you fellows so scared of theory? Seems to me that we could use something well-founded in science instead of making it up as we go along. Besides, the thing is studded with practical examples.'

'Oh come now. We have a large body of management theory already. And the examples seem a bit contrived to me.'

'There are many indications in the text that the examples actually happened. As to established management theory, where's it got us?'

'OK. But I expect theory to account for reality. Theory can't be right if it doesn't.'

'So what are you thinking?'

'I'm thinking of those three black boxes — the square, circle and fuzzy area — and I'm thinking of the four channels connecting them. Anyone noticed that the management unit has no contact with the outside world? It's allowed only to interact with its own operations. That's got to be daft. I had lunch with a customer only today.'

'You mean there should be arrows going straight from the management to the environment? Yes, I'd wondered about that.'

'Probably they're taken for granted.'

'That wouldn't be very scientific. Besides, I'd like to see a discussion of the transducers involved.'

'They would be alcoholic transducers.'

'No, hold it. There's got to be a reason for this. After all, its perfectly obvious that managers do interact directly with the environment. They don't have to go through the operation.'

'Don't they?'

'Well, I certainly don't. Dammit, I live in that environment. And I deal directly with customers and suppliers and politicians, and so on.'

'Yes, so do I. This is pretty strange. What's the answer?'

'Let's test it out. What do we do when we see a customer, for instance?'

'With a bit of luck, I'll sell him something that the salesmen haven't thought of, or couldn't clinch.'

'Then you're acting like a salesman. You've changed your manager's hat for an operational hat. You emerge as a supersalesman from the circle, not from the square.'

'Yes, it's a possible argument. But does it follow that whatever I do as a manager to interact with the environment is necessarily done as an operations-man in disguise?'

'That's an unprovable statement. What we need is a counter example to disprove it.'

'Well, let's say that I go out with an explicitly managerial hat — I mean saying out loud that the operational activity has gone wrong, and that I'm over-riding that relationship. That's got to mean that I am going round the circle, and not through it.'

'How could you do that? Let's have an example.'

'*Actually, that's not difficult. Only this week I met with the managing director of one of our customers. I told him frankly that the difficulties we had experienced were due to our own operational failures — inside the circle, that is. I said that I would use my managerial authority to honour any new agreement we made. We made the deal: I personally have promised him that we will deliver his three hundred sets in March. To keep that customer, I ignored the operational whining in the circle; and now I have given it direct instructions that this order has to be met — regardless. It will happen, I assure you.*'

'*It will happen because you will now work through your operational circle. You couldn't do it alone.*'

'*Of course not. The point is that I by-passed the operational circle in setting up the deal.*'

'*Then how do you know that your operation can fulfil your promise?*'

'*Of course I know. I know what our capacity is, and I know what our existing commitments are. I know about material supplies, and I know exactly how to achieve the objective.*'

'*In other words, Gareth, you did the deal with confidence because you carried the operational facts in your head.*'

'*I should hope I did. Otherwise I might commit the factory to an impossible outcome.*'

'*Then obviously the square is working through the circle — even if the circle exists only as a model-in-your head for the purpose.*'

'*But I am dealing directly with the customer, using my authority as the manager.*'

'*You are. But you do not ignore the constraints of your own operation. So in a sense you enter the circle to brief yourself, and emerge from the circle fully informed. You've got one of these regulatory models that contains the operational variety.*'

'*It sounds as though Bill's saying that we cannot perceive the environment, except through the eyes of the operation.*'

'*Well can we? And if we did, wouldn't we be hopelessly out of touch with the realities of our own firms?*'

'I find this conversation very ingenious. But so what? If Joe has made the somewhat technical point that in some sense or other the management can't go to the environment except through the circle — real or imagined — maybe the diagram is adequate. But I'm left with the uncomfortable feeling that I myself actually do deal with the environment direct.'

'Why do you say 'uncomfortable'? Is it because you are seeing that the operational circle is always in the way — as the diagram alleges.?'

'Maybe that's the positive point. We can't see the external world — except through the eyes of the operational facts that we understand. You know, if we really did detach ourselves from the operational facts in making our deals, no amount of authority exercised in the return loop would make the unworkable workable.'

'But this is thoroughly alarming. You are saying that my variety is all cut down, just because I am a realist about the operational facts?'

'It's got to be. It is the price of practicality.'

'But if there is an alternative answer lying outside the scope of the existing operation, I should expect to spot it.'

'The diagram says you won't.'

'Then I take issue with the diagram.'

'Suddenly the burden of proof is reversed. The diagram says that none of us can deal directly with the external world. We have to go through the operation, or else through our simulated understanding of the operation.'

But that's dreadful. I don't feel blinkered by the fact that I know the operational facts.'

'Requisite variety says that you are. The would-be amplifier is turned into an attenuator.'

'What am I supposed to do? Turn the factory into a machine for manufacturing eggs out of wire netting?'

'If necessary. But because the diagram is right, you won't succeed. Going through the operational circle will convince you that this new prospect is inadmissible. It can't be done.'

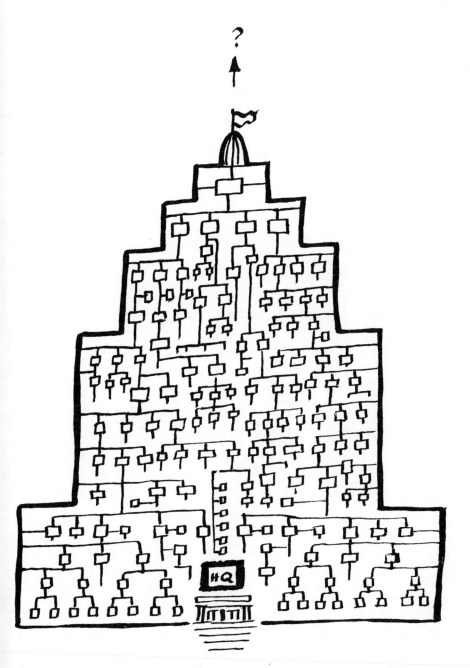

Figure 22. An exhibit: piece of paper discovered by barman after closing time, beside recumbent manager. Both were appropriately disposed of

'Well, I don't think that any of us round this table is as unlikely to see the world differently, and to make changes, as you're insisting. It's my round: same again for everyone I presume... '

'Not for me thanks. I'm off to read this chapter again. I can't solve the exercise — I can't even see the relevance of this exercise — and I don't like that.'

'Good for you. I can't either. Tell me about it at breakfast.'

'That's real management for you... '

CHAPTER FIVE

Bases of viability

The Oxford English Dictionary says:

Viable: able to maintain a separate existence.

There are a great many ways of characterizing an enterprise. The law has one way, economics another, the financial press has a third, and so on. From the cybernetic standpoint, I think that the most useful characterization of the enterprise is as a viable system.

All managers are familiar with the phrase 'economically viable'; but this simply means that some project is financially sound. Financial soundness expresses no more than one *constraint* on the viable system, and there are others. In particular, as we have begun to find out, there are very fundamental constraints that can be perceived and discussed in terms of variety. Our account of the enterprise as a viable system will indeed be written in these terms.

After all our enquiries into the subjective nature of systemic structures and purposes, and our discoveries about the role of implicated observers in their recognition, it ought at first blush to sound suspicious to hear said: all enterprises can be characterized as viable systems. Who says so, we may well ask, and by what authority? The answer is a very special answer: *they* do. Now it will be remembered that we defined the purpose of a system as 'what it does'. What we observe the enterprise to be doing is maintaining its separate existence. Of course, it has all manner of declarations to make, in public and some in private, about what it is doing. But it will change its declarations, if what they say becomes inconvenient; it will erect new norms of every sort, so that it looks like a different enterprise altogether, if that is convenient; but it will — if it can — *survive*. It will maintain its separate existence.

The purpose of survival is a very special purpose. It cannot be compared with purposes which say: 'I want to be a rock star', or 'our object is to reform society', or 'double the profits', or 'Mars or bust'. These, the usual formulations of purpose, involve squaring the shoulders, lifting the eyes to the horizon, and charging forth. But survival is something different. It is a purpose that closes in on itself; it is a matter of preserving identity. It says, albeit ungrammatically: 'whatever else may happen, *I am me*'. To use personal pronouns in this way may jar, since we are talking about institutions; and yet there very definitely is such a phenomenon as corporate identity in every enterprise: managers are quite aware of it. They refer to the enterprise as if it were a self-conscious entity and, under some fairly cautious definitions of terms, that is just what it is. We shall come to some strange consequences of all this much later, and may well begin to turn them over in the back of our minds. But it seems orderly to work out the structure of any viable system first, which is the task of Part Two.

Of all the observers of that viable system called the enterprise, the most significant is inevitably itself. This is because of the reflexive nature of the affirmation of identity. The enterprise spends a great deal of its effort in this preoccupation; and if we bring Ashby's Law to bear on the need for a viable system to do just that, we can see why. If a certain variety is generated in the pursuit of 'let's go' purposes, then an equivalent variety must be devoted to self-maintenance: otherwise the system is going to disintegrate. That issue will emerge in precise terms once the model is built. Meanwhile, however, the enterprise is telling not only itself, but everyone else, that *it* exists. Society has various means of checking on this: they belong to the rule-books of the law, of economics, of financial journalism, and so on. As was said at the start of this chapter, there are many ways of characterizing the enterprise, and here they come. Each of them embodies a model of enterprise which is of course intended to be regulatory. But we have already examined the cybernetically proven fact that the regulator is as good as its contained model of the system regulated, and no more. None of the models mentioned has anything like the variety necessary to play a regulatory role. The enterprise is tough and virile; it is concerned to survive. It will obey legal constraints, therefore — but it will engage in all manner of activity which would probably be illegal if the law's model had requisite variety. Its economics are expressed in balance sheets that satisfy the financial regulator, and its public stance is expressed in public relations exercises that satisfy financial journalists. But neither accountancy nor the press has requisite variety in its regulatory model. In the last ten years alone, Britain has seen all manner of manipulations in company law, financial abuse, and public scandal, on the part of major concerns. We may deplore such misdemeanours, and we may point to the cybernetic reasons why the alleged regulators failed for so long to regulate. But we can (as it were) only celebrate the toughness and virility of the viable systems that we observe to maintain themselves. As to those which crashed, their misdemeanours having become public, what has usually happened? It is that the enterprise blew itself up: that is to say it failed to obey the *internal* criteria of viability. The so-called regulators outside finally acted, but they were alerted only by the sound of the bang.

It is these internal criteria of viability that a theory of effective organization has to establish. The next problem is to decide what are the rules that will satisfy us that we have discovered the criteria of viability. The classic approach to this problem is to say that we must first determine the conditions that are necessary, and then we must further show that these conditions are sufficient. This is an exacting task. It is very likely an impossible task, if as would be preferable, necessity and sufficiency are to be demonstrated in a fully rigorous way. But let us break the problem down. It should not be too difficult to demonstrate that certain features of a system are necessary to its viability. 'Without this particular sub-system or mechanism', we should be able to say, 'no system is survival-worthy'. By the same token, it should be possible to eliminate features of viable systems that we often notice, and which therefore appear to be typical concommitants of viablity, but which do not appear to be essential to survival. Very well: we shall carefully scrutinize each feature of the emerging model before invoking its necessity as a condition of viability. The question of sufficiency is much more difficult. I can think of only one test that the final model is sufficient to account for viability, and I have been using it for many years. It is to ask all and sundry, but particularly those to whose enterprises the model has been applied, if anything necessary to viability has been left out. So far, this has evoked a nil reaction. Well, that is not a logically rigorous test; it is merely an empirical verification. But it is much better than nothing. Perhaps the rigorous test would be to build an enterprise on the model, and to see whether that enterprise survives. In fact, this has been done, and the test worked. But all the rigour was lost in the evident fact that all the people engaged in building an actual enterprise are constantly pumping variety into it. They may conscientiously be adhering to the model, but what *else* are they unknowingly supplying? Even so: our method will be to aim for a statement of conditions that are necessary and sufficient. As a good philosopher, I am bound to declare the inadequacy of the rigour; and that means that I shall fall short of the target — like any good manager.

The chapters we have so far shared were intended to equip us with a language in which to address the description of a viable system. Already, precepts are beginning to emerge. The three Principles of Organization educed in the last chapter make a start on viability testing, because if those principles are flouted, then variety is certain to proliferate to overwhelm the system — and it will cease to be viable. So far, however, we have been looking at a little embedment of black boxes which may seem to be remote from the large, thriving enterprise with which each of us is most familar. How do we get into those?

The standard tool (if it can be dignified as such) for examining the structure of an enterprise is the organization chart. It is a terrible mess. It proliferates variety in all directions, and indefinitely — since it continuously attempts to reflect the adaptations that its senior management effects. New departments are formed, and new chains of command are delineated. Whether this continually changing account of the enterprise adds up to a viable system is not testable. However, we have already worked out some ideas (in Chapter Two) that will permit a massive variety reduction of the huge and proliferating organization chart.

The basic device is to divide the notion of the viable system into two, and to form a **logical** hierarchy of these two parts. One part consists essentially of the *operational elements* (see Chapter Four) of the viable system. An operational element exists to undertake one of the system's basic activities: it consists of an operation (circle), in which is embedded a management unit (square), and an environment in which all of that is embedded. In short, the management system examined at the end of the last chapter, the one from which the three Principles of Organization were educed, typifies an operational element of any viable system. The *collection* of all the operational elements in the viable system exhausts its basic activities, namely those which exist to do what the system does.

What is left? It is a collection of subsystems that exists to look after the collection of operational elements, so that they cohere in that totality which we called a viable system. Remember that the management unit so far described exists to manage an operation. Whatever else is needed to manage the *collection* of operational elements is METASYSTEMIC to that. It is something logically beyond (that is, meta) the logic of the operational elements combined. In ordinary managerial parlance, the metasystem thus defined is called 'senior management'; and this term carries the connotation that it is superior to a 'junior management'. But that is only to invoke the language of command, which we have foresworn.

It is worth wondering if the logical requirement for a metasystem (which will emerge later, in the search for the necessary and sufficient conditions of viability) is in fact equivalent to the political supposition that there must be policy bosses of the operational bosses. I do not think that it is. In fact, there is a major confusion here in our inherited thinking. And it leads to all manner of nonsense when it comes to the discussion of such essentially socio-political issues as to whether workers' representatives should sit on directorial boards. For the moment, the point is to understand the language we are setting forth: the relationship between the total operational system and its metasystem (which, in a sense we shall proceed to display, is to 'look after' it) is a *logical* relationship, whatever social form it is given.

The next point in this development of an organizational language is to handle the variety proliferation implicit in the hierarchy of operations themselves. Are *all* operations, some of which report to more inclusive operations, to be listed in the 'collection of operations'? Not so: otherwise there will be an arbitrary variety explosion, and we shall be back to the orthodox organization chart. What has to be added to the vocabulary of this organizational language is the notion that operational elements are those *fundamental* to the viability of the system that is actually under discussion. They do not extend to dependent units of those fundamental units — in which they are subsumed. Because the dependent units are included in the operational elements, they are certainly not ignored. On the other hand, they are not specified. It is this convention that attenuates operational variety in our model. Each operational unit is to be treated as a black box: we do not enquire what dependent units it may contain.

In practice, then, we might talk about the viability of the transportation system. Its operational elements would be (say) roads, railways, rivers, canals, airways: no further breakdown is needed. Attention is instead directed to the metasystem that looks to the coherence of these elements in a viable transportation system (although we shall be lucky indeed if we can find one, having chosen this example). Thus we have defined the total transportation system with minimal — yet requisite — variety. It has, as we intended, just two parts: a system of operational elements, and a metasystem. The requisite variety is implicit, because any actual piece-of-transport (such as a bus, or a barge, or an aeroplane) is necessarily contained within one of the system's black boxes.

Suppose you were then to say: 'Look, I am in charge of airways, and I have a very high variety system to handle. I resent being treated as a mere black box in your model. In fact, my operation is elaborate, and not all *that* muddy'.

Then I should reply: 'it is very muddy indeed from the standpoint of the viability of transportation as a whole. But if you want to look at *airways* as a viable system, let's do it. What are your operational elements?' Then you would list airlines and airports, perhaps; and from the standpoint of your airways model, *these* would remain as black boxes. This list of operational elements would constitute the airways system. And again there would be a metasystem dedicated to their coherence.

Next, of course, the chairman of a whole airline will complain to you that he too is more than an interaction between a few boxes. And you will explain to him in turn that a model will be constructed of his airline, and that this will identify its own operational elements. And so on.

It follows from this arrangement, this nested set of descriptions, that the metasystem of any one viable system is an operational element in another viable system *at the next level of recursion.* We saw how this concept derived from the variety analysis made in Chapter Three. Now it is possible to state a theorem, like this:

Recursive System Theorem

> In a recursive organizational structure,
> any viable system contains, and is
> contained in, a viable system.

This is an alternative version of the Theorem as stated in *Brain of the Firm,* which expressed the same point from the opposite angle: 'if a viable system contains a viable system, then the organizational structure must be recursive'.

Theorems, no doubt, ought to be proved. The proof offered later will be a topological proof. Not only shall we find that all viable systems have necessary and sufficient conditions of their 'independent existence', which means that when drawn out as systems diagrams they will all look alike (they display the topological invariance discussed earlier); we shall also find that the topology whereby viable systems are interconnected as between levels of recursion is invariant too. A start has already been made in demonstrating this as between management units themselves in Figure 17.

Assuming that this variety-attenuating approach to the problem of analysing organizational structures cybernetically has been made clear (it is, as it were, to depict a large organization as a set of Chinese boxes or Russian dolls, wherein each is contained within the next), a difficulty certainly remains. It troubles many who have already made use of this work and says:

> If a viable system is one 'able to maintain a separate existence', how is it that a viable system *contains* viable systems which are clearly NOT separate from the viable system in which they are contained?'

The answer lies in the word 'able', in the first place. For example, consider a large chemical corporation that has divisions dealing with fertilizers, with dyestuffs, with inorganic chemicals, and so on. Each of these divisions is a viable system. It could in principle be hived-off as a separate business. The corporation, however, sees no merit in this. The accounting system that prepares the group accounts, on the other hand, is clearly not a viable system (in fact it is a function of the corporation's metasystem), since it could not conceivably operate independently of the corporation whose accounting system it is. The same is true of the sales department.

Confusion creeps in when people notice that the actual group of people and their facilities that I should call metasystemic to the collection of operational elements (each of which is a viable system), could go away and construct a business. The accountants just mentioned, for example, could doubtless leave the organization en masse, to set up a firm of 'company doctors'. The operational research department, or the computer department, or the market research department: all these could leave the corporation, and set up as independent consultants. They would then *become* viable systems. But they are not viable systems *now,* because their role is to serve the corporation, and to service the viable systems that constitute the operational elements of that corporation. It may help to make this point clear if we distinguish between, on the one hand, the knowledge and experience and comradeship of the people who staff such departments (which are the attributes that would enable them to found a viable system in the market place), and, on the other hand, the content of their work. Every system that they operate, every statistic that they handle, every conclusion that they reach, is in aid of the elemental operations of the enterprise. Therefore they are not themselves, in their corporate roles, viable systems: they simply cannot maintain a separate existence.

In the second place, we have to note that any viable system exists in an environment, and that this environment may be a precondition of viability. For instance, no-one would deny that *you* are a viable system, 'able to maintain a separate existence'. You achieved that status at the moment when you could operate without your umbilical cord. But there is now a particularly nasty bomb which exhausts the oxygen over a wide area. If that bomb were dropped near you, you would cease to be viable, because you cannot operate without oxygen. In short, the concept of 'a separate existence' is a relative concept.

For these two reasons, applications of the cybernetic models unfolded here have to pay attention to the managerial realities which they attempt to reflect. It has been argued strongly that all systems — their natures and purposes — are subjective. Therefore the managerial consensus as to what the firm or institution really IS will always be critical to the decision as to what is and what is not allowed to count as an operational element, or contained viable system. And this may change with time. For example, a large computer installation may start off as part of the regulative activity of the metasystem. Then it grows, and becomes a frighteningly large component of the 'head office overhead'. Therefore a decision is taken to allow this unit to offer services outside the corporation as a Computer Bureau. So far so good. But it may happen that this Bureau becomes a major profit centre for the firm, and that its internal services becomes a minimal part of its activity. At this point, the firm should begin to wonder whether it has not changed its role, and become a viable system — an operational element, rather than a metasystemic activity. If the firm does not ask itself that question, be assured that the managers of the computer undertaking certainly will ask the question of themselves. They may then give the firm a sharp lesson in the nature of viability. (The current pages are intended to demonstrate this lesson by reasoning, and in advance of any internal coup.)

Here is a further example of the difficulties that are met within nominating contained viable systems. It frequently happens in the enterprise that somebody's brain-child, which has attracted financial support as an experimental undertaking, begins to flourish and to earn money. It is *on the way* to becoming a viable system. It will *eventually* become an operational element of the firm. But at which point? This example will be reconsidered when we have established the mechanism that can handle it. So much space is being devoted to the correct identification of operational elements at this stage, because it turns out in practice to offer the worst problems, and the most traps to intending users of these cybernetics. It was a memorable day when I was presented with an application of the viable system model to an entire industry, in which *not one* of the nominated operational elements answered the criteria of a viable system. All of the functions nominated were in fact activities of the metasystem. Well, anyone can make a mistake. But it is clearly not too early to urge that the nesting process put forward here requires much thought. We live in an hierarchical culture, and the notion of recursion in the form advanced is foreign to our ways of thinking.

With these explanations of what is going on, we begin cautiously to put together the elements of which the operational system is constructed, and to see how the system that they then comprise relates to its metasystem. We are working towards another conceptual tool that will be needed. Now surely we can claim that it is a necessary condition of a viable system that it should have operational elements. If it did not, it would not be a system at all; it would just be a *thing*. Therefore we may draw the diagram shown in Figure 23.

Here is an enterprise, of whatever kind, that has three operational elements. They cohere; because although each is itself a viable system, they all perform as distinctive parts of another viable system (which is the one that we are modelling).

The metasystem exists to undertake whatever functions are required to procure coherence. For the time being, we shall take it that the three elements have no relationships with each other (which is a temporary simplification), and we shall take the metasystem to be a logical construct (which indeed it is). Call it 'senior management' if you must; but then beware of all the connotations that this phrase will necessarily import into the logical situation. Its real nature will emerge as these chapters proceed.

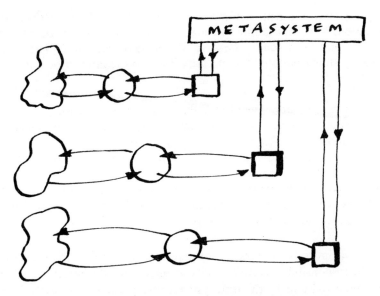

Figure 23. Three operational elements in their relationship to a
metasystem (but without relationship to each other)

The first issue to examine is clearly the relationship between any one of these
operational elements and 'its' metasystem (that is, the metasystem is in fact
shared between all three). The cybernetic logic of this relationship has already
been exhibited in Chapter Three: but now we must look at the variety
equations that dominate it, in more human and more empirical terms. Then let
us redraw the above diagram insofar as it stands for any one of the three
dependencies indicated.

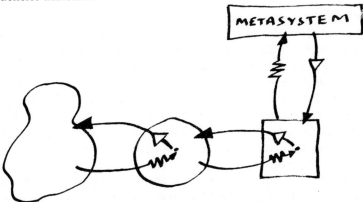

Figure 24. The relationship between any one operational element
and its metasystem

The operational element, subject as it is to the Three Principles of Organization, is by now familiar enough. Then consider the relationship of its managerial unit (the square box) to the metasystem itself. The diagram immediately shows attenuators and amplifiers on the interactions: is this too *necessary?*

Assuredly it is necessary. The metasystem cannot possibly assimilate the total variety generated by (even this single example of) an operational element. Nor can the metasystem exhibit requisite variety towards the operational element, without amplifiers. To do either of these things, it would have to descend into the black box, and effectively to police every action across the horizontal domain. Therefore the vertical link above is as much subject to the three principles as is the horizontal double-link. Let us observe how those principles work in practice on the vertical linkage.

The first principle relates to the law of requisite variety itself. In practice this is met by the responsibility-accountability arrangement. Resources are allocated to the managerial unit by the metasystem, in response to proposals from the managerial unit that are quintessentially attenuated in their variety. Those proposals are declarations of intent, supported by minimal operational data. The resources are provided — under amplification. For it is not simply a question of saying: 'here is the money you want'. There are amplifying rules attaching to those resources. If there were not, the managerial unit could simply say: 'thank you for the money', and pocket it. The rules are basically terms of agreement as to what is accepted as accountability: that is to say, the amplification sets the parameters of the *returning* attenuator. As usual, we are dealing with a dynamic system, and the vertical loop on the diagram is indeed continuous.

There are many other forms of amplification to be found on this vertical loop, and not all of them are neutral in their effect on morale at the operational level. Good higher management will provide variety amplification that is supportive of the operational unit's amplifiers. For example, if the management unit decides to start a special publication aimed at its operation as a means of increasing its variety, and if it has no budget for this, then the higher management might make a special grant, and provide an amplification of its own perceived states to be floated on this vehicle. Unfortunately, however, many standard forms of amplification on the vertical loop are damaging to the performance of the operational unit. For by amplifying its own variety in the form: 'thou shalt not do this, that, and the other — as a matter of company policy', the higher management seriously attenuates the variety of the managerial unit. As has been seen, that unit has by definition a major task in amplifying its own variety on the twin horizontal loops. If its local autonomy is curtailed by instructions from above, its task will be all the harder. Let us pay particular attention to this point, as very strong use will be made of it later on.

The second principle relates to the channel capacity of the vertical loop. This has to be capable of transmitting requisite variety, given whatever agreed system of attenuators and amplifiers is in use. Again, the formal arrangements seem to work well in practice, and they are usually perceived as neutral in human terms. But experience suggests that these formalities provide only an *average* variety balance. *Requisite* variety may well entail that huge surges of variety must be transmitted along these channels at particular moments. It is standard practice that this marginal variety is made available by straightforward human interaction. And, since conditions of virtual crisis obtain so familiarly in modern management, this often means that a large proportion of the total time available is spent in extremely inefficient variety absorption of the marginal variety (that is, the difference between average and requisite variety), using either formal or informal *ad hoc* confrontations. So I have observed.

Informally, we find that the formalizations providing the *average* variety absorption have broken down, and have to be supported by *ad hoc* procedures that are tantamount to inquisitions. For example, I have seen an entire budget procedure (that took the entire financial year to implement) superceded by a 'court of enquiry', conducted by directors of the firm, moving round every division of the corporation — two days at a time — and overthrowing the corporate plan in ten days. At the time, this was regarded in political terms as 'horse trading'. In terms of management theory, it has to mean that the procedures set up to prepare the budget were simply defective. But in cybernetic terms, it is obvious that the variety balancing apparatus built into the formal procedures was taking out far too little of the variety engendered. It was working, as it were, on the lowest common multiple rather than the highest common factor exhibited by the variety equation. Consequently, the marginal variety was ninety percent of the problem — instead of (say) nine percent.

Thirdly, there is (from the third principle) the question of transduction. Here again the formal-informal dichotomy is critical. Once the encoding and decoding of information has been taken into account on the formal network that represents the vertical loop, people assume that the transduction problem is solved. If it is not, then (they think) it will be overcome by the informal network. They have good reason for this belief, insofar as people honestly consider that eyeball-to-eyeball confrontation presents no serious problem in transduction. Yet it does. If two statesmen confront each other in person, and do not happen to have a language in common, then official interpreters are supplied in the role of transducers — and onlookers assume that the transducers are infallible machines. But they are not. Nor should anyone versed in cybernetics conceivably accept that they are.

The matter is straightforward, but not perhaps as straightforward as it immediately looks. The two statesmen dispose very high varieties, on each side. Do the interpreters dispose an equivalent variety? Surely not: the interpreters are variety attenuators, because they do not at all comprehend the nuances (states of the system) that they seek to interpret. I came to understand this myself long ago. At the age of seventeen, I was a student of philosophy; and I grappled in *English* with Bergson's book called *Matière et Memoire*. The book made no sense at all. Therefore I was moved to read it in French. I discovered that the English translator — my transducer — was rendering the French words *l'esprit, l'âme,* and even *le cerveau,* by the same word: *mind.* Now this was a variety attenuator operating in the transducer — *par excellence.* Since then, at a maturer age, I fell into the habit of listening to a conference speaker with one ear, and listening to the transduction of his speech through the second ear — through the earphones that were alleged to provide 'simultaneous translation'. This experience was shattering. I wish no harm to those who undertake the onerous task of simultaneous translation. They are excellent linguists. For the sake of the argument, let us call them *perfect* linguists, and then they cannot be hurt. The fact is that they do not have requisite variety as transducers. The immediate result of my experiments was to understand why it was, when my own turn came to speak, that no-one laughed at my jokes.

Now comes the point: this is not a problem of 'translation' as such, as everyone thinks. It is very precisely a problem of requisite variety. The translator is (I just admitted it) a perfect linguist. But does the translator personally comprehend — not my *words* — but the number of possible states that I intend to evoke by my words. No: neither he nor she, in my experience, deploys that much variety. To continue (for a moment) in personal vein, I record the experience of correcting my interpreter. Had I enjoyed a mastery of the language involved, no interpreter would have been needed; as it was, her capability as a translator was not in doubt — she was superb. So what happened on that occasion was not a matter of linguistic subtlety. It was a failure of requisite variety in the transducer, because I wanted to draw a distinction that did not exist for the interpreter. It existed in the language, and she knew the language. But she did not know that I wanted to draw a distinction.

These anecdotes point to grave difficulties in the conduct of world affairs. What concerns us in the management context is that although there is no problem of translation, there may yet be a problem of transduction. The boss may perfectly well hear, and perfectly well understand, the words he hears. But if those words are attempting to draw a distinction that he cannot recognize, then the transduction lacks requisite variety. Once the point is taken that there may be a problem here that is deeper than the obvious semantic issue ('what does he actually *mean*?'), one may well become extremely alert to the risk. Again, my own experience is that vertical loop transducers often fail in this way, and no-one is quite sure what has gone wrong because the very existence of the transducer is not recognized. 'But I *told* him': how often one hears that cry of despair.

Having taken this preliminary look at the nature of the vertical loops that connect each operational element to the metasystem (which we are still treating as a logical construct), we should think about other likely connexions in the vertical dimension. To do this, it is necessary to redraw the diagram so far used, and to introduce certain diagrammatic conventions. First of all, let it be clear why we are using two dimensions — the horizontal and the vertical. It is NOT to pay attention to 'seniority', as on the orthodox organization chart. The task is to construct a necessary and sufficient model of any viable system. The system contains major functional parts, the operational elements, which are themselves viable systems. These have to be spread out, somehow or other, on these two-dimensional pages. If there is no intention to call any one of them 'senior' to any other, then maybe they should be strung out across the page like this:

Figure 25. A first attempt to diagram three operational elements of a viable system

But if we do that, we are faced with insuperable problems in trying to indicate relationships between them. The diagrams would soon be covered with lines and arrows, and would look like a piece of knitting that had been entrusted to the family cat. Therefore these operational elements are turned into *a list*. Lists are arranged, by agreement, vertically on the page. We see the answer in Figure 26.

Here is a *list* of three operational units, of equal 'seniority'. The point must be stressed, because it conflicts with the conventions of organization charts. Please: this is a *list*. (No-one supposes that Mr Aaron is senior to Mr Zacchary in the directory.) Each of these units does its own job on the horizontal axis. The vertical dimension is used to indicate logical relationships between them, and between each of them and their shared metasystem. So the first convention used here is the simplification of Figure 23, as far as the three managerial units (square boxes) are concerned. *The two diagrams are meant to be equivalent* in this respect. Therefore it is not contended that the lowest operational element in the list has to communicate with the metasystem *through* the two elements listed above it. We simply cannot afford all the lines that would be needed to connect each one separately (as we did in Figure 23) to the metasystem. Nor can we afford to move the metasystem to the right-hand-side of the diagram, which would be very attractive — since it is a logical construct and not some kind of authority. That is because we shall need that space on the page for other purposes.

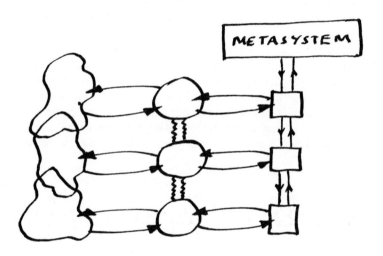

Figure 26. Three operational elements in their relationship to a metasystem, and (compare Figure 23) in their relationship to each other

The diagrammatic limitations that apply to the square boxes apply to the other symbols as well. Look at the 'environments': the first intersects with the second, and the second with the third. But most certainly the first intersects with the third as well. This cannot be shown without introducing confusion to the diagram later on. Again, there is a postulated connexion (the squiggly lines) between operations (the circles). And the diagram again appears to contend that there is no connexion between the first and third operations. There is. We cannot afford the white space to show it.

Finally, all the amplifiers and attenuators have been omitted, again in the interest of simplification. But let us not forget about them, nor about the three principles of organization that apply to *all* the loops that are implicit (though not explicit) in the picture. If the conventions adopted are to be properly understood, it is well worth counting the number of loops that the diagram depicts; otherwise the simplifying conventions may fool us into thinking that life is less complicated than it is. So: how many loops are intended? There are *eighteen* loops connecting the three operational elements (exclusive of the metasystem): maybe you forgot the connexions between the squares and the environments. They exist, even though managers who explore their environments may perforce work through their operational models at the psychological level. Then we have to add the three loops connecting the metasystem to the managerial units, as was shown in full in Figure 23, to reach a total of *twenty-one* loops. And of course it is a mere convention that only three operational units are depicted. Had there been four, the number of loops would have been *thirty-four*. Thus does variety proliferate. And if there are three principles applicable to every one of these loops: then, for four elemental operations, there are one hundred and two cybernetic checks to make. I have dwelt on the simplifying conventions of Figure 26 for that reason. It conceals, for reasons of draughtsmanship, much that is of deep concern. And by the time that it is embedded in the full-scale model, people tend to forget all about its innate complexity. We are faced with serious issues of variety engineering in studying this whole organization — without actually entering a single black box. . . .

Consider now the 'squiggly line' connexions between operations. These connexions may be either strong or weak; but in any viable system, they certainly exist. In a conglomerate, to take the weakest linkage, there may be no superficial relationship at all. But even in a conglomerate, where the viable system itself is a kind of holding company, and the operational elements hardly seem to know of each other's existence, the vertical squiggly loops are still there. For example, the separate divisions are at the least competing for capital. They may also be competing for managerial talent, trained within the metasystem. It is within these special circumstances, whatever they happen to be, that the three principles need investigation. If the management does not attend to this, it could well be that organized labour will. Managers always seem to be surprised when faced with a strike called 'in sympathy' across the squiggly lines, for example; and, if they are not surprised, their representatives usually claim *force majeure*. It is not 'their fault'. But of course it is their fault. The likelihood of sympathetic action is implicit in the organizational structure of the *operational* linkages, of which senior managers are often unaware, and if the workforces involved 'understand' the three principles to better effect than does the management (although neither side has encountered this analysis by cybernetics), then the management is undeniably at fault. It has to be remarked that organized labour often appears (to me) to act with an instinctive understanding of cybernetic principles that is lacking in the boardroom. To account for that observation is not so hard. It is inordinately easy to annihilate variety in the boardroom — it can be done by clearing the throat. On the shop floor it is much more difficult.

The squiggly line connexion may, on the other hand, be very strong. For example, if the total model related to a steelworks, the list of operational circles might stand for an ironworks, a steelworks, a cogging mill, and so on — a succession of processes feeding each other with hot metal. In such a case the vertical loops between operations are all-important, and the variety interactions ought not to be confused with those that appertain between the managerial units (although those are important too). There is a clear difference. The states of the operations are directly matched with each other in terms of the physical product, rather than in terms of a management system. The channels involved are extra-managerial: it is extraordinary the degree to which a receiving operation *knows* about the states of the delivering operation (and this is very hard to measure in practice). The transducers, in the case of the steelworks, seem to be the interprocess stocks: they contain coded information about probable next states of the delivering operation which can be read at the receiving end. I have often noticed that the variety-exchangers at the operational linkage are far richer, more accurate, and speedier, than the bureaucratic variety-exchanges between the managerial units — which are supposedly 'controlling' the action. Of course, the reason is that the operations are their own representation: like the bricklayers of Chapter Four, they furnish their own requisite variety. That variety is necessarily attenuated in the office representation of operational reality.

Next we come to the loop connexions between the environments, where again the Three Principles apply. That generalization can be made with confidence. But examples must necessarily vary widely, because organizations 'parcel out' environments to their operational elements in highly arbitrary ways. For example, an enterprise that works from 'coast-to-coast' may divide environments primarily by geographic divisions. In that case, the overlaps shown in the diagram may look incorrect. It would appear that there are sharp demarcations, coming at the county/province/state/country boundaries, which negate looping interactions. But even in this extreme case, the argument does not hold. Adjacent territories overflow into each other, at the very least to the extent that people living near the territorial boundary are perfectly well aware of the reputation that the enterprise has in a neighbour's house on the other side of that boundary. And in general, we must expect that the viable system projects a personality, which is read (under whatever local transformation) within each environment — even though each distinctive operational element is doing its utmost to project a divisional and territorial image. But the more usual picture is the opposite of this. Large sums are spent in trying to secure a corporate image of the enterprise that will transcend all environmental boundaries. It has to be noted that, in this cause, many lies are told. The large sums become justified in the eyes of the enterprise insofar as the lies are believed.

As soon as the nature of the environmental overlap is identified in any given case, the Three Principles can be used to examine the relationship between any two operational elements in those adjacent environments. For example, the product, the sales force, the advertising activity — all are likely to be operating in geographic contiguity, despite the separation of their management units. And if geography is not used to make environmental distinctions, but rather functional divisions are employed, the logical intersection of environments will be greater still. In *all* cases, there is an environmental classification that runs right across the board, for any viable system: consider, for example, the financial prowess of the whole enterprise, or its employment policies. No amount of separation among operational elements, undertaken as a matter of management policy, can separate those environments as seen from the stock exchange, from government offices, from banks, from the committee rooms of political lobbies, or even perhaps (dare it be said?) from the employees themselves.

The integral nature of the viable system *may* be concealed from the general public, and especially from the consumer. Thus pharmaceutical companies, publishing companies, chemical companies (for instance) may well succeed in marketing virtually the same product in different environments as if they were completely separate. 'Different environments' does not necessarily mean *geographically* different. It is noteworthy that the enterprise has the facility to define environments at will — for the appropriate expenditure. For example, electrical appliances are mostly manufactured by giant monopolies. They are marketed under a variety of names, and the only feature that distinguishes them is the price. Then the environments that are set up are a function of social class. Sufferers from back-ache may buy the same remedy, differently packaged, from the same supplier, differently organized; the same is true of down-market magazines; the same is true of household detergents. However, the rise of consumer protection movements means that all run the risk of exposure; and it becomes increasingly prudent to look at the looping interactions between environments. Where more overt operations are concerned, in transportation, social agencies, or government itself, the need to study those loops is paramount.

Probably the most compelling illustration of these arguments is to be found in any enterprise dealing in information. Such enterprises include government itself, broadcasting, the press, telephones, and all financial operations such as insurance and brokerage. Just because information is a basic commodity, the issue of variety transfer within and between environments is crucial. This is usually attended to in terms of the second principle: the requisite variety of the channel capacity. Were it not so, the enterprise would probably not operate at all. But people rarely distinguish the transduction from the transmission; and (since they have not even heard of it) they do not look at the underlying requisite variety at all.

Here is another example which is quite familiar, and it comes from marketing. Suppose that the basic division between the elementary operations is territorial, so that there is a minimal overlap between environments. All the operations are selling essentially the same set of products, which is the company's standard range. But the company also produces a few very special products, the marketing of which demands specialist technical knowledge. Therefore the operation that handles these specialities covers *all* territories. Here is a picture of this situation:

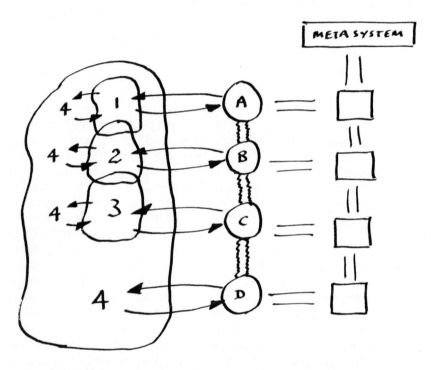

Figure 27. An example of elemental operations (A,B,C) that deal with specific territories (1,2,3), while a specialist element (D) is trying to cover the whole ground (4)

For example, the country is exhaustively divided into three territories 1, 2, and 3, and three management groups conduct the three operations A, B, and C that service these areas. All of them are dealing in (say) mild steel, or (say) individual insurance. Operation D, however, is the specialist activity, dealing in (say) high-alloy and stainless steel, or (say) group insurance; and D representatives handle these products *wherever* they are required, at home and abroad.

There is an obvious managerial problem on the right-hand side of the diagram, insofar as operations have to mesh together (squiggly lines), while costs and revenues must be apportioned (a matter for inter-square box discipline). But what is going on in the inter-environmental interactions? Consider as typical the 1 → 4 → 1 loop. A-men in environment 1 do not have requisite variety in environment 4 (they lack the requisite variety of technical states). D-men in environment 4 do not have requisite variety in environment 1 (they lack requisite variety of territorial states). This may be all very well from the representatives' point of view, especially if they are friends; because they then have the chance to amplify variety to each other, they have the channels, and they can perform the transductions. But from the point of view of the customer, the situation is quite different. He may be completely mystified, and his view of the company's persona may be hostile. The point is that the customer is right in the centre of this environmental convention, and in practice may be forced into the role of variety transducer on the left-hand-side loops. The company is not paying its customers for any such service; and it may be totally unaware that it is demanding it. (I have observed this many times.)

To conclude: we need to study the variety connexions on all three vertical relationships under the criteria provided by the Three Principles. The first common fault is to forget about the environmental interactions, on the understanding that the variety has been taken out by attenuators organized on the horizontal double-loops. It may have done so successfully in terms of internal housekeeping; but the world outside continues to proliferate variety. That has to be modelled, maybe in great detail: the tracing of loops and the assessment of variety balancers is more difficult in the environment than in the part of the organization that is under direct regulation. The second common fault is to forget about the operations interactions — the squiggly lines — on the understanding that variety has been taken out by attenuators called 'established practice'. That may well be true for any normal circumstance. But the capacity for variety proliferation is still there; if the confidence of operational staff is lost, this variety will rapidly recrudesce. If these two issues are not attended to, the viable system attempts to handle all vertical variety equations through their surrogates in the muddy-box models of the management units. That is a recipe for bureaucratic fun-and-games — which will not be effective in cybernetic terms.

We can see this diagnosis coming to its full pathological fruition in the growth of bureaucracy wherever government activity impinges on the individual citizen. This growth, which is so notorious, is generally regarded with resignation as some kind of natural law. It is not: it arises from total ignorance of the cybernetic realities, and therefore a total managerial failure to apply the Three Principles that have been unfolded here. The growth occurs, as was noted in general before, because the law of requisite variety asserts itself. In the absence of variety engineering, it does so without any regard to managerial effectiveness.

The whole of the model developed in this chapter appears to be a NECESSARY component of a viable system. For we have done no more than trace the relationships that must exist between the tripartite operational elements as originally defined. The *collection* of operational elements (that is, including their horizontal and vertical connexions) will be referred to as SYSTEM ONE. As will soon be discovered, System One is not sufficient as a condition of viability. But it is necessary; it does constitute a conceptual tool; it does have concomitant percepts in the managerial world; and it does acknowledge some powerful precepts — as this chapter has tried to show.

LATER IN THE BAR...

'How is it that systems are subjective, while some of them can be singled out and declared to be viable?'

'Once you have defined them, you can tell whether they are viable or not.'

'And those criteria are suddenly supposed to be objective?'

'Well, it's all about necessity and sufficiency within a stated frame of reference.'

'Yes, remember the argument about favoured environments. It said that the concept of viability is relative to that. Nothing would be viable in a vacuum.'

'Isn't this a Humpty Dumpty business of paying the words extra and having them mean what you like?'

'We do that all the time in any case. All the terms we use drag around a lot of connotations, and I suppose that systems are the same.'

'Conventional thinking is positivist.'

'What's wrong with being positive? There's too much negative thinking around as it is.'

'Not positive — positivist. It has to do with illusions of objectivity.'

'Oh damn all this high-falutin talk. We make an hypothesis, and test it. It may be false. That's an objective fact.'

'Not if its built into the system as defined, because that definition itself is subjective.'

'I just don't understand the argument.'

'Hang on: somewhere here I've got a little piece of Anders Munk that I'd better read to you.'

'Who's he?'

'Biologist. Dane. Professor in Copenhagen.'

'*Biologists are* proper *scientists. Don't tell me he doesn't believe in objective facts*. . . .

'*Wait for it: I've found the thing. This is what he says:*

> '*Melbourne and Toronto are two cities of about the same size and about the same car density.*
>
> *The number of traffic accidents per year is four times higher in Melbourne than in Toronto.*
>
> *In Australia, 'everybody knows' that even the most timid and civil person will turn into a roaring monster as soon as he sits down behind the steering wheel of a car. Whereas in Canada people are 'ignorant' of this 'fact'.*

'Ignorant *and* fact *are in inverted commas. So is* everybody knows.'

'*Well, you've got an objective fact in Melbourne, and not in Toronto.*'

'*Is that likely? People are much the same everywhere — especially at similar levels of so-called civilization.*'

'*You mean that the fact is a function of the subjective account of the system*. . . .'

'*That won't do. If there are all these accidents in Melbourne, then there* are. *It can be* verified.'

'*Put verified in quotes too. That's what a positivist fallacy is.*'

'*Let me tell you what Anders Munk says about it: 'there is something wrong in the Australian set of expectations'. But they don't change them because 'Lo and behold! They see it coming true every day'.*'

'*All that matters is that the expectations* do *come true. Those accidents are the objective facts.*'

'*The difference lies in what you are going to do about it. Are you going to spend more on policing traffic, or on changing expectations?*'

'*Will someone please tell me what all this has to do with the bases of viability?*'

'*Well, it seems to me that a system will not be viable unless the relationships between its operational elements in the three vertical planes conform to the three principles of organization — just as the relationships between the three elements on each horizontal plane must conform.*'

'*So what if they don't. Does the company fall apart?*'

'*I don't think it's easy as that. We keep hearing that these cybernetic laws assert themselves* anyway.'

'*Then what are we bothering about?*'

'*It's the same argument in the vertical plane as it was before in the horizontal plane. If we just wait for nature to do all the variety engineering for us, we shall lose out on effectiveness.*'

'*Nature* is *effective. That's the whole meaning of a 'natural law', as I understand it — it's something that always works.*'

'*Hey, John, I'm just getting the point. It's that business about the purposes of the system. I don't know what nature's purposes are, but I don't see why nature should care whether my firm makes a profit. That's a subjective criterion that we lay on top of nature's attitude to viability.*'

'*You mean that we can muddle through with nature, but that we need to design our own amplifiers and attenuators if we adopt subjective criteria of purpose that go beyond just surviving.*'

'*Well, that's obvious, Bill. If you strip that remark of all this jargon, it just says that managers manage. Of course they fix on purposes, and of course they implement those purposes in the enterprise.*'

'*Don't throw the baby out with the bathwater, John. The issues — like subjectivity and the traps about purpose — that the jargon is trying to express are real enough. Remember all that business about the switching of the electric light bulb.*'

'*I was in Montreal last month — *'

'*No, but Tony, we weren't talking about subjectivity. I want to get back to the three vertical planes. We've got variety being sponged up by environmental, operational, and managerial interactions. Right. How do we know that viability is consistently served by all three? They might be inconsistent in terms of purpose.*'

'Just a minute, John. Sid was trying to get in about Montreal.'

'Oh, its nothing much. It was Tony talking about the switching of those light bulbs reminded me. I was staying at my favourite hotel, the Bonaventure. The mirror in the bathroom was surrounded by light bulbs, like a star's dressing room, and there was only one switch. I counted the bulbs — fourteen. On the glass was pasted a notice which said: Conserve Precious Energy. Sorry to spoil the flow.'

'That's real life for you, I must say. Only one switch, so no requisite variety for conservation.'

'More than that. If we've got a real life example here, lets apply it to the question John just raised. Didn't you say that the three vertical planes were at war, or something?'

'I said they might be inconsistent in terms of purpose.'

'Right. There's an environmental interaction — to do with the competition for business and so on — which says that we must flatter Sid by equipping his bathroom like a rock star's. But the management loop has an energy conservation policy that it wants to promote. . . '

'What's the operational loop doing?'

'That's easy. Fourteen bulbs with one switch.'

'So the three planes are behaving inconsistently.'

'See it all the time.'

'Don't he lugubrious, Bill.'

'Some businesses don't even survive, you know.'

'According to this theory, that must mean that the management is so bad that it actively prevents the natural laws of viability from operating.'

'Come off it: we can't be that bad.'

'Well, I can credit it. Look at some of the messes we get into with union negotiations. We have lunatic postures taken up on both sides, and the place grinds to a halt.'

'What's that got to do with it? We all know that human nature can be turbulent. That's no discovery of cybernetics!'

'No. But if we look at a problem like that through the three principles, I can see that variety is being blocked off all round. Probably we never designed the amplifiers and attenuators in the first place — then it's just another example of the variety laws taking over, without regard to the subjective criteria we would like to apply.'

'Tell that to my shop stewards.'

'Bill, that's what they're telling you.'

'What are you guys TALKING about? I'm up to my neck in problems of wage differentials. That's hard social graft. Can't you see it? People don't like their differentials eroded, and they call it unfair. It's got nothing to do with all this stuff.'

'Hasn't it? 'Variety is the number of possible states'. When wage differentials are compressed, we are losing variety in the number of states of payment.'

'That's it! Then there is a mismatch between the variety of the work structure and the variety of the pay structure.'

'Hell, that's just to name the problem. It doesn't help to answer it.'

'I'm not so sure. If that is the nature, as well as the name, of the problem, we are up against Ashby's Law — and it means that we should never have adopted pay policies that make uniform changes across the board. It drives down the variety.'

'Then somehow we have to get the variety back.'

'All right. Meanwhile there's a strike. You can't deal with human beings as if they could just be computed with. It doesn't work, and its immoral — technocratic.'

'No-one suggested that. Look, if there are cybernetic preconditions to a successful negotiation in human terms, they'd better be met. The argument is the exact inverse of the one you used. You want to blame human beings for behaving badly when you set up conditions in which they can't possibly behave well.'

'This is all very tedious. We don't do so badly.'

'Well, we're not doing so well, either. Think of the public services. We're always hearing about the tendency of things like Health and Education to collapse under their own weight — or their own cost. And I would certainly like to see this variety engineering applied to them. How do you think the vertical interactions stand up under the Three Principles?'

'What would you have? For Health, the operational elements would be hospitals, general practice, and local government. That's three horizontal double loops. So where are the relevant vertical loops? Or where are they for primary, secondary, and tertiary education, in the second case?'

'Well, they exist. The environments are interactive for a start. there are some squiggly line connexions between operations. And the management units confer.'

'Yes, and all you get is confusion plus a thundering great bureaucracy.'

'We're not going far enough into it. The point surely is that if the whole set of loops were examined in terms of the Three Principles, we ought to find out what's wrong. In the meantime, the natural law takes over — so that viability is purchased at enormous cost.'

'How could we get that done?'

'You can't. You'd just get another committee.'

'That's nature's way of absorbing the variety of any change agent.'

'I'm just thinking about that business about accidents in Montreal and Toronto... '

'So?'

'Well, maybe the bureaucracy works as it does because, quote, everybody knows *that it does.'*

'Hmmm. Here are the drinks, people. I propose a toast to Anders Munk.'

PART TWO

THE VIABLE SYSTEM

Summary of Part Two

Equipped with a basic armoury of cybernetic concepts, percepts and precepts, we are ready to explore — in Part Two — the nature of the enterprise conceived as a viable system. But the basic building-block has already been established: it is called System One. In this Part, the main concern will be to elaborate its metasystem.

Some sixth sense of caution checks the immediate postulation of the metasystemic subsystems, however. There are four of them; and before this Part of the book is finished they will be familiar names to us. The check, or the pause comes in the first of these next chapters, numbered Six. The sheer force of cybernetic analysis has already become clear in the unfolding of System One; and it is necessary to consolidate its meaning in the face of dauntingly new descriptions. In particular, if the human being stands at the heart of enterprise, can that person prevail in a morass of theories, theorems and diagrams? And if so, then how can those cybernetic phenomena also stand at the heart of enterprise?

Truly, there is no antinomy here. Humankind has by no means been excluded from the preliminaries of Part One. The subjectivity inherent in systems theory, and the observer's role, attest to that. There have been many examples quoted that demonstrate the human predicament as central to the theory. But that is not to deny the existence of the theory itself, which we continue to evolve. The role in the enterprise of the people who actually constitute the organizational structure is paramount; yet we proceed to investigate the regulatory principles that necessarily bind them together, so that the enterprise maintains its identity in the face of all disturbance.

Chapter Six does not advance the structural properties of the viable system. It uses the pause to reflect on the questions of freedom that the above remarks propose. These are not grandly philosophical; they are specific to the organization of any enterprise. (Even so: it is doubtful, surely, whether the basic notion of freedom can legitimately be considered outside the confines of some institutional framework, even if that 'institution' turns out to be just 'me'.) The autonomy of the elemental operational unit is in question here. The stance of the book is now poised on the end of a spring-board. Then take a deep breath for the dive; because 'freedom' is an emotive word. . . .

... What is more, as Chapter Six explains, the concept of freedom is relative to the purposes of the system in which the unit seeks to exercise it. When its 'absolute' character is abandoned, as it must be, then Chapter Seven must confront the issue of its constraint. It does so with some delicacy, as human rights demand. We are not necessarily dealing with constraint as an oppression, but with constraint as a service. *Liberty is not altogether untrammelled: that is called licence — an overblown 'freedom' which people, in their own interests, wish to constrain. They often talk of the constraining boundary as the point where the exercise of one person's freedom impinges upon another's. But that is a static concept, and we are concerned with dynamics. Cybernetics has an answer to this perennial problem, that is set within the framework of the viable system. It is regarded as important, but as difficult to master — because it has no name in orthodox management theory. Here, it is firmly nominated as System Two of the viable system. Its unfamiliarity surely deserves the space it attracts. It is wholly concerned with the damping of oscillations within System One.*

Returning to the building-block called System One, we find that it is embedded in a metasystem. In Chapter Eight these two systems are teased apart, in the vertical dimension of the model as it is depicted on the printed page. The process exactly parallels the teasing-apart of System One in the horizontal dimension (which was accomplished in part One), and inevitably the same three cybernetic principles of organization apply. Precisely how *they apply is now our topic; and the arrangements that we find in real life provide the answers. A great deal of this 'vertical' variety is absorbed by happenstance. The enterprise is as it is. The* environments *of its elemental units interpose conditions on each other, curtailing variety explosions to whatever extent may be found in any particular application. In the same way, the strongly or weakly connected* operations *impose constraints on each others' variety. In the* management *domain, we find that the stamp of the manager's personality on his own elemental unit, coupled with the attempt of all System One managers to act as a team, constrains explosive variety in its turn. All of this variety absorption (in three different planes) arises from the nature of System One itself, given what the enterprise is actually doing, and without considering the metasystemic role. But this containment of variety is not enough. It is only when System One is synoptically reviewed as a whole that its potential synergy can be understood, and the need to contain residual vertical variety (left over from happenstance) can be perceived.*

Thus Chapter Eight determines the existence, within the metasystem, of System Three. This is the component of the metasystem that is synoptically and synergistically concerned with the optimal operation of System One — the inside *and* now *of the enterprise. Again, three channels of its operation are detected. They do not occur by happenstance, and must needs be designed. The first is obvious: it is the command channel. But we have already learned to minimize its variety attenuation. The second is System Two: but (as we know) its absorption of variety is by definition limited to oscillatory behaviour. Thus the necessity for a third metasystemic linkage is established: it may be called auditing.*

In this way, six variety loops are nominated on the vertical plane of the model — three determined by the nature *of the enterprise, and three designed for metasystemic, managerial reasons in accordance with the* purposes *of the enterprise. These six vertical loops (of which only one, the command loop, is customarily acknowledged in management theory) must absorb the total variety generated by the horizontal loops of the elemental units, according to Ashby's Law. This requirement leads to the designation of* The First Axiom of Management.

By this point, we have established the conditions whereby the internal *environment of the enterprise is stabilized. The* external *environment is so far being handled only through its impact on System One, for which it constitutes a disturbance — a threat to internal stability. But for the viable system itself, the external environment is more than this. It includes all the environments of the elements of System One, but much more. In particular, it includes the problematic environment that the future represents: the playground of opportunity. Then it becomes a necessary condition of viability that there should be a system within the metasystem that can deal with this. System Three is debarred, because it is dedicated to the internal environment, and System Four is born.*

In Chapter Nine the basic requirements of an effective System Four are explored. This is the weakest component of the viable system in existing management orthodoxy. System Four exists — it has to: but it is disseminated, and lacks integration. The models of the enterprise that it necessarily contains are locked in the heads of senior management as paradigms, and they are inaccessible to interrogation or to testing. The chapter considers how the elements of System Four may be focussed. The use of an operations room is discussed, and the managerial problems involved in inventing the future are seen to be intense. Solutions founder on human factors, and this is why these issues are so poorly handled in contemporary society.

The model of any viable system is nearing completion. If we understand the subsystems called Three and Four, dealing respectively with the internal and external environments, then we certainly perceive the necessity for each to absorb the other's variety. In practice, this is hard to accomplish, because each is a dedicated subsystem: they do not share the same managerial nor technological languages, and their criteria of success necessarily consider different spans of time. In Chapter Ten we are led to a fourth principle of organization; and also to a reconsideration of the operations room as a general management centre. Above all, we are led to the concept of closure, whereby the viable system 'turns in on itself' to become an identity. To achieve this organizationally, it becomes logically necessary to identify System Five.

This is synonymous with 'corporate management' in the managerial vernacular. Because of the route by which System Five has been encountered, however, we find that 'the boss' is a rather different entity from his customary image — except in a total autocracy, which turns out not to be a viable system in the long run. The role of System Five is publically ambiguous; cybernetically, its key role turns out to be as monitor of the variety sponge between Systems Three and Four: the administrator, as it were, of Ashby's Law in the metasystem.

The model is complete. It is closed. It has identity. Then is the viable system floating in space, untouched by any further influence than has yet been discussed? Certainly not: the logical framework that we have used shows the viable system as embedded in another viable system. The notion of recursion embraces the notion of local closure. But this will become finally clear in Part Three, when we shall try to understand the cohesiveness of an indefinite recursion of viable systems. For the comprehension of the next five chapters, it is well to think of the viable system as an independent entity, capable of survival in an as yet incompletely defined milieu.

CHAPTER SIX

Freedom

Maybe this is the most emotive word that could be written at the head of any page today.

Systematically, it seems, during our lifetimes, the world has become less and less free. More and more people have died for their devotion to the *idea* of freedom. Those deaths appear to be in vain.

I do not know, nor do I here intend to speculate, whether the turmoil and the sacrifice will pay dividends to humanity in the longer run.

Then why not get on with the book? If System One on its own does not provide the necessary and sufficient criteria or viability, then *why* does it not? What more needs to be added? What is the role of the metasystem in all of this? What is the point of interjecting the notion of *freedom*?

The point is very clear. As far as the evolving model of the viable system model is concerned, the dear question of freedom is locked into its orthogonality. There are series of horizontal loops in the picture of System One; there are series of vertical loops too. Thus these two-dimensional pages are committed to a presentation or organizational theory that sets the part (the operational element) at right-angles to the activity of the whole (the connectivity between operational elements). According to the conventions so far adopted, no meaning can be ascribed to any directionality *between* these two axes; they stand at right-angles; they are orthogonal.

Historically, in terms of this model, the reasons for this orthogonality derive from the neurocybernetics from which the model was itself derived (and these neurocybernetics may be consulted in *Brian of the Firm*). But in this book, neurocybernetic justifications have been forsworn. It is therefore a serious methodological question, in the present exposition, as to why we now find ourselves dealing with orthogonality as between the part and the whole. And the answer has everything to do with that emotive word 'freedom'.

When first we considered an operational element, the double-looped horizontal chain, it was FREE to act. Recognizably, the management unit (square) had things to say to the operations it managed (circle), and the operations had things to say to the environment. We analysed the conditions under which all this happens, and we discovered the three principles of variety engineering which govern those interactions. But as soon as we talked about *several* operational elements, cohering within a larger unit (the next level of recursion), and thereby involved with a *metasystemic* activity, we found ourselves drawing orthogonal diagrams.

The reason is that the coherence pattern of the whole affects the free action of the parts in a way which *cannot be translated* into graphically horizontal terms. The horizontal axis of the operational element is totally dedicated to its own activity. Whatever impinges on that free activity (since environmental shocks are already allowed for in the horizontal model) must arise in a different DIMENSION. A good definition of a dimension is 'a condition of existence'. It is a condition of existence for the operational element (*element*) that it subsists within a larger whole, containing other elements. The impact of those other elements, and of the metasystem that contains the whole, cannot be depicted in the horizontal, because they do not speak the elemental language. This impact is therefore orthogonal. There is again therefore, a purely graphical reason for depicting System One on two orthogonal axes, as has been done, and remembering that these diagrams tell us nothing about hierarchical seniority.

It turns out, however, that they do tell us something — and perhaps a great deal — about freedom.

Time was taken in the last chapter to consider, with some care, the interactions of the elements of this model on the vertical plane of the diagram. But that was to study particularities, or indeed peculiarities, of the connexions that necessarily subsist between boxes, circles, and amoeboid shapes, when the horizontal elements are *listed* (vertically) on the page. There is a more profound version of all this orthogonality. It says that AT ANY POINT in the space that the two-dimensional diagram occupies, two organizational forces are at work. The one depicted on the horizontal axis is the *operational* force (concerned with the effectiveness of elemental operations). The other is the *coherence* force (concerned with systemic viability). At any point on the diagram, then, these orthogonal forces interact. It is that interaction which DEFINES FREEDOM within the viable system.

The emotive word rejoins the argument. And yet we must hold back emotion, at least until our definitions are clear. The argument now stands thus: some account of freedom is to be found at *any* crossover-point on the horizontal/vertical axes of our two dimensional diagram: because elemental effectiveness and systemic viability continuously interact orthogonally, and because each is primarily concerned with contrasted requirements of viability.

The thorough understanding of what this really means entails some delay in devising metasystemic subsystems with which to surround System One, as defined in the last chapter. In any enterprise, the elemental operations themselves constitute the activity that defines systemic purpose; and it is precisely on the territory of System One that (for this reason) the practical issues of freedom must be settled. As many nations, as well as smaller enterprises, have discovered: no amount of metasystemic declaration of purpose can over-ride the operational facts. In pursuit of further understanding, then, the System One diagram is now redrawn — with a superimposed indication of an infinitely applicable orthogonal grid.

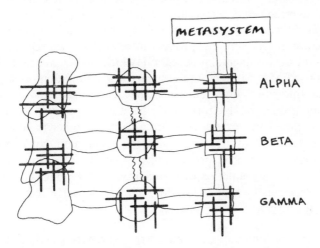

Figure 28. An indication of the infinitely applicable orthogonal grid that overlays the diagram of System One

Wherever a *point* is considered in a portion of the diagram that deals with horizontal-vertical interactions, the grid may be conceived as running through that point.

Starting from the notion that each elemental operation is autonomous, namely a free agent inside the enterprise, a given quantity of variety is available on the horizontal axis at this chosen *point.*

Then the question is: what effect on that variety does the vertical grid line passing through that point exert? Is the net effect of the vertical component adding variety to the horizontal component, or is it subtracting variety from it?

Consider the environmental interactions between elements. The policies 'in the field' that are adopted by one autonomous element may either add or subtract variety at a given point in the field or another autonomous element. If element Alpha makes a high-variety effort in its own territory to market a particular company product, thereby amplifying the possible states for that operation as it impinges on a particular geographical region (since no-one buys a product that does not exist for them), the variety grid will generate an effect in any intersecting portion of the environment of element Beta. At a particular point, this may add variety to the horizontal component in Beta. For although this point may exist in another geographical region, it could be that a thousand people there who did not know of the product's existence suddenly become aware of it — through no action at all on Beta's part. Then we should rightly regard this result as a bonus, or spin-off, of the original marketing effort. But suppose that Beta itself has invested heavily in a variety amplifier for a second company product, aimed at increasing the number of possible consumer states in a geographical region of its own. It could be that element Alpha has made a technical failure in servicing this product in one of its own regions, and that the effect of the environmental intersection (which we saw to be separate from divisions of terrain) is to block the element Beta's amplifiers as some *point*. For example, this point could represent a particular individual in the market for whom the promotional effort would have proven seductive, if his mind had not been closed by hearsay emanating from the other region. Then this ought to be regarded as negative spin-off: a common concomitant of unsuccessful investment or effort, to which attention is uncommonly drawn. In any case, the variety equation of the environmental loops betwen elements Alpha and Beta can be viewed as the sum of the net effects of the grid interactions for all *points* in the intersect.

The environmental domain is not exhausted by marketing activities, even in a manufacturing enterprise, however; and the same arguments apply to any other environmental concern. The point is *that there will be interventions* in elemental autonomy that arise in the environmental domain for any enterprise. This is extremely clear, for example, in the case of a political party and in the case of conducting a war. And those examples may lead us to suppose that the whole problem can and must be handled by interventions by the metasystem, acting in a Senior capacity.... .

The difficulty here is twofold. First of all, if environmental interaction entails intervention in elemental autonomy by its own nature, there is already a loss of freedom involved. To invoke a metasystemic solution, is to exacerbate the difficulty. If the nature of the enterprise and the management style is such that there is no perceived difficulty in this, the second and more covert difficulty appears. Does the metasystem deploy requisite variety to do the job? The answer is probably not, in practice. The metasystem will have sufficient problems in containing a regulatory model of the enterprise conceived as a collection of management units. Its models of their environment will usually be generated through the muddy box models contained in the elemental management units themselves. And this is why, even in the conduct of war (in which acceptance of metasystemic regulation, intervention in autonomy, and even loss of individual freedom is commonly accepted), many solutions to the environmental variety equation are necessarily generated within the environmental domain itself. Nelson put his telescope to his blind eye: 'I see no signal'. He saw the cybernetic point, instead, which is why he made sure that he did not see the metasystemic signal. And, in the second world war, we experienced the emergence of Commandos, of the Chindits, of Popski's Private Army — all variety absorbers operating within the environmental domain with little metasystemic direction in the absence of metasystemic requisite variety.

Next consider the operational interactions between elements. The squiggly line connexion between circles have been discussed before, and it was observed that those connexions may be strong or weak. In terms of freedom, the strong connexions are easy to discuss, since they not only intervene in autonomy — they dominate input and output activity. If element Beta necessarily accepts its raw material from element Alpha, and necessarily passes on its entire product to element Gamma, then its operational variety is heavily constrained. But suppose that it is open to such an element as Beta to purchase materials from outside, and to sell part of its product outside, then any *point* in its operational space that marks such an interaction with either element Alpha or Gamma can be represented as a grid point: and again it is clear that the vertical component of variety may increase or diminish the horizontal component.

These are operational phenomena. By this I mean that the interventions in autonomy exercised by vertical components across the squiggly lines are a function of the operational facts: we are not yet discussing 'management decisions', for these are 'square box' matters. But the management units can agree on policies between themselves only within the operational matter-of-fact, and we are arguing that this *of itself* offers a variety intervention at any shared point in the operational space. In a production situation, the relevant issues may well be technological. Suppose that an operational element has indeed permission to buy raw material from outside the firm. It may decide, then, to buy cold steel bars from outside (as part of a bulk purchase agreement, for example, which reduces the price of the bars below the firm's internal transfer price), although those bars are available inside. But this same element can hardly exercise its option when it comes to feeding a hot metal process. Where would it buy liquid iron for its foundry, except from the smelting furnace next door?

These considerations of course suggest that it may be worth while to make technological changes which would free an element from operational interventions of a vertical kind in its horizontal variety engineering. For example, the hot metal process *could* have its own smelter. But these sorts of proposition are looked upon, piecemeal, as ideas to be examined serially by a team of development engineers. It is not until the total pattern of vertical operational interconnexion is examined in terms of the variety equation, that the particular activities which cost too heavily in terms of horizontal variety can be pinpointed. Moreover, in these matters of technological intervention in autonomy, there is often an industry-wide technical culture which accepts the loss of freedom involved without even recognizing that it occurs. It is taken for granted that materials used in a particular process are of a certain delimited variety.

For example (and to stay with the metal-working illustration), a steel billet may be, say, ten metres long. To propose the use of billets that are, say, a hundred metres long, thereby adding a great of deal of vertical variety from the billet mill to the horizontal variety exercised by the bar and rod mill, runs straight into the cultural block that such a length of steel would not *be* a billet, according to accepted usage. (Remember the tiger of Chapter One.) This is not to say that people are incapable of coming to grips with an innovatory idea once it has been stated (although there are notorious problems even then). It is to say that the idea of a hundred-metre billet may never come up, because the bar-and-rod operational element knows that billets are more like ten metres long, and knows moreover that it could not (in its present technological format) cope with a hundred metre length. therefore *no erosion of liberty is even perceived*. Nevertheless, the loss of variety is a fact. Anyone who has ever tried to cut lengths of any material into a number of measured pieces knows about the loss involved in the wasted pieces left over. The longer the length, the less the incremental waste: the cutting-up schedule has more possible states.

Now we are speaking about the operational phenomena that necessarily make vertical interventions in horizontal variety manipulation for any element of System One. They need not of course be technological, but human. And again I think that erosion of liberty in the operations plane may not even be perceived. The most obvious case where it is perceived, and where that perception causes endless trouble, is in the case of a demarcation dispute. Here again it is the technical culture, now backed by the social culture to which it once gave rise, working up and down the vertical domain, that makes inevitable the subtraction of variety on the horizontal plane. One element cannot do as it would like, because another element is attempting to do as it would like, and because the contradiction is reflected through the grid to a focus at any *point* of the shared operational space. Attempts to solve such problems run into the fact that to enhance the autonomy of one element erodes it for the other. Thus the analogue of technical innovation in the previous example is human reorganization in this example. To effect either is difficult;

to effect both together may be much easier, since the technological change may unfreeze the human deadlock. This has often been attempted; it has often succeeded, and often failed. But usually it is attempted at a *point,* and without regard to the remaining points that constitute the shared operational space. That would account for those failures that I personally have seen. We have to study the whole variety equation involved in every shared domain.

If we require an example of the erosion of liberty in the operational plane that may *not* be perceived as such, two are readily available in the average firm. It is inevitable that (a) the incomes and (b) the fringe benefits of employees in any one operational element take away from the variety at (horizontal) disposal of any other element. This is so usual that it is not perceived, in the typical case. Now it is true that this intervention between operations is usually perceived as a metasystemic intervention; and the fact is that the metasystem *does* intervene. We shall examine that precise situation shortly. But our examination will not be understood to be metasystemic at all, unless the operational matters-of-factness of the interconnexions in the operational plane are fully understood in advance.

Any manager is accustomed to work within the imposed framework of a salary and wages 'policy', and other whole sets of 'policies'. They range from the provision of motor-cars for senior people to Christmas parties for operatives. He takes this framework for granted. Now what would he do with his horizontal authority, as the management unit of an operational element, if no such framework existed? It would mean that, for the first time in his life, he would consider himself FREE to deploy requisite variety towards the variety proliferation of his own employees. This scenario challenges the manager to match his total employee variety with his own. If he has only a few total staff, he may be able to consider the circumstances of each person, and to match each of their varieties with his own understanding. But he has to take into account the effect of his decisions about each one on all the others (and vice versa). We saw much earlier that n people generate $n(n-1)$ relationships. Once his staff exceeds about seven people (42 relationships to consider), he starts to make rules. He attenuates input variety by lumping people together into classes. He amplifies his own output variety, by favouring young people or women (or older people or men, as the case may be). Even so, he may well devise startling reward systems, which might be startlingly successful, because his horizontal variety is not trammelled by a vertical component.

But now this manager, still untroubled in this example by a company-wide convention, or set of metasystemic 'policies', becomes aware of vertical interactions in the operational plane with other elements of the enterprise. Indeed, he is *forced* into that awareness. Because his people will come to him and say: 'why is x, in another division, doing so much better than I am? He has a higher salary for the same job, or a better car, or a more advantageous overtime agreement, or a wealthier sports club'. These are the connexions in the *operational* intersect that will rob the unit manager of horizontal variety. Therefore he will be compelled to engage in negotiations with other unit managers, in order to establish the conventions which do not yet exist. But obviously, once any such process begins, the metasystem will become involved. In practice, the metasystem always has been involved — hence its well-known 'policies'. The argument is that because this is indeed the cultural status quo, few managers of operational elements have ever considered how they would behave in these affairs IF they were autonomous. Moreover, they have not (therefore) noticed a vertical intervention in their autonomy in the operational plane, which robs them of immense variety. If they have been upset by a loss of this freedom at all, they have automatically blamed autocratic metasystem management for it. They have not recognized that the difficulty resides in the operational intersect, and in the effect of the grid on any chosen *point* therein. If they had, their attitude to this unperceived erosion of freedom would not have been silent.

This brings us to the interconnectivity of the third vertical domain, the managerial: and that is the only variety engineering that is normally perceived as happening. However, we have seen that the grid applies both in the environmental and the operational domains. It follows that much of the discussion that goes on about vertical variety interventions in the managerial domain is not altogether to the point. Much of it merely reflects the matter-of-fact interventions that are implicit in the other two vertical domains. If that is so, much of the dissention about overcentralized decision-taking is irrelevant. The loss of autonomy, the erosion of liberty, is already implicit in the total system, that is to say System One as it is preceived — but the fact goes unrecognized, and is blamed on autocratic corporate management.

This is the beginning of an explanation of a common malaise in modern enterprises. People do not think that it is common; they suspect that it is unique to their own organization: therefore they are embarrassed about it — as one would be if he contracted an unpleasant disease, and assumed that he was the only victim. Then how can the fact that it is common emerge, if no-one wants to mention it? There are few satisfactions in the process of consultancy: it is part of the job that any credits should go elsewhere. But one satisfaction lies in the enrichment of experience that enables the consultant to become aware of common patterns. On the other hand, because his information is both subjective and confidential, it is difficult for the consultant to present proofs of such discoveries. Therefore I shall drop into a personal mode of discussion for a moment, and simply ask the reader if he does not perhaps recognize something familiar in what I shall say — even though it is condensed to the level of caricature.

I am having a meeting with the Board of a company. All of the members are executive officers in the firm, and I have come to know each of them quite well at the personal level. We are now talking, very freely, about their perception of the organization, and of their own role in it. This picture emerges:

'We hope that we are a modern and progressive management team. We have put ourselves through business schools. We have studied, and tried to understand, behavioural theories of management. We had much discussion of Theory X and Theory Y, and we have used consultants in personality testing, managerial grids, and so on.

As a result, we have abandoned autocratic methods. We have made it clear that we expect our operational elements to work autonomously. We just hope that they can do it... . However, we have embarked on a very elaborate management development programme for our people, and spent a lot on sophisticated recruitment techniques, so we have some confidence that all will be well.

As far as we board members are concerned, however, and to be perfectly blunt, there is something of an 'identity crisis'. What are we ourselves supposed to *do*? If we were to give rulings about things, that would be autocratic. So we have reduced ourselves to the role of advisors — benevolent, avuncular holders-of-hands.

That would be all right if anyone *took* the advice. They don't seem to do that. They ask: is that an instruction? We say: no, of course not. So they promptly do something different.'

These people are clearly rather unhappy. But, never mind: they are all beginning to take more interest in extramural activities, and will adjust themselves. They set out as young men to 'reach the top', and they did it. They may have been robbed of some of the fruits of office, the ego-tripping ones; but that may be good for their souls.

Well, meanwhile I have also been making friends with the heads of divisions — the operational elements of the firm. And so I embark on a tour of divisions, to meet *their* management teams. What is the typical picture that emerges here?

'The fact is that we are at our wit's end. There is a lot of talk around here about modern management methods. But just try and DO something without getting six signatures first!

As you realize, everyone is very amiable. Nowadays, the bosses 'make suggestions' instead of giving orders. But God help anyone who doesn't act on that so-called 'suggestion' instanter.

Then there are all these damn committees. We have a 'matrix organization' now, with the result that none of our senior people is ever available to do any actual work. If he's wanted, he's miles away, sitting on some committee or other. It would not be so bad if the committees ever came to any conclusion. But, oh no, that would be autocratic. Besides, they cannot. In committee, you can only reconcile conflicting views through a strong chairman. But the strong men among us are never confirmed as committee chairmen, because they have been evaluated as not balanced enough (5-5, and all that, or 9-9, or whatever it is).

Frankly, our most talented people are on the look-out for new jobs. Don't be surprised if you catch them reading the classified ads.'

Both sets of people are talking about the same firm or enterprise, which is their own. Both believe that they are making fair and considered judgments about the same 'objective reality' (as both call it). Then what has gone wrong? Obviously, for a start, there *is* no objective reality, as has been argued *passim* already in this book. We can account for a major discrepancy of outlook simply by saying that each group has its own subjective impression of the total system. Even so: well-intentioned people are capable of making allowances for their own — and others' — bias. The answer must be more profound than this.

It is. Both groups are failing to observe that huge variety constraints are being applied in the vertical plane that crosses the environmental and operational domains. Because the metasystem has abandoned 'giving orders', it assumes that each operational element is now autonomous — whereas that autonomy is already heavily mortgaged in a variety debt to adjacent elements. And the operational elements assume that this is because the total organization is still autocratic. Why should they continue to believe this, in the face of protestations from above to the contrary? It is because the metasystem, having consciously abdicated the autocratic role, is now engaged in trying to guarantee 'fair play' for the operational elements that they wish to help, and for whom they seek to secure autonomy.

Fair play: it is clearly an issue of freedom, once again. It would not be FAIR if one operational element were paying an executive, aged 30, with a wife and three children, and the qualifications $x, y, z,$ fifty percent more than another operational element was paying to another executive, also aged 30, also having a wife and three children, and also the qualifications x, y, z. Therefore, says the metasystem, we must invent ·a salary .... . *policy,* yes, that's the word. Policies are guidelines. Policies are not ukases or instruments of oppression.

Memorandum to Everybody:

The Board, in the interests of fair play, has adopted a Salary Policy, which is embodied in the attached note (of 200 pages). This policy is not an instruction, and divisional directors are free to use their discretion within the guidelines of this policy.

on page 137:

an executive, for instance, havine qualifications *x, y, z,* aged, for example, 30, and having, let us say, a wife and three children, might be expected to earn £8000 p.a. ±£250.

This is where the misunderstanding will surely start. Now consider the matter-of-fact interactions in the other domains. Smith and Jones are 'indistinguishable' executives (both aged 30, and so on) from operational elements Alpha and Beta. They operate in the same *environment,* in which Smith is producing twice the business that Jones produces. They know each other, in the *operational* domain, wherein Smith has been sent on a course for potential directors, and Jones has been warned that 'he may have to be let go'. Their respective managers know each other, and also both know Smith and Jones. Then in the vertical plane management unit domain, Beta says to Alpha: 'there is no hope for Jones. Because of the Salary Policy, I'm paying him more than he's worth. I can't afford it, and I can't make a new deal with him.' Alpha says to Beta: 'that's really strange. Because of the Salary Policy, I can't give Smith any more than he's getting, and I fear he's going to emigrate'. The two managers agree that both Smith and Jones have proper roles in the firm, which each would accept for a proper remuneration. But the firm is going to be without either Smith or Jones in six months' time. It is a tragedy. And obviously the Alpha and Beta managers themselves regard the probable outcome as another typical result of autocratic management from higher up. So they are both considering the prospect of leaving as well. Meanwhile, the metasystem is congratulating itself on the Salary Policy, which has assured fair play: that means freedom for all concerned.

Now it is no use asking the question what, alternatively, the corporate mangement ought to have done within the confines of this story. It is the confines themselves that need to be recast. The dilemma is inherent in the variety equations of this particular orthogonality, and that could be CHANGED. But it cannot be changed without any insight into the cybernetics of the situation. If that sounds like an evasion, let me say that organizations *can* be recast to meet the cybernetic facts, but that it has to be done from a particular model of the institution, and cannot be done from a general model.

It is totally necessary to know how the laws of variety are actually operating. Let me also say that in two different business incarnations (at the metasystemic level) I have been able to *double* the salary of an employee, without recourse to performance bonuses or similar chicanery, because the 'salary policy' was recast in terms of other domains than the purely managerial. That left the elemental autonomy intact.

The developing theory, then, is not without answers to practical problems. The question is whether the answers are audible to those whose perception of the system is overly constrained — those who may be organizationally 'deaf'. They will blame 'the system', or they will deny 'the answers', or they will do both together — which is reinforcing for them, and for their problems too.

So we come to the reality of the problem of freedom within any institution. It lies, not in the subjective impressions of the people involved, but in what the institution DOES to them by way of variety constraint. The subjective impressions follow from that; they are not paranoid delusions. Suppose that within a given institution you are a manager who actually has the possibility to deploy a variety measured in the eyes of your boss as 100 units. Suppose that your subjective impressions of the system is such that you reckon your disposable variety to be 10 units. Then you will be *seen* as inadequate; and you will *see* the institution as oppressive — but that oppression is in your own perceptual failure. Now suppose that the situation is reversed: you try to use 1000 units of variety, while the system reckons, as before, that it is granting you 100. Now you will be *seen* as rebellious — an anarchist; and again you will *see* the system as oppressive, from your own perceptual failure. This statement seems to account for the mismatch of belief in the elemental autonomy of the institution, as observed between its two orthogonal planes.

In my opinion, drawn from observation, most people get this personal variety equation wrong. Even given a statistical slippage, a 'just noticeable difference', in his reading of the 100 units of variety that a manager has to deploy, he does not have an even chance of doing well, because the system will brand him if he comes down on *either* side, while he will call the system oppressive in *either* case. The reply to this of orthodoxy might be to argue that this situation provides an excellent test of the manager's judgment. This reply would be more impressive if it had been thought out in advance and used as such, which it certainly has not, instead of being a riposte to a cybernetician. It is again my opinion that the solution lies in offering the manager *elastic* variety, which the boss proposes to monitor with that manager's connivance. The notion is a revolutionary one; although people argue that it is not, if only the cybernetic jargon is replaced by behaviourist jargon. I repeat that it is. The organization chart with its boxes, the job description with its demarcations, and the accounts of personality used in management with their diagnoses, all predispose the system to award inelastic variety to the manager. And I think it is true that junior management is, as a result, feeling very frustrated. This view may be set alongside the seemingly universal belief that any such frustration is pecuniary (which is what comes of viewing the world through its own low-variety economic model of enterprise).

These are considerations taken from observations made *within* the enterprise, and have to do with handling the problems of individual freedom that derive from organizational structure. The discussion came up in the vertical plane of the managerial domain. It could equally have arisen in the horizontal plane of the operational unit, in which case we should have spoken not of the boss-manager relationship, but of the manager-worker relationship. The arguments are identical. What is strange is that in the latter case progressive opinion already acknowledges that the practices of mass production and its variants, spread throughout industry, have delimited the freedom of the individual: it is even acknowledged in offices and homes. The cybernetic contribution, maybe, is to expose a similar loss of liberty at higher levels of recursion, where its effect is less damaging to the individual in material terms (because his rewards are at least compensatory) but more damaging to society (as it becomes less competent).

From within the enterprise, all these matters are relevant to viability; and they ought to be studied on site. But from outside the particular enterprise, and looking for the invariance that we expect to obtain in the cybernetics of *any* viable system, there is something more, and in fact much more, to say. This argument should be taken very carefully, both by me and by you, because of its explosive conclusion. It goes like this:

(i)   For the management unit, handling horizontal variety in the elemental operation is very difficult, since it has less variety than its own operation — which has less variety than its own environment in turn. It must design amplifiers and attenuators in order to regulate the double loop, if it is to meet the Three Principles of organization.

(ii)   Since the elemental operation is part of a whole, which is a cohesive system, its related elemental operations within System One *intervene* (in the vertical plane) in these horizontal variety equations. This intervention is a mark of the total cohesion, but it tends to vitiate elemental autonomy.

(iii) If the metasystem, in its turn, intervenes in the interests of fairness, it is likely (on the whole) further to diminish the variety disposed by the management unit of each operation.

Therefore

The metasystem should make minimal use of variety attenuators in its dealings with management units in a downward direction. But this is difficult, since even 'policies' and 'guidelines' tend to be preceived from the other direction as massive constraints.

This is the cybernetic argument for autonomy (or freedom), as distinct from the ethical, political, or psychological arguments. Unlike these others, it has no emotive content. It is basically mathematical.

(iv) If *minimal* variety attenuation is desirable, the question arises whether there need be *any* metasystemic intervention in elemental operations. The minimum is in principle zero.

(v) However, if there were *zero* metasystemic intervention, elemental operations (in pursuit of their individual targets) would inevitably exhibit activities that were not consonant with each other — and which might be downright contradictory.

Therefore

The metasystem must make some intervention, and should make only that degree of intervention that is required to maintain cohesiveness in a viable system. For a viable system cannot disintegrate without losing its viability.

(vi) Cohesiveness is however a function of the *purpose* of the system. Viable systems of concentrated purpose will be closely-knit, highly cohesive. Viable systems of general purpose will be more loosely coherent.

(vii) But systemic purpose (as we saw) is a subjective phenomenon, rather than a property of the system independent of its instigators, participants, and observers. Thus the mathematical extent to which the metasystem will minimally vitiate elemental variety disposable, above zero subtraction, is determined within the total systems framework as earlier described.

THEREFORE

Freedom is in principle a computable function of systemic purpose as perceived.

That is the explosive conclusion. It is explosive precisely because it sounds heartless, whereas the dear question of freedom is full of heart. The trouble seems to be that people do not like to believe that any matter of passion for them could possibly be bound by scientific rules, forgetting that the passion itself is limited by the scientific rules of their own physiological capability to endure it.... .

In any case, the 'heart' comes firmly back into focus when we consider the conclusions 'as perceived' clause, in conjunction with item (vi) of the argument. For, if the systemic purpose is subjective, only agreement of the heart will justify a given level of cohesion in any institution. The committed member of a conservatory commune cannot accept the degree of cohesion exhibited by a multinational corporation; the committed member of a conservative community cannot accept the lack of cohesiveness exhibited by its own eccentric deviant. Both are misled to think that they are discussing ethics. Once the heartfelt committment is made, the rest is a cybernetically foregone conclusion.

It may help to discuss item (vi) a little further. Suppose, for example, that a group agrees on a plan to rob a bank. Each member of this gang (an operational element) begins with his ordinary human autonomy — and even that has to be considered in the context of another level of recursion. But it is a condition of the commonly perceived purpose of the gang-system that this freedom must largely be sacrificed. Each element must do its own job exactly as agreed in advance, otherwise every element is in jeopardy, and the gang-system's viability is threatened. Therefore there is (a computable) massive intervention by the vertical domain in the variety disposed by the horizontal domain of management. If this group, on the other hand, set out to be an organization for loving others instead, massive intervention is not required. There are many ways of loving others, and all members get on with doing it. Even so, there is a minimal vertical intervention in individual freedom. For it is part of the human prerogative to hate another human being, whereas to join this organization is to forego that component of autonomous variety — and to submit to the group's sanctions in that one regard.

This kind of argument (meaning that examples of it could be multiplied) seems to me to settle a hotly disputed question. That asks whether there are not many types of viable system, where the type depends on the *form* of cohesion. Surely, says the objection, and to take extreme examples, there are institutions that exist to satisfy the elements of the institution (and nothing else), and other institutions wherein the elements exist to serve the institution (and nothing else). This being so, there is every expectation that the appropriate organizational structure will be totally different in the two cases. So runs the argument. But it ignores the one issue that we address — the issue of viability. Each of these institutions shares identically with the other that precise characteristic. Thus the counter-argument proposes that there are always *elements* in a viable system, and that these are *always* organized orthogonally to the metasystem. That is all; and it seems to be necessary (though not yet sufficient). Then the way in which we account for the difference between the two institutions just mentioned, is in noting that they are no more than extreme points on a continuous scale of variety intervention in the vertical domains.

This explication of elemental freedom within an institution, which can be extended to cover individual freedom within a society (since we are dealing with the identical cybernetics exhibited at a different level of recursion), hinges on the operational requirements of item (i) in the argument. The conclusion that minimal intervention by the metasystem in the vertical plane is essential to viability, save only that this minimum is compatible with systemic cohesion, must be examined further. For how does this intervention take place, and what does it mean in the *corporate* management context?

When the metasystem intervenes so as to attenuate variety disposable by the management unit (in the interests of cohesion), it is in fact amplifying its own variety downwards. The 'policies' discussed, for salaries, motor cars, and so on, are amplifying basic statements of the kind: 'yes, people should be remunerated'. Such a statement chooses between two possible states: the job is honorary, and the job is paid. The two-hundred page salary policy amplifies this two-state system to a (say) two-thousand-state system by its 'policy' elaborations. We see this happening all the time — in the tax law, for example, and in the administration of social security, as well as in the management of firms. That is how the intervention happens. What it *means,* however, is that the metasystem is disobeying the conclusion relating to minimal intervention — and there must be a reason for this. There is; and it ought to be evident in light of the reasoning in Chapter Five. What we are observing is a struggle for requisite variety in the *vertical* management plane.

That is to say, the corporate management has a variety equation with its System One (the totality of operational elements) which is consistently denied by the arguments, be they never so heart-rending *or* cybernetic, in favour of elemental freedom in the horizontal plane. This is why it increasingly tends to 'grow' amplifiers on the downward path. The answer to the paradox will emerge a little later, when further characteristics of viability have been disclosed. For the moment, it is well to confront the paradox, and to perceive in it the root cause of so much institutional pain and dismay.

After all, the argument was that if Ashby's Law demands that amplifiers be in place, then they must be designed — or they will disadvantageously 'happen'. The latest argument was that there really should be no amplifiers at all on this metasystemic downward pathway. That argument carries much weight in the current managerial culture, because of the evidence of behavioural science, and requisite variety is lost. Then of course the necessary amplifiers will 'grow'

— and they will grow outside the perception of the senior people, who would otherwise have their noses rubbed in the whole paradoxical mess.

It is worth drawing attention to this very directly, because there is at hand a nutrient medium for this forbidden yet inevitable growth of vertical intervention in horizontal autonomy. It is a nutrient medium that is largely beyond the perception of senior management, who regard it as a normal part of the contemporary management scene, and therefore pay little attention to it. If they did, they would come to understand the paradoxical position in which they stand, as they address their elemental subordinates on their desire to preserve freedom on the horizontal plane. The nutrient medium is the computer.

This is the first but not the last mention of this machine. It is, in my view, one of the greatest innovations of the human culture, and one of the greatest inventions of the human mind. Yet its capability is perverted — firstly to imitate an incredibly fast adding machine, whereas it is truly a logical engine; and secondly to enshrine in incredibly expensive technology those very methods of hand, eye, and brain which were the limitations of the manager before computers were invented to transcend them. So much is self-plagiarism, since I have been using variants on those two statements in published writings for twenty-five years; it is also self-mockery, since no notice was taken of them. But the third statement is added, in this immediate context, that computers are now the nutrient medium for the growth of cancerous vertical amplifiers — in the firm, and in society.

Two paradoxes with which to end a chapter are enough.

LATER IN THE BAR...

'Hello, John. Am I interrupting?'

'Oh, hello Bill. No, no — sit down.'

'Saw you all alone in a brown study, and drinkless... .'

'Thanks very much. I didn't hear the bar open.'

'What gives?'

'Erosion of personal freedom, that's what. I've been trying to use this stuff on the police problem we were all talking about last night. You know: how the friendly copper who tells you the time seems to have been replaced by someone more sinister. I've been trying out my ideas on the question of handling dangerous driving.'

'Drunks?'

'That's a bit of it. But there are plenty of non-alcoholic maniacs on the road.'

'Ah, here come some of the others. Keep thinking, and I'll get them over.'

'Hello John. What's all this about driving then? Tell us all.'

'Well, I was thinking that the management of the car driving operations on the roads, which is in the hands of the police, poses a hell of a problem in requisite variety.'

'Hung on. The police are simply agents of the legislative, the public at large, and so on.'

'OK, David, but don't be touchy. There's a lot involved — for instance, the attitude of insurance companies — but the police are at the sharp end. They know what to do if there's a crash. But they want to stop potential crashes, and those exist everywhere, continuously.'

'Didn't we have all this before somewhere?'

'Yes, I looked it up. There was a times-500 amplifier mooted in Chapter Four. But that was general. This is particular. Driving. Dangerous driving.'

'What about things like traffic lights?'

'They're sure as hell variety attenuators.'

'Yes, I know. But they are on the environmental loops. I'm thinking about the management task of the police, and their effect on personal liberty.'

'All right John. Let's stop interrupting, fellows. What have you done?'

'Well, I came up with two sets of operations — dangerous and normal.'

'All driving is dangerous, bloody dangerous.'

'Be quiet, *Alan.'*

'No, I take Alan's point. I'll just change my diagram to 'very dangerous' and 'normally dangerous'. O.K.?'

'Yes. Except we don't know which is which until it's too late.'

'That's just what I'm investigating. Let me table my bit of paper. Here, I'll tear it out.'

'Hmm. I still think that the division you've made John — I mean between two operational elements — is fictitious. We are all ... just drivers.'

'That's because the culture doesn't enable us to recognize the difference, Bill. I think I can see what John is driving at. There really are *dangerous — I mean especially dangerous — people on the roads. And lots of them have a long series of convictions to prove it.'*

'But no-one is allowed to know who they are.'

'You could paint their cars with purple spots.'

'Unnecessary. When I see a car with a crumpled offside wing swinging across my path, I brake.'

'And when I see a car with a smashed boot I increase my distance. It means that he *brakes. And how.'*

'So there are purple spots already.'

'Damn the purple spots. Will someone let John tell us what he's doing at last?'

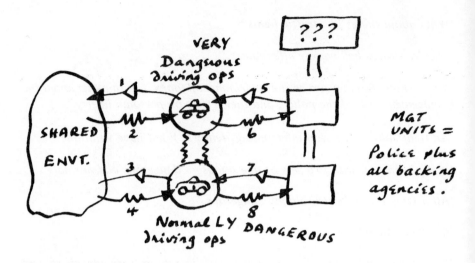

Figure 29. John's (augmented) model of the 'dangerous driving' problem

'Thank *you, Sid. These two operations share the same environment. That's the reason why you are all saying that they can't be recognized as separate. But they ARE separate.'*

'*But give or take the odd crumpled wing, there are no purple spots.'*

'*Purple spots?! Can't we settle that? Painting people's cars with purple spots would be an erosion of liberty. The cops would be down on them wherever they went.'*

'*They asked for it.'*

'*Seems to be my role to pray silence for John.'*

'*Sid I'll buy you a drink for that. Now look. Because the environment is* shared, *it treats both populations the same. Look at attenuators 2 and 4. How could they differ? They are your traffic lights, Bob — variety attenuators as George said. Same goes for the highway code, and so on. This 'general culture' of the driving environment provides, well, a sort of* disguise *for the two operational elements, so that you are able to say that my distinction is fictitious.'*

'*How would* you *separate them?'*

'*By the amplifiers they use. Amplifier 1 is, for instance, a fast burst of speed. Put your foot down in a tight corner, regardless. Amplifier 3, on the other hand — the prudent driver's amplifier — is, for instance, attention to the white lines. They're amplifiers because they tell a driver, in a sense, what's round the corner that he can't see.*'

'*But the white lines — you mean long dots, double solid, and so on, don't you? — are part of the shared environment.*'

'*Bill, I didn't say 'the white lines', I said* 'attention to *the white lines'. Your very dangerous driver just isn't looking — or else caring.*'

'*So he carves you up.*'

'*That's an attenuator from his point of view.*'

'*No, don't laugh. It really is. The danger man solves his variety equation, just like anyone else. It was my first conclusion that it's the way he does just that that constitutes the danger.*'

'*Well, John, that does distinguish your two operational elements in a theoretical kind of way. But how are the police — so long as they are standing for the management units involved — to make the separation?*'

'*Purple spots.*'

'*Erosion of liberty.*'

'*If someone will* drown *those two in beer, I shall continue. The police are supposed to use attenuators 6 and 8. Take for instance 'quality of driving'. What we usually call careful driving is a variety attenuator for the police. The driver concerned isn't making use of more than a fraction of his possible operational states. The police can then recognize the fact, and cut him out of their scene. Filtration.*'

'*But a cop once told me that a careful driver — someone hugging the pavement at 15 mph — just after the pubs close, is bound to be drunk.*'

'*Filtration takes out the middle band of 'normal' people. There are such things as high-pass filters and low-pass filters, you know. The police will get their requisite variety like that. After all, it's only the facility to notice something odd. 15 m.p.h. is odd. So is 100 m.p.h. Those boys have requisite variety to deal with the oddities. The rest of us are driving in between.*'

'*Right, Sid — that's what I think. So what's the problem? How do you bring it home? If a guy is speeding, you use two police witnesses to his one denial. RV.'*

'Where is this rendez-vous?'

'Not *rendez-vous, Tom. REQUISITE VARIETY.'*

'But then we get to the subjective judgments. 'The man was staggering, yer honour, and I formed the opinion that he was drunk'. How do you handle that?'

'Green bags.'

'Bill, if all you can say is 'purple spots' and 'green bags', you'd be better employed in buying the next round.'

'Bless you all. Will do.'

'Bill's right though. Green bags: the breathalyser is an amplifier of policy variety.'

'Exactly. Hey, John! I just got the message. In the case of a drunk, it's the breathalyser amplifier on 5 and 7 that enables the police to know which of your two apparently inseparable operations they're managing.'

'Well, you said it, George. And now I want to follow up that point, if everyone has taken it. As a matter of fact, I had been thinking in terms of seat-belt legislation as an erosion of personal liberty — but maybe the breathalyser will do better. I'm thinking aloud now ... .'

'Bill's back with the drinks, John. Collect yourself. But before you go on, kindly blow up this bag.'

'Laugh away. I have a hunch that John is getting to his point.'

'I hope I am. All right, let's try ... .
Is it or isn't it true that evening visits to the local pub have been part of the British way of life for donkey's years?'

    'True,'

        ' — true,'

           ' — true.'

'*Right. Some people got drunk, and got into difficulties — accidents. Nasty. What do you do?*'

'*Legislate. So many millilitres per whatsit.*'

'*Yes. You put a variety amplifier in the hands of the police.*'

'*But it isn't well designed. It's inaccurate. What's more there can't be a standard measure — we are all so different.*'

'*Exactly. The breathalyser hasn't got RV.* Eh, *David?*'

'*Fair dos. It's better than nothing. And it leads to a blood test, which is far more reliable.*'

'*In my case, they ought to consider my body weight. Absorbs alcohol, you know.*'

'*General agreement is signified to* that, *Bob.*'

'*Thanks very much.*'

'*What are we talking about? I got breathalysed because I had no rear light — bulb gone. What's that got to do with being drunk?*'

'*Nothing. But I can tell you that if you commit a misdemeanour of that kind, the police are entitled to breathalyse you.*'

'Is that right, *David? Then (thank God) I can see how to complete my point.*'

'*Yes, it's right. We're all waiting for the point.*'

'*Please look again at my diagram.
We said that the police get the breathalyser as one of their amplifiers 5 and 7. The idea is to separate dangerous from non-dangerous driving operations. But NOW David says that they can use it in any case of misdemeanour. My first point is that this denatures the 5/7 amplifiers. They were supposed to be designed to IDENTIFY the operational group of the very dangerous driving operations. No longer.*'

'*What's more, John, not only doesn't it work in that way, it's likely to stop amiable and self-contained people from visiting pubs. As you said — 'part of the British way of life'. It's a pity.*'

'*A PITY? It's a disaster! We're victims of bureaucracy.*'

'Victims of growing fascism, you mean.'

'Even so, I don't want to be knocked off by a drunk driver.'

'Hey, you blokes — keep it cool. Let John make his second point. What is it, John?'

'Well, don't you see?'

'We have not only denatured the 5/7 amplifiers.'

We have created a variety interaction in the operational intersect between the two circles. It's the grid business. Suddenly we are operating on the squiggly line connexions.'

'That's mind-blowing, John. I just don't get it.'

'Well, now. The methods we set up as amplifiers 5 and 7 precisely to separate out the first operational group are impinging on the second operational group.'

'Not only can we not tell them apart — which was the object of the exercise. The 'grid' is operating in the operational plane to reduce the horizontal variety of the normal drivers. And no-one realizes it.'

'Sorry. I've forgotten what I was going to say next.'

'Never mind, John. I've got it.'

'The operational matter-of-fact is eroding personal liberty in a way that was not intended, and is not perceived.'

'Phew. Thanks Sid. You did get it. I almost lost the flow.'

'What could be done?'

'Purple spots.'

'Oh no!'

'Stop treating me like an idiot. If, in some way, all those people who had proven themselves irresponsible drivers were identifiable to the police, that would be a design for attenuators 6 and 8. Amplifiers 5 and 7 would then be redesigned to deal with — not any old citizen — but the citizens identified by *the attenuators. It's bound to be a combination that is four times as strong (rather than twice as strong) as the two devices operating separately.'*

'... I notice the silence. Bill was quietly doing the mathematics, I suspect.'

'But all this has appalling consequences for personal liberty — for freedom.'

'Yes. Even at the operational level. No-one thinks about that *grid interaction when they make their management decisions in the unit boxes.'*

'It's self-interest.'

'Probably. Even if it's well-intentioned.'

'But if the squiggly-line is interconnecting the operational circles anyway, *so that crazy drivers are crashing into innocent citizens in their shared environment, what has happened to* their *personal liberty? All they can do is write to the papers about it from the hospital.'*

'This personal liberty business isn't as easy as it sounds.'

'And in the enterprise? — yours and mine?'

'I think I'll go to bed now.'

'Me too. But thanks, John. I'll think about this.'

'What now? You're still here John.'

'Well, so am I. Is it worth going on with John's police thing?'

'All of that is horizontal talk as far as the management *domain is concerned. John's only looked at the vertical plane in terms of environments and operations.'*

'True — I realize that. But to say anything about it I have to decide what is the metasystem of the police, who are here considered simply as System One managers. I just don't know what it is.'

'Yes, we have to be careful. I think John's wary of a trivial statement that the metasystem is just a senior copper back at HQ.'

'Exactly. It's something to do with society as a whole ... .'

'I have lots of problems with this metasystem idea altogether. When we're speaking of public matters like policing, well, in a democracy, the metasystem ought to be the public.'

'I'll buy that definition — because it means that all matters, in a democracy, are public matters. The Internationals should be under public control in our country, just as much as our police.'

'I've got the feeling that we are confusing dozens of levels of recursion.'

'Well, we might get there yet. Obviously, we're only just started on that stuff in the book.'

'But we are invited quite happily just to talk about 'the metasystem' without any more theory about recursion.'

'He doesn't tell us how the metasystem works.'

'He?'

'Oh, come on — our benighted author.'

'He hasn't got to that yet. The analysis will doubtless come later.'

'Well, he's said quite a lot about it already, black-box-wise. What was all that about giving variety elasticity to the System One manager. As one of those, I quite liked that.'

'You would, Gordon. But I wonder if he's ever tried it himself. It sounds just great. But, look, if I assure a subordinate that he can ... enlarge his variety as it suits him, how do I as a senior manager maintain any control?'

'He *says: by monitoring the process with the guy's connivance.'*

'I mightn't have time.'

'Mutual confidence, old man.'

'Could I say again: I wonder if he's *tried it* himself.'

'Well, he says often enough that he's used all his own theories, so he's probably used this one too.'

'Then he probably had some nasty shocks.'

'Suppose he did. It might have been worth it.'

'Not to him, *surely.'*

'Who's he?'

'I see what you mean.'

CHAPTER SEVEN

Constraint

In discussing the dear concept of freedom, that emotive word, we saw that its institutional synonym is autonomy, a less emotive word. And indeed it seems impossible to discuss freedom at all except within an institutional context. There is no 'absolute' freedom, in short, for there are institutional barriers to every kind of action and every kind of passion — even within ourselves considered as protein machines. I can neither leap to the moon, nor contain my anguish for the human condition for very long without diversion. There are limits, in this case physiological. And, if we are more than protein machines, we are still institutionally bounded: by the vocabulary of our culture, by the theology of our religion, by the metaphysics of even our most outlandish thoughts and spiritual encounters.

The paradox that we encountered in the last chapter, showed that the most impassioned urge to freedom at the level of the operational element of whatever institution, is countered by a necessary call for institutional cohesion that inhibits the variety disposable in the horizontal plane. In cybernetic terms, we call this simply *constraint*. Of course, the contrary of 'freedom' in the vernacular is 'oppression'. Not only is that another emotive word; it says too much. To be constrained within the context in which we seek to deploy variety is not necessarily oppressive, although it may become so. The constraint of which I speak here is that directed to the cohesion of the system of which the elemental operation is part.

Hence there needs to be a distinction. Constraint within the institution that *exceeds the minimal* variety reduction that is needed to ensure the cohesion that betokens viability, is oppressive. Compulsion *to remain* an element of a system of whose purposes one disapproves is oppressive. But these are very different things, and they ought not to be confused. They commonly are confused. In continuing to examine the necessary and sufficient conditions of viability in a system, we shall speak of constraint only in terms of minimal cohesion. It is, therefore, something that is not oppressive, by definition. Drawing such distinctions may be boring, but it is necessary: in no other way can the other paradox that this book inherits from the last chapter — concerning the computer — be resolved. But that is for later.

Meanwhile, we have System One. It is conceived as the set of operational elements of any viable system, where these are the largest elements (which is to say, we remain at one level of recursion). System One inheres in a metasystem, whose role has been touched on, all the way through, but whose full nature remains to be unfolded. At this point, then, it is appropriate to ask whether this account is *sufficient* to determine viability in a system, as well as being *necessary* to it. The answer is no.

Consider three operational elements, arranged as a list on the page as they have been drawn here several times. Bear in mind that they are elements of a cohesive viable system, and that the metasystem seeks not to constrain their autonomy. Each of them does its best to perform its role; or, to use modern jargon, we might say that each management unit strives to 'maximize its pay-off functional'. In so doing, each unit has in its hands a battery of scientific techniques, derived over the last thirty years by Operational Research, and covering the key areas of management responsibility for pay-off — from stock control, through linear programming, to the theory of games and econometrics. Again, this exposition will take the form of a caricature. Matters will never look as absurd as they will now be depicted (it is to be hoped). However, caricatures must be recognizable .... .

Unit Beta completes its planning process for the next period, reckoning that its plan will maximize its profitability in its own horizontal plane. The system is strongly connected in the operational domain, on the vertical plane. Therefore it communicates to Unit Alpha that (say) it requires an input of raw material of a hundred tons a day, broken down according to a schedule of qualities and sizes attached; and it tells Unit Gamma that it will deliver its Beta output — five hundred tons — each Friday.

Meanwhile, Unit Alpha and Unit Gamma have each been calculating their own most profitable plans. Unit Alpha decides to send Unit Beta 250 tons on Tuesday, and another 250 tons on Thursday, according to a schedule of qualities and sizes attached. Unit Gamma decides to ask Beta for a hundred tons a day, according to its own schedule. All these plans are put into envelopes, and are mailed on the same day to the respective suppliers and consumers.

On receipt of the others' plans, each division recognizes the needs of the others. They are members of the same viable system. Therefore, although each has his own autonomy (which he began by exercising), he resolves to recast his own plan — treating the plans of the other two divisions as operational constraints. Note: *each* division does this. It takes some time, and again the new plans cross in the post.

Then the whole process must obviously start again, with each division accepting a new set of constraints. And again the new plans that result cross in the post. *This process will continue indefinitely,* because there is no provision in the System One that has been described whereby the process could be expected to converge on a stable solution. It is not surprising. Because each operational element is exerting its freedom, in order to discharge its individual responsibility; and it is also behaving cooperatively with the others, in order to discharge its corporate responsibility; and we have seen that its own activity is of very high variety.

This sketch is a caricature only because sensible human beings endeavour to reach an agreement 'behind the scenes', and because attempts to reach that agreement are not phased into time epochs when contradictory plans are interchanged according to the ritual just described. In principal, however, the sketch acknowledges a reality — and there are many wildly oscillating interprocess stocks around our manufacturing organizations to illustrate it. Who, in industry, has not seen raw material stock bays overflowing, and then completely empty some little time later? Both conditions are difficult to handle and potentially damaging. Now *oscillation* is indeed the word for what is happening here. It threatens to occur whenever inter-related subsystems having disparate criteria continuously interact. In short, the necessary System One of our viable corporate entity will go into uncontrolled oscillation — unless a sufficient element of 'damping' is introduced.

The mechanism of damping was introduced and discussed in Chapter Three. Out of this was supposed to grow an understanding of how feedback is used in the elemental operation to regulate oscillations in the horizontal system that would otherwise cause that system to explode. The mechanism was seen to be related to time lags in the system. Now the problem that confronts us is exactly the same problem, again very much related to time lags (as the caricature displayed), except that it is turned through ninety degrees in the graphics of our model. We are now talking about oscillatory behaviour in the vertical plane. But the cybernetics are identical. (That phrase recurs in this text, and with good reason. For, as has been argued before, we are dealing with natural laws that exert themselves in every situation where there exists a systemic invariance.) Reference should now be made to Figure 17. We need, effectively, to turn the mechanism exposed in the central box through ninety degrees, in order to apply it transversely and metasystemically across the three horizontal boxes of System One.

This is a high-variety operation. We cannot damp this kind of oscillation with a few simple regulatory rules. The reason is that the oscillation derives from vertical interactions in the *operational* domain. In the caricature, mention was made of 'plans'. Well, of course: the three managers could meet and agree upon the broad pattern of supply across the divisions during the week. The reality behind the caricature relates to the hour-by-hour implementation of those plans. The variety of each operation is extremely large, and is certainly not fully predictable in its unfolding through time. Therefore a system is required to handle potential oscillations between the operational units, and it must be HIGH variety with respect to interactions in the operational domain, on the vertical plane. The only available vertical channels that so far exist in the model are the three vertical linkages. But the environmental and operational linkages are the *matter-of-fact* interactions. The current problem is managerial. But the vertical linkage in the managerial domain, which runs to the meta-system, must operate with minimal variety in relation to corporate cohesion, if autonomy is to be upheld. This was clearly demonstrated in the last chapter. The anti-oscillatory apparatus carries by its very nature HIGH variety — and all Three Principles (requisite variety, channel capacity, transduction) clearly apply . . . .

Thus is demonstrated the need for a System Two. Its function is anti-oscillatory with respect to vertical interactions within System One in the operational domain, but it necessarily operates in the vertical plane of the managerial domain — OUTSIDE the channel that is often called 'command'. Here is its diagram, displaying a new graphic convention:

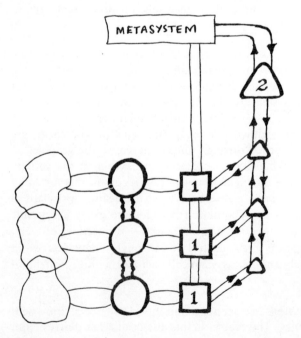

Figure 30. The genesis of the anti-oscillatory System Two. It is necessary to any viable system. Therefore it can always be discovered; but usually it goes unrecognized

I have displayed System Two heavily, with its triangular symbols, because it is so far unfamiliar. As displayed, it looks *dominant* in the entire model. The cybernetic fact is that it is not dominant; but it is necessary. Any contributor to a viable system that is logically necessary to it exhibits some kind of dominance: if it were not in place, the total system would not be viable. But people readily assume that this vital importance betokens a role in the game of *power,* and that is a mistake. The game of power, if there has to be one, is played on the direct vertical linkages between System One and the metasystem — which is a portmanteau name for the next level of recursion.

System Two is logically necessary to any viable system, since without it System One would be unstable — it would go into an uncontrollable oscillation. Could not the metasystem itself regulate the potential instability of System One, by damping its oscillations? Yes, it could; but in doing so it would necessarily be an autocratic controller, because it would have to deploy high variety on the channel that intervenes in the freedom of System One to manipulate its own horizontal variety. But System Two, as described, will also intervene in that freedom — if not, what can it do? That also is true. But System Two has the highly specific function of damping oscillations, and nothing else. In fact, then, System Two is a **service** to System One.

All services, surprisingly, at first, inhibit variety to some extent. If I have my hair cut, for example, to a particular style, then several other styles that were immanent in my unkempt hair have been lost: variety has been reduced. I do not however consider that I am being oppressed by my barber, because I gladly *expected* that he would reduce my hair's variety in this way. Equally, the viable system engages the services of System Two to cut down the variety of its operational interactions insofar as they are inherently oscillatory — and *only* to that extent.

It seems that this is not at all well understood in the managerial culture. Many so-called services, many so-called advisors, become dominant in terms of power — and they should not. This is because they are allowed to become manipulators of their bosses, wheeler-dealers behind the scenes, and (in general) the *politicians* of management. But if we can clearly identify the role of System Two as simply and solely anti-oscillatory, very little scope is left for such opprobrious activity. It is not generally done; and our institutions suffer the consequences.

In the example with which we began, whereby supplies are transferred between divisions, and oscillation is felt in the misbehaviour of interprocess stocks, the System Two role is played by 'production control'. This is a bad name, for a start. I was once a Production Controller, and I know. The very name suggests that all System One bosses are in some sense being told what to do. The Production Controller does not (correction: need not, and should not) subtract from the disposable variety of a System One management unit, except to constrain those states which would — in conjunction with certain states of other units in the operational domain — lead to uncontrolled oscillation. To attend to this is a service to the management unit, because it does not have requisite variety to know about the states of parallel units in the horizontal plane. It needs its disposable variety, all of it, to do its own job.

A completely different example, which might help to make the point clear, is to be found in a large school. System One consists of operational elements called forms (or classes, or grades). Each of these forms, under a form master, is intent on maximizing its own learning. But many facilities of the school, from specialist teachers, through laboratories to the gymnasium and sports fields, are shared in common. Therefore there is a strong interaction on the squiggly lines — in the operational domain. What happens if three different classes arrive in the French language laboratory for the same school period? What happens if the only teacher who knows Russian is booked by three different forms on Wednesday afternoon? The result would be chaotic, and therefore a booking system for facilities is started, and the Russian teacher is invited to take a class with due respect to his or her engagement book.

So far, so good. But what happens is that there are many clashes; and therefore A asks B for a switch, while C is asking D for a switch, while D is asking A for a switch, and so on. The result is: uncontrollable oscillation. Yet somehow or other, schools operate. They have an anti-oscillation device, a System Two. It is called *the school timetable*. By reference to System Two, you can propose a change in your own class timetable that will not induce oscillation. And even if it does, the keeper of the school timetable will shortly damp it. I do not think that any pupil or any parent or any teacher confuses the keeper of the school timetable with the Head Teacher or the Board of Governors of the school. Indeed, if these people have any sensitivity at all, they will be *sorry for* the keeper of the school timetable.

In short, the lot of System Two is not a happy one, in human terms, insofar as those who play the Two role are often accused of destroying horizontal variety — whereas their proper function is merely anti-oscillatory, as the school timetable example makes clear. And yet, because of a general failure to understand the nature of the System Two function, it could well be that there is a basis of truth in the accusations that are so often made. Let us take two further examples, in both of which there is often cause for complaint; although the anti-oscillatory function is not well understood in either, with the result that there is general unease and no resolution of the bickering to which that unease gives rise. The misunderstanding of the System Two function arises in each case because the function itself has not been identified in standard managerial thinking, and is therefore confused with other functions performed by the people involved. In the case of production control and the school timetable, there is no other function than to be a System Two. That is not true of either personal secretaries or company accountants.

The personal secretary of an executive is an amanuensis. She (how rarely is the pesonal secretary a man) provides two more hands in the service of the executive's own two hands. She takes dictation and types, which saves the executive hand-writing. But she does much more than this. She posts the letters that he does not post, waters the office plants that he does not water, makes the tea and coffee that he does not make. So the complaint arises among militant feminists (and I agree with them) that she is a multipurpose servant. But if we look at all these activities in cybernetic terms, we may identify the anamuensis as an *amplifier*. And this amplification extends to much more than the posting, watering, and tea making. 'Mr Ponsonby cannot see you today.' Can he not, indeed? Even more amplificatory: 'Mr Ponsonby won't like *that* idea'. Are we sure? Or, the other way round, Ponsonby may say to his secretary: 'Draft me a list of the appropriate guests (or recipients, or addressees), and I will amend and approve it'. In the event, he does not have the time to do a thorough job; his managerial role has passed to the amanuensis. Meanwhile, much more obviously, the personal secretary is acting as an input attenuator: she is filtering the boss's information, and she is deciding what and whom he shall see.

There are many cybernetic issues built into the above description, and System Two is not one of them. Small wonder then, that the Two role of the secretaries is not readily identified within the institution. But these people *between them* (which is to say, vertically) constitute an anti-oscillatory device across the horizontal elements of a very powerful kind. 'Mr Ponsonby will be available on Tuesday but not Thursday', and so forth. Now it is perfectly possible to argue that the set of secretaries is acting in the role of 'the keeper of the timetable' in the school example, and so it may well be. On the other hand, the timetable keeper has no particular axe to grind. He does not 'prefer' physics to gymnastics. Mr Ponsonby, however, may indeed receive preferment in his weeks' worth of engagements, vis-à-vis other executives, if his personal secretary is a powerful character (or high-gain amplifier).

The point is not that 'executives are run by their secretaries, and don't know it' (most executives are well aware of the extent to which that may or may not be true). The point is that the *firm* is employing a damping device, a System Two, of which it is not truly aware — since it has never thought about the necessity for a System Two. Even then, there is not necessarily anything ominous about what is going on. It is just that there might be better ways of solving the problems that System Two addresses, which will never be recognized since no-one knows that System Two exists.

The problem with the company accountants is more severe. They have charge of the entire measurement system in the firm, and they translate their measures into monetary terms. Since profitability is the lifeblood of the firm, everyone from stockholders to managers to employees comes to fear what they may say. Often they achieve the godlike status of the medical man, who appears to wield the power of life and death. Moreover, unlike anyone else involved in the day-to-day management of the firm (which is to distinguish them from the legal advisors), the accountants have appeal to a body of law that transcends the power of the board itself. Thus the constraints that they exert on each horizontal management unit have the hallmarks of metasystemic authority; and the units receive bound copies of 'the accounting manual' to prove it.

In the last chapter was discussed the problem as to how the perceptions of senior management and divisional management units about unit autonomy could possibly be so different in the typical practical case. The accountants personify this problem institutionally. And they add another dimension to the human puzzle, because they are usually such extraordinarily amiable people. They do not see themselves as ogres; and yet they themselves are often aware that they are targets of bitter resentment 'down the line'. The fact is that no-one recognizes that a large part of their activity, perhaps eighty percent of it, is *purely anti-oscillatory*. But all of that becomes confused with, lost within, the small amount of their activity, say ten percent, which imposes mandatory constraint and wields demonstrable power.

I propose a division of the entire machinery of management accounting into three components. These are, using the terminology of the emerging model:

(i)   Interventions on the vertical line from the metasystem to System One which constrain horizontal variety for legal reasons.

These interventions, to put matters crudely but still correctly, reduce the variety of the operational element quite precisely to eliminate those possible states that are *crooked* — which is to say, illegal.

Managerial units in System One, be they never so tenacious claimants to individual freedom, can scarcely complain about that.

(ii) Interventions on the vertical line from the metasystem to System One which constrain horizontal variety for the sake of institutional cohesiveness, as judged from the *purpose* of the institution.

These interventions relate essentially to the handling of resources. How is each managerial unit within System One to requisition resources, to have its intentions for using those resources approved within the context of systemic purpose, and how is it to be held accountable?

Again, proponents of freedom would be hard put to it to deny that the absence of such arrangements would lead to the collapse of the firm.

Therefore this is an invocation of the principle whereby at any point on the orthogonal grid in the vertical plane of the managerial domain, variety may be *minimally* constrained in the interests of systemic viability.

(iii) System Two activities, which are purely anti-oscillatory.

The demands of the system of management accounting which deals, for instance, with the preparation and format of information are serious, and must be met. But why? Simply because without a large number of agreed conventions, the system would oscillate. We should be forced to spend vast amounts of uneconomic time in 'correcting' information from elemental operation Beta, to put its facts into line with the conventions 'freely' adopted by elemental operation Alpha, and so on.

And, of course, we should find the notorious salary 'policies' and motor-car 'policies' listed under this heading. Were they not instituted in the name of *fair play* — that is, precisely to prevent inter-unit oscillations?

But naturally, once these things are listed under System Two, they may be called 'policies' no longer.

My second proposal is that all documentation dealing with the accounting functions (i) and (ii) should be distributed on (say) red paper. This is the sign that they relate to mandatory interventions in elemental variety. Functions relating to System Two activities — item (iii) above — would be dealt with on (say) green paper. The immediate result of drawing this distinction would be the perception of all concerned that a tiny proportion of the total paperwork machinery is red: and that is the only aspect of the system that genuinely reduces freedom.

Then we have begun to solve an important example of the cognitive dissonance that exists between the 'senior' and 'junior' management about the degree of autonomy exerted by the operational elements vis-à-vis the corporate management. For the red items (i) emanate from two sources, namely government and the accounting profession at large, which belong to a different level of recursion. They may be in dispute; but the dispute belongs elsewhere. The red items (ii) derive from the argument for cohesiveness within the viable system. They therefore *must* exist, although (since they belong to this level of recursion) there must be machinery whereby they can be challenged.

And so we are left with the massive green bureaucracy, of which we know (a) that it is essentially anti-oscillatory, and (b) that it can not only be challenged, but is open to total redesign. And that is just what we should do with it, in most cases that I have ever studied. That is because it is masquerading as a red system, and therefore giving rise to much anguish. In necessary-and-sufficient cybernetics, it is a subsystem of the metasystem, provided as a service to System One. Now there is a strong behavioural case for *participation* in all management processes. That is to say, there is every reason why the System One view of all metasystemic intervention in its autonomy should be put forward by each of the management units. In the case of the red system, this participation can hardly result in the basic redesign of whatever is mandatory — although it may certainly affect its form, and that has considerable importance (especially when it comes to machine-driven procedures). But the green system should effectively be designed *by* System One, since it is a service; and the role of experts residing in the metasystem is fundamentally advisory.

This is to turn the notion of participation on its head. We think of participation as a plea for freedom from the oppressed System One, because our standard models of management are hierarchical (in the pyramidal sense). But the model emerging here is not hierarchical, except in the logical sense of its recursiveness. Therefore there is no reason given in some imagined 'seniority' whereby the metasystem should magnanimously permit the participation of System One in the design of its own anti-oscillatory System Two. There IS reason given in the recursive logic why System One should seek the participation of the metasystem in that design. Because the metasystem, *in its role as an operational element of the next level of recursion,* may know something affecting oscillatory behaviour in our System One that we do not know.

Contrast the following two statements:

> 'I am the boss, and therefore in the nature of things I am entitled to tell you what to do about your System Two. But I am also an enlightened boss, and therefore I shall allow you to have a say in the matter.'

and

> 'You need a System Two as a service, and it falls to you to design it. However, I have views on the matter, since I belong as an operational element to the next higher level of recursion. Moreover, and because of this, I can make expertise available to your work which you do not have.'

These are radically different appproaches to the matter, and they do not at all reflect the orthodox division of approaches. For this accepts the authoritarian, hierarchical model in advance of seeking participation in that predetermined authority. Thus are we led into absurdities. The idea that the board of a firm should necessarily consist of a given proportion of workers' representatives does not address the problem of System Two (for example), which is one degree of absurdity. The idea that those workers' representatives should necessarily be officials of Trade Unions introduces (in any context, and not only that of System Two) a second degree of absurdity; since the *purpose* of the Trade Union's own viable system is *antithetic* to the purpose of the firm. ('Antithetic' is not synonymous with 'contradictory'.)

Then how, in practice, can System One design its own Systems Two (for there are many of them, ranging from the problems of the secretaries, to management accounting, and taking in such issues as the anti-oscillatory 'house style' of the firm on the way)? Again, the standard answer would be to form a committee. But this is never the answer to any problem of design. There is a precise reason for this. A particular design of anything at all, including a System Two, involves the SELECTION of one configuration out of a vast population of configurations. That is, the invention of the design is best regarded as the annihilation of a myriad alternative designs. For instance, in carving the *Pieta* out of a block of stone, Michelangelo PREVENTED his statue from being anything else — including Epstein's *Genesis* or the Lincoln Memorial. This act of selection involves procedures of incredibly high variety, and a committee by its nature does not deploy requisite variety to handle that. This is why the horse designed by a committee turns out to be a camel: this classic outcome has nothing to do with the competence of the committee members. It has everything to do with the disposable variety of the committee as a body, and *that* is condemned in advance to meet Ashby's law with incompetent attenuation of the possibilities. There is not enough time; and what time there is presents itself sporadically, and with the absence from committee of key members (see the secretaries problem).

All of this applies to all problems of design. Committees can do other things successfully. In particular, they can review the purposes for which a design is commissioned, and they can monitor the results of the design process against those purposes. Then if the committee is not itself to prepare designs for System Two, who is? The answer must be a working group of people who are committed to the task full-time until it is done. Well, we know how to select a balanced team of such people. The criterion is not (as so often happens) that some person is such a nuisance in his or her present role that he or she can be 'spared' with a great sigh of relief. The first criterion is the contrary one: he or she must be so good (for System Two is a necessary condition of viability) that it will be agonizing to make the contribution available. But the second criterion is even tougher. All members of the group must know what System Two is FOR. It exists to damp oscillation, and nothing else.

Even acknowledged management cyberneticians sometimes forget this. Especially they forget that the oscillations that we are discussing arise from the freedoms exerted by the operational elements comprising System One. System Two has nothing to do with 'command' functions, since it is a mere service to System One. Nor has it anything to do with the regulation of the metasystem (which will be discussed later), of which it is a subsystem dedicated to System One service. Some commentators have been convinced that it does have a role of this kind, and have amended the viable system model accordingly. But that manoeuvre denatures System Two. Finally, System Two is *not* dedicated to the performance of routine procedures of whatever kind, but only to those routines that are anti-oscillatory. Most routines constitute variety attenuators on the vertical loop of the management domain. Attention is drawn to this point, because several simplified accounts of this viable system model have appeared in print which, in laudable attempts to make the work more (and more quickly) accessible to general readers, have identified System Two with the general clerical task. Further, there have been specific applications of the model by others which have made the same mistake. It is not to be either fussy or proprietorial that I draw attention to it. If we lose sight of the essential nature of System Two as a damping function, then we rob the model of its diagnostic power. There are two reasons why the issue is of such importance, and they explain why a whole chapter is now being devoted to System Two. Firstly: although every enterprise dedicates much effort to anti-oscillatory activity, under all manner of guises, there is no orthodox managerial correlate available to match it. Not to put too fine a point on it, System Two is a cybernetic discovery. By trying to match it with some standard managerial activity (such as 'clerical' or 'routines') this discovery is vitiated. Secondly: much diagnostic work has convinced me that System Two failures are extremely common — and this is not surprising if the nature of System Two is not properly understood. But if these failures are to be corrected this whole question of oscillatory behaviour as endemic to System One, and of System Two as the antidote, must become crystal clear. The oversimplifications destroy the major point.

In thinking about System One, there was no difficulty in understanding the existing correlates of elemental units: these *are* the basic operations of the enterprise, just as we know them. We shall later find that there are direct managerial correlates of Systems Three and Five. It is just because such correlates are not readily identifiable for Systems Two and Four, that these two Systems present problems of cognition and recognition. But they are *necessary* components of the viable system, and they comprise (such is the diagnosis) the big failures of current managerial performance. Therefore it is essential to learn how to perceive and how to recognize them in practice. Note, please, that there has been no problem in *defining* System Two as the damping mechanism that serves System One, because its necessary existence was demonstrated by cybernetic enquiry. It is always there, beyond doubt; so this is not an advocacy that 'maybe it should be there'. The advocacy is on the part of recognition, and thence of enhanced design and performance. The issue is so serious that two further examples of System Two activity are now offered, from contexts as different as possible, as exercises in the comprehension of this chapter. When they are finished, it is much to be hoped that you will examine your own experience, and contrive your own exercises, in order to become alert to the nature of System Two in your own milieu.

The first exercise concerns the development of the Christian church, which is chosen partly because it is a fairly familiar topic in a 'Christianized' although un-Christian culture.

The totally amazing feature of the brief public ministry of Jesus, expressed in purely cybernetic terms, was its capacity as a variety generator. There is surely no need to argue that proposition out: a little reflection upon it would be a better use of your time. For as long as the apostles themselves were alive, then (as is clear from the *Acts,* and also I think from the *Gospel of John*) there were successful managerial efforts to contain this variety. This was done by 'interpretation'; it was a kind of interpretation then seen, and seen to this day, as authoritative. But already the variety generator was working: whatever was going on among the gnostics by the Dead Sea escaped the specific attention of Paul, for instance; it has become available to us only recently through archaeological means. I refer explicitly to the *Gospel of Thomas,* which already had higher-variety things to say than Paul, maybe, would have let pass unremarked. But then hundreds of years went by, during which the variety generator continued to proliferate variety; until the forms of Christianity, geographically dispersed, seem to have been multifarious indeed.

And yet there was a metasystem. Its wordly manifestation, which is all that can concern us here, is called The Church. There can be no doubt (for this exercise is not at all polemical) that for a milenium at the least the Church was authoritarian: probably it remains so, although the purpose of the system is in the observer's eye — as we know. Through a succession of great oecumenical councils, and many other devices, variety was attenuated. The anathematization of heresies is as good an example of variety attenuation in the vertical managerial domain as can possibly be imagined. And now it becomes clear why this example appealed to me: the Church is the only institution I know that actually *calls* its metasystemic recursions 'the hierarchy'. On the face of it, we are confronted with a totally autocratic enterprise, in which the autonomy of System One is non-existent. All the horizontal variety is (at some point in history, perhaps the Middle Ages) quite consumed by the vertical variety in the managerial domain. Or so it appears. The fact is that, even within so devastatingly rigid an hierarchical structure as could implement the Inquisition, System One variety was not yet fully contained. And, because of that, the inherent propensity to oscillation was always immanent. (Sometimes it totally exploded; and the protestant churches, for instance, were formed as a result. But this exercise remains within the system that could by now be identified as the Roman Catholic Church.) Oscillation: yes; because there are operational elements that 'maximize their pay-off functional' around the notion of poverty, while others are building Gothic cathedrals and filling the Vatican Museum with treasure. And so on. The incipient oscillations necessarily — for a viable system — invoked a System Two.

My reading is that System Two was (and remains) embodied in the monastic orders. Now any one of these may well *look like* a viable system, which is to say an element of System One, in its own right. They have lasted for a very long time, a fact that betokens 'survival power'. Yet none of them has, or conceivably could have (unless it changed its present identity), an independent existence from the metasystemic Church. What do the teaching orders teach, if it is not the Church's teaching; on what do the contemplatives contemplate, if it is not the mystical union; for whom do the mendicant orders beg, for *themselves?* Above all, what does that order, called Jesuit, dedicated to the service of the Pontiff do with itself, aside from its incorporation in the Church? These are no more viable systems than are the computer department, the sales department, or the accountancy function, of the firm (as was argued earlier). The lesson, so far, is that organizations are not necessarily viable systems because they have been around for a long time, or because they are powerful, or because they are internally organized in an (apparently recursively) hierarchical fashion. There is a very strong warning here. And I have often been asked to model an enterprise as a viable system, only to say: sorry, but you are *not* one of those; you are somebody else's System Two (or System Four). Once I was compelled to tell a huge governmental organization that it was 'a nervous system for someone else's body'. If the criteria of viability exist, and can be precisely stated, then we must be very jealous of their integrity. We must not pervert them, as a matter of mere convenience, to try to describe any organization whatever.

To return to the monastic orders: if they are not viable systems, namely operational elements of the Church, what are they? They are anti-oscillatory devices. They are a System Two. Observe, then, another reason for choosing this example. The orders have my tremendous admiration, for they have discovered (and I have learned from their *Rules)* so much about the regulation of human communities. It is ridiculous to suppose that they should here be *denigrated* because they are called System Two. System Two is a service, and it is necesssary to the viable system. Both attributes are statements of commendation to which no monk of my acquaintance will, I think, take objection. (That goes for Buddhist monks too.) The fact is that the monastic orders have damped the incipient and actual oscillations of System One, that is comprised of the parish, the diocese, and so on, at all levels of recursion. They do not exist as such elements themselves, nor do they exercise hierarchical authority. It is their quiet insistence on the particular aspect of the Christian message that they nurture with so much love that makes their anti-oscillatory service so very acceptable. Explicitly: it works.

The denouement of the argument is very powerful indeed. Earlier reference was made to the great oecumenical councils of the Church as massive variety attenuators in the vertical plane, in the mangerial domain. The latest of these, held in 1962, was the Council known as Vatican Two. This is not the place to rehearse the whole story of that affair. It is however, a matter of record that the Abbots and Generals of the monastic orders, who have 'rank' it is true (which is why they were there), but who exercise no hierarchical authority whatever in the general business of the Church, played an enormous — and totally unexpected — role. I read it as *anti-oscillatory*. I read it as a service to System One. (Even so, we should not forget that System Two is a subsystem of the metasystem .... .)

All of this goes to show that System Two is a very important part of the viable system, and that its recognition is not easy within the familiar managerial culture. But at least we knew, when we started on that exercise, that the Church is a viable system. Would you call 'traffic' a viable system? This is an interesting question, and it begins the second exercise. The physical existence of networks of roads bearing moving vehicles is clearly an operational reality embedded in an environmental reality of countryside — and a great many of those famous places, A and B. And its management unit surely projects the rules and regulations by which that operational variety is contained, whomsoever is regarded as custodian of those rules and regulations (they are many; and they confuse all the levels of recursion involved). But to what viable system does this elemental unit of road transportation belong? It is just because no-one has said whether it is the geographical area or the multi-faceted transportation system at large, that difficulties arise: of course, it belongs to *both*. Therefore the dilemmas entailed can be treated only at the national level of recursion — and no-one is willing to face up to that fact. But when we drop down a few levels of recursion, we may certainly recognize a viable unit called 'the family', encapsulated in its motor-car, and launched into the environmental and operational domains of *some* next higher level of recursion. (What a pity, then, that this refuses to be identified. Our examplar family would be far safer if it were.)

At the lowest level of recursion of the motor transport system, in any case, our car-encapsulated family is an elemental unit. The driver has autonomy. That is: the driver is free to do as s/he pleases (such as going from A to B) within the traffic regulations, which exist to maintain the cohesiveness of the road transport system (regardless of where it belongs). Note the form of the regulations: Drive on one side of the road; Observe traffic lights, white lines, parking restrictions, and all the rest. These are colossal variety attenuators, poised with legal force on the command channel of the system. But, after all these commands have been observed, the driver of our car — and the driver of all those other vehicles too — has still an almost limitless capacity to generate variety. He may start or stop; he may join or leave any road at will. Long may he enjoy the freedom to do so. But we can see the results in, for example, the miles'-long 'tail-backs' which the popular radio stations warn the motorist to avoid. At one moment the road is empty; a little later there is a gigantic traffic jam.

Now all this is highly reminiscent of the over-full and too-empty materials bays in our production control example. The free interacting elements of System One (vehicles now), each with its own purpose and pay-off function, each moreover attempting to behave with courtesy and consideration to other operational elements, naturally produce local oscillations in the system. Some of these 'explode' — and a traffic jam is the result. Then obviously the informational loop that involves the police and the radio station, and which announces directly to the drivers of vehicles in the area: *avoid junction Zeta,* is a System Two device. It is trying to damp the oscillations. What a tremendous advance this is! We have policemen, helicopter pilots, disc-jockeys, engineers ... all engaged in System Two activity, without any one of them understanding what a System Two really is. This could be regarded as a triumph of human insight — until we note its total failure to do the System Two job properly. No oscillation has been damped; only the disastrously explosive consequences have been observed, a great deal too late, so that people are warned not to help that explosion along. If this warning system, as it would like to call itself, did understand the role of System Two, then the traffic jams would not occur in the first place. The car-encapsulated elemental unit would be diverted in time. But — wait a minute — that would intervene in the driver's autonomy. But — wait another minute — it would be in the interests of general efficiency. And — an afterthought, perhaps — the car-encapsulated family might get from A to B much sooner, though by a longer route.

It ought to be clear from this example that management simply does not know about System Two. If it did, it would design these systems effectively. Surely, the Church did not design the monastic orders from any such insight: their actual origins are well known. On the other hand, the Church *evolved* that System Two: but it took roughly a thousand years to do it. Automotive technology does not make contemporary society the gift of evolutionary time on that scale. If we evolutionists are allowed only a decade or so to cope with our own technological follies, then we shall have to get down to some cybernetics.

What is going to happen next is perfectly obvious, not because the powers-that-be will indeed embrace cybernetics, but because they will as ever follow their technological noses into the *next* unresolvable piece of nonsense. This will be car-borne microcomputers. The car-encapsulated elemental unit of System One will declare its origin, position and destination, and 'the system' (which, note carefully, no-one has properly defined) will then *tell it what to do*. This will be construed by all concerned as a service; with a little good luck, the result may approximate to a System Two — even though no-one knows what this is, and even though no-one knows which is the metasystem to which he is obedient. With a little bad luck, however, our motorist will be arraigned in court. He exceeded the speed limit between A and B; he took an unauthorized detour to visit his sick aunt; he has leave of absence from work today because he is bedridden and claiming social benefit — so what is he doing on the road anyway; and he probably committed that unresolved major crime, because he is known to have been in the area at the relevant time, driving a blue *Pezaz*.

Thus is freedom eroded, and we may well weep for its loss. The prophecy that I made (and I care for my as yet unsullied reputation as a prophet, which is based on predicting only the inevitable) is that (a) the car-borne microcomputer will come, because it is so evidently technologically feasible, which means (look at history) that no-one can stop it; and (b) that no-one will use this moment to design System Two to make cybernetically valid use of the innovation, because no-one understands what that is. Whether we shall get an approximation to System Two by accident, as did the Church, or wether the whole development will define another step to fascism, I explicitly do not prophesy. It is in the lap of the gods.

The effort of this chapter, to disclose the logical necessity for System Two in any viable system and to define its characteristics, has been especially intense. We have argued that 'no system is given in nature': it is *recognized* by the observer. It is worth repeating that those subsystems of the viable system that have obvious correlates in standard management thinking prove easy to recognize. System Two does not have such neatly-packaged correlates, although (as I have tried to show) it has a host of unrecognized exemplars. To those who, having used this model, determine to explicate System Two differently, I say: then go ahead. Whatever in this chapter appears overtly didactic is not intended to restrain scientific progress. There is however an obligation on any innovator to make clear what the terms he has invented are actually supposed to mean. If there is no agreement about the way these cybernetic words (of mine) are being used, then everything will fall apart.

Equally, and this fact is by far the more important to the enterprise, if appropriate Systems Two are not designed to take up the proliferating variety of oscillatory behaviour between the horizontal units of System One, then the institution itself will fall apart. To put the point more cogently: it will explode.

To avoid explosion is minimally to constrain freedom.

That is a cybernetic fact. How often is it used to excuse tyranny.

LATER IN THE BAR...

'What the devil did that last bit mean?'

'I don't know. It seems to be saying that tyrants can excuse themselves for thuggery by saying that the institution — or I suppose society itself — will explode, if its oscillations are not damped.'

'That means repression.'

'Wait a minute: the last bit didn't say that tyrants can *excuse themselves, but that they* do *excuse themselves.'*

'So what is *excusable?'*

'Evidently whatever is required minimally to damp down oscillations. That might allow for the banning of a march in explosive conditions, but it couldn't possibly explain away the wholesale incarceration without trial of political opponents.'

'I thought we were supposed to be discussing our firms?'

'Oh, it's much the same thing. You can see that from this use of the words 'freedom', which I'd call 'autonomy' in the business, and 'constraint', which I'd call 'oppression' in politics.'

'Hell's teeth: we can't mix up the serious management issues that worry firms, with the illogicalities of politics.'

'Why not? Nationalization and strike action are both serious management issues, and both are political.'

'They should keep politics out of it.'

'Who should?*'*

'Bill said: 'they should*', didn't he?'*

'They are *us, and everyone else. Bill wants a conspiracy theory somewhere, whereby it's all someone else's fault.'*

'No I damn well don't. I just don't see why politics should be dragged in to the management of a business.'

'It's not dragged into the business: it emerges from it.'

'Sounds like Marxism. "Capitalism contains the seeds of its own destruction": all that.'

'Look here. I'm not going to get into an argument of that sort. All I said was that politics arise out of the way we conduct our business. We create wealth, right? Then the question of how the wealth is divided comes out of that, and so does the question of who controls the business.'

'That's politics, man.'

'Exactly.'

'Why so pensive, Bob?'

'Well, it's not that I mind talking politics, as you know. I'm really grabbed by this System Two business, but I can't sort it out yet. Did you notice that bit about 'house style'?'

'I did. It went clean over my head.'

'Well, not mine. It's the company image, you see. Ours is a mess. The divisions are each promoting a different public stance, and those stances are unreconcilable. It's got to stop. So I have been interviewing three people — two men and a woman — who, I'm told, are leading designers. I've got to choose one of them to design a 'corporate image'. It will cover all our letterheads, all our advertising, and so on.'

'Good for you, Jack. You're the Managing Director, so what's the problem?'

'I didn't think that I had one, until now. But, you know, this stuff is right. The reason why we are in a mess is that all our divisions have been doing their own thing. I thought it was time that I moved in, and took a lead. Hence the incipient appointment of a consultant designer.'

'So? What's wrong?'

'Don't you see? I'm planning a great big (what's the phrase?) metasystemic intervention. But the whole problem arises because each division is doing something different — to the point where expensive promotional efforts are counterproductive. Oscillatory, then. I'm suddenly wondering whether this isn't a System Two problem, which I ought to leave System One to resolve. With metasystemic participation, and offering System Two as a service.'

'Sounds sense. You don't have to abdicate, Jack. After all, you've appointed the artistic consultant.'

'No I haven't. I'm looking at three of them. Maybe System One should make the choice, like the book says.'

'Are they qualified?'

'Am I?'

'Got the point. Jack: that criterion of the least-spareable guy. Who would be your least spareable guy?'

'Arthur Newsome. But he knows nothing about design, as far as I know.'

'But neither do you. Forgive me.'

'Touché. Arthur is a retired senior manager. He got to be redundant, because of a reorganization, technologically based. I didn't want to lose him, and he's only 63. He's a sort of Minister Without Portfolio — I rely on him for so much, now.'

'Maybe that's your answer, Jack. My situation is more easily identifiable. It's the production control problem.'

'Well, Joe, that's classic by now. And if its a System Two issue — according to this confounded jargon — you know what to do. System One resolves it. Some sort of committee, if I dare use the word. But who would be you're Arthur Whatever?'

'Newsome.'

'Yes, well, that's just the point. If I took the argument of the least spareable man seriously, it would be Cyril Gates. But he's a chargehand — nothing to do with the office, the planners.'

'Well, that fits. You're General Works Manager, right? Naturally you know a chargehand when you see one.'

'Of course he does. But what do I know when I see it? I know that I've got a System Two problem as well. It comes out of the interaction of a hundred and twenty-three retail shops. I'm just appointing consultant accountants to sort it out. But the person I can least afford to loose is Nancy. She's the best shop manageress I've got. How would she interact with consultant accountants? I can't imagine.'

'*Better start imagining then. But what am I supposed to do in Government? If I accept this modelling, which I'm not sure I do, everything around suddenly turns into a System Two problem.*'

'*We haven't read the rest yet, David.*'

'*And even so. . . David, who is* your *most spareable man?*'

'*The Prime Minister. Don't quote me.*'

'*That's got to be a signal for more drinks. . .* '

'*Action taken. But I want to get into the basis of David's endless evasions. I can see that most problems in government are System Two problems — just because it's the biggest bureaucracy we've got. All right, David: be honest. Who is* your least spareable *man?*'

'*Yes: it was supposed to be 'least' spareable, and not 'most', wasn't it?*'

'*Did I say that?*'

'*You did.*'

'*More Freudian slips. . .* '

'*Come on, David.*'

'*Well, I suppose my least spareable man is a woman. Statistician. I think you know who I mean.*'

'*And this is regardless of* which *System Two problem you're talking about?*'

'*If I've got the System Two message right, yes.*'

'*Good for you, David. Even so, gentlemen: what are we doing? We're supposed to have a working group to design System Two. We've used the criterion of the least spareable person. But you can't have a working group of* ONE.'

'*Well, it was for purposes of illustration.*'

'*We've also ignored the second criterion. Each of these people is supposed to know what System Two is* FOR. *None of them has even heard of System Two.*'

'We could teach them.'

'What 'them'? They are all separate.'

'Hey. I've got an idea. Get these new drinks organized, and I shall hold forth — if you permit.'

'All yours, Sid.'

'Well, then. The emphasis is on 'least spareable' people, right? That simply means that names and qualifications and status — all the things we normally rely on — are irrelevant. We are not challenging our friends around this table for any proof that their nominees are any good. We automatically trust our friends to know what they're doing.'

'And so?'

'We have heard about four people of discernment. Let's see: there was Arthur, the retired manager, Cyril the chargehand, Nancy the shop manageress, and the statistician.'

'Felicity.'

'Thanks. And the System Two problems were concerned with house style, production control, something, and government.'

'The 'something' was retail management.'

'Sure. Of course.'

'Get it together. Sid.'

'I'm trying. Take your four managers: Jack, Joe, Bob and David — finance, production, retail, government. You all have System Two problems. Your least spareable people are Arthur, Cyril, Nancy, and Felicity. They respond to the 'least spareable' criterion, and incredibly none of you have argued that this criterion is inappropriate.'

'I reserve my position on that.'

'All right, David. But you didn't. All of you have implicitly acknowledged that someone you trust is good. So why shouldn't Arthur design Felicity's System Two, and Nancy Cyril's?'

'Good grief — they know nothing about each other.'

'But Arthur knows nothing about design. Etcetera. 'Knowing about it' wasn't the criterion.'

'Sid, aren't you really saying that we could make a team out of these four men and women, who would design all four *Systems Two between them?'*

'Why not? It doesn't seem to be a matter of technicalities, does it? All four of you are nominating people who don't know the details in *your own show. Why should it matter that they don't know the details in someone-else's show?'*

'I'm hanging on to this argument by the skin of my teeth. You seem to be relying on the judgment of we four managers in people — *and nothing else.'*

'Why not? They are supposed to be the heart of enterprise.'

'Well, Sid, there has got to be some technical competence around here somewhere.'

'Ah, but that's not the technical competence that you're accustomed to.'

'What's that?'

'I mean that the people who really know the job.'

'What else is there?'

'Well, if I may interject, that's now perfectly *clear. You need to know the history of the monastic orders.'*

'I could tell you a funny story about the Jesuits.'

'Bet you heard it from a Jesuit.'

'How did you know that?'

'Never mind. But I'm sure that I could summon a Jesuit into the group. He'd die laughing. Who knows a traffic expert?'

'What are you talking *about, James?'*

'I'm just looking for all the experts that this chapter expects. No-one understands System Two it seems. Except Jesuits, and traffic cops, and.. '

'Look, it's easy enough to have fun. But I must say that the whole point of those exercises was to demonstrate that neither the monastic orders nor the traffic controllers had any idea that they constituted System Two.'

'And nobody else has any idea what constitutes System Two either. That came across with some force.'

'So the folk we need to design System Two don't even know what it is. Great.'

'It needs explaining to them. But how do we do that?'

'Give them the book.'

'It's not necessary. We have confidence in our people. All that's necessary is to convey a little bit of the jargon, so as to explain... '

'... that System One will oscillate if there is no properly designed System Two.'

'Felicity doesn't know that.'

'Nor Cyril.'

'Nor Nancy.'

'Arthur probably does — but he wouldn't recognize the words.'

'None of them would.'

'We could teach them.'

'Phew — what a team.'

'But to create a team on these bases... well, it's unheard of. How would we do it?'

'You'd constitute yourselves a metasystem.'

CHAPTER EIGHT

Inside and now

The ability of a system to maintain a separate existence, which we call viability, depends on a number of necessary conditions which, in sum, will also be sufficient. That was the proposition that we set out to explore, using the language and the insights of cybernetics. Let us briefly recapitulate on progress so far.

In order to discuss the organization of vast institutions as well as small ones, the principle of recursiveness was invoked. We should depict the organization as a set of viable systems contained within a set of viable systems, and so on. That decision was perhaps not a necessity; but it did offer a convenient and powerful convention for our work.

From this point, it certainly was a logical necessity to identify the operational elements of the viable system that are themselves viable systems, and to understand how they work in cybernetic terms. From these discussions emerged the three principles of organization, dealing with requisite variety, channel capacity, and transduction, as necessary tools in the establishment of equilibrium around the loops that connect subsystems together. All of this became explicit in terms of the horizontal plane of the model, in which the operational elements have their autonomy.

It soon became clear, however, that 'autonomy' does not stand for separateness — otherwise the system would not be cohesive, and could not therefore be viable. A diagrammatic convention of orthogonality was set up, so that the connectivity of operational elements could be examined in a vertical plane. This was done for each of the three domains exhibited by the horizontal model: environmental, operational, and managerial. The three principles of organization were applied in each case, and we began to see how the set of elemental viable systems hangs together within the 'parent' viable system. Its name is System One.

Implicit in all these investigations was the notion that System One is embedded in a metasystem, which is in fact an operational element of another viable system at a higher level of recursion. I say 'embedded' advisedly, because the metasystem is the *managerial context* of System One activity. Diagrammatically it was convenient to pull System One and its metasystem apart, in order to examine the connectivity of the embedding (just as was done in the case of the horizontal plane; where the embedding of the management unit in its operation, and the embedding of that in its environment, is the same topological notion.) It was inconvenient to depict the metasystem *above* System One, since this carries connotations of seniority and autocracy. However, this was done; and we relied on the fact that the vertical dimension of the page, in which operational units had already been 'listed' with explicit denials that this ordering had relevance to seniority, has logical but not organizational implications. Indeed, a strong case was developed to say that metasystemic intervention in System One activity should be minimized.

The important principle was deduced that freedom for the operational unit is a computable function of the purposes of the system as perceived.

The question then arose: are all these necessary conditions of viability, in sum, by yet sufficient? No, they are not. Cybernetic factors of the model as so far elucidated indicated that the system is vulnerable to uncontrollable oscillation as between its operational elements. In light of this, it was necessary to nominate a regulatory mechanism which was named System Two. The meaning of this name was examined in the last chapter. But now I wish to emphasize the logical status of the name within our developing language.

It is not possible to conceive of System Two as a subsystem of System One. The only practical modality for damping inter-unit oscillations *within* System One, would be some sort of committee set up within the managerial domain in the vertical plane. But the cause of the oscillatory behaviour lies in the matter-of-fact interactions of units in the environmental and operational domains. These are very high variety interactions; and no committee structure could possibly absorb their variety. This is proved by one argument alone. The interactions are continuous in time; the committee (using ordinary definitions) meets sporadically. No: in order to deploy requisite variety, System Two must be continuously in being. Moreover, in achieving its total view of System One operations in respect to the managerial dimension in which it is an anti-oscillation regulator, it requires criteria which can be formulated only by *this* viable system conceived as an operational unit (part of System One) of the viable system at the next level of recursion.

For example: if System Two is a production control function damping oscillations in the build-up of inter-process stocks, then the money represented by the stock investment is a quantity for which *this* viable system is accountable to the next level of recursion.

Thus we have to regard System Two, which is a service to System One, as a subsystem of the metasystem in which System One is embedded. Our diagram already shows this connexion. But it so far makes no discrimination about metasystemic activity: the metasystem, so far, is a black box. In order to improve the diagrammatic conventions of the model, I propose a System Three as a logical necessity.

Now this may sound like an unjustified leap. But it is not. We already know (a) that System One is embedded in the metasystem, and that the diagram pulls the two apart in order to expose the modalities of their connectivity. We have just seen (b) that System Two is a regulatory activity that must have its roots in *this same aspect* of the metasystem — namely its role as an operational unit at the next level of recursion. All that now happens in the naming of this box as System Three.

Then you may think that System Three is actually the name of the metasystem. But we do not yet know whether the metasystem has *other* roles to play in viability than the two we have so far discovered — (a) and (b) above. Then the diagrammatic convention ought to be as follows:

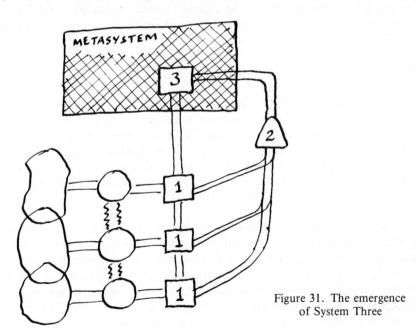

Figure 31. The emergence
of System Three

where the shaded area might or might not turn out to be EMPTY.

Thus System Three *is* the metasystem as we have already come to know it. Its box is embedded in the metasystem. And, if the metasystem has no other functions than Three functions, then the box marked 3 will in fact exhaust the metasystem. The concern of this chapter is not to answer that question, but to examine in further detail the role of System Three.

System Three is first of all typified by its metasystemic nature, and by the SYNOPTIC SYSTEMIC viewpoint from which it surveys the total activity of the operational elements of the enterprise. It is aware of all that is going on *inside* the firm, *now.* This is because it has direct links with all managerial units, which exist simultaneously and in real time. It is also aware of the anti-oscillatory activity of System Two, since System Two is its own subsystem. Then whatever managerial functions at the corporate level that relate to the continuous activity of the firm's internal operations (with which the culture is familiar) are rightly seen as System Three functions. Whether they are rightly seen by that culture as *command* functions, is an entirely different matter. The cybernetic fact is that we have encountered, for the first time, a subsystem of the viable system that can see all operations simultaneously, and therefore has a *logical* role to play in the process that promotes viability. How it discharges that role is a matter of managerial style, which will be discussed later. It is an important matter, because the style affects everyone's perception of freedom; but so long as we adhere to the logical role in this chapter, we have the opportunity to see what constraints on freedom derive from the structure of viability rather than from whim or ideology.

If we firstly note what some of these functions are, it will help alert the potential user of this model to some of the traps that lie in wait for him. The example taken is a manufacturing organization, having a set of divisions as System One. These divisions make and sell products on the horizontal plane, as operational elements of the firm. Each of them contains, in its own management unit, a financial manager, a production manager and a sales manager, say. (And if we wish to know what those people do in the process of obeying the three principles of organization, we shall have to drop a level of recursion and model each division separately as a viable system.)

In System Three we find among others a Financial Director, a Production Director, a Sales Director. Each of them is setting out to *integrate* the work of the respective divisional managers. Leaving aside, as promised, the question of personal style, what is the logical intention of 'integration'? If the word meant: 'you all do exactly as you are told by me', then the operational units would not enjoy any degree of autonomy, and their managers could be replaced by slave computers. As has been argued consistently, this word integration refers to the minimal metasystemic intervention that is consistent with cohesiveness within the purposes of the viable system. These purposes are not of course objective properties of the system; they are formulated by those people who have charge of it, which include its initiators, its owners, its employees, its customers, and its observers.

The question as to what actually are the minimal interventions, depends in each case on what actually are the purposes. But we can be fairly sure that one purpose will be to get the most out of System One (under some definition, such as profitability) as that systemic machinery can deliver. This is different from saying that we want the most out of each operational element that it can deliver, and will then collect the proceeds into one bag. The systemic machinery is supposed to do better than that: the product is called SYNERGY. This refers to the margin of profitability that derives from having a viable system, rather than a collection of parts.

Synergistic behaviour derives from the recognition of mutual support between the operational elements. It is intended to lead to a higher total pay-off for the total system than the sum of independently acting elements could produce, *even if* one or more of the elements is thereby rendered less profitable than it might have been without invoking synergy. It is this fact that determines the metasystemic location of synergistic planning. And it is this fact that determines the minimal degree of metasystemic intervention in System One. This does not necessarily entail submission to command. Consider: the heads of all management units might observe that they were failing to achieve the synergy of which they suspected that System One were capable. They might club together to hire an operational research consultant, who would study their problem by (say) linear programming. They would abide by the solution. If they did all that, they would have undertaken a *System Three* function. It cannot be too often stated that we are constructing a viable system, and not an organization chart.

Nevertheless, it usually falls to the corporate directors to fulfil these functions — precisely because they have the synoptic view, and do not find themselves preoccupied with divisional affairs (or should not do so). Hence, and bearing in mind the general requirement to minimize metasystemic interventions that inhibit the variety of management units, the logic of viability demands some intervention in the interests of corporate synergy. The director of finance is working with the managerial units entirely within the vertical domain. He is trying to achieve a synergistic use of capital, and also seeks the corporate synergy of optimal cash-flow. As far as the production director is concerned, he is working with the unit managers to obtain some kind of synergy across the squiggly lines that indicate the matter-of-fact interactions of the operations (this being a manufacturing company). The sales director is working with the unit managers in search of synergy in the interactions of the environmental domain. All three can produce results, either by improving the attenuators and amplifiers that govern the relevant loops in their vertical domains, and thereby mounting synergistic programmes around those loops; or by altering conditions within the muddy boxes (contained within the managerial square boxes themselves) in the synergistic interest — which they should not be altering, outside the autonomy of the management unit, for any other reason. Here is a diagrammatic account of this (see Figure 32).

It may have been noticed that this manufacturing company has no *operational unit* called 'sales'. Its selling is done on the environmental loops of the manufacturing operations, and its synergistic regulation is a function of System Three. This is because the purpose of the manufacturing company is to manufacture. It must sell what it makes; but this activity is a function of its interaction in the world wherein it seeks its viability. We could however consider a marketing company, in which all the operational units were doing nothing other than selling. Such a company might contain a large department making boxes of all shapes and sizes, in which to pack goods purchased outside under the company's emblem. But this production department would not constitute an operational unit. It is not a viable system within *this* viable system, although it might become one if we sold it: for it would then change its purpose. This is the argument already considered (in terms of accounting, market research, computers and so on) in an earlier chapter, when we considered what ought to count as an operational element. The argument comes up again here for two reasons. Firstly, just as we do not want to label a function wrongly as System One, we do want to label it rightly as System Three. Common services that contribute to synergy are always Three functions (and the box-makers contribute to synergy because their boxes are of similar and publicly-recognizable design, for whichever division they are made). However, such Three functions may often be mediated through System Two (since the process of the design of these boxes is an oscillation damper) — which is easy to conceive given that Two is a subsystem of Three.

The second reason why the argument as to what constitutes an operational element comes up again now, lies in the severely practical business of applying this model to an actual firm. The model we newly develop here has been publically available in a variety of forms for a long time, and I myself have been using it for much longer. It is perfectly clear to me that the model has no power, predictive or diagnostic or prescriptive, if its logic is perverted. It is a major and fundamental perversion of the logic to confuse the subsystems of the viable system with its constrained viable systems — which between them constitute System One. This is why I am pressing the importance of that identification. It can be done only through the critical application of the rules of the logical language, supported by an understanding of recursiveness itself. I have seen many an alleged use of the model that confused two, if not three, levels of recursion. But the most common mistake is to seize on the existing organization chart of the institution, and blithely to assume that every division or department shown as depending from the boss is a viable system in its own right — and therefore an operational element in System One. The confusion induced when 'engineering maintenance', for example, is depicted in this role is unimaginable. In general, the traditional functional breakdown of senior

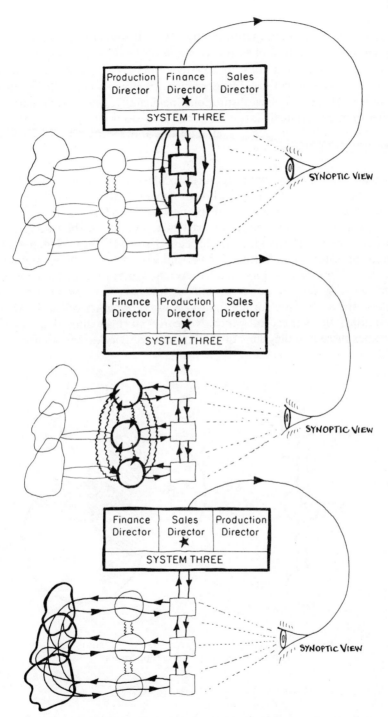

Figure 32. Sample operations of System Three, acting synergistically
to the benefit of System One

management in manufacturing industry (production, sales, finance, engineering, research, and so forth) can *never* be directly transposed into the listing of elements that constitute System One. By the same token, if such a mistake is made, it will never be possible correctly to identify the components of System Three in a given institution. Incidentally, the traps in mapping the model onto government institutions are even deeper dug, since there is not even the notional difference that industry draws between cost centres and profit centres to use as a guide.

But I digress from the main argument in offering practical hints which may themselves sound daunting — although they pose no threat to the thoughtful reader. We had reached a point where the synergistic function of System Three was apparent. And this places no particular burden on the variety equation that links the metasystem (and in this case System Three) to System One. The search for synergy is a matter of logic; and although the elemental units to be 'synergized' are each of very high variety, the synergy must lie in a low variety statement — however powerful and lucrative the synergy may be. This is because the synergistic formula must lie in the *intersect* of all the elemental operations, the variety of which is clearly much smaller than their sum. Consider these two diagrams of the interconnectivity of operations:

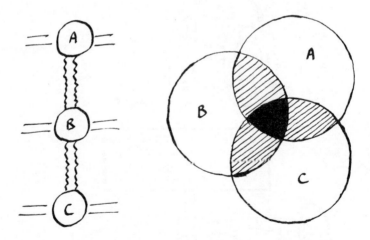

Figure 33. Alternative diagrammatic versions of the interconnectivity between operations

The diagram on the left is the one with which we have become very familiar. It is the squiggly line connectivity. If we now ask ourselves about the *variety* deployed by the three operations, we may well find that only a small subset of the number of possible states available to each impinges on another. This is simply a question of the matter-of-fact relationships on the squiggly lines. The diagram on the right measures variety according to the area of the circle, and the white spaces indicate possible states that have no bearing on the operational states of the two other operations concerned. The hatched areas show where two operations intersect: A and B, B and C, A and C. In these hatched areas, oscillations are likely to occur, and System Two is automatically involved in damping them. But it is only in the shared variety of the dark area, which is the intersect of all three operations, that true synergy for System One can lie. It is the area in which all three operations can agree upon a state that could increase synergy. (It could — it will — increase oscillation too; but System Two will monitor that, especially if it has a synergistic plan conceived by System Three to guide it.)

Thus the System Three role, conceived as fundamentally synergistic, offers a powerful (to the firm) yet minimal (to System One) metasystemic intervention in elemental autonomy. It is worth repeating that this intervention could reasonably be made by System One itself, acting in concert, and adopting a System Three role. This fact suggests that the loss of freedom entailed by adopting synergistic policies in the cause of corporate viability is no particular hardship, providing that the reason for it is fully understood at the elemental level. Then that fact in turn suggests that the most effective managerial mode in which System Three may apply synergistic policies, is to co-opt the heads of the managerial units in System One as members of System Three *to that end*. Those three words are italicized, because there is no good reason to co-opt System One into System Three for any other purpose. So often there is a 'general committee' in Three, constructed to make System One 'feel good', which merely induces frustration in the heads of the management units. This is because there is nothing they can contribute, except in the negative sense of complaining about their lot. But if instead of a 'general' or 'executive' committee of this sort, the firm would empanel a Synergy Task Force, comprised primarily of System One operating in a System Three role, it would draw on the knowledge of the A-B-C intersect which those people share, and on the positive psychology entailed in constructing synergy.

Well: in elucidating the role of System Three in synergistic terms, it has been possible to adhere to the cybernetic 'rule of freedom' that does not overload the Three-One channel with inhibiting variety amplication. The minimal metasystemic intervention needed is indeed small, as the last diagram showed. But if this is to constitute the whole story of System Three activity vis-à-vis System One, there is a rather embarrassing consequence. I display this as an impressionistic picture (rather than a true diagram) of the current position, in Figure 34.

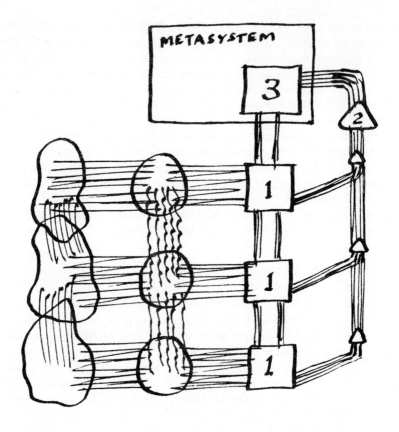

Figure 34. An impressionistic picture of the variety interactions
so far (and inadequately) obtaining within Systems Three-Two-
One

This diagram is a picture of variety interactions. It is impressionistic because
we are not able to provide proper *measures* of variety, since these are unique to
each institution. However, it is possible to look upon the lines I have drawn as
if they were blocks of colour in a picture — which tells us something, even if
we have not measured their sizes or the light intensities that they absorb. It is
easily possible to justify this picture, in those general terms, as a reasonable
representation of reality as it has so far been depicted in the model, in terms of
the variety deployed.

We know that horizontal variety is massive, and that the variety exchanged in
the matter-of-fact connectivity within the vertical domains of environments
and operations is also massive. This massivity is depicted by a lot of scribbling.
It looks from the picture as though the interchanging varieties of the six
muddy boxes on the left of the picture could well exhibit requisite variety

between themselves. I think that is a correct reflection of the world that I know. And if it were not so, that world would be even more unstable than it is.

Now look at the 'measure' of variety scribbled into System Two. It has to be *much* less than the variety interchanged between the six muddy boxes, since System Two deals *only* with those aspects of the interchanged that threaten oscillation. On the other hand, it has to be substantial; because *within* those oscillatory dimensions, Ashby's Law must apply.

Thirdly, then, look at the vertical channels in the managerial domain. These scribbles depict a variety interchange that is meant to represent the cybernetic policy of freedom: minimal intervention, in aid of cohesiveness plus synergy. I think that the scribbles correctly show far less variety commerce than we see in System Two. Of course, the whole picture *is* impressionistic; yet the relative 'weight of colour' in all the loops seems to reflect the truth.

It might be worth pausing a moment to detect the 'embarrassment' to which I referred. Remember that the metasystem is the System One of a higher level of recursion, in which this whole system is embedded; and that therefore (in some sense or other, depending on style) System Three must have the capability to absorb the variety of System One — by Ashby's Law.... .

According to the current diagram, System Three does not deploy requisite variety to succeed in this. The sum of variety interconnectivity between Systems Three and One (the direct channel, plus the channel monitored through System Two) is far less than the total variety deployed throughout the interconnectivity of the six muddy boxes.

Again it is worth pausing a moment to realize how the existing managerial culture deals with this embarrassment.... .

There is no question about it, to my mind. The existing culture *grows a cancerous activity* on the vertical axis. This was mentioned before; and it was said that computers provide the nutrient medium for that cancerous growth. In terms of our picture, in short, the scribble on the Three-One axis becomes virtually SOLID BLACK. That is what happens. It is the final answer to the paradox about cognitive dissonance between senior and junior management.

Now if we adjust our picture, according to reality, so that the main axis is depicted in solid black, it will be evident that Ashby's Law has been met. System Three will then be seen to deploy requisite variety. And so it does — because Ashby's Law always exerts itself. *But if we do this, we deny everything we have discovered about freedom.* The solid black central axis will annihilate the horizontal variety of System One. We should be depicting just that tyranny of which so many of our existing Systems One complain — to the astonishment of their metasystemic 'superiors'. There has to be another answer to the problem, and there is. The clue to that answer lies in the matter-of-fact high variety of operational interaction, which is the source of the problem, and over which we have some control — since these operations ARE (after all) the very elements of the viable system.

If we allow for direct interaction between System Three and the *operations* of System One (which of course would need the approval of the management units), the variety equation between Three and One can be built up without recourse to the notion of command that exists between the metasystem and the units in the managerial domain. Is this new notion a mere quibble? No; because the loop proposed will not in fact exert any command function at all. It is quite specialized, as we shall see — just as System Two is specialized in a service capacity to System One.

The impressionistic picture would then look like this:

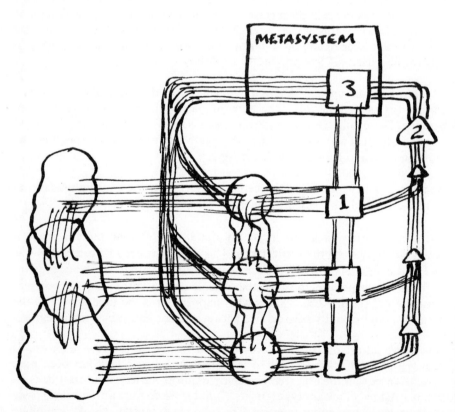

Figure 35. An impresionistic picture of the variety interactions that must necessarily obtain within Systems Three-Two-One, if Ashby's Law is to be vindicated

— and it is evident that the new channels between System Three and the unit operations can be transmitters of variety interchange such that:

The *sum* of variety deployed by System Three in the
vertical plane
= the sum of variety deployed by the elemental
operations in the vertical plane,

without the illegitimate use of the variety-minimized interactions in the vertical managerial domain that is customarily treated as the axis of command.

In this way is Ashby's Law vindicated by good design, rather than by cancerous growth in the form of a solid black managerial axis.

Now I have introduced this new loop as a matter of good design, rather than by eliciting its existence from the available evidence. For, if it is a matter of logical necessity, then we may predict its existence, and then examine the empirical facts for verification of this hypothesis. There is in fact plenty of evidence for the existence of this high variety channel — which does not exist to command, but to inform System Three (and, reciprocally, System One) in the cause of equilibrium in the vertical plane.

An outstanding example is the AUDIT. This refers to current accounting practice; but it could equally well refer to other audits — such as those conducted by the personnel department in System Three. In order to conduct an audit, direct access is necessary to the operations themselves — a fact that is conceded by the management units of System One. This is because no filtration (especially by the square box) of operational variety is legitimate. There are laudable aims to an audit, concerned with synergy, that do not carry sinister overtones. Nonetheless, the original purpose of the audit is to prevent fraud. This fraud is imagined as perpetrated by the management unit of the elemental operation. Thus it is pointless to conceive of auditors who go to the square boxes and ask whether they are fraudulent, and pointless to look through the *managerial* records to see whether the fraud has been 'properly recorded'. The audit is an operational matter; and it can be successful only if *every* transaction in a sample of activity is inspected. If some invoices, for example, are missing, then obviously they may be the fraudulent ones. The audit itself is a superb example of the application of Ashby's Law, regardless of the present arguments as to its location in the logical diagram.

Now the audit, as conceived on the new routes of the diagram, is a two-way loop between the operational matter-of-fact and the accounting subsystem of System Three. Much of what happens is contained within that loop: and very high variety it is. However, there seems to be (in quite normal circumstances) a continuous output of the audit that calls for the modification of System One behaviour. If so, then this output will inevitably reach the management units by way of instruction — that is, by metasystemic intervention. But this inhibition of variety is totally expected, and belongs to the minimal intervention category; because it is an intrinsic part of the operation of the accountants' red system (i) — which deals with mandatory requirements determined by the next higher level of recursion. In this way, System Three obtains, uses and filters requisite variety in the vertical plane. If the outcome involves the use of the metasystemic intervention loops in the managerial domain, they will be of low variety. For example, an auditor's explication of the rules that ought to govern the distinction between 'capital' and 'revenue' items does not need to list every conceivable state of the system and the outcome of each such state if it ever happens to materialize. All that is left to the amplifiers on the horizontal plane.

Admittedly, the effect of those amplifiers is to expand the simple rule to cover the eventualities met with in practice: that is the whole intention. It is precisely what ultimately restores requisite variety to System Three in its relationship with System One. The point is that the vertical channels in the managerial domain are not overloaded with variety. People have difficulty with this distinction (hence the earlier remark about 'quibbles'), and so a homely example is offered by way of clarification. Most of us are motorists. If it were not for an instruction — a metasystemic intervention — which says: 'drive on *this* side of the road', the traffic system would surely, and finally, stop. The driver continually applies this rule, which is a low variety statement, and thereby amplifies it infinitely (or for as long as he continues to drive). Thus it is true that his liberty to drive wherever he likes is massively impaired. Even so, he has no sense of oppression resulting from an overloading of his channels to System Three. Now suppose that no-one had been able to think out this low-variety rule. How could System Three possibly achieve its purpose of keeping the traffic moving? It would have to ask a driver to submit a plan of his route in advance; it would have to plot a route on a map showing the driver's movements on *this* side of the road for every inch of the journey; and the driver would need to carry a passenger to read him the continuously unfolding instructions. The resulting loss of freedom would be identical; but the *sense* of loss would surely lead either to emigration or to walking.

This distinction is by no means trivial. Part of the autonomy which the elemental operation must feel that it exerts resides in the knowledge that it is trusted. It is trusted to invent amplifiers that enable it to handle its own horizontal problems. It is also trusted to apply simple rules, that are handed down in the interests of either legality or synergy, in an appropriate way. It is its own variety amplifier, despite the simple rules that largely constrain its variety deployment once they are amplified. Yet the reasons for this are understood, and there is no sense of oppression. The sense of oppression arises when there is no trust, and therefore every move is predetermined from above.

Many people have reported the subjective impression, from their own experience, that there is little difference *in practice* for an honest citizen to live in a country of totalitarian ideology, and one supporting 'absolute freedom'. Perhaps the foregoing examination of the puzzle resolves it. For it could be that the citizen in each of these countries undergoes an equivilant diminution of variety, in the interests of societary cohesion. And while one of them is trusted to inhibit his own variety by amplifying low variety rules, the other has the same amplification done for him. The result is the same. But the feeling for freedom that eventuates might be quite different. Such is the human condition. Interestingly, the outcome for the two governments concerned is also quite different. We began with 'the honest citizen' in both cases. In the 'absolutely free' country, where the honest citizen is trusted as an amplifier of simple rules, the pressures upon him make him dishonest — to a greater or lesser degree. In the totalitarian case, he will suffer severe penalties if he is dishonest, and sufficient variety is deployed to catch him in the process. Thus he may feel oppressed. Is that feeling the price of moral rectitude? Is moderate immorality the price of feeling free?

These debating points are extreme; and they certainly have nothing to do with the political realities in which arbitrary imprisonment, routine torture, and hideous death are involved. Even so, the debating points are worth that very debate in the context of the cybernetics of organization. For much of the argument that goes on in our managerial culture about 'industrial democracy' is piffle. These writings have not only made concessions to subjective impression: they have already gone so far as to contend that the system itself *is* a subjective impression. Then it is not too much to repeat an earlier contention that what counts as freedom in our institutions is in practice mainly a matter of psychological manipulation, and that the nearest we can get to objectivity is to observe what the system actually DOES to the individual's natural variety deployment. (Of course 'natural' means what is left of his variety after upbringing, education, training, and the mores of his employment, have finished eroding it.)

To phrase these essentially scientific issues in debating terms is highly contentious. But our society does so debate them, and there *is* contention. I am trying to build a bridge between this reality of the managerial world, and the cybernetic account of organization which — without such risky efforts — could sound altogether arid. Using the impressionistic picture approach, let us look at the foregoing argument in terms of a cybernetic model of the two kinds of management involved. This is a picture of the variety disposed downwards from System Three to System One, in circumstances such that System One has itself to dispose horizontal variety towards its operation of an amount equivalent to that directed to the operation by the environment.

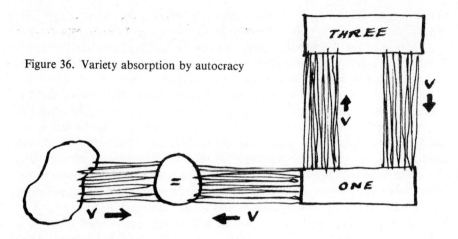

Figure 36. Variety absorption by autocracy

This is the autocratic mode of management. System One has requisite variety on the horizontal loop; System Three has requisite variety on the vertical loops. The management unit has no freedom: its requisite variety in the operational circle is supplied to it by Three.

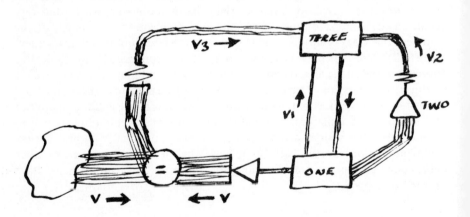

Figure 37. Variety absorption by autonomy

This is the autonomous mode of management for the same problem, minimizing metasystemic intervention. System One has requisite variety on the horizontal loop: it is achieved by the amplification of its own variety plus the variety stemming from System Three (which is a variety inhibiter for System One itself). System Three has requisite variety on the vertical plane, since the sum of $V1 + V2 + V3 = V$ itself. Now the management unit has maximum freedom to deploy its own variety, since it has minimum metasystemic intervention. But part of this freedom is illusory, since it is committed to the component of the V it generates that derives from amplifying low variety rules from System Three.

I hope that this analysis is indeed a bridge-building device between the contentious world and the scientific world of management. If it does fulfil that expectation, it helps to show how managerial cybernetics can be used in explosive situations. But of course the underlying purpose is to illustrate the workings of the composite Systems Three-Two-One in our model — it is the composite dealing with what is INSIDE the firm, NOW.

It would be wearying to list all the activities, other than auditing, which use the new System Three channel that runs directly to the operations. Auditing is common to all enterprises, whereas other examples are not. The fact is that any activity that is not an elemental operation, not an anti-oscillatory device, and of corporate range, will be using these channels. Therefore it must be SEEN to be using them, or it will be confused (certainly in the minds of System One) with metasystemic intervention in the sense of command. In fact, such command intervention as it generates will come down the central axis in low variety form, *thanks to good design of the attenuator* shown on the left-hand side of the last picture.

Doubtless it would be helpful to the reader to think out those functional uses of this channel in his own institution. Here is one example, to get him going. In the manufacturing firm we considered before there exists a Central Work Study Department (the elemental operations cannot afford their own). Using the criteria of the last paragraph, we can see that the functions of this department are located in System Three. Any enquiry made by these people 'across the board' in System One will gain high variety access to all operational circles. The findings will be heavily attenuated, by the expertise of engineers and statisticians within the department, before they are submitted to System Three. IF there is any conclusion that a new rule would contribute to corporate synergy, that formulation of the finding as a rule should be a further variety attenuator. Thus the metasystemic intervention added by command will be very small. Contrast this recommended practice with the practice (which I have seen) whereby a manual of piece-work rates and overtime payments in four volumes, each three inches thick, is delivered as an edict down the vertical axis. . . .

In conclusion, should we not reflect on the utility of the model we have so far constructed in reflecting the complexity of management — the magnitude of which was pressed home with some drama in an early chapter. After all, the problem of running the enterprise, internally and now, is usually perceived (and in particular is depicted by the organization chart) as having *one* formal vertical channel — the 'command chain'. This delegates authority downwards; in return, it demands the acceptance of responsibility, and the flow of accountability upwards. For the rest, we talk about informal networks, interpersonal relationships, and so on. We talk about the responsibility itself in terms of 'line' and 'staff' (and there will be much more about this later). We talk about style. Of STRUCTURE there is almost nothing to say, beyond the 'machine for apportioning blame' that the organization chart comprises.

Our cybernetic enquiries, on the contrary, have elicited SIX interactive elements in the vertical plane, all of which appear to be necessary to a viable system, all of which can be identified with logical precision, all of which can be measured in terms of variety exchanges under the three principles of organization. All six are indeed present in every viable system that I have ever encountered; normally five of them are not formally recognized or studied as vertical components of the system. They should be; and unless they are, there will be no knowing whether System Three has requisite variety or not.

The first three are the variety-interconnections in the vertical plane of the ENVIRONMENTAL, the OPERATIONAL, and the MANAGERIAL domains. Regardless of the very existence of System Three, proliferating variety is absorbed by the interactions of elemental units among themselves. Environments can never be disconnected. Operations are invariably connected, although their interactions may be strong or weak — and therefore may absorb much or little of each others' variety. In the vertical managerial domain, managers necessarily curtail the variety of their colleagues as the stamp of their own personalities on the behaviour of the elemental units becomes manifest, and as each learns to tolerate the resulting performance profile of adjacent units in a willing spirit of teamwork.

The second three are the channels of METASYSTEMIC INTERVENTION (normally confused with the inherited 'chain of command'), the ANTI-OSCILLATION CHANNELS that innervate System Two, and the OPERATIONAL MONITORING CHANNELS of System Three. These are all management activities that result from the embedding of System One in a metasystem. Unlike the first three variety absorbers, which are given in the nature of the enterprise for that particular System One, these three variety absorbers are subsystems of the metasystem itself. They are there to contain the residual variety not absorbed by the first three, given the *purposes* of the enterprise as a corporate entity. The first three variety absorbers just happen, but must be recognized. The second three must be recognized, and then designed.

Then because of the cybernetic laws that govern the embedding of System One in its metasystem, which we have been calling the principles of organization, it becomes possible to make a definitive statement concerning the internal and continuous stability of the enterprise. It is this:

The sum of horizontal variety disposed by n operational elements
= the sum of vertical variety disposed on the six
vertical components of corporate cohesion.

This is **The First Axiom of Management.**

LATER IN THE BAR...

'What do you mean — 'Beer's Razor'? From what I hear, he doesn't own one. Bearded fellow.'

'I was drawing a comparison with Occam's Razor. You know: entia (or some say essentia) non sunt multiplicanda praeter necessitatem.'

'No, I don't know, David. What's it mean?'

'It means that things (or some say essentials) should not be multiplied without necessity. In short, take the simplest hypothesis.'

'Yes; I know it, anyway. It was William of Occam who thought that one up. But surely that was hundreds of years ago? And it only seems relevant to logical theory.'

'Oh, hello Bill. You missed the beginning. I was trying to invent the concept of Beer's Razor. It would say: don't use the central command channel without necessity.'

'Well, that's plain common sense.'

'Then just how commonsensical are we? Personally, I'm totally overloaded with the stuff that comes up to me.'

'Then why don't you stop it?'

'I don't know where to start. It all LOOKS essential. But it can't be, because — frankly — I don't read most of it.'

'Neither do I.'

'Nor I.'

'Confessions all round. I don't either. How do we use the downward central channel? I didn't think I did, much; but I'm beginning to wonder.'

'Well, it seems to me that that's just the point. We don't think we do, but we do. So all our Systems One get their vareity inhibited. What's gone wrong?'

'It's amplification. The case is that we're all rotten amplifiers, and don't realize it.'

218

'It has to be said that just to be a boss is to be an amplifier. People are inclined to take note.'

'Not in my case.'

'Come off it, Tom. These are human affairs we're discussing. When the boss speaks, things happen — even if he's only thinking aloud.'

'I don't believe it. We five aren't actually Little Tin Gods whose every whim is amplified by the organization. It's just not true. All I do is to offer my people suggestions. They don't have to take any notice.'

'Put that way round, no. But no-one who works in a particular organization, with particular people, and a particular boss, just IGNORES the set-up he's in. He does his best, unless he's an idiot, to 'read' the situation.'

'Sure. And that isn't the same as saying that the boss-box is amplified downwards.'

'Isn't it?'

'Yes, it IS.'

'I see what you mean .... '

'Well, I'm not sure I do. But I'm quite prepared to use this Beer's Razor of yours, David. I like it. But where do I start?'

'No idea.'

'You're intellectualizing, as usual.'

'Probably.'

'Give it up, you two. I get the message, and I know where to start. I'm going to review our whole management system, to see where the vertical variety is being absorbed. I want it under those six headings. And if most of it is in the vertical channel, I'll use Beer's Razor on it.'

'Then according to the theory, you'll have to reinstate it in one of the other five domains — or whatever they're called.'

'Why reinstate it? Throw it away.'

'Then you won't have requisite variety. The cancerous growths will begin.'

'It's all very well to call computer developments cancerous, Sid, just because they're on the vertical command channel. Where the hell else would they be?'

'Nowhere else. The question is: just how much of this is necessary anyway? There are five other vertical planes absorbing variety. The message is that we're not paying any attention to the other five. We behave as if it were all command.'

'Well, three of them can be designed. That I see. But the three that exist by happenstance ... why doesn't he make it more clear what they exactly are?'

'What they are depends on the purpose of the particular system. He said that. He can't generalize.'

'That's an easy way out, Tony. Give me an example.'

'All right. But I'm going back to World War Two.'

'Groans all round.'

'Do you want the example, or don't you?'

'Carry on, Tony.'

'All right. The Army runs courses to train its specialists. Around 1940, the people sent on those courses were volunteers, supported by their Commanding Officers. Very few of them — twenty percent or so — passed out. But, given a war, all that democracy couldn't be afforded. So tests were instituted. A man acquired a simple psychological profile. It gave rough measures of his general intelligence, his verbal and numerical skills, his manual dexterity, and so on. The profile, instead of volunteering and support, decided whether he should join the course. Result: something like eighty percent passes.'

'Fine. Sounds effective. What's that got to do with anything?'

'Never mind that, Bill. Is Tony telling us that the high variety of the human being can be reduced to some 'test profile'? I am disgusted by the very idea.'

'That's exactly what I'm illustrating. Of course the man can't be reduced in this way. He does have high variety. But the course does not. The purpose of the system is not at all to acknowledge the humanity of the man, but to maximize the efficiency of the course. Result, success. There's a war on.'

'So you're dealing with an operational variety match, conceived within the context of an environmental variety match.'

'Exactly. It is a happenstance for sure. But it is determined by the purpose of the system — in this case, to create as many specialists as possible.'

'That's reasonable, Tony. And once you've set up mechanisms for that happenstance matching, you are not taking command decisions any longer.'

'That's fine, unless you are using the whole mechanism to duck the personal responsibility of saying NO.'

'We do that all the time, Joe.'

'Then better recognize it.'

'Yes, I see. Look here: is it possible to make all these variety measurements, and to compute these equations? Looks impossible to me.'

'Oh, don't let's get into that loop again. It's not the point. Look: if you have an old-fashioned weighing machine, and you put a heap of carrots on one side and a damn great metal weight on the other, you soon see whether you're out of balance. No-one counts the carrots, and you don't have to know what figure is marked on the metal weight.'

'You do when it comes to paying for the carrots.'

'Trust an accountant! We're not talking about economics. We're talking about variety balances in the regulation of a surviving system.'

'Which won't pay my salary.'

'Won't it? You get it all wrong, and the firm won't be viable. No salary.'

'Well, I'm still paid — and no-one knows anything about all this in my patch.'

'Exactly. It's a mixture of intuition and Ashby's Law that does it. As soon as you hear how it all works, you complain that you don't know how to do the variety arithmetic.'

'Isn't that supposed to be important?'

'Not number-crunching, surely. The idea is to understand the mechanism behind the intuitions.'

'Why?'

'Oh — to oil it, or something. Speaking for myself, I'm quite clear that my horizontal-vertical balances DON'T, quite clear that this is inducing cancerous growth on the vertical channel, and quite clear that this new System Three channel for audits and so on isn't properly understood or designed. And I haven't counted *anything yet*. There's more to measuring than counting things — I can see that.'

'We have a convert. I shall pour this beer over his head in baptism.'

'Shave it, with Beer's Razor.'

'Cut Beer's throat with the razor instead. What was all that about free societies being dishonest?'

'Yes. I didn't go for that either, I must say.'

'Yet according to the papers, we're up to here in young drop-outs claiming six times their due social benefit.'

'I agree. That's disgraceful. And *it's* dishonest. But these are people knocking the social order; so it's no use saying that the social order is itself dishonest.'

'The social order produced the drop-outs.'

'Oh, I'm not buying that argument. That's what they'd like *you* to believe.'

'Who?'

'The drop-outs. And the do-gooders.'

'And the rest of us are honest citizens?'

'Well aren't we?'

'Heard a man in the pub the other night expounding on this. The wickedness of youngsters on the SS. He had all the figures. Ten minutes later I heard him haranguing another group about the wickedness of the taxation system, and how he was evading most of his.'

'Well, at least you can say it in this country.'

'There'll be a right old political flare-up in a minute, and we shall have missed the entire point.'

'Which was?'

'That society has to have a lot of variety absorbed, one way or another, or there'd be bedlam.'

'All very well. But which way it's absorbed is relevant. I don't want my variety absorbed by a secret police.'

'Nor do I. But I don't want it absorbed by television producers who slant their stories either.'

'Take your choice.'

'There isn't any choice. The variety has been absorbed already. Let's face it, we're institutionalized.'

'That's just like Tony's personnel selection example. He claimed that it was justified by the purposes of the system. Maximize the number of men who passed the course.'

'Well, that might be justified in a war, Bill. But who is it who says that we can reduce variety of the individual like that in peacetime?'

'Advertising agencies do it. They have a low-variety model of the individual, and they apply positive feedback to reinforce it.'

'Never mind them, Joe. If people fall for that stuff, it's their own affair. Universities, for example, have a more serious responsibility.'

'What do you mean, Tony?'

'Take post-graduate admissions. There's no war-time pressure to say that the course must maximize its success rate. The university is supposed to e-ducate. Latin for 'lead out'. Instead of producing the highest number of specialists, it's supposed to offer the individual the chance to proliferate variety.'

'And so... ?'

'Well, it's all a matter of the purposes of the system, isn't it? In the war, we needed selection techniques to maximize the productivity of courses. In education, that isn't the purpose of the system any longer. So why do we administer selection tests for graduate candidates?'

'It reduces the variety in the operational domain, refers back to the environmental domain, which it in turn conditions, and ...'

'... *and finally lets the university managers off the hook of taking a responsible decision.'*

'But we, as managers, do exactly the same thing.'

'Well, that's exactly what I was arguing. A devil of a lot of variety absorption goes on in the first three domains, before you ever get to managerial decisions in the second three domains. We are indeed institutionalized.'

'Maybe. But I'm free to play golf and wash my car on Sundays.'

'Call that free? You haven't any choice. Have *you?'*

'Hmm. Conversation stopper, I notice. We don't have much choice about anything, really. I used my vote in the last election, but I found myself wondering why.'

'Democracy.'

'Choosing between two twits?'

'Politics again. Watch out.'

'Well: the cybernetics *of it is that variety has to be absorbed.'*

'Exactly. But I like *the way that it's absorbed here.'*

'How many years is it to 1984? They *'liked' it.'*

'Not many.'

'Seems to me we're bang on course.'

CHAPTER NINE

Outside and then

We have arrived at a structure whereby a firm, or any viable system, must necessarily be organized to handle its own internal regulation. The necessity arises from cybernetic laws given in nature, once they are described in the language created in this book. If any particular institution does not at first sight look anything like the last diagram of Systems Three-Two-One, it is because the conventions used to describe it (such as the organization chart) are different. If you will adopt the cybernetic conventions offered here, you will be able to translate from one language into the other, whereupon the particular institution will indeed 'look like' the model. This is unfailing; because the principles of analysis that were used are scientifically rigorous. And it is at this pont that the model becomes useful as a diagnostic tool.

These straightforward statements may sound overweening. But it is not a question of 'making claims', and still less a question of prescribing how a business 'ought to be run'. It is a question of creating a language that will discuss a viable system, and then of using that language to describe how enterprises actually *are* run. Diagnosis of the ills of any particular institution becomes possible simply because the language is also competent to express the principles of effective organization that are embodied in the science of cybernetics.

It is interesting that the search for necessary and sufficient conditions of viability has first of all consolidated a model devoted to internal regulation, but it is not surprising. The famed biologist Claude Bernard, who should certainly be regarded as a precursor of the group who first called themselves cyberneticians in the early nineteen-forties, uttered a dictum on viability more than a hundred years ago which has become extremely well-known. 'La fixité du milieu interior est la condition de la vie libre.' 'La vie libre' may certainly be translated by our 'independent existence' criterion: and Systems Three-Two-One are dedicated to the process of internal regulation that will indeed conduce to stabilization of the inside, now.

The primacy of this requirement in a viable system is not misunderstood by biologists, but is often misunderstood by managers. For, they feel, it is an advocacy on behalf of the status quo. They do not want their enterprises merely to survive. They declare: 'we must progress'. I agree (although there will be all manner of difficulty in defining what is to count as 'progress': witness current arguments as to 'zero growth' economies). But the manager who entertains this particular doubt at this particular point is *confusing several levels of recursion*. Suppose that we are modelling the energy industry. Then we have operational elements called coal, gas, electricity, oil, nuclear: and all of these are muddy boxes. If we are not to break all the rules of our language, we must leave them alone — except insofar as they need to cohere in our energy system. Otherwise we are making the wrong sort of metasystemic intervention in their horizontal variety equations. The call for coherence is precisely a call for the stability of the interior milieu. Given that stability, the energy industry can begin to decide what it means by 'progress'. Does this then condemn each of those five Systems One to 'mere survival'? Certainly not. For if we drop one level of recursion, we may construct a viable system model of each. The nuclear energy model, for instance, will have operational elements called nuclear plants. And from the point of view of the Atomic Energy Authority, those are muddy boxes which are expected to cohere in a stable interior milieu — while the Authority gets on with whatever *it* defines as 'progress'.

To use this work, in short, it is VITAL to know at all times at exactly which level of recursion one is operating. And since many managers operate at different level of recursion, in different roles, confusions often occur. For example, it is very familiar in our managerial culture that the Heads of System One *constitute together* System Three — which is an operational element (or part of it, as shall be shown) of the metasystem, one level of recursion higher. But they forget their roles. And this is why System Three discussions about corporate synergy sometimes end (to take an example that I witnessed) in two hours of argument as to whether a particular youth was or was not entitled to a tea break... . It might well pay to appoint a Recursion Monitor to each management committee. He would be authorized to stop the discussion if it wandered outside the appropriate level of recursion. Did you imagine that this is the job of the committee chairman himself? Then you have forgotten that he also is human, and that he also has other roles in the enterprise... .

These reflections on the recursive nature of the model lead to the next step in its construction. Systems Three-Two-One are necessary components of a viable system, which between them account for the stabilization of the internal milieu. But that CANNOT be a sufficient organizational structure for viability. This stability is a precondition of viability: but it takes no account of 'progress' at the level of recursion for which this set of systems constitutes the internal milieu. Then we have to come to understand this notion of 'progress' — not in terms of its politics and economics (which are matters for the particular enterprise), but in terms of its cybernetics (which are universal).

The enterprise is embedded in an environment, which is full of challenge and opportunity. Now we saw a model of that much earlier (the square in the circle in the amoeboid shape); but we were then discussing the operational elements of the viable system. Now we are discussing the viable system itself, and it is necessary to hold on to the level of recursion of that argument. The environment of the viable system is the environment that it has *has considered as an operational element of the metasystem* — a level of recursion higher. Thus the environment of the viable system is by no means the sum of the environments of its own contained viable systems. But the viable system that we are modelling must respond to this larger environment. System Three cannot do this, because (under our definitions) it is concerned with inside and now. Thus we clearly need a new system, dedicated to the larger environment, and to regulation in its regard, which environment I call the OUTSIDE AND THEN. So this will be System Four. Again it is worth remarking that these numbers (in this case Four) do not betoken 'seniority'. They are the numbers of the logical steps we are taking in constructing a necessary and sufficient model of viability.

There are two senses in which System Four has to deal with 'the larger environment' called Outside and Then. In the first place, there is the *accepted* environment of the corporation — which is OUTSIDE the collection of System One environments. Take the Energy example recently considered. Coal, gas, electricity, oil, and nuclear energy all have expanding environments of their own. But Energy itself, of which these five constitute the Systems One, has something more to consider. It includes, for example, new sources of energy — solar, wind, tidal; it includes, for example, the rapidly changing social opinion of the environmental issues involved in using energy at all. All of this is already apparent to any concerned citizen. But, in the second place, there is the *problematic* environment of the corporation. This is also outside the collection of System One environments; but it is especially concerned with a future that it is the specific duty of the Energy Corporation to advance. That is to say that there is an area of concern in the Outside and Then that belongs — in a creative sense — to the viable system's responsibility. I am drawing a distinction between environments in which there is general interest, and in which managerial interest is largely reactive, and those which are highly specific to the viability of the enterprise itself, in which managerial interest ought to be wholly innovative — as deriving from special knowledge and dedication, from research and flair. Reflection will reveal that the Energy example is by no means special, or peculiar to that topic. *Every* viable system is involved in an environment that is wider than the sum of System One environments. *Every* viable system distinguishes between the problematic component of this wider environment that 'belongs' to it, and the accepted wider environment in which it is contained.

The situation may be depicted like this:

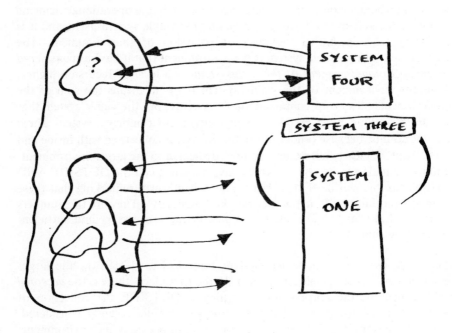

Figure 38. The emergence of System Four. It is determined by a larger environment and an unknown future

Obviously the System Three-Two-One diagram already established fits into the above diagram, in the undiscriminated space of the lower right half of the picture. The present concern is with the two loops drawn between System Four and the wider environment, one of which interacts with the accepted environmental domain (the total envelope above), and one with the problematic domain (included in the envelope, but special to System Four, and marked with the interrogation sign).

Now if System Four is a logical necessity in the development of our model of any viable system, because System Three is preoccupied with the inside-and-now executive management of the organic whole, it will be useful to acquire some 'feel' for its universality. And since we have lately referred to the Three-Two-One composite as related to the stability of the internal milieu (with acknowledgement to Claude Bernard), it may help to look at System Four in biological terms too. Introspecting, first of all, it is surely evident that the human being has a System Four. It deals with the wider environment; that is, it takes account of a perceived cosmos that is much larger than the sum of its organic environments. We humans are more than survival machines that operate to keep the internal milieu stable, although that activity is indeed a precondition of everything else that we do (and it was noted earlier that the same is true of the firm). Human beings take account of the wider environment that we all share, which is the envelope environment of the last diagram. Each of us, individually, also takes account of a problematic environment embedded in this envelope. It is peculiar to ourselves; it is the environment in which each of us debates: 'shall I do this, or that?' To this end, we are prone to say: 'we have foresight'; meaning, not that we have prior knowledge of events, but that we may well contemplate the probable consequences of alternative actions. To this same end, and under similar conditions and constraints, the firm may well say: 'we engage in business forecasting'.

But how is this reflected in general biology? It is hard to conceive of a tortoise planning next week's activities, and yet more difficult to imagine a microscopic organism entertaining alternatives. Both the tortoise and the amoeba clearly have Three-Two-One composites that regulate the *internal* environment. But their accommodation of the *external* environment appears to be purely reactive. And in all conscience, most firms appear to be purely reactive too. For although they may 'engage in business forecasting', many firms do not believe in the answers — and maybe they are right not to do so.

The biological answer to this paradox appears to me to involve an invocation of the recursion theorem. I spoke of an amoeba as an individual. But it is difficult to bring home this concept of individuality in a creature that DIVIDES twenty times while you are formulating any such question. The System Four of the amoeba, I submit, is amazingly ingenious. It copes with the wider environment by *dropping a level of recursion*. It divides. In this meiosis it amplifies its variety vis-à-vis the wider environment. In short, the whole notion of biological evolution, of 'survival of the fittest' (with however many neo-Darwinian refinements) involves a System Four that manipulates recursiveness.

There is confusion between two notions of Nature. One says that it is profligate, the other that it is parsimonious. This dilemma is easily resolved if we use the language of cybernetics. Take profligacy: so *many* acorns, so *many* spermatazoa. . . they are simply variety amplifiers. Yet so many acorns and so many sperms die. Of course: we need variety attenuation around here, or else we would be overwhelmed by oak trees and animals. The ecology is parsimonious in this. So what is happening? The expansion and contraction of variety in the reproductive process is not absurd. It provides the degree of freedom needed to promote survival-worthiness, mutation, learning, adaptation, evolution.... .

If this argument holds, then what about System Four in the human being (his 'foresight'), and in the firm (its 'forecasting')? The answer is that both are using a different survival technique, or think that they are, which does not resort to recursion. They expand variety by *contemplating* rather than *creating* alternatives. They reduce variety by the mental elimination of those alternatives. Thus: I do not say to my children: 'quick — run across the road... oh, too bad, they didn't survive', and then replace them by further breeding. Nor do we say to a firm: 'quick — here's a money-making opportunity... oh, too bad, we are bankrupt'. In both cases, we hope to acquire the degrees of freedom needed to promote mutation, learning, adaptation, and evolution (in a word survival-worthiness, or in another word VIABILITY) by *simulating* the amplification and attenuation of variety.

Intellectually, I submit, these arguments solve the paradox of System Four in various circumstances. 'Higher organisms', such as men and mankind's institutions, simulate the variety engineering that 'lower organisms' achieve by manipulating recursions. Intellectually, I submit, this is a great discovery. Certainly it will satisfy the needs of the viability modelling process in which we are engaged.

Objector: Then why all this defensiveness? Why the 'intellectual' qualifications?

Honest Reply: Because, cybernetically, the manipulation of recursion levels is far more powerful. No wonder the coelacanth has been on earth for millions of years, while Rolls Royce went bankrupt.

Objector: And as to humankind?

Honest Reply: Just what *I* was thinking.

This discussion was supposed to provide a universal 'feel' for System Four. It raises more questions than it answers; even so, the System Four 'feel' is there. And now we have to consider what the firm does about it, bearing in mind the mental reservations about the forms of variety engineering that may be appropriate. It could be that our institutions have *totally* misconceived the System Four activity. For the moment, the onus is sufficiently great to argue that the System Four activity has been merely misconceived.

Consider, first of all, what counts in the enterprise as System Four activity, dealing with the Outside and Then. Obviously, Research and Development counts. Market Research counts. Corporate Planning counts. Economic Forecasting counts. Management Development counts. Very well then: consider how all these managerial activities are integrated to constitute System Four — to respond to the 'feel' for that survival-worthiness that our excursion into biology provided, or that our search for necessary-and-sufficient conditions demands.

The truth is: THERE IS NO SUCH INTEGRATION.

Activities concerned with the Outside and Then, which were identified as System Four activities, are disparate, are disseminated, are active all over the organization in the cause of special pleading. . This is my universal experience, in every kind of enterprise, large and small, all over the world. Assuming that this allegation is true (and is it not?) the question arises: does it matter? I think that it does, for two distinct and powerful reasons.

The first of these reasons is the change in the rate of change. Dealing with the Outside and Then, in the traditional enterprise (whether public or private), was a simple matter — before the Second World War. The boss was primarily preoccupied with the stability of the internal environment. And rightly so. He could deal with the problems of System Four in the bath-tub: such as once a month. But the exponential expansion of technology in all fields (and surely the exponential expansion of *electronic* technology has affected *all* fields, apart from any other advance) has meant that System Four is in continuous action. This is surely the reason for the invention of 'corporate planning'. The term itself is of recent currency. It is, in short, generally recognized that much more attention must be given to the Outside and Then. This has led (we shall argue later) to a managerial fiasco of monumental proportions. Meanwhile, the need is sufficiently real.

The second reason why the diffusion of System Four matters so much is that **responsibility** for adaptive behaviour has shifted, whereas this fact has not been recognized within the institution. This responsibility (like all others) belongs in the first place to the boss. But of course, the boss has (rightly) been taught to *delegate*. Now he has delegated responsibility for System Three (with its Two-One) to an executive directorate, carrying authority with its responsibility. But he has delegated . . . *what* has he delegated? . . . the System Four function to various and disconnected teams of 'advisors'. This was an option apparently open to him, because of the division between 'line' and 'staff' management that became established after the Second World War, when military usage in the matter was embraced by civil management. It had worked well in the armed forces; it worked well, for perhaps twenty years, in business and industry. It works no longer, and I think that it should be abandoned.

The notion of 'staff' is supportive. The staff officer undertakes those activities which the boss could in principle undertake himself, if he had the time. The responsibility of the staff officer is essentially advisory, since the boss may quickly review the staff report and approve it, or quickly choose between alternatives presented in that report as appropriate ways of implementing the boss's own intentions. When the contemporary activities of System Four are examined, however, it soon becomes apparent that these staff characteristics no longer apply. The reason is that all sub-systems of Four are using new technologies that are probably outside the competence of the boss to evaluate. Unless the boss happens to be a mathematical statistician, he simply has to put his trust in his market researchers. Unless he happens to be a physicist, he has to put his trust in his R and D department. Unless he is a real expert in input-output analysis and stochastic simulation, he has to place trust in his corporate planners. Of course, the boss has various ways of checking up on all these people: he may, for example, employ outside monitors of their work. But that is not the point at issue. The fact is that, whether they wanted it or not, System Four people have acquired a great deal of *power* in the modern enterprise. They must be held accountable for the exercise of that power. The 'staff' man has no power at all that is not simply a reflection of the boss's power; these people have.

Putting together the two arguments, that of the change in the rate of change and that of a new assumption of responsibility, it is evident that System Four is a continuous and powerful subsystem of the metasystem. Insofar as it is not properly integrated, then, the viability of the enterprise is at risk. Moreover, if the line-and-staff dichotomy is no longer serviceable, new managerial concepts are needed to effect this integration. Let us think over the typical state of affairs, to understand the realistic starting-point of this enquiry.

It is quite normal, in a large enterprise, for the elements of System Four to have virtually no knowledge of each other's activity. Thus to the visitor from Mars it would surely seem an absurdity that the R and D department is following its technological nose without much regard to market research findings, that both departments are unaware of the general framework provided by corporate planning, and that this department itself conceives of corporate plans without much knowledge of the technological thrusts in R and D or of the expectations of the market. Yet I very often find that this is the stark fact; and I also find two reasons for it. The first is that, thanks to the line-and-staff dichotomy, each of the elements 'belongs' to the staff of some director or vice-president. They are engaged (supposedly) in a supportive role to different men of power in the organization. Then it is not culturally surprising that the existence of System Four as a condition of viability has not been recognized. And, if it has not, it is not altogether surprising that these Four elements may actually be used by their bosses as tools in the jockeying for power that goes on between them. This jockeying is usually apparent, and I have seen many situations where it should really be described as a power struggle (conducted according to polite rules) to the finish. In such a situation, the elements of System Four may not only be unintegrated, but actually at war between themselves. For instance, I recall a firm in which the market research department did indeed make itself aware of every report issued by the operational research department; but it did so only to mount immediate studies seeking to disprove any OR finding that affected Marketing!

The second reason why System Four integration is often ineffectual, is that the top people (directors, vice presidents) believe that they are effecting the integration *themselves*. Thus, at a board meeting, or a meeting of the executive committee, one may perhaps hear: 'according to my market chaps, this trend will not continue'; 'Oh, but according to my R and D people, there will be a technological breakthrough in this area'. The meeting then tries to piece together the jigsaw of advice. Cybernetically, however, it is evident that his process *does not have requisite variety*. The two statements are highly attenuated in variety. The trend projection and the break-through expectation are each dependent on a mass of conditional clauses that are not being expressed. They are saying (in the small print) 'other things being equal'. Not only are other things rarely equal, but in this example the conditions affecting each statement are directly juxtaposed in terms of the assumptions each is making about the whole set of possible states that underly the other statement. Each of these sets has very high variety. And if those varieties were allowed to absorb each other, the final filtered statement to the board could easily be the reverse of the judgment that it finds itself making.

It follows that to speak of the 'integration' of System Four entails an involvement between its elements at the level of their own variety generation. This is an important conclusion; not least because it seems to point to an obvious solution that I believe to be mistaken. That solution would be to amalgamate all the elements of System Four in one integral department. I think it is mistaken, because it would involve a colossal proliferation of variety that no management could handle. There needs to be a new notion to capture the essence of System Four integration as revealed by our enquiry, and I shall call it 'Focus'. This is intended to mean that all elements of System Four (as it were, optically) 'project' their activities, in full variety, onto the same screen. At once the optical metaphor breaks down: detailed pictures focussed onto the same screen would obscure each other, and the image viewed would be a blur. Then an instrumentality is needed that achieves the logical need to focus, without having a blurring effect. Then I propose that the 'screen' on which the elements all focus is none other than the model of the viable system whose System Four they comprise.

At the conclusion of this book, the model of the viable system will be complete; and an attempt will have been made to guide readers in mapping their organizations onto it. Then (as we said earlier) a diagnostic tool will be available, to examine the organizational health of the enterprise. But further: if this is done, the elaborated model provides exactly the 'screen' on which to focus System Four activity. In that case, the optical metaphor can be rescued. I visualize a room in which is exhibited a large-scale representation of the firm, fully developed according to these cybernetic conventions, for all levels of recursion. This room would be a kind of club-house for all System Four people and their bosses. Means would be needed to indicate work in progress on any aspect of the model, by any element of System Four. Then obviously the variety interactions we were seeking could take place — on a continuous basis, in a club-house atmosphere.

I hope that this proposal comes across as 'a good idea', since it needs to have psychological verisimilitude. In fact, it embodies that cybernetic reality which has already been thoroughly discussed. It is stated in terms of the principle:

> *Every regulator must contain a model of that which is regulated.*

Reflection on this principle pays off in every regulatory situation. We have reflected upon it before, and must needs do so again. Unless the enterprise *as a whole* contains an adequate model of its total environment, how shall it be viable? And of course the notion of environment must itself contain a regulatory model of the range of possible futures. This is precisely an explanation of the necessity for System Four. We may re-examine the issue in human terms.

An excellent paradigm of regulation is to be found in the learner-teacher relationship. Each component of this sytem is trying to regulate the other. There is no point in the teacher's uttering wisdom, if the pupil cannot comprehend what he says. There is no point in the pupil's floundering reactions, if the teacher cannot interpret them as defining the pupil's difficulties. Now the doyen of cybernetics in this situation has always been, and (thankfully) remains, Gordon Pask. More than a quarter of a century ago, he had built a teaching machine: it taught mechanical skills, such as the punching of punched cards. Whenever I had the opportunity, I used to stay with him, and we worked together. Because Pask was dealing in machinery, the human pupil had inevitably to communicate with the machine electrically — by pressing buttons. There was monitoring equipment in another room, showing how the teaching machine and the human pupil were interacting — with a resultant skill for the pupil. One day, I was watching this equipment; and, with a sense of panic, I realized that I had forgotten which screen reflected the actions of the machine, and which the actions of the pupil. I tried to identify which was which: *there was no way.*

Here was a sharp lesson. A good pupil is trying to imitate his teacher (in the matter of a skill). That is, he is trying to build a model of what his teacher would do in given circumstances. A good teacher is trying to imitate his pupil. That is, he is trying to build a model of his pupil's processes, in order to understand his difficulties, and to correct his mistakes. What I learned on this occasion was that the success of relationship of learner and teacher is to be measured *meta*systemically. When the two models of each other converge, learning has occurred.

This anecdote is intended to press home the point that any would-be regulator must contain a model of that which needs to be regulated, and that if this model has a given level of variety, it will handle only that equivalent variety in the outside world. So many of our would-be regulators in society have low-variety models of what has to be regulated. As a result, and recapitulating our previous discussion on the point, as soon as the system to be regulated adopts a possible state that is not allowed for in the model embraced by the regulator, regulation fails. Parents should acknowledge this. Every kind of social worker should acknowledge this. And management needs to see the point as well, as we have seen in several contexts already. But although the theorem is completely general, that is to say that it applies in any regulatory situation, it has a very special application in System Four. This is because System Four houses the viable system's whole apparatus for adaptation. It follows that System Four must contain a model of the viable system of which it is the System Four. In current managerial practice, System Four is hardly recognized: still less does it contain this model. Thus the proposal that would use the model as a 'screen', to obtain the 'focus' that would manifest 'integration', has sound cybernetic underpinnings. The model is indeed a *corporate model*. But it is necessary to be very careful with terminology here. The current notion of a corporate model is of a set of simultaneous equations fed into a computer, which then optimizes the values of controllable variables under some maximizing functional. Instead, we are discussing a cybernetic model of the necessary and sufficient conditions of any viable system, as illuminating the managerial structure and behaviour of that organization.

Examining in more detail how such a Development Directorate ought to work, the following diagram (Figure 39) may be consulted. In the square box, denoting System Four, are the elements (four are shown: there may be more). The box includes the model of the entire system, as advocated above; and the 'scribble' again indicates the requisite variety that must exist between the elements and the model, whose FOCUS it is.

Next, we observe the two classes of the wider environment, delineated earlier. For the moment, the diagram depicts interactions only with the *accepted* (envelope) environment. As usual, the three principles of organization have to be considered. How does the firm establish requisite variety between System

Four and this envelope environment: that is, what are the amplifiers and attenuators involved — and have we *designed* them? Secondly, are the channel capacities adequate? Thirdly, are the transducers in good order? It seems that it is not difficult to satisfy ourselves about these conditions — once the integral nature of System Four is recognized. The elements reinforce each other — once it is understood that this is the intention. if there is a Development Directorate, all these matters can be properly considered: otherwise not.

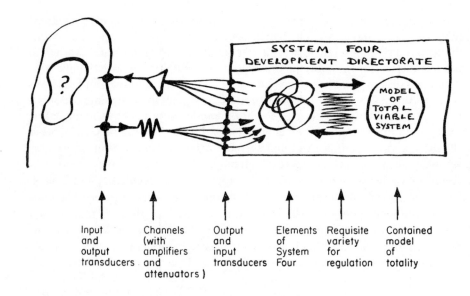

| Input and output transducers | Channels (with amplifiers and attenuators) | Output and input transducers | Elements of System Four | Requisite variety for regulation | Contained model of totality |

Figure 39. Key components of System Four

The reason why the bold statement is made that the three principles of organization cannot be properly considered in the (usual) absence of any entity that counts as a Development Directorate, is that each element of System Four will make its own arrangements to meet the cybernetic demands of natural laws. Then it would be a sanguine expectation indeed to suppose that the arrangements made by the elements were mutually reinforcing — or even compatible. What should be expected, and what is normally found, is a mixture of vast reduplication, and vast gaps in those arrangements, as far as their mere coverage is concerned. Their combined capacity to meet the conditions of the three principles in the most effective way is hardly a question worth raising. They have no such capacity.

Before considering further the managerial issue about System Four, it will be useful to look more closely at the problem of the contained environment, defined as *problematic* (the shape containing the question mark in Figure 39), which is related explicitly to the *creative* capabilities of the enterprise. The distinction was drawn earlier, and on sufficient grounds. But when we consider more precisely what are the consequences of that distinction, we may well be inviting a cultural shock. For, despite all protestations to the contrary, the best that our contemporary management can do is indeed to react to the stimuli that reach it from the environment. Of course these stimuli include intelligence reports about possible futures; thus policies may be formulated that take up new options, and these may be represented as more than reactive. But we ought to draw a distinction between this range of responses to stimuli and the internal creative urge. It is easy to recognize the distinction in the individual human being, and more difficult in the enterprise. Yet the enterprise does generate creative ideas, usually at junior levels, and these conflict with the paradigm held at the senior levels. They are usually squashed. This is clearly because System Four's contained model of the whole viable system (which we have shown *must* exist) is held in the heads of the senior people: it is not made explicit, and cannot be interrogated or tested. Consequently, occasions when a genuinely creative impetus is supported are rare. But they do happen. Consider the most famous incident of this kind: it was the declaration of intent, made by President Kennedy, to reach the moon. Then of course it was done: I repeat, of course. Without disparaging the achievement of the Apollo programme itself, it may be said that this demonstration of the capability of humankind to do whatever it determines to do might have been directed to a more useful cause. There is, for example, the problem of nourishing the undernourished two-thirds of the world. Unfortunately, more stands between us and that target than empty space... .

Whatever the merits and demerits of that example, we enter the arena (not of reactive, but) of creative management. It is the arena called by Denis Gabor: **inventing the future.** And this is a most valuable phrase. Because most people appear to believe that 'The Future' is something that *will happen to us,* whereas it is certainly open to humankind to take charge of these events. As far as our modelling is concerned, this means considering the interaction between System Four and its *problematic* environment. This was defined as special to the concerns of the viable system whose model we are entertaining: how will it invent the future?

We could easily redraw the last diagram at this point, showing the two environmental links as continuing into the problematic, contained, environment that is marked with the interrogation mark. That diagram would be perfectly legitimate; but it would add nothing to the discussion. For we now face an issue that has not reared its head before. It is the issue of *initiative*. System Four is involved in containing environmental variety, as we recently saw; it is also concerned in generating that variety. This being so, it is appropriate to begin the next diagram with a double amplification of variety.

The symbol, as usual, is a conventional device. It relates not merely to the reciprocal absorption of variety proposed to the viable system by the envelope environment, but to a questing variety generator, seeking the raw material of innovation itself. In doing this, System Four must be ready to handle the variety input thus generated — and therefore to *design* the attenuating filter that conveys that variety home.

Such an arrangement is included in the next diagram, Figure 40, which is taken to include the details (which are not shown) of the contents of the System Four box already indicated in the previous diagram. What is now added is a new model: the model of System Four itself, the innovation generator. The need for such a model follows from previous arguments as to the need for regulatory models of that which is to be regulated. Insofar as System Four is now depicted as penetrating into the *problematic* environment, then, it will need a special model of that domain. The diagram shows this new model as transmitting its messages through the transducers that it has already established to communicate with the envelope of the accepted environment. These are the only devices that it understands. But it must be prepared to receive replies of a different sort; it must devise new input transducers, and (a fortiori) a new attenuating filter. Here is the diagram:

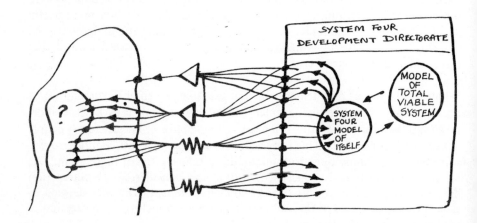

Figure 40. The System Four mechanism for interrogating the problematic environment

Now this is a very special activity, and one that is little understood. Innovative variety generation is generally understood in our managerial culture to be a matter of flair, of inspired guesswork. But in the above diagram exist the beginnings of a model of what is really going on. Successful innovators are not in fact acting as if possessed by occult powers. Invariably, they use existing channels and transducers through which to stimulate and interrogate the problematic environment. What is different about these innovators (and I have studied their strategies, my own included) is precisely the design of the input returned. Innovators are impelled to use the existing arrangements for addressing the Outside and Then, because those channels and transducers are available. But if they are to 'hear' the answers, they cannot rely on the existing arrangements — because they are designed *to filter out* exactly that novelty which may inhere in the replies.

Therefore innovators devise new attenuating filters and new transducers, in order to understand the novelties which (by definition) they are not aware of in advance. How may they do this, in the state of ignorance which (by definition) is their starting point? It can be done only by a feedback mechanism, because the new filters and attenuators have to learn by their own experience. In trying to portray this mechanism, which is of course an expansion of the 'problematic' part of the preceeding diagram, we immediately discover that the simple loops that are our customary convention are totally inadequate, since they take no account of those very feedback devices which are essential to the mechanism portrayed. Thus the following network diagram is advanced:

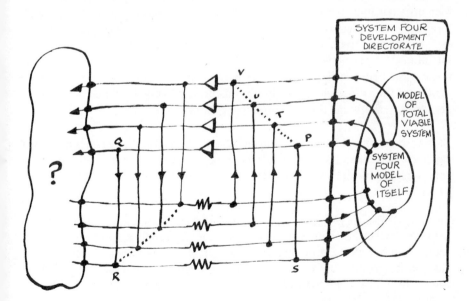

Figure 41. An elaboration of Figure 40

This diagram seems to be the minimal statement of a self-organizing network for the 'problematic' aspect of System Four. It looks far more rigid than it will be in practice; and that is because it does not show the *interactions* between the four loops that are generated by the four elements originally considered as comprising System Four. But if the advice about creating a focus for System Four is accepted, such interactions will occur.

To explain this further: consider the loop PQRS on the diagram. This loop shows one of the System Four elements launching itself (P) towards the problematic environment, through a variety amplifier. The intended impact is fed back through R and S to the System Four model of itself. However, the *result* of the *total* System Four impact on the problematic environment is being picked up at R as well. Thus the message at A has two components, one of which is rich in information from the problematic environment. That message (in addition to returning to the System Four model of itself) is fed back to P. The purpose is to modify the design of the amplifier between P and Q. That is an explanation of the rigid diagram, and it applies to all four loops, originating from all four elements in System Four. System Four itself however, is by these means integrated, insofar as it is provided with a focus. Then the four loops, with their feedbacks, are not to be conceived as independent. For example, in the case of the PQRS loop, we expect a spin-off feedback to the other three loops. This spin-off makes its effect (on the diagram) at the points T, U and V. A full version of the diagram would be well-nigh incomprehensible, because it would show these feedback spin-offs for each loop onto the others — not only on the self-regulating amplifiers, but on the self-regulating attenuators too. So this is why the total arrangement was introduced as a 'network'. It is very complicated, because of the variety absorption between System Four elements that it entails, thus meeting the condition that those elements should absorb each other's variety — even in, perhaps especially in, this self-organizing situation.

This abstract model has made considerable demands on the reader's analytical capacity, and his impatience would be understandable. What are the practical consequences of all this cyberneticizing? Fortunately, they are very simple — or so I think.

The last diagram created a complicated situation in the diagrammatic space between System Four and the problematic environment; it would be yet more complicated, if all the dotted lines of the P-T-U-V type were included for both amplifiers and attenuators. Then what is the situation back in System Four, where the focus was created? To answer this, we may revert to the picture given in Figure 39, where the four elements (there might be more) of System Four were shown as intersecting. These are the activities of R and D, market research, corporate planning, and so on. Please look at this situation more closely, considering it as a *logical* diagram as shown in Figure 42.

The hatched area now marks the phase space in which all the elements intersect. We could call this hatched area the **kernel** of the focus.

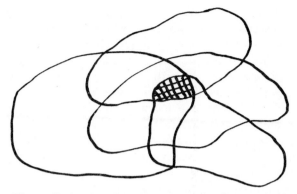

Figure 42. Logical diagram of the interactions between
the elements of System Four

It is here that the managerial reality for System Four resides. System Four management has to handle the (supposedly) four elements in their normal interactions with the accepted envelope environment. That is straightforward. It has also to handle those four elements in their penetration of the problematic environment. That is not straightforward, because of the variety proliferation implicit in the interactive learning systems that are involved. Back at the focus, however, there exists a logical intersect of all such activity — which we called the kernel. It is right here that the management task exists; and these models define it. Then *who* should undertake these managerial duties, and *how?*

When, in the last chapter, we understood the internal-and-now responsibilities of System Three, we nominated it an Operations Directorate. I doubt if that nomination caused a raised eyebrow. Given a few variations that might have been inspired by the model, the idea is sufficiently familiar. Now the responsibilities of System Four are equally complicated — and equally important, as the next chapter will show. Then surely, there ought to be a Development Directorate. This idea usually causes more than a raised eyebrow: it leads to expostulation. For (please remember) our arguments placed System Four in the corporate *management* (and not the merely advisory) domain. Hence a Development Director, in these terms, is not a 'Chief Boffin', a tame intellectual. He is a full member of the senior management. The arguments for such an appointment, as advanced in this very chapter (and enhanced in the next) appear to me inexorable.

After the last few pages of abstract thinking, it is well to get down to earth again, and to consider political realities. I have often advocated an appointment of Development Director in this full sense. The advice has never been accepted (except in the two cases where I personally received that appointment). That is a very interesting fact, because I have never met any *intellectual* resistance to the argument. The problem seems to be this. A Development Director (as defined) has to be knowledgeable in the development arena: he therefore knows more than anyone else about the future into which the enterprise is heading, and about the technology that is taking it there. This is a very threatening stance within senior management — unless the person holding the position 'has no teeth'. Now this is why the line-and-staff dichotomy is so convenient. Were the Development Director 'merely' advisory, he would not constitute a threat. Thus most people who putatively hold this role have, indeed, no teeth. But a toothless Development Director (as defined) is not a Development Director at all. . . .

Next, there is a practical problem that I have often encountered. Since a Development Director belongs (by definition) to a *future* managerial culture, he is unlikely to be found in the ranks of the *existing* management — for that is dedicated to the existing technology and mores. There are always people within the enterprise who are future-oriented; but they are inevitably junior. To find a Development Director capable of undertaking the System Four role, and of recruiting and mobilizing those more junior in-house people, probably means 'going outside'. Well, this book is about managerial cybernetics. The top management group in any enterprise exists in unstable equilibrium. Equilibrium is maintained only by the internal high-variety absorption of the group, which is based on intimate knowledge of each member by the others. It is therefore usually unthinkable to this group that a total stranger should be introduced at their level. Such a reaction is entirely reasonable. Unstable equilibrium is a very uncomfortable state. Even so, it is evident that the enterprise needs a Development Director. In my experience, and not surprisingly, the man who usually gets the job (under whatever title) is the one who — his colleagues think — has the least chance of accomplishing change. This is an appalling dilemma. I wish to attest to my sympathy. Even so: enterprises that do not grasp this nettle are unlikely to remain viable indefinitely, as the arguments of this chapter reveal.

The second question was: *how* should the managerial duties of System Four be discharged. The answer, we saw, was through a mode of integration described as a focus. A room was described, in which the whole model of the viable system, at all levels of recursion, would be displayed. It was to be a club-house. It is difficult to enlarge on this concept, because each institution must needs adapt the idea to its own conditions. In *Brain of the Firm* I outlined the design for an Operations Room. This was subsequently built for President Allende in Santiago, Chile. Most sadly, the experience of using this technique did not outlast the date of 11th September, 1973, which saw the overthrow of democracy in Chile, and the death of the President. I say 'most sadly', let it be clear, not because of the loss of the scientific outcome (which was sad enough), but because of the calamity that overtook our hope of civilized progress in every aspect of national life.

An Operations Room, considered as the physical manifestation of our focus — in which in particular the kernel of the System Four model of itself is displayed — might take on any form. But outstandingly it must be an ergonomically viable locale. The people who use this club-house are human beings constrained by their own neurophysiological limitations. Therefore it is absurd to overload them with data that they cannot ingest, absurd to present those data in ways that actually suppress their inherent patterns, and especially absurd to maintain data that are out of date. With so much absurdity as is here invoked, it might seem that these warnings are unnecessary. Unfortunately, they are necessary. There has been considerable interest in the Operations Room concept, and I have visited many. Without exception, they exhibited at least one — if not all three — of these absurdities. Then naturally enough, the Operations Room concept itself falls into disrepute; and that is a pity. At any rate, I seek to revive it under the name of focus, and shall return to the topic in the chapter on quantification. For the Operations Room is a tool of total management, and arises in the context of each of the subsystems of the metasystem. But it has a very special *developmental* role. System Three, after all, if there is no Operations Room, can go and look at the operations themselves. But System Four has no operations to examine; it has only its creative facility to visualize alternative futures, and to invent them.... .

... Outside and Then.

LATER IN THE BAR...

'Well, I think it's monstrous. If all our bloody intellectuals, scientists, and so on start thinking of themselves as managers, they'll get a darned sight too big for their boots.'

'I think it was Churchill who said of scientists that they should be 'on tap and not on top'.'

'He would. In practice, he thought the same about his Chiefs of Staff — sending for them in the middle of the night, and all that.'

'There goes that word 'Staff' again. Weren't the Chiefs of Staff precisely the people who actually conducted the war? Managers, that is.'

'That's because they were Chiefs, not because they were Staff.'

'Remember Flanders and Swann? "Chief assistant to the assistant chief?" I liked Flanders and Swann.'

'You fellows are making it sound as if it's all a matter of semantics. Is the System Four notion as described a revolutionary move, or isn't it?'

'Just what I was saying. If those people start thinking of themselves as managers, where are we? Revolutionary it is — especially as so many of those boys are Leftists.'

'The Marxist infiltration of management, eh?'

'Oh come on now. Bill can find himself some right-wing scientists, I'm sure. This isn't to the point. We are being asked to consider whether System Four people play a management role or not.'

'Of course they don't. Right now I've got a problem. There are only two basic courses I can follow — call them A and B. I've put together a task force to evaluate them. In a month's time I shall take a decision, note. System Four is a helpful notion, I think, because of the focus idea as a mode of integration. But the stuff about line-and-staff is crazy.'

'All right, Frank. Let's follow this through. What do you think your System Four, your task force in this case, is going to come up with?'

'I told you. They'll come up with an evaluation of courses A and B. Relative merits.'

'Then suppose they say this. Following Course A is likely to make half a million by Christmas. Following Course B is likely to lose a million by Easter. What would be your decision?'

'Oh, for heaven's sake ...'

'No, go on, what is your decision?'

'You can be damned offensive when you want to be.'

'I'm not being offensive at all. Please: what is your decision?'

'Well — obviously A.'

'And that is your decision?'

'Yes.'

'What Bobby means, Frank, is: is that your *decision?'*

'Certainly it is.'

'What alternative have you got?'

'Course B.'

'But Course B is likely to lose you a million by Easter.'

'So I decided against it.'

'— I give up.'

'Frank, don't you see what these two are trying to say? The decision has been taken for you by your task force.'

'I could always disagree with their findings.'

'Let me come in again: you didn't. *When I asked you what would be your decision, you didn't question anything at all.'*

'Look, for God's sake, I appointed the task force, and I trust them.'

'Fine. It was the appointment of the task force that was the decision. It was a decision to delegate the decision between A and B to them. Now they're managers.'

'Rubbish.'

'Can I interrupt?'

'Good idea, man. Just lower the temperature, that's all.'

'Suppose we have an Operations Room, the focus, the kernel of the focus, and everything.'

'How can a focus have a kernel? It's a mixed metaphor.'

'No it isn't. You're thinking of cameras and nuts. These terms are both pinched from mathematics.'

'Get on with it, George. You have your Operations Room.'

'Well, I was thinking that if all the senior management went to this club-house, the Operational people and the Development people, and listened to the task force explaining themselves in terms of the model of the viable system that is supposed to be there, maybe there would be a real decision.'

'Meaning?'

'Well, I guess Bobby was implying that there might be prior decisions implicit in the task force's report. This exercise would expose all that.'

'It might. But it might not. How would it do it?'

'Simply by the explosion of variety that comes out of my scenario. After all, the report we heard on A and B is a very low variety report. That's why the decision appears to be pre-empted.'

'Even so, there could still be a lot of special pleading in the club-house.'

'Oh, I don't deny it. I think the System Four people are indeed managers. The merit of the Operations Room scenario is that everyone would notice the fact.'

'You mean that people would see how they were fanagling evidence.'

'No, no. We have Frank's word that this is an honourable task force. They are not 'fanagling the evidence'. They are reaching decisions.'

'*So?*'

'*Well, I think that if I were in Frank's situation, I would say:* 'O.K., chaps, you have convinced me that you are right. But if we're going to do Course A, you have to be responsible for it.' *Then System Four has to put its money where its mouth is.*'

'*But the task force is* advisory!'

'*Hell's teeth, Bill, that's exactly what we're arguing about!*'

'*Well, it ought to be.*'

'*That's your conditioned reflex working. The argument is that NO WAY are you going to get a 'purely advisory' task force.*'

'*It's an illusion.*'

'*So you had better face up to the realities.*'

'*Dammit all. You* can *get advice. I get advice from my doctor.*'

'*Do you? I don't. I do what he says.*'

'*When did you last over-rule the 'advice' of your doctor?*'

'*In my case, when he said I had to give up smoking.*'

'*Do you want to defend that as a* decision, *Joe? That's just a weakness of character.*'

'*Thanks. But you're right.*'

'*Good Lord!!*'

'*What's the matter, Jim?*'

'*I've recently turned down a proposal from what I suppose I have to call System Four. Was* that *character weakness?*'

'*In your case, Jim, never.*'

'*Well, at least I need a drink.*'

'*And so do we all. Charge it to System Four.*'

'Management?'

'*Let's not start it all over again. I'm convinced. Wait till I work this one out with my so-called Management Services Department. Those boys and girls are in for a shock.*'

'*How come?*'

'*He's going to call them all Senior Managers, double their salaries, and do whatever they tell him.*'

'*Ha-bloody-ha.*'

'*Well, what is in your mind?*'

'*I'm going to drop the 'Services' word, for a start. If those devils have all this power, they'll damn well answer for it. I'm going to put my System Four together, and* call *it the Development Directorate.*'

'*Don't over-react. That phrase was intended simply as a name for the* concept.'

'*Well, its a perfectly good name. I'm going to use it. Because if all this cybernetic fun-and-games is for real, and I think that it is, I might as well get right into the terminology.*'

'*Hang the terminology. The crunch issue is: will you have a Director of Development?*'

'*Yes. And I know just the guy.*'

'*According to this chapter, you have just thought of the man who has least chance of effecting actual change.*'

'*No, I read the chapter too.*'

'*Who is he?*'

'*Hands off. He's outside the business. And he's an innovator.*'

'*So what are your colleagues going to make of that?*'

'*It's a good question. 'Unstable equilibrium', remember? But I shall handle it. That's what I'm paid for.*'

'Hm. Maybe that's what management is all about.'

'Management is about delivering the goods. Profits. Satisfy the shareholders. Happy, well-paid work force.'

'Very nice. Meanwhile you're all ignoring the epistemological problems in all this.'

'The what problems did you say, Doctor Rowell?'

'Don't stand on ceremony, Frank, and neither will I. All I'm saying is that there are huge distinctions between the way we acquire knowledge in the internal and external environments. There is a reality for System Three to interrogate in System One. System Four has no reality to interrogate in its problematic environment. So the interactions are quite different, and the theory doesn't point to that.'

'One set of loops is affective, the other is cognitive.'

'And the creative urge bit is conative.'

'What are you three talking about? Do any of these distinctions matter? I don't get it.'

'They matter. This chapter introduces different epistemological concerns, Jim, from those we were handling previously — and the author doesn't admit it.'

'But I'm interested in managerial concerns. So what's the problem?'

'The differences shouldn't be glossed over.'

'O.K. But are you saying that the principles of organization that I'm finally mastering are not applicable any longer?'

'Not really; but we should note these differences. For one thing, the variety generated in the problematic environment is strictly infinite, whereas it couldn't be in the interior milieu.'

'But we've still got to filter it down to manageable size.'

'I agree, Jim. Seems to me that providing requisite variety to absorb the variety of an unknown future is a hell of a task.'

'Well, "sheer ignorance" was offered as a variety attenuator once before.'

'*I think that the creative urge is a better way of attenuating variety than just not knowing.*'

'*Tony: the creative urge has* got *to be an amplifier.*'

'*Oh no. It* selects *from a range of possible futures, and says: this we are going to do. If you're in business to invent the future, that's going to inhibit the variety that would otherwise churn away and finally tell you what happened.*'

'*Politicians do it, don't they David?*'

'*You must be joking.*'

'*But surely you could use this System Four idea, and its focussing in government?*'

'*Who wants to know? This lot we've got now are entirely reactive. Come to think of it, so were the previous lot.*'

'*Is the government viable then?*'

'*You're speaking of the party in power, Frank. Their viability is their own affair. David's department goes on, regardless.*'

'*Oh* he's *viable alright, aren't you David? Come on now, cheer up.*'

'*Have yourself an operations room.*'

'*Focus things.*'

'*You must be mad.*'

CHAPTER TEN

Metasystem

All Systems One are viable systems. At the level of recursion that we are considering, they are treated as muddy boxes.

They inhere in a metasystem. This is itself a System One of the next higher level of recursion.

We discovered the logical necessity for System Two, *outside* System One, to damp oscillations internal to System One, and said that it must be a subsystem of the metasystem.

We discovered the logical necessity for System Three, superior (though not necessarily senior) to System One, in the sense that it has a synoptic view of all Systems One; and it exercises this *logical* superiority in terms of synergy for the corporate whole, in terms of the Inside and Now.

We discovered the complementary channels between System Three and System One, required to endow System Three with requisite variety — given that its so-called 'command' channel could be used only to ensure the coherence of System One. The first of these complementary channels is System Two itself. The second is the System Three channel that has unfettered access to the *operations* of System One.

We noted that System Three would display requisite variety vis-à-vis System One when the total varieties interchanging on the horizontal and vertical planes were equal. (This calculation has to include the variety absorbed by the vertical environmental and operational connexions, as well as the managerial connexions.)

Finally, we have observed the necessity for a System Four subsystem of the metasystem, to deal with the Outside and Then.

Thus the picture of the necessary conditions of viability that now emerges, shows various components of the metasystem that are required to handle the regulation of System One within the corporate whole — together with those other components of the metasystem that are required to handle the larger environment. The question yet remains as to whether the catalogue of necessity has reached the status of sufficiency (as moderately defined earlier) in accounting for the viable system.

The diagram at Figure 43 incorporates the structural findings to this point. It includes (a) the 'scribble' convention that indicates the variety flows necessary to maintain requisite variety, and (b) the conclusion of the last chapter that System Four is, in reality, a *line* function. It begins to display the necessary subsystemic aspects of the metasystem in which System One is embedded. It also exhibits a spectacular weakness within the internal structure of the metasystem as so far elucidated. In fact, the system depicted could not possibly be a viable system. Since the cybernetic reasons for this ought by now to be abundantly clear, the reader is invited to pause for a moment to appreciate why this is.

Figure 43 is a new edition of the diagram exhibited in Figure 35. The variety balance within Three-Two-One, which attests to the First Axiom of Management, is clearly shown, as is the variety balance between System Four and its two environments — the general and the problematic. All this gives rise to a massive horizontal variety flow through each of the Three and Four components of the metasystem. But there is no diagrammatic convention, nor has anything yet been said, to account for their interaction in the vertical plane. The metasystem as shown is schizoid — torn between present and future preoccupations.

The theoretical argument is immediately apparent: the attenuated channels between Three and Four cannot carry requisite variety between these two subsystems of the metasystem. To provide that variety on the so-called 'command' axis on which both exist would necessitate a huge block of black scribble that would evidently overwhelm the proper functioning of both subsystems: it would lock them together in a solid embrace. Every action of Three would have to be invigilated by an observer in Four, and vice versa. Let us also remember that System Four is in no sense senior to System Three: they are accountable *to each other* for the huge variety that each disposes in carrying through its own activity. But they are not in business to attenuate each other's inputs, nor to inhibit each other's disposable variety. The channels of the vertical axis must therefore remain tenuous connexions. Nevertheless, the Law of Requisite Variety will exert itself between them.

Theory, then, points to a dilemma. And that dilemma is devastatingly evident when we leave theory and look at any actual institution. All those that I have examined so far, at any rate, have exhibited the practical pathology that the theory expects. Let us lead our thinking gently into this reality.

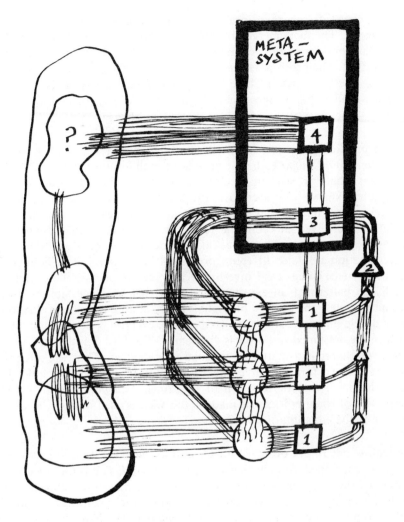

Figure 43. An impressionistic picture of the balance necessarily existing between the system and the metasystem. But the internal structure of the metasystem is variety-inadequate ... why?

Every institution, be it a firm in the private sector, a government agency, an industry in the public sector, or a department of government itself, has a certain *investment* to make in its own viability. This investment certainly involves the expenditure of money. But this is the least scarce resource with which the viable system is concerned. Money can be made available, one way or another, sooner or later, so long as the system remains (and is observed to remain) viable. That is why I have previously described the availability of money as a constraint rather than as a condition. No: the really scarce resources needed for this investment are those of time, talent, care, attention.... The fact emerged before, in relation to System Four itself. But now we are considering the investment in viability that the viable system must make in itself. The problem is that a finite amount of investment, as defined, has to be *divided* between Three activity and Four activity. It is very, very difficult to judge this balance correctly; it is increasingly difficult to judge it correctly — because of the change in the rate of change.

How in practice is the division made, and under what criteria? In the first place, the criteria *ought* to be the criteria of viability for the CORPORATE system (at whatever level of recursion is being considered). But no-one in management knows what are those criteria: indeed, this book is addressed to managers to the end that they should find out. In the meantime, the concept of viability is perceived in economic terms: it has to do with estimations of relative Return on Investment. But this approach *does not work*. Methods of ROI estimation are quite different for System Three and System Four. In the case of System Three, cash investment can readily be assimilated into the established pattern of an existing technology that has an established set of accounting rules. In the case of System Four, and even if the evaluation of future development is correct (which it is not), everything depends on the rate at which the presumed cash flow is discounted. The former is a matter of legal norms; the latter is a matter of speculative judgment. Thus the attempt to compare the two forms of investment in economic terms cannot hold. Even more: the belief that the division of investment *will* be made in this way, irrespective of whether it *can* be made in this way, is itself illusory. It takes no account of the equation of power.

The reality that I have observed hinges on the evident truth that exists in the eyes of all concerned: *System One must produce itself.* This is the one criterion of viability that everyone seems to accept. It means that the existing enterprise has to go on being itself. Therefore, it follows, the investment required to enable System One to produce itself is **mandatory.** Now it is true that individual operations may be called in question, and may indeed be axed. Thus the components of System One may change. But System One as a whole is guaranteed in survival. (This is the moment to understand why the language developed here lumps together the collection of operational elements, whatever they may be from time to time, as System One. It is a fictitious entity, as is 'the average man'; but it has the utmost credibility — as has 'the average man'.)

Thus it comes about that System Three, which sees itself as 'managing' System One — whereas its true role in terms of viability is to look to the synergy of System One — claims whatever share of the available finite investment capacity it needs. What is left is, grudgingly, available to System Four. This seems to be a correct account of observed behaviour. It is well reflected in the statement that one often hears (I use my own terminology, which may be replaced by any appropriate institutional terminology) which says:

'System Four constitutes the group of people
who spend the money we make in System Three.'

Too bad. But it is undertandable. And thus it is that System Four acquires whatever investment capability remains after System Three has taken what is needed for System One to produce itself — *plus* whatever further capacity it is permitted to raise from outside. Again: this refers not only to money, but to people. So the question arises whether System Four *will* be permitted to raise the 'capital' it thinks that it needs. And we are back to the Power Equation.

Wherein resides the power to determine the balance of Three-Four investment? In some sense, it resides in the requisite variety equation that must subsist (somehow) between Three and Four. But, as we have seen, this equation cannot be manifested in the links available on the central axis, because these are low-variety links. Therefore, logical necessity compels the modelling of new loops connecting Three and Four, which do not belong on that axis. Let us draw them as shown in Figure 44 — remembering that (under such a convention) the Three Principles of management must be applied to the problem of managing relative investment in the Inside-and-Now and the Outside-and-Then.

In this diagram, System Three originates messages (which it seeks to amplify) to System Four, which will make clear the needs of the existing business, and in particular elucidate the difficulties with which that existing business will be faced in trying to assimilate new developments that do not conform to the known technology and the established culture inside it. For its part, System Four originates (and amplifies) messages to System Three which will illuminate future prospects that it expects the enterprise to confront, and in particular it will elucidate the threats and opportunities which it considers that the existing business must face. These efforts to amplify variety are often formal, and pass through channels that have been designed to carry them (situation reports) and transducers (committees) that are charged to decode them. But these formal arrangements are woefully inadequate, usually, and they do not generate requisite variety. Less formal methods may then (self-consciously) be used to enhance the variety absorbed on both sides.

For example, in 1966 I was Development Director of a business that I considered had badly misjudged the Three-Four balance of investment, in favour of Three. (This probably sounds biassed, but the view was later vindicated.) All the research and development facilities, as well as the management science groups, were located out in the country — heavily labelled 'staff' rather than 'line'. I divided my time, each day, between that location and the centre of power in London. It is probable that I personally was regarded as a mixture of staff and line — which is an ambiguous position to be in. In trying to apply the Three Principles in this situation, I soon discovered that the formal procedures could not possibly cope with the variety generated by my Division. The reasons for this are sufficiently common that it is worth proceeding with the anecdote.

The whole of the senior management, other than myself, were children of the technology of the existing business. They were highly capable people, well able to consider new ideas — and not at all hostile to them in principle. It is often supposed that there is an automatic unwillingness to contemplate change, but I cannot verify that supposition at the highest levels of management (either in this example, or any other). No: the problem is that the transducers fail, and the channels are exiguous in variety. Because the high-variety activity of the Division was being generated many miles away, the best arrangement would have been to immerse my colleagues in that environment — but naturally they did not have the time. Therefore much-attenuated reports were the formal channel. These were found 'interesting', but they did not have the requisite variety to induce a change of state. As a result, I adopted informal methods back at headquarters; and the first point to note is that this reduces the variety of several hundred people to a channel consisting of one man. Social psychologists have referred to this person, in general, as the 'gate keeper'. The only such gate keeper whom I can envisage as generating the requisite variety for such a job is St. Peter.

Now we pass to the problem of transduction. My office at headquarters fortunately lay on the corridor that led to the Most Senior dining room. Therefore it was relatively easy to waylay colleagues on route to lunch, or to bring them back after lunch. Imagine the problem (to take two actual examples) of trying to explain, in 1966, how to make money out of on-line real-time computer terminals, or holography, to perfectly well-intentioned people who had no conception of either. In both cases, the transduction totally failed. It was not, I think, that I could not explain these technologies, nor that the colleagues were stupid. *They thought it was all science fiction.*

Accordingly, and despite the cultural shock that any such plan must induce, I introduced into my plush suite in this corridor of power, firstly, an on-line real-time terminal, and secondly, a laser apparatus. Then I proceeded to waylay colleagues, one by one. They actually communicated with the computer about their own stocks and shares. They actually smashed glass holograms (although it is always difficult to persuade a civilized person to smash anything, as I learned in trying to demonstrate the cybernetic potency of redundant networks in automation), and observed with their own eyes that the holographic picture remains whole when laser-illuminated in a fragment of the original glass. Note that the channel variety is now equivalent: brain to brain.

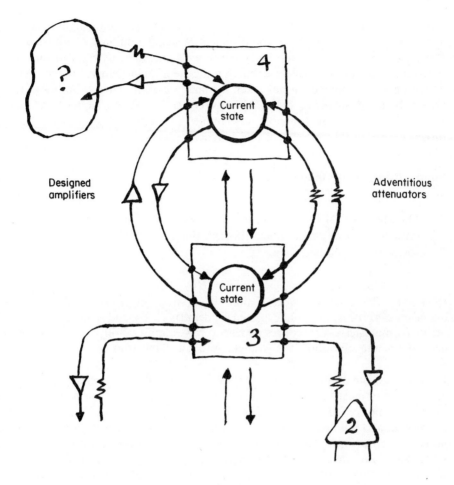

Figure 44. The Three-Four Balancer

Note that the transducer — apparatus plus persuasive exposition — now has requisite variety.

It was a triumph for cybernetic analysis, because now my colleagues really did understand. It was not, however, a triumph for psychology. They *still* thought it was science fiction. I got the feeling that they thought it mighty clever to be able to do such tricks ... 'but I have to get back to the office', and 'one day it will be possible'.

I am trying throughout this book not to indulge in anecdote for its own sake. There is surely a clear lesson here. The three variety equations were finally satisfied, but they were *momentarily* satisfied. They were not distributed through time. The Zen Master may shock his pupil into *sartori,* enlightenment, in a well-judged instant. But in management, a steady familiarity with what is going on in System Three and in System Four seems to be essential. Hence it seems that we should postulate a fourth principle of management. It was there all the time, but somehow it has taken the analysis of the Three-Four loops to exemplify it with sufficient force. Perhaps reference back to Chapter Four will now show that the new principle was entailed in the formulation of the first three — we just did not recognize it as crucial (did we?). Here it is:

Fourth Principle of Organization

The operation of the first three principles
must be cyclically maintained through time,
and without hiatus or lags.

Breaks in flow, and especially time lags, are dangerous to the entire management process (as will be argued, in detail). This sounds truistic; and yet orthodox managerial procedures appear to rely, almost wholly, on 'snapshot' accounts of the situation. It is strange. And it is dangerous.

Returning to the analysis of the Three-Four loops, it seems evident that the easiest way to meet the requirements of all *four* management principles is to extend the notion of the Operations Room. Let it become the Three-Four clubhouse, and not merely a development-oriented place. The argument, be it noted, is moving towards the provision of a *management centre.* It would replace the Boardroom, the Executive Suite, and all of those committee rooms. Here System Three and System Four would exhibit themselves to each other, in a continuous mode, and absorb each other's variety.

More about the loops devised in the last diagram will follow. The mechanics may become more clear when we discuss measurement; the implicit systemic interaction may come more sharply into focus when we discuss planning. Meantime it is important to see how vital an issue the Three-Four interaction constitutes. And maybe some heart-searching will reveal that — in your own institution — some (possibly all) of the principles of organization are betrayed in this regard. If so, the correct balance of investment, where 'correct' is determined by the criteria of viability, can hardly be found. In the absence of cybernetically valid management machinery, it will not be a matter of the mutual absorption of variety between Three and Four, and the settling on an equilibrial state. It will be a matter of Three *versus* Four and Four *versus* Three — and one of them will WIN, as a matter of power. It usually happens. It is a signpost to disaster.

Some pages ago, the question was posed:

wherein resides the power to determine
the balance of Three-Four investment?

Came the answer:

in some sense, it resides in the requisite variety
equation that must subsist (somehow) between
Three and Four.

Since then we have examined the meaning of that qualifier 'somehow'. It comes down to this. Because of Ashby's Law, the requisite variety equation between Three and Four will indeed subsist. In practice, there are no clear regulatory means for ensuring that this happens effectively — and we are back to the rule that we ought to design those mechanisms, before they just 'happen'. In the Three-Four case, they normally 'happen' by a massive variety attenuation between the two subsystems — so that for each of them the rich reality of the relative investment problem is attenuated to the rule: 'it's *them* against *us*'. The Operations Room, grown now to a Management Centre, might well ameliorate such a dangerous mess. However, as long as we adhere to the logical 'razor', to the establishment of necessary and sufficient conditions of viability, we have to admit that — though the Three-Four looping arrangements are necessary — they are not yet sufficient. What happens if they do not work; if they (in their turn) result in uncontrolled oscillation? System Two cannot reach into the metasystem: it is dedicated to damping oscillations in System One.... .

We reach the final argument as to the logic of viability. There has to be a System Five. That will do it. System Five will monitor the operation of the balancing operation between Three and Four. The argument is complete: Three-Two-One *plus* Three-Four-Five is a viable system — where the second group is metasystemic to the first. Should anyone ask: 'what happens beyond System Five? Is it System Six?', the answer is, no. What is beyond System Five is the next level of recursion, of which *this* fivefold viable system is an operational element. The logical recursion finally worked. Because, out of many necessities, we have reached sufficiency (in the moderate form of that concept adopted at the start).

What is this System Five? Throughout the argument attention has been paid to the likely confusion between the logical structure that the book has built, and the orthodox notion of an hierarchy of increasingly 'senior' people. Well, it is not altogether damaging that the two tend to reflect each other, because that correspondence lends the verisimilitude of practical affairs to the rigour of the logic. Even so, this is a final appeal to everyone not actually to confuse the two versions of what a managerial structure truly is. In some ways, it will seem strange to *stumble* on 'the boss' in the role of a systemic monitor. But, truth to tell, they must, in scientific terms, be the same thing. Would that typical 'bosses' (I mean the people who enjoy just that appellation) understood why. The answer lies in the mathematical notion of 'closure'.

The role of mathematics is minimized in this whole story of the viable system because it 'puts people off'. Even so, the concepts are too potent to be ignored. We entered gently into *recursion,* for instance; let us enter equally gently into *closure.*

Closure is the snake that is eating its own tail. Closure is what makes the language complete, self-sufficient. Closure stops the entire system from exploding in shattered fragments to the ends of the universe. Closure turns the system back into itself, to satisfy the criteria of viability at its own level of recursion. Closure is the talisman of *identity.*

> (The philosophical implications of these assertions can hardly be ignored. A full discussion would perhaps begin with the monadology of Leibniz; but even then it would have to take account of 250 years of reaction to Leibniz. It would have to take account of all the logical problems that the idea of closure generates, and the relevance of Gödel's theorem to their solution. Even so, it is proper to note that the viable system as defined here has much in common with the self-conscious monad, conceived of by Leibniz as a self-contained system, with no 'windows'. By being part of a larger whole, it somehow expresses that whole; its relationship to the whole is dynamic, rather than spatial or mechanical. In these respects at least, recursions of the viable system reflect the monadology. They do not reflect the categorization of systems into those that are 'open' and those that are 'closed', which has in modern times been written into so much of General Systems Theory. I do not find these categories helpful, since I cannot identify any system that is either completely open or totally closed. Nor do I think that attempts to rescue the categorization by distinguishing between systems closed to energy but open to information (or vice versa) will avail, since both commodities are expressions of a common entropy. This parenthesis is necessary to avoid misunderstanding: by 'closure' I mean a *self-referential process,* and not the isolation of the system within an adiabatic shell.)

If that is 'closure' what is 'the boss'? Sometimes he is depicted as the draconian, autocratic, repository of all power. He may, indeed, be just that. But such a boss is ruler of a highly unstable situation, unless he uses his power fervidly to repress the variety generated in the viable system — as military dictators are wont to do. Sometimes he is the representative of that very variety. This is supposed to be true of democracies; but usually that picture is illusory. The interesting fact, in cybernetic terms, is that *however* we depict 'the boss' (however calmly, however emotionally, however politically), this boss *supplies the closure.* That is his cybernetic function.

The autocrat supplies the closure by saying: 'that's enough; I have heard all the arguments; THIS is how it will be'. Then high variety generated between Systems Three and Four, and not absorbed between them, is CLOSED by System Five. Thus:

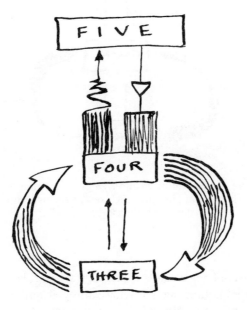

Figure 45.   The emergence of System Five:
conceived as an autocracy

Such an arrangement may be thought (ethically) to be immoral. Certainly (cybernetically) it is extremely vulnerable, unless the boss (Five) is God Himself. Sooner or later, Five will make a destabilizing mistake. That is because his requisite variety (in administering closure) depends on a much attenuated input. It must so depend, because Five cannot deploy sufficient variety to absorb the variety of Three-plus-Four, which is multiplicative, without that enormous degree of filtration. Perhaps students of the regime of Stalin in the USSR will recognize the point. Perhaps anyone who has worked for an autocratic boss will recognize the point too. Perhaps any observers of the Nixon Administration in the United States will also understand.

Closure does not have to be applied in this way. *The power to balance the Three-Four investment resides in the equation of variety between Three and*

Four. That can be a delegated power, IF the (four-principled) machinery is in place. Variety absorbs variety. All that remains for System Five is to monitor the regulatory machinery — to ensure that it does not embark on an uncontrolled oscillation. Thus the cybernetically perferred solution is:

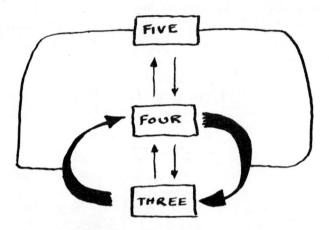

Figure 46. System Five conceived as the monitor of Three-Four interaction, in which their respective high varieties are deployed to absorb each other

The boss is still supplying closure — in a logical sense. He is not applying it by massive variety inhibition: he is leaving variety absorption where it belongs, between Three and Four. His role is metasystemic. Note that (therefore) the boss's intervention on the 'command' axis has minimal variety, and that the mechanism in use is the familiar one whereby the monitor listens to the 'I'm all right' messages flowing round the loop. It is only the interruption of those messages by a cry denoting imbalance and incipient oscillation that will lead to intervention. Precisely how this occurs will be discussed in Part 3. But anyone who has sat on a (System Five) Board will recognize the scene depicted here.

The last two diagrams are as different as could be, especially if you happen to work under either of the two regimes. But both representations identify 'the boss' with 'closure'. It is the role of System Five: the last of the *necessary* conditions, and that which provides *sufficiency*.

Just as the theorem of recursiveness entails a metasystem within the viable system, so the theorem of closure entails a metasystem within that metasystem. That is the end of the line; because any further opening of the closure lifts the argument to the next level of recursion. And there the whole process begins again. The very notion of recursiveness embraces the notion of *local* closure at any given level of recursion. Within any one viable system, System Five is the metasystemic administrator of Ashby's Law. It necessarily absorbs the residual variety of the Three-Four interaction.

Perhaps I should stop now, for I regard the previous paragraph as the very dramatic conclusion of all our endeavours to elucidate the organizational structure of viability. But three more comments, at the risk of bathos, seem wholly relevant to this chapter. Especially so, because each of them is severely practical. If you will settle for three practical points, then I shall feel comfortable to sneak in a final theoretical remark of principle at the last moment.

The first practical point is this. The Inside-and-Now was found to depend on Systems Three-Two-One. The Outside-and-Then was found to require Systems Three-Four-Five. System THREE is the common element: it is the managerial fulcrum of viable organization. This is emphasized by the evolved theory, and it very much accords with practice. It is natural that the role of Chief Executive should reside at the fulcrum. With great respect to System Five (for there sits 'the boss'), System Three in practice really runs the enterprise. With that obeisance to observed facts, I rest my case that the cybernetic model is not congruent with the hierarchical model. For, in the cybernetic model, 'the boss' (System Five, 'where the buck stops') is not the *actual* boss (who is to be found at the fulcrum (System Three), around which the power revolves).

Then who *is* the 'boss', that is, System Five? The point again is practical, but it is deeply mysterious. In the case of autocracy, which is an extreme case, we know his name. Even so, he is likely to be 'run' by System Three — which controls his access to internal variety. Under more democratic conventions, System Five consists of many people. The list probably includes the Heads of Systems One, and of System Three. Probably it does *not* include the Heads of Systems Two and Four, because they are mistakenly labelled 'staff.' It may consist primarily of the shareholders, with only the Managing Director/-Company President from inside. In that case, he becomes the gate-keeper at the metalevel — a most unattractive role, in cybernetic eyes (just think of the requisite variety that he is supposed to embody, to channel, and to transduce, *all* the time — according to the Four Principles. . .). In a nationalized industry, a 'consumer's council' may embody the role of System Five; or a nepotistic group of the élite may constitute a Board of Governors — as it does in some schools, and in the BBC. In such cases, the closure is administered with an almost total lack of requisite variety. Such schemes cannot possibly work, for cybernetic reasons: nor do they. They are ostentatiously farcical, in the eyes of all concerned. The viability of such systems is supported by the metasystems of which they are Systems One. The situation is highly interesting, because everything depends on the power structure of the recursion itself. For example, nationalized industries are subservient to the governmental recursion (which is exceedingly powerful), while the BBC has a Royal Charter... .

I am anxious to show that the language here developed applies to any given situation. We may use that language, and exercise this model, regardless of the alleged purposes of the viable system, and regardless of the culture in which it operates. There was a strong lesson awaiting me in this respect in the Chile of 1971. The story must be told here, with apologies to anyone who read the book *Platform for Change* — and has heard it already.

Salvador Allende, the Compañero Presidente, was a physician by training. Therefore I used the neurophysiological version of this model in expounding it to him. In this version, System Five is the cortex of the brain. Having explained how Systems One, Two, Three, and Four are entailed by the criterion of viability, I drew in (on the piece of paper between us) System Five. Taking a histrionic breath, I wrote in '5'. Before I could explain that *this* was *he* — namely 'the boss' — he leaned back and laughed. 'At last!' he cried: 'El pueblo'. As I said, the understanding of System Five is difficult, and its nature is mysterious. Its *role* is not mysterious at all. That role is closure.

At the very least, we can say that (except for genuine autocracies) System Five includes many people — which is contrary to popular belief. In many firms, this group includes representatives of management, of shareholders, of investors. Maybe, in the future, it will include trade unionists — or better still, simply workers. In government enterprises, the constitution of the group may be even more convolved. Therefore it becomes very difficult to see where the power of closure resides. It is less difficult to see that the power over *this* power resides elsewhere. It may be in System Three, since System Five is, in a very real sense, deriving from superior knowledge, its puppet. It may be in another level of recursion where System Five is a mere System One, and therefore, in a sense, a puppet again.

Probably System Five's main problem is its belief that it is *not* the puppet of some other system, whether subsystem or metasystem. But it always is. The logic of the fulcrum, the logic of recursion too, dictates it. Regardless of these cybernetics, System Five is often supremely arrogant — incognizant of its fundamentally subservient role. Insofar as I quoted the higher functions of the brain as the neurophysiological version of System Five, these few remarks may well be provocative. I stick by them. The cortex has no direct connexion with either the external or the internal environment: all its input is mediated by Systems Three and Four. The same is true in both industry and government. If the President (of the industrial enterprise, or of the country) were vehemently to declare that this is not his or her situation at all, then that is because he or she operates normally in the System Three mode, despite the Five label. That cannot be said of the Chairman of the Board, nor of a constitutional monarch.

Such people *are* aware that they are in the business of closure role-playing. The Three-Five ambiguity of the presidential role confuses the issue — both for the President and for his interpetors. The point demonstrates that in actual situations, the nature of System Five is crucial, is not agreed, is mysterious. It requires much thought and debate. I have called it The Multinode, and have tried to analyse its role in *Brain of the Firm*. The analysis seemed to reveal the essentially disseminated character of System Five, and the strength that closure gains from that very dissemination. Beyond that kind of thinking, we are locked into the power equations of any particular institution. Principles there certainly are; the realities of power spawn variety through time in wholly unpredictable ways.

Here is the third practical point. A substantial case was made out in the preceeding chapter to show that System Four is often, indeed usually, virtually empty. This was because its components are scattered, are not in communication with each other, are labelled 'staff' and 'merely advisory', and so on. Then what may be expected to happen (see the last diagram) if System Four, on line, is void? Especially, what happens given that the role of System Five is, to say the least, ambiguous?

Without a System Four clearly in place, and with a System Five whose very nature is ambiguous, there is no Three-Four interaction, and no Five monitoring of that interaction. Then the whole metasystem collapses into System Three. I called this a practical point, and so it is. Everywhere one turns, the reality is the same. In terms of the neurophysical model, however, and this is the theoretical point, the institution is a decerebrate cat.

You can take a perfectly good cat, anaesthetize it, and remove the cerebrum. You can pin the decerebrate cat to the table, and keep it fed. It lives on; its viability is ensured by a bogus environment, and is sustained by artificial sustenance. If you prod its leg, it kicks back. And this is called 'living'. If we think this through in institutional terms, we diagnose a major pathology of our times.

It is not too surprising that this so often happens, devastating as the results certainly are. The two reasons have already been given. First: the organization's people of established power are unwilling to admit a Development Directorate that would constitute a legitimate System Four. They do not want to acknowledge the power that System Four already exerts, nor to make it accountable for the responsibility it exerts. They do not want to take in people from outside, at their own level of senior management, who might turn out to be antibodies. Second: the constitution of System Five is ambiguous. But in general, the most visible System Five individuals are people soaked in the technology of the existing business, and comfortable within its culture. They have achieved the appearance of immense seniority, because they have been steadily promoted out of the realm of the existing business, and of all those contretemps that they (used to) understand so well. And now they feel uncomfortable. Because of their 'immense seniority', they have little to fear. But as good men and women (they mostly are) they are uncomfortable, because of the ambiguity of their new roles. Thus it happens that, as soon as some great crisis occurs in the Inside-and-Now, a member of System Five cries out: 'I know all about that' — as indeed he does. Then he dives down from System Five straight into System Three, or (worse) straight into a muddy bog in System One. He is never seen again. We saw the *risk* in a very early chapter. Now, from the eminence of System Five, we can see the *reality*.

Thereby do our institutions become decerebrate cats. Management is noticeably failing the world, in the absence of metasystem. It can just manage to say *miaow*.

LATER IN THE BAR...

'Cigarette?'

'No thanks.'

'You know the one about the man who was about to be executed? The commander of the firing squad offered him a cigarette. He replied: no thanks, I'm trying to give them up.'

'Well, I am trying. So don't tempt me.'

'I suppose we ought to jack it in. The report of the Royal College of Physicians says that on average every cigarette shortens your life by five-and-a-half minutes.'

'Oh, for God's sake!'

'Well, that's what they said.'

'Aren't we learning anything from this dreadful book?'

'How do you mean?'

'Well, that statement about the five-and-a-half minutes has got to be meaningless.'

'Why?'

'It's devoid of system content. Remember the remark about 'the average man' — who, like System One, is a fictitious entity? The five-and-a-half minutes applies to no actual person. Not to me. Not to you.

'Even so: smoking isn't good for you.'

'How do you know? Without it, I'd be dead by now — from sheer frustration.'

'Some folk are vulnerable to cancer, and some aren't. I think that if you are vulnerable, then smoking might settle the site in your lungs.'

What I want to know is why I should seek to prolong my life by five-and-a-half minutes — or even a year's-worth of five-and-a-half minutes's.'

'Yes. You could fall under a bus tomorrow.'

'Looks like we're short of a systems outlook on every front. The doctors don't have any conception of the body as a total system, they carve it up between specialisms. So there's no way of saying what's good for it and what isn't. Second, there's no understanding of the metasystem: perhaps there are trade-offs between all the things we do that aren't good for us. I mean, when I gave up smoking for two years, I put on an enormous amount of weight — started sucking sweets all the time.'

'Extra weight equals heart attack.'

'Exactly.'

'Then there's the third systems thing that Joe mentioned. Who says that the object of life is to prolong it? I'm a fairly religious man myself — there's more to the total system than that. Why stick with one level of recursion?'

'Well, I'm not religious at all. I'm an atheist, and my wife's an agnostic. We couldn't agree how not to bring up the children.'

'Very good. But what's that got to do with prolonging life?'

'If you don't believe in an after-life, it makes no difference. You might as well enjoy what you have. I smoke. What's the point in staying alive longer, to be miserable?'

'There's a story about a Canadian industrialist who equipped himself to go up-country at the weekends. On one of these trips he encountered an Indian, sitting in a canoe, fishing. The man was poor, and the industrialist set out to explain that the Indian bands should organize themselves — to get ahead in society.'

'And so they should. Poverty is the common enemy, and the failure to do anything about it is just an excuse for laziness.'

'Quite so, Tom. Can George finish his story?'

'Well, the Indian asked a lot of questions as to why he ought to get ahead in this way. The wealthy man said: look at me — I got ahead, and now I can afford to spend my weekends out here fishing. The Indian raised his rod — and his eyebrows.... '

'Phew.'

'It's right, isn't it, that all these points are systems *points. I mean, there is no agreement about what the system is, nor what its purposes are. So the smoking business can't really be resolved, and no-one can say whether Indians in Canada ought to 'get up and go' or not. Why isn't it understood?'*

'The whole educational set-up is reductionist. It doesn't allow people to understand systems. Least of all, it seems, the Royal College of Physicians.'

'Never mind them. What about System One as a fictitious entity? I thought that those operations were the one thing that we were sure about.'

'We are sure about them in principle, not as individuals.'

'What the hell does that *mean?'*

'That the Systems comprising System One will continue to be viable systems. Some may be added, some subtracted. The others may change, and become unrecognizable. But there is always System One. Its identity is assured by its role in the viable system.'

'That's a pretty queer statement.'

'It's a metasystemic *statement.'*

'You seem to have 'bought' this whole business.'

'I'm not sure. But I'm beginning to see how to use the language. At least it's internally consistent.'

'It's not like any other language that management uses. Just look at all that stuff about profits.'

'Well, I'm going to spend some of mine right now. Same again, I take it?'

'There aren't any profits in government. Must say, I've got pretty interested in the way the language seems to work for any *institution.'*

'That's because it's the language of viability, David. Even government is interested in that.'

'Too interested, *if you ask me. Nothing matters but staying in office.'*

'You're talking about political government. I was talking about the civil service.'

'Hey, there's an interesting point. The elected government and its policies change. The Civil Service goes on being viable — doing the same old thing. It's the same set-up as System One.'

'Producing itself — in both cases.'

'There goes another metasystemic statement.'

'Look here: the Civil Service can't be a System One. It's not a viable system; it has no independent existence; it's a service.'

'That's right. It obviously has a System Two role, which is anti-oscillatory, and it obviously has a System Three channel — the one that intervenes in operations. Just think of the taxation audit.'

'Then what the hell is it doing masquerading as a viable system in its own right — busily producing itself?'

'Perhaps it's a System One at another level of recursion?'

'Oh you'd sure like that, David, wouldn't you — an operational element of the godhead.'

'Who's got it in for the bureaucracy, then? It isn't a System One at all.'

'Then why is it preoccupied with producing itself?'

'I don't think that it is. Everyone's got to live. It's quite reasonable that people should preserve their own jobs — and their own kind.'

'It goes far beyond that.'

'And so it should. The government machine preserves the good order of affairs — and, yes, our traditional value structure — while the politicians come and go.'

'Too much! Who elected all these functionaries to do any such things? No-one. They just stand in the way of progress. Pretending to be a System One of the eternal verity, as Bill just said.'

'It seems to me that exactly the same thing happens in the firm. You get some entrepreneurial character sticking his neck out. Maybe he succeeds — and he gets to the top. Maybe he fails — and he's out. It's all one to the accountants.'

'Why pick on them? It's all one to the bulk of the organization men.'

'But that says there's no incentive for anyone in the firm to do anything that isn't merely glueing the place together — the 'minimum intervention consistent with coherence' argument.'

'Well, is there?'

'What about you, Fred? The papers are full of this massive reorganization that you're going through. The middle management is 'alight with expectation', I read in someone's column yesterday.'

'Huh! We are all standing with our backs firmly against the wall, keeping very quiet. The whole place is a hive of inactivity.'

'What about all the new thinking?'

'Don't confuse reorganization with anything new. When it's all over, everyone will just have moved round a place. It's the Mad Hatter's Tea Party.'

'But what about the structuring of the metasystem? Is it supposed that your Three-Four-Five is all right?'

'What metasystem? What Three-Four-Five? Like the man said, we're a decerebrate cat. The whole thing has collapsed into System Three.'

'I reckon it's not surprising that the people we usually call the bosses operate at a Three Level, since it appears to be ambiguous as to what System Five really is. At least in the Three role they know that they are taking a total approach to System One.'

'That's all very well. If they did their job properly, they would set about defining System Five, as it is supposed to be for the particular institution of which they are The System Five — or part of it.'

'But that would involve value judgments. And it would be a political hot potato.'

'So? Haven't ... leaders, or whatever you'd call them, always made some value judgments? People funk it now, in case someone calls them political names. It has discredited the system.'

'Not the fault of industry. The system is already discredited, and that's why they funk it.'

'Who's responsible, then? No-one seems to deny that the system's discredited. Some say management, some unions, some government ...'

'Oh, its discredited all right. People just don't believe in it any more. I'm inclined to blame the cynicism of the financial sharks and speculators.'

'You can apportion blame *as much as you like. But no-one's mentioned WHY the system is discredited.'*

'Over-exposure by the media.'

'That's blaming *again, Bill. I asked the question* why.*'*

'I don't know why the system's discredited.'

'It's in the book.'

'Why is it, then?'

'It doesn't work.'

PART THREE

VENTURES IN VIABILITY

Summary of Part Three

Having established the basic model of the viable system, the book next undertakes an exploration of certain consequences. Naturally, the logic of necessity and sufficiency is behind us now: the primary orientation of the next five chapters derives from fundamental managerial concerns — measuring performance, planning activities, and so forth — as seen through the eyes of cybernetics. It would neither be possible to express the views that follow, nor is there any hope that they could be understood, without the use of the special language that has been painstakingly developed in the first two Parts. It is the value of the language, rather than the precise lay-out of the model (which could have been drawn some other way) that justifies the effort of understanding. And of course, claim must be made to the discoveries, the principles and axioms, that have already been made by the analysis that has been using the developing language. Given the complete language, there is another discovery to come — although it was implicit in the earlier analysis — which is perhaps the most significant of them all.

The need for all this background becomes immediately apparent in Chapter Eleven, which deals with measurement. It is not at all the kind of discussion of that subject that a manager would, without this book, either expect or entertain. The contention is that most managerial measures, as they are commonly understood, are worthless in the actual task of managing. Of course they are required, often legally required, as statements about viability. But they are elastic, and can be manipulated. In other words, they are projections of good health intended for public consumption. What the manager needs to know in the course of managing is not what has always been quite evident to him — namely that most things are as he knows them to be. He needs to be alerted, instantly alerted, to any evidence of incipient instability in any of the loops that are supposed to display equilibrium. But nobody is measuring stability. It can however be done.

The key to the problem is statistical filtration. This sounds quite obvious; but it is not actually done, at least not in the sense proposed. Perhaps the reasons have to do with psychological blockage. If so, this would be the result of continuing to use the hierarchical model of organization ingrained by orthodoxy. And yet, by now, we have a completely different model, based on logical recursion. But it is all too easy to be trapped, even now, into using the notion of recursion as if it were just 'another way' of looking at hierarchy, and this is a mistake. It is because of these psychological barriers that Chapter Twelve ploughs through the process of demonstrating recursive isomorphism. It is hoped that the hard work involved in following an essentially mathematical argument in terms of complicated diagrams will be compensated in terms of practical applications — when attempts are made to put the model into use. Much more importantly, however, the objective of Chapter Twelve is to make sure that the recursive nature of the viable system is properly understood. It is only then that the proper managerial consequences can possibly be drawn, either for measurement or for planning, to which Chapter Thirteen is addressed.

Planning, it is alleged, is a much misunderstood topic. It is seen by most people as a professional activity which results in products called plans. In fact it needs to be seen as a continuous, managerial, process of decision, whereby allocations of investment are made now, so that the future may be different. And, since at any moment more information is available than at the previous moment, it is madness to implement plans — those considered as professional products — at some date later than they were conceived. They will necessarily be mistaken. Hence it is necessary that plans should always abort before their time is due. In cybernetic terms, plans should be continuously adaptive to fresh information. The viable system model is deployed in Chapter Thirteen to examine how this contention is plausible, and how it works in practice. The notions of closure, of recursion, and of all that has so far been disclosed about requisite variety, are needed to make sense of the planning process — which is perceived as the cohesive 'glue' that holds the embedments of viable systems in place. This examination leads to the ennunciation of the Law of Cohesion for multiple recursions of the viable system — the discovery referred to earlier.

Filtration and cohesion: these are essential notions. But of course if everything is made so tightly integrated and so well-regulated that we attain to a state of perpetual peace-and-quiet, we may very soon be dead. If the job is being well done by the operation of cybernetic laws, operating through management systems that have been cybernetically designed, the manager may go to sleep. It is better that he should do so, than that he should interfere with a perfectly smooth operation just because he feels that he should earn his keep. What, then, is his job? It is to be alert to incipient instability — and to take action about that. In Chapter Fourteen, this problem is carefully examined. How is the manager alerted, and how can he react in a sensible way? A fresh model is devised to account for the manager's state of psychological calm, the alerting system that disrupts that calm, and his reaction. This model contends that the manager must choose both a response and a style of response, which are not independent of each other, and which jointly succeed in suppressing incipient instability within an appropriate time-scale. Several different kinds of filters *are detected in such a system, and the model indicates where the feedbacks need to be positioned in order to keep those filters properly tuned.*

Finally, Chapter Fifteen turns to the very remarkable property of the viable system that it retains its identity. The enterprise may last for hundreds of years, changing all of its component parts many times, and assimilating many kinds of change on the way — and yet it is recognizably itself. *The human being shares this property of identity preservation, through all the vicissitudes of life; and it is in biological cybernetics that managerial cybernetics finds illumination. The primary characteristic of a viable system is not the power of self-reproduction, but of self-production. It is continuously in business to produce itself, to be what it is, to preserve identity. This mechanism is discussed; and it becomes clear that some organizational pathology is due to abberation of that machinery. Too much organizational effort may go into maintaining the status quo as an end in itself, so that the job that the enterprise is supposed to do becomes almost a by-product. This is the last of our diagnoses.*

The Chapter (and the Part) ends with a lengthy exercise whereby the reader may gain insight into the regulatory activities in his own enterprise that bear on the maintenance of identity, and summarize its power to act as an effectively integral whole.

CHAPTER ELEVEN

Measurement

To *know* something properly, you must *measure* it.

Most managers would nowadays agree with that, although it is a fairly recent idea in the conduct of practical affairs. Lord Kelvin's reputation has been dining-out on this dictum (although he expressed it with far less punch) for the whole of my working life as a scientist. That must mean that there was once a degree of novelty in what now sounds perfectly evident; and therefore it is reasonable to ask how managers ever conceived that they knew what was going on in the absence of much-measuring.

The question proposes the issue as to what is to count as a measurement — and was intended to do just that. Today, management operates in a welter of figures; and that suggests that a great amount of measuring is going on. In turn, we may argue back through the Kelvin dictum that we do indeed know things *properly*. It is all most comforting. But I should think that Lord Kelvin is turning in his grave.

Consider this accusation against our contemporary habits with figures. The comfortable feeling that we 'properly know' what is going on is a delusion occasioned by our ability to generate figures, in overwhelming spate, out of computers. But this experience of floating on numbers is not a real experience, because the variety is not really there. What we are experiencing is the *process* of the proliferation of variety. Usually, a few basic figures are being manipulated: they are summed under various heads, aggregated and disaggregated under various categories, divided into each other, multiplied by each other, and in general made to work to an oppressive degree. This is not necessarily wrong, and may be extremely convenient. But if we have measured, let us say, ten independent variables, and differentiated between ten states of each, then we have a measured variety of one hundred. From this basis, we could keep a computer going for a long time in making convenient presentations of the figures involved: there is a vast number of ways in which the 10×10 matrix can be partitioned. But our variety measure never exceeds 100. Now if the managerial requisite variety measure is 1000, what we need is a times-ten variety amplifier. Merely to re-process the hundred measurements in ten different formats does not do this. And if we experience the feeling that it does, *there* is the delusion.

Secondly, there is the very challenging question as to what *counts* as a measure. Often some aspect of a matter is measured because that is the easiest aspect to slap a number on, and by now it is the traditional and the accepted thing to do. Thus output may be measured in tons, regardless of the mix of sizes which makes tonnage-per-week totally incommensurable from one week to another. Attempts to deal with such incommensurability result in complicated formulae and elaborate statistical weighting systems, to which many definitions have to be attached, and into which many exceptions and annotations are introduced over a period of time. Thus nobody is quite sure what trends in such statistics as the unemployment figures or the retail price index really mean, and we have recurrent scandals as to the 'loss' of millions of pounds sterling from the statistics for reserves or the trade balance. Note that in such cases what counts as a measure is not a measure of the *variety* of the matter considered. The measurement taken may count as a proxy for the matter concerned (as when absenteeism is considered as a measure of morale), but whether it can reflect the variety involved is a different matter — while the question of the variety of available response is a different matter again.

Thirdly, it is idle to pretend that we can always attain to objective measures in practical affairs. By this I mean that different observers of the same event would measure with measuring-rods that somehow include something of their own personalities, so that identical results were not obtained. Suppose that 40 per cent of school-leavers are in fact illiterate (supposing that this were a figure that could be objectively measured, given problems one and two above). Two observers try to measure this proportion. Are they in conflict if one reports proudly that 'most school leavers can read and write', while the other mourns that 'nearly half of school leavers are illiterate'? Note the words 'proudly' and 'mourns'. When people use figures, they have purposes to fulfil. And they do not have to be dishonest; the slant comes sidling in. There is nothing dishonest in saying that the dentist kept us waiting for half-an-hour, and that we spent five minutes on the way back chatting to his pretty receptionist, even though our wristwatch was dividing out the total loss of time evenly between the two.

The philosophic issues involved in this preamble to a chapter on measurement are profound. I wish neither to minimize them, nor to immerse in the self-indulgence of discussing them at length. But if it is necessary, as I suggest, to take a *totally new* look at the problem of measurement in the context of the viable system, we must first suspend belief in the hallowed habits of measurement that we inherit. The object so far has been simply to stir up sufficiently disquieting thoughts as to make that suspension temporarily possible. Surely thoughtful managers are aware of these problems; they just hope that good advisors will eliminate them, that bigger computers will solve them, or that in general the expenditure of more money will sooner or later make all things plain. But it is not so. The whole of the inherited approach to measurement for management is flawed.

Please work through those three points in the reverse order, testing them against honest experience, rather than looking for incontrovertible evidence that the case is made. Here is the guide:

(i)   figures are useful only to the extent that we use them. When we use them, we shall import our personalities into the numerical facts. It is probable, then, that subjectivity has penetrated into the selection and the mode of the measurement — along with historical respectability and bureaucratic convenience;

(ii)   the measures we use do not have requisite variety to absorb the variety of that which they claim to measure. The missing variety proliferates on . . . the missing variety *may* be the crucial managerial material, even if it was not when these traditional measures were first conceived and handed down to us;

(iii)   figures that are embellished by computer processing embody a hallucinogen: we conceive that their effective variety is that of the number of modes of presentation, whereas in reality their effective variety is the variety of the raw measurements on which the computers are performing their pyrotechnics.

If belief in the whole machinery is, as a result of this exercise, duly suspended — what next? Shall the cybernetician wave a wand to correct this disastrous scenario? *No-one* can do so. The cybernetics required is not available, precisely because of cybernetic laws. Perhaps the whole message of this book can be summed up in this context:

No-one can conjure-up variety from thin air

— least of all the cybernetician for whom variety itself is the stuff of management.

The argument so far has scrupulously avoided (was it noticed?) the major terms used in managerial measurement. I have spoken about 'numbers' and 'figures' — naively — to mean, say, 317 or 5, 482, 721. But now, working on the foundations provided much earlier, and incorporating the experience of this preamble, we may conveniently turn to the definition of some important words that are very much confused in the contemporary managerial culture. These are the definitions offered; and a cybernetic commentary is appended.

Fact:

That which is the case.

This is a very precious word, because it incorporates requisite variety.

If

'I was in London on 26th August'

is a *fact,* then I was there, regardless of where in London I was. For 'London' absorbs the variety of all my movements through the City, and Kensington, and Soho.

We **must not say** 'I deny the fact that. . .'
It is an internal contradiction.

I often saw a proforma letter which said:

'The company would not like you to believe the fact that your order is not receiving our closest attention.'

The customer should have changed its supplier.

Noise:

A meaningless jumble of signals.

Noise, as the name implies, is worthless — and often counter-productive because it is mistaken for information.

Much of the measurement that reaches management is **in fact** noise.

However, what is 'meaningless' to one person may convey meaning to another — N.B.

It follows that it is worth suspecting *noise* of being *data* in disguise.

Thought for Today:

If management were to inspect the noise thrown up by industrial disputation, they might therein discover data.

Data:

> *Statements of fact.*
>
> *Data* is the plural of *datum:* 'something given'.
>
> Whatever is 'given' is a fact.
>
> Data are therefore quite as precious as facts, but they are consistently misused; for instance:
>
> > after data have been reprocessed through a computer ninety times, they become — *noise.*
>
> Then simply to say: 'get me the data' invites the reception of noise —
>
> — because a human being cannot deploy the computer's variety.
>
> The human being cannot normally discover the facts in the data, which become noise for him at the point where Ashby's Law is putatively (but to no effect!) over-ridden.

Information:

> *That which CHANGES us.*
>
> Noise becomes data — when the **fact** in it is RECOGNIZED.
>
> Data become information — when the **fact** in them is susceptible to **action.**
>
> How can I possibly know that I am **informed?**
>
> — Only because I have *changed my state.*

Armed with these definitions, we obtain a new vision of the arena of 'management information'.

Noise is a problem all right; but it may conceal riches — and usually does, if it can be turned into data. Data are an excrescence, for which managers gladly pay an enormous price, because these data are not geared to action. Information (since it is what changes us) arrives only when we are changed. Then, recognizing that change when it occurs, let us ask *what happened?* It often happens that the change arose from the distillation of noise. The noise changed into data on route, of course, but we hardly noticed that. For data are the components of the information-that-changes-us, whereas the data for which the high price was paid changed us not at all. These seem to be the facts of the matter, bizarre though they undoubtedly are.

What is going on? Try fixing your mind on the image of two friends: we could call them Dick and Harry. How *tall* is Dick? How *tall* is Harry? Can you please assess those two heights? If you can, then you have abstracted data from the noisy impressions you have of your two friends.

These data can now be manipulated. It should be possible to get the answer right: which is the taller, Dick or Harry? By how much? The problem is very difficult. Few people have the confidence to say that Dick is taller than Harry — never mind by how much — unless they have picked on extreme examples. And yet, if Dick and Harry were here together, side by side, there would be little difficulty in knowing which was the taller, *nor* in knowing roughly by how much.

The human brain turns out to be very good at recognizing patterns, comparing key characteristics of such patterns and making judgments based on those comparisons. We do it all the time. Remember the arguments of the early chapters about our handling of variety; remember the Just Noticeable Difference. Now how about *this* definition of a manager:

> a manager is a human being who has refined the brain's ability to recognize patterns, and to compare the key characteristics of such patterns, in the context of extremely complicated systems comprising men, materials, machinery, and money;

> he has become skilled in recognizing a change in his own state, by recognizing information in the data flowing around him *and* in the ambient noise;

> he has the motive, and has cultivated the style, necessary to transduce his own change of state into a change of state in the extremely complicated system of which he is the manager.

This definition is a cybernetic definition. It is based upon the analysis of the human capability to handle variety. The expectation of many liberal-minded people is that cybernetics de-humanizes the individual. On the contrary, it makes him finally human. For this definition does not describe the manager by his role in the organization, by his 'job description', by his character 'weakness' (compare the management grids, Theory X and Theory Y, and so forth), or by his 'track record' (which is the most de-humanizing description of all, because it applies subjective criteria, without any regard at all for Requisite Variety). The definition acknowledges the manager as especially skilled in human *cognition,* in that he refines a particular human ability, to recognize patterns, in an unusual situation. It acknowledges the manager in his human strength of *conation,* in that he applies his *will.* It recognizes his human ability to control his behaviour in the mode of his address, which is a person's style. Above all, it points to that ultimately human capacity, which is reflexive, applying closure, which is metasystemic, to *know himself* — which is to recognize his own change of state.

This chapter is called 'Measurement'. Does it seem to have gone off course? Should we not be talking about Return on Investment, and Profit/Earnings Ratios? These are delightfully sophisticated measures. But a good manager can and does manipulate the ROI. It does not have Requisite Variety, and its definitions of component variables are elastic. Then the manager, as I have just defined him, will of course make sure that the ROI indicates what it is expected that it should indicate. And he can readily do that, within the limits of any system *that is in fact viable,* regardless of embarrassing accounting conventions. As to the *P/E* Ratio, the situation is so complicated that the managerial task is less complicated. 'Profit' is a conventional term, and so is 'Earnings'. Both lack Requisite Variety; both are elastic. The ratio between them is therefore a meta-convention applied to two conventions. In the result, a good manager (as defined) will be able to demonstrate that it is a very good thing that the *P/E* Ratio has gone up, or that it has gone down, in any given set of circumstances — providing that *the system is in fact viable.*

The academic economist knows very well how such outrageous outcomes are possible in theory. The skilled manager knows very well how to manipulate events to procure such outrageous outcomes. The financial director, with his expertise in accountancy, straddles the two worlds, and makes it all work. And your author, sitting on both of all three sides, has seen it *happen,* over and over again. Therefore does he retreat into his cybernetics, the science of effective organization, to say to you: the sole limit on all these goings-on is the *viability of the system itself.* Given that, all delightfully sophisticated measures will do as they are told. Without that, the conventions, however skillfully manipulated, will break down. This is the definition of something called: 'Scandal in the City'. Once that has been declared, you can watch all concerned flying their Flags of Convention in a stiff breeze, and proposing toasts to Business Rectitude. The poor fellows who got the answers wrong go to the wall. The issues, we can be sure, will be lost in the froth of the scandal; because no-one knows what they are. The issues are the criteria of the viable system, which are the targets of all our understanding, and which this book is trying to make explicit.

Then let us be constructive. What is measurement to do with, if not with these conventions? What is it *for,* if not to determine the cause of the effect?

Readers of this book are familiar by now with diagrams that look like this:

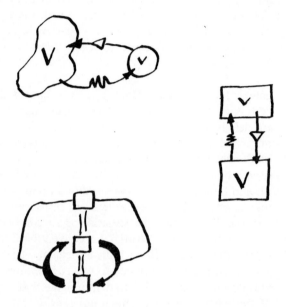

Figure 47. Three of the variety-absorbing devices developed as diagrammatic conventions in this book

What are they all about? What do they ultimately mean?

These diagrams are embodiments of Ashby's Law. They say: *only variety can absorb variety.* But we begin to perceive the managerial role in all of this.

The managerial role is META to all of this.

The manager's job is three-fold:

(i)   *to set the CRITERIA of stability;*

> then —
> having allowed autonomy to work,
> Requisite Variety to do its job,
> the viable system to settle down,

(ii)   *to detect instability;*

> or —
> recognizing that settling-down
> is not to viability
> but to coma
> to death

(iii)   *to change the criteria.*

We suspended belief in the inherited modes of measurement. We defined the manager. We assaulted the conventions of mensuration. We now detect the NEEDS of the manager to do his job...

> The manager's requirement of measurement is
> that it should measure stability and instability
> in the system that he (this being his role)
> has subjectively defined.

Many management scientists, and I was one of them, have written about the collection of the information that the manager needs to 'take a decision'. The manager's information, however, is his own recognition of his own change of state. The problem is therefore beyond (meta) the problem that was at first detected. Moreover, decisions themselves are not taken *in vacuo*. They simply reflect the manager's detection of his change of state, and his capability (again, in his own eyes) to transduce that change of state into the system that he manages. This is why the measurements he needs have to do with stability. It is not at all difficult, once the cybernetic bases have been established.

If we take any one of these three diagrams just recapitulated, but in this case the first, we may propose the following arrangement:

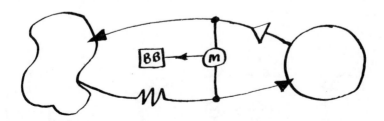

Figure 48. Measurement for management conceived as the detection of instability in a normally satisfactory operation (and see Figure 49)

288

'M' stands for 'Meter'. This meter detects the messages that are flowing in the loop. These, please recall, are **not** messages about the details of all that is really going on in the two essentially muddy boxes on either side of the diagram (representing, in this example, the environment and the operation, as the notation conveys). The messages are simply saying either 'I am all right', or 'I am not all right — DO something'. The messages are continuous; therefore something more is added by a knowledge of the *rate* at which the messages flow. This *rate* is a kind of measure of the ease or unease experienced inside the muddy boxes that are generating the messages.

The meter, then, is performing the measuring that most matters to the management — despite the fact that its 'perception' is at one remove from the data themselves (which are invisible in the mud of the muddy boxes). After that, however, more has to happen. The meter is detecting disbalance in the loop; but this disbalance answers to statistical criteria as to how much deviation *counts* as disbalance. This means: how LOUD is the cry 'I am not all right'. Moreover, the *rate* of the shouting is relevant.... .

Figure 48 subsumes these rather elaborate notions in a little, square black box (BB), which is the management tool for understanding what is happening. Sooner or later, this black box will have to be mastered as a tool — even though its activity remains black, un-transparent, opaque. The management (remember the black-box 'aphorism') does not need the details; it needs to know whether the system it manages remains 'sane' or has 'gone mad'. Then it has to set criteria for the meter; and it has to **teach** the black box when to speak — not to shriek with pain at the slightest discomfiture, nor to die stoically without uttering a word. In scientific language, then, the problem is not so much to design and build the black box, as to find the relevant black box and to *tune* it.

The management needs all this; the management has to set up the machinery. Yet the management is outside, beyond, this system that is or is not equilibrial in terms of its requisite variety. Thereby we observe, for the first time, that even System One management is *metasystemic*. The new diagram is completed like this:

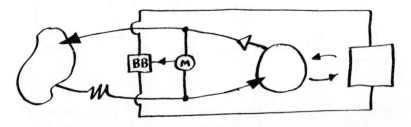

Figure 49. Completion of Figure 48

The basis of this idea was proposed, in a somewhat different context, in my first book, *Cybernetics and Management* (1959), when the principle involved was called **Completion From Without.** You can see why. The managerial control is indeed operated metasystemically, since it does not deal with the *stuff* of the system at all — it deals only with the managerial consequences of what the system does. Conversely (it would seem) I have also argued (there and *passim*) that the *controller* of a system is embodied in the system itself, and does not stand outside it. These two points are mentioned to exemplify confusion for which I seem to have been responsible, and therefore wish to resolve.

The *stability* of the system, in which we are acutely interested, derives from the ability of its subsystems to absorb one another's variety. To this extent, control is **intrinsic** to the system (this being another of my terms); it derives from the automatic operation of Ashby's Law, and is not embodied in a controller. However: the criteria to which the system answers, in terms of its *degree* of stability, derive from the criteria of systemic viability in the context of the total viable system — and in particular they derive from the understanding of cohesion, in which (as we saw earlier) freedom and constraint are balanced to provide a workable level of autonomy.

Then the business of measurement that is under discussion here relates not to intrinsic control within an interactive set of subsystems, but to metasystemic management within the criteria of which the intrinsic control is expected to operate. For System One, this metasystem is the Three-Four-Five concatenation. But the System One management, we now observe, is metasystemic to its own operational reality.

When these arguments are applied to the vertical dimension of the viable system model, there is an interesting outcome. In Figure 47 we looked at a vertical diagram, which is reproduced in Figure 50 (on the left). Let us choose to nominate this as relating System One to its Three-Four metasystem. If the construction that has just been worked out (Figure 49) in the horizontal dimension is now mapped onto the vertical dimension, we obtain this rotation (at Figure 50 on the right).

This is none other than the rediscovery of System Five ...

This time, however, the topology is pointing to the fact that System Five, in its role as providing the final closure for the viable system, needs to monitor the variety absorption between System One and the Three-Four activity. This is a reminder that there are many, many concealed loops on the diagram of the viable system. That diagram is necessarily a simplification; it becomes an over-simplication at the moment when we forget to study the loops that are not made explicit — to all of which the cybernetic managerial axioms and principles apply. The rotation experiment reminds us also that management, when correctly conceived at the appropriate level of recursion, is concerned to measure stability and instability between muddy boxes. System Five must not immerse itself in the muddy boxes themselves. It follows that the measurements appropriate to System Five management have nothing to do with weighing the mud.

These approaches effectively repudiate the **causal** view of the world on which existing managerial measurement is based. It is two hundred years since the philosopher Hume made his profound criticisms of the very concept of causality; it has been strictly necessary to replace it ever since; yet our culture to this day continues to propagate the belief that 'every event has a cause'. Thus, when it comes to the management of very large systems, we still look for a **unique cause** of systemic failure — and this is not at all the appropriate methodology. Complicated systems fail because they are potentially unstable, and because some concatenation of circumstances has made the potentiality actual. No unique event is *the* cause; and when we look for one it often seems that if the total system had been in a different state, that event would not have led to disaster. Even when the event is intrinsically disastrous of itself, it is not feasible to isolate it from its systemic milieu. For example, if the President of a country that has nuclear armaments finally 'presses the button', would he be *the* cause of the war? The war is the evidence of destabilization; and that occurs when the trajectory of the representative point of the system leaves its 'I am all right' circle — as the outcome of changes in the *relationship* between systemic components.

The body is a complicated system. When it goes wrong, Western medicine looks for the cause. It speaks of the etiology of disease. As a result, it is always advising people to avoid what it takes to be the causes of illness; and its therapy is directed to treating symptoms that are concomitant with these alleged causes. Eastern medicine, it seems, does not do this. It aims at re-stabilizing the total system through the harmonizing of *relationships* between the parts of the body. It is systemic medicine, as is homeopathy for example. But such an approach is viewed askance by all who are committed to the concept of causality; and when such people refer to the total system (and Western physicians do this) it soon becomes clear that they do not understnad what a system really is. This is nowhere more evident than in the field of psychiatric medicine. If you are sure that there is a *cause* of depression, for example, you can be persuaded that it is localized in the frontal lobe of the brain. But even that is itself a very complicated system; and to administer a convulsing electric shock to it is the equivalent of kicking a television set in the hope that the picture will improve. Sometimes it does.

There is a story told of Ross Ashby himself. In 1965 there occurred the famous 'black-out' of a large portion of the Eastern seaboard of the United States. Now the stability of the loop that connects electrical generation, through

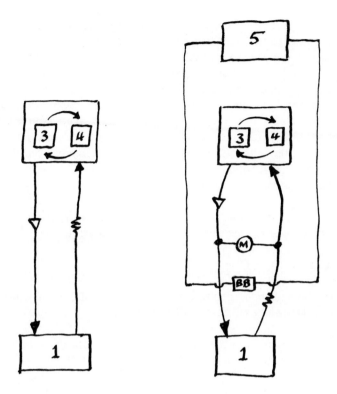

Figure 50. The rotation of a System One map (see Figure 49) onto a Corporate map

supply, to consumption, in an area that makes the most massive use of electricity for every purpose under heaven (including the cleaning of teeth and the carving of meat) might well be upset as the result of a change in the set of relationships connecting any set of variables in any subset of the system. It happened; indeed, it happened again in 1977. At any rate, in 1965 Ashby was working in the laboratory of another greatly distinguished cybernetician at the University of Illinois at Urbana — namely Heinz von Foerster. Ashby was discussing the potential instability of the Eastern electrical system which had just become actual, and referred to the inevitable public outcry. He said that the public would not be satisfied until someone had identified 'the cause' of the blackout. A few days later he returned to von Foerster's office beaming, and waving a newspaper. Blazoned across half a page was a photograph of 'the cause': a fused little relay.

Improvement in the management of complicated systems will not occur until managers give up the dysfunctional concept of causality, and the search for the unique cause. The consequences for the measuring systems that they use are severe. As I have tried to show, it is necessary to create measurements that detect instability, rather than to track the parameters of muddy boxes. Now the method, in practice, for doing this is *appallingly* easy. I use that adverb because it would be more convincing if the recommendation were demonstrably difficult and revolutionary. We need metasystemic measurements suited for a managerial metasystem: if this meant that all serious managers ought to put themselves on a three-year course in higher mathematics, the idea would be seen to have some real substance... . The truth of the matter is that the mathematics have already been done by the cybernetics. And what follows is appalling because it will look so trivial that it may not be taken for the serious solution that it is.

We need to meter the messages on any muddy-box loop. Then what does it mean, in terms of some measure, to say: 'I am all right'?

It means to say:

- 'we *normally* produce, sell, make a profit (or whatever else) when we have *17,000* (say)'.

- 'our *plan* is to produce, sell, make a profit (or whatever else) when we have *18,000* (say).'

- 'we *wish we could* produce, sell, make a profit (or whatever else) of *20,000* (say).'

These three versions of 'I am all right' respond, obviously, to different criteria. The first accepts the status quo. The second announces an intention. The third expresses a will to advance. But in any case, 'I am all right' if we have 17,000.

Then what does it mean, on behalf of the other subsystem in the loop, to say: 'I too am all right'?

It means to say:

- 'responding to your criterion of ACTUALLY, we have/have not done it — to *this* extent.'

- 'responding to your criterion of CAPABILITY, we have/have not done it — to *this* extent.'

- 'responding to your criterion of POTENTIALITY, we have/have not done it — to *this* extent.'

And in any case it means:

> 'I am all right, because I have met your criteria —
> *without denaturing myself:* I am still in being.'

Well, if the two halves of any loop are saying such things to each other, what is the meter expected to measure?

The meter simply measures the *ratio* between the declaration and the response for each of the three criteria.

If the meter registers ONE under the first criterion, the *situation* remains stable.

If the meter registers ONE under the second criterion, the stability of the *plan* is assured.

If the meter registers ONE under the third criterion, the *normative expectation* is stable as well.

THE RATIO OF

- *actuality* to *capability*
  is called PRODUCTIVITY,

- *capability* to *potentiality*
  is called LATENCY,

- *actuality* to *potentiality*
  is called PERFORMANCE.

So much for the meter. The role of the black box in the preceding diagrams is to **filter** the information that the meter produces. Management has already assumed its responsibility by declaring the precise value, for any important variable, of actuality, capability and potentiality. Now it takes the metasystemic responsibility of setting criteria as to *what is to count* as a destabilizing admixture in productivity, latency, and performance.

The simplest way to start thinking about this is to visualize a precise rule set into the Black Box (which in fact makes it transparent). All the indices we are using will turn out to have values less than unity, and each of them will tend to an average value that represents the current performance of the subsystem under consideration. This is to say that the relationships within the total system propagate themselves in such a way that, for example, the productivity index for *this* loop, in *this* subsystem, is running at (say) 74 — instead of 100.

Actuality is not attaining to the managerial criterion of Capability by 26 percent. There is no unique reason for this: pressures within the total system are modifying the behaviour of the subsystem. If we seek to improve this productivity, we shall need to make a systems enquiry. The old approach said: 'people will have to work harder. Devise an incentive payment scheme'. But any industrial manager could regale us with anecdotes about the grotesque outcomes of incentive schemes that he has experienced; and it is a safe bet that the study of his experience will reveal systemic fallacies in the thinking behind the scheme — which was envisaged as a simple cause-effect arrangement. I have known workers push a productivity index up to 300 (which says little for the management's understanding of the subsystem, in that the criterion of capability must have been wrongly set), and receive an increase in take-home pay equivalent to one packet of cigarettes a week. I have known salesmen to adapt themselves so well to an incentive scheme that they earn more in a year than the Company President (which tells us that the scheme did not have Requisite Variety). In both cases there was total failure to understand the system in which the incentive intervention was made. But, to return to the productivity index of 74, we shall ignore the problem of improving this for the moment, and return to the question of monitoring it — assuming that this is the value normal to the subsystem in its present systemic milieu. What *rule* could be laid down to make the Black Box transparent?

The rule could say: since 74 is normal, 73 or 75 is destabilizing to the subsystem — then send a message to the metasystem. But 74 may be 'normal' because the typical experience day-by-day runs like this: 74, 70, 76, 75, 71... in which case the rule is ridiculous. So the rule could instead say: report any deviation of more than 5 points, or of 5 percent, or of 10 percent. Managers often use this kind of rule; but where these arbitrary values for what is to count as destabilizing come from is a mystery. They are mere conventions deriving from the causal approach.

Two points should engage the mind as a result of this discussion. The first is that we are not dealing with a simple numerical scale of deviations from a norm, because that scale has no *operational* significance. It just 'sounds bad' to hear that today's figure is 10 percent worse than normal; maybe tomorrow's figure will be 15 percent better. In short, the concern is not for these raw measures, but for the *likelihood* that something has really gone wrong. The truth of this was appreciated on the shop-floor a very long time ago, with the result that Statistical Quality Control, based on the theory of probability, has been a familiar feature of production management for at least thirty years. But exactly the same truth reveals itself in the board-room and in councils of state. It is well-nigh incredible that it should have been largely ignored in these high and mighty places. The first system of *management* control to be based on the mathematical theory of probability that I installed was begun at the end of the 1940's, and I have not heard of an earlier one. Once computers became available, it was possible to run such a system much more easily, and to incorporate much more mathematical finesse. Yet how many management information systems have, to this day, incorporated such ideas? They are regarded as essentially 'forecasting' techniques, and as such have been widely used in marketing activities: that much is true. But I was referring to *management* systems. Then obviously the question arises: if these ideas are so powerful, and have for so long been demonstrated to work, why has management not seized on them with avidity? The arguments of this whole chapter are meant to reply to that question. Thus the practical manager who found those arguments 'too theoretical' has answered his own disparaging question.

From 1971 to 1973 I was engaged in the endeavour to build a real-time regulatory system for the social economy of Chile, under the direction of President Allende. By then, extremely ingenious methods of handling the filtration problem in terms of likelihood were available, using Bayesian statistical theory; and this was done. The theoretical means are fully available to any mathematical statistician, and the computational means are fully available wherever an electronic computer is to be found. What, it seems, is not available at all is the managerial realization of the truth that senior management is dealing in likelihood. The model from causality is so ingrained, that managers are extremely uncomfortable with a system that does not provide them with the familiar raw figures, and the familiar 'variances' expressed in raw terms. No-one is training them to think in terms of ratios (apart from the delightfully complicated ones criticized earlier), and the probabilities that ratio movements should reveal. This has to mean that senior managers are trying to do the job in their heads. I am a great believer in intuition, and am inclined to trust in it far more than most management scientists. However: managers simply *do not have* an implanted knowledge of statistical theory, on the lines of a Platonic foreknowledge gained in heaven; *nor* does the cerebral computer work well enough with numbers even to solve a simultaneous equation in two variables without pencil and paper as aids. Managers therefore **guess** the answers that can so easily be provided for them. It should not be too surprising that the guesses are so often wrong. At any rate, I have demonstrated by experiment that a probability-plus-computer monitoring system can detect a change (= information) in the movement of a performance index long before a human being can detect that change by eye in a graphical time series.

The second point that engages the mind is that the Black Box **is** black; it needs the endowment to operate, not on simple rules, not only on complicated rules such as mathematical statistical theory can provide, but on *its own experience* of destabilization in the loop. The black box is a filter; but it is a filter that **learns.** The cybernetics of learning are well understood, thanks principally to the work of the British cybernetician Gordon Pask. But in the case of a learning *filter,* the issues are much more simple than an understanding of Pask's whole corpus of work entails, and a great many scientists in many fields know what is involved. Essentially, the point is that the filter sets its own parameters by experiment, and does not have them thrust upon it. The experiments are automatically provided by experience, which can be regarded as a succession of unplanned experiments. This is also contrary to the view of science that is based on the notion of causality, because one is supposed to define 'the cause' in advance of determining its effect. Under the protocol of causality, that is indeed good advice: otherwise, it is easy to be trapped into nominating any adventitious relationship as causal. But if we forget the teleological neurosis altogether, which is to give up the search for 'the cause', and look instead directly at the relationships that are seen to occur, we may succeed in reinforcing those which lead to outcomes that we deem satisfactory and to extinguishing those which do not.

It is foreign to the purposes of this book to supply *recipes* for doing these things, because the best way to extract information about destabilizing trends in any system must depend on a study of that system itself. The principles need to be understood; the availability of an instrumentality has to be expressed. These matters have been aired; and there is more detail about the learning filter in the companion volume *Brain of the Firm,* under its name of the 'algedonode'. At this point in the general argument it seems more important to look back to the source of power behind these appallingly simple yet evidently revolutionary ideas, and then to generate the further principles of measurement in the viable system to which those ideas inexorably point.

As to the source of power, it is to be found in the variety engineering involved. Thinking back to the early chapters, we may recall the emphasis on designing filters, attenuators and amplifiers, that obey the cybernetic laws in advance of their being foisted onto the system by Nature herself and in the sublime ignorance of the management. We may also recall the aphorism that declares it unnecessary to enter a black box in order to understand the nature of the function that it performs. And to this a new clause may now be added: *or to monitor the stability of that performance.* Thus, preeminently, is proliferating variety contained.

Consider: the nature of the measures involved in this approach reduces the variety of the vast number of *factors* involved in any one measurement to a single statement of all-rightness. It reduces all many-digit variables to a common pure measure — a ratio, having two digits; and this in turn reduces the variety of the actual *numeration* involved. The factors, the variables and the actual numbers involved in what starts as a huge proliferation of variety, have all been slashed — without the slightest loss of information (= what changes us). Many data have been lost; but data in excess of information are irrelevant to the management process. They may be needed for other purposes, as a record; to this extent they may be data-banked. But it is only when the banking requirement is clearly separated from the operational requirement that a management information system begins to engineer its variety.

Consider next: by using statistical filtration to report on the likelihood of incipient change, we remove a lot more variety from the system that is concerned with the generation of raw data. It is of no interest to a manager to know that everything is carrying on much as usual, as this chapter has strongly argued. If so, then it is ridiculous for him to spend prodigal sums on computer systems that will tell him what he is not interested to hear in ever greater detail. Messages about stability are meta-messages; the absorption of variety to which the raw data refer can safely be left to the intrinsic control manifested by systemic interaction within the operational loops — provided that the four principles of organization have been correctly directed to their design.

Consider further: *routine* reports amass data day-by-day to the point where they become mere noise. It is fundamental to this approach that management is informed by an instantaneous alerting signal. Not only does this slash the variety of the reporting system as such; it also totally expunges the variety generated in the traditional system by *time-lags*. Time-lags have to be allowed for; they are differentiated with respect to each other, and are confounded statistically; they make the projection of trends almost impossible. Under the new arrangements, they are simply dispensed with.

The computing capacity required to do all this is minimal. The scheme should probably be mounted on micro-computers, because they are already so cheap, thereby obtaining the maximum available advantage from the decentralization that bestows autonomy (consistent with cohesiveness). It should certainly, for cybernetic reasons, be designed as a network which maps onto the informational structure of the viable system. This means that main-frame computer capacity may be required to assemble the synergistic components of the metasystem, but the demand is very light. In the Chilean work referred to, we were (at the time of the coup on 11th September 1973) monitoring 75 percent of the social economy on a single IBM 360/50 — down to plant level. The illustrious people who have, in good faith, denied the very possibility of this have clearly not understood managerial cybernetics. They must have been thinking in terms of the classic information systems that require vast data-banks, and do not work. For the variety reductions listed above are not only excellent ends-in-themselves, they permit the design of a single filtration system that can be applied *anywhere* in the viable system, at *any* level of recursion. And that is yet another variety attenuator in itself. Critics of the Chilean work who, perhaps in less good faith than their data-bank colleagues, complained that the use of a single computer was centralizing and oppressive, and in manifest opposition to the declared views of myself and of the Chilean government on autonomy and freedom, conveniently ignored the fact that only one computer was available. We could not buy small computers and the teleprocessing interfaces that are really desirable, because Chile in those days was a seige economy. But we could (and did) ensure that data processed on behalf of plant managements sent the alerting signals back to them, rather than to anyone else.

This commentary on the source of power in the measurement scheme and information structure ends the discussion on measurement itself. But it is the moment to enunciate the further principles to which, as I said, these ideas inexorably point. They logically belong to the previous chapter; but could not then be set down there without the explanation of these recent pages. They are extremely important, but they can now be stated quite briefly.

The metasystem of the viable system consists of Systems Three, Four, and Five. *Within* this metasystem, System Five is itself metasystemic — as we observed in the last diagram. Then it is necessary for Systems Three and Four to absorb each other's variety: System Five cannot do it. The monitoring role of System Five demands a set of measurements based on the arguments of this chapter. Thus these two consequences follow:

The Second Axiom of Management

> The variety disposed by System Three, resulting from
> the operation of the First Axiom, and the variety
> disposed by System Four, are equivalent.

The Third Axiom of Management

> The variety disposed by System Five is equivalent to
> the residual variety generated by the operation of
> the Second Axiom.

It is difficult to know what more can be said to elucidate these two axioms, because everything has already *been* said in the exposition of the viable system and the measurement processes that are appropriate to it. But it is evident that a great deal of thought is required before the full meaning (never mind the implications) of these two axioms is, in the opening words of this chapter, properly understood. 'To *know* something properly, you must *measure* it.' We have arranged to measure; and so we have arranged to have knowledge. But a metastatement about a statement is always logically possible, and is even invited by a logic (such as the viable system's logic) that is innately recursive.

That metastatement was virtually 'thrown away' at the start of the chapter, but may by now be more seriously considered:

how do you *know* what it is that you know?

This is above all System Five's problem, and it has to be resolved within the terms of the Third Axiom. Of course it is in fact resolved, by every System Five, for the old (by now boring) reason that cybernetic laws 'will out', even if you do not know what they are. But when you *do* know what they are, the information system can be *effectively* designed.

Here is another way of stating the point, as a guide to the thinking-through process just recommended. Some way back it was asserted that **transduction** is more than **translation;** and in this chapter the manager was depicted as someone who could transduce the change in himself (that is acquired by receiving information as defined) into the system that he manages. This facility seems to be necessary in every manager. But the manager in System Five is metasystemic within the metasystem. Thus the System Five manager must not only undertake this managerial transduction, and supply himself with the measurements he needs to effect it; in addition the manager in System Five must **listen** to himself doing the job. Here is closure for the viable system. It also is a form of measurement. But it is self-referential, and there is no objective measure for a measurement so defined.

In the viable system called 'the human being', this function is usually called *conscience.*

LATER IN THE BAR...

'*Listening to myself sounds a trifle narcissistic to me.*'

'*I don't know what he means at all. Does he mean analysing one's own motives?...*'

'*... or being the conscience of the company? Sounds pious.*'

'*I don't think he means either. The talk is of closure, at a particular level of recursion. Both of you are talking reductionist, causatory talk — using all those concepts that we're supposed to shuffle off.*'

'*It gets a bit too much.*'

'*I think not. It gets all too easy. Hell, I know all about ratios — did when I was a schoolboy. I'm not going to learn any more about it just because of all this pretentious stuff.*'

'*Well, that's the crunch, isn't it? Either this is pretentious, or it isn't — it's for real. We have to decide for ourselves.*'

'*Yes: and I'm keeping an open mind, because I don't want to write myself off as an Establishment fellow who can't hear anything novel.*'

'*There goes the 'hearing' again. What does it mean to listen to oneself doing the job?*'

'*I've got a slight clue on that. I suppose all of us learned French — and for all I know someone here's bilingual. I cart around this little French piece that I copied out of a book.*'

'*Funny place to acquire a little French piece.*'

'No, come off it. I'm going for another round, seeing as it's my turn. I'm seriously asking you — anyone who knows French — to look at this card while I'm away.'

> Un petit d'un petit
> S'étonne aux Halles
> Un petit d'un petit
> Ah! desgrés te fallent
> Indolent qui ne sort cesse
> Indolent qui ne se mène
> Qu'importe un petit d'un petit
> Tout Gai de Reguennes.

'Well, if I'm supposed to hear that, I can't.'

'Nor can I. Who the devil is this 'little one of a little one'?'

'I've been to Les Halles, before they moved it. Full of vegetables, like Covent Garden.'

'— Before they moved that.'

'Has anyone heard of Gai de Reguennes? Some troubador?'

'Well, I haven't. This looks to me like a load of rubbish. I can just about translate it, but it doesn't convey any real meaning ...'

'Then we're not expected to translate it, but to transduce it.'

'Here he comes. Tony, why did you produce this wierdo?'

'We were talking about listening to oneself, remember. Read it, but listen to yourself reading it.'

'... OK: I did it. The meaning gets no clearer.'

'There you go again, talking about meaning. You're supposed to listen.'

'I'll listen, if someone will volunteer to read it out loud.'

'All right: I'll do that...'

'*Impeccably read Henry.*'

'*What's got into you, John? No, come on, stop laughing and tell us.*'

'*Didn't you* hear *it? Especially you, Henry.*'

'*Ah, but Henry was too busy reading it to hear it.*'

'*Well,* I'll *read it ...*' *... Hm. Now everyone's got it but me.*'

'*There's a lesson in that. Yes, I see, Tony: we can operate all the information systems, and do a good job of manipulating them — and rectifying the results in the boardroom, but maybe we don't* hear *at all. Is that it?*'

'*Well, that's what I was getting out of the chapter. So I gave you the French piece — some data. It was all noise to you. Then you* heard, *and you got information. I knew when you had performed the transduction, because you changed your state. You exploded into laughter.*'

'*Where did you get this pleasing thing?*'

'*It comes from a book called* Mots d'Heures: Gousses, Rames, *allegedly by Luis d'Antin van Rooten, and published by Angus and Robertson.*'

'*That may well be. But I was doing the reading — and I haven't changed my state yet.*'

'*Sorry. The whole book is in English, not French: it consists entirely of familiar nursery rhymes.*'

'*Well, now we've* all *had the laugh, what next? I'm completely confused about the business of management being intrinsic — and metasystemic at the same time. Can't be both.*'

'*I don't see why not. Take those four principles. Someone has to set up the amplifiers and attenuators, and see to it that all the black boxes absorb each other's variety. That's metasystemic — it's outside the system that will then proceed to regulate itself. That's the intrinsic control argument.*'

'*And someone has to set the criteria too — metasystemic again.*'

'*Then, I suppose, we can all go home. I don't believe it.*'

'*No, no. We listen out for alerting signals, don't we? The signals of instability.*'

'Is that really supposed to be all? I'd be lost without my routine reports. I want to see the actual figures, not a mixed bag of ratios.'

'You wouldn't see those ratios either, under this scheme. Only instabilities.'

'But you'd have to know what the indices were — when they are stable. No use telling me to shut up, everything's stable, if productivity is 50 percent. I'd do something about that.'

'Obviously. But that's a completely different matter from the dynamic reporting system we need. The state of all the ratios in a stable situation is a sort of base — a datum. I take the point that you don't need a daily report saying 'productivity is still 50 percent'. You've got figures like that on the wall, and you're working on them. But you do need to know if that figure changes significantly.'

'That's just our old friend, management by exception.'

'The pejorative use of 'just'. You might as well say that the penal policy of locking up criminals is 'just' management by exception. It's a different scene altogether.'

'What's so different here?'

'The instability business. Has anyone here ever measured an instability?'

'No. And I don't think I'm going to.'

'I don't know: if you see a line wobbling about on a graph that's normally smooth and flat, you are detecting an instability.'

'Yes; and if the line is sytematically going up or down, you're detecting a trend. I think trends are more important than exceptions — which after all may just be freaks.'

'But both sorts of detection are done by eye, and the brain behind it must be making what are essentially statistical judgments. We're being asked to use probability theory to make the statistical judgments automatic — a routine screening.'

'Both exceptions and trends are departures from a norm, and a norm is only a static statement about a dynamic equilibrium between bits of the system — hence we are to measure instabilities.'

'All this is just statistical quality control.'

'The pejorative 'just' again. As the book says, we've used SQC on the shop-floor for years, but it hasn't got into the boardroom. It hasn't. That can't be dismissed by the word 'just'.'

'And if it got into the boardroom, it wouldn't be *SQC either — just or otherwise. The application to stabilities has nothing to do with quality. Besides, the whole statistical apparatus would be different.'*

'You mean Bayesian short-term forecasting? I have used that, but specifically on market trends. It never occurred to me that you could run a whole management information system on such lines.'

'Say, rather, management filtration *system. We are aiming for requisite variety, not inundation.'*

'Did this Bayesian stuff work?'

'Oh yes. I got into it through an article by Harrison and Stevens in the Operational Research Quarterly *— the last issue in 1971. They have developed the techniques since then, and so did the work in Chile this chapter mentions.'*

'Well, Bill, don't give us a lecture on the technicalities, but what's so special about this?'

'Hm ... in a funny sort of way it enables you to break the time barrier, as I heard our present author say. You see, our ordinary notions of measurement are essentially historical. It's all over by the time you have found anything out.'

'Yes, but we're improving a lot. We have *got the weekly figures out by the following Tuesday.'*

'But in big organizations, really big ones, like governments, there's still a shocking lag. The report on information industries that I'm using was published by the United States government in 1977. It uses the latest available complete set of statistical data — and that was for 1967.'

'Ten years! But what was that about breaking the time barrier?'

'Look: it doesn't matter if it's ten years or yesterday. It's over. You can't change what happened — only learn from it. But Bayesian techniques pick up the instability as soon as it begins, and not after everything has gone BANG. Then you may be able to avert *a disaster before it would otherwise have happened.'*

'I guess that does burst through the time barrier. You're talking about anticipating events, aren't you?'

'Indeed. But don't confuse that with predicting the future, which is known only to God. If the kettle is on the fire, it's damn well going to boil — and you had better be ready with the teapot. Probably that's why the chapter avoided the phrase "forecasting techniques", and talked instead about Bayesian filtration.'

'I can accept that. I read the neurocybernetic version of this stuff in Brain of the Firm, *and the physiological model makes Bill's point very clearly. The nervous system, in any regulative situation is poised to act. Take playing tennis. You'd never hit a single ball if you couldn't anticipate — and then pounce. That's not crystal-ball futurology, it's simply awareness, alertness.'*

'And yet it does break the time barrier in some sense.'

'The idea that measurement is directed to measuring the future event rather than the past event is pretty hair-raising to me. Aren't we at all concerned with measuring what already happened?'

'Of course we are. But why? *We aren't historians or archivists. We measure what happened so that we can* do *something — and that something is in the future.'*

'Where does the famous data-bank stand in all this? It sounded like a good idea: all knowledge is here — retrieve whatever you want to know.'

'That's fine, isn't it, if you are a re-manager of history. But time goes one way. None of that record is of any value unless it helps us anticipate the future that we still have time to manage.'

'So what would you say is the real purpose of my data-bank, Tony — in a nutshell?'

'— To build the profits of computer companies.'

'Ah, so. Let us measure ourselves a final pint.'

CHAPTER TWELVE

Plots...

Plots refer to measurement also. Familiarly we say that a position may be plotted on a map. This means that a point is selected within a space of two dimensions, and identified by a set of co-ordinates. If we take all the houses, say, in a country district, and plot the position of each one on a large-scale map, then we have a *mapping* of domeciles onto the map. Mathematically, this would be called an isomorphic mapping: for every house there exists a plot. Thus the terrain and the map have the same (Greek *isos*) form (Greek *morphos*). But if we were making a smaller scale map, and ran into a whole suburb of houses, we would be unable to plot each house separately. The smallest mark we could make would represent a whole block of houses. This also is clearly a measurement, although clearly approximate: 'your house is somewhere in this block'. It is also a mapping in mathematical terms; but instead of mapping every element (the house) into a unique element (the plot on the map), the process maps a number of elements (the block of houses) onto a single plot. This is known as homomorphic mapping. The Greek derivation is much the same as before, since *homos,* like *isos,* means 'the same'. But the lexicon also says: 'belonging to two or more jointly' in the case of *homos,* which is perhaps why mathematicians use the word homomorphic for many-to-one mappings, while reserving the word isomorphic for one-to-one mappings.

In a book dealing with management, this may sound like a communique from the department of useless information. The facts are, however, that we have arrived at a basic structural model for a viable system, and that our theorem of recursion declares that all viable systems contain, and are contained in, other viable systems. To make the model 'stick', then, it is necessary to show that each level of recursion exhibits the viable system as an *isomorphic* mapping of that same viable system at the levels of recursion above and below it. Only if this isomorphic mapping exists can the claim be made to have delineated a necessary and sufficient recursive model of any viable system.

Earlier (in Chapter Three) we gave the notion of recursion a trial run. The hope then was to create a preliminary but clear impression of isomorphic mapping as between recursive levels of organization. By now, however, the likelihood is that the phrase 'level of recursion' has lost its value in the linguistic currency of this book. Because everyone in management is so accustomed to thinking about 'the corporate level', 'the divisional level', 'the company level', 'the plant level' (or whatever the appropriate terminology may be), it seems likely that readers will have become accustomed to tacking on the words 'of recursion' to every mention of the concept of organizational level as well. Many scientific words lose their necessary force when familiarity or hubris leads to their casual, name-dropping use: for example, the terms *catalyst, entropy, feedback,* and indeed *information.* If the term *recursion* is allowed to become a meaningless appendage to the term *organizational level,* then we do not have a valid model of a viable system. The levels of recursion in any such organizational model answer to mathematical criteria. But, since this is not a book for mathematicians, we have to discuss the issues in words and in diagrams, and must needs take time off to do so.

First of all, please remember why the issue is so important. The Recursive System Theorem states that any viable system contains, and is contained in, a viable system. Then if we can properly define a viable system, that is to say define it with scientific exactitude, we have to hand a tool of organizational description and of variety engineering that is a vast attenuator of the variety proliferated by any large organization. In Chapter Four we reviewed this proliferation, in terms of an arbitrary scattering of managerial boxes over an 'organization chart' that would cover the sides of the building housing head office. The methodological alternative advanced here has been to treat a viable system as consisting of two levels alone: the level of the operational elements of the system, and the level of metasystem that organizes those elements. Then in order to encompass a large organization using such a descriptive device, we need the concept of recursion; thereby every viable system contains, and is contained in, a viable system. Now that the main (not quite all) characteristics of a viable system have been laid bare, the image of the Chinese Boxes or the Russian Dolls may achieve more verisimilitude. But it is not just an image that we need, helpful though this is to comprehension; we need an isomorphic mapping of a recursive model.

Given that isomorphism can be understood as a one-to-one mapping of elements from one level of recursion to another, we are faced with the problem of identifying the elements to be mapped. But that has been done, in the by-now-familiar diagram of Systems One-to-Five — *with* all their vital linkages. Next comes the problem of where to begin, and where to end; and it is this problem that requires a fundamental understanding of what recursion, the mathematical concept, truly means.

The concept of recursion derives from a branch of mathematics called Number Theory. Suppose that we consider the number FIVE. Everyone knows what *that* means. But do we? It is a very complicated idea (note that it is not a thing — not *any* thing). On analysis, it seems to refer to whatever it is that various *collections* of things have in common. Faced with five beans, five men, and five spaceships, the child in us may not recognize any commonality at all. The trained adult in us recognizes the 'fiveness' in them all. So much, then, for the notion of invariance, which we discussed earlier. This 'fiveness' is invariant to *all* collections of five things. Again, the child in us comes to know this because it makes an isomorphic mapping across the three collections: *this* bean maps onto *this* man onto *this* spaceship. Having mapped in this way five times, the child in us finds that no bean, no man, no spaceship, is left over. Therefore 'everything is accounted for'. The 'fiveness' is invariant, says the adult in us; *that* is what 'five' actually *means*.

So far, so good. This insight shows that a number, just like a viable system, refers to a collection of things that are all alike — given a purpose. The things in the collection are not identical: beans, men and spaceships are very different entities; and so are the corporation, the division, the company and the plant. But the collections have an invariant in common: in the first case, the numeral 5; in the second case quintuple subsystems with their linkages. But it is unavoidable that the *purpose* of saying so be acknowledged. In the first case, the purpose has to do with counting, with the ability to reckon. In the second case, it has to do with viability, with the capacity to survive.

If we are now swimming hesitantly in these mathematical waters, we suddenly find that the ground has gone from under our feet — and that we are out of our depth. Why so? Because all that has been said as appertaining to the numeral 5, or the term FIVE, or the concept of a quintuply-based viable system, *also* applies to the numerals 3, 7, and 21,497, and to the concept of any system (however defined) which shares with other systems a set of elements and a set of connexions.

It is an old conundrum: 'how many beans (or men, or spaceships, or subsystems of systems) make FIVE?' This problem is the one addressed by *Recursive* Number Theory. It relies on the elementary notion of identity, of oneness. We know how to recognize *a* bean, *a* man, *a* spaceship, and indeed *a* viable system. If we did not know how to recognize these entities, we should not be talking about them at all. (Please allow me to note that there are huge epistemological problems that arise in saying that; for the moment the concern is Number Theory.)

Very well: if all we know about FIVE is that it shares 'fiveness' across collections of any five disparate entities by isomorphic mapping, and if SEVEN says exactly the same thing about 'sevenness', we shall proceed to **define** FIVE — by recursion. This is it:

FIVE = FOUR + 1.

What is this 'FOUR'? Well, we can define FOUR by recursion too. It is: THREE + 1. Of course, that enables us to define FIVE = THREE + 1 + 1.

The end of this recursive logic, obviously, defines FIVE as = $0 + 1 + 1 + 1 + 1 + 1$. Or, perhaps, it is not so obvious; because it would equally be true to say that FIVE = $(-1) + (-1) + 0 + 1 + 1 + 1 + 1 + 1 + 1$.

Mathematics, 'queen and servant of the sciences', can be great fun; but what has all this to do with management?

Pause to think, perhaps?

Here, at any rate, comes the answer. We cannot define FIVE as if it were a *thing*, because it is not a *thing*. But we can **define** it as a PROCESS by which that which we seek can be found. Thus recursion is a process, which homes in on the numeral — once we know the purpose of the exercise. This process will distinguish between FIVE and SEVEN perfectly well. It will also distinguish the fifth from the seventh level of recursion in the Chinese Boxes of viable systems perfectly well — once we know the purpose of viability, namely to survive.

This use of Number Theory in managerial cybernetics has something crucial to demonstrate at this moment. In Number Theory, contrary no doubt to expectation, we find that we are not concerned to examine The Number, but to look at the rules whereby the *names* of numbers are transformed into each other. It is exactly the same with viable systems, as we first saw in the big diagram of Chapter Three.

The problem will be to specify the transformation rules whereby one level of recursion defines those on either side of it; and this problem will shortly be solved diagrammatically, in terms of structural isomorphism. But before we move to diagrams, let us allow mathematics to make a final point — since the maddening question that it poses may have already occurred to the mind schooled in management.

In managerial terms, the question is: 'how do I know where the recursion begins or ends, or where is its main focus?'

In mathematical terms, the question asks the difference between the following expressions:

$$0 + 1 + 1 + 1 + 1 + 1 = 5$$
$$(-1) + 0 + 1 + 1 + 1 + 1 + 1 + 1 = 5$$
$$(-1) + (-1) + 0 + 1 + 1 + 1 + 1 + 1 + 1 + 1 = 5$$

Mathematically, the 'origin' of these equations is taken to be zero; and clearly plus and minus units can be added indefinitely on both sides of the 'origin' while still procuring the equivalence FIVE. In other words, both the location of the 'origin' and the extent of the recursion on either side of it are quite arbirtary. It is the same in management. The focus of our recursions is wherever our interest lies. The series extends indefinitely in both directions — until we reach the universe, in terms of pluses, or the quark, in terms of minuses — for both (it seems) are viable systems. What happens then is a mystery, not only for physics and for management, but for humankind. This utterance can be understood only in terms of our 'nesting' logic; it cannot be understood in terms of reductionism.

There is a second, and difficult, comment — which the manager may conveniently ignore. Aside from either physics or management, one might wonder whether there is any end to the piling of metasystem on system, so far as mathematical theory is concerned. The answer (which really is interesting) is No. As to the evidence of Number Theory there can be no formal categorization (it means *no closure*) of arithmetic. This was the discovery of Skolem. The consequence is given in Gödel's Theorem, which shows that in any system of logic there is a verifiable proposition that cannot be *proven* within the canons of that logic. This is known as 'Incompleteness'. I discussed its managerial implications in *Cybernetics and Management* (1959), but these need not delay us here. In terms of the human understanding, however, Gödel's Theorem points to God: the name of final closure.

Hastening now to the managerial consequences of all this, which arise because of the methodology chosen at the beginning, we see straight away that there is NO 'basic' level of recursion on which the manager can afford to focus. Whichever level of recursion we may now be considering becomes arbitrarily and temporarily, the 'origin' of a series of recursive models that extends into the distance on either side.

Now the argument, from the very first chapters, has been that systems are to be recognized subjectively; and that their purposes exist only in the mind of an observer (or a group of observers, who have between themselves agreed on the conventions of their joint observation). Consider then the ease with which it was possible to say just now: 'the corporation, the division, the company, the plant', and to speak of these as four levels of recursion of any viable system. It is true that these managerial entities *are* viable systems, and that their recursivity will be established if we can (and we shall) take the step of demonstrating an isomorphic mapping across the four levels. But we ought to despair of the ease with which this is accepted. The sense of ease derives from the inherited model that this work has challenged. We *know* that those four levels of organization exist, and we *know* that they jointly encapsulate our managerial universe. But it is not the case. The corporation belongs to an industry, to a community, to a shareholding ownership, to a society, to a political entity, to a country, to an international market, to a world trading partnership... you name it. Moving in the other direction, the plant contains the viable systems of departments, of sections, of men and women themselves, of their families, of their brains, of their body cells, of their trade unions, of their operatic societies, of their clubs... you name it.

In short, the recursive logic on which this approach to the science of effective organization is constructed admits of no 'origin' and no 'limits'. What counts as the origin, at any given moment, is the focus of our attention at that moment, which could be called Recursion Level x. The modelling of organization moves away from any x towards the microcosmic in one direction, and towards the macrocosmic in the other. As managers, we need to be extremely wary of cutting short the PROCESS thus defined, and of saying: my responsibility ends *here*. How could anyone possibly know this? He does not; but he imagined (from the classical models of organization) that he did: we have dust bowls, pollution, city decay, starvation, violence, social revolution, and international warfare to prove it. These are not simply evils that the flesh is heir to; they are consequences of the artificial delimitation of responsibility for a recursive process that was not acknowledged.

To bring this argument straight down to the level of practical and human affairs, see how it illuminates the role of actual *people* in organizational cybernetics — with all the technocratic overtones carried by the connotations of those words. The general answer to the implied question is sufficiently clear: the sabbath was made for man, not man for the sabbath. Knowledge, which includes science and technology as well as philosophy and poetry, is part of every person's inheritance. Ask rather why the capital-intensive part of this birthright comes to be sequestered, and its power the perquisite of unordinary folk... But the particular answer, derived from recursion, is concerned with the managerial focus of attention.

Suppose that this focus, namely recursion level x, happens to be upon the corporation itself. Its operational elements are its divisions. Now both the corporation and the division are *managerial constructs*. If they have to do with people at all, these are the senior executives who inhabit the elegant buildings that epitomize those constructs — and they (in my experience) are well able to look after themselves. The questions that relate to *people* arise in the context of a level of recursion several steps down from that of the corporation and its divisions, where the work happens, where the wealth is created. It is inevitable that people, when considered from the corporate level of recursion that has no successive mappings onto a recursive organizational series of viable systems, should be viewed as a homogeneous statistical mass — like the molecules in a gas. It is the only way to attenuate their variety. The network of people working on something may be relied upon to do so with less than perfect effectiveness. Therefore the corporate executive may measure productivity in the group, and select various other measures of ineffectiveness — such as absenteeism, or the number of days' work lost through strike action. Such measures obey statistical laws. Meanwhile, any understanding of *why* these things should be so is to be found at the (say) sixth level of recursion down from *x*. If the recursive model exists, and if we understand its isomorphic mappings, then the facility to move focus also exists. That is why these few pages are being written. In the absence of any such model or facility, the tendency noted is for top executives to cut off the model of their responsibility early in the recursive series. Then 'the people' becomes a statistical artefact, and the individual worker is perceived to be exactly identical with any other, as measured by average ineffectiveness. The top executive then feels fitted to pontificate on television panels about the problems of his labour force. Certainly the more perceptive and humane of the top bosses will seek direct contact with the men and women down there: but he is prone to detect in them a naivety and ignorance that he feels he would share if he were not so successful a man himself. His is the reductionist model; it is not the nesting model.

This excursion into a hard reality (of which I personally have been intimately aware for so long) is provided not to insult, but as a motivational inducement to work through the exercise in recursive maping on which it is necessary to embark — if the power of this tool is to be grasped. The diagrams will become complicated, but they are less awesome than pages of mathematics. Once the recursive connectivity has been properly understood, we shall be able to discuss the cohesiveness of any whole enterprise, and its manifestations in planning and alert behaviour — which seem to be critical matters in management today.

The *idea* that each level of recursion that constitutes a viable system contains viable systems, which can in turn be examined as viable systems themselves — rather than be left as muddy boxes — was firmly established early on. In the next diagram (Figure 51) we see an exemplification of this *idea* of recursion. In actual analyses of actual institutions, such a diagram has often proven helpful. Firstly, it makes clear which particular organizational units belong to each level of recursion: their actual names are written into the various circles. Secondly, it indicates that the institution believes itself to consist of this set of recursions, but that these are part of a continuous series of viable systems — extending in both directions. (In this connexion, it is useful to model at least one more contained and containing viable system than the management considers it has responsibility for.) Thirdly, it emphasizes the invariance of the structure of viability at every level. Fourthly, it can readily be expanded to indicate how many models must be constructed. In the diagram, there are (for the sake of simplicity) three operational elements in each system. So there will be one model of the first level of recursion, and three at the second — one for each of the three divisions. If each division has three operational companies, there will be nine company models. By the same token, there will be twenty-seven plant models. The total number of departmental models will be eighty-one. But it is very necessary to resist the 'family tree' impression of this expansion, which is reductionist: that leaves us with a hundred and twenty-one models strung up the side of the building, which is too many — even if the models are structurally identical. These models are nested; therefore each level of recursion is connected only with four models: its own, and its three models of contained operational elements.

So the diagram well exhibits the *idea* of structural recursion — a word italicized because it is no more than it says: an imagining. The connectivity of the logic, that is to say the isomorphic mapping itself, is not shown. The same is true of the depiction of the total model portrayed at Figure 27 in *Brain of the Firm,* in which again the *idea* of recursion is conveyed by implanting the total model within each operational circle of the next higher level of recursion. (This device is of course equivalent to that used in Figure 51, which amplifies that very operational circle into the total model.) It is well to mention that these devices are not more than indications of recursiveness, since both have been widely reproduced by other workers — some of whom have been misled into incorrect conclusions about the mapping that is strictly involved.

Please think through what the difficulties of iconic representation are, because they are concerned with dimensionality: and dimensions (which are conditions of existence) offer the enrichment of this model which its full comprehension requires. The fact is that each recursive step moves the model into a new dimension; so that a model involving six dimensions, representing six recursions, is impossible to depict geometrically. Indeed, it is difficult to represent a model of even two recursions, although this page has two dimensions available, as we shall now see.

We need to illustrate how one viable system is embedded within another, so that its logical connectivity is preserved. The problem became vivid for me during work some years ago for the Government of Alberta in Canada. This government, like any other, is traditionally divided into departments — which are its operational elements. But, also like any other government, its practical agencies for communal activity are grouped territorially. This is the meaning of the two-dimensionality of recursiveness. The first problem, which ought to be mentioned in passing, was that there were too many departments and too many constituencies — as is usual. 'Too many'? Oh yes: the proliferation of variety determined by a matrix of departments-by-constituencies was way beyond the capacity of the human brain, however redoubtable the chief ministers undoubtedly were. Some variety engineering was needed, before any kind of sense could be made of *any* model. The departments of government were grouped into categories which I called 'foci of concern', while the

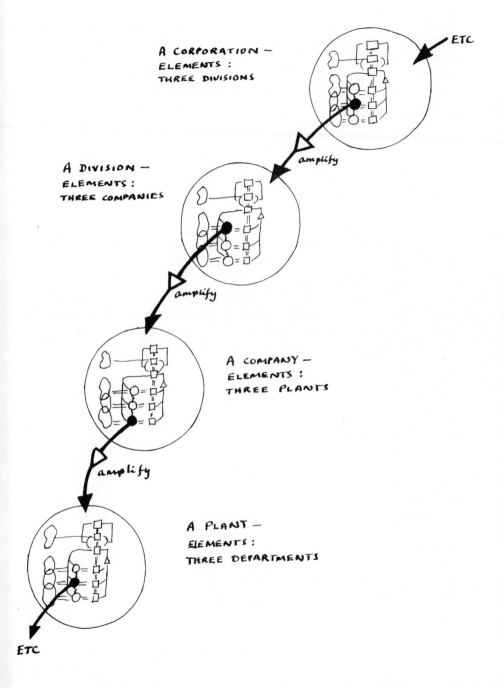

A CORPORATION —
ELEMENTS :
THREE DIVISIONS

ETC

amplify

A DIVISION —
ELEMENTS :
THREE COMPANIES

amplify

A COMPANY —
ELEMENTS :
THREE PLANTS

amplify

A PLANT —
ELEMENTS :
THREE DEPARTMENTS

ETC

Figure 51. The organization of the corporation conceived of as a recursive *process*

constituencies were grouped into categories of territory, which I called 'planning regions'. This having been done, however, the *orthogonal dimensionality* of the mapping remained. That is to say that the administrative and the territorial models of the viable system, representing two levels of recursion (provincial and regional), stood at right-angles to each other.

In the next diagram (Figure 52) appears a reduced version of this manner of recursive representation. To read the diagram, it is necessary first to look at the page as it is printed, and to assimilate the model at the first level of recursion. Then turn the page through ninety degrees, and assimilate the model at its second level of recursion. This done, check the logical connectivity of the two systems. They are identical.

This exercise begins the process of moving from the *idea* of recursion to its isomorphic mapping. What has now been done, in particular, is to differentiate the components of the system and the metasystem at the second level of recursion. After all, the metasystemic systems Three-Four-Five belong to the management box depicted as a System One at the first level of recursion (and System Two is an appendage to System Three). Meanwhile, the operational elements (circles) of the second level are simply *parts* of the total operation (big circle) appropriate to the first level of recursion — and those parts include their System One managements, *and* their System One environments. In other words, what we now see within the big circles of the diagram offers an optical resolution of the first recursion operation; and what we see in the big boxes offers an optical resolution of the first recursion's elemental management. From the viewpoint of the first recursion, for instance — and quite importantly, each System One has its own System Four.... .

Next: what is the enormous box that appears surrounding the metasystem of the first of these two recursions? We have not seen this box before. Well, *this* is the managerial System One of the level of recursion *above*. It is worthwhile to study this diagram carefully, because it begins to make the dimensional transition that we need. It does so geometrically, by using the page both ways. It does so mathematically, by repeating all connexions of the viable system's model isomorphically. But it conspicuously fails to reflect one aspect of the embedding of one recursion in another; and it would be a pity to proceed with this explanation without detecting this fault.

Please pause again, and find it.

Evidently, the limitations of our graphical means have left us with an *environmental* confusion: anyone could be forgiven for reflecting that the facts of our society have produced the same result.... .

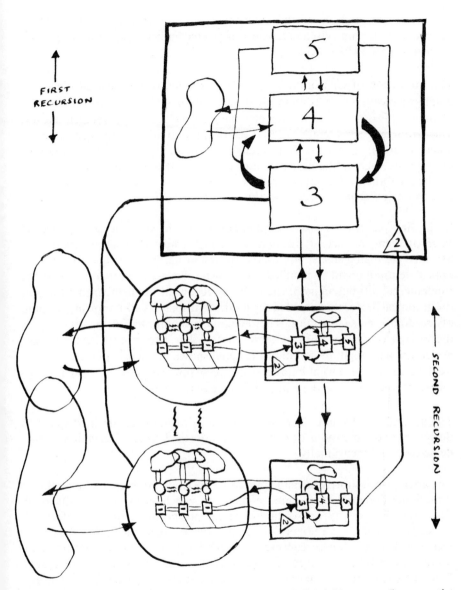

Figure 52. One method of depicting two recursions of the viable system (but note the misplacement of environments)

Diagrammatically, the failure lies in the 'clouds' that represent environments. The cloud representing the probabilistic future environment for each System Four is trapped within its own metasystem; it is not shared with its own recursion entire. Moreover, the clouds portraying the environments of System One at the second level of recursion are not — as they should be — embedded in the clouds portraying the environments of System One at the first level of recursion. The nesting of the environments across recursions is quite as necessary as anything else; and, as was indicated earlier, this is forgotten (as it is) at our peril (which it is).

This confusion of environments can be overcome, if we can find means — graphical means — to contain all the environmental clouds in one vertical domain. This is possible, if we change the pictorial account of recursion itself. The orthogonal representation, that requires the rotation of the page through ninety degrees, leaves us with clouds in both dimensions: they cannot be brought together. In the next diagram, Figure 53, this problem is resolved. As can be seen, the environments are all embedded inside each other. But at what cost to our other perceptions has this been done?

In the first place, both levels of recursion are depicted in the same plane: all *three* of them, in fact, if we include the large, heavily marked square as a System One management box of the recursion before 'the first'. Well, that optical delusion might be handled for its own sake — except that it betrays the fundamental orthogonality of the viable system itself. Remember that this was the graphical device that enabled the model to display its all-important account of freedom-versus-constraint. The dilemma is manifested in the diagram by the existence of two pairs of large circles. The two empty circles on the horizontal axis ought to be full of the detail shown in the occupied circles. But we have already seen what happens when recursion two is itself swung through ninety degrees: we lose the embedding of environments.

The dilemma is absolute. The two dimensions of the page are inadequate to depict the two dimensions of recursion because *each* level of recursion is *itself* depicted two-dimensionally.

The attempt will shortly be made to resolve the iconic problem by 'inventing' a third dimension on the two-dimensional page, which means using its diagonal. This trick is used by artists in indicating perspectives, and our device is basically the same — although it is not intended to create the optical illusion of receding distance, but to capture the recursivity of the model. Beforehand, however, it will be helpful to take a new look at the representation of System Two. This is partly for diagrammatic reasons (as will become clear), but also because we are approaching a definitive diagram of the total model of any viable system.

System Two is anti-oscillatory: it performs the damping function. If it is to do this effectively, then it had better be understood as the *transducer* of operational information into the managerial box. Of course, the regulatory centre (depicted as a triangle) at each horizontal level in the basic model is an 'office' function of the management at that level; therefore the next diagram must not be interpreted to say that management is isolated from its own

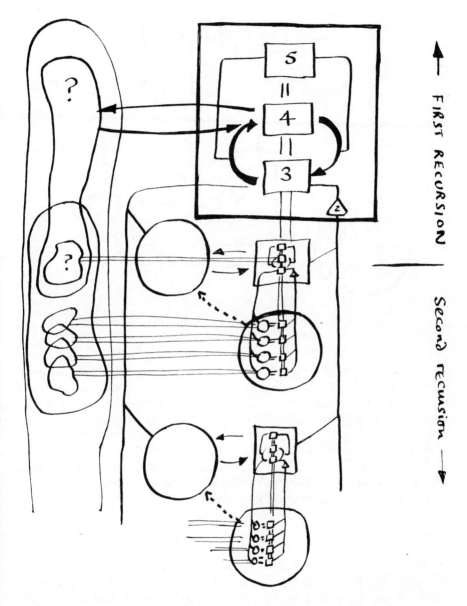

Figure 53. A second method of depicting two recursions of the viable system (but note
the misplacement of operations)

operational reality. The triangle 'belongs to' the square, for which it
transduces, despite the role it also plays in the vertical domain as a
disseminator of filtered information within System Two. Thus in Figure 54, we
replace the familiar shorthand of the top diagram with a more elaborate
version in the lower diagram.

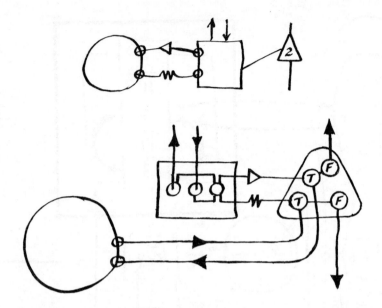

Figure 54. Replacing the familiar convention for System Two
with a more elaborate one

The two small circles inside the regulatory centre marked with T are the
managerial transducers of information to and from the operation itself; and
the circle in the management box to which they are connected stands for that
part of the managerial function that is concerned with directing operations (it
is the System *Three* of the next level of recursion down). The other two circles
in the box (its inward System *Five*) are shown as maintaining this box and its
horizontal operations in the vertical domain on the central axis of the model
whose System One it is. The small circles in the regulatory centre marked with
F are filters of the information flow, which feed only such information as is
needed for systemic damping purposes into the vertical domain of System
Two.

Using this device, we now redraw the general model that has been twice
attempted already. The familiar picture is called Recursion x: it is the one on
which we are focussed. Then Recursion y is the contained viable system. By
drawing y at right-angles to x, it proved impossible to embed the y
environments in the x environment. By drawing y in the same dimension as x,
thereby embedding the environments, two images of the operational circles
were created, and could not be forced into alignment. In the next diagram,
then, Recursion y is included at an angle of 45°. Because of the new
representation of System Two, it is possible to make the isomorphic mapping
between both levels of recursion complete.

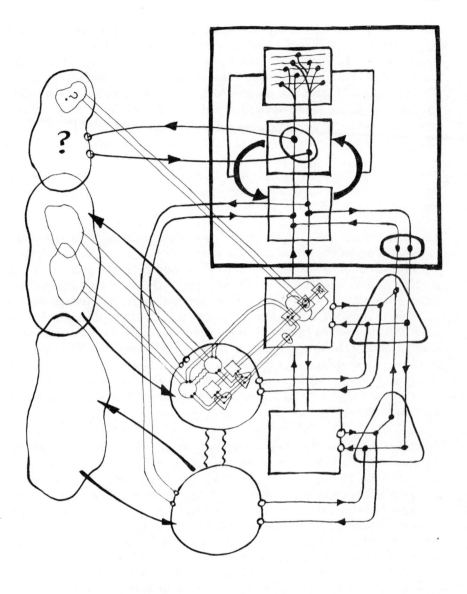

Figure 55. Definitive model of two recursions of the viable system (the diagonal of the page being used as the second dimension)

As before, Systems Three-Four-Five are encapsulated in a heavily-marked square Box: and this is the managerial unit of System One belonging to *Recursion w.* Then, if the isomorphic mapping has been successfully accomplished, the rest of this diagram is the *operation* of that management. That means that it should be possible to draw a circle around this remainder, so that the whole detail then depicted within that large circle *exactly reproduces* the detail already shown within the smaller circle of Recursion *x.* Close inspection will demonstrate that this is indeed the case.

Thus the new diagram (Figure 55) of Recursion *x* isomorphically maps the embedded viable system of Recursion *y*; and also has the potentiality to map onto Recursion *w*, in which *x* itself is embedded.

The flat, square pages of the book have almost yielded their maximum capacity to depict the isomorphic mappings that it is so important to grasp. The problem of dimensionality has been sufficiently exhibited: there is also the problem of sheer size. However, the next diagram (Figure 56) will illustrate the three recursions, *w, x,* and *y,* that were under discussion — although there is no room to complete the drawing of Recursion *w,* and although double lines have been dropped in favour of single lines, and other simplifications have been introduced. Before studying that, however, it is worth recalling clearly to mind the stark methodological contrast between established organizational theory and managerial cybernetics. Certainly both approaches speak about levels. But it seems that the notion of hierarchy and the notion of embedding are totally different.

When we draw the 'family-tree' type of organization chart for (say) the corporation, its divisions, their companies, and *their* plants, we are certainly demonstrating an hierarchical structure. The four levels of hierarchy are characterized by dependency: they hang from each other. Thus however much autonomy is delegated down the three, it is based on the concept of command. It is not surprising that in large organizations the ultimate bosses seem totally remote to the people on the shop floor and their managers. The pious talk about delegation and participation goes on; the reality is perceived to be otherwise. Earlier on we discussed the absurdity of referring to motor-car 'policies' and salary 'policies' which turned out to be rules offering very little latitude to those implementing these so-called policies. In government it is the same, as is nowhere more evident than in the so-called 'prices and incomes policies'. To refer in libertarian tones to 'pay guidelines' which turn out to be absolute barriers in any circumstances whatever, is at best a gross misuse of language; and at worst it is misrepresentation. But the use of the hierarchical model makes the command structure explicit; and, give or take a few dotted lines to indicate the so-called 'staff' activities and 'liaison work', there is no way of understanding the institution as operating in any other mode.

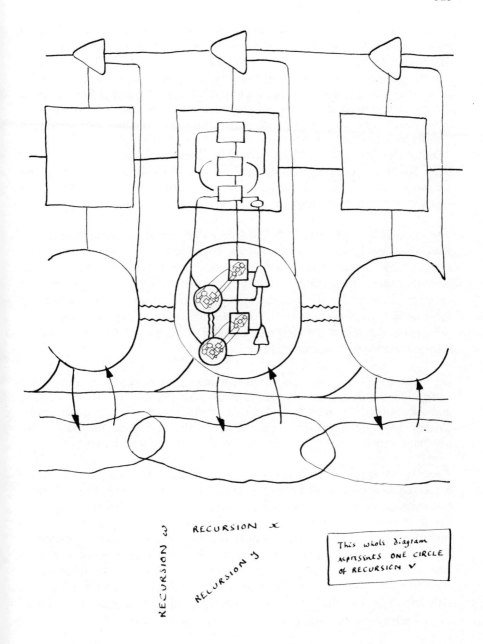

RECURSION ω

RECURSION x

RECURSION y

This whole diagram represents ONE CIRCLE of RECURSION v

Figure 56. Definitive model of three recursions of the viable system. Recursion *w* (to be viewed under a 90° rotation) shows only Systems One and Two. Note that the whole diagram represents *one circle* of Revursion *v*

Secondly, because that approach has no structural invariance of any kind (and least of all in terms of what structures conduce to viability) it remains a purely descriptive device that can offer no guidance as to how new boxes should be added, and with what relationships to everything else. The innovators have to guess: they add a box or two, declare that it 'reports to' another box (meaning 'here is your commander'), compose another box containing representatives of likely people who may be affected and label it 'steering committee', and then wonder whether that is enough and who is going to be upset. At this point it is common to connect a few boxes at the same hierarchical level with horizontal lines. No-one is sure what this means, because lines indicate dependency, but are supposed to be vertical. I have made sufficient enquiry into this practice in many institutions to be convinced that the ambiguity is intentional.

The cybernetic approach, I should like to recapitulate, depends upon the structural invariance of viable systems, conceived as an operational system regulated by a metasystem. Since the arrangement involves five subsystems in intimate connectivity, I dispute that this is an hierarchical structure in the sense defined. *Powers* in the viable system derive from *concatenations of information*. They do not derive from the allocation of dependencies, which grow exponentially as the hierarchy extends upwards, and for whose holders information is not concatenated but attenuated.

Secondly, one of the five sub-systems, namely System One, is itself a viable system. This is recursively embedded in the viable system on which we focus; and that in turn is embedded in another viable system of which it constitutes System One. The recursivity is guaranteed by the isomorphic mapping of the invariant structure in both directions from the focus, indefinitely.

These recapitulations of the two approaches point to the fact with which you are asked to wrestle in studying the final diagram (Figure 56). The process of this chapter has been a process that succeeds only if it changes the mind-set about the nature of organizational structure. By 'mind-set' I mean the inherited outlook that all of us familiarly use in thinking about organization. The mind-set is embodied in a pattern of thought applied to such matters which may well be called a *paradigm*. Then Figure 56, intended to complete the process of the chapter, is anti-paradigmatic; and it will not be understood as it is intended to be understood unless the mind-set is released .... . Please look at it carefully.

LATER IN THE BAR...

'He had a mind-set, that's all. And the symphony was his orchestral paradigm.'

'So when he kept on rewriting Fidelio, and all those Leonora overtures, he wasn't writing an opera? Come off it.'

'He hoped he was writing an opera; but he was writing a symphony — and that's why he kept rewriting it. Because it wasn't coming out as an opera.'

'Just listen to Mark: he's got poor old Ludwig van B straightened out at last.'

'No, no; I'm just quoting Stockhausen.'

'Well he was anti-paradigmatic enough. He should know.'

'Is that sort of thing what 'paradigm' means?'

'Sure. Stravinsky: looked what happened to The Rite of Spring — booed off.'

'The Beatles.'

'All that suggests that when the paradigm is overthrown, a new mind-set develops which creates a fresh paradigm. So we're no better off.'

'Oh, I don't know about that, Bill. The times change, and a fresh paradigm may be needed. I couldn't help thinking that we've been stuck with the hierarchical paradigm of organization for a hell of a long time.'

'That proves it's right.'

'Does it? You want to go on with serfdom, with sacrifices to the Minotaur, with Inquisitions, with a feudal industrial revolution? We ought to do better.'

'We can't get away with it.'

'Very droll. Our values have changed, and we need new models to accommodate that. How can you map 'participation' onto 'dependency'? It doesn't work.'

'Talk like that lost us The Empire.'

'It wasn't the talk that did it, but the emerging facts of evolution.'

'And now look at them. Most ex-colonial countries are far more authoritarian than they were under imperialism.'

'Perhaps that's because our idea of education was to sell the authoritarian paradigm.'

'And we're still at it. Public schools, the Army, now even the police. All dressed-up with woolly words proclaiming freedom. . . .'

'Well, if this is the new paradigm, at least it recognizes that. Just look at those 'pay guidelines' — he's right about that.'

'Yes; the 'policy' version of ordering people about really won't wash.'

' "It is our 'policy' that you be shot at dawn." '

'Got you. There can be no complaints about that, if it's simply a matter of policy.'

'Nonetheless, fellows — come on now. How are we supposed to get anything done?'

'By, and I quote, 'the concatenation of information'.'

'Oh, fine. What a phrase!'

'Being a well-known masochist, Peter, I looked up that word and transcribed it into my notes — right here. It means: 'union as of a chain by links'. Sounds linear.'

'What about chain-mail? That's not a linear chain, it's a whole. . . well weaving of links.'

'Trouble is: where does one get hold of the pattern for weaving this union?'

'Well, you idiot — that's exactly what all those wretchedly complicated diagrams purport to be. The information pattern, the invariant structure.'

'I guess that's right. Wow. Same again?'

'Thanks John, I'll stick with lager. But tell me this. If that is the pattern, the one in the last diagram, why not just set it down, comment on it, and have done? I must say that I found this chapter very heavy going.'

'*The argument was that we had to get through the process, so as to get rid of the mind-set, and overthrow the inherited paradigm.*'

'*Patronizing. I'm quite capable of looking at an argument on its merits, and so are you all. We don't need all this fancy stuff about mind-sets and paradigms: mysticism, not science.*'

'*Mind-set comes from psychology, I think.*'

'*And 'paradigm' is philosophy-of-science, David.*'

'*There you are: as I said,* mysticism.'

'*Here's the tray, men. What's been happening?*'

'*Nothing much. David just got hoisted with his own petard.*'

'*Well, I'm prepared to say that I see the point about going through the process. This really is very different from . . . .*'

'*. . . oh all right. But why give two wrong versions of the diagram before giving the right one?*

'*None of them is* wrong. *The earlier versions were not sufficiently tidy, that's all: they didn't fully convey the isomorphisms involved.*'

'*But if the last one does, why not junk the other two?*'

'*It's for the* process. *You look at a diagram, and you say 'oh, I see', but you don't really see. I think I see now, having flogged through it all.*'

'*What in particular do you reckon you see, Henry?*'

'*— That it really is different. These womb-like enclosures of identical structures are not hierarchic in any sense that I have previously recognized.*'

'*What about System Two? Why does that suddenly turn into a snake-like affair?*'

'*Well, it exactly matches the neuro-cybernetic account of System Two that appears in* Brain of the Firm, *I can tell you that much.*'

'*I don't know whether to be impressed or suspicious. I understood System Two way back — the oscillation damper. Suddenly it's got the role of transducer too.*'

'If you had understood, you'd have realized that before.'

'Oh, heavy stuff!'

'Well, it makes perfect sense, doesn't it? But it would have confused all those 'necessary and sufficient' criteria to go into these details earlier. They emerge from the total pattern — once you've seen it whole.'

'Personally, I found the first account quite satisfying. This disturbs my picture of the diagram — it seems unnecessarily complicated.'

'Hm . . . maybe it's that reaction which accounts for the contention here that most Systems Two don't work very well.'

'It certainly emphasizes its role. I think I'm getting the feel for all this . . . . But what's the matter with you. Tom? You're poring over that chart and looking suicidal.'

'. . . What in heaven's name is Recursion v?'

'The next above w, that's all.'

'Well, I was focussing as suggested on Recursion x, and identifying myself with its System Five. OK. I'm Divisional General Manager brackets Electrical. There is also a Divisional General Manager brackets Mechanical, and a third brackets Hydraulic. OK? Each of us is a viable system, Recursion x. OK?'

'OK, Tom. So what are your operational units, viable systems all? These are your Systems One, OK?'

'Right then, here goes. There are five of them, and I suppose that each is a viable system at Recursion y. There's Fulsome Generators; D.B. Jones and Co. (making transformers); the Switchgear company, Lever and Nobb . . . .'

'Hold it, Tom. Where do your stand in these companies?'

'I'm Chairman and Managing Director of all five.'

'Sorry. Let's have the other two.'

'OK. Refractory Refractories deal in insulation. Then I have the infant electronics company, Fischern Chips Ltd.'

'They don't sound as if they were in the same family as generators, transformers and switchgear.'

'Well, they are. All electrical.'

'How is insulation electrical?'

'You can't have electricity without insulation, dolt.'

'Let Tom answer. The whole technology of refractories is quite different from the heavy electrical engineering of the first three, surely, Tom?'

'Well, yes. But it isn't mechanical or hydraulic, is it?'

'Faute de mieux; I see.'

'If you've finished insulting Tom in Greek or whatever, Bill, I'd like to know what this 'infant electronics' is doing in there. So it's electrical. But I doubt that people who deal in bloody great generators know much about integrated circuits or micro-computers.'

'They don't have to. Fischern Chips is a separate company.'

'But you are Chairman and Managing Director just the same.'

'Tom's the only board member who knows Ohm's Law.'

'Oh, stop the mickey-taking chaps. Let Tom go on.'

'OK, the lot of you. I agree it's a pretty odd arrangement — and I did come from the heavy electrical side myself.'

'Then there ought to be a reorganization.'

'But at least I know more about refractories and electronics than the mechanical and hydraulic Divisional GMs. And I trust that I know how to delegate. I'm the father-figure, really, for those two companies. My job is to nurse the crystallographers in Refractory Refractories, and to make myself un-square to the whizz-kids of Fischern.'

'Reorganize.'

'Shut up, James. How can they do any better?'

'The whole set-up has come about by accretaion from a' bygone age.'

'If you don't mind, we did reorganize. Fischern Chips started out in the Hydraulic Division. We rationalized that.'

'Hydraulic?'

'Well, yes. It was historical, you see. Something to do with fluid logics.'

'Will you let Tom get on with his problem?'

'Thank you, David. If these five companies are sited at Recursion y, because they constitute my Systems One, then Leviathan Engineering itself is Recursion w.'

'That's it. You are a System One of Leviathan.'

'Read Hobbes.'

'Who?'

'Quiet, Bill.'

'I was saying that my parent, Leviathan itself, is Recursion w. I can cope with that: dammit, I'm a director myself.'

'So are the other two Divisional General managers, I'll be bound. System Three at w Recursion is made up of the Systems One; and then they erect themselves into System Five as well.'

'Cheer up: it's normal. Let Tom finish.'

'All I was saying was this. I'm the boss of Recursion x. My five companies are System One to my System Five; they are also five viable systems at Recursion y. Leviathan is Recursion w. Now that takes me one recursion each way away from my own Recursion x, which ought to be enough. So what is this on the diagram about Recursion v — which is alleged to be an operational circle around that whole diagram, with (presumably) all the rest of the recursive equipment that goes with it?'

'Look, Tom, you are not only concerned with Recursion x, where you are System Five: the Division General Manager. You are also System Three there, I bet. In addition, you are System Five, or part of it, throughout Recursion y. Moreover, you'll be into Three, Four, and Five at Recursion w.'

'If that's right, what's the point of all these distinctions? I'm the same fellow, after all.'

'That's the problem. How the hell do you know which hat you're wearing at any given time?'

'It's easy, in the old model.'

'I wonder if your subordinates and colleagues find it easy. How do the shop-floor people in the switchgear company know in what capacity you are speaking? Board director of Leviathan, Head of Electrics, their own Chairman — or what?'

'Yes, Tom: and which of them are you at a Leviathan board meeting?'

'Oh, we all understand each other.'

'Do you indeed. When I was in a similar situation, it was obvious that no-one on the main board knew whether I was speaking as a board colleague, or grinding one of several other axes.'

'Typical of you, Tony: not levelling.'

'Levelling *is a fine word to use, amid all these recursions. But if Tom is involved in all recursions as he says* — x, y *and* z — *then he should be reviewing the contained and containing viable systems on both sides.'*

'That's got to be right, except that Tom is focussing on Recursion x. *So you mean that he's involved in* w, x, y, *and ought to be reviewing Recursions* v *and* z.'

'That's where we came in. With Tom worrying about Recursion v.'

'Thank you. *As I said hours ago, what* is *it?'*

'Hell, Tom, Leviathan isn't the whole engineering industry. It is System One of that Recursion v. *You need to contemplate where you stand as an operational unit of that.'*

'Perhaps I do. I've just been studying a whole pile of paper about Engineering Standards, issued by our Nomenclature Committee: it covers the whole industry.'

'Exactly. Recursion v, *System Two.'*

· *'But they're telling us what to do.'*

'In that case, they're using the wrong channel, in the wrong vertical domain.'

'Well, it's only fair to say that we do have a representative on the Nomenclature Committee.'

'*Don't tell me it's you. I couldn't bear it.*'

'*No, it isn't. All right: I understand about the* v *Recursion. And the* z *Recursion takes me down to the plants of my* y *Recursion companies, OK? I'm not a complete idiot, you know.*'

'*Just as well, Tom. You'll soon have taken over the whole universe.*'

'*No, I'm simply looking towards the actual people that were mentioned somewhere in all that theoretical stuff.*'

'*Well, laying off Tom for a moment, I didn't get that. It appeared to be saying that there were no people* except *on the shop-floor. The rest of the organization consists of 'managerial constructs'. Nuts to that. Why, I should think that a quarter of our whole staff is employed at recursive levels above the shop-floor.*'

'*A quarter? I actually heard a lecture from our present author that sought to demonstrate mathematically that one HALF of the people in the orthodox organization can be expected to be found above the shop-floor level — spread over the hierarchical levels in the total pyramid. Minus one.*'

'*Minus one?*'

'*Yes — must be accurate.* n over 2 minus 1 *was the formula.*'

'*Ridiculous.*'

'*Is it? I'm not so sure. Bureaucracies proliferate.*'

'*Well, that's what he proved. Sounded convincing.*'

'*Even if it is true — or rather* because *(he says) it's true — I resent the argument that real people are only to be found on the shop-floor. Our head office is stacked with real people .... .*'

'*... and you have the Christmas party to prove it.*'

'*All right, you two: fact is, if half the folk in the organization are not on the shop-floor, what are they doing?*'

'*Serving the umpteen levels of hierarchy that are needed, by way of attenuation, to construct the organizational pyramid.*'

'*Government please note.*'

'*Good Grief, I'm lost. And it's my round. How many now? One, one, one, one, one? OK. Five beers. I'll get them.*'

'*— And a better lecture on Recursive Number Theory I've never heard.*'

'*Not that again. Could we really save half the staff of a large company or a government institution by changing the . . . paradigm, I suppose the word is?*'

'*Changing the paradigm is only the start. The presumption is that you would need to IMPLEMENT the recursive model of the viable system*'

'*Has it ever been done?*'

'*I believe it has. But in fairness, you can't expect a total reversal of the mind-set, and of all the ways of doing things that are concomitant.*'

'*And you, friend, are a proponent of the exercise. Is that the best you can say?*'

'*Well, I'm a Libran. See both sides of the question. You know: can't take a decision.*'

'*So* that's *why you are the Chairman of a nationalized industry!*'

'*It's the other way round, Joe. It's because Chairmen of nationalized industries aren't allowed to take decisions that there's a top-secret Whitehall committee searching for Librans.*'

'*That's all I need — to hear that Whitehall bases the whole thing on astrology.*'

'*What's wrong with astrology? Look here: it's had a cultural influence for five thousand years, and sixty percent of people can't resist 'consulting the stars' in their newspapers. In my book that gives astrology quite as much credibility as the Church, for instance.*'

'*One could say that astrology offers a long-standing paradigm.*'

'*— And managerial cybernetics offers a short-standing paradigm.*'

'*I don't think I* like *paradigms.*'

'*You can't afford them, but you can't avoid them.*'

'Even so, Tony, if the best you can do is to compare the cybernetic paradigm with the astrological paradigm, I don't think you're making much of a scientific case.'

'Ever heard of Newton? — Sir Isaac of that ilk? He had a lifetime's interest in astrology.'

'Well, that was hundreds of years ago.'

'So what? A great scientist. He overthrew a paradigm with his Principia. *Yet he was also prepared to question the rationalist paradigm that said 'astrology is bunk'. Must say I'd like to have known what his view of cybernetics would have been.'*

'Do either of you know what happened when the bright young scientist — I think it was Halley, no less, of Halley's Comet — upbraided Newton for his consideration of astrology?'

'No, I don't.'

'Nor I.'

'Well, Halley said: 'how can a great scientist possibly take such rubbish seriously?' The Establishment people often pose the same question about cybernetics.'

'Newton was Establishment enough. What did he reply?'

'He said: 'because I have studied the subject.'.'

... and plans

Cohesiveness is the primary characteristic of organization.

This fact derives from the very purpose of organization which, as was seen earlier, exists to contain the variety proliferation that arises from the uninhibited interaction of the elements of a system. In breaking down that interaction, the process of organizing itself creates a problem of fragmentation which only its capacity to provide cohesion can offset.

Hence any model of organization that we may adopt must exhibit a mode of cohesion: it is possible to identify the 'glue' whereby the parts that the model postulates hang together.

The hierarchical paradigm, by its delegation of authority and demand for an antithetic accountability, uses the resulting chain of dependencies as its 'glue'. Even when allowance is made for the horizontal linkages that often indicate cohesion between units at the same hierarchical level, there is — in the long run — no other 'glue' than dependency. Because the basis of horizontal linkage is a cross-over point occurring at a *higher* hierarchic level, form which units that are said to be functionally linked are all dependent. The dependency of each from the common cross-over point at a higher level (even if this point is the box of the ultimate boss himself) is invoked to prescribe the need for liaison. It does not normally arise naturally, since each unit at the same level is basically competitive rather than collaborative with the others. In practice, the liaison arises because the higher level authority is 'knocking those heads together' lower down.

This authoritarian 'glue' is nothing to the purpose in the paradigm of managerial cybernetics. It was made very clear in the chapters on Freedom and Constraint; and the recursive models elucidated in the last chapter show that the process of embedding could not rely upon authority for its 'glue'. In this model, the 'glue' is the recursive logic itself. Yet it is fair to ask what is the practical reality, the translation of recursive logic in managerial terms. Well:

recursive logic is a *process*. So its managerial embodiment must be a process too, rather than any such static bonding as dependency. It seems that this process is none other than PLANNING.

Many a treatise has been written about planning; but I do not know of any that contends that it is actually the 'glue' of organizational cohesion. However, treatises on planning usually assume from the beginning that planning is an activity carried out by professionals called planners, that this activity results in products called plans, and that these plans will then be either implemented or not by those in authority. (Please reflect for a moment: is that not indeed the common belief?) Then however much may have been said to the contrary, and much has been vehemently said, there is a cognitive gap between the common belief and the reality that leads to planning as organizational 'glue'. It is not so much a gap, as a chasm. We must try to cross it.

There are two points that a number of real thinkers have been making about planning for many, many years.

The first is that planning is a *continuous process*. This notion conflicts violently with the stereotype of a plan based on the next month, the next year, the next five years, or 'the year 2000'. Nature does not have a calendar, except insofar as the primroses will surely appear where I happen to live next February. The primroses have to do with a systemic cycle that is nowhere reflected in the affairs of business or government. Especially it is not reflected in arbitrary time epochs as decided by administrative convenience.

It is surely evident that some events are more predictable than others. Suppose that I set a kettle on the fire, sit down beside it with a crystal ball, and then solemnly declare: this kettle will shortly boil. No-one will be terribly impressed. If I were to say: you have confronted the unions, offering them two choices — knowing that neither is conceivably acceptable to them — and I have seen in my crystall ball that there is going to be a strike, then that is not very impressive either. To say that solar energy will replace other forms of energy by year 2000 *is* impressive: but you may not believe it. To say that world governments are being secretely manipulated by extra-galactic powers is even more impressive; but you are even less likely to believe that. There is, in short, a continuum of prediction, set against a continuum of probability. In attempting to *plan,* we engage in a continuous process. The continuity arises from the constant readjustment of rational expectations against shifting scenarios — in circumstances where some sorts of expectation are more rational than others, and some sorts of scenario are more credible than others. But *plans* are supposedly set across the board — on which all expectations are equally rational, and all scenarios are equally credible. Only thus is there any meaning (never mind sense) in chopping up future time into planning epochs.

Any such assumption is false. Not only is there no logical validity in the entailed premises that everything develops at the same pace, or with the same degree of likelihood, but there is no chronological validity in the notion that epochs are somehow marked out to notify the requisite changes that would denote any need for managerial action.

For these reasons, most of the planning systems that may be inspected are nonsensical, on the preliminary ground that they do not relate to a *continuous process*. And the specific conclusion is that their use of arbitrary time epochs is absurd. That is because some features of the projected system are, like boiling kettles, virtually certain to reach a specific state next Thursday; while other features may or may not attain to a specific state by the year 2000. Then, if this is so, let us remember that global systems are extremely complex, and that we have no idea how the probable boiling kettles and the improbable extra-galactic intelligences will interact. Perhaps those people can *stop* a kettle from boiling. If so, I predict that it will not be in the year 2000, but in the year 2001 — on the 25th September, if that is interesting. It is much more interesting to anyone who adopts these ridiculous 'planning tools' (as most people do), to know that this particular prophet expects to be dead by then, and to note what a convenience his own death must be to any long-range forecaster.

Secondly: just as most people really do imagine that it is in principle possible to forecast and to plan in the above sense, so they also believe that plans are products of advisory groups that are submitted to competent authorities for decision. But this is equally ridiculous. The main arguments against the idea were set out in Chapter Nine, when we discussed the proper role of System Four, and they will not be reiterated now. What needs to be reiterated is that planning happens only when there is an act of decision. This act commits resources now, so that the future may be different from what would otherwise have simply happened to us.

It follows that the only planners are managers, namely those people who are entitled to commit resources. And it follows from the preceeding argument that this must be done (that is to say adjusted) continuously — because rational expectations and probable scenarios are both constantly changing, so that the decision taken yesterday is very probably and ostentatiously wrong today. More information has arrived, and 'information is what changes us'.

Out of these two arguments, it seems to me, emerges a third. It is that plans must continually abort. Produce a plan, dated so-and-so, which has today been implemented in every detail, and you will see a stupid action. This is just because more information must have become available since the so-and-so date and today. There is nothing more hair-raising than to see an implemented plan — unless it is to see honours and awards heaped on the idiots who went through with it.

This is a strong contention. But if the reader wants evidence, he needs only to look around him. The tribute to Sir Christopher Wren in St. Paul's Cathedral in the City of London does indeed say: *si monumentum requiris, circumspicere* — 'if you want a monument, look around you'. I do not deny the achievement, nor do I deny the movingly poetic quality of the memento. I do not deny the supreme technological glory of the aeroplane Concorde, nor do I deny its aesthetic appeal. But from the point of view of 'planning', of enshrining the plan of yesteryear in the practical reality of a different today, it has to be noted that Concorde loses a great deal of money for every mile; and it has to be noted that the dome of St. Paul's would have collapsed without the last-minute emergency action that put a vast chain around its circumference to hold it together. The argument is not against St. Paul's or against Concorde: people may argue for or against such projects as they will. The argument is to say that planning is a continuous act of adaptive decision that continually aborts. If it were not so, the cathedral would have fallen down, and Concorde would not have flown into New York. The pay-off to civilization of either is a matter of debate over a glass of beer; the notions of planning involved in both are matters of simple fact.

So planning is *not* an activity carried out by professionals called planners; it is an act of decision carried out by managers empowered to commit resources to a different future. Planning is *not* an activity resulting in products called plans: it is a continuous process, whereby the process itself — namely that of aborting the plans — is the pay-off. The plans do *not* have to be implemented or not by those in authority: what the authority **does** constitutes the plan — and its realization.

With this analysis of the planning activity, we are well-placed to consider what — if anything — all this has to do with the 'glue' of organizational cohesion. Well, the fact is that the endless flux of the planning *process,* undertaken by *managers,* and constantly *aborted* by their own *decisions,* is the reality of management. The rest is illusion. To sit behind a big solid oak door, at a big desk, on an expensive carpet, is to play a role. To deliver rulings, as if one were God himself, is neither here nor there (except to those who are ruled for or against). But to partake in the continuous managerial process of aborting decisions — that is to direct the company. It is to plan. And in that planning process the manager dispenses the cohesive 'glue'. The institution hangs together because, and only because, plans are constantly aborting — and, in so doing, realizing the actuality called profit and loss, success and failure, reward and punishment, happiness and misery, and (in the long run for the viable system) life and death.

Insofar as this has not been understood, and insofar as people have so often considered (and written about) planning as an activity in its own right — replete with a modus operandi that is conceived as separate from the business of managing, nonsensical rituals have evolved. Managers and ministers, being far from stupid, are aware of this; but they are impotent, because there is no credible way of denying that 'we ought to plan'. And if planning *means* to engage in such rituals, then there is no escape for them. Thus managers and ministers become helplessly entangled in immensely high-variety estimations about performance in future epochs that have been arbitrarily selected, well-knowing that their effort will be wasted. They know this from experience. They have found that the attempt to plan consists mainly in rationalizing and updating plans that are being constantly falsified by unfolding history.

To avoid all this means recognizing planning as a continuous process within the viable system embedded in a viable system; and now we have the recursive logic available to make clear how this is possible. We also have the tool of variety engineering with which to examine the cybernetic validity of the activity. Then, taking a fresh diagram that is an abstract from the previous ones (that is to say, all the missing parts are presumed to be there), the examination can begin. Unfortunately, it has to begin somewhere — although it could begin anywhere: a continuous process is a total loop, however complicated. In short, and naturally, the planning process involves organizational *closure*. Then do not be misled into supposing that the starting point has any special status; we could have ended with what follows just as well. The commentary relates to Figure 57.

Consider System Three of Recursion x. It is concerned to know what is going on in System One, its operational elements. It knows about this on its central axis of information, where the report is 'all is well' as viewed against the criteria currently in force, to be sure. But System Three also wants to know about the intentions formulating in System One as to inventing its future and accommodating incipient change in its local environment. This is not an appropriate question to launch on the command axis, which would instantly be overloaded with variety (and this is precisely what happens in most organizations). To make high-variety interrogations of the operational elements, one must go to the operations that are generating variety — to the circles (by arrangement with the square management boxes, of course). Now the data generated on emerging from the circle is part of the information that the System One management itself exacts from its own operation, and it is being filtered *and* attenuated at the regulatory centre appropriate to each System One. So what is System One's activity in this, and why should System Three intervene?

System One (we were speaking of Recursion x) is the whole viable system of Recursion y. Its system Three wants to know about the intentions formulating in System One as to inventing the future and accommodating change in its local environment ... of course, one may now repeat the remainder of the previous paragraph. Even so, the data being collected and shaped into information for the one purpose is not the same as for the other purpose. This must be the case, because the perspectives of the management box in the centre of the diagram are different when it is behaving in the horizontal domain as the metasystem Five-Four-Three of an operational element, and when it is behaving in the vertical domain as System One of the next higher level of recursion. We have seen the truth of this in many ways during the building of the recursive theory. But in particular, each Recursion y totally lacks the synoptic view of the whole System One of Recursion x, which they together constitute: so this is why System Three must intervene.

To what end, then, is the intervention, given that the command axis is not in use, and that therefore nothing is to be done to attenuate the variety of System One? For a start, it is clear that no uniform planning rubric can be imposed. This would very seriously impair the autonomy of the System One management, whose own needs (horizontal) are quite different from the needs of the metasystem (vertical) — a fact that will become much clearer by the completion of this examination. Despite this conclusion, it is normal practice to impose a planning rubric in the supposed interests of homogeneous planning across the institution. It is with this mistake, in my observations at least, where the troubles already mentioned usually start: there is a mismatch between the two roles of System One, and the resulting perception of itself (and its plans) is not the same as the metasystem's perception of it (and its plans).

Now the intervention that these arguments have so far allowed is solely that of requesting the operational circle to generate data. What data, if there is to be no rubric? The first position (which will be modified later) is that 'you ought to know what data are to be generated, because it is *your* purpose (not ours) to project to the metasystem an accont of your intentions — so that they may be approved and funded. We in System Three are concerned with the allocation of resources, remember; so make sure we understand your case'. Please suspend disbelief in this over-simplification until the end of the examination.

System One has its warning here. It knows that it must generate more variety for *this* purpose that it needs for its metasystemic role in Recursion y. It has its own regulatory centre, which will filter the data into information for both purposes, and in the process attenuate the variety engendered for both regulatory loops — the horizontal and the vertical. It would be as dangerous to equate this with having two sets of plans, as it would be to have two sets of books; but it is perfectly right to expect the one plan to be projected in two different formats. In particular, we expect the Recursion y version to have much higher variety (because it has to supply requisite variety on the horizontal axis) than the Recursion x version — otherwise System Three will be unable to generate requisite variety to handle that variety. And this again conforms to observed facts in reviewing normal practice. Incidentally, the

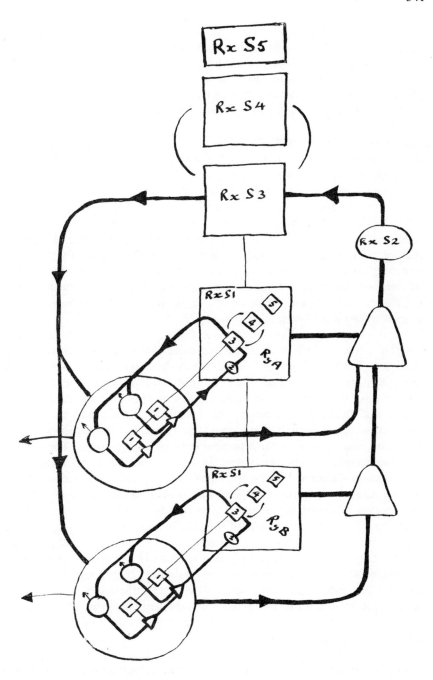

Figure 57.   The start of a planning model for Recursion *x*, showing the routes
of its interaction with Recursion *y*

lesser variety of the recursion x information is not simply a matter of aggregating numbers, so that 'the breakdown' is available in the other plan. Look back at the last figure: there are management boxes in System One of Recursion y, and the people in them have to be capable of implementing the plans. Handling this human problem (just as an example) injects variety into the horizontal plan — unless, for instance, it involves massive new recruitment or total retaining.

The plans now emerging in the vertical plane are being generated by different Systems One in different formats; and they are being forwarded by the regulatory centres to the corporate regulatory centre. Here further filtration will occur, so that the variety returned to System Three meets the first and second axioms of managerial requisite variety. The second of these axioms involves System Four, which we have not yet brought into the planning picture; and again it is needed to apologize for this necessarily step-by-step approach to a systemic continuum. For this is also the reason why it may not be clear why the plans are said to be moving via System Two, which is an anti-oscillatory device, rather than on the return loop of the channel which was chosen to begin the examination.

Well, it is now possible to say something more about the *continuous process* of planning. The planning loops delineated in the diagram and discussed above are meant to be *dynamic*. They do not stop or start; they are indeed continuous. It is difficult to understand how this may be, given that our managerial heads are cluttered with epochs, horizons, and last dates for submission, even though these unhelpful concepts were denounced at the beginning. But let us try. The argument is based on two points. The first arises from management cybernetics and its view of (all kinds of) measurement, discussed in Chapter Eleven. We look to a balancing process, operating against adaptive criteria, to operate according to Ashby's Law. Then 'to measure' is to detect instability in that process. So let it be with planning. Plans should not be created out of thin air, because when they are, they don't work. Plans are the embodiment of the intentions subscribed to at each level of recursion: since these intentions are constantly changing, and not in a homogeneous way with respect either to time or to probability (as we saw earlier), they must continually abort. The only characteristic worth detecting, measuring, reporting, or doing anything about, is incipient instability in the system.

Then what actually *is* the system? This invokes the second point, which is severely practical. Suppose yourself a manager, working within the orthodox framework of a planning rubric. Then you must have a staff 'working on the plan', collecting evidence, and struggling to meet the deadline for submission. What will they come up with, when you receive the draft? Will it be that your finance house should start building aircraft carriers, that your engineering company should start publishing pornography? No, it will not. Is there ever the *slightest* innovation that will totally surprise you? If there is, you are a thoroughly unapproachable person, and should put yourself on a course of some kind. Because your people are constantly checking-out with you, mostly in the most informal of ways. 'We know what the boss wants', they can be heard saying. What they mean is that they have a very clear idea by now what you will and will not stand for. After all, is this not true of you and *your* boss? You move across to his table, where he sits alone at the coffee pot. 'Syd', you say, 'I've been thinking ... .' Soon you will know whether to keep at it, or to stop thinking quite those thoughts.

All of this *is* the planning system. It goes round and round the delineated loop in a basically informal fashion. And then it becomes enshrined in documents, because someone needs a signature, or security demands a record. These documents are free of surprises: if not, someone has made a bad psychological error. Institutions really run like this, and it is high time that the 'planning system' be drafted to recognize the fact. There is one huge and important exception, it seems to me, in this contention, and that is the institution called the State. The general public are daily shattered to hear that some plan or other has been 'adopted by the government'. The man-in-the-street had not an inkling that any such idea was in the air. As to why this should be an exception, I will have a guess. It is because the State does not know that the public is the Boss. If it did, it would be as circumspect as the rest of us.

In order to see more clearly how this 'continuous loop' works in any particular institution, it should be helpful to introduce a new diagram. I have found it impossible to show this much detail on the basic model, but the labelling should make clear what is happening. Note: we now lose altogether the layout of the different vertical domains, which need to be understood with reference to the viable system model itself. In particular, we lose the routing via System Two.

On this new diagram, Figure 58, the impetus so far discussed begins at point A. The jogging of System One, to fulful its obligations to the metasystem *and* to itself, is registered at point B, and this provokes enquiry at point C. The enquiry causes Recursion *y* to change state: so that is the meaning of the vertical line and the new dot, accompanied by a tiny arrow. Information has arrived, and 'it changed us'. The results of this adjustment return to point D, where again this represents the receipt of information. So, after changing state, the loop returns; whereupon there is another change of state, and point E returns the message to point F. Thence we return to point B — and the process is continuous. Now all of this is best regarded as a Recursion *y* phenomenon: that is the loop B-C-D-E-F-B.

The new diagram is as yet incomplete. But because a double, interacting, loop has been *closed,* we are ready to resolve one mystery, and to comment on another.

Since there are several operational elements comprising System One, there will be several points Y in the System Three space. This situation will be modelled later. Meanwhile, however, it is apparent that the repetition of this diagram several times (on behalf of all Systems One), and the generation of several points Y *which do not map onto each other* (why should they? The subsystems generating them are autonomous), coupled with the fact of continuous interaction on all several loops, means that oscillation will inevitably settle into the total System One. At least, that must be the expectation, unless System Three **forces** all points Y to occupy the same position. It could do so by ukase: orders issued on the command axis. But this is (cybernetically) forbidden. Then *this* is the full explanation as to why System Two is the X to Y channel: it exists to damp oscillation. And of course it can do so by using its own double loop to the Systems One, without diminishing managerial variety, but simply by agreeing the meaning of the conventions used by their low-variety planning formats in the vertical plane. This is not as ominous as it sounds. Remember that the whole process is continuous; there is plenty of time to converge on linguistic conventions. On no account should System Two issue a book of rules — (a) because there is no need for a *uniform* language, but only a need for System Two to speak *all* the languages of System One: (b) because any such manoeuvre would be perceived as the introduction of a planning rubric on the command axis. This resolves the mystery of the use of System Two.

The second mystery involves the uncharacteristically simplistic 'suspension of disbelief' at the start of the examination, which said (in effect) that System One could tell System Three whatever it liked about its intentions. Well, so it should: it is autonomous. But, in a viable system, it must not be robbed of feedback. When B 'first' received the message from A (just as if there ever was or could be a first time), it could do as it liked. A was taken to be an innocent enquirer. But now that the double loop is closed, A does not look so innocent at all. Every point marked is influencing every other point marked to change its state — because of **information** (not edict). And that certainly includes A's effect on B, via the double loop. Do not, pray, sourly call this authoritarianism in disguise. Notice, rather, the cohesive 'glue'.

The examination must now make a fresh start, since the double loop is closed. The start already made was at an arbitrary place, it was admitted; but it came about from my own preference to discuss autonomy — freedom if you will — whereby System One (or the whole Recursion *y*) should have its full variety available to *manage,* accepting only the constraint that cohesion must be maintained within the purposes of the viable system. A whisper of such constraint was discovered in the feedback from A to B; but that is no more

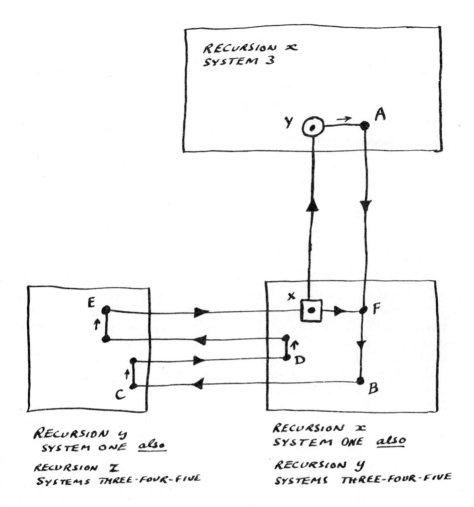

Figure 58. The continuous planning process that provides cohesive 'glue' between two levels of recursion at their intersect

menacing than the man with the coffee pot in my example. The cybernetics of this seems sufficiently protective. What cannot be allowed for, by any such routine treatment whatsoever, are the human and cultural factors in the ambience of which the viable system seeks to maintain itself. If you *know* that to ignore the slightest hint from the coffee-drinking boss means dismissal, you have to accept that in your planning (or you leave the enterprise, which — if possible — is a better idea). And if the ambient culture consists of patrols armed with machine guns, then again: *sauve qui peut*. Management cybernetics can readily discuss such situations, in any particular implementation, by the simple expedient of examining higher levels of recursion. From the insights gained, it may be possible to see how to change the boss. On the other hand, it may not. But you cannot knock out a machine gun post with a few accurate words, however insightful. All this is the human condition, and you can kill a cybernetician as easily as a yogi. But a richer understanding of the systemic character of the viable system, and its recursive embedments, in which any particular set of human factors constitute a major problem cannot possibly make the situation any worse.

Turning to the fresh start: whoever supposed that planning theory should begin with System Four has got a case. Then the next diagram (Figure 59) will model the planning activity of the metasystemic managerial activity that deals with the outside and the future. Given Figure 58, the new diagram is stark in its originality! Please take comfort in the value subscribed to the economical handling of variety in this isomorphic mapping of Figure 58 onto Figure 59; but contemplate the labels and the explanation with more care.

It is the primary task of System Four to interrogate the outside world of the whole institution of which it is System Four (and not of some other Recursion: a very common error), and if possible to invent that institution's future. It cannot possibly do this properly by the mere aggregation of the development plans of the constrained viable systems at all lower levels of recursion, because *this* level of recursion is a different beast. The topological diagrams of the last chapter make this fact abundantly clear. Secondly, we should remember from earlier discussions that the nature of the interrogations undertaken by System Four into a problemmatic domain is different from that of System Three, despite the isomorphism of their respective diagrams — which comes about because of the need for logical closure, and the need for reiterative enquiry.

The diagram at Figure 59 is marked as Recursion x, because that is the focus. But since it does not (as it stands) involve another level of recursion, being contained within itself, it represents any level of recursion at all: it is a statement about part of the metasystem of any viable system.

Given the preceding explanation of the topology, there is no need to label all the points. Starting arbitrarily at point M, we find System Four addressing the unknown. There are many ways of doing this, and they were commented upon in Chapter Nine. What matters to us now is that in completing the complicated loop from M to N, and round again on the horizontal axis continually, many changes of state will be induced — both in System Four itself, because of the learning process, and also in the putative environment. This latter expectation may sound odd, unless the name 'Heisenberg' is instantly recognizable. The great physicist showed that to examine, to measure, to interrogate, something changes its state. And this is even true of that which is yet to be, because what is yet to be is conditioned by its present. Those who recognize the word 'karma' will also understand. But to the manager who has interests in neither

RECURSION x

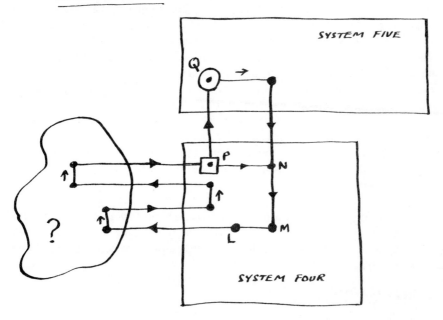

Figure 59. The continuous planning process whereby Systems Four and Five are 'glued' together in any one recursion

physics nor vedantic philosophy, it is necessary to say only: think it through in terms of a practical example. If a company with no interests in electronics begins a System Four activity, however discreetly, that indicates a potential interest in electronics, then the whole state of any future market that links this company with all electronic concerns will change. (Having once done just this, I could write a book about the effects.) It is obvious. Thus the horizontal loop, in this case M via P and N back to M, is not only present, not only continuous: it operates at a high metabolic rate. Or it certainly should, in a rapidly changing environment. That is not to say that rapid change inside the institution is inevitable; it is to say that since such rapid change *might* be urgently demanded, the System Four consciousness of that institution must be extremely alert and active. Look around: the first System Four you meet probably is not. Most probably it is engaged in overlording the System Four activities at lower levels of recursion, imagining that this is its function.... .

Now obviously System Five will wish to be aware of the activities of System Four, because the latter's perception and presentation of the putative future should have a profound effect on policy (*real* policy, that is: not internal edicts masquerading as policy). Then P goes to Q in a continuous way, in the mode of 'sounding out', just as happened between Systems One and Three. And in that same mode, Q then changes state, and modifies its input to M. M, in turn changes state — not because System Four has received instructions from System Five, but because it has received information. That statement presupposes that System Five has access to data that are not flowing on the horizontal loop of System Four, and that it is also capable of converting such data into Five-type information. It is necessary to wait for a few pages to see how it does this, just as we are still waiting to see how System Three manages to add anything in providing feedback to System One. The mechanisms are wholly different, but the cybernetic need is the same. But before we can perceive a planning closure for the whole viable system, it is necessary to close the gap between System Three and System Four. In order to examine this, a revolutionary diagram is necessary; but it will not prove difficult to master if you lie on your side.

The next part of the examination, then, based on Figure 60, picks up point L in System Four as depicted in the previous diagram. This point L was not mentioned in the description; but it is obviously a point of access to the closed double loop just considered.

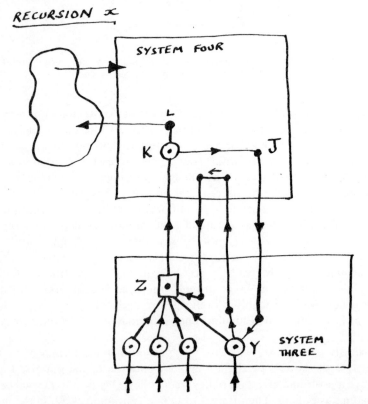

Figure 60. Closure of the Three-Four loop conceived as a continuous planning process

It has long been established that there has to be a powerful balancing arrangement between Systems Three and Four. The Second Axiom declares that their respective varieties are equivalent. Moreover, the four Principles of Organization apply to the above arrangement. The diagram offers a minimal explanation as to how these conditions are fulfilled insofar as planning is concerned.

Whatever System Four understands, at any given moment, about its institution's posture towards its external environment and its potential future is accessible at point L. Whatever System Three understands about these same attitudes as expressed by any System One is accessible at point Y. Then, in order to meet the cybernetic criteria listed just now, the information available at point L is passed (through points K and J) to point Y. The information accessible at point Y is passed to System Four, thereby causing a change of state, and asjusted information returns to System Three at point Z — following a change of state in System Three. The feedback loop from Z in Three to K in Four closes the Three-Four loop. The feedback from J in Four to Y in Three closes the Four-Three loop. And the whole loop, having been closed, operates continuously.

There is a complication. Several other 'Y' points, originating in the several other operational elements of System One, must be taken into account. (Three others are shown in the diagram, on a line with Y itself.) Since all Y points are created from information supplied *via* the filtration of System Two, we can assume that they are not in mutual oscillation. They do, however, represent quite different operations, therefore they are shown separately. The point Z provides their synthesis, as their synergy is understood by System Three. And so we see (on the diagram) that the channel Z to K needs to carry all the variety of each of the Y double loops, plus the variety of the K synthesis itself, *plus* the variety added to the loop from point L which is affecting the entire process. (Remember here the Second Principle of Organization, as to channel capacity, and the Third, as to transduction.)

The demands on the Three-Four stabilizing system are formidable. It might be wondered whether it is necessary for System Four to receive the total variety of every System One as represented (and therefore already System Two filtered) at all points Y, as well as the synergistic variety of System Three as represented by point Z. According to the cybernetic criteria, the answer is unfortunately yes. The Four-Five double loop, recently examined, is continuously producing new information at point L — which may affect each Y loop in a different fashion. Although System Three is capable of creating the synergistic statement at Z on behalf of information arising from System One, it is in no position to evaluate the impact of System Four information, arising at point L, on each of them separately. The whole of the interaction just described (which, in the diagram, should properly repeat the double loop shown three more times) is in the grip of the Second Axiom, that demands variety equivalance between Systems Three and Four.

There is moreover a reciprocal argument in the reverse direction. We know that there are several Y points in System Three, and may count them as equal to the number of operational elements in System One. But there are probably several points supporting K in System Four as well, which could be counted in a given situation. These differentiations of K would derive from a multiplicity of environmental loops (whereas we showed only one) directed towards different targets of opportunity in the outside and future. In that case, the point K shown would be the synergistic outcome of several L points. The reverse argument would then be that it is not enough for System Three to receive K information (which is developmentally synergistic) for each point Y. It would need feedback from *each* point L, to *each* point Y, as well as the synthesis represented by point K. The diagram is impossible to draw; but its huge variety equation is not surprising.

It is worth noting, in that light, that System Three is the fulcrum of the viable system. It represents (Three-Two-One) the synergy of the inside-and-now; it also represents the metasystem (Five-Four-Three) to the system. Thus the Three-Four balance is not only as crucial to viability as has been repeatedly argued, it is necessarily a very high variety interchange. We have now studied the cybernetic why and how of this; the practical consequences will be examined in another chapter.

It remains to connect the new 'planning' diagram together, and to supply one missing linkage, before the full conclusions can be drawn. The final picture, shown in Figure 61, which connects any two recursions called x and y (and therefore all recursions in successive pairs according to the Theorem of Recursion) is, as can be readily checked, a simple assembly of the preceeding diagrams — plus the addition of the omnipresent System Five loop that has not previously appeared. It is this that supplies the final closure in which System Five assumes its full role as the metasystem of the metasystem. This loop is shown in heavy lines, and will be properly traced through in words in a moment. But let us first rehearse the fact that what is now manifested is not the ultimate source of planning, despite all the 'metas' imputed to it by the logic. It is still right to think of planning as a continuous, dynamic, closed system (closed, yes, although closure moves its trajectory through all environments); thus it is still right to say that there is no beginning and no end, no superior and no inferior authority. But since we have to start and finish somewhere, it is still my preference to choose System One in that dual role. Please note, especially, that in Figure 61 only one operational element is shown in full, although inputs from three others are indicated. But suppose that there were (say) eight operational elements, and that all were shown in full, reproducing the lowest part of the diagram, the page would need to be three times its existing height; in that case the system would not look top-heavy in the metasystem, as it misleadingly does.

Even so, the metasystem Five-Four-Three is necessarily complicated; and the cybernetic laws that govern its requisite variety go beyond the three axioms already enunciated. This is because, although we have come to understand something about the cohesive 'glue' of the recursive viable system, we come only now to the complete evidence that supports the variety equation for cohesion itself. When the definitions were established, the contention was that autonomy should be passed to System One, and the command axis minimally used, consistently with maintaining *cohesion* of the viable system: it must not fly apart. But the variety equation that would govern inter-recursion cohesiveness was not obviously in sight at that time; and that was because the recursive logic displayed in this and the previous chapter was not yet fully available. (A rereading of this book would surely make evident the fact that the Law to which we are leading up could have been stated, though perhaps not clearly understood, much earlier.) Then let us approach the end of this examination with these needs in mind. To understand cohesion well in cybernetic terms is most important, because it governs the question of **identity** in the viable system, and because its practical application is potentially valuable. To explain this latter belief, let me explain that I started searching for the Law of Cohesion some ten years ago in bizarre circumstances. As the director of System Four in an international corporation, I suddenly discovered that the divisional chairman of a vast division (a System One) was secretly moving to *sell* his division. Autonomy is one thing, but... .

Looking at the assembled diagram of planning, Figure 61, which might have been entitled 'the regulation of the totality of intentions in order to maintain cohesion according to the purposes of the institution', we see that the double loops connecting Z in Three and K in Four are high-variety balancing devices. The mechanism is there: high-variety L inputs to K, high-variety Y inputs to Z. The cybernetic facts are there: they exhibit the second axiom of managerial requisite variety. Thanks to this axiom, we expect the balancing of Three-Four to work, and we have spoken of the need for System Five to handle the 'residual variety'. This means that System Five must be able to detect instability in the Three-Four loop. That necessity is embodied in the third axiom. If this is all that System Five has to do in order to monitor the Three-Four loop, it will not be overloaded with data flowing from the balancing device — so long as instability does *not* set in. The expected message is 'I'm all right.'

Despite this, there is a profound problem in designing a System Five regulator that will preserve cohesion. System Five must have *requisite variety,* even if it manipulates few data. Without a measure of variety that matches the interactive variety in Three-Four, System Five cannot (by definition) understand what that interaction is about, cannot set the criteria of stability for the loop, and therefore cannot detect instability. Amplification of variety from Three activities and Four activities would in principle solve the problem: but this will not work, because System Five does not have sufficient variety to assimilate the almost infinite number of possible states of the Three-Four interaction in real time. Indeed, Three and Four are set to absorb each other's variety for precisely this reason.

The resolution of this difficulty is to be found in a cybernetic discovery that has already been noted and discussed (namely the Conant-Ashby Theorem). Every regulator contains a model of whatever is regulated. This *model* must have requisite variety. If it had less variety than the system under regulation, that system could undertake activities that were incomprehensible to the regulator. *Model* is italicized, because it must not be confused with the variety in the information that happens to be flowing. For example, your son may perhaps start taking drugs. If you are not alert to this possibility, and if you cannot recognize the symptoms, your regulatory model does not dispose requisite variety — even if the symptoms are never presented. And if your son never engages in drug-taking, you will not be inundated with data.

System Five, then, must necessarily contain *models* of System Three and Four — answering to the criterion of requisite variety. To continue with examples: if System Three is talking about the plant in Medicine Hat, System Five needs to know that the company has such a plant. Moreover, it needs to know enough about that plant to give meaning to System Three's statements about it. That involves requisite variety: even if the only message ever received says 'we just sold it'. And if System Four starts talking about the potentialities of micro-telepathy, what then? Is System Five supposed to be omniscient? Certainly not; but System Four will have to ensure that requisite variety is added to the Five model that will absorb this micro-telepathic variety — before it begins to inject data concerning the potentialities of micro-telepathics.

The System Three and Four models that System Five must needs contain are shown in Figure 61 in mini-boxes marked 3* and 4*. The interaction between the real Systems Three and Four is also modelled in System Five. It is noted on the diagram by the double arrows that were earlier associated with the real Systems Three and Four; and the balance that betokens stability is marked in a small circle between them. Then the learning experience of stability and instability undergone by System Five can be thought of as stored in that small circle. Meanwhile the actual state of the Three-Four balance at all times is informing the models held in System Five; because there is direct input from Z in Three to model 3*, and from P in Four to model 4*.

Now the store of learned experience held in System Five about the balancing behaviour of Three-Four, together with any current tendency towards

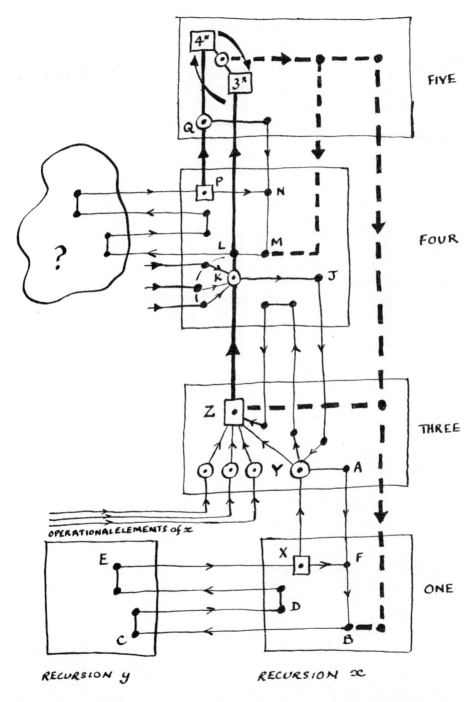

Figure 61. The definitive model of the planning process that provides closure (and therefore cohesive 'glue') between two recursions of the viable system

instability, creates the policy ethos pertaining in System Five. The feedbacks (marked with heavy dotted lines) pervade the whole viable system with this ethos. As before (compare the argument about the response from A to B, or from J to Y), these feedbacks are not instructions. The word 'ethos' relates to the constant interactions that occur between System Five and everyone else, continually. The ethos provides implied answers to the questions that people are asking (from their quite different perspectives) at M in Four, Z in Three and B in One. These questions are not requests for permission; they are of the form 'is this idea a starter?' The implied answers are received via the continual closure of the total (heavy print) loop. For once the implied answers are linked into the double loops that are made accessible at points M, Z, and B, their *variety* is injected into the whole system via three filters — and continuously flows, re-emerging as part of the variety reaching its own 4*-3* model. This is not information of which we speak, but variety. The injection may add to or subtract from the variety generated within the subsystems. It has the effect of encouragement or admonition, of reinforcement or depletion. And because it **returns,** in whatever 'mixture' with internally generated variety, a built-in tendency for System Five to converge on stable policies is exhibited.

The full diagram provides a dynamic model for cohesion, including (as has just been seen) a cohesion-conducing, positive-feedback, mechanism. Then let us search for the variety equation that supports this cohesiveness in the following way.

(i) The variety of the whole metasystem under discussion, which was conceived as the metasystem of Recursion *x,* is *also* the variety of the System One management box that it constitutes in Recursion *w.*

(ii) We know (First Principle of Organization) that the variety of any System One management box tends to equate with the variety of its operational circle and in turn with the variety of its perceived environment.

(iii) We also know (First Axiom of Management) that the sum of vertical variety equals the sum of horizontal variety, as presented at System Three.

(iv) It follows that the sum of the variety disposed by all the metasystems of Recursion *x* is equal to the System One variety accessible to System Three of Recursion *w.*

(v) If this relation holds between the recursively successive pair *w* and *x,* then (because of the isomorphic mapping) it holds between any other such pair, for instance *x* and *y.*

Thus, using Recursion x as focus, we may state

The Law of Cohesion for Multiple Recursions of the Viable System:

The System One variety accessible to System Three of Recursion x = the variety disposed by the sum of the metasystems of Recursion y.

There is a very important point to note about this law; and it applies also to the axioms that were stated earlier. The variety balances that have been expressed as equalities (to make clear the notion of balance) require some *extra* variety, which is called redundancy, to deal with noise in the system. Let us suppose that we could measure cohesiveness, as defined by the law that has just been stated, by an index labelled C. Then we should find that

$$\frac{dC}{dt} > 0$$

It is this fact that makes the viable system not only cohesive, but *self-organizing*.

To some, this statement may well look trivial, and to others incomprehensible. But 'he who has ears to hear, let him hear'. What I have said is due to the cybernetic discoveries of Heinz von Foerster, and their explication to me by Gordon Pask. It is necessary to make these two attributions.

We come now to the expectation mentioned before that a second reading of this book would reveal that the Law of Cohesion was implied before its formal elucidation here. In fact, it is an implicit consequence of the First Axiom. However, it seemed necessary to take our fences one by one. The First Axiom is explicitly concerned with cohesion inside any one viable system. That is to say, it is addressed to the inexorable operation of Ashby's Law within a single level of recursion. It is an important result in understanding the cybernetics of *the* viable system, with the characteristics of which we were primarily concerned in parts One and Two of the book.

However, we have also to wrestle with the recursiveness of the viable system model. Consider paragraph (iii) of the above demonstration; then consider paragraph (i). The Law of Cohesion was logically entailed all along. But it seemed maladroit to focus attention on the cohesiveness of multiple recursions at the moment when attention was primarily directed to a single recursion — a moment, moreover, before the full account of the recursive model had been given, as it has been given in these two chapters.

A final point ought to be made, in the light of this explanation, about the choice of terms in which to discuss the discoveries that our explorations have made. Recently in the text we have chosen to call the viable system to which we were primarily attending: Recursion x. It is here that we find the three Axioms of Management, so-called. Axioms are statements 'worthy of belief'. In the viable systems contained by Recursion x, which belong to Recursion y, we find the four Principles of Organization, so-called. Principles are serious matters too: 'primary sources of particular outcomes'. Of course, those four principles apply to all loops in every recursion; but they were unfolded on the 'horizontal axis' of Recursion x that became Recursion y. When we come to the embedment of Recursion z in w, of w in v, and so on indefinitely, the concept of cohesion becomes outstandingly important. That is why it is dignified as a Law, so-called. Perhaps that could be described as 'something invariant in nature'; although the *caveats* that could be entered on that would fill many pages.

It is easy to imagine a group of philosophers of science dining out on their disagreements about these distinctions. It is easy, also, when armed with a copy of the Oxford English Dictionary, to defend the use of any of these terms in any of these senses. I believe all eight propositions that I have enunciated in this book to be **facts** about the management of variety in those viable systems that we call enterprises. The choice of three different terms was decided upon as a matter of expository convenience.

LATER IN THE BAR...

'Why haven't we been given any names for all the forms of planning that are involved in all these loops?'

'Probably because there are too many names flying about already. No-one agrees on their definitions. And what do names matter anyway? They're just labelling devices.'

'That's true: it's more important to understand the processes that go on. But we need ways to refer to the various bits and pieces.'

'Why not just refer to, say, 'System Five's role in planning'? That's a better reference than a label, because it has much more variety than a term with no agreed definition.'

'I don't know: System Five's planning role is clearly normative. It says what the top direction reckons should be done. Hence — Normative Planning.'

'If that's so, System Four's planning role speaks about what can be done. It surveys opportunities, without saying that they should be done — something deferred to System Five — or that they will be done. Call that Development Planning.'

'Who says what will be done?'

'Obviously, within the existing organization, System Three does that. That's where the action is. No planning is involved: just get on with it.'

'But the book of words says that planning IS action — nothing else. So why shouldn't System Three be planning? It's right there at the fulcrum of all the loops.'

'Doesn't mean to say that System Three is planning. It looks more like switching to me.'

'But switching, by definition, is selective. The whole account implies that the moderating of planning concepts is achieved by a continuous... negotiation is probably the word.'

'Then there must be a strategy behind the negotiation — and then the switching.'

'Well, everyone talks about Strategic Planning: maybe that's it. System Three needs a strategy to generate all the feedbacks, upwards and downwards, that this fulcrum role entails.'

'You can't call that 'strategy'. As an ex-Army man, I would unhesitatingly put Strategic Planning into System Five. It stands for the grand conduct of the war.'

'Oh no it doesn't. System Five in a war concerns moral imperatives — such as do we have a war in the first place, do we continue it... It was right to call System Five's role normative. Strategy is the function of the generals, who work within normative rules.'

'It ought to be. But many generals go beyond that.'

'Then they are calling themselves part of System Five — as they often manage to be.'

'And what if System Five in a war stops being purely normative, and starts dictating strategy?'

'Then it is putting on a Three hat, that's all. It's often done. Look at Churchill in the Second World War. Look at Viet Nam.'

'The existence of power struggles at the top doesn't prevent our identifying who is playing which roles in the viable system.'

'Well, if strategy is indeed a System Three job, and System Three is concerned with the allocation of System One's resources, as we've been told, what is the 'strategic' element in that?'

'Oh — to find the best allocation. There are many more or less inefficient ways to allocate resources (we're not just talking about money, you know), and there is a most efficient way. The strategy incorporating all resources spread over time, has to determine that.'

'That's 'optimazation', man.'

'Then we'd better fill up System Three with mathematicians doing linear programmes.'

'Maybe they should be there; but I don't believe that mathematical optimization gives what Jim called 'the best' strategy.'

'Optimum is Latin for best.'

'Many thanks, David. Look: I've had quite an experience of optimization techniques, since I used to have an OR group in my division. The strategies we need are n-dimensional, since they have so many parameters, and it's very hard to envisage an optimal point in an n-dimensional space.'

'What the hell are you talking about?'

'Give me a chance to explain, Tom. Let's say that profit depends on sales volume. You could make a graph of that — two axes on a bit of paper.'

'Yes, but profit also depends on a great many other things.'

'Exactly. My point is that although you can graph each one separately against profit, the best stragey has to mix them all together and discover — through all their interactions — what is in fact best.'

'But we know all that. All you're saying is that profit is a mathematical function of a, b, c, d, etcetera, and we have to find its optimum. That's perfectly possible to a mathematician armed with a computer.'

'But that's not all I'm saying. OK — take a look at this — half a minute, while I tear this page out. Now I'm making this graph in two dimensions, on the supposition that we actually know the function that connects all the variables — now I'm asking you, Dick, where is the mathematical optimum?'

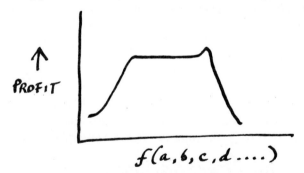

Figure 62.   Bar drawing of the relationship between profitability and some function (supposedly known) of some variables (supposedly known). What is *optimal?*

'It's the value of the function corresponding to that little peak on the end.'

'Yes. And if we go and perch ourselves on that, and if our information system makes the slightest mistake in measuring one of the variables belonging to the function, we'll as likely as not come sliding down that precipice to land with a thump at zero profit.'

'What's more, and far worse, is that the same catastrophe would follow if we didn't formulate the function correctly.'

'Speaking as a layman, I wouldn't buy that in any case. I'd want to be half-way along that plateau. Then a lot of mistakes could be made in information, or in formulation, but I'd still have a mix that made a respectable profit. You could keep your refinements.'

'Just my argument, Tom. No sane manager wants that extra half a percent profit at such a risk to his operation's stability.'

'There's that word again.'

'Sure: it's a key cybernetic notion. The 'best' strategy must include the stability of its own results.'

'Well, that's a meta-notion. But it seems to be right. That's why Chapter Eleven was arguing for measurements that picked up instabilities — it's beginning to sink in.'

'OK. So System Three finds the best strategy — continuously, I take it — for resource allocation, and we agree to call that Strategic Planning. Then who does the tactics?'

'System One. It's got its agreed plan, and now it works out its own tactical implementations.'

'Hen-er-y... you just dropped a level of recursion.'

'How so?'

'What System One does about its own planning is done on the horizontal axis — it's a Five-Four-Three function ut the next level of recursion.'

'So who do you reckon does tactical planning at this level of recursion — the one we've been discussing?'

'Well, I think it's System Two.'

'But it can't be. We've been warned over and over again that the concept of System Two should be limited to damping oscillatory behaviour. What's tactical planning got to do with anti-oscillation?'

'Didn't we just say that the best strategy is not the mathematical optimum, and that its criterion is its own stability? Then all we're worried about tactically is a *planning procedure that will continuously detect and damp down* instability. *System Two.'*

'Good God.'

'That's a conversation-stopper.'

'We're in difficulties because we're not used to this strange notion of what measurement in the system is really in aid of . . . '

'But we do have some units of measure, at least: actuality, capability, potentiality — and the indices arising therefrom: productivity and latency.'

'Yes. . . and, look it all fits. Strategic Planning in System Three (with its tactical planning offshoot in System Two) has to do with actuality. That's where constantly modifiable resource allocations are decided in line with what's actually *happening. Developmental Planning is a System Four function, dealing with what the organization is really* capable *of doing. And the Normative Planning of System Five is dealing in* potential *futures. Wow.'*

'It all sounds a bit too convenient to me.'

'You remind me of my eldest son Simon, Bill. If I'm making something at home, like a corner cupboard, and it all works out, he says: 'Gosh, what a stroke of luck!' I could kill him.'

'Well I can see a snag. Something has been worrying me ever since you said it, Peter, and now the penny's dropped. If Developmental Planning in System Four is about what the organization could *do . . . well, didn't you suggest, Peter, that this means to 'survey opportunities' (I think was your phrase) — meaning without committing resources, or deciding anything? And then if 'normative' means 'should', just as 'capable' means 'can', then the only decision-taker around here is the 'will' man in System Three. And this whole approach to planning says that it just isn't happening unless a decision is taken.'*

'Yes, I think I did say something like that. You're right, you know. There's a dreadful inconsistency here.'

'What rotten bureaucrats the pair of you are! You think that no decision is taken unless it's written on a form or somesuch!'

'How do you mean, Bob?'

'System Four is surveying opportunities — and so is System Five, although

they seem to be of a more ethical nature. What do you mean, 'surveying'? It can't possibly mean that people are just looking around and saying how interesting the scenery is. Seems to me you've forgotten the whole business of variety.'

'Oh, that again.'

'But it's the whole story. Think of an R & D manager. There is a virtually infinite variety to his possible projects — he could cook up a story to support practically any research. But he decides which to do, and which not. He chops out massive variety. You can't call that not making allocations of resources. And what's more, he's more likely to be continuously aborting his projects than any of you lot.'

'You're telling me. System Three makes the money, and System Four spends it.'

'Oh rubbish. Don't you remember the crack against that very phrase earlier in the book? It is in the nature of scientific research to get negative results. If the experiment was well designed, no negative result is ever wasted — again because it reduces the variety of ostensible alternatives.'

'But, even on your showing, and granted that Four and Five are really making planning decisions, it's all terribly airy-fairy, isn't it?'

'Of course it isn't. Those fellows are 'committing resources now that the future may be different', as the books says. Just now you were complaining about the money they spend.'

'Yes, but they spend it to reduce variety, you said. System Three spends money to do something positive, like building a plant. Who is controlling these blighters, I should like to know?'

'Now calm down fellow: your nasty experiences are getting on top of you. First you forget about variety and the regulation of complexity. Now you've forgotten the very chapter we're talking about. That big diagram builds up a picture of the way in which all subsystems of a viable system control each other.'

'All right: I'm not losing my hair. I suppose it might work. You're very silent, George, what do you think?'

'Well, I'm thinking that the whole contention is that this is how it does work, and trying to test that against my own outfit. We are using a lot of new words,

and — yes — I guess a new paradigm. So it needs reflection. But I don't think we're being told 'this is what you must do'. It isn't a prescription.'

'Then what's the point?'

'About understanding, I suppose. After all, we *have* to take the decisions in any case. You can't lay that responsibility on a book that's never even heard of you.'

'But there are plenty of management books that tell you exactly what to do.'

'Ah.'

'He's gone quiet again. Can anyone tell me how System Four in Recursion x organizes its relationship with System Four in Recursion y? Or isn't it allowed to?'

'That's in the diagram, surely. The lower level of recursion is shown on one side as a single box. I take that box to represent the lower recursion's System Four. Once that set of dynamic loops enters into Recursion x, it is totally implicated in the closed loops of its planning systems — or, if you like, that's exactly where the cohesive glue sticks.'

'The box indicating Recursion y isn't System Four on its own, or it would be marked as such. I think it stands for a reduplication of the whole planning system we've been discussing all evening.'

'Yes, that must be right. If you imagine the whole of the diagram reproduced in Recursion y, the cohesion gets very strong. I like it: it makes operational sense of the 'Chinese box' image of recursion.'

'Yet apparently it's too damned complicated to draw.'

'What would be gained by that? Real life *is* complicated; and this notion of embedding simplifies as neatly as realities allow. Don't forget that once we really understand the implications for any one recursion, we've understood the lot.'

'How do you know that?'

'Because the logic is the same. Each recursion maps isomorphically onto the next, remember? So if we get the System Four connexion clear — the one we've just mentioned — between Recursions x and y, it follows that we understand the System Four continuity right through the corporation, from *top to bottom, no matter how many recursions there may be. A is to B, as B is to C, as C is to D, and so on. Recursively.'*

'And then we have to go through the whole exercise again, to understand cohesion between all Systems Five and all Systems Three.'

'It's just not necessary. Don't you see that the entire metasystem is implicated in the recursive mapping of any one of its subsystems?'

'Just study the diagram.'

'Well, I'm going up to bed now, and maybe I'll do just that.'

'Me too. I seem to have a tendency to look at diagrams, say 'oh yes', and pass on.'

'These diagrams aren't just illustrations, you know. They are trying to exhibit a whole mathematical theory without using incomprehensible algebra.'

'So we get incomprehensible diagrams instead: great. Why has no-one mentioned this damned Law of Cohesion? How comprehensible is that?'

'That's just why I said that I'm off to study the diagrams of the last two Chapters. If this Law really guarantees the cohesive glue, it's vitally important.'

'Goodnight; I'm tired. Would someone remind me why planning thus conceived is supposed to be the only *cohesive glue?'*

'Because planning thus conceived is the only *managerial activity that is not purely reactive.'*

I'd like to think that I'm not a reactive manager; in which case everything I do is planning?'

'That's the message. And whatever isn't *done by you — within your area of competence — isn't planning.'*

'Come on you three: let's go. Leave these two night owls to finish off.'

'Night.'

. . . .

'Anything in that paper, John?'

'Nothing much.'

'Why do you reckon it is that we have such trouble in thinking through a subject we know so well in novel terms? I know that coping with any new language isn't easy, but I can just about manage French.'

'It's not the language problem, I think. It is as you said: we know the subject so well. We've got the subject confused with the language in which it's usually expressed. I doubt that we understand the subject — because it's too familiar.'

'See your point. Probably that's why we end up with counter-productive systems, as we argued earlier on.'

'Maybe. I almost despair at the sheer incompetence of all our efforts. Things go the wrong way. So much effort goes in, too. Very ironic.'

'Hm. Irony is quite a feature of our world. But people bustle on blindly, and don't even notice the irony — never mind the incompetence and still less the counter-productive systems.'

'There is *something in that paper, I can sense it.'*

'Well... do you remember Gray's Elegy, *by any chance?'*

'Elegy Written in a Country Churchyard. *Yes I do. It was at Stoke Poges. I had to learn the whole thing at school.'*

'It's just that I was trying to remember a passage from Gray about 'animated busts' Can you get it back?'

'Hold on... '

> *'Can storied urn or animated bust*
> *Back to its mansion call the fleeting breath?*
> *Can Honour's voice provoke the silent dust,*
> *Or Flatt'ry soothe the dull cold ear of death?'*

'Well done.'

'What about it?'

'Well, it says here that the National Trust has raised £10,000 to save the monument to Thomas Gray at Stoke Poges. A reinforced concrete ring-beam is being installed by the Cement and Concrete Association to replace badly corroded iron supports to the sarcophagus. Free of charge.'

CHAPTER FOURTEEN

Calm and alarm

Sometimes advice takes the form: 'there are really only two basic courses of action open to us now. The first leads to success; the second is suicidal'. I have mentioned this kind of advice before, in trying to demonstrate that System Four lies on the central command axis of the model of any viable system. But this chapter is all about the business of managing: what can managers *do* with the advice contained in this book? Then please consider the managerial reaction to advice of the kind mentioned.

In reality, this kind of advice takes the manager's decision for him. 'The expensive study we commissioned clearly entails. . . ' The fact is used in business and industry to justify organizational change, and especially to escape responsibility for the 'murder of the innocents' that such change quite frequently involves. In practice, as one watches the inexorable consequences of the new organizational design, as to which many guarantees have of course been given, it quickly becomes obvious that some luckless individual — despite his position of privilege and despite the guarantees — was born with a silver knife in his back. In government, one may observe the same inexorability, although it has an extra twist. If the major enquiry becomes politically inconvenient, it can be shelved. Otherwise, it is again used to justify unpopular conclusions.

However it goes, this kind of advice is called **practical** advice.

There is another kind of advice; and the advice contained in this book is of that second kind. It is meant to open the insight of the manager and the minister to the real nature of the problems that he confronts. This means, to be precise, that he will recognize the decisions that *he* ought to take. This situation is onerous. It imposes the burden that the range of alternatives is suddenly enlarged, because the success-versus-suicide dichotomy is never an adequate account of the matter. Secondly, it means that he must do the job he is paid for, and back his judgment: there is no scapegoat.

This kind of advice is called **theoretical** — by managers.

So much for the ironies of the impasse that has to do with the application of insight, and the turning to practical use of theoretical constructs. The reality is quite different, if all concerned keep their heads. The model we now have, contemplated at any one level of recursion, comprises two hierarchical stages — and only two. There is the Three-Two-One stage of operations inside and now, and there is the Three-Four-Five stage that constitutes the metasystem.

The first of these, it should by now be clear, poses no problem. It is that muddy box with which the metasystem deals, but into which it does not descend. If we really want to know more about it, we must consciously address the viable system at the next lower level of recursion — where it is the metasystem. For the viable system at present in focus, then, we are concerned only to discuss the articulation of the metasystem Three-Four-Five. This is the problem of so-called 'senior management' for *any* level or recursion. And it should be characterized by calm.

The calm is engendered by the fact that the Three-Two-One component of the two stage hierarchy is autonomous. Subject only to the Law of Cohesion, which coheres all levels of recursion, that muddy box will adjsut to its own (horizontal axis) pressures. Then if there is no calm in the metasystem, it is because Three-Four-Five admits to a continual buffeting from the muddy box, and accepts the role of continual intervention. Let it not do so; let it be calm. The admitted problem of its articulation can indeed be tackled calmly — subject to one human constraint which will be acknowledged in a minute.

Articulation means the process of jointing, or the mode whereby jointing is made possible. In the previous chapter we argued that the jointing process is all about planning. But what is its mode? That question asks how actual managerial structures can be formed so that they are properly jointed, or in articulation. It is no accident that the word 'articulated' has come to mean something like: 'openly expressed in a set of words'. The words that we articulate, join together, are meant to express the articulation or jointing, of the metasystemic organizational structure. Unfortunately, there is no simple recipe for the articulation of the metasystem; and that is because the individual circumstances of any senior management are unqiue. But, although it is proper to recognize the individuality of each of those men and women, and of their special inter-relationship, the cybernetic laws that underlie the *functioning* of the metasystem cannot be dispensed.

It was for this very reason that we separated out, or teased apart, the peculiar functions of Systems Three and Four and Five as distinctive logical components of the metasystem. Nevertheless, it has been reiterated that these logical components need not be embodied in organizational units called (for instance) the Operational Directorate, the Developmental Directorate, and the

Policy Directorate. It might be useful, depending on circumstances, so to distinguish them; but even if this were done we should not expect the three directorates to be mutually exclusive of key people. Any executive director of the institution necessarily wears each of these three hats. He must contribute to policy formulation; he can deny neither a concern with developmental issues nor responsibility for the current management of the business in hand. But he can apportion his attention to those three component duties in various ratios. He can urge more, or less, formalization of the necessary support systems for the three activities. And he can make, or help to make, the consideration of each component more or less ritualistic in terms of committee work, explicit reporting, and personal accountability.

There is, I submit, an assumption made by senior management (at every level of recursion) that the three components are each being adequately handled between the team. But in fact, as my researches invariably find it, this is not the case. Still less is it true that System Five's monitoring of the balancing arrangements between Three and Four is being carried out. Each member of the senior management team devotes most of his time to System Three, and therefore (as a consequence) to Five-activity at the next level of recursion. Hence at *this* level of recursion, the second and third laws of managerial requisite variety are ignored. But, since they are indeed laws, they will assert themselves; and the senior management is then in disarray.

You may wonder how I dare to make such a statement: where is the evidence? Confessedly, it is hard to present. However, I have always made estimates (albeit subjective) of the time allocations made by senior managers to the roles allocated to them by the metasystemic model. In ideal circumstances, I have asked each member of the senior management team to nominate his own apportionment of time. That is again subjective from his own standpoint. But what happens when his colleagues are asked to adjudicate on his behalf? The answer invariably shows a chaotic dissonance of mutual perceptions. For example, if all the others say that Mr A devotes 90 percent of his time to System Four, whereas Mr A himself allocates his effort 40 percent to Five and 50 percent to Three, with only a 10 percent involvement in Four, we can conclude that System Four is not adequately considered.

Articulation of the metasystem has to do with agreement about how the various roles involved are being discharged. It has nothing to do with titles displayed on office doors, nothing to do with the organization chart and who reports to whom, and nothing to do with liaison committees charged to keep the various roles in touch. It is a continuous negotiating process — or, if you prefer a more realistic phrase, it is a continuous struggle for power. This was referred to just now as the human constraint. There is no point in expostulating about our common humanity: power is undeniably a critical factor in organizational mores. The concern of the management cybernetician, engulfed as he usually is in the ebb and flow of these very tides of power, is to see whether the regulatory roles of the metasystem as defined are being discharged or not. If they are not, there is highly predictable trouble ahead: it can be deduced from the viable system model. If they are, then praise to the cosmic forces that impel viability are in order, and supportive advice is in order as well. (And in that case, the cybernetician who cannot help feeling that it was all accidental should perhaps be ashamed of his own cynicism.)

Let us make explicit the dilemma that the senior management faces in the attempt to articulate the metasystem. There is a need for *comradeship* at the top of any enterprise. This expresses itself internally to the metasystem as a confidence in mutual loyalty, agreement as to institutional identity and behaviour, and determination in a common intent — whether that be expressed in terms of profitability or fun, whether its criteria are directed to short-term goals or to long-term aspirations. Any such comradeship is understood within the enterprise as a whole quite differently. It is moreover understood by the outside world, to which it is projected by diverse media, quite differently again. This is because the metasystem we discuss speaks an appropriate metalanguage, many of whose propositions are not decideable in the languages of the systems mentioned. To put this logical point in everyday terms, it means that observers of the metasystem in action cannot understand the basis of the comradeship that the senior management group continuously generates: what they observe is the net outcome, which they recognize in terms of apparent leadership. It often happens that the metasystem is so preoccupied with its own articulation, the continuous negotiation of the terms of comradeship, that it fails to notice the effects on morale within the firm and in the business community of any inadequacy in the projection of leadership. The negotiation certainly involves conflict; and this looks different to people outside the metasystem from the way it looks to the metalinguistic negotiators themselves. But omissions or obfuscations of leadership do not constitute a dilemma. The dilemma arises because the requirements of the negotiation (the shifts of attention, preoccupation with power) cause those involved to deal in the balance of *interpersonal* variety, rather than in the balance of managerial variety as between Systems Three, Four, and Five. If the most effective organizational arrangements for meeting the demands of the laws of managerial variety do not match the arrangements continuously emerging from the negotiations (and why should they?) there is a dilemma indeed.

In practice, senior managers do not seem to confront this dilemma, because they do not know it is there until they have mastered a cybernetic analysis of the articulation problem that the metasystem confronts. Nonetheless, the variety laws continue to operate; and in my experience managers sense that something is wrong. If the viable system exhibits pathological symptoms from such causes, the alert manager can hardly fail to notice them — even if he has no understanding of the etiology. The result is that he decides on what is known as a reorganization. I take this decision to be an implicit recognition of the dilemma just discussed: if the dilemma is real, then the decision is predictable, since the mismatch between the solutions of the negotiation (to the interpersonal variety equation) and the solutions of the intrinsic regulatory mechanisms (to the managerial variety equation) produces an institutional tension too great to be borne. Either the comradeship is blown apart, or the leadership function is finally abdicated, or both. Now the commentary offered in the first pages of this chapter was confessed to be subjective; it derives from thirty years' experience, as both a senior manager and a consultant, set alongside the insights provided by theory. But now the predictions at which we have arrived can be compared with raw facts. It is a matter of record that great companies engage in reorganization of the metasystem — often with an almost obscene frequency. And this repetition is predictable too, because the reorganizations no more acknowledge the cybernetic laws than did the original organization.

We might take a brief look at an example: British Leyland. This is not a book of case studies, and there is no need to enter into immense detail to make the cybernetic points that the story well illustrates. (I use this example because I had the relevant information, but no particular axe to grind.) In 1961 Lord Stokes was running a relatively small company — Standard — that proceeded to grow by acquisition. By 1968 it had acquired Austin Morris. Because I knew the financial director, I suggested that the time had come to make a careful appraisal of the company's effective organization. He was sympathetic to that proposal; but it was soon answered by the flat statement from Lord Stokes that he had no need of advice. In the early seventies, I had (in a professorial capacity) many discussions with Leyland middle management representatives. One of them said to me: 'we are all standing silently, with our backs to the wall, waiting for the outcome of the senior power struggle'. (At this point, we might note the 'leadership projection' of the comradeship negotiation.) In 1974 the partnership of Lord Stokes and his financial director abdicated. The Government sent in Lord Ryder. As it happened, I knew Lord Ryder quite well; and therefore made no approach to him about the reorganization that he immediately engaged upon. Predictably, he decided on a total centralization of the whole enterprise; and he subvented three hundred and fifty million pounds of government money to this end. The outcome was disastrous, and in 1977 Mr Edwardes took over. Predictably again, he decided to decentralize.... .

There is no desire here to pillory individuals. There is however an obligation to refer to the fact that the consequences of cybernetic theory are in practice inexorable. The theory of the viable system demonstrates that the articulation of the metasystem depends on cybernetic laws that cannot be gainsaid. Reorganizations, so called, that ignore those laws will not work. I have mentioned one specific case; I could mention ten more without further research. What they all have in common is the necessity to resolve the interpersonal variety equations, to which problem many consultants are willing to address themselves, and no perception on the part of any of the actors concerned (including those consultants) that the cybernetic laws exist and 'will out'.

This book is, in its way, a testimony to the need for a more subtle mode of thought and a more elaborate (but by no means incomprehensible) language than managers and ministers and their consultants customarily adopt. If I have seemed to harp on the absurd dichotomy that is normally drawn between centralization and decentralization in these pages, it is because these are kindergarten concepts compared with the theme whereby freedom is a computable function that determines the degree of autonomy. And if I now seem to dwell too long on the mismatch between the solutions to interpersonal and managerial variety equations, it is in protest at an equivalently crude understanding of the metasystem and its delicate variety balances. For the match that we need, as distinct from the mismatch that we perenially experience, is certainly computable too.

No-one concerned has the motivation to become involved in that computation, because no-one stands for the viability of the viable system. There are those ready to stand for the economic property of the viable system. There are those ready to stand for the legal status of the viable system. There are supporters of the outlook of owners or shareholders, of workers and their families, of communities and their ecological interests. There are those ready to stand for the System One role of this viable system in the next higher level of recursion (but watch their interests). But who is supporting the *viability of the viable system?* I shall tell you in the next chapter, and you will not like the answer. Meanwhile, we may well decide that when the contest of viability arises — so that **reorganization** is in prospect — the very last interest to be considered is the viable system's viability. This reorganization will take account of economics, of legality, of vested interests, of the posture of the trade unions, of the views of minority groups, and of the manipulations of power-people in the next higher level of recursion. We can be fairly sure that it will not take account of viability itself.

The trouble is that the few impressive words that are available in the managerial vocabulary, and 'reorganization' is such a word, carry on their backs so vast a connotation that they mean all things to all men. In short, this word does not have requisite variety to label the solution to the quite precise dilemma that we set out to discuss. If reorganization means primarily that what is now centralized should be decentralized and vice verse, and that all the chief characters in the drama should change places, then the dilemma is not addressed at all. The model for this kind of reorganization was beautifully delineated in the Mad Hatter's Tea Party; and over and over again, at least in

Britain, we may observe that the necessary qualification to take on a new top job is to have made a resounding and conspicuous failure in the last one. No: if the objective is to solve the equations of managerial variety without disturbing the continuously adjusting solutions to the equations of interpersonal variety, then we are explicitly seeking an articulation of the metasystem that is *self-conscious* with respect to its cybernetic, as well as to its psycho-social, adequacy.

Now it seems likely (and this is a contention of neurocybernetics as illuminated by mathematics of a most advanced kind) that the point of self-consciousness is reached by a system that has developed the power to recognize itself at the infinite recursion. This is not as daft as it sounds, although to talk about infinities in words — rather than to use the mathematical apparatus that handles them with facility — usually leads to confusion. People tend to think of infinity as a definite location (where all sorts of strange things may happen, such as the meeting of parallel lines in Einstein's universe) that is always further away than you can possibly go. On the contrary, infinity is a *process;* thus to understand the process is to understand infinity without going there. This is like explaining the statement 'the earth is round' by specifying the process: 'keep flying in the same direction for long enough and you will eventually land where you started'. To a Flat-Earther, and there are still some of those about, this specification would sound absurd.

It is clear from this book and from experience that a management may define a number of levels of recursion in the insitution, that it may move deliberately between them and take decisions that are appropriate to this level or to that, and that it is reasonable and also useful to speak of 'the highest level of recursion' in referring to that largest (most inclusive) viable system in which it has any power to effect outcomes by edict — should it wish to do that. It is also a useful rule of thumb always to consider this 'highest level of recursion' as a System One of the recursion further on — in which the power of edict is lost. But to be fully self-conscious, as distinct from being aware of a System One role, is a larger matter. Consider, for instance, the corporation as the 'highest level of recursion', and that we belong to its System Five. Then our corporation is System One within our Industry, *and* within our community, *and* within the political framework that makes regulations for corporations such as ours, *and, and, and...* All of these next higher recursions are themselves the Systems One of some other viable system. There are of course geographic and geopolitical aspects to all of this. Well: we can make a finite model if we wish. For instanee, we could conclude that the whole planet is the highest level of recursion; and then our rule of thumb would alert us to a possible galactical system in which Earth would be a System One. And now we really have reduced the modelling process to absurdity. We no longer know what we are doing; and even on route to absurdity we shall have made some extremely arbitrary judgments as to which mammoth systems are incorporated in which. The multinationals, and the governments of nations, and terrorist groups, not to mention the perceptions of men and women everywhere, may entertain very different notions as to how this series of Chinese Boxes 'really' evolves.

Note that as long as we are dealing with that level of recursion to whose System Five we belong, we have only ourselves to blame if we are absurd — because we still have the power of edict. Even if we do not choose to use that power to instruct our System One in its supposedly autonomous activity, we cannot avoid setting climates of opinion (see the previous chapter), nor can we avoid establishing the language in which the institution talks to itself. So two points emerge. First: there is a very real barrier to modelling the recursivity of viable systems more than one system beyond that over which we have authority. Second: no *finite* model is possible, because we do not have requisite variety to make it; and all we can do is to contemplate the *process* whereby such models are endlessly capable of generation. And that is to define the infinite recursion; and that is to explode into self-consciousness.

This undoubtedly difficult argument is the case for saying that any organization that is to count as an appropriate articulation of the metasystem should conduce to a shared awareness within the senior management group of the infinite recursion of their institution.

It sound like the briefing for a spiritual meditation, and perhaps it is. But I can say this much for it: all sorts of practical consequences follow, and all sorts of common practices are contra-indicated. (Nor, since the argument is already set out, can I resist taking these parentheses to remark that the World Models that many scientists have run as computer simulations are arbitrarily finite designations of the infinite recursion, and will remain of little value until they are commissioned by a genuine System Five (power of edict) of a genuine United Nations (viable system) which is not at all in prospect.) Then what are the indications and the contra-indications that flow from the notion of infinite recursion, where the articulation of the metasystem is concerned?

In the chapter called 'Measurement', the case was set out to say that we are primarily interested in the detection of instability. Instability is the opposite of calm; instability is inimical to the contemplation of the infinite recursion, and therefore to corporate self-consciousness. Then we must be alert to it, rather than to routine reports of the 'I'm all right' variety. There are two features about instability that need a lot of careful consideration. The first is that instability may set in anywhere in the behaviour of the organization, and at any time. The second is that there are always pre-symptoms of the fact. Unfortunately, the typical management information system, in both Three and Four, is repetitiously reporting on stability — it is in fact challenging the manager to find evidence of this crucial instability in the welter of routine data. If, nonetheless, he finds it, he does so because instability has already set in — it is in fact too late to avert it.

Now it is customarily said in any institution that the time base on which reporting is done is a function of the nature of the business. If you are running a betting shop dealing with horse racing, then the information you receive about the three o'clock race becomes more and more precious, by the second as the hour of three approaches — and it is worthless after three-fifteen when the race has already been won. But if you are underwriting an insurance policy on the life of someone who is actuarially expected to live for another fifty years, you do not enquire after his health every day. All this is true, and managers quite correctly look at their informational needs in the light of the speed of response that is possible to the special nature of the business in which they engage. There is no problem in understanding this, nor do I seek to refute it. Indeed, I recall the argument about appointing a director of operational research in a publishing company in the shape of a man who had made a national reputation working for a nation-wide bakery. What did *he* know about publishing? Nothing. But to sell yesterday's newspaper is as difficult as to sell yesterday's cake — and when that point was made the battle was won. But such considerations, real as they are, have nothing to do with the problem of the onset of instability, which may happen at any moment in any business of *whatever* kind. Moreover: if there are presymptoms, that is to say if instability is a 'telegraphed punch', then we are certainly not concerned with epochs that are normal to the business, but only with the interval between a warning and a disaster.

The fact is that the nature of the business and its natural rhythm, or the articulation of the metasystem designed to cope with that, have nothing at all to do with the issue of instability considered in terms of viability, since that has invariant features. We face instead a **time barrier** — through which we needs must burst. If our information is six months' out of date, then (since information is what changes us) we are ready to deal with a world that is past and gone. If our information is a month, or a week, or a day out of date, then we are talking in terms of a progressively more realistic world — but that world is still past and gone, and there is nothing that any of us can do about what happened even a second ago. That is to say: historical information may well change us, but it cannot change history. The only advantage in making such information more 'timely', as they say, is to put us into a better position to clear up the mess. But suppose that we can acquire data about stability that can be transformed into information (which changes us) about the possibility, the likelihood, of *incipient* instability: then, and only then, do we have a chance to avert it. You have heard this argument before.

For example, the value of real-time data was discussed in the chapter on Measurement in terms of the treatment of management systems as probabilistic rather than causal. Indeed they are probabilistic, and causality has to do only with the post-mortem on disaster. But if we have real-time data; and if we use them to measure the likelihood of instability, instead of trying to impute necessary results from an unsound theory of causality, then we have the opportunity to break the time barrier. Action may be taken now, in order that incipient instability shall not become actual. That was, briefly, the argument about the design of regulatory systems used within the system-of-managing. The argument is equally efficacious in considering, as we now are, the self-consciousness of the viable system itself. The distinction is equivalent to the difference between monitoring presymptoms of ataxia and of psychosis. If incipient instability is not detected and corrected, ataxia will manifest itself in a shaking disorder of the limbs; in the case of psychosis, *you* go mad.

To use the appropriate terminology is important. If we say, from the assumption that causality in the system is understood, that since the current situation is like *this* therefore the future situation will be like *that,* and our managerial action is clear, then this is self-delusion. The causal model in a complex, probabilistic system does not have requisite variety to predict the future. This can be said with confidence from many theoretical standpoints: epistemological, logical, even theological, as well as cybernetic — wherein the causal model cannot possibly exhibit requisite variety. Much more convincingly for the manager, is the incontrovertible fact that such predictions are never correct (which is to say that they are correct only to the extent that the throw of a pair of dice 'correctly' guesses a number). If, on the other hand, we say that the behaviour of the system as evidenced by real-time data is incipiently unstable, and that therefore we shall take action to increase the probability in favour of stability, we have changed ourselves (acquired information) which may make the future other than it would otherwise have been. There is no available satisfaction here in declaring: 'look how clever I was', because no-one can possibly know whether matters would have been better or worse without that managerial action. And that is why managers prefer to use a causal model, however defective, precisely to show how clever they were, rather than a probabilistic real-time praxis that can in principle break the time barrier, while leaving them with no credit as Gods of the System.

It seems, may we not then say, that calm is a function of alertness. It comes from being *poised* to read the signs of incipient instability, in the quiet confidence that instability can be averted. This contention applies to every kind of planning, moreover, as can be understood from the previous chapter. If the intention is to be poised to detect incipient instability, then the cycle-time within which that can be measured is determined by the dynamics of the system that we have subjectively recognized to be the system of concern. As System Three tunes in to stability in System One, it will find short cycles (such as the overloading of machines which may result in their breakdown, or the overloading of human emotions which may result in wildcat strikes), and it will find long cycles (such as the inadequacy of a preventative maintenance scheme in which some renewals are made every ten years, or a growing disbalance in the age, race, or sex profile of, say, middle management). Thus the 'inside-and-now' system is not simply concerned with short-range planning. Nor is System Four simply concerned with long-range planning; for although some development trends are of a kind that will necessarily take many years to mature for good or ill, rapidly generated instabilities may occur in the very short term indeed (tax changes, unheralded competition based on different systemic conceptions, local wars in foreign markets, riots on the streets at home — these are obvious examples).

So in terms of the articulation of the metasystem, which is the search for self-consciousness at the infinite recursion, it becomes clear that we cannot make functional divisions, nor geographical divisions, nor planning divisions based on time horizons, and then propose to join them again in a metasystemic articulation; because none of these sets of categories maps onto the criteria of viability. Please (for both our sakes) do not turn that long sentence into a misquotation robbed of content. Certainly we can make functional divisions: the probity of professional life turns upon them. We cannot undo the knitted fabrics of engineering, or accountancy, or works' management, or company law. Certainly we can make geographic divisions: the marketing strategy of all large firms depends upon attaining to requisite variety locale by locale. We cannot suddenly declare that a village in Wales will in future be serviced from Tokyo instead of Cardiff, and we would be trying to abrogate the laws of autonomy if we did. Certainly we can make planning divisions by time horizons: the provision and servicing of capital doubtless required that we do so. We cannot ignore the economic implications of discounted cash flow. But the first sentence of this paragraph did not deny all this. It began, with deliberate caution, by referring to the articulation of the metasystem; and when it went on to say that we could not have the conventional functional, geographic, and time-horizoned divisions, it continued: 'and then propose to join them again in a metasystemic articulation.'

How, in heaven's name, *are* the accepted divisions of the enterprise to be metasystemically articulated? The popular answer, at the time of writing, is by something known as the matrix organization. Some theorists have very reasonably contended that all ways of dividing the managerial task are equally legitimate, and that if each orthogonal axis of categories is set against the others, then matrices will be formed whereby the bearing of any x on any y may be taken into account. Well: We were considering a simplified case, which took note of three typical ways of dividing the management task. Then how shall these be divided? We might say that functional management includes: legal, financial, production, sales, maintenance, research (that is six functional divisions, minimally). The geographical divisionalization (let us merely guess) involves six major territories. The time-based division yields (say, for the sake of symmetry): the immediate; the pending; the short-term, the medium term, and the long term plans; and 'blue sky' thinking. Then our matrix organization consists of a cube, with six divisions on each axis. $6^3 = 216$ elements. Well, this is indeed minimal. There might be twelve functional divisions and thirty geographical divisions. There might be six axes to the 'cube' instead of three — and a six-space is difficult to comprehend, except mathematically. But while the more imaginative reader is working out the possible permutations, we may well sit here stoically and ask how the metasystem — comprising perhaps ten people — is going to divide its time among two hundred and sixteen committees.

This is the second time in one chapter that I have used the device called *reductio ad absurdam,* and perhaps that in itself calls for apology. If it were merely an intellectual ruse, I would apologize forthwith. But it is not a ruse at all. The matrix approach *in practice* reduces to absurdity. The trouble is that managers are expected to take the approach seriously (which is all right), and to follow through its organizational consequences (which do not work). In one of my managerial incarnations I was appointed, via the matrix approach, to twenty-seven bodies — boards, committees, working parties, task forces, steering groups. The boards met once a month, which involved nearly two board meetings a week. The remaining bodies met weekly ... It really should not be necessary to invoke Ashby's Law, appropriate as it is, to observe that someone who already has several jobs of his own does not dispose requisite variety to handle all of this.

This (so far) reflective chapter began with an ironic definition of the kind of advice that managers are prepared to call 'practical'. It said that practical advice takes the manager's decisions from him. I still remember hearing Bertrand Russell defining the 'practical man' (see my discussion in *Decision and Control*). Russell said: 'I define the practical man as the man who has no idea what to do in practice'. Since then, the experience as to how the metasystem may be articulated has repeatedly reinforced Russell's view. Then let us now creep up on some sort of practical articulation of the metasystem, which *would* map onto the viable system, which *would* respond to Ashby's Law, and which *would* make a practical man practical. But do not expect that what follows will take the senior manager's decisions for him.

The senior manager *is* a manager, and his task was described in an earlier chapter — especially in terms of his humanity, and the variety that he can dispose. The senior manager (at whatever level of recursion) is also a member of a comradeship, that in its own activity articulates the metasystem. It does so, not by edict, not by expostulation, but by what it **does** in the process of its internal negotiation. The senior manager must alert himself to the interpretation that will be placed on this, in terms of his leadership, by all those internal and external systems to which his metasystem is metasystemic.

The senior manager stands as he humanly is: a very finite person. But he holds many privileges, that can extend his human faculties: in expertise, through his staff and advisors; in space through telecommunications; in time through a monitored alertness to incipient instability — whenever it may come. He operates within a metasystem which, though its currency is conflict, generates a special and indeed unique comradeship.

Then what is he to do?

In Chapter Nine, we saw that although his roles in Systems Five and Three were probably clear to him, there would have to be a new *focus* to create an effective System Four. The kernel of that focus was to be the intersect of many fields of interest. Thus while matrix organizations indiscriminately identify all the elements of interaction between all the dimensions of management, and all the dimensions of possible advance, the viable system must needs procure a variety-attenuating means of focussing, and even of identifying (for this man) the kernel of the focus. To this end, the appropriate environment of decision, for this lonely but comradely senior manager, was discussed. He needed some sort of Operations Room in which to work — with his comrades. But the Operations Room as currently envisaged in the culture becomes a fiasco; it is not the nerve-centre of activity that I have hitherto described under this heading (and actually created in Chile). It has become instead a tarted-up public-relations exercise. Therefore, it was said, something more like a *clubhouse* is envisaged. Its precise form, however, would depend upon the cultural conditions of the enterprise whose metasystemic clubhouse it ought to be.

In Chapter Ten, we found the Fourth Principle of Organization, with its insistence on the continuity of time. And it became clear, at that point, that to focus on developmental activity would not be enough. The Clubhouse would have to be a Three-Four meeting place. Thus it was renamed a Management Centre — to replace the Boardroom, the Executive Suite, the Committee Rooms. And in this Management Centre, the boss (or the partial boss now being called the senior manager) would administer **closure.**

In Chapter Eleven, we obtained a first insight into what closure means: the senior manager must *know himself.* Control in the metasystem is *intrinsic.* The job of System Five (to which all metasystemic activity is in fact dedicated) is to *listen to itself,* as it goes about the tasks of setting criteria of stability, detecting instability, and changing the criteria of success.

In Chapters Twelve and Thirteen we took time off to complete the theory of the viable system and its recursivity. But in this very Chapter Fourteen, the notion of closure returns — at the macrolevel. It is only in the *infinite* recursion that self-consciousness occurs. It occurs for the man himself, of course; but the present discussion concerns the self-consciousness of the enterprise. The senior manager has to embody the self-consciousness of the institution; even if, unhappily, he does not yet know *himself* . . . And that self-consciousness relies on a set of sensors, emanating from the management centre like nerves to reach as far as they can effectively sense — and especially in the dimension of time. Some issues are impenetrable up until next weekend, while others seem to be transparent for years ahead. Let the nervous system of the management centre then be highly selective as to the *quality* of sensation. There is no uniform prescription; everything depends on the circumstances for which the design is drawn. But one feature of the management centre that is quite general has to be provision for the intercommunication of the senior managers that reflects the comradeship.

It is on this that the articulation of the metasystem depends. Assuming that negotiations go well, but applying the law of requisite variety to them, we must expect that each senior manager spends a large proportion of his time explaining to his colleagues what he is doing. In successfully viable systems, experience bears this out. The time consumed is huge. On the other hand, when senior management attempts to economize on this apparently profligate use of the most scarce resource of time, Ashby's law operates: the system quickly loses its viability. Not only experience but probability theory also attests to the cybernetic expectation. The metasystem is an intercommunion (in *Brain of the Firm* it is called the 'multinode', and some probability analysis is provided). But obviously good design of the management centre could save time — as compared with those verbal encounters that last all day, and those confabulations between pairs that last for half the night. The impossibility of providing a uniform prescription for this aspect of articulation, is something even more particular than 'the circumstances': it is founded absolutely in the question of **style.**

There seems to be a preoccupation in the behavioural science literature, and its consulting practice, with style conceived as a commodity that is measurable — and understood in its effects. Thus certain styles are 'known' to be good, and some bad; while 'preferred' styles can be taught. Successes have been claimed; there have been notable failures (for instance, at International Harvester). But does a two, or even three, or even four-dimensional account of a manager's style really account for his effectiveness or lack of it? The models seem to lack requisite variety. And practical observation again poses questions. Different leaders use different styles, yet through some other magic are equally effective. People respond to cajoling — though not from leaders whose nature it is to be authoritarian. People respond to authority — but not if their leaders do not appear to know what they are doing. It seems likely to me that people are very accommodating to a wide range of styles; what they reject in leaders is especially insensitivity and insincerity. A harsh command that has a twinkling eye behind the noise may be acceptable. A feeble lead that has manifest logic behind its directions may be acceptable too. We cannot legitimately talk about managerial style independently of circumstances — nor of (let's face it) the conditioned responses of the people managed, which are based on their previous experience of those circumstances and of that manager. The dynamics are loaded with positive feedback. Moreover, the very high variety, in human and cultural terms, of each particular system at each particular time, can hardly be attenuated to match a cardboard cut-out manager — bland, all-purpose, preconditioned. He is an illusion, although some (certainly not all) trainers offer him as a panacea. And if they succeeded in creating him, he would not know *himself* — only what he is supposed to be, according to models that lack requisite variety.

If we are to gain any insight into the stylistic factors that undoubtedly affect the design of a management centre and the articulation of the metasystem that it houses, a systems approach to the matter ought therefore to help. It necessarily takes account of the varieties being generated and, although those quantities cannot be measured (according to the recent argument), it can postulate *structures* which have at least the possibility to absorb the variety of related subsystems. Secondly, by presenting the total system as *dynamic,* it offers the chance to detect the existence and likely effect of the feedback channels that are needed if equilibrial behaviour is to be attained. The diagrams presented here begin to develop a model that beings together all the considerations that were rehearsed a few paragraphs ago.

The first diagram, Figure 63, shows the 'psychological space' of the senior manager who has metasystemic responsibilities — which all managers do have, at some level of recursion. The metasystem as such (of whose comradeship our manager is a part) is seen as setting the criterion for a meter that is measuring a point of stability within the system.

The point of stability is one of many. It represents some feature of the system regulated by this metasystem that is adjudged important to viability. The location of the dot within the amoeboid shape that is the system exhibits a stable performance, within physiological limits indicated by the circle surrounding the dot. That is, the dot may move in its systemic space, but only within the confines of its circle. If the representative point moves outside the circle, the system is incipiently unstable. So the nature of the criterion set by the metasystem into the meter is to specify the critical limits on the dot's location in systemic space.

The psychological state of the manager, if he is assured that the dot is within its circle (I'm all right'), is to approve of that. He is at his own point of calm. But, to revert to a question discussed earlier, how does *he know that he knows* that all is well? The system is generating massive variety, as usual; the manager must have some confidence in whatever set of devices it is that attenuates this variety. After all, anyone (with practice) can enter into a state of calm — by blocking off all input. Unfortunately for the manager, to do that might enhance his knowledge of himself, but the manoeuvre is managerial abdication.

Well, the first filter (called the *resolution filter* on the diagram) that is assuredly being applied has been designed by the metasystem of which our manager is a member (see dotted line). It has everything in common with an optical device which, by a system of lenses, determines the degree of optical resolution at which we are prepared to look. The human eye cannot see a virus; the resolution filter (in the diagram) does not know whether John or Mary is operating that machine today (nor whether Bill Sykes has his hand in the till). This is because the filter is designed for *this* level of recursion. Please note: this set of diagrams depicts a single level of recursion. Hence, if someone 'sees a virus', he is indulging in gossip. That would be quite normal. But the design of the filter should make the fact evident.

To hammer this point home: it is essential to recognize when we *are* using filters, so that they will be properly designed — or, if design is impossible, that the limitations that their inevitable existence imposes be recognized. As was said before, there is no bigger or more damaging variety filter than sheer ignorance. Both these admonitions apply to the second filter in the diagram, called the *perceptual filter*. This is designed, perhaps from a lack of self-knowledge, by the manager himself: as the picture shows, it is generated out of his psychological space, which is in turn contrained by his physiological equipment.

This perceptual filter, is something whose design should be considered and reconsidered daily by the manager (and by those around him too). It accepts an input which is already attenuated by the agreement, or merely the fact, that optical resolution is as it is. It then proceeds either to attenuate variety further (for example: 'this is of no interest to me'), or to amplify it (for example: 'I'll handle this, if it's the last thing I do'). In either case, the design of the perceptual filter may be determined by ignorance, prejudice, brainwashing, laziness, incompetence, dependency — or any other nasty characteristic to which human inadequacy and arrogance is prone. It is hard to reach hyperbole here; because we all 'know' so much that we may fail to read signals, however urgent they may be.

Then we reach the third filter, of which the manager *is* conscious, although he may well have done nothing about its design, called the *variety filter*. This is the formal way of attenuating variety: it houses the bureaucracy. Attenuations range from standard forms that aggregate information into nothingness — that is, we do not change — to informal decisions of the kind: 'we need not

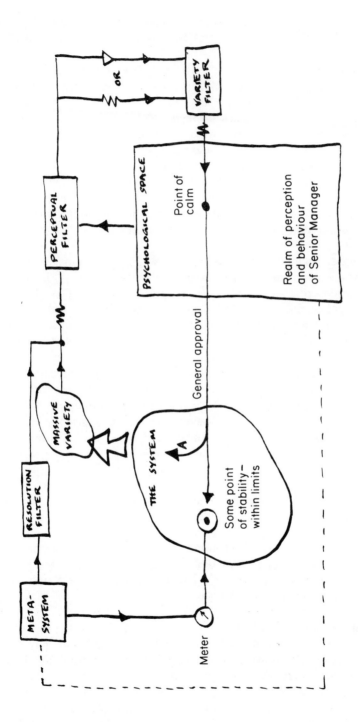

Figure 63. Handling incipient instability, stage 1

bother the boss with this'. A responsible manager ought surely to be able to explain (to himself) exactly what this filter is doing to him, and why.

Given that the data generated in massive variety have passed through these three filters (none of which the manager may have seriously reviewed) by the time they reach him, it is not too surprising if he maintains his point of calm. His general approval flows back through the circuit, via the arrow marked A. Nothing is happening in relation to any point of stability in the system — yet. And if it were, his three filters would probably ensure that he did not hear of it. Well: congratulations on that, *if* he has designed or at least overhauled those three filters. The point is, however, that a *special mechanism* is required to deal with the crucial question of alertness to incipient instability, because the likelihood is that if there is no such device the triple-filtration will take out the vital signal along with all the others that are trivial.

If this special mechanism is required by a viable system, in the cybernetic sense of logical necessity, then it surely exists. (To repeat: our enquiries are directed towards discovering how viable systems actually work.) It looks as though the special mechanism that alerts the metasystem to incipient instability anywhere in the system is normally triggered by personal observation, and transmitted by personal communication. It seems to come down to this: 'I say, Harry, have you heard what's going on down at . . . ' This must mean that the triple-filter already discussed cannot recognize the signals indicating incipient instability: perhaps they occur below the level of optical resolution that the official reporting arrangement sets, perhaps the perceptual filter is so designed that there is no machinery for perceiving them, or perhaps they are lost in the process of data-aggregation in which the variety filter is bureaucratically expert. Very likely all three inhibitions are applied to the alerting signal; so the function of the human network is to by-pass all that.

Well, we could say, that is marvellous: the human being is still ruling the roost. But let us enumerate the disadvantages:

- we have installed at immense cost (time, talent, money) a management information system that eliminates the most important of the data that we need to convert into the information that changes us;

- we are relying instead on the perceptual filters, the acumen, and the institutional models of individuals who may not know themselves, may have personal axes to grind, and may not share the conception of the system on which the comradeship is homing. (And in that case, why bother with the investment in the management information system at all?);

- we have to devote vast amounts of time to distinguishing between real and bogus signals carried on this human network;

- these signals may come from *any level of recursion*. Thus, unless a model of recursivity in the enterprise is available, and unless it is ruthlessly applied, the metasystem will (as usual) be seduced into floundering about in black boxes that it has no hope of making transparent.

This syndrome is omnipresent. I am familiar with it, and my guess is that you are too. If we want to nominate an experience that we share, it is that of being world citizens. There exists an enormous and expensive bureaucratic triple-filtering system administered by international bodies (UNO, UNESCO, FAO, WHO ...). This system is manifestly incapable of detecting incipient instability: its ponderous structures filter out the alerting signals. Instead, instability is signalled in direct human terms — usually by sudden violence. The process of instant diplomacy begins. This leads to instant alliances, instant wars, instant revolutions, instant threats — in all — to the survival of humankind (so far). But all of this activity is generated *wholly outside* the regulatory system for world brotherhood to which everyone subscribes. It has to be, since that regulatory system refutes every cybernetic canon in the book: it does not constitute a viable system. In particular, as far as the present discussion is concerned, its triple-filtration is guaranteed to suppress all signals that alert to incipient instability. That is an analysis of information available to us all; it is confirmed in my own case by (small) work in three international agencies where (in each case) it was completely impossible to discover anything of the remotest interest about the issues alleged to be addressed. It was enough, apparently, that a group of experts should sit in a cellar in the dark and tackle the problem of what it is like to be an expert.

If we apply these arguments, and the foregoing checklist, to national problems, we shall find the same thing. It takes the intense and unsavoury human disclosures of a 'Watergate' enquiry (and these occur in all countries) to reveal that the official regulatory system is systematically filtering-out the signals of incipient instability. In the enterprise, the same is also true; and most people know it, even though it comes to light only in the form of a scandal. But the scandal is not altogether scandalous, in the sense that people have been misbehaving themselves in a moral sense. The more profound scandal is that a firm operates a regulatory system, backed by an information system, that cannot possibly work.

Then it should be worth while to look again at the last diagram, and to note that the problem arises where the calmness of the senior manager is routed back to him through channel A. The more iterations of this loop occur, the more often the three filters operate, and the calmer he becomes. This will impart a positive feedback to the filtration properties of the filters: their activity is reinforced by approval. Please remember what was learned at the outset about the way in which transducers become denatured: they are learning systems, and may easily learn the precisely wrong thing (they get the sign wrong). Now this chapter constitutes an appeal for calm; but if calm is simply a matter of making sure that you are not even told that you should be in a rage, then the calm is spurious because the viable system is robbed of its metasystemic component — which is a coma.

In the next diagram, which builds on the first, there is an assumption that the special mechanism required by a viable system to alert a senior manager to incipient instability can be designed to be independent of human intervention of the 'I say, Harry' variety, which ranges from gossip-mongering to panic-stricken incapacity. This would be a device, operating in real-time, that monitors chosen points of stability by statistical methods, and aims at breaking the 'time barrier' in the sense earlier described. The technology is freely available: that is not the issue. What is at issue is the human role in all this, for there had better be one, or we shall remain for ever (as we are now) powerless in the grip of inept automation. The strange thing is that people *will* try to do themselves those jobs that can be much better dealt with by computers, and insist on leaving to computers those responsibilities that they can discharge only by themselves. (That is not said with hindsight: it was entirely predictable — see 'The Irrelevance of Automation', my plenary address to the Second International Conference On Cybernetics in 1958, *Proceedings.*)

To understand this second diagram, Figure 64 (which takes the missing portions of Figure 63 for granted), look first at the point of stability in the system that has suddenly been blown out of its (small circle) limits — as determined by the criteria laid down by the metasystem, and monitored by a meter. The meter moves, detecting instability. In fact, this moment is diagrammatically dramatized; the meter should initiate the process *before* the point actually leaves its circle, thus breaking the 'time barrier'. This action generates the *alarm signal*, which impinges on the manager's calm. Then the manager must needs react. He has to move his position in his psychological space to somewhere more comfortable. The model proposes that this necessity takes him through a three-phase trajectory, before he returns to his point of calm (which has by then another meaning, because the situation will have changed). The three phases of this trajectory are marked in his psychological space as T1, T2, and T3.

The trajectory T1 is the trajectory of judgment. A range of responses is conceived as open to the manager, and he *chooses between them.* The objective is of course to do something, the substantive nature of which will cause the incipient instability to be damped. The trajectory T2 is the manager's *choice of style* as to the projection of his judgment into the system. Now the effectiveness trajectory is a product of T1 and T2, and will result in the return of the representative point of the system to the circle that determines its limits of stability — if indeed the manager's choices have been well-considered. In that case the alarm signal will disappear; if it does the manager returns, on trajectory T3, to his (newly defined) point of calm.

Before discussing the manager's personal situation further, it is highly relevant to look at the extra loop that has appeared on the outside of Figure 64. The meter that detects instability has acted: it has a norm, set about with limits, and has detected the change that gave rise to the alarm signal. Thus the comparator (a circle marked by a cross) that knows firstly what that difference was, and *how long it took* for managerial action to restore stability, is in a position to send information back to the variety filter. As we saw, if the variety filter had been properly designed in the first place, and given that the alerting signal reached it (through the resolution and perception filters), the standard bureaucratic system should have warned the manager. It did not — or it typically does not. Then the feedback modifier, which we met in the initial chapters, should be organized to affect the design of the variety filter. In this way, the bureaucracy could be arranged to become more and more, instead of less and less, effective to its supposed purpose of informing management.

According to this description, managerial effectiveness is a product of the manager's judgmental and stylistic *preferences*. The diagram so far suggests that these two choices are independent of each other — but certainly they are not. And yet the diagram reasonably reflects much management training, in which style can be taught in its own right. By drawing the whole picture as an integrated system, we may observe a potential trade-off between judgment and style. The loop must necessarily be closed. Then to choose a substantive response and an innappropriate style to go with it, will not lead to an effective product. Equally, to place every emphasis on a 'good' style (that is one determined by criteria not settled by *this* system at *this* time) will necessarily attenuate the variety of judgmental response. In both cases, distortion will be induced in the T1-2-3 trajectory, and effectiveness will be lost. Consider why this is so.

Draconian measures are sometimes necessary, especially if there is no filtration system for detecting incipient instability. Such measures are, by definition, not benign. It follows that a benign style, chosen only because we approve of benignity, renders the draconian measures ineffective. It results in confusion, and usually in what is called 'lash-back'. To choose a draconian measure entails the attenuation of the variety of available style. Conversely, responses to incipient instability may be chosen that are by their very nature light and delicate in their touch. If so, the variety of style is again attenuated: we ought not to use sledgehammers to crack nuts. If we do so there will be a different sort of lash-back; in any case effectiveness will suffer. The problem is that managers are themselves, and tend to use the response they see fit and the style they see fit as if these two things were unconnected. The variety analysis leads to the conclusion that this is not so. Then managers should recognize these trade-offs in judgmental and stylistic variety.

Machiavelli understood the point very well, but we have lost the sense of his teaching — which was systemic. It was also amoral, and our generation has noticed that. Thus we find an explanation of the inadequacy of those accounts of style that were criticized earlier. The bland, all-purpose, benign manager that some of our development and training schemes try to produce does not understand the nature of system: to do so would retain his options in the matter of style, which would be attenuated later — but only according to circumstances. He is not so much amoral as immoral, because his unnatural style attenuates his judgmental variety. The most preposterous managerial failures in general effectiveness that I have known have always fallen foul of these alternatives, while the successes — which can often be quite as preposterous — have ignored them. Successful managers are never bland.

The two immediate consequences of these arguments are, first that it is better to teach a manager to know himself than to know what someone supposes (without knowing the circumstances) that he ought to be; and, second, that he should understand the systemic nature of the viable system in which he participates. It is to the second of these intentions that this book is primarily dedicated. It is notable, however, that a strong movement is developing in regard to the first — and I have gladly involved myself in such activity. (Having said so, I am perhaps entitled to add that I am not speaking about twenty minutesworth of unstructured meditation a day. If Instant Nirvana were thus attainable, the Zen apprenticeship would not take fourteen years.)

Returning to the diagram, it is therefore essential to delimit the freedom of choice indicated in selecting judgemental and stylistic preferences: each inhibits the other. In the next and final version of the picture, a web of interactions between these choices is intended to convey their mutually inhibitory effects. It will be noticed too, that in putting the first two pictures together, a further feedback from the experiences of the meters should modify the design of the variety filter. Assuredly so: but a comparator measuring discrepancies between the existing variety filter and the feedback modifier should tell us a great deal about the inadequacies of the *perceptual* filter. It is highly probable that the signals of incipient instability in which we are most interested are not reaching the variety filter at all.

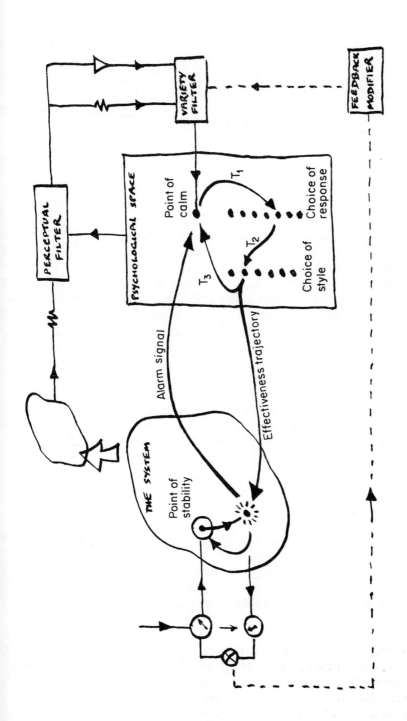

Figure 64.   Handling incipient instability, stage 2

The final diagram (Figure 65) shows us how everything is modifying everything else. Its contemplation is rewarding, because it finally demonstrates the foolhardiness of reductionism in senior management. No piece of this picture can be analysed and improved without instituting MAJOR effects everywhere else. If we attempt an explicit articulation of the metasystem, if we set out to design a management centre, without understanding this, then there can hardly be a worthwhile outcome of those endeavours. Although those statements are true, they are negative in tone. What then is the *positive* conclusion? Here it is.

If we want to classify the situations in which the manager finds himself, they are dependent on two major parameters. Neither of these is commonly nominated in management theory, but both are strongly implicated by our new model. The first is of course variety, and the second is relaxation time. Now we have just been looking at the effects of Ashby's Law on judgmental and stylistic response — within the psychological space of the manager. But as this book has demonstrated *passim*, every transaction, everywhere in the system, can best be considered in terms of the variety equations that bear upon it. How many points of stability in the system shall be nominated? How shall their states of incipient instability be graduated? We have seen how the manager's point of calm is disturbed by a signal of alarm: but suppose that eighty-seven alarm signals fire at the same moment. Variety engineering, using the major (viable system) model must attend to this possibility. Then, looking more deeply into the nature of the systemic problem that promotes the instability, some of those situations will dispose much higher variety than others. All these sources of variety have to be *channelled* and *transduced* and *accommodated* on a *time scale*. The four principles of management were addressed to these four aspects of the matter; they must not be forgotten. Thus in designing a regulatory system for any given situation, the first rule is to follow every significant loop through the systemic diagram, applying the variety rules that have been elucidated.

The second rule is to attend to the relaxation time of the system. Once a loop of incipient instability is activated, how long will it take for a return to stability? This problem has been discussed here several times. The key point to note is that if the system has not returned to stability before another shock drives it once more towards instability, then regulation is impossible. So is learning impossible, so adaptation, so evolution.

These two parameters, of variety and relaxation time, enable the classification of situations when the articulation of the metasystem is in prospect. We are not concerned with the technical complexity involved, nor with bland styles of management that are so often unreal — and are perceived as such. The real concern is with the proliferating variety that must needs be absorbed; and with the time that must needs elapse before the iterative loops of the managerial system can assimilate that variety and return the representative point of the

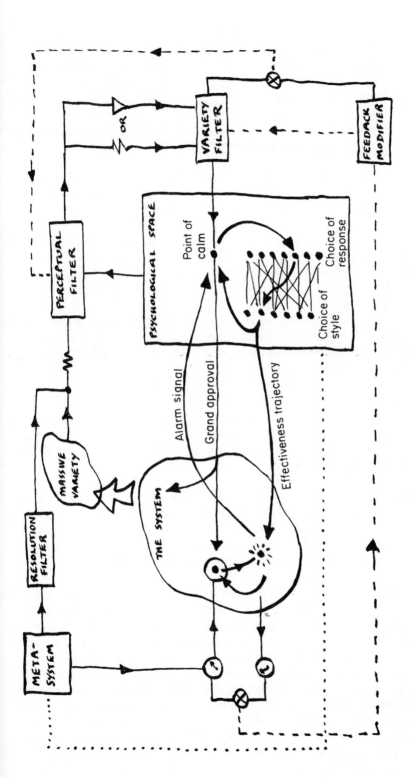

Figure 65.   Handling incipient instability, stage 3

system to stability and the psychological state of the manager to its point of calm. Now it would be ridiculous to claim that these two parameters of managerial effectiveness are independent of each other. The reason is that the judgmental trajectory (which we already saw to be closely associated with style) is itself a way of talking about relaxation time. This lag in effectiveness is implicit in our diagrams, since closure is indicated in the iterative loops. What the lag really is in any given situation surely governs the judgment.

This analytic conclusion is well borne out in managerial realities, but it is not an issue to which managers normally address themselves realistically. When people ask which among alternative actions they should take, they look to the minimization of duress in the immediate future — or so I have observed. This criterion ignores both the stylistic constraints under which the manager labours (because he is himself, and not the creature of a training programme), and also the relative time lags in restabilization that the alternative strategies determine (because some actions metabolize the system faster than others).

In the next diagram, Figure 66, which is given all in words, I offer a way of classifying the situation in which a manager, faced with incipient instability finds himself. It is of course based on the model just unfolded. I think that this model works, because I have used it myself many times. Frequently, the initial procedure leads to failure. In that case, it is necessary to 'cancel all engage-ments' and to address the second procedure in a life-or-death spirit. That usually does work. It has failed me four times in my life. On each occasion I omitted to resign until later, because I simply could not believe that there was no way out. There *was* no way out, with hindsight. Thus I now believe in the reality of the model to its final conclusion, and will not ever be caught again.

The parameters of effectiveness enumerated — judgment, style, and relaxation time — are not nominated casually. They derive from the model proposed in this chapter, certainly; but it should be remembered that *this* model derives from the model of any viable system, with which we have been concerned for so many pages. We are very close, now, to the heart of the firm.

Management texts try to replace judgment by decision theory. They talk about style as if it were independent of what you are, and what you are trying to do. They ignore the relaxation time, which may well be the most importance parameter of all. Even so: this is not intended to denigrate the work of anyone else, nor management training approaches as we know them. If cybernetics offers new insights, as I am sure it does, let them add rather than subtract. But it is surely a strange fact, and something that might well alert us all, that the three parameters on which *this* decision model focuses are not the three that are conventionally regarded as critical; and also that they do not find any reason to make money a central argument at all. Let me say it for the last time: money is a constraint, no more, no less. As things are, all our wise men —

HOW TO CLASSIFY MANAGERIAL SITUATIONS AND TO DECIDE

Criterion of Effectiveness:

A representative point of the system, becoming incipiently unstable, must be returned to stability (within acknowledged physiological limits) within a time-scale that does not allow immanent disaster to become actual.

This satisfactory conclusion is to be recognized by the return of the representative point in the manager's psychological space to its POINT OF CALM.

Procedure:

Consider the range of alternative actions that are addressed to the problem.

Eliminate those possible actions that cannot meet the criterion of effectiveness within the time-scale available: leaves n alternatives.

Estimate the relaxation time for each of these n alternatives, and match each to a stylistic mode that would most meet the criterion.

Eliminate those possible actions for which the **effective** style is not available or is implausible.

If more than one solution remains, choose between the stress of adopting an unnatural style (given the psychology of the manager and the culture of the situation) and the speed of the effective response (given the degree of threat imposed by the incipient instability).

In Case of Failure:

Recast situation.
Look especially for new alternatives, not hitherto considered.
Entertain new styles, not hitherto envisaged.
Contemplate new relaxation times, which means changing metabolic rates.
If all this fails, it is necessary to resign.
Therefore consider under what terms (fundamentally changing available alternatives, plausible styles, and conceivable relaxation times) it might be possible to continue.
Propose such changes.
ACT.

In Case of Failure:

RESIGN. (And do not fail to do so.)

Figure 66. Handling incipient instability, final stage — a procedure for using the model

from the most sober statesmen to the whizz-kids of the City — are making a career out of money, as if it really mattered. We know in our hearts that this golden calf has nothing to do with human happiness. It should also become clear that it has nothing to do with the heart of the firm. When that happens, the world of enterprise will be a different place.

An earlier chapter attempted to show that the senior manager — whom we now see as a member of the comradeship at his own level of recursion *behaving* as an articulator of the metasystem — must listen to himself.

In this long, difficult, and diffuse chapter, we observe him as personifying the self-consciousness of the enterprise. The clue was that he operates in the awareness of the infinite recursion.

If the senior manager succeeds in understanding, and legislating for, his own ambiance of calm and alarm; and if he also succeeds in classifying managerial situations and his own decisions according to the tripartite model here set out, then he may operate closure in the sense defined. And if he does *that,* in full awareness of *what* he is doing, then he may embody the infinite recursion as a living process.

Henry Ford did this, I think. Salvador Allende did this, I know. Most managers and ministers, admired as they are for whatever reasons (but usually because they treated or treat the constraint of money as a goal), did and do not.

Perception of the infinite recursion is always the goal. Perhaps the problem is that once a man or woman has reached that perception, nothing matters any longer.

If the human race is to survive, some of those people must continue to care.

LATER IN THE BAR...

'Yes, I'll buy a ticket. It's rather pathetic though—'proceeds in aid of Third World charities', isn't it?'

'Don't you think those are worthy causes? Think of your cup of tea that you're stirring right now, piling in more sugar than is good for you. Do you realize the degree of poverty that sugar cane workers and tea pickers have to suffer? I think it only decent to support charities that help those people.'

'Of course you do, Tom; you're a nice man. But only yesterday you were carrying on about huge increases in the price of tea.'

'Government ineptitude, that's what it is.'

'Very likely. But you want to keep down the cost of living in Britain — point A — and you want to be a nice man, so — point B — you raise money for Third World charities.'

'Well, I should have thought that they were both good ideas.'

'Damn it, we're here learning about systems. *Can't you see that if well-intentioned people understood systems theory, they would get up a petition to the government to* **increase** *the price of sugar and tea.'*

'Neatly said, Alan. But if Tom can't answer that, I will. If you understood Systems theory, you'd realize that the price increase would not go to the sugar and tea workers, not on any account. It would be dissipated through all the intermediary systems, middle men, owners, tax gatherers. So neither the British housewife nor the workers would be any better off.'

'Well, they ought to be. Is it beyond the wit of man to short-circuit some of these all-too-complex systems? If all these well-intentioned people — like Tom — knew that the whole of the price rise was going to the cane-cutters and the tea-pickers, I'm sure that they'd cheerfully pay double for both commodities. Most people have the right attitude.'

'What about fixed income people, and our own poor? They also have the right attitude. But they don't have any money. And they belong to the system too.'

'Seems to me, then, that 'having to right attitude' has no bearing on anything.'

'*That can't be right. If we had a return to Christian values, which means having the right attitude, all would be well. Just look at what the unions are doing in my industry ...* '

'*Oh, they say the same about you. Attitudes are all very well; what counts is* behaviour. *Choose your strategy and choose your style, then act. That's what the book says, anyway. If you make instability yet more unstable, you got it wrong — and it makes no difference what your 'attitude' was.*'

'*This the cane-cutters and tea-pickers already know.*'

'*Touché.*'

'*Anyway, I don't see how you can choose a style. The leopard cannot change his spots, training schemes nothwithstanding.*'

'*Encounter groups, and so on — they make people change, don't they?*'

'*Not* change, *exactly. They make people observe themselves. That has to increase their stylistic variety to some extent.*'

'*If they don't go crazy at what they see. That happens.*'

'*It's the role of art to do that.*'

'*How do you mean, Tony?*'

'*Picasso said that art is a lie that shows us the truth.*'

'*In that case, I've wasted a lot of money on pictures for the boardroom — they are supposed to be decorative.*'

'*So much for self-awareness, David. What do you think, John?*'

'*Well, the book goes into the knowing-yourself and observing-yourself angles, but it doesn't tell you how to do it.*'

'*Load of mysticism.*'

'*It would be, if it told you how to do it. Standing on your head night and morning, for instance, is not the answer. The contention seems to be that if the informational system is properly designed to recognize incipient instabilities, and if there is a management centre in which requisite metasystemic vareity is shared between comradeship, then the senior management can become aware of what it is really doing.*'

'What a pretentious statement!'

'On the contrary, it's trivial. We all do exactly that anyway.'

'Well, you can't both be right.'

'Yes they can, Charles. Look, if this book is right about viable systems, then John is correct to say — yes, it's really what we do. But to make a clear statement about that can easily sound pretentious ...'

'... then there's no need to say it.'

'But there is. Most of the formal systems we have are totally divorced from the real systems we use. Those are the ones that conduce to viability. Take the lunch of a few of the top people that goes on, with various changes of venue, until midnight. I get involved in those occasions sometimes. My secretary can't find me. And the whole thing is indefensible — to people who have been stood up, to wives, to the tax man. But I get the feeling that those affairs **work,** *that suddenly we understand each other, and know what we are going to do.'*

'Me too. And if this book succeeds, we won't need all that any longer, which would be a pity, because it will have ... as it were, formalized the informal.'

'That's exactly what it's trying to do, you know. As to you, David, you're a sybarite.'

'You might at least get my sex right. I'll settle for Epicurean.'

'I've never seen either term on a management grid.'

'Well, we now understand the problem with those things. Ah, here's Jim — move over. Where have you been?'

'I've just returned from the infinite recursion.'

'No wonder you sound sepulchural. What was it like?'

'Look here — seriously — just what is all that stuff supposed to mean. It's asking a lot, isn't it?'

'I've got a glimmer about it. You've heard of Heinz von Foerster? He's one of the founding fathers of cybernetics, and I once heard a talk of his on these lines. It was an informal occasion, but it had quite an impact on me.'

'Try and tell us.'

'Well, you take a mathematical statement that is supposed to be an expression of the state of affairs, and you operate on it. That's equivalent to a manager taking action, because everything is changed as a result. You go on doing this — mathematicians do it, and so do managers. Both of them find that the initial statement (or state of affairs) vanishes in the process.'

'Well it would, wouldn't it? At the end of the line, everything has changed — certainly it has in management.'

'Yes. The point is that you have to operate an infinite number of times to get there.'

'That's impossible: you'd never finish.'

'Wait a minute; the book says that infinity is a process.*'*

'So we have to imagine *the end of the line?'*

'Something like that. At any rate, 'the end of the line' stands for a total transformation of the initial state of affairs — which is of course what managers like us are after.'

'I'm trying to do the imagining. But how *do we get there?'*

'Well, that's just the point. You get there by experiencing the process.'

'The book said that about planning.'

'So?'

'Let me break this ghastly silence. How do you **know** *you've got there? What* **is** *this goal?'*

'The goal generates itself, I think. As I understood him, Heinz von Foerster said that the final expression computes *itself, so that the infinite recursion generates self-representation.'*

'Then we finally know who we are.'

'That's it.'

'As individuals, or as an enterprise?'

'The book makes that comparison... I guess it should be both.'

'OK for the individual. But that's a very private matter. This sounds to me like mathematical Buddhism.'

'Perhaps it is. But the book argues that the metasystemic comradeship is a sort of individual — it certainly says that the metasystem cannot be fully understood by the system. And surely there has to be a joint awareness of the metasystem.'

'This Heinz man sounds a very dry stick.'

'On the contrary, he is the most vivacious man I've ever met. It was a hell of an experience that I'm trying to convey. Everything was very clear at the time, and it was such fun too.'

'Maybe you were hynoptized. Bert, you are *a mathematician, but you're very quiet. Does this make mathematical sense?'*

'Oh yes. I'm trying to get at its managerial sense.'

'So are we all. But do tell us, are there really mathematical expressions (as the book seems to claim) that state the situation at the end of the line — although it is only a process?'

'Sure. They are called eigenvalues... '

'They would *be. Please don't explain.'*

'All right.'

'Apparently there is a theory of self-consciousness in this whole picture of calm and alarm.'

'That's what I'm getting through. Together with a process of self-organization towards viability.'

'Who's in charge?'

'Of self-organization? It would be hard to say, wouldn't it? What is the real nature of System Five, in fact?'

'The book said that first.'

'Then just hold everything for a minute. We are sitting here talking about self-consciousness and self-organization, and someone wants to quote this book. It says, in this very chapter, that the limits of stability are 'laid down by the metasystem'. That sounds like the ultimate authority to me. Surely System Five is actually running the show.'

'No doubt it is. The real question is: what is System Five?'

'The trouble with you, Bill, is that you are a natural authoritarian. Because you read that limits are 'laid down by the metasystem', you feel happy. If only someone will point to the door of the room where this is done, you will know how to manipulate the situation. But the whole teaching shows that the system and the metasystem are in intimate interaction, and that neither does anything except as a perpetual response to the other.'

'You mean a continuous response.'

'Very likely. The whole point is that there is no beginning and there is no end. Everything is process.'

'Yes: it leads to continuous self-organization, continuous self-consciousness — and, of course, to continuous viability.'

'Thanks, Tony. I'm only trying to say that a phrase such as 'laid down by the metasystem' can't possibly be interpreted in hierarchical terms. We are not dealing with hierarchies, except in a logical sense. What the metasystem 'lays down' is simply the result of the requirements of the total viable system, which are expressed metalinguistically, and must therefore be uttered by the metasystem.'

'System Five is everywhere, then.'

'Like God.'

'Is that what you believe, Tony?'

'I would not risk owning up to anything as unreliable as belief.'

'Oh, come on now...'

'What you call my belief, Dick, is that part of my knowledge which I don't succeed in communicating to you convincingly.'

'How patronizing can you get! Meanwhile, Mark is slumped in his corner over there, saying nothing, and drinking a foul concoction. What on earth is it Mark?'

'It is a mixture of vodka and creme-de-menthe.'

'Disgusting. Why this thusness?'

'All right, I'll tell you. I am absolutely and completely fed up. The talk is a pain in the neck, and I do not like this job.'

'What job? I thought you had your life thoroughly well organized.'

*'This job. You are idiots, all of you. Don't you realize that we are **figments**.'*

'What do you mean — figments?'

'We are figments of this book's imagination. And I resent it.'

'No wonder, if you drink that stuff. The rest of us are perfectly self-conscious about our role, observing what we are doing.'

'That must be nice for you. If we are not figments of the book's imagination, what are *we?'*

'An articulation of its metasystem.'

CHAPTER FIFTEEN

Life and death

The viable system is organized recursively, and maintains its independent existence at each level of recursion. This independence, at any one level, is conditional on the cohesiveness of the whole — or, as we should now prefer to say, simply on cohesiveness. 'The whole' is simply an arbitrarily defined chunk of an infinite recursion: that part over which we consider ourselves to have power of edict, should we care to exert it.

It is small wonder that the enterprise, which has legal status as such 'a whole', but which partakes in several intersecting infinite recursions, suffers typically from recurrent crises of identity.

Repeatedly here, criticism has been levelled at what were called 'management slogans'. They do not have requisite variety to handle the complexity of real-life issues. But one such slogan became popular which posed the question: *what business are we in?* This is a slogan that the cybernetician can approve. It addresses the problem of identity, and — since it is not bounded by preconceptions as to the reply — implicitly disposes requisite variety. It does so, that is, provided that there is no automatic answer built into the managerial culture that says: 'my grandfather's', or 'read the Articles of Association'.

Even within the arbitrary whole, each level of recursion is likely to answer the identity question differently. When, thirty years ago, I asked the manager of the cold rolled strip department in a steelworks what business he was in, he said that he made materials for razor blades, for jet engines, for chronometer springs... When I asked the men and women who worked the machines in that department, they said that they made cold rolled strip. But that was thirty years ago. *Today,* the manager would have the sense to explain the point; *today,* he would erect a large glass case containing examples of the customers' finished products, so that everyone could understand their societary role. Well, that manager was a little ahead of his time. Thirty years ago, he actually had that large glass case. Irregardless (as the chief clerk in that department was fond of saying), those workpeople made cold rolled strip. They were proud of it.

Of course, when I asked the directors of the steelworks what business they were in, there were as many answers as directors. And of course none of them thought to mention cold rolled strip. I used to wonder what the shareholders thought: did they necessarily know that the block of shares in their portfolios labelled with this company's name had anything to do with steel? At this point the industry was nationalized. The government must have known that the company made steel, or its name would not have been included in the Schedule. But what *business* did the government think my company was in? If there had been a clear answer, at that level of recursion, the next government might not have denationalized steel. For that matter, the government after that might not have nationalized steel for the second time. At some level of recursion, these activities must have made some sort of sense. At my own level of recursion, there was no perceivable difference of any kind between being private, being public, being private, and being public again. Meanwhile, the enterprise was viable: it survived. Therefore it must have had an identity — even if there was no agreement as to what the identity was.

Life forms share this property. You and I reckon that we are alive, and we reckon that we are ourselves and not anyone else. Where is the evidence for this? Outwardly, we are, in scientific fact, more dead than alive. Our hair and our nails are inert; our visible skin is all dead, and flaking off. Our whole bodies are infested with parasites: our innards are a factory for maintaining the viability of vast numbers of micro-organisms, and the roots of our eyelashes are colonized by mites. In ten years from now, every cell in our bodies will have been replaced. Who *are* we, you and I? And what *business* are we in? In microbiological terms, it is impeccable to say that we are environments for vast populations of viable systems. And incidentally, we shall continue to be so in our graves. Assuredly, at the level of recursion of the myriad life forms that my body supports, that is all there is to it.

The moment of birth (as we call it) and the moment of death (as we call it) are not moments recognizable to the individual *E. Coli* in our gut. Our birth and our death is recognizable at another level of recursion, where criteria of 'being alive' have been agreed by the metasystem. We rely on these criteria when we talk about the deaths of parents and the births of children. As to ourselves... well, we had better respect the criteria we use to assess the viability of others, had we not? For the purposes of this book: yes. (For other purposes, certainly not. But that is another book, for which there is no publishing contract.) At the level of recursion at which we normally speak of *ourselves,* we are born and we die. And somehow we remain viable systems within these temporal limits — despite the continuous process of death experienced by ourselves at lower levels of our own recursion — in the cells. How is it done?

The answer is that viable organizations *produce themselves*. This is something different from self-reproduction, which involves changing the level of recursion. Cells are born, and cells die. The parasites run through countless generations. But 'the whole' that we call 'me' goes on. At least, that is the picture between the conventions (at this level of recursion) of birth and death. Of course, this 'whole' is an arbitary designation of 'me' selected from the infinite recursion, to be called 'a system'. But let that pass: again I am in danger of writing the wrong book, and it will not happen again.

The enterprise, that arbitrary 'whole', *produces itself* too. That is to say that its staff may come and go, its departments may be closed down or opened up, it may be nationalized or denationalized — and still it has and retains its **identity**.

In cybernetic terminology, this enterprise is called autopoietic. The word derives from the Greek: *poio* means 'to make'. So an autopoietic system makes itself — continuously. What business is it in? *It is in the business of preserving its own organization.*

Look at any great institution: a hospital, a university, a multinational company, a social service, a country. All these things change, insofar as their elements are replaced; all these things change, insofar as some features disappear while others are invented. But Guy's Hospital, Oxford University, the steel industry, education, and Britain itself, are recognizably themselves. There is, as in our bodies, every kind of change. But there is no alteration.

In the concept of autopoiesis we have the final testimonial to viability. The viable system is directed towards its own production.

Now the quintessence of the cybernetic thinking that demonstrated autopoiesis was due to Humberto Maturana and his associates, notably Francisco Varela. Maturana is a biologist; in autopoiesis he found, he reckoned, the principle of life itself. Life is not primarily characterized, as most people would say, by the process of self-*re*production, but by the process of self-production. Life is devoted to the preservation of its own organization. As long as the living organism can maintain its organization, despite the living death of its cellular elements, and the behaviour of its parasites, through lice, amoebae, and viruses to its pathological protein chains, then 'I' am still 'me'.

For each of us, this cynosure of life is cause for celebration. For the enterprise also, we can at once see that autopoiesis is a mode of solidarity, for all levels of recursion. Come hell and high water, the show must go on. Somehow in the maelstrom, identity is preserved. We shall take a close look, now, at how this happens — in the viable system as we have studied it, that is to say; since what follows cannot be attributed to Maturana, although his concept of autopoiesis is central to the argument.

Consider *one* recursion of the viable system.

The state of calm envisaged in the last chapter is the outcome of much filtration. It has been seen that all the lines connecting together the five subsystems of the viable system carry variety (in accordance with the Second Principle of Organization) to a management unit — and of course this principle applies between the system and the metasystem too. But on these lines are the variety filters that perform amplifications and attenuations designed to meet the First Principle of Organization, that deals with requisite variety itself. Now although System Two is dedicated to damping oscillation between the autonomous components of System One, it is clear that *all* systems have a damping role in respect to oscillatory behaviour in the viable system itself. Witness, for example, the mutually 'calming' effects of the system on the metasystem and the metasystem on the system that were closely examined in Chapter Thirteen. The viable system, which is autopoietic, must maintain this general calm if it is to preserve its own organization.

Management information systems, as conventionally understood, exist to exercise this function. They are massive attenuators; and they promote the calm that ignorance of 'little local difficulties' underwrites. In the limit, however, this whole design will send the organism to sleep. If we take one period with another, for department alpha, and ally that to the same treatment of department beta, and for department gamma; if we then do the same for their higher divisional recursions, Alpha, Beta and Gamma; if we then, taking all these aggregates as representing the corporation entire, proceed to take one *year* with another... then at the level of System Five, nothing much will ever appear to happen. Therefore sleep supervenes. If we are not very careful, sleep turns into coma; and coma becomes death.

It was to deal with this lethal calm that the measurement of instability was introduced. Calm we must have, but not lethal calm. Then the alarm signals proposed in the last chapter do not belong to the family of management information systems at all. These systems are maintaining calm; but they do so by every kind of aggregation — thereby supressing the signals that point to instability. The alerting system is orthogonal to the calming system, in fact.

The theoretical basis of this distinction has been discussed at length in *Brain of the Firm*, just as its practical basis was discussed in the last chapter. But it will be useful to borrow nomenclature from *Brain,* to call these alerting signals **algedonic.** This word derives from the Greek words for pain and pleasure. Alerting signals are triggered by the same basic data that are turned into information by the calming filters; but a different set of filters is required to awake the enterprise from sleep, to disrupt its coma, to ressuscitate it from death. The data are the same; the information is different. It is because the two types of filter act in different ways. The traditional set of (MIS) filters says: 'take no notice, it will all come out right in the end'. And this is true, even though the MIS filters are looking for 'variances', and even though managerial action be taken to 'correct the variances'. The algedonic signal screams: 'ouch; it hurts!' No wonder that the enterprise awakes.

All this is said, remember, about one recursion of the viable system. But viable systems are nested; and the lower recursion is autonomous (as defined) with respect to the higher. Thus the lower recursion is seen by the higher as a muddy box, into whose management information system it will not enter.

Thus in the infinite recursion, or even in the arbitrary chunk of the infinite recursion that the enterprise calls its 'whole' system, the metasystemic state of calm is on this showing likely to be well-nigh absolute, namely dead. Not only does the viable system at each level of recursion induce its own calm, but the nest of viable systems is likely to induce a 'metacalm' in the whole. This could be interpreted by the statement: 'we are calm because all known points of calm are calm'. But this description does not apply to any actual enterprise, because algedonic signals are constantly by-passing the official MIS filters. They need to, of course, because of the extremely lethal risk of a spurious 'metacalm'. So, as always happens in these pages, the call goes out to design them properly.

The postulate is that algedonic signals, alone of all the signals in the enterprise, are organized to *break through* recursivity. Again, the theory is debated in *Brain*. But again, the practical exigencies can be seen as fundamental to actual managerial experience. Indeed, so strong are the algedonic signals from recursions lower down that (if they are not blocked off by effective management action at their own level of recursion), they cause mayhem at the senior management level — the 'top' recursion. And this is seen when board meetings discuss tea-breaks, as was mentioned earlier. Now we see *why* boards discuss tea-breaks. If they did not respond to unblocked algedonic signals at lower levels of recursion, the viable system would *lose its cohesiveness*.

In the Law of Cohesiveness we found the variety equation that stops the enterprise from blowing apart. Now we have its mechanism. But as usual: just because the mechanism is there, it does not mean that its cybernetic design can be disregarded. To understand the mechanism, and the cybernetics of the viable system, remains the route to effective organization. It is extremely important, when contemplating what is to count as the management centre, to consider the inter-recursive algedonic signalling equipment. Otherwise: either the management centre will go to sleep in trance-like contemplation of the self-consciousness of the infinite recursion, or it will be overtaken by anarchists from lower recursive levels intent on alleviating their personal pain. And why not? The senior management owes a debt to those people, for their agreement to 'belong'. And if that sounds 'soft', let the senior management consider the alternative in terms of total viability.

If all this still sounds complicated and theoretical, please apply the thinking to national government — whereupon it is all blatantly obvious. There are many levels of recursion involved in the nationwide bureaucracy. It is an absolute fact that lethal 'metacalms' are induced as the level of recursion rises: the citizen seeking action at a local level is familiarly told that the regional level is 'considering'. But (in Britain, at least) the bureaucracy is not even intended to be a viable system, but part of a political process that is a viable system. It is not surprising, then, that the inter-recursive algedonic signals turn out to involve politicians rather than bureaucrats. When a bureaucracy is allowed to become a viable system in itself, although in societary terms to do so is to be pathologically autopoietic, it is not surprising that algedonic signals do not get through. The citizen is reduced to a cipher. It is a state of affairs that can be observed in many parts of the world.

It is with the algedonic mechanism, which has been implicit in the model for a long time, that the final clue to viability lies. For the viable system cannot remain viable if it goes to sleep. *A fortiori,* it cannot remain viable if it dies. But if a system has all of the necessary and sufficient conditions of viability, which we set out to discover and have now listed, it will live. Most enterprises respond to these cybernetic criteria, and continue to be the enterprises that they are. Some do not respond, and are observably crashing. But, again, most enterprises are at risk; because they *barely* meet the criteria. They do not understand what the cybernetic criteria are, and remain alive by 'feel' for the situation. And so we have a diagnostic tool.... .

Well, the pathological traits of the five-part viable system have been sufficiently discussed. For instance, it should be very clear by now why Systems Two and Four are normally vulnerable subsystems, why the monitoring devices of the Three-Four balance often fail, why System Five often collapses into System Three, and why the metasystem often lacks a capabilty to speak the metalanguage. But all these traits, or symptoms, relate to any one level of recursion. The ultimate pathology of the viable system concerns the failure of its cohesiveness, and of its inter-recursive algedonics. This turns out to be an aberration of its autopoietic function.

The viable system is autopoietic: it produces itself. Thereby it maintains its living identity. It preserves its own organization.

BUT TO WHAT END?

This book began by demonstrating the subjective nature of systems, and by calling in question how their purposes should be defined. But for any enterprise, there is supposed to be some sort of concensus about the nature of the system, and about its purpose. If this analysis has severely damaged these notions, leaving both disputable for any enterprise whatever, then I think that is proper. There really is an identity crisis in every enterprise, and that crisis really is associated with what purpose is alleged to be upheld.

Meanwhile, you may say, the enterprise goes on — so why worry? Well, there is good cause to worry. The autopoietic system produces itself, by preserving its own organization. If both its identity and its purpose are in doubt, it still remains viable. That is the whole point of Maturana's biological principle. There is great divergence of opinion about what constitutes the human being: whether, for instance, it is an environment for micro-organisms, the vehicle for a mind, or the vessel of a spirit. There is even more divergence about the purpose of this system: whether, for instance, it is an entity to play a role in ecological balance, or to achieve perfectability, or to see God. But while people debate these issues, even concerning their own persons, the biological principle keeps them in self-production: they retain their identity. Just what they are, or why, can be decided later — perhaps *much* later.

Now apply these points to the enterprise. A hospital, we tend to say, exists: it is a defined system, and it is there to heal the sick. A university, too: we know all that. So with the firm, the social service, the government. When systems-theoretic notions are applied to any part of these organizations, however, the stereotypes fall apart. We are no longer sure of their boundaries (what is the boundary of medicine, if it is to be preventative; of the university, if all life is a learning experience; and so on). We are no longer sure of their purposes, either. Some fifty percent of illness turns out to be iatrogenic, that is, caused by treatment. Universities teach people how we always failed to solve the problem in the past. And so on. But cheer up. Using the concept of autopoiesis we can at least say that the viable system produces itself. Yes, indeed: that works. The hospital is still recognized as a leading eye hospital, after two hundred years. Oxford University is palpably Oxford, after a thousand. And so on. All the elements of these institutions have changed: we are still not sure *what* they are; we are still not sure *why*. But they *are* viable systems.

The suspicion dawns that the enterprise may not only be a system that produces itself, but that this is both its definition and its purpose. If, sometimes, someone leaves a hospital, not dead, and not iatrogenically worse than when he went in, this is simply a by-product of the hospital's primary activity — to produce itself. If, sometimes, someone leaves the university, not brainwashed into creative sterility, but being a little wiser and not just knowing more than when he went in, this is the by-product of the university's autopoietic function. When the election comes, the citizen tries to decide whether he has been better or worse off under the departing government. It is not easy; but the government will try to help him understand, as part of the exercise called staying in power. It is entirely an autopoietic exercise. As to the firm: well, it is still quoted on the stock exchange, after all... .

It is very much to be hoped that all these suspicions are false. If they were justified, however, we should be delineating the pathology of viable systems. We need a thyroid gland; its pathology is to become a goitre. Enterprises need to be autopoietic; their pathology is to turn self-production into an end-in-itself.

Now there ought to be plausible tests to determine whether the autopoietic function of the enterprise is healthy, or diseased. And these are not difficult to propose. The people in the hospital are all replaceable — are indeed replaced over the years: consultants and surgeons, matrons and nurses, administrators and patients. All are supposedly united in the cause of healing the sick. The simple test is: what proportion of everybody's time is spent on healing, and what proportion on the autopoiesis of the medical profession? The hospital is ritualistic; and it is not difficult to examine these rituals to determine the effort that goes into keeping all concerned in their appropriate places, a process whereby the hospital produces its own organization.

The same applies in the university. Huge amounts of time, on the part of professors and lecturers, administrators and students, are apportioned to the maintenance of 'academic standards'. (Well, the degree has to be worth *something,* does it not — in everybody's interests.) This is done by an elaborate network of committees, in which we may well note that everyone (and especially the student) is careful of the correct rank and precedence of everyone else. First names are used, these days, to obscure the realities, but no-one is fooled by that. Some time is spent by teachers and students in sharing enlightment, but not much. And in any case, that is not to be confused with the autopoietic lecture room in which *I* teach and *you* learn.

It would be extremely boring to rehearse these arguments in every context. What is Social Security for? What is the Post Office for? And what is government itself engaged in doing? Each of us may muse on the autopoietic balance of each enterprise that happens to interest him. The autopoietic content invariably looks alarmingly large. And yet the autopoiesis of the viable system is essential to its viability. We saw it coming, quite apart from Maturana's biology, in the notions of System Five closure, in looking at oneself acting, and in the infinite recursion of self-consciousness. Thus, although it is easy to propose a methodology to distinguish between pure autopoietic activity in the enterprise and activity devoted to whatever the consensus alleges to be 'the system's purpose', and although it might not be too difficult to measure this proportionality in terms of time consumed, we do not know at what proportion the viable system resides. Naturally, as a cybernetician seeking natural invariance, the first thought is to suspect that the balance is a constant for all viable systems — including the individual human being. Then any viable system that devoted more time than this constant proportion of time to autopoiesis could be declared to be pathologically autopoietic. The idea is attractive. I feel as a citizen that it is pathological autopoiesis of the institutions that makes me frightened of hospitals, so that nothing would induce me to enter a hospital if there were any other choice. As a professor in two universities, I stay only for so long as is required on any visit to hug those at all ritualistic levels who reckon that being hugged is worth the candle, and leave the august portals as fast as my legs will carry me.... .

But when we look for this 'constant' in terms of a measure that says x-percent of all available time is required for necessary autopoiesis, and that the rest of the time consumed is pathologically consumed, we encounter a difficulty. Such a constant could exist if and only if every viable system acknowledged a similar purpose. But purposes vary; and, as we have seen, the balance of freedom and constraint varies in proportion as a consequence. Therefore to seek a numerical constant of the x-percent kind for the maintenance of necessary autopoiesis, is to pursue a chimera.

It behoves the cybernetician seeking invariance to move slowly at this point. The constant under discussion is not a *numerical* constant at all, but a *structural fact* of any viable system. The proportion of total time that needs to be devoted to maintaining necessary autopoiesis is exactly the time required to maintain System One — which is the viable system at the next level of recursion — whatever that may be. Numerically, the proportionality will vary, because purposes vary; and therefore the law of cohesion will generate different relative varieties in different cases. But the expected invariance is there.

Because this problem of pathological autopoiesis was approached through mensuration, the result could sound disappointing: there is no magical x-percent. To the contrary, this is a final lesson in the precept that 'there is more to mensuration than numeration'. For if we had an x-percent firmly established, it would still be very difficult to measure the actual percentage with which to compare it in a given case — a matter of scientific ambiguity and political contention. But the structural invariance to which the analysis points is easy in its implementation as a detector of pathological autopoiesis.

Only a viable system exhibits autopoiesis at all, since autopoiesis is defined as a 'characterization of life'. Therefore the whole of 'this' recursion is autopoietic, but through and only through its System One which constitutes the *whole* of the next lower recursion. Systems Two, Three, Four, and Five are not in themselves viable systems at any level of recursion: therefore they should exhibit no internal autopoietic behaviour whatever. They often do; and *that* is the source of the pathological time-usage that has been noted. Hence, instead of seeking a chimerical numerical constant as an invariant in detecting pathological autopoiesis, it is necessary only to study the actual behaviour of Systems Two to Five, conceived of as services to the autopoiesis of System One.

It is precisely when these subsystems of the viable system exhibit internally autopietic behaviour (whereupon the total viable system becomes pathologically autopoietic), that people start to talk, grimly, and glumly, about 'The Establishment'. Such pathologies do not exist in the world of plants, it would seem, until such a mechanism as symbiosis goes wrong. (When an ivy-clad tree crashed across my path recently, I recognized a System Two failure when I saw it.) But an ordinary plant, just like an ordinary amoeba, is devoted to autopoiesis: Systems One are, as argued earlier, incipient progeny. We do not find a daffodil, as Jennifer Adie pointed out to me, doing anything *other* than producing itself. And yet there remain examples, in the biological world, of pathological autopoiesis beyond failed symbiosis — and I suppose that a cancerous tumour is one of them.

Returning however to the Establishment, as it is known in social systems, this chapter does perhaps throw more light on its scientific nature as a pathological growth of the viable system than many informative but picturesque disquisitions that have hitherto been addressed to this fascinating subject. For here is an actual definition:

> 'The Establishment' in any social system comes into being at the point when the vital principal of autopoiesis consumes energy greater than that needed to maintain cohesiveness through the appropriate number of viable recursions that mark its claim to organizational identity as a set of embedments of System One.

> 'The Establishment' presents autopoietic activity on the part of Systems Two, Three, Four, or Five; and this constitutes a pathological symptom of the viable system.

Strong arguments were advanced in early chapters to show that the 'purposes of the system' are imputed by the observer. The system's purpose, we said, is simply what it does. It is in this cause that we observe System One to be autopoietic; it is in this cause that we observe Systems Two to Five not to be so, in a healthy enterprise.

Hence if all the patients entering a hospital depart (to take the limiting case) in coffins, there is no need — and in fact no justification — for saying that the hospital is not 'achieving its purpose'. It is we who impute the purpose of the hospital as being to cure the sick. It is quite clear that this particular hospital's purpose is to kill people. It is quite clear that the purpose of Jenny's daffodil is to be a daffodil. If the hospital turns out not to be a viable system much longer, it will be because it is expelled from System One of the next higher level of recursion, because of its pathological autopoiesis. Happily, daffodils are still with us.

How often has this book declared that it does not pretend to make managerial discoveries or to offer prescriptions, but only to elucidate how things are the way that we know them to be.

I do not disclaim having made *cybernetic* discoveries here, for the record. But the intention of the book is to provide useful insights for the business of management.

Then let us return to an enterprise, namely the firm, that was carefully excluded from the examples used in the argument just completed. No industrial manager of my acquaintance would fail to recognize The Establishment at its pathological work in government, hospitals, and universities. But does he recognize it in his own concern? If it exists, of course, he will be part of it. And so will his shop stewards be part of it. The Establishment includes everyone who plays a role in the ritual of pathological autopoiesis.

That rough allegation concludes this enquiry into the nature of viable systems — with a very strong question:

Is your organization viable, survival-worthy, live?

Or is it pathological, and nearly dead?

LATER IN THE BAR...

'*Evening, barman.*'

'*Good evening, Sir.*'

'*Where's everyone, then?*'

'*I don't know: they've just sort of vanished.*'

'*How do you mean, **vanished?***'

'*Well, I don't know. Closing time last night, that Mr Solipsus called for a toast on the last round. 'To figmentation', he shouted. I was pulling down the shutters from in here, and they were all laughing and drinking up. Haven't seen hide nor hair of them since.*'

'*That's a pity. I wanted to give them this little document.*'

'*Then why not pin it up here, beside the dart board. If anyone turns up, he'll find it.*'

'*Good idea. There it is then.*'

'*I'll keep an eye on it for you. Perhaps it was **pigmentation. Or fermentation.***'

'*No, I don't think so. Look, as I'm here, I think I'll have a large Scotch.*'

'*Oh, I'm sorry Sir, you can't.*'

'*No?*'

'*Well, you're not a member of the club, are you?*'

Figure 67. *Timeo Danaos et dona ferentes* — Virgil: I fear the Greeks when bringing gifts

IDENTITY: AN EXERCISE

Identity: an exercise

How do managers know that they are any good?

This question troubles some managers in the silence of the night.

Probably the question troubles good managers more than poor managers.

This document is a guide to help managers work out whether they are any good. It is founded on a serious scientific approach to organizational analysis, and it proceeds to ask questions that may well reveal deficiencies in the nature and working of the organization itself. It does not use any jargon, and aims to help the user come up with a fresh view of his own organization.

So this is why the leading question was posed in such a casual way. It is easy enough to plunge into verbiage that would set any computer buzzing with the recognition of keywords: the question is, what do those keywords actually *mean*?

Each organization has its own notions about such matters as economy, efficiency and effectiveness, and it has instituted regulatory systems with these notions in mind. It is not the present purpose to interfere with any of this. There is no reason to try and impose uniform definitions on all organizations when we are trying to understand how they really work. The fact is that they all work differently, because each organization has its own culture.

The question that this guide seeks to unravel is this:

Does the organization have the *power* to do what it says that it will do — given that it has done its best to define its terms, state its goals, and set up regulatory systems to these ends?

Let us first see what the use of the word 'power' in that context means. Certainly it does not refer to legal or financial capability; nor does it refer to the potency and flair of the management team. It refers to the ability of the organization to gather itself together into an **effective identity,** to act as a unified whole.

We are pretty sure by now that we have the components that make up a viable organization. That is like saying that we are pretty sure we have all the pieces of a jig-saw puzzle spread out on a tray.

But there is more. We have made terrific efforts to connect these components together, with information systems, committee structures, interdepartmental task forces, and the like. That is like saying that we have assembled the jig-saw, making sure (for example) that the top of a wall extends in an unbroken straight line across as many as thirty pieces of the puzzle.

The problem of **identity** is this:

have we seen the picture on the lid?

This expresses the issue quite well. The difficulty for managers is, of course, that the jig-saw puzzle came in a bag instead of a box — and there never was a lid. No peeping at the solution, then.

Management has to recognize the picture in the completed puzzle itself. But (to finish with the analogy) in the large organizations with which we are concerned, the jig-saw puzzle is about five miles square. So we all say: stand right back, to see the total picture. But when we have stood back far enough to bring the whole picture into focus, our eyes are not good enough to pick up the pattern. The identity has eluded us again.

It follows that we have to understand the identity from within. This is surely why there is so much emphasis, these days, on the notion of *consensus*. What one person could recognize the pattern?

Consensus is usually thought of in terms of the agreement to particular policies. But because of the foregoing arguments, it really has to begin with a common view of the identity itself. Are we, in senior management, agreed on what it is that we are managing?

This is not a trivial question. To wave an arm out of the window, or to point to the organization chart on the wall, does not count as an answer. Clearly we are managing 'all that'. But what **is** all that?

What happens when we ask senior managers, separately, the by now traditional question: 'what business are we in?' Experience shows that this is still not a matter of consensus, despite the attention that has been directed to it. Under questioning, we still find that there are different answers. But there are other questions, by no means traditional, on which there is no consensus at all.

Please try this experiment.

Divide the organization into the main blocks which everyone recognizes as constituting the organization (operating divisions, territories, departments, provinces, or whatever). These will be referred to as **elements**. The list is not meant to include service activities, such as accounting, maintenance, the computer. These elements cohere in a **whole**, which is precisely the organization that we are investigating.

Questions follow on the next pages, and we need some sort of 'scoring system' to help in providing a 'feel' for the outcome. But we are entering ground where it would be bogus to pretend that proper measurements can be made. These are subjective judgments for which we ask. Moreover, the questions are important — but which are the most important will depend on the particular weakness of any organization. Therefore there would be no authentic way of weighting scores, even if scores were available.

The plan is to make a stack of cards, fifteen of them, each marked with a simple scale (as shown in Figure 68 A). When responding to a question, take a card, and mark it clearly (as shown in Figure 68 B). Try not to think in terms of numbers. There is however a judgment of proportionality. Put the card face down, once it is marked, and try to forget about it as you address the next question. All this is to avoid 'halo' effects, whereby one rosy answer leads to another, as far as possible, although revision is not excluded.

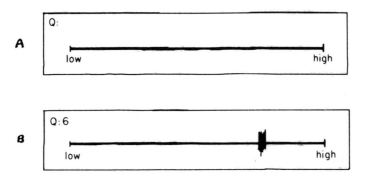

Figure 68.   The original and completed card

420

QUESTION 1:

To what extent do you think that the people who constitute the senior management team *share* **a picture of what it is that they manage?**

Perhaps these diagrams will help.

Is the agreement high, as in the first picture, or low, as in the second?

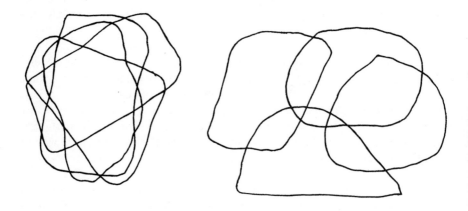

Figure 69.   Consensus diagrams

Remember please: this is not the time for wishful thinking, corporate solidarity, and so on.

Think instead: suppose that a new type of activity were proposed. Would there be instant agreement about whether it 'belonged' to the enterprise or not?

Or: suppose that a proposal were made to get rid of one of the Elements. Would there be instant agreement (tempting offers excluded) that it is disposable, or an intrinsic aspect of the enterprise?

Now mark a card.

QUESTION 2:

Suppose that you took Question 1 around each of the management teams of the Elements.

To what extent do you think that they agree with each other about what is being managed by the Whole?

The answer to this question will depend rather strongly on the representation of each Element in the management of the Whole.

In some organizations, the management team of the Whole is comprised very largely of Heads of Elements. In others, there may be no overlap at all. One could hardly expect the answer to be the same in both cases.

Again, there is a difference between the identity picture that is projected by the Whole to the Elements, and the Identity picture received by the Elements, because the Whole and the Elements stand in different relation to the outside world. This has to be taken into account.

Moreover, each of the Elements is probably receiving a different understanding of this projection from each of the others, because their own circumstances are different from each other's.

Reflecting on all this, then, it would not be surprising if the honest answer to the question is that agreement between the Elements on the Identity of the Whole is lower than one might have expected.

Instead of making a hopeful guess at the answer to this question, it is a good plan to go and ask each of the Elements for its picture of the Identity of the Whole. This had better be done by 'casual' interviews. Otherwise you will get back the ritual statements that were projected by the Whole to the Elements in the first place.

Mark a card.

QUESTION 3:

Taking the degree of agreement marked for Question 2, whereby the Elements agree or not with each other about what is the Identity of the managed Whole:

to what extent do you think that their agreement coincides with the Identity picture retained by the Whole?

This is a very different question from the last.

For instance: if everyone in the room had an hallucination — one that bears were present, another that everything had turned green, and so on — they would debate their hallucinations with mutual interest. But if everyone present had the *same* hallucination — say that they had seen a unicorn — then it is likely that unicorns would become part of reality for them.

In management terms, the degree of agreement among the Elements as to the Identity of the Whole may be very strong, because it is self-reinforcing at that level, and still be very much at variance with the Whole's Identity picture of itself.

As time goes on, because of self-reinforcement between the Elements at the elemental level, and of self-reinforcement at the level of the Whole as it communes with itself, the Identity itself may well be shattered into schizophrenia. How far along this path have we gone?

At this point it is probably necessary to ask again what is the Whole's Identity picture; because we are no longer considering the extent to which its management team *shares* it (Question 1), but the extent of disagreement between what that picture is and the Elements' consensus on this.

Mark a card.

QUESTION 4:

Assuming that you have not been so foolhardy as to mark both scales in the previous two questions at their highest points, there will be a gap between the points marked and 100 percent in each case.

Please contemplate those gaps, and reconsider their relevance to the organization. Then:

to what extent do you think that the management team of the Whole correctly assesses the magnitude of those gaps?

It would be quite wrong to *assume,* if the gaps are large, that the senior management is unaware of them. Machiavellian management works on just that principle. Pure-minded managers, however, may be doing nothing about those gaps because it has never occurred to them that they might exist.

At this point it is a good plan to go and ask the management team of the Whole, using the examples that you have probably unearthed, whether they are aware of the gaps or not. This obviously helps to answer the current question...

... but, note: it may also lead you back to revise your marking on Question 1, because you will have asked the senior management individually.

The fact is that this Question 4 is very potent (we could call it a meta-question). It touches on the issue of the ability and honesty of the Whole to observe its own behaviour correctly and in context. This is difficult for any human being to do, since so many mechanisms of self-defence are built into his and her conditioning; and we have to recall that the 'corporate image' apart, the senior management team is no more than a collection of human beings.

Mark a card.

On the supposition that there are divergences, however large or small, between the Whole and the Elemental view of Identity, we should try to track down their causes.

The most obvious (also the most naive) is poor communication.

How is anyone *supposed to know* what it is that the enterprise constitutes?

Perhaps there exists:

- a declaration on the subject
  ('nature and purposes', 'our objectives' ...)

- an organization chart

- pamphlets, films, annual reports
  — in that case, directed to WHOM?

- an annual statement by the boss

- something else.

Then these things should be studied:

— Are they consistent with each other?

— Are the views of Identity projected to different
parties consistent?

— Especially, what do the Elements think of them?

Much may be learned from these enquiries, but we should not be sidetracked. The objective is to see if some component of divergence in Whole and Elemental comprehensions of Identity can be accounted for in this way.

QUESTION 5:

Therefore please indicate the degree to which you think that Identity as perceived by the Whole is properly transmitted to, and received by, the Elements.

Mark a card.

A deeper reason for the divergencies between Whole and Elemental perceptions of Identity is organizational.

No enterprise is either completely centralized or completely decentralized; there is some kind of balance between the authority exerted by the Whole over the Elements, and the authority left to the Elements to exercise themselves. Let us label this balance 'Degree of Autonomy'.

The Degree of Autonomy is a crucial factor in Identity: it results in the application of epithets to the organization — which may be called 'authoritarian' or 'liberal' by the people in it. These are emotive words already. If there is tension about the issue of Autonomy, the epithets may become more emotive still — say 'fascist' or 'anarchic'.

It is not worth looking for 'objective truth', because the Degree of Autonomy is strongly a function of what people **think** it is. The Whole interferes without realizing it. The Elements respond to interference that does not exist, because they *expect* interference.

Then it is most unlikely that the Whole and the Elements coincide in their view of the Degree of Autonomy; and this cognitive dissonance could account for a large component of the divergence in perceived Identity that we are studying. Then:

QUESTION 6:

What is the extent of the agreement between the Whole and the Elements on the Degree of Autonomy?

Note that this can be discovered only by depth interviewing. The attitudes that people demonstrate to this question are usually complicated, because of the expectations mentioned above, because of reinforcing interactions between the Elements, and because questions of loyalty arise. People differ greatly in their willingness to say what they think on this matter more than most: should they be disloyal? And then, should they be *seen* to be disloyal?

Mark a card.

We might take it as a principle that the amount of intervention necessary in Elemental operations is only that required to support the **coherence** of the Whole.

What is the evidence that there is enough, or too much, intervention to this end?

First, we should look at the information flowing between the Elements and the Whole:

— is there enough, or too much?

— what is *done* with this information at either end?

Second, we should look to see what information reaches the Whole about Elements *of the* Elements (and even Elements of Elements of Elements, etcetera).

Evidently, our discoveries on this point bear on the reasons for the answer to the previous question.

The fact is that if the Degree of Autonomy is adjusted to the coherence principle (above), lower level information should be suitably aggregated at the Elemental level for the purpose of managing the Whole.

When it goes well beyond this, not only do we interfere with the perception of Autonomy, we *invite* actual interference in Elements of Elements. It is well established empirically that management groups are more comfortable taking decisions at a level below their own appropriate level.

QUESTION 7:

Then to what extent is the information passing between the Whole and the Elements correctly judged: in terms of volume, and in terms of its appropriateness to the level of decision concerned?

Mark a card.

We have been studying the *structural* features in Identity; the last question begins a movement towards examining the *behavioural* features of that structure.

How are decisions that bear on Identity actually made?

Note that we remain focussed on Identity. The fact that all manner of decisions are taken for various purposes lies within the province of the regulatory systems set up to provide them. We are here speaking of decisions that **lead to** establishing regulatory systems, or **integrate** the activities of regulatory systems, or **result from** outputs of regulatory systems.

What are the mechanisms in use?

Are they

— committees?

— task forces?

— interdisciplinary investigations?

— arbitrary judgments of the boss?

— or what?

There is usually a collection of such mechanisms, and they are not usually articulated as a *system*.

We shall call this system Identity Regulation.

Thus the task is to identify this system, to see how well it is articulated, and to try and express it more clearly. (The organization chart format is not well adapted to this task, since the reality is usually not an hierarchy but a network.)

Then try to answer

QUESTION 8:

To what extent is this network adequate to the need for Identity Regulation?

Mark a card.

And *certainly* —

it is worth taking time

to pose

to reflect upon

to answer

this crucial

QUESTION 9:

To what extent is the Identity Regulation Network understood by the Elements?

> Note: It *will* be understood by the Whole.
> Then why did they not articulate it
> better?

Mark a card.

Now consider an Element that takes a decision bearing on Identity.

How will the Element know this?

And, having regard to the answer to the last question, if it does know it, how will it have access to the Identity Regulation Network?

In most organizations, in short, such Elemental decisions are usually taken with incomplete knowledge of the total picture (expressed, of course, by the Identity of the Whole).

Procedures have to be designed that will lead such decision-events into the Network.

What these procedures are must depend on how the Network is articulated, described, and understood.

Meanwhile, we ask

QUESTION 10:

To what extent is the Element about to be involved in a decision bearing on Identity likely to recognize this, recognize the Network, and have recourse to the Network?

Mark a card.

The Identity Regulation Network itself usually operates on signals from the organization that it calls (for instance) 'key variables'. It is alerted to activity in the enterprise that bears on Identity (such as flagging profits, loss of cash flow control, and all manner of failure in the internal regulating systems; such as investment plans, budget performance, and so on, on the positive side). It then takes appropriate action, and that is fine.

But its continuous experience of doing all this ought to be fed-back *into its own design.*

Remember that you will not find the Identity Regulation Network on any organization chart. It is more like a living thing.

It should be

- LEARNING

- ADAPTING

- EVOLVING

continuously.

QUESTION 11:

To what extent is the Identity Regulation Network SELF-ORGANIZING in this sense?

Mark a card.

In every enterprise, time is devoted by all concerned, not only to the job that appears to be what the enterprise is for, but to the preservation of the enterprise's Identity. Many rituals are engaged in, the effect of which is to preserve accepted structures in the organization.

These rituals have to do with the exercise of power. They may relate simply to questions of seniority, but are often much more complicated. For example: the task of maintaining 'standards of excellence' in the hospital, in the university, and on the product line, clearly have to do with *both* the accepted job of the institution (which genuinely needs high standards) *and* with the preservation of relationships between roles (between people who would be highly insecure unless those relationships were ritually reinforced).

Again: how much of negotiation, at the business lunch, at the trade union bargaining table, between employers and government, or at the office party, is ritual rather than substantive?

How much of the total effort is honestly addressed to the intended job (as distinct from ritual in all its forms).

QUESTION 12:

by the management?

QUESTION 13:

by the work force?

QUESTION 14:

by you personally?

Distinctions are very hard to draw, you will notice.

But mark three cards.

Finally,

QUESTION 15:

To what extent do you think that the enterprise is aware of the issues discussed in this guide?

This question is again worth considerable reflection.

The enterprise will not be familiar with the theories expounded in a book called *The Heart of Enterprise*. That is why jargon has been excluded from this exercise (although readers of the book can surely translate the exercise back into the jargon). But the enterprise will not be familiar with the thoughts advanced in the exercise either, although there is no jargon, because these are not issues which management consciously confronts.

Yet if the theories are correct, the issues are being deliberated all the time. The results are being worked out under our noses — in terms of power struggles, morale at all levels, and ultimately of viability itself.

Perhaps we should think of institutional failure less in terms of an unsupportable balance sheet, or industrial unrest, and so on, and more in terms of the collapse of its identity.

At any rate, the question as posed is not about the language used, but about the reality. You will need to translate.

Mark a card.

THE EVALUATION

Just as the value of planning lies in undertaking the process of planning, rather than in a product called 'the plan', so the value of this exercise lies in working through it. That is especially true if it is undertaken by a group of colleagues who can then argue about their experience of this process. However, we did set out to make some sort of measurement, by marking cards; and now it is possible to see if that has any pay-off.

Take a piece of paper laid out as in Figure 70, and taking each card in turn transfer the mark onto the appropriate horizontal bar. The result should look something like this:

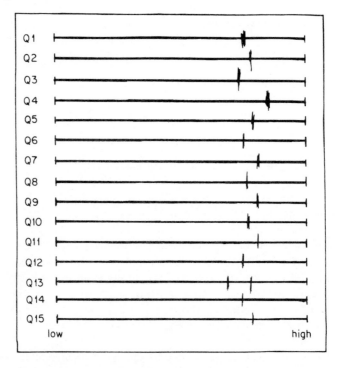

Figure 70.   An impression of the power of the enterprise to
act as an effective integral whole

The result shown in Figure 70 is obviously rather satisfactory. More importance is attached to uniformity of the fifteen 'measures' than to the displacement on the horizontal scale, for any one marker. His view of the identity system may be more or less jaundiced; but if the system is consistently as it is, then a certain kind of identity is already recognizable. If there is an almost random scatter of marks across the diagram, then the integrative system is quite probably out of control. But it is usually very interesting to compare the charts independently prepared by a group of colleagues; and again the making of the comparison is of more value than any spurious averaging of totals.

There is more to mensuration than numeration.

How much more? The answer lies in the **patterns** that any such comparison makes. To find these patterns, it will be necessary to run the results through a computer, since the human eye is not very effective in this task. Hence, and despite all earlier disavowals about quantification, it is worth considering the transformation of the analogue data generated by this exercise into digital data. This is easy enough: make a transparent graticule that can be laid over the answer-card (Figure 70), and read off the respondent's answers to each question as a two-digit number.

Suppose we ask a group of twenty managers in the same enterprise to undertake the exercise. Then we have twenty answer cards, each dilineating a 'profile' of response. After the graticulation of Figure 70 in each case, we have some *approximate* digital data, in which may well reside some *accurate* information. This is the information about patterns — which would be entirely lost by merely averaging the replies within or between the different answer-cards.

The patterns we seek are those which reveal, from the replies, how the twenty managers are grouped. They may group themselves into clusters, by providing similar profiles on the answer-cards. They may group the *questions* into clusters; and this might be revealing, since the questions relate to various levels of metasystem in the viable system model. In short, since the exercise relates to corporate identity, we need to examine the degree of *coherence* within a group's replies.

To find out how the managers group *themselves*, we compare (from one manager to another) the shape of the profile of the fifteen answers which he gave to all the questions. All twenty profiles must be compared simultaneously, and that problem is readily solved by multivariate statistical analysis. Each manager's answer-card is transformed into a string of thirty numbers, representing two digits from the graticulation for each question in order. In statistical terms, each manager's answer-card is now a vector, and this delineates a point in a fifteen-dimensional space created by the fifteen questions that they shared. Managers who produce similar *patterns* of answers will appear as points in this space which lie close together. This is how we may recognize a cluster; and surely it is clear that the inexactitude of the original measurements that has been acknowledged at all time does not matter. We are not attempting to pin a manager down to a point on a fifteen dimensional scale, but simply to find out — with a measurable probability — to which cluster of colleagues he belongs.

Using an up-to-date computer, with a keyboard present in the room of the exercise, the necessary statistical calculations can be performed within seconds. The correlation of views between any two managers can be expressed as the cosine of the angle between their two vectors. This cosine will be zero for unrelated patterns, plus one for identical patterns, and minus one for opposite or reversed patterns.

Taking a different perspective, but using exactly the same statistical approach, we may turn the matrix representing managers and questions through ninety degrees. Now we have a twenty-dimensional space (created by the replies of twenty managers) in which there are fifteen vectors (conceived of as the questions). A point in this space is defined by twenty replies to one question, and there are fifteen such points. So now the profiles under study are those of the questions as interpreted by the managers, and it is the questions that fall into clusters. A cluster will form when all the managers tend to agree that the questions in it are related. Naturally, some managers will be marking high, and others low. That does not matter, so long as they are consistent about it, because we are looking for correlations between questions and not between managers. The correlation coefficient is again measured as the cosine of the angle between each pair of vectors that stand for the questions.

Why should we expect to find these clusters, and what can be learned from them if we do? The managers belong to the same organization, in whose corporate identity we and they are interested. Clusters formed by managers clearly indicate differences in perception between different parts of the enterprise as to its cohesiveness. Clusters formed by questions are the product of the managers' shared perception of the relevance of those questions to the enterprise's structure — and we know (from the viable system model on which the questions are based) what is their structural significance in cybernetic terms. So it ought to be possible to discover through this exercise and its evaluation just how successfully the law of cohesiveness is working in a given enterprise; and maybe (one day) thresholds will be established, to exceed which will predict collapse.

At the time of writing, only preliminary experiments have been made with the digital quantification of data during the course of sessions that used the exercise. In the very first trial, the twenty managers concerned belonged to the same company, but to different divisions — and, in the main, to two such divisions. The group members cheerfully asserted that they shared a corporate identity. But Dr Sidney Howell, having digitized the replies and manipulated the correlation matrices while the session was still in progress, succeeded in identifying clusters that distinguished between the members of these two divisions. A little later he disclosed that one member of the group stood apart from all the rest. The experiment was deliberately anonymous; but the respondent was asked if he would care to identify himself, and he did so. His colleagues concluded that the reason for his separation was that he was a relative newcomer to the company. He denied that this was the reason, said that he knew what was the real one, but vexingly declined to disclose it.

THE LONG AND THE SHORT OF IT

NOTES ON IMPLEMENTATION

Summary of Part Four

This book contains a theory, despite the fact that it also contains much material to show that this theory is not just theoretical. Even so, we must move on to answer the obvious question: what happens when one tries to make some use of the work — for that is the long and the short of it.

There follow some notes about this. Some are long and some are short. They are not proper 'chapters', and are not presented as such. The first note discusses the problem: what is to count as success in using managerial cybernetics? Unsurprisingly, we find that no practical meaning can be attached to the idea that the whole content of this book is exhibited in some particular enterprise, as if it were a new kitchen. Even new kitchens are exhibited only in exhibitions of the 'ideal home'. In practice, actual kitchens embody some of the ideas, some of the furniture, that was on show at the exhibition. And that has to suffice — so long as it works.

In the second note will be found a discussion of the graphics used in mapping the model of any viable system onto reality. The facts themselves dictate how this is done; on the other hand, the model must not be denatured in the process of mapping. It follows that graphical distortions, which arise because that is how things really are, coupled with faithfulness to the cybernetic principles of the model, often reveal glaringly obvious discrepancies. These contrasts display the model's use in its primary, diagnostic, mode. Three major examples are cited; each is actual, but each is chosen to exemplify a typical diagnostic class.

Moving on to the detailed use of the model to explore a particular subsystem, actual examples are taken for every one of the five. In this third note appear hints on the detailed development of each subsystem, using different applications for each. Please note that this is done to spread the relevance of the examples; no attempt has been made to tell a complete story in recounting work on Systems One to Four, although in the case of exploring a System Five this fuller treatment is unavoidable. The whole point of this note is to provide clues as to how deeper investigation of the subsystems, with which by now the reader is familiar, may be approached. It is particularly important to realize that none of these examples could conceivably be transported as it stands into some other context. If the model is to be used in a professional way, then real research must be done.

Finally, Note Five does record — in considerable detail — a case study. It is meant to be read where it stands: after the other four notes, and particularly in relation to the first. That note discussed the question 'what is to count as success?' Note Five is one such answer, not at all of the sort that some readers would expect, and moreover unfinished. That is a good way to leave the book.

On success

No-one in his right mind would expect a management suddenly to submit to the revelation that management cybernetics provides a miraculous solution to the problems that beset any complex organization. Nor do we expect that management to assert that 'as of next Thursday' the institution has been handed over to cyberneticians.

But if the arguments that there are laws governing the structure and dynamics of *any* viable-system are valid, then *all* successful enterprises will be found to respond to those laws. They may nonetheless respond too slowly, too hesitantly, too uneconomically; too formally or too informally; too aggressively or too anarchically.

What is the meaning of all those statements of 'too'? Too whatever for *what?* Why, too whatever for maximum benefit — whether of profitability, satisfaction, or general ease: in a word, of eudemony (or well-being). Everyone has had the personal experience of achieving something that works: with satisfaction, but with the realization in hindsight that it could all have been done with much less stress and strain.

In the continuing process of organizational reform, this is where theoretical cybernetics and practical cybernetic experience each has something to say. It is both silly and agonizing to reach successful organizational outcomes by trial and error, **if** the rules of the game are already known. And, in the limit, it is perfectly possible that the trial-and-error approach (which is itself good cybernetics, given a suitable learning framework) will blow the institution apart (in the absence of that learning framework). After all, one of the trials may result in an error so great that viability is altogether lost. In private organizations, this is called bankruptcy. In government organizations, it is called PSBR: the Public Sector Borrowing Requirement.

For these reasons, managerial cybernetics ought in the first place to be seen as diagnostic. By mapping both the organization and the developmental process in which it is engaged onto the viable system model, it is possible to understand strengths and weaknesses in terms of the axioms of viability. In the second place, it is almost possible to prescribe for whatever turns out to be pathological.

The use of the word *almost* is of exceptional interest to all managers concerned with the proper use of these tools. In talking about the pathology of organizations, about diagnosis, about prescriptions, we are using a medical metaphor. It is noteworthy that, in our culture, doctors take it upon themselves to determine treatment. It is a case of 'mother knows best'. Many commentators on the medical scene now think that physicians have over-reached themselves: only the patient (or the comatose patient's representative) has the ethical right to say what is to happen to him or her. Of course, this presupposes that the physician is able to explain the issue to the patient, while medical autocracy is based on the benign assumption that the patient is a fool. Be that as it may, the manager who consults a cybernetician is certainly not a fool. It should be taken as read, then, that the institutional 'patient' is going to prescribe for himself.

The cybernetician *almost* prescribes in this sense. The collaboration between the patient and his physician, that we would like to see in medical practice, is well modelled by the collaboration that often exists — and certainly ought to exist — between the manager and the management scientist. Only the manager is entitled to take the decisions. It is the duty of the cybernetician to press his expert views; but he must not bully or cajole beyond the threshold of the manager's personal accountability.

All of this, so far, ought to be self-evident to anyone engaged in managerial work, from whatever standpoint. Thus I find it surprising to be asked so often: 'where can I see 'all this' in action?' The questioners appear to be using what I have called the Joshua model of success. Jericho, it seems, really was a closed system, which is something very hard to find. We may read in *Joshua* 6.1 that 'none went out, and none came in'. If a system can be envisaged as truly closed, it is possible to believe that there exists a unique algorithm that would lead to 'success'. At any rate, Joshua had such an algorithm. His people had to process around Jericho once a day for six days, and make seven such processions on the seventh day; seven rams horns had to be blown by seven priests, and the people had to give a great shout. The walls of Jericho then fell down flat. It would be highly satisfactory if this model of success were generally applicable. But we do not confront closed systems, and we do not have the algorithm; nor is it easy to rally the great shout, unhappily, since that might be enough on its own. But the people are going about their business, or watching television; and when the people do show any strong signs of working up to the great shout there are all too many agencies keenly interested in stifling it — as we have repeatedly seen happen in our own lifetimes in country after country.

If the Joshua model of success is inapplicable, we are left to ask ourselves whether things are in some way better or worse than they were before we started, or whether the processes that we initiated have led to something worthwhile that would otherwise not have happened. In short, the expectations ought not to be too high (perhaps we lack support of the class that Joshua had), but nor should they be too low (or we are timeservers). As far as my own experiences are concerned, I have said much already and will say more later. But from time to time I receive reports from others who have set out to 'implement the viable system'. One such report came to me in a vivid form, which is reproduced in Figure 71. I had nothing to do with any of this personally.

Robert Bittlestone first encountered managerial cybernetics because of an uproar in the press that attended the publication of my work for President Allende in Chile. He studied that work and the viable system model as presented in *Brain of the Firm*. He then joined a major company, Roneo Vickers, and set out to 'implement'. His diagrammatic report is self-explanatory, but he did provide some more detail in the following commentary.

Some Ideals: a cybernetic company, an operations room. . .

Models and Forecasts: We installed APL-based systems on time-sharing terminals.

Courting Catastrophe: We had

- technical success

  — systems dynamics simulations over ten years,

  — Bayesian short-term forecasting,

  — results consistent with experience, with some exciting counter-intuitive exceptions

- psychological failure

  — 'This is all very interesting, but if you'll excuse me I must get back to my desk to take some decisions.'

Rethinking: What are we doing wrong?

So then the diagram follows two routes.

THE IMPLEMENTATION SYNDROME

(or : 'Spot the Critical Path')

A GAME OF SKILL

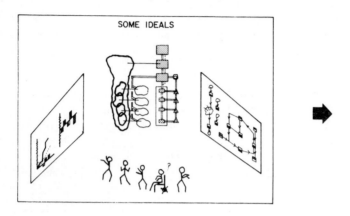

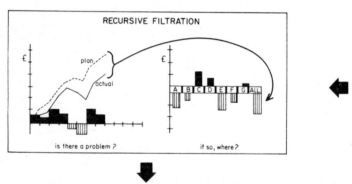

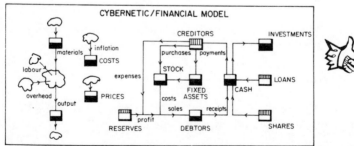

Figure 71. The Implementation Syndrome, a report by Robert Bittlestone

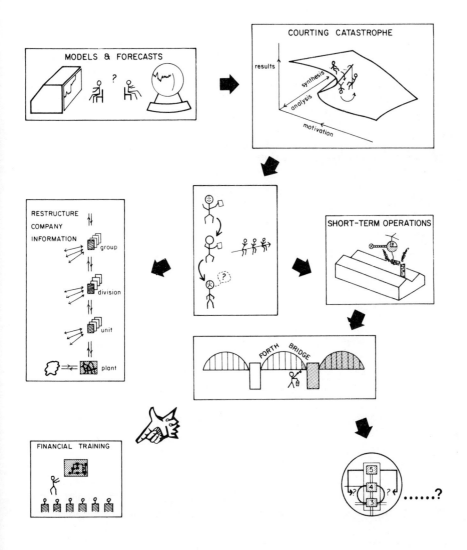

Short-Term Operations: which resulted in

— cost savings

— improvements in efficiency

— better credibility

'Painting the Forth Bridge': a possibly endless revamping of existing systems as a maintenance activity...

... and thence to the decision that the Board is misunderstanding the Systems Three/Four interface, which they may not even realize it is their job to monitor.

Secondly, to

Restructure Company Information:

— financial operating statements

— accounting codes of practice

— definitions and standards

(System Two work; note recursive)

Recursive Filtration: at last some real cybernetics!

— hierarchically independent suite of analyses depicting the state of the whole and the contribution of the parts.

But puzzlement: after all this, why isn't the company more successful?

Ah! nobody understands the rules!

Cybernetic/Financial Model: development of generalized financial model, leading to multi-recursive system (personal, corporate, national, global).

Both routes lead to financial training, so doing it.
The issue of the metasystem is still in the air.

Well, that is the Bittlestone report. It gives a very good feel for the way things actually develop. As to 'success'. . . perhaps it is enough to say that, as I write, Bittlestone is still there, and that his report can hereby be made public.

Managers who read this will probably smile with understanding. The tale will sound familiar, and there will be feelings of empathy for the Roneo Vickers managers who have been trying to cope with this cybernetic intervention, and get something useful out of it. There will however be some academics reading this, who have never taken a full-time job in industry, who will be rather shocked. They tend to use the Joshua model of success. After all, they send their students out into enterprises to do a job in the summer vacation, and the job is written up as a dissertation. It all *looks* very crisp, clean, and effective. But of necessity the job is a small job, and self-contained; and if one asks the manager at the other end of the dissertation he is likely to say: 'Oh yes, I think we got something out of it'. If one goes to look at the scene of action, where the charge-hand responsible for holding stocks of spare widgets has 'got a new system', one finds that not even the walls of his little cubicle have *actually* fallen down flat.

The major business schools have understood this very well. They promote programmes that work systematically with individual enterprises in various modes over many years. Unhappily, there are many other academic institutions that have not understood; these house the professors who, it was predicted, will be shocked. Our hearts need not bleed for them, but for their students. These people enter business, industry, and government with high qualifications and high expectations. But it was not Jericho, and they could not even find Joshua. My shoulder is wet with their tears. If any such are reading this, let them be heartened. Robert Bittlestone looked very chirpy the last time that I saw him.

Finally, a comment for the managers — who got off rather lightly in this analysis of 'success'. Let them take rather more care to use the resources of management science as good stewards, and to work out what would count as success for applications within their own enterprises. Above all, let them take rather more care of the people concerned. Here are four messages about that:

- What you are calling his arrogance, may just be his insecurity coming out at the seams;

- he is probably as loyal to the enterprise as are you: criticism, which is endemic to his job, is not disloyalty;

- it is, when you really consider the matter, most unlikely that he is after your job.

● You, the manager, and not he, the management scientist, are responsible for his 'success'. By all means, therefore, take the credit — but earn it first.

For 'he' and 'him', of course, read 'she' and 'her' as well. But I have witnessed the firing of a number of people under each of these four headings, and all of them were men...

Graphical distortions
of the model

Armed with these cybernetics, and noting what counts as success in any given situation, the approach to a fresh enterprise is essentially diagnostic. If the enterprise is there to be examined, we should regard it provisionally as viable. But it may not be in full good health; it might be really ill; its structural condition might actually be pathological. In the limit: the enterprise we approach may not be viable much longer. Every enterprise, however ostensibly successful, runs the same risk as the viable human being: maybe disaster lies around the corner. And, as with the human being, the pressures of success may make the enterprise the more vulnerable: witness some great and unexpected crashes of major British enterprises in recent times. When people have doubts about their health, maybe they have a medical check-up. Enterprises also entertain doubts about their viability; but they think of this usually in economic terms. Thus, if they can be satisfied that their finances are in good order, they think that all must be well. Maybe they should call in a consultant cybernetician.

To quote a recent experience of my own: someone had drawn up an elaborate schedule of work that needed to be done in reviewing the organization of a certain enterprise, and called me in to do it. But when I met the boss (with whom I had worked in another of his managerial incarnations) he laid this schedule aside. 'Never mind all that', he said. 'I have a gut-feeling that something is wrong. Your assignment is to find out why I feel like that'. That was all. It was a classic statement of the diagnostic approach.

Everything in this Note relates to the use of the model of any viable system as a diagnostic tool. Here, and in Note Three, are some indications, every one of which is drawn from actual applications in real life, as to how the tool can be used in the diagnostic mode. They relate to experiences with the model in many government departments (in both western and developing countries), in social services, in companies both large and small, in universities, and in a learned society. Except in the two nominated cases, the diagrams have been slightly changed so that the organizations concerned may not be recognized.

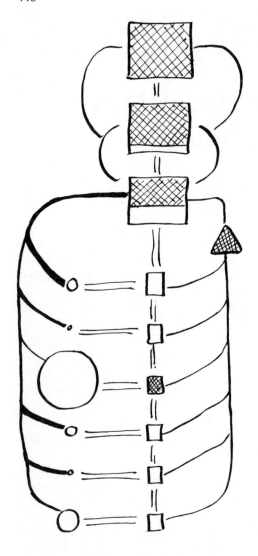

Figure 72. Using the model to show how one company dominates a consortium. In terms of variety engineering, can this be a viable system?

The first indication, which is the topic of this Note, concerns the mapping of the model onto reality. There should be no hesitation in drawing a diagram of affairs as they actually are, rather than as we should like them to be, using the model as a convention for making the description, and using the language that has competence to talk about the model in diagnostic discussion. This is like displaying an X-ray of the human body, on which is shown a dislocated shoulder, and saying: 'it should not look like that'. That is what is meant by the title 'graphical distortions'. In some applications of this model that I have seen, in several parts of the world, people have found such 'dislocations', and have simply *changed* the model to fit them. That wastes all our effort to discover the nature of any viable system, and is a denial of cybernetic science. We do not say to the dislocated-shoulder patient: 'look at this X-ray; it seems that this is how you are; goodbye'. (Note: this criticism does *not* apply to many excellent uses of the model that have been made by others, but only to some.)

It is a useful device to draw some components of the model so that they are roughly proportional in size to some parameter of the system that is regarded as important. This is, diagnostically speaking, instantly revealing. In Figure 72 we meet a very large company which purports to be a consortium of several companies, and presents itself to the general public and to its own government as such. It exists, acording to its publicity, to satisfy 'the public interest' in terms of a national though privately owned service. But in the diagram, the operational circles are drawn in rough proportion to the business transacted by each of the component companies. Moreover, the dominance of the major company in the management of the whole is indicated by the hatched areas in the relevant System One as reflected in the total System. Note also how the diagram brings out the relative weight of System Three intervention in the various Systems One on the left-hand channel: how light the touch on the home base!

As the diagram clearly indicates, the direction of the consortium is virtually under the command of one component company, the measure of variety used here being the number of executives with dual roles. It is hardly surprising that this should be the case; but the fact is not generally understood. It is surprising that the dominant company's top brass, being well-intentioned people, had not really understood it themselves. They were shaken by (the original version of) this diagram. This is not a viable system, but a fiasco: because the consortium disobeys the canons of viability in terms of variety engineering. It survives, but only because it is the will of the dominant company that it is convenient for itself that the consortium should survive. And although they were shaken, the management did nothing about it; which is why their anonymity is preserved here. If I were the responsible Minister, they would need to do something about it rather quickly.

Figure 73 illustrates another attempt at iconic quantification. This is the result of using the technique (as mentioned elsewhere) whereby each member of a senior management team estimates the amount of time that s/he devotes to work on the three components of the metasystem, and to their integration, and then estimates the time devoted by each colleague to those four components. The top two portraits are typical senior managers' self-images. The bottom portrait is typical of how his colleagues see such a senior manager.

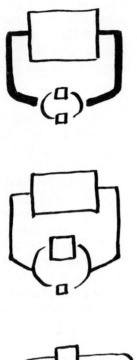

The Delusory Me
others are handling Four and Three
I'm Mr Big
and I am *monitoring* them

The Self-Regarding Me
I apportion my time appropriately
to my station
(well done, Me)

The Me my colleagues see

Figure 73. The apportionment of a senior manager's time between Systems Five, Four, and Three, and to monitoring, as perceived by himself and by his colleagues

As the main text has argued, everyone in the senior management team tends to believe that someone else is devoting time to System Four, with the result that its actual care and attention is vanishingly small. No single member of the team believes that he spends much time on System Three, because that clearly is not his job. But all his colleagues think that he is interfering in operational control for most of his time. Each man thinks that he takes a major interest in System Five, and in the monitoring of Three-Four, but his colleagues dispute this. Working this through, and giving the same weight to each man's belief about himself as to the sum of his colleagues' beliefs (since he willingly takes their views into account, but only as a bloc), it is understandable that the *team's view of itself* is well balanced as between devotion to Five, Four, and Three, and everyone believes that the Three-Four monitoring occurs. But of course a better appreciation is realised by summing the team's view of each other as a measure of the total team's care and attention, and disregarding all the self-images altogether.

When this is done, the metasystem's time is seen to go largely into Three; Four hardly exists as an object of affection; and although Five is well represented, it is floating in space. Naturally enough, the sum of colleagues' views is an amplification of one colleague's view (see Figure 73), except for the *isolation* of System Five. Each member of the team gives so little weight to his colleagues' attention to Three-Four monitoring that, in sum, the team's view is that this function simply does not happen. They ought to notice this, but do not; and this is usually due to the existence of a 'Delusory Me' in the team. He is making a lot of noise about the balance of Three-Four activity, but everyone knows that there is no effective corporate machinery whereby this delusion is made real.

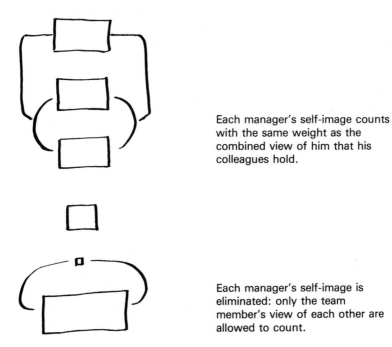

Each manager's self-image counts with the same weight as the combined view of him that his colleagues hold.

Each manager's self-image is eliminated: only the team member's view of each other are allowed to count.

Figure 74. The managerial team's view of its own devotion of time to Systems Five, Four, and Three, and to monitoring. The top picture (because it includes self-images as half its weight) accords with Axioms Two and Three. The lower picture, excluding self-images, is a better estimate of the facts, and challenges the Axioms

The metasystemic diagnosis is summed up in the (very damaging, very threatening) Figure 74. The mismatch between the shared belief and the facts should be a cause of such concern that any senior manager who reads this ought to instigate an enquiry along these lines into his own management team. For, after all, the facts are in attempted disobedience to both the Second and the Third Axioms of Management (check with Appendix 1), whereas there is an unfounded belief that these axioms are being met. But the concerned manager will find this enquiry very difficult to undertake if he faces his colleagues with a direct questionnaire. I have done that (see, for example, Note Five) and have discovered that people panic in the face of so obvious a challenge to their joint managerial skill and to their team cohesion. Then how may a measurement (these measurements are certainly approximate, but quite proximate enough) be obtained — how were those reported here obtained?

The answer is, by patient enquiry and surreptitious recording. This is not as ominous as it sounds. It was remarked earlier that Heisenberg showed how, in physics, the recording of an observation altered the system being observed. The Heisenberg Effect is even more drastic in social systems (and public opinion pollsters should remember that). In the case of a senior management team, direct enquiries of this kind can be destabilizing, or lead to nonsensical conclusions. On reflection, surely, that is to be expected. Data may however be obtained by keeping a private chart, such as that depicted in Figure 75. The object of the consultant is of course to insert numbers in every box, which he may do over a period of time, as a result of individual interviews, and casual questioning as to 'who does what' and 'how much'. The numbers, written as percentages, will be subjectively gauged estimates (but see previous arguments as to the measurement of variety); but they *are* open to verification by further checks — especially if inconsistencies make themselves manifest. It is clear that exact figures are not required to establish such diagrams as those portrayed in 73 and 74: the diagrams themselves are loosely drawn — but they make their point.

In fact, it is just as unwise to produce the finished chart (Figure 75) as it is to confront managers with a questionnaire in the first place; because this is an affront, and can lead only to statements of self-justification. But to investigate thus surreptitiously is no more ominous than to undertake any other kind of behind-the-scenes work in the client interest with which that client will not be directly confronted — *provided* (see Note One) that the manager-scientist relationship is full of trust. Hence, if any of those many good managerial friends on whom I have urged metasystemic disbalance (and they are many) read this exposé, I should expect them to be pleased to know that there was some cybernetic science behind the apparent flair, and not to complain that they had been spied upon.

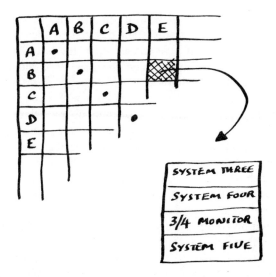

Figure 75. A research chart in which each manager of the metasystem assesses (but see text) the percentage of time that he and each of his colleagues devotes to the four activities delineated within each cell. His own self image appears on the diagonal

As a final example of graphical distortion as a means of exhibiting a diagnosis, consider the case of 'superenterprise'. It is very familiar in the current managerial world. A group of (already large) companies comes together as a conglommerate: will *that* be a viable system? A group of governmental ministries is brought together under a single minister (called, in Britain, the 'overlord' system); will *that* be a viable system? Undoubtedly, in all the cases mentioned, the development is possible, in cybernetic principle. Given that the very large systems to be agglomerated are themselves viable systems, and supposing that each of them constitutes a viable Recursion One according to the historical scheme of things, in which each has well-established second, third, and so on, recursive levels, then the huge new enterprise can be regarded as Recursion Zero. The real-life problem is that this perception is never attained — or so the diagnostic inspection of these huge beasts (in all three examples, and in several countries) suggests. Thereby do they normally fail. It is because the 'huge beasts', now supposedly comprising System One of the superenterprise, are strongly autopoietic; and no-one is using cybernetics to assert the Zero level of recursion. Instead, there is erected an alleged boss of the superenterprise, who has a staff. After that, it is simply a matter of hard bargaining as to where the real power resides. The boss and his staff have legal powers on their side; the components of System One have their autopoietic strength on theirs — and a long history to prove it.

Consider, firstly, the cybernetic viewpoint on all this. It is very simple. Recursion Zero needs an entire metasystem devoted to the *zero* recursion. What it has, instead, is a System Five consisting of the heads of all Systems One (that was part of the deal), in which the new boss and his staff are encapsulated (or entrenched). There is absolutely no Zero System Four, because that is regarded as the sum of Systems Four within the System One — at the first level of recursion. A committee of these people is set up to provide the Zero System Four; but all the committee does is to squabble about which components of System One are to get the money allocated to Zero Four. The needs of that entity are not considered — because it does not exist, except as this committee — each of whose members has other fish to fry. System Three is also a committee, dignified as an *executive* committee. The boss of Zero presides over this (whereas — by the Regulatory Alphorism (see Appendix One) — he should not be even present), because this is where the horse-trading will occur — and unless he can get control of that auction he will be lost. System Two, which is supposed to depend from System Three, is therefore grabbed by the Zero boss, in a vain attempt to assert this control — which he cannot do through System Three, because that is simply a committee of autopoietic components. In well-merited despair at his predicament, the Zero boss also grabs the left-hand channel that ought also to depend from System Three, and threatens System One with his legal sanctions — which are his only strength.

This is not a viable system at all. It describes, in one paragraph what happened in Britain in:

- the Ministry of Defence

- the Ministry of Technology (Mintech)

- the Department of the Environment

- the Ministry of Transport

- the Ministry of Fuel and Power

- the (nationalized) Steel Industry

- the (nationalized) Electricity Industry

- the (nationalized) Gas Industry

- the (nationalized) Railways

- the Health Service

- the Education Service

- the Police Force

- the Prison Service

— to mention only some superenterprises of which I had (at the time of diagnosis) direct knowledge, since I was in some minor degree a consultant to them all at one time or another — though in *no* case on the topic of organizational design, I hasten to add.

This diagnosis offers good mileage for one paragraph, although it takes an understanding of the whole book to comprehend it. And this was just what was lacking in my attempts to draw attention to Zero recursion problems in the cases quoted: in British management, at the highest levels, there is no such thing as management science. 'It is an *art,* dear boy.' Yes; and it virtually depends on membership of that club whose art it is.

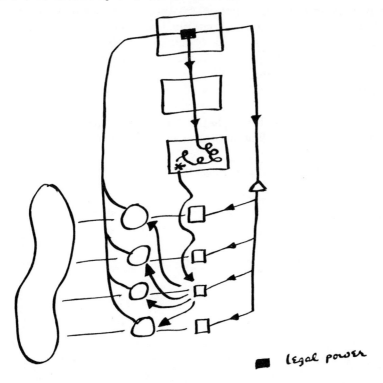

legal power

Figure 76.   Graphical distortion of the model to illustrate diagnosis of non-viability in a superenterprise (see text)

Therefore do I turn, in Figure 76, to another country, and to an actual diagram that exhibits this diagnosis in terms of a graphical distortion of the model. This is part of the commentary I wrote for Figure 76 at the time (omitting words that would betray the anonimity of this superenterprise):

> It is attempting to exercise a System Two damping function from System Five.
>
> Because this is cybernetically unworkable, it seeks a COMMAND route to specific action within System One.
>
> This involves discovering a pressure point (marked *) in superenterprise System three, from which to seek out a particular component of System One which has the potency (= budget) to act on the whole of System One.
>
> This is not a viable system.

The report enshrining this diagnosis was entitled (as mentioned in the main text): 'A Nervous System for Someone Else's Body'. The solutions are obvious, once the diagnosis itself is understood. Create the appropriate Zero level metasystem. Get System Two properly organized. And so on. It is not relevant to this Note to thrash through all the recommendations, which the thorough reader could certainly provide for himself, given the diagnosis.

Oblivious to such advice, the horse-trading normally goes on. This Note is a diatribe against horse-trading, and an advocacy of cybernetic science.

Figure 76 is a supreme, but altogether familiar, pathological distortion of the model in the superenterprise.

Is anyone listening?

Substantive elaborations
of the model

Throughout the main text we have been looking at the model of any viable system, at all levels of recursion, in terms of a particular degree of optical resolution. That is to say that, because we were in search of invariant principles of organization, no distinctions were drawn in the diagrams between one kind of enterprise and another. We stood sufficiently far back that only invariances were optically resolved. In any actual application, however, this degree of resolution is not adequate. Simply to draw the enterprise so that it looks like the model may tell us a great deal, through variety analysis, about its viability. But in practice it may be necessary to make a more detailed elaboration of one or more subsystems of the five. In this Note, indications are given as to how this is actually done. But now the degree of optical resolution is much higher, and we discuss invariance no longer. Therefore, a warning: these examples cannot be transferred, as can the main model, to *any* viable system. They are here to demonstrate how more detailed analysis may be applied in particular situations.

An Elaboration of System One

This example is taken from a business school, because that is an enterprise with which most people in management (be they managers or management scientists, to each of whom this book is addressed) are by now likely to be familiar.

At the school in question, there are four major (plus a variety of minor) operational elements. That is: there are two post-experience courses, one for 'high-flying' managers, and one for senior executives; and there are two post-graduate courses, one leading to a master's degree (MBA) and the other leading to a doctorate (PhD). In terms of the model as we already have it, that is, given its usual degree of optical resolution, the school's operational elements would be shown according to Figure 77.

458

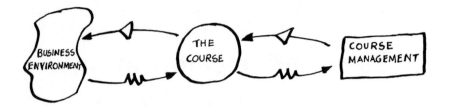

Figure 77. The operational element of a business school: a course

The course management is clearly involved in amplifying the school's resources towards making a high-variety impact on the members of the course. It must attenuate the course-members' feedback; for if it did not, then a unique programme would be needed for each course member, and this is simply not possible (although doctoral students may approach this asymptote). In general, the school's facilities have to be *shared* amongst members of the course, a fact which entails a degree of attenuation in their individual variety. In turn, 'the course' is clearly intended to be amplified, through each individual member, into the business environment, where the variety expansion ought to be orders of magnitude higher than the course content variety, because each member's variety has enlarged, but in a different way from any colleague's. The attenuation of the variety of the business environment vis-à-vis the course is also implicit; because 'the course' (as distinct from the faculty management of the course) constitutes a filter of that environment, the variety output of which is equal to the sum of the experience of course members. Thus the familiar model (Figure 77) fits the situation perfectly well. On the other hand, it does not tell the course manager much about the way in which all this *happens,* and is therefore not much help to him.

The course manager is, in fact, in an experimental situation. There is no proven rule as to the running of courses in business schools. If there were, all courses would be very similar all over the world — and they are not (Laus Deo); although they all do, and necessarily must, obey the dictates of Ashby's Law, as just explained. Then let us pursue our cybernetic analysis of this System One. What follows is taken from my own report.

Here is a picture of the experimental situation. It takes nothing for granted beyond the fact that the school exists and must do something to people outside itself. It is a kind of minimal model.

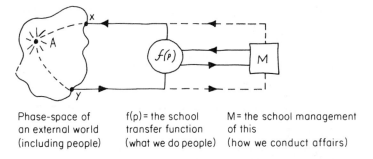

| Phase-space of
an external world
(including people) | f(p) = the school
transfer function
(what we do people) | M = the school management
of this
(how we conduct affairs) |

Figure 78.   A first elaboration of Figure 77

Caricature of a False Interpretation

M says: The school's transfer function *f(p)* is obviously a course. This I
devise with all the skill, thought, effort, and assistance at my
command. It must be *someone's* job to fill it (even if my
nominee for this job says it is not). I shall have to run it though
— which will hold up my research, stop my consulting, interfere
with my family life, and earn me a pitifully small honorarium.
Never mind: I shall move on soon. Better keep asking the
students what they think of the lectures by the way: must
provide some feedback.

New Script (with Exegesis) for the Management Function M

M says: There is a situation (called A) of some kind, a state of the
external world, which it is the school's job to influence for the
better by enhancing managerial capability. So A could be a firm
in distress; or it could be a set of problems which are currently
defeating the managements concerned with them; or it could be
a set of dispersed managers characterized by ignorance, or by
lack of incentive, or by lack of opportunity; or it could be a set
of difficulties to which no answer exists at all: and so on.

It should be possible to identify a whole group of situations A,
specifying in each case the parameters which locate A in its
phase-space. If I have those parameters, then I should be able to
devise measures of performance in A.

So what? Three things. (a) Measures have statistical
distributions, and I should be able to attend to the homogeneity

460

of my sample of A-like situations. (b) I should be able to rank my own priorities by tackling low-performance A's first. (c) Most importantly, when I have done whatever I shall do, there will be a way of calculating the effect — back in A.

Exegesis:

If situation A is defined by default as that set of locations which, for all manner of reasons, contain simply someone willing and able to attend the school, then there can be no homogeneity with respect to the A-performance measure. Then (a) does not hold: so (b) and (c) cannot be implemented.

Secondly, it is now clear that what the School does cannot be assessed elsewhere than in A, since change at A is the only objective we have. Responses of the school to the school at the school may have pedagogic value, but say nothing at all that bears on that objective.

M
continues: But this is a major research job; no-one has ever managed to do what I perceive ought to be done. Moreover, to the extent that any situation *A* is changed, this turns out to have been a major consulting assignment.

If I set off from my M-box and approach the external world along the upper line in the diagram, I shall reach point X — a point of transduction. Here I change my academic form of energy into whatever fits me to operate in the external world. Does that make me a salesman? Am I marketing seminars? Clearly not. More appropriately, I am setting up a management laboratory for doing field work, and enormous effort must go into its design.

If I follow the trajectory from X through A, I emerge from the external world at transducer Y, where the form of my energy is changed back into academic terms. And so my loop closes: I can get back into my M-box.

By circulating round this closed loop, I become the instrument of change at A (some call that consulting) and an expert in X, Y transductions (a powerful research activity in academic terms). Moreover, this is a learning system: because, thanks to the attention I must give to both transducers, the stimulus-response time across both X and Y, and at A from X to Y, ought monotonically to decrease.

Exegesis:

M is a management function, although personified in this soliloquy. Let us see what can so far be said about this function.

First, there could be a range of M's (M1, M2, M3 . . .), all performing in this way. The only limitation is the supply of classifiable A's (A1, A2, A3 . . .). That is, there is scope for **specialization** — not in techniques or the classical divisions of management — but in A situations.

M-work is high level, sustained, and it must be led. What leadership characteristics can be inferred? It is not an appointment for a tyro in the external managerial world. Academically, it is a top research activity, suggesting the minimum status of Reader. In both worlds a programme capable of achieving measured results over a range of A situations would surely last five years at least, so this is not an appointment for a Visitor. It is a post with tenure.

Especially: the lead appointment over each M-staff is for someone who sees this task *as* his research, *as* his consulting, and *as* his source of remuneration. His staff must be similarly inspired.

M is a fully-dedicated activity. The M-staff would include assistants, and a cadre of doctoral students, for whom this work itself is the research vehicle. Since M is about fulfilling the school's objective of enhancing managerial capability in A, the publications and dissertations of this M-staff would be about that task. Promotion would derive from successful work in performing that task. Academic reputations would be earned in terms of studies of that task. And the livelihood of the M-staff would be earned in doing all of this. There is no need, industrial or academic, to do anything else; there is certainly no time.

NOTE 1 These inferences derive from reflecting upon the model and its component implementation. There is no proof that no other scheme could be devised to meet the needs of the situation so far laid bare, to be sure. And yet I do not feel I am making proposals, but rather exposing the conditions of a viable school operation.

NOTE 2 Earnest enquiry in the market-place reveals that M-staff at all levels would earn much higher than academic rates if they worked in industry. It is axiomatic that the School needs to select from the best; it cannot afford to deal in throw-outs or refugees from industry. Hence we must carry forward from this point a requirement sizeably to increase academic salaries for all M.

NOTE 3 M's soliloquy and his exegesis have travelled all this way without mentioning 'courses' until now.

M
continues: So what is a course?

It is something done to people who spend time at the School.

I have some control over what is done to them, because I stand for the management function. But they will do things to themselves and to each other over which I have little or no control. Then there is (School minus M) the rest of the School's influence: not the part I can formally bring to bear, but the part operating through the School's ethos.

Lord Frank's Report, which set up the School, says:

'The general atmosphere of the School, and the teaching methods and organization it adopts, are likely to be at least as important as the content of the syllabus in developing managerial skill'.

I see what he means, by studying a new loop of the original model. That is the left-hand loop, which includes the transfer function. Round this, I now observe, students themselves move, and the transducers X and Y take on new roles.

Transducer Y is an input filter. Course members must be selected — and quite clearly *in relation to the need at A*. Then this Y must be very specially designed. We cannot possibly accept people just because they arrive, or because we need the money, or even because an academic board or a zealous employer 'thinks they would benefit'.

Transducer X is an output filter. Course members must be transduced back — quite clearly again *in relation to the need at A*. So, for instance, X cannot possibly be an examination geared to School-oriented standards of attainment — at least, not on its own.

Next, the model needs enriching. If $f(p)$ is the School transfer function, it applies through time for the duration of a course, and we may think of the student as a variable continuously passing through.

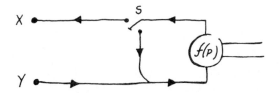

Figure 79. A *dynamic* version of part of the
model: time is brought into the picture

That is, we capture a student at Y and inject him into the system,
closing switch S so that he can be regarded as a continuously
variable input for the duration of the course. He goes round
and round that loop for that amount of time. Then we throw
switch S, and shoot him back to X.

Now the function *f(p)* produces a different effect on every
student — he is a unique input. Then I need continuous
corrective feedback in order to maintain a stable output.

This seems to be an important inference. One thinks of a *course*
as being adaptive: but each of its students is unique. Better to
say, perhaps, that there is adaptive feedback intended to adjust
each student to the benefits of the course. It looks like this:

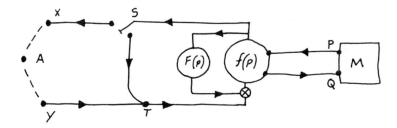

Figure 80.   The fully dynamic model, operating in time, from the School's
standpoint

Two new transducers (P and Q) have arrived, because in
managing this course with its feedback I shall have to interpret
events continuously at Q, take decisions, and somehow operate
P to influence events.

Exegesis:

It has to be said that at present our understanding of A, our operation of X and Y, and our knowledge of the trajectory X-A-Y are all very weak at the School — even by current standards and available methods. We are course oriented, not need-system oriented, despite the existence of home-based projects by students meant to sustain the loop. These projects arrive, after all, as characteristics of the student, and remain so — like the colour of his hair.

Secondly, and this is the main illumination of the model, we need to ask whether we are not treating our School activity on the loop $f(p)$-S-T, instead of the loop $f(p)$-X-A-Y as clearly we should.

If we really talk about the larger loop, then we have no feedback.

This word 'feedback' is used far too loosely, which is why I have given the 'course' model in terms of a transfer function. It *is* possible, with a captive course, to design an $F(p)$ operation (though we have not gone far towards it yet), and that, as modelled, counts as feedback. Note that the concept depends on continuous variation over a time epoch. So to say that we have an association of past students, or to say that we check up on what happens after the course, entails follow-up — not feedback.

On the larger-loop scale, where our objectives lie (at A), the model offers the clear suggestion that a one-off course for the student cannot possibly be the answer. He should be circulating round the larger loop as well as the smaller. We need to discover ways of doing this; and this need, more than any other, could totally change our modus operandi (for all kinds of student. This model is meant to be general to the School).

Finally, there are interesting problems at P and Q. These are the problems currently solved by course directors, and they take up most of their time. Now we have identified the task of the leader of function M, and it seems quite clear that he has far too much to do to be his own course director. He should be monitoring and researching the f(p)-P-Q loop, along with the other loops, but he cannot embody it.

Thus is identified a major cause of current difficulty. If course directors ought to be embedded in an operation M, whereas they exist *in vacuo,* and if course directing is a full-time job, whereas there is so much else to be done, the School is structurally deficient on a large scale. And I take this chance to say that, insofar as criticisms are beginning to emerge, they are directed at this structural deficiency, and certainly not to hard-working individuals.

M concludes: It must be time to think about that X-A-Y trajectory. Why did the cybernetician call the external world a phase-space, and define situations of class A as states of the external world? Why, for that matter, a trajectory?

All I know about A is that we intend to define it with care as a homogeneous population of something about which something needs to be done — in terms of enhancing managerial capability. We are due to determine its parameters and create measures of performance.

In that case, then, it is understood that this is an *equilabrial* state. If it were not, there would be no A susceptible to all these processes. Moreover it must be, by some criterion, an *unfavourable* state: yes, the idea was to improve something.

Hence state A must be changed to state B, defined as less unfavourable. We can hardly say 'favourable', just like that, or we shall make the situation unstable — for the situation is characterized by human fallibility. Then we could move to state C, and so on, keeping watch for instabilities generated by change as we go.

Let us say we reach 'favourable' by state F. Not only could we not short-circuit A-B-C-D-E-F by saying A-F (because that would cause instability), we cannot even risk saying that A-B-C-D-E-F will lie on a straight line — notoriously the shortest way there. The fact is that we must expect to circumnavigate difficult issues, not just plough through them. Let's re-draw that part of the picture.'

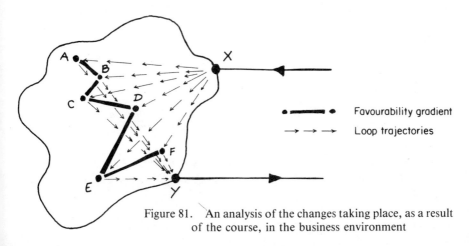

Favourability gradient

Loop trajectories

Figure 81. An analysis of the changes taking place, as a result of the course, in the business environment

466

Exegesis:

Now M has uncovered the mechanisms of the major loop. And we see again why our notion of 'course' *must be iterative*. All of this has to monitored: it takes time, and it takes research.

It also takes feedback:

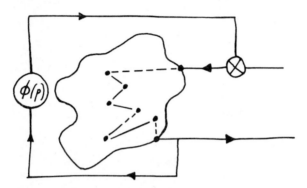

Figure 82.   Feedback, and a further transfer function,
added to Figure 81

With thanks to the thoughtful M, here (at
Figure 83) is the completed model, which will in
future be called:
SYSTEM ONE

This System One analysis affected the outlook of many people at the School. But it was only part of the application of the total model; and the purpose of this Section is not to provide a total case study, but to exemplify the elaboration of System One. Those interested in an objective comment on the entire project should consult References 2 and 3.

REFERENCES:

1. Beer, Stafford, *The Organization of the Manchester Business School from Nineteen-Seventy,* Manchester Business School, 1970.

2. Cooper, Cary L (Editor), *Organizational Development in the UK and USA,* MacMillan Press, 1977, Chapter 1: 'Tracking Down the Middle' by John Morris.

3. *Ibid:* Chapter 3: 'Reflections on OD American Style', by Larry E Greiner.

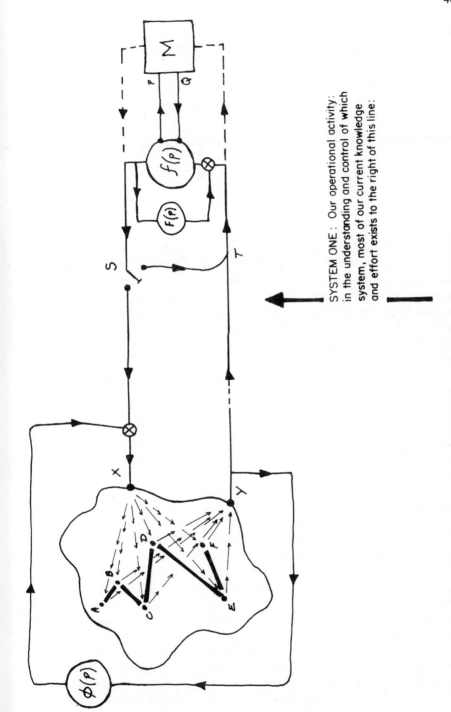

SYSTEM ONE : Our operational activity:
in the understanding and control of which
system, most of our current knowledge
and effort exists to the right of this line:

Figure 83.   The completed model of an operational element of System One — a course

An Elaboration of System Two

System Two is anti-oscillatory, and that is its only function — as educed by the necessary and sufficient criteria of the viable system. Thus it is not a 'cover story' for any or every kind of bureaucracy that shields behind the title of 'the office'. It has often been cited in this way by others; but if we lose sight of its special damping function, then our diagnostic ability is impaired. In working on its detail, we face the problem that it deals in many dimensions, whereas the general diagram offers only one (namely, the single line running through a set of System One 'triangles'). In practice, then, we shall need to disentangle the various dimensions of management in which System Two operates.

Here is a very useful classification for any enterprise that is a straightforward commercial firm. We can consider System Two in terms of the company's four major resources: materials and machines, money, people and time. Each of these four classes may have subsidiary classes. And so we shall not have *one* System Two, but at the very least four of them. There is no diagrammatic difficulty in drawing four or more parallel vertical lines on the right-hand side of the model, all of which depend from System Three, and all of which enter System One. Nor is there much difficulty in seeing (and recording) that each line depends from a subsystem *within* System Three, where these subsystems are virtually independent of each other in administrative terms. After all, the maintenance engineer (machines), the accountant (money), the personnel officer (people), and the planner (time), do not in general need to coordinate their policies in these respects, although they are all members of the operational directorate.

Difficulties arise, however, because all four (or more) of these regulatory activities, independent as they may be in the System Three perspective, have simultaneous impact on each component of System One. In fact they compete for the One manager's attention. Moreover, they are mediated to him through his own regulatory centre (his local triangle), which has no machinery for discriminating between them. The problem is depicted in Figure 84, with which Figure 54 (in Chapter Twelve) should be compared. Here is a clear recipe for overloading System One with variety — in the guise of a variety *damping* function! The attenuator marked A will have to work overtime; the System One managers will become confused; and quite typically the senior managers of specialist functions (W,X,Y,Z) will complain vigorously that their anti-oscillatory efforts are being undermined at the System One level. Equally obviously, System One managers will rise in a body to complain that 'Head Office is round our necks', while it is at the same time pretending to be no more than an intra System One anti-oscillatory device. . . .

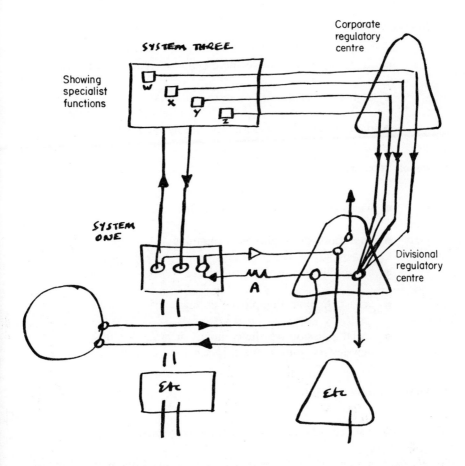

Figure 84. Predictable System Two overload on the operational element in
System One

Now let us take an actual case, and observe what is really going on, in terms of
Figure 84. We have System Two regulation, emanating from System Three, as
follows:

W: Materials and Machines Resource:

- engineering damping of machine variances

- quality control of major raw materials

- quality control of hygiene

X: Money Resource:

- damping systems to regulate debtors/creditors/stock

- cash flow regulation — anti-oscillatory

- damping of idiosyncratic accounting methods

Y: People Resource:

- wages-damping across System One

- conditions of employment damping

- anti-oscillatory works procedures

- across-the-board employee surveys

- social cohesion for the company at large — clubs, newsletters, joint ownership schemes, etcetera

Z: Time Resource:

- Tactical Planning (see Chapter Thirteen)

So there are, minimally, twelve Systems Two, grouped under four functions, to be considered. In the case under review, every one of these twelve had some kind of question mark hanging over it; in three cases, the functions hardly existed at all, since there was no real accountability for them. Well, it is clear that (such a diagnosis having been made) each of the twelve Systems Two could become the subject of special study and recommendations could be made as to its improvement. That is an orthodox managerial undertaking, provided that all this anti-oscillatory activity were recognized as such (which it was not). But however satisfactorily these problems were solved from the point of view of functional specialists W,X,Y,Z in System Three, each working from his own domain, System One would be left with the problem of variety overload — all in the cause of damping, and therefore variety reduction.....

Then a yawning trap opens beneath our managerial feet, and it is all too easy to fall into it. It consists in the idea that the WXYZ configuration that is appropriate in System Three should be reproduced in every elemental operation as a wxyz configuration, so that W has his local w, X has his local x, and so on, in every System Two. Admittedly, there may sometimes be a case for this local reproduction: for example, in the accounting function. But to yield to the pressures that each functional specialist in System Three may exert to create mini-departments when the variety equations do not support any such need is to fall into the trap.

Leaving for a moment the example under discussion (since that management were well aware of the trap, even if they did not altogether avoid it), consider for one paragraph the case of a small band of North American Indians. Now the government departments that deal with the survival problems (that is, the viability) of the Indin culture are concerned with many bands; further, they must necessarily be organized to relate to other government departments, and they must accept the organizational norms of the bureaucracy in general. Thus it is not surprising to discover that the department has an administration section, a finance section, a planning section, and so on. The Indian band, however, consisting of a few-hundred-strong community that is attempting to maintain its own heritage, is organized quite differently. It has a Chief, who sits in Council, and a system of Elders. 'Do you ever consult the Elders, these days?' I asked a Chief. 'Most certainly'. 'Do your Council members consult them?' 'I don't know, and I don't *want* to know.' Clearly, this is an organizational mode that differs radically from the bureaucratic mode, and it is precisely that Indian culture to which this government activity is dedicated. Then consider whether it makes sense to instal within the band an administration assistant, a financial assistant, a planning assistant, and so on. But there they are — or are fast becoming — because there has to be a damping function. The rationale of System Two will not be repeated here. It is enough to remark that damping relates to incipient oscillations between Systems One, and that it is not intended to suppress the very purposes of any System One itself. . . .

The example originally under discussion concerns a manufacturing and retailing company in England; its Systems One consist in Divisions presided over by Divisional Chief Executives, and not Indian Chiefs. It would seem that the parenthetical example just quoted has not the least relevance. Instead we hear (as to Figure 84): 'we are over loaded with System Two variety, which does not damp oscillations, but interferes with our intentions'. We also hear: 'those people at Head Office have no idea how we actually conduct our affairs'. It is, as they say, a small world.

The company, long before it encountered cybernetics, had found a cybernetic solution to these problems. It is depicted in Figure 85. They had, in the person of one of their senior officers, a man who virtually epitomized a 'Corporate Regulatory Centre'; a man who massively attenuated the variety of the

472

specialist functions within System Three as they asserted their impact on the elemental operations. He also knew, through his own virtue and expertise, that most of the variety engendered by System Three should not be transmitted to System One on the 'command' channel, but on the other vertical channels that subscribe to the First Axiom of Management (see Appendix One).

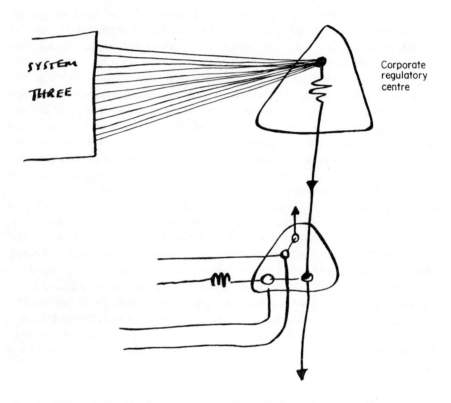

Figure 85.   Assimilation by the Corporate Regulatory Centre of the System Two
variety overload generated within System Three

However, no enterprise should rely on serendipity to handle its System Two concerns. The Corporate Regulatory Centre must be properly designed, *and* it must be projected to System One as an anti-oscillatory device. Because System Two remains an obscure notion in the managerial culture (which is also the reason why it is normally defective) the task of its design and its projection is abnormally difficult. Any person set up in this role requires especial gifts of understanding and compassion and patience. He should have (to put the point somewhat melodramatically) no paranoid tendency within him. The reason is that System One will always be alert to the risk that the anti-oscillatory system has been handed over to a power merchant.

The task, as Figure 85 makes fairly graphic, is to *meld* the variety generated in the direction of System Two by WXYZ components of System Three (which have no functional bearing on each other) by the use of a 'house style' which exists to attenuate variety. The phrase 'house style' is often taken to refer to the uniform design of paperwork, to the damping effects on idiosyncracy exerted by newsletters, and the like. But this is no more than a beginning. System Two should present the anti-oscillatory activities of the enterprise (despite all their diversity) as a homogeneous package with which System One may feel comfortable. The impression of variety overload normally experienced by an operational element assaulted by twelve different Systems Two is more due to the unnecessary diversity in presentation than to the inevitable diversity of content. After all: the divisional manager knows perfectly well that the twelve matters listed earlier are indeed aspects of his managerial responsibility, because he handles them all the time. What is oppressive to him is the fact that he is required to handle each matter with System Two using utterly different conventions: different terms for the same thing, different expressions of the same measure, different codes, different formats, different categories of praise, blame and excuse.

The phrase 'house style' covers the variety attenuating activities of System Two's own design — but only when it is fully understood. House style as graphic art is very much part of the story: it is a massive variety attenuator. And it is fascinating that artists rather than managers have deeply understood this role; managers see frills here, where they should see more basic garments. Even then, however, the visual designer depends upon the manager's conceptualization of the total cybernetic attenuation that System Two ought to exert. The manager has a great ally in the artist, but he needs the scientist too. If he fondly believes that these two cannot work together, have nothing in common, the odds are that he understands neither — or has chosen inadequate representatives of both.

REFERENCE:

Henrion FHK and Parkin, Alan, *Design Coordination and Corporate Image,* Studio Vista, London. Reinhold Publishing Corporation, New York, 1967.

An Elaboration of System Three

Systems Three-Two-One are concerned with the 'inside and now'. System Three is the first managerial location that the model of the viable system encounters where there exists a synoptic view of the 'inside'. It follows that any elaboration of System Three must include an account of every general activity that encompasses the whole of Systems One and Two.

In Figure 86 we see a typical first picture of a System Three. The attempt is made to identify the functional components of System Three (Marketing, Accounting, Personnel, and so on), and to notice the main interactions between them and System One. The variety that they generate towards System Two is noted (see last section), and the variety that they dispose on the left-hand channel is noted too (see main text). There will also have to be some preliminary consideration of the varieties generated upwards on the diagram, towards Systems Four and Five. Putting the whole of this together is a matter of corporate concern: it amounts to the application of the three Axioms of Management (see Appendix One), and that is a Three-Four-Five task.

There are two major issues that always confront System Three, considered discretely. The first is its inner-connectivity. Thanks to the conventions that apply to management, all the little boxes shown in Figure 86 will certainly exist; *and* each demands a certain autonomy, which is underwritten by national, professional, and international organizations. The main job of the Chief Executive, as he sits in the Three box, is to explore the connexions insofar as they effect his own enterprise. The relationship between production and marketing will usually be a major concern. In the case quoted, and quite unusually, there was no production director within System Three: production was a System One activity, answerable to the Managing Director — so that he effectively doubled as production director. Marketing had to be regarded as a servicing function to System One, otherwise the operational elements would have been robbed of autonomy: thus marketing should have been making full use of the System Two pathways in particular (which it was not). If it is surprising to see market research appearing in Three rather than Four, it is because this research was explicitly undertaken on behalf of the components of System One: it had no relevance to the higher level of recursion constituting the Company embedded in the industry. As so often happens, no-one could be entirely sure of the total range of the Personnel function: it sometimes seems to be in on everybody's act. The role of Finance, which is also ubiquitous, tended to be dominant — which of course it should not be, although no-one succeeded in bringing home this point: those people were entrenched.

In explanation of the box marked 'other', it is always advisable to keep track of activities that are not an obvious or monolithic part of the enterprise. For example: consultants move in and out, and the role that they play is not often well understood. Again: the company may employ the part-time services of many specialists (a doctor, a chaplain, a scientific advisor), and such people may well figure significantly in the variety equations that support the First Axiom. leaving aside the 'cosmetic' explanations for the appearance of all these 'others', which have to do with an alleged (and may be genuine) concern for *people,* it is significant that all of them are variety attenuators. It is not necessarily cynical to observe that management may use this kind of attenuation to conceal the use of the command channel, because the management may not even realize that it is doing just that. The disinterested cybernetician cannot afford to be similarly misled.

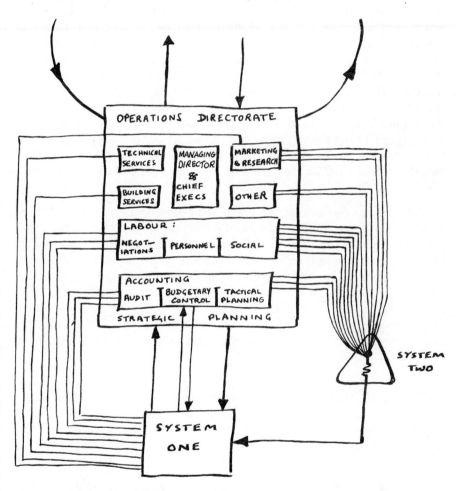

Figure 86.   An example of a preliminary elaboration of System Three

This Note draws attention to that first issue, but does not pursue it further. The reason is that, although the cybernetics of the situation are evident (and therefore do not even need to be pursued), any actual case-study turns out — at this point — to be a psychological study and not a cybernetic study.

Everything will turn out to relate to the characters of the human beings involved, especially because many (perhaps more than half) of those concerned in System Three will prove to be Heads of System One in disguise. This is the reason why the main text offers such advocacy for better techniques than the monthly meeting can dispose, such as the creation of an operations room or better still a management centre. In the absence of any location and protocol for a continued debate, psycho-political issues are likely to be paramount; and they will not be ameliorated by the fact that functional specialists within System Three are in constant professional contact with System One, because much distortion will be introduced into messages carried on those circuits. At the time of the periodic meeting, the motives of all concerned are often in doubt, and no-one can be sure (because of so many dual roles) who is disguised as what. It continually amazes me that Chief Executives seem quite prepared to believe in the masked ball that the Executive Management Committee so often constitutes. They have my sympathy, but lose my respect, at the moment when 'the masquerade is over', especially if they ignored so many algedonic signals in advance. These are always there.

Hence: turn now to the second major issue that confronts System Three, because this is not purely emotive. Looking at Figure 86, we see iconic representations of the right and left-hand channels to System One. But the *direct* channel, so-called the 'command channel', is not iconically represented. Well, the main text argued (forcibly enough) that this channel should be not-much used: correctly so. But that contention does not respond to the question as to *what System One constitutes*. It is entirely a System Three concern to decide exactly what is the configuration of System One. And it is in this, perhaps because of its psychiatric preoccupations with its own infrastructure, that System Three so often fails.

On the fact of it, the enterprise consists of a number of viable systems, jointly denominated as System One. These are the operational elements of the corporate identity. But they are the deposit of history. Therefore System Three poses (or ought to pose) three questions:

- is any one of these operational elements non-viable?

- is there any activity going on, or is there any activity that should be going on, which is not yet recognized as a viable system — a component of System One?

- how many components of System One are there; and does System Three dispose requisite variety to cope with that number?

The rules of the game that apply to the first question are known to readers of this book. They are not known to most Systems Three, who continue to answer the question in terms of attachment and antipathy: it is a matter of affection. The rules that apply to the second question are determined by System Four. Most Systems Three have too little rapport with System Four: often for the very good reason that System Four does not have a proper focus for its very existence. But there is no escaping the third question. It is to this, having resolutely cleared the ground, that this section of Note Three is now addressed, and a new example is selected. It comes from government.

National, provincial, regional, and local governments, despite the differences in their size, power, competence, and budgets, are all dealing with one (at the least) invariant measure of variety. It is the variety generated by the lives of all the people who live in a society of our age. Having pursued variety analysis of government in various countries at all these levels of organization, I feel strongly about this invariance, which is surely counter-intuitive. At first sight, especially, it would seem that there must be a major variety disbalance between administrations in the first and third worlds. It is not so. Remember that variety measures possible states of the system, and not numbers of bureaucrats; these possible states are a function of the aspirations of the people and of the current state of technology. It is certainly true that the latest technology is more available in some places than others, and that therefore similar technological aspirations are more plausible in one place than another. Nonetheless, they are there, and governments must handle them. The reason, of course, is that modern communication systems have spread the cultural norms of the developed nations all over the world like butter. Since these norms are in my opinion unavailing to human happiness, and lead to the degradation of the human spirit, the outcome is tragic. But that is a private judgment; it does not alter the fact that people cram into the cities of India, Africa, and South America, demanding public utilities, and private ownership of cars, refrigerators, and television sets.

The growth of government machinery everywhere reflects the worldwide use and abuse of technology, independently of the pathological autopoiesis whereby the bureaucracy produces itself. This is a distinction that it is necessary to draw. Pathological conditions may be cured; but the number of *distinctions* between facets of government as it reflects the lives of all the people is fundamental to the structure that the government adopts. Now if System Three is responsible for that System One structure, it needs to think again about the distinctions that are customarily drawn. There are two quite separate reasons for this contention, although each is based in considerations of variety engineering.

Firstly, consider government growth in terms of the accretion of newly recognized responsibilities. There could have been no ministry of telecommunications before the invention of the telephone; thereafter, such a ministry had to be created. Departments of the Environment have sprung into being only with the sudden awareness that such a concept as environment has a real-life denotation suffering real and often irreversible damage. In short, the world at the end of the twentieth century looks very different from the world at the end of the nineteenth century — at which time the major departments of government were all well established. And there they remain. Evidently it would be wise to reconsider the scope of government responsibility in terms of the requisite variety it needs to deploy in absorbing the variety generated by *modern* society, given the availability of *modern* technique and *modern* paradigms. Then (to create an hypothetical example) it might be decided that a human being has a micro-ecology in which it is both absurd and technologically unnecessary to distinguish between health, welfare and education — as if these three had no bearing on each other. Redefinitions of structure, then, might be expected to flow from the application of the four cybernetic principles of management (see Appendix One) to the horizontal loops whereby people are micro-ecologically embedded in their environment. Evidently, also, it would be enormously difficult to implement any such findings, because of the autopoietic tenacity of the three departments concerned. However: government is used here as a generally understood illustration, and in other kinds of enterprise it is much more familiar to undergo regroupings of established System One components. The trouble is that these are normally undertaken as political (small *p*) measures, rather than as cybernetically valid consequences of variety engineering.

Secondly, the growth in government arising from the drawing of new distinctions has obvious consequences in the vertical domain, whereby the multiplicity of departments inevitably robs System Three of requisite variety to manage them. As usual, we find that attenuating filters that have not been designed simply come into being, in response to Ashby's Law. The solution whereby 'superministries' are demarcated, under ministerial 'overlords' has been criticized earlier in this book. This cannot be allowed to count as designed attenuation, because it predictably cannot succeed — thanks to the autopoiesis of the original ministries, with which the so-called design has no policy other than harmless exhortation to deal. Since a particular example is in mind in this as in all these Notes, some actual details will be given now. They relate to a government of provincial or state level, that is, the level just below federal or national level. Once again, however, the example exists because it will be generally understood: it can readily be mapped onto the problems of many firms. For instance, I joined a firm in which thirty-six people reported to the managing director personally in System Three; and this is a practical impossibility.

In the governmental example, the figure was ninety-three. That is to say, this number of major projects (for this was an advanced, project-based, organizational structure) were all dependent from the Executive Council in System Three. To visualize what this entails, consult again Figure 86, and imagine ninety-three lines connecting Systems Three and One (where four lines are drawn). In practice, and of course, these major projects could be grouped, so that eighteen ministers each could absorb the variety generated by about five of them. But the question yet remains as to how System Three handles the variety of 18×5: the eighteen is sufficiently difficult; the amplifier 'times five' cannot be simply ignored, since any major government project may suddenly become the focus of public attention at any moment.

Recognizing the impracticality of working from the contemporary needs of this society *inwards* to determine (through the four principles) a view of government structure that would meet the criteria of viability, I determined to work *outwards* by seeking significant groupings of the eighteen groups that would simulate the preferred methodology without presenting an impossible challenge to the status quo and to its autopoietic institutions. There resulted six 'foci of concern', each capable (on average) of absorbing the variety of thirteen of the major projects. (There were sixteen left over, which were already regarded as the absolutely direct responsibility of System Three; and it did not seem at all feasible to disrupt this understanding.) This compromise analysis in the horizontal domain was of course an attempt to reach a significant perception in the vertical domain, and the requirements of the first Axiom. The six foci of concern came out as follows:

- Land

- Work

- People's Welfare

- People's Growth

- Communications

- Law and Order

These details are given because they make clear the extent of the compromise necessary under practical constraints (that is, the distinctions drawn still reflect historical accident); but they also show how it remains possible to reach a variety attenuation that can be contained *both* by System Three *and* by the public whose projects these are. To sum up: six foci of governmental concern will fit into the human head; eighteen will not; ninety-three are beyond contemplation.

It remains true, however, that the media of mass communication may at any moment select one from ninety-three possibilities on which to attack the government or to arouse the public. S/he in the street may never have heard of the issue before; the government may be otherwise preoccupied, although it has a sufficiently firm grasp on the six foci of concern. Hence it can be said that the media have an amplification factor of 'times fifteen' up their sleeves, which they do not hesitate to use. This is called a democratic right, which sounds satisfactory. Its unrestrained use can, however, totally disbalance the stability of agreed societary policy. If the intervention amounts to a 'Watergate', everyone approves. If, as is more usual, it amounts to a mare's nest, then society is the worse for it; and no-one should forget that there are interests capable of triggering the media into this kind of action for their own ends.

In terms of the ordinary firm, all of this also applies. In particular: union militants on the one hand, and shareholder activists on the other, both have an amplifier (which may very well be about 'times fifteen') up their respective sleeves. Firms constantly discover this to their cost. Let them get their cybernetics right. If System One is properly structured, then the enterprise can be managed in terms of Axiom One in the vertical domain in relation to System Three. The four principles of management will nurture that properly structured System One in the horizontal domain in relation to its environment.

Until then, and in every application, we must look out for squalls.

An Elaboration of System Four

Detailed consideration to the design of System Four was given in Chapter Nine. But again the question arises as to how the existing facilities should be investigated in systemic terms, how the cybernetics of that system may be disclosed, and how any missing components may in practice be identified.

The following example is, once more, an actual study. As before, it is anonymous; and in this case (so that the work may be understood) a pseudonym is invented for the industrial process in which the company is engaged. It shall be called 'fambling'. Fambled products are, in their reality, in wide use and familiar to everyone. Now one of the major fambled products can be put to use only through a second process. This is accomplished on a special type of machine, of which there are many varieties: it shall be called a fambler. Originally, the company concerned fambled; but users of this major product purchased their famblers from suppliers of such machines. At the time of this enquiry, the company had seized on the opportunity to gain control of a fambler manufacturer. It could henceforth make its own machines, and also of course sell machines to other concerns. In short, it was in the process of vertical integration.

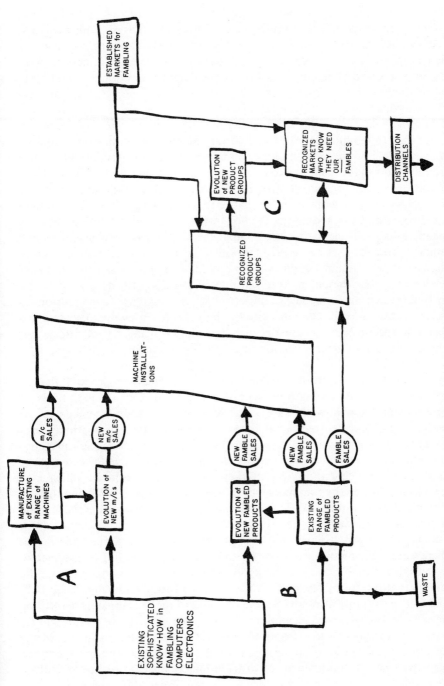

Figure 87. The perceived situation on vertical integration. Acknowledged System Four activities are marked in the loops A, B, and C

Figure 87 is a picture of this situation, which was established by investigations made on the ground. The Company was proud of its System Four activities, although it acknowledged (and see Chapter Nine) that they were so far disseminated. The machine-making part of the enterprise had a well-established R and D activity, marked on the diagram as Loop A, and so had the original fambling company, where it is marked as Loop B. Each of these units was drawing on the latest fambling technology, and also on its own pool of knowledge in such fields as computer and electronic technology, insofar as these relate to fambling. It was clear to everyone that new selling opportunities were available, in that installations of *their* machines for users of *their* major product allowed the company to press these buyers of machines also to buy-in fambled products for use on those machines. Indeed, it might in principle be possible to design the machines so that only the company's fambled products could be used. Thus, looking at the box in Figure 87 that is labelled 'machine installations', it is clear that the company *actually* sells both machines and fambled products to the enterprises in which the machines are installed. But as far as the two Systems Four are concerned, if Loop A can devise better machinery, it has the potential to sell that. As to Loop B, there are two new possibilities. One is to encourage sales from its existing range to new customers (because they have bought machines); the other is to evolve new fambled products specifically for use on such machines — and to sell those too, whether by technological coercion or merely hard-selling.

As to Loop C, this concerns the development of new fambled products that do not belong to the product group just discussed, nor do they require the use of sophisticated know-how. In short, this activity is a market-oriented type of development, aimed at traditional markets. As the diagram shows, there are in reality two Loops C. The more contained proposes to introduce new products to the market in which the company is already well-known and accepted. The larger loop considers the wider market for fambled products, which may perhaps be seduced (by the emergence of new products) into becoming such an acknowledged customer. One diagnosis made at this point was that the C Loop of System Four had consistently failed in its task of radical innovation, although much pedestrian R and D in *process* improvement was undertaken. There were many plausible reasons for this, but the outstanding one seemed to be that all the innovative people involved in the original company, from the Chairman down to the research staff, put most of their effort into Loop B. It is of course the more attractive option, because of the excitement generated by the use of more advanced technology.On the other hand, System Four ignores major development of the established business (on the right-hand side of the diagram) at some peril. It can be seen from the diagram that the limiting factor might well be the containment of distribution channels to orthodox outlets; such indeed the diagnosis contended. The challenge thus posed is always severe, because the very existence of an orthodox business virtually prescribes its outlets. It probably requires the use of specific techniques (such as 'brainstorming'), aimed at the metabolizing of creativity in the enterprise, to dislodge the thought-patterns that obstinately insist: 'but *this* is how famble products are distributed'. Once a breakthrough has occurred, it all looks very natural — with hindsight. Witness the marketing of records under the 'Music for Pleasure' label through supermarkets, at a third of the price paid in the (then) orthodox music emporium with its cathedral ambience. But it took a Paul Hamlyn to do it.

In Figure 88, the cybernetic mechanisms that are implicit in the first description are pinpointed. Look first at the feedback amplifier, whereby the existing range of fambled products might well gain a 'new sales' momentum by working through machine installations set up by the acquired subsidiary. This possibility was mentioned earlier; and the company had certainly taken it into account in making the acquisition in the first place. But no System Four activity attended to the strategic consequences, perhaps because the boost to sales on this loop was expected to arise automatically. Not so; and to identify the mechanism is to focus attention on it. The extreme example was taken earlier that perhaps machines might be built that would accept only this company's products — a policy which might well be commercially counter-productive. But it surely ought to be considered; and during that consideration more acceptable, but still effective, uses of the feedback amplifier might occur to the management. For instance, a contract to instal a machine might be tied to a different contract to use a minimum quantity of the company's other products on that machine. And so on. These are System Four considerations: precious little happens 'automatically' just because we are aware of a potentiality.

Secondly, Figure 87 shows a sink whereby waste (which in the fambling industry is a major cost component, since raw materials are very expensive) simply 'goes to earth'. Systems thinking does not like to see open loops — especially when high money values are attached to them. The immediate question, as raised in Figure 88, is to ask whether this waste cannot be recycled. The managerial answer given during the course of this work was a flat no: it is quite useless. But, as with the problem of distribution outlets, an orthodoxy is involved in this reply. Therefore the issue is put on ice until the investigation has gone a little further.

Next we come to the three feed-forward loops, which had not been recognized (at least, not with any precision) at the time of the machine company's acquisition. The existence of machine installations in other enterprises over which we have a certain control as designers should have implications for the *traditional* market. For if it is difficult to change the market image of the fambled product on our own, it may not be so difficult if other enterprises acknowledge a new product group, and new sectors of the market might thereby be penetrated. If that sounds like a recipe for subsidizing competitors, it is not the case. Take a look at the feed-forward *amplifier*. If Loop C of System Four tackles its job in earnest, with the amplification derived from the positive feed-forward arising from the new machine installations, it must always remain 'ahead of the game'. In that case, the putative competitors perforce become props.

The fourth cybernetic pinpointing is the most important of all. It concerns the interaction of the two evolutionary activities supported by advanced technology (Loops A and B). There was no interaction: dissemination again. Well, it could be argued, the vertical integration was as yet fairly new. Agreed: but there ought to have been ideas as to the closure of that loop. In fact, the two locations were widely separated geograhically. Then should they be moved together, so that the A and B Systems Four would create a 'critical mass'? Could the closure be made by establishing a committee, by an interchange of directors, or what? None of these solutions is anything to the purpose: they do not have requisite variety. At this point we face up to a loss of potential synergy, exacerbated by geographical distance, and the fierce loyalties of two developmental staffs to their original colours.

Then it is appropriate to move on to the third stage of this System Four analysis. Every excellent managerial device (such as the divisionalization that was inherent in the history of this example) carries its own antithetical risk. The issue was argued in general in the main text; we have just confronted an exemplar.

Looking at Figure 88, one can at least say: 'that is very tidy'. The reason, probably, is that the diagram shows an organizational structure for System Four that is centripetal, rather than centrifugal. So far, so good: no-one wants to blow the enterprise apart. The antithetical risk to this tidy arrangement can be understood by replacing the nice-sounding, scientific word 'centripetal' by a synonym that has pejorative connotations. For instance, we could say that the system depicted in Figure 88 is busily contemplating its own navel. How does that come about, when so much growth prospect is already in sight, and the company (newly-integrated) is so well activated? It is that everything is set to operate within the existing universe of discourse, as so far defined. It would be necessary to make a quantum jump to lift the company's eyes from navel-contemplation into a *different* universe of discourse. But this might be exactly a necessity in order to solve the problems so far disclosed.

Quoting from the report of this investigation:

> 'Why bother? Is that not actually dangerous? Would it not invoke possibilities that could not be securely financed? And anyway: did we not prove that we could do it, when we 'went into machines'?

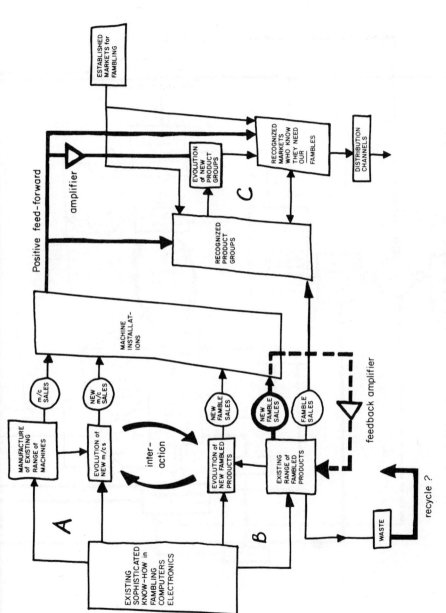

Figure 88. Pinpointing some cybernetic mechanisms implicit in Figure 87

486

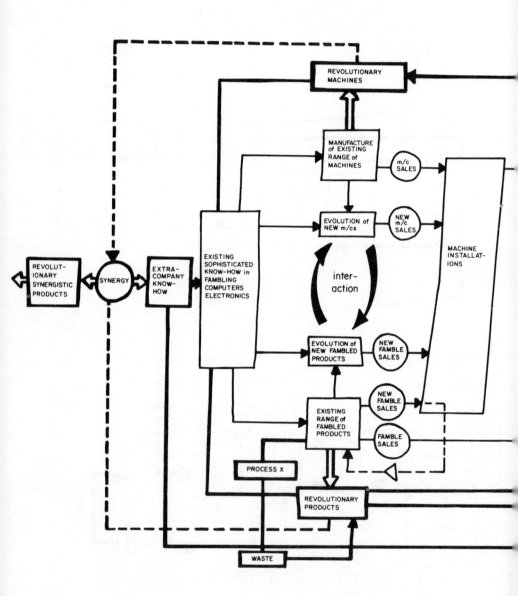

Figure 89. The completed analysis of the institutional System Four, in a particular example

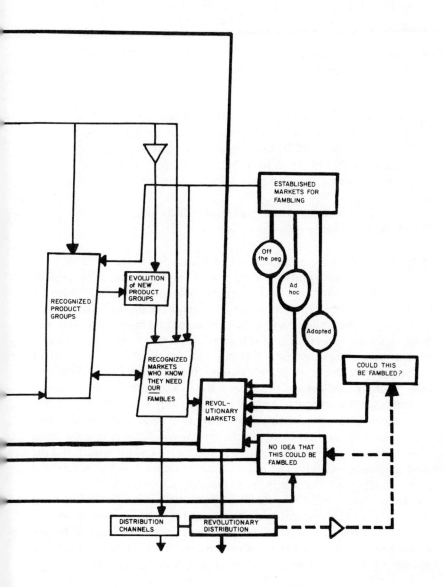

> As I read the story, the machine development was (as the Gunners say) a 'target of opportunity'. I am delighted that such a target was (a) spotted, and (b) hit. But the Company cannot rely on repeat performances by the goddess Serendipity. Thus my answer to the question 'why bother?' would be that there ought to be machinery for hunting down targets in this other universe of discourse.'

The boss took exception to this account of the acquisition: and it could well be that the verdict quoted was too harsh. But the report had already gone on to say:

> 'I propose that the answer to the dilemma posed is that whatever has extra-systemic potential does not *have* to be floating in space (like the target-of-opportunity, or the winning number in the casino), but is really part of a second system in which the existing situation is embedded.
>
> This encapsulating system calls for identification, and systematic surveillance'.

These arguments led to the establishment of Figure 89. It was an attempt to identify the missing and unifying elements of System Four. The existing 'sophisticated know-how' could be augmented by additional scientific knowledge and managerial insight not yet in evidence; or (at the least) it might be enhanced by further *attention* to such knowledge and insights, should they already be in the mind's eye. From this augmentation, the existing A and B loops might well be spurred into 'revolutionary' activity: the creation of revolutionary (by which was meant simply 'beyond present perceptions') machines, and revolutionary products. By comparing these emerging developments (see the feedbacks shown in Figure 89), a wholly new synergy might well spring into being, creating products of a totally new kind. These imaginary inventions are indicated on the left of the picture, and fantasies about their probable nature were indulged in for the sake of the report. But the cybernetic diagnosis was this. The *revolutionary* machines and products that might be hovering in the company's unconscious were unlikely to be recognized, as things were (Figure 88). New ideas were inevitably being channelled in the other direction — because of the centripetal system — towards the *evolutionary* boxes. Meanwhile, the revolutionary boxes did not receive any stimulation along the arrows emanating from the new box labelled 'revolutionary markets', because these themselves went unrecognized.

Now the 'recognized product groups' of Figure 87 were created and sustained by the established markets for fambling. In Figure 89 these were distinguished:

there were known calls for 'off the peg' fambles, for 'ad hoc' fambles, and for 'adapted' fambles. Any one of these, once distinguished, could in principle lead into a revolutionary market: indeed, all three of them *have* done so, both before and after the time when this analysis was made, but not by this company. In more innovative terms still, it was evident that there might be a population of potential customers wondering whether something-or-other unknown could be fambled or not. But there was no poised listening-post awaiting any of these algedonic signals. The recognized markets of Figure 87 absolutely defined potentiality, just as they were in turn defined by the acknowledged channels of distribution. Hence to identify a revolutionary market within Loop C entailed the discovery of a revolutionary channel also; and since neither was within the compass of the managerial mind, each potentiality negated the other. As to the possibility which (if feasible) would lead straight to a revolutionary new product, as the diagram educes, it was non-existent, even as a gleam in someone's eye. Note that the model clearly indicates the importance of investigating revolutionary distribution channels: because if these were found, there would at once come into being a feedback amplifier to support the two sorts of potential customer just described. But the existing distribution system works for the existing notion of the fambled product. It could not possibly work for a revolutionary fambled product in the second universe of discourse. *Therefore* revolutionary markets cannot be discovered; *therefore* revolutionary products cannot be invented; *therefore* synergistic products (those involving the revolutionary machines) are not even possible.

To pick up once again the cost of waste: the recycling loop could not be closed under the protocol of Figure 88. Everyone said so, and it seemed to be a fact. The waste was unusable. But under the protocol of Figure 89, waste becomes the potential raw material of a revolutionary (so far, then, unknown) product. And if the form of the waste is (as it was) apparently intransigent to *any* kind of recycling, it is at least possible to hypothesize a Process X (unknown) which would make it a suitable material for the (equally unknown) revolutionary product.... .

This 'double take' about the waste loop brings home the entire problem that surrounds the specification of a competent corporate System Four. Every development waits upon another: nothing seems real. If the waste loop is studied carefully in Figure 89, and the eyes are then drawn back to take in the entire new circuit of boxes and arrows that by now surrounds the original diagram of Figure 87, the waste loop is structurally reduplicated in a massive way. Revolutionary markets wait on revolutionary distribution channels that would feed those markets, which would in turn help to generate revolutionary products — if only extra-company know-how were put into the interaction that links the evolution of machines with the evolution of products, in which case the theoretical synergy released would sponsor an undreamed-of synergistic output. It is a beautiful scenario; yet, looking again at Figure 89, it is like a bracelet on the arm of Figure 87. There are connexions, it is true: bracelets are not suspended in space around the arm, with an anulus of air (or in this case vain imaginings) in between. But these connexions have not been made real.

Before real connexions can be made, however, it is essential to *become aware* of the hypothetical System Four that surrounds the existing system like an ethereal bracelet, and of its cybernetic structure. Having become thus aware, the only practical advance lies in devising ways of mobilizing and metabolizing the arcane powers of the so-far invisible bracelet. Then, perhaps, the bracelet can be turned into a reality, its powers unleashed, and its institutional embodiment fitted into the existing organization. In fact, the expected problems of financing anything labelled 'revolutionary', and meaning 'beyond present perceptions', was daunting to the management. But it is pointless to worry about capital requirements for a development that is defined as unknown. Once a development has been at the least identified, sensible talk about financing it can begin. It must be noted that the *recognition* of the full scope of Figure 89 costs nothing whatever, and that the attempt to metabolize it by mobilizing latent creativity demands a minimum investment in people's time.

At any rate: here is an elaboration of System Four.

An Elaboration of System Five

The main text describes System Five, some may have thought perversely as 'mysterious'. But indeed it is. From one point of view it consists of the bosses, the people who made it to the top, whose only problem is to maintain their own power and privilege. But this view is slight and dangerously paranoid. There is always some sense in which System Five is the embodiment of the whole enterprise, and answerable to it.

This is easy to recognize, at any rate in principle, in the case of *elected* Systems Five. They are quite explicitly charged to represent the will of the electors, and there are many protocols under which this responsibility is recognized — from parliamentay democracy to bloc-voting by the trade unions. The members of a Board of Directors, under a capitalist system, are there to represent the interest of the shareholders; although nowadays a director presumes that the shareholder accepts the legitimate demands of the worker, and is not intent on grinding his face into the dust. The difficulty, and hence the mystery, arises from the fact that none of these arrangements considered formally disposes requisite variety. Therefore other arrangements, informal and often reprehensible, spring into being to validate Ashby's Law.

In the case of *non-elected* Systems Five, where people have by one means or another (some merely ingenious, some violent and bloody) seized what is called control, the situation is in some ways even more mysterious. This is because, if such Systems Five do not by some means satisfy the will of the entire enterprise up to some threshold of dissent, they will be overthrown. It is again a question of requisite variety. Stupid dictators (from the firm to the government) amplify their own variety by brute strength, using the authority and facilities of their offices. They are quickly overthrown, because the variety generating capacity of a united opposition overwhelms them — though with many casualties. Clever dictators use in addition the counter-availing device of attenuating the variety they face by legitimizing much of what they do in the eyes of a large part of the enterprise. Hitler and Mussolini did this; but the attenuators they chose to use were of a kind whereby national aspirations were amplified: these systems would have gone out of control whether their masters had willed it or not, and the synergy generated by 'the Axis' made the explosive outcome quadruply sure. But there were no cyberneticians in the British Foreign Office. Franco and Salazar were more clever in their choice of public attenuators of variety, and each lasted out until the dictat of a higher recursion set the final limit. There were still no cyberneticians in the British Foreign Office. There were no cyberneticians in the United States' Department of State, either; otherwise there could not have been so protracted and obscene a war against Ashby's Law in Viet Nam.

The expansion of these thoughts would be the content of a different book. But anyone who wishes to think deeply about the nature of System Five, and especially those who are labelled in that way, must try to penetrate the mystery surrounding his or her activity as an embodiment of the will of the whole enterprise. The basic rules of mangerial cybernetics, as promulgated here (see Appendix One), ought to be of major assistance in that task.

To choose an example of the elaboration of System Five for this section is a difficult matter, since it must not be too recondite, nor so involved as to demand very lengthy treatment. The choice therefore falls upon the affairs of a learned society in the year 1970. Most readers of this book will have had dealings with a learned society: the expectation is that they will quickly appreciate the points that need to be made, without elaborate diagrams this time. The other advantage in using this example of an 'elaboration' is that the president and council of the society, in all the above fullness of a System Five, is using management science to advise, not others, but itself; and it alone has the resonsibility for implementation. Therefore we may see the entire process in the round.

On becoming president of the Operational Research Society, I found myself surrounded by an especially distinguished and well-balanced Council. There were three leading government OR scientists, three eminent consultants, three full university professors of the subject, and six heads of OR Groups — two of whom ran central OR services for the great industries of coal and steel respectively. In March 1970, we held a twenty-four hour meeting at Marlow in Buckinghamshire 'to examine the Society's responsibilities afresh'. In preparation for this meeting, I naturally prepared and circulated a version of the viable system model, together with a diagnostic commentary. Moreover, I had a decision model whereby I hoped to help the meeting to focus on its own conclusions. The current purpose is to provide a System Five elaboration, rather than to indulge in historical anecdote; and therefore most of what is said here will be said by direct quotation from the document that Council subsequently published: *Marlow Seventy* (Operational Research Society, London, April, 1970). Of course it will be necessary to add a commentary in terms of the viable system *language,* which was not used in the document itself.

> 'Many learned societies have always run themselves on the basis of an exclusive cadre at the top. The same old faces reappear in different jobs, and the influential positions are somehow 'fixed'. Today, this kind of procedure is a talisman for alienation of the membership: it will not do. But of course all such procedures survive, willy-nilly, if paid-up members do not do their job. For years this Society has had a democratic procedure for the election of a president. There has only once been an election, and I was the losing contender. This surely qualifies me uniquely to say that losing does not count as a disgrace. I stood because an insistent group of members did not want to be deprived of their franchise, and I thought they were right to ask for a choice. If I read the signs correctly, there is likely to be another election this year. This is healthy and entirely as it should be; let us count it an honour to be nominated. Any participative society is likely to be run this way in the modern world, and as Augustine (who often got in first) said: *securus judicat orbis terrarum.*'

> (page 3)

In Britain, many learned societies had been run by cliques. There was agreement at Marlow that the presidential and associated offices, which are after all a formal embodiment of System Five, should in future be seen to be open to every member. Elections would be held, and we would ensure that they would not be turned into a farce by seeing to it that alternative nominations were put before the membership. This was done; and ever since then normal democratic procedures have been followed.

The Council itself, which is the full embodiment of System Five, had always been properly elected — by the votes of the memberhip. Leading personalities in the field, whose names were generally known throughout the country, were therefore those nominated and duly elected. But the Society had a number of regional 'subsidiaries', and also a number of study groups centered on particular managerial topics or particular scientific techniques. These networks were the real substance of the Society's activity; and yet they had no specific representation on Council. Only by accident could the 'leading personalities' on Council speak knowledgeably about them. Note the variety attenuation implicit in this arrangement. It was possible to have a System Five which hardly knew what constituted System One. Therefore:

> '... we consider that each region should have a seat on the Society's Council. Thus a number of 'constituency members' should be appointed to Council, in addition to those directly elected by the national Membership.'
>
> (page 5)

> 'We note also the very effective growth of Study Groups, and will continue to support these as needed. It is not proposed to attempt a systematic classification, since the success of Study Groups appears to us to rely on the spontaneity with which they spring into being as a new focus of attention makes itself manifest. Nor should there be any barrier to the closure of a Study Group that finds there is no more useful work to do in its area for the time being. We applaud the heavy managerial involvement in industry-based Groups and the professional zeal of the technique-based Groups alike. The Study Groups have indeed proven to be a home-grown system for solving the dilemma with which this report began. However, it is certainly necessary to change the system whereby a single member of Council concerns himself with (currently) seventeen Groups, and we are providing for a broader Council interest.'
>
> (page 5)

> 'The plan so far envisaged radically changes the organization of the Society, the regular conduct of which will become heavily decentralized by regions.'
>
> (page 5)

Eight years later, an officer of the Society, Hylton Boothroyd, wrote (OR Newsletter, August 1978):

> 'By any account, the regionalization of the Society some years ago must be reckoned a success. The Yorkshire and Humberside OR Group has this year not only run national one-day events but is taking a significant part in organizing the Annual Conference. Both these contributions stand in what is being established as a tradition within the Society.

At meetings of Council, too, there is a sense of strength in the sheer number of representatives who arrive from all parts of the country.'

In eight years, it seems, the revolutionary proposals of Marlow had become nearly 'a tradition'.

But there was a big difficulty in the way, before System Five could be 'regionalized'. This is of considerable cybernetic interest, because it very well illustrates the confusion between System Five and System One that is part of the mystery earlier discussed. The argument can be left to *Marlow Seventy* to elucidate:

'We begin with the question of national meetings, held in London, which well exemplify the problem and are not well attended. They are mostly interesting: but the programme as a whole is inevitably designed to be all things to all men. This is not a criticism of the programme but an acceptance of the inappropriateness in the 'seventies' of traditions inherited from and suitable for the 'forties'. The national Society will not continue to hold these meetings after the current session. Instead it will convene a few national meetings, each designed with a specific and attainable purpose, and armed with a proper organization to assure its success. A working group has been established to recommend the basis on which this should be done.

This decision leaves a lacuna in London and the South East of England. A forum will be needed for the OR professionals who live and work in this region, a forum organized by themselves to suit their own needs. We note the healthy and successful growth of regional Societies in all other parts of Great Britain, and consider that this natural development has not happened in the South East simply because frequent 'national' meetings were held in London. Accordingly, we intend to foster the creation of a regional society, and to make facilities available to its organizers. The OR Society will then become a federation of regional societies. Another working group is now looking into the consequences of this decision, since all members ought in future to have the opportunity to belong to a regional group, and will pay special attention to the financial links.'

(pages 4 and 5)

Obviously, the regional System One located around London was identifying itself with System Five — even to the extent of not actually existing... ·

Eight years later, Hylton Boothroyd commented, in the article already quoted:

> 'Yet there has been some cost to regionalization, perhaps nowhere more so than for the London and South Eastern Society. There our fellow members have in effect been required to discover a regional identity and purpose separate from the natural gravitation of national events and study groups to the capital. This is apparently now being achieved at the cost of wearing out each set of officers in twelve months!'

With apologies to those officers, it has been worth the effort. Something has been achieved which answers to the First Axiom of Management. And the process begun in 1970 proved to be properly adaptive, since it continues now. For Hylton Boothroyd (*op. cit.*) goes on:

> 'Elsewhere there are hints of possible further condensations of affiliated societies out of inter-societal space — the hint of a little thickening around Oxford (or is that just a result of being on everyone else's boundary?) and a much more definite looking condensation in the East Midlands.'

These fairly massive changes on the vertical axis of the Society, recognizing fully (and even, in the case of London and the South East, creating) a regional basis for System One, to be reflected in System Five, at once raised the question of the effectiveness of Systems Two and Three.

> 'We have already announced our intention to strengthen the permanent staff. In particular, appointment to a post senior to that of secretary called Chief Executive (hitherto referred to as 'Director') will now proceed. It becomes important to delegate authority to a full-time paid official in many matters if the Society is to grow and flourish. A major responsiblity of this post will be the promotion of professional-managerial interaction, as well as the provision of more services to members.'

> (page 7)

It has to be admitted that this System Three appointment did not work out as we had hoped. Probably the misjudgment was that the Society's budget was inadequate to the calibre of the person needed at that time. Even so, and just because the new organizational design was cybernetically sound, System Three gradually (and long after my time) found its proper level. The post of 'Chief Executive' was too grandiose; and the excellent man in the System Three chair now signs himself 'Secretary and General Manager'. So be it.

As to System Two, it was evident that the new Five-Three-One arrangements would lead to oscillation which could not be handled by part-time activity on the part of elected officials. Some publication was needed. The Society already had the *Operational Research Quarterly,* the oldest (and surely the best) professional OR journal in the world. *Marlow Seventy* made proposals about it, which were duly implemented. But a quarterly and scholarly journal could not possibly provide a System Two. Accordingly, the step was taken to inaugurate the OR Newsletter.

It could of course be said that this innovation was commonplace. However, it had never been suggested; and I record that the inspiration for it did not come from easy comparisons with other societies, but from the contemplation of the System Two problem. The Newsletter has been a great success: it set out, of course, to make the cross-matching between the regional network and the study group network. It still does.

Finally we come to the issue of the recognition of Systems Three and Four. On this, *Marlow Seventy* shall speak again:

'Here then is the new structure of the Society's general management. Hitherto, every committee of the Society has reported directly to Council. Standing and ad hoc committees have often been numbered in double figures, and the practice has generated a huge volume of business. In future, Council will meet as a whole essentially to receive and debate the reports of three Committees of Council. These will be as follows:

(i) The Policy Committee (consisting minimally of the President, the immediate Past-President, the Hon Treasurer and the Hon Secretary) will manage the Society's full-time Executive staff, constitute the Council's steering group, manage the Society's Benevolent Fund, and attend to recommendations for the Society's most senior awads.

(ii) The External and Future Affairs Committee (elected, with its own Chairman, by Council from its own membership) will be concerned with fostering Education and Research, with national Society Affairs, and with Publications — each of which topics probably requires a sub-committee.

(iii) The Internal and Current Affairs Committee (elected, with its own Chairman, by Council from its own membership) will be concerned with Society Membership (admissions, standards and awards), with the Co-ordination of Regional Groups and of Study Groups (in both cases to ensure that standards are maintained, needs met, and financial arrangements equitably made) and with the integration of programmes held by all Groups under the Society's auspices. Again, these four endeavours probably involve four sub-committees.

Terms of reference and methods of operation have to be worked out in detail by those who will be appointed, but the intentions are sufficiently clear. We have (a) reduced the total number of committees, (b) organized them at two levels to increase participation, and (c) structured them into a design which co-ordinates the outword-looking planning function and the inward-looking operational function.'

(pages 5 and 6)

The organizational intent here, quite obviously, was to define Systems Five, Four, and Three. IFORS, by the way, stands for the International Federation of Operational Research Societies.

For six years after Marlow, these three Committees operated as planned. But as Marlow receded into the distance, and as successions of new officers in the Society took over, further changes were made. In July 1976, the External (System Four) and Internal (System Three) Committees were formally abolished. Quite certainly, at this point, no-one serving the Society knew in any detail the history recounted here: they were simply being adaptive. What they did about it was fascinating. They created two new appointments: Vice-Presidents of the Society. And the then-Chairman of the two Committees were appointed in these roles. Each of them (as this is being written) continues to report, through the Newsletter to the Membership under the names of EFAC and ICAC.

It remains to say, going back to 1970, how the progenitors of the Marlow plan proceeded in the matter of implementation. As was mentioned at the start of this Section, it is a remarkable moment when a group of management scientists find themselves advising *themselves*.

It is normal, when the basic organization of a learned society has to be changed, that an Extraordinary General Meeting is called to approve the changes. Hardly anyone attends. The proceedings have legal force; but the procedure does not have requisite variety.

Accordingly, at Marlow in 1970, revolutionary tactics were adopted. The report from which these quotations have been drawn was written. It was sent personally to every member of the Society (*Ashby's Law: ONLY VARIETY CAN ABSORB VARIETY*).

'This plan has been formulated and is being developed with much effort by the Council which holds your mandate. There will be an Annual General Meeting on 10th June 1970 when the views of those present will be sought on the Marlow Plan as the main item of business. It is our intention, with your agreement, to complete our proposals and to hold an Extraordinary General Meeting to give them legal effect by the year's end if humanly possible. Although we urge your attendance in June, we know that many members will not find it possible to come. We do not wish to ignore these absentees, since the future of the Society is at stake, and we therefore ask for your involvement.

In the first place we list below the main areas of concern covered by the plan, and nominate a Council Member for each area who is prepared to receive your written views. He undertakes to have them properly considered by whichever working party is concerned. If members do write will they please assist by separating their comments according to this scheme.'

(page 7)

There followed the names and addresses of Council Members prepared to deal with the six major aspects of the new plan. Members, as the last quotation shows, were invited to write to them with their views. They did so, in abundance.

Next, the President visited every regional society (save one) to explain the proposals. Members of Council also visited regional societies. But in particular, a Council Member was attached to each of the (then) seventeen Study Groups, in order to gain their understanding. Note the quite explicit use of this tactic in the left-hand System Three channel.

In the outcome, the Annual General Meeting of 10th June 1970 approved all these changes unanimously. None of them (*mutatis mutandis,* as explained above) has since been contravened.

The Operational Research Society subsequently saw other upheavals. But they were not part of these cybernetics, and nothing to do with this elaboration of System Five.

What this Section of Note Three tries to convey is, above all, the involvement of the entire enterprise in any System Five appreciation. It is one exposition of 'the mystery'.

It cannot close without incorporating salutations to my fellow Council Members of 1970, who constituted one of the best teams with whom it has ever been my privilege to work.

Cyberfilter and the
time barrier

The idea of managerial measurement as being dedicated primarily to the detection of instability was discussed in detail in Chapter Eleven. In terms of implementation, it is worth recording exactly what this involves.

'Exactly' is an unhappy word, because there are many possible approaches to the problem; as we said before: 'it is foreign to the purposes of this book to supply recipes ... (we) must depend on a study of that system itself'. This is perfectly true; there can be no claim to a unique solution. But it is possible to be exact about a proposition that is not yet unique. In doing so, it is well to be as general as possible.

The postulate therefore begins by saying that most systems of management accounting operate in arbitrary time epochs. There are daily, weekly, monthly, quarterly figures (and so on), and these epochs are not necessarily standard for any one enterprise. Some data lend themselves to collection by one epoch, some by another. The collection of data in *real time,* which is to say that data may be registered in the information system continuously, just as the events that give rise to the data occur, is already possible — in technical principle. It is also prohibitively expensive for many enterprises, and maybe quite unnecessary for most of them. As to the expense, however, the situation is changing rapidly: electronic microprocessors are becoming more capacious, more flexible, more reliable, *and* withal cheaper, year by year. Thus what is agreed to be unnecessary now, as far as real-time sensing is concerned, may yet turn out to be perfectly convenient in the short-term future. Such shifts between necessity and convenience, price and value, should be under constant review.

For the time being, however, spasmodic input of data to the managerial information system is assumed, as is also the institutional process and plant by which these data are captured and secured. The existing arrangements will be referred to as SASWIMB: this stands for the Standard Accounting System Whatever It May Be. (Maybe Saswimb should be changed; but no assumption is made here in advance.)

In Figure 90, the basic Saswimb is outlined. The managers determine their own data needs, although they may call for professional help in this. From the operations under their control, these data are selected, and put into the information system — where they constitute some sort of file (whether on paper or inside a computer makes no difference). These data are extracted from their files under standard rules, aggregated in some way (monthly totals, moving annual averages, and so on), and become the content of the periodic reporting system. In addition, it is usual for the management team to design certain indices of performance, which Saswimb computes, and also enters into the periodic reporting system. These are such indices as return-on-investment, profit as a proportion of sales value, and so on. Eventually, the periodic reports are made to the managers, who then proceed to act — and also, if necessary, to adjust their data needs and their design of indices, thus closing the loop which the diagram delineates for informational services as it also does for action (the double line).

However up-to-date the periodic reports may be, they refer to matters that have already occurred. Thus managers find themselves concerned mostly with holding post-mortems, with clearing up the remnants of catastrophes, and with trying to create conditions (through their 'double line' actions) in the enterprise which will preclude further disasters of a similar kind.

Some effort, on the other hand, will surely be devoted to examining the periodic reports for evidence of that instability which is incipient — in the hope of averting disasters that have not yet happened. It is in this sense that managers hope to 'break the time barrier'.

Two factors militate against them. The first is that their data are needlessly out-of-date. Evidence of instability has been stored in Saswimb, awaiting the proper moment for the periodic report. Even if it would be too expensive to relay this information the instant it occurred (namely, in real-time), it is wasteful — given that it is already on file — to conceal it until 'the second Tuesday in the month'. Secondly, and although the human brain is good at spotting patterns in data generally, no-one can be sure that the evidence of incipient instability will be noticed as soon as it appears. It is the province of mathematical statistics to detect such a tendency.

A variety of methods is available for monitoring data in this way. Bayesian statistical theory, and the techniques of Harrison and Stevens (references 1 and 2), are not unique to this end. They can, however, be specified exactly. Moreover, having used them, I feel confident in their efficacy. What is more,

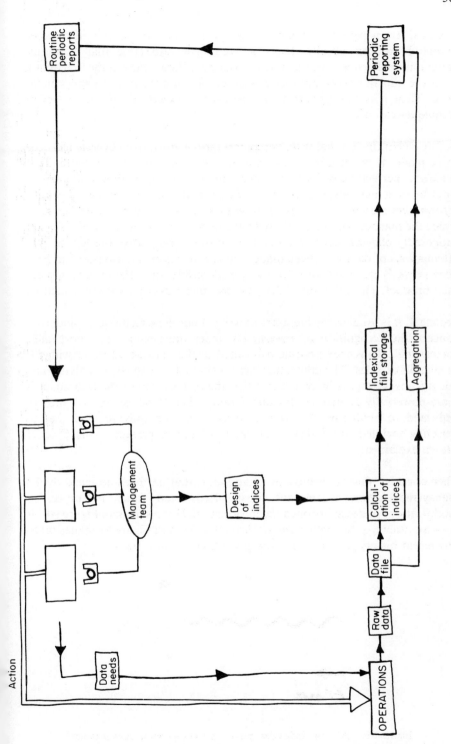

Figure 90. SASWIMB—the Standard Accounting System Whatever It May Be

it is clear (from experiment) that they detect instability earlier in time than the human brain can usually detect it; and it is also clear that a routine computational system can examine thousands of data points in the time that it takes the human to pick out the relevant graph from the pile of papers on his desk. Then it is appropriate to try to express exactly what such a set of techniques can do.

Before embarking on that task, two points (also learned from experience) need to be made. If we deal with raw data, we face a monumental exercise. That exercise is perfectly possible; if it is necessary to control ten thousand items of stock by such methods, it can certainly be done. But in terms of a *management information system,* this is quite unnecessary. The incipient instabilities to which the manager should be alerted have to do with the variety loops that are supposedly obeying Ashby's Law of Requisite Variety **after** the appropriate attenuations of data have been made. Those attenuators are supposed to have been properly designed: therefore we need consider only the indices that are their product. This criterion of design constitutes a massive variety reduction.

Secondly, it is usual in the literature to write about these techniques (since they concern the recognition of *tendencies*) under the heading of 'short-range forecasting'. Thus they become associated in the managerial mind with the prediction of sales. The contention here is that all management activity, and not just marketing, is involved; and that the competence of the techniques is more powerfully defined as 'filtration' rather than 'forecasting'. We are not dedicated to predicting that future which is known only to God, but to detecting incipient instability in an all too insecure present — as Chapter Eleven explained.

Then consider now the behaviour of an index, that has been designed by the management team as relevant to its needs (and which is subject to modifications in design through the informational loop shown in Figure 90). It is — inevitably — 'wobbling about' through time, and Figure 91 relates (a) to this recent history, and (b) to a new point that has just arrived.

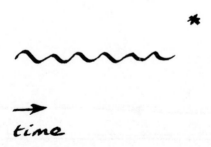

Figure 91. A new indexical point arrives — what does it mean?

Cyberfilter addresses the problem as to the meaning of this new point. On the face of it, and as far as Figure 91 can tell us anything, a substantial change is indicated. There is a number of preliminary questions to be addressed... Does this datum point arrive in good standing? (It might be a perversion of the system; but statistical subroutines can be contrived to declare whether Cyberfilter should accept the new arrival as legitimate, or question it.) Or, for a second instance, is the datum point a *statistical* freak? (It might be an artefact of a skewed distribution; but again subroutines can be contrived, using trigonometrical functions, to 'normalize' skewness.) Suppose, then, that the problem posed in Figure 91 is recognized as genuine. What does the new datum point mean?

According to the Harrison-Stevens model, it might mean one of four things. These are exhibited in Figure 92. In interpreting Figure 92 it is important to notice that these four probability assessments refer to only one index (and not four) and to only one new point (and not four). The recent history of the one series is established, and in regard to that the new point looks suspiciously high. If we then search past history, matters are more confused. The *actual* time series is still a fact, although it is drawn differently in each trial on the diagram. This is because its meaning is ambiguous; so what the program is doing is making trials of the actual past data in search of evidence that each of these four effects may exist. When the four probabilities are assessed, then the program makes a judgment (based again on statistical theory and the manager's capacity to cope with alerting signals relatively infrequently) as to whether it should notify incipient instability or not. There is no point in notifying a chance result, nor the existence of a transient pulse unless its effects have been causing concern. But a probable change in slope may indicate a burgeoning trend, while a probable step function in the data may indicate an incipient catastrophe. The program will not make any notification about these risks, however, until it has established a certain degree of confidence that the risks are serious; and it is a noteworthy cybernetic feature of the Harrison-Stevens model that the filter responds to the increasing uncertainty which surrounds change by increasing its own sensitivity whenever change is signalled.

Now suppose that there is a stream of data emanating from the enterprise, and being used for some purpose of management; then we might route that data stream through a statistical program inside the computer — without interfering with the managerial purpose that was at first in mind. In this way, we should expect to recognize incipient instability in whatever process is generating the data stream. The difficulty is that Saswimb (see Figure 90) does not deal in continuous streams of data, but in periodic reports. Furthermore, the periods involved are not all the same. Thus we have a powerful tool to hand which is not yet adapted to the typical management information system.

504

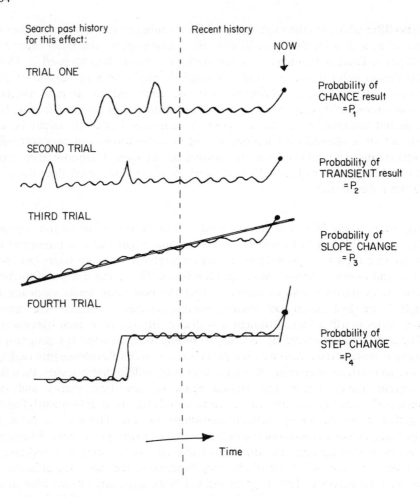

Figure 92. The Harrison-Stevens statistical program examines the new indexical point four times, searching past history for evidence that one of four effects is present, and assessing the probability of each

To deal with this situation, we may create a concept called *bogus real time*. Saswimb is not sensing events in the enterprise in real time, but it can be made aware of its own activity in real time. In particular, it can be made self-conscious about the updating of its indexical file.

In Figure 93 we consider an unchanged Saswimb that produces a duplicate copy of its indexical file. Whenever this file is updated, bogus real time is in being; whenever the file is inactive, 'time stops'. And whenever the file is in use, whatever index is being consulted is automatically submitted to the

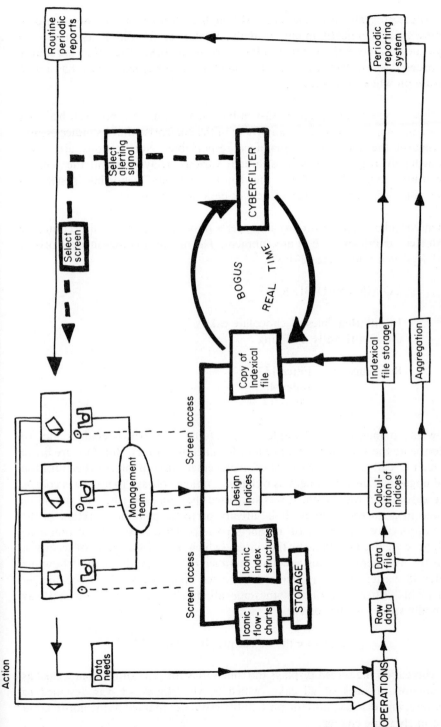

Figure 93. CYBERFILTER, and the invention of Bogus Red Team (compare Figure 90)

statistical program just described. Although each index has its own periodic nature in real time (it might be daily, weekly or monthly), its points are equivalent to those of any other index in bogus real time. The points are simply an ordered set of data: as far as the computer is concerned, it now has a data *stream* on which to operate.

So this is Cyberfilter. It makes Saswimb self-conscious. As soon as it becomes aware of incipient instability, anywhere in the enterprise that its indices sense, it reports the fact to the manager responsible. Notifications are made immediately they are sensed, although various delays exist in the sensory apparatus itself. Meanwhile, the routine periodic reporting system as originally designed continues to deliver periodic reports.

Then consider a screen on any manager's desk. This screen will become live with alerting information at any moment. The manager comes into his office, and sees such a message as this:

TO MR FRED BLOGGS

I think that sales of chocolate cake
are significantly declining

References: Filter 137
                Index 48
                Chart 14

Now the manager has a simple device at his side, which enables him to interrogate the system. It could be a little panel of buttons. But if we are brave enough to embrace the new style of management that involves cyberfiltration and bogus real time, we might as well have enough courage to invoke *accoustic interrogation* of the screen. It was suggested that the cyberfilter file should be stored in a microcomputer. It is already perfectly possible to retain in the microprocessor a memory of anyone's voice pattern, to the extent that s/he will be recognized by name by the system (which provides a degree of security), and to the extent that an adequate number of commands of the 'show me Index 48' variety can be recognized and acted upon. Thus, when the manager enters his office and finds a message about chocolate cake, he may say (literally speak) to the screen:

'Show me the actual graph of Filter 137'

— whereupon the screen displays the time series for sales of chocolate cake as a function of sales of all cake, which is what Index 48 was designed to measure, and displays also the probability estimates that led to the notification of a likely slope change.

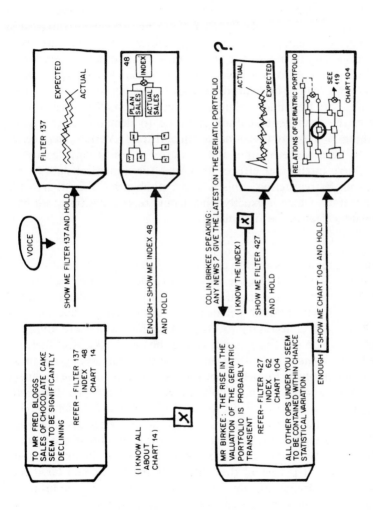

Figure 94. An impression of Cyberfilter from the manager's desk. The upper picture shows Mr Bloggs being alerted, as he walks into his office. The lower picture shows the response of Cyberfilter to a question from Mr Birkee, who has a suspicion. In each case, security is protected by the recognition by the computer of 'his master's voice'

If the manager has forgotten precisely how Index 48 is constructed, he will ask the system to show him; and if he needs to recall exactly in which bakeries the chocolate cake is being made and by which shops it is sold, he will ask the system to show him Flowchart 14. In the diagram, the storage of these two types of back-up information is referred to as 'iconic'. Not everyone is familiar with this word, which is the adjective from 'icon': it means that the information is a portrait. Examples are given in Figure 94. Again, variety engineering is in action. A great deal of useful information can be conveyed by the use of iconic representations, because they indicate structures directly to the pattern-recognizing facility of the brain which would otherwise need to be transmitted by paragraphs of verbiage or by mathematical equations. Iconic representations can readily be quantified, too, by making the sizes of boxes and the widths of flow-lines relativley larger or smaller than others. Unfortunately, the managerial culture is prone to demand actual figures (before anything is allowed to count as 'quantified'). Variety engineering declares this to be a waste of time and a source of confusion, because — having made huge intellectual efforts to master the numerical data — the manager ends up by registering: 'this is about double that', or 'that is less important than this', which is exactly what iconic representation could have made immediately clear in the first place.

In general, the indices are designed to monitor basic business information. The dramatic example of chocolate cake was used to demonstrate the system's flexibility. For if there is a new product launched, it is a good idea to create a special index to monitor sales performance until that product is well established. Then it is unnecessary to keep asking how things are going, or (worse) forgetting to do so. The example of the chocolate cake is, in fact, not merely quixotic: it is true. Much attention, care and support were given to the launch of this new product. In fact, a few mistakes were made. The decline in the initially booming sales was not spotted (because people were busy with hundreds of other products) until it was *too late* to repair the damage. The mistakes could easily have been corrected; but by the time when declining sales had been noted by Saswimb, the product had lost its credibility in the market. Perhaps this makes clear the contention that Cyberfilter 'breaks the time barrier'. In this case, it is evident that those few mistakes could have been corrected *before* the decline in sales became significant, if the appropriate manager had received an alerting signal of incipient instability.

The technology for Cyberfilter is readily available. If Saswimb is already using a large computer, then the 'duplicate copy' of the indexical file is simply that file itself, switched into another mode of operation. If Saswimb is using simple accounting machinery, then the duplicate can be entered into a micro-computer — at very low cost. It is not the technology that is in question, nor the statistical theory, nor the cybernetic design . . . It is perhaps the willingness of the manager to enter into a novel encounter with data which, in the process of being transformed into information, changes him.

Maybe, though, 'willingness' is not the right word. We are dealing with changes that are culturally repugnant to anyone trained in Saswimb. A very senior manager to whom all this was recently elucidated said something like this:

> 'It is very compelling. It is a fine idea. I shall support it. But I can tell you this much. Making the biggest effort of the imagination of which I am capable, I simply cannot see anyone at all in this company actually using such a system.'

Yes, *that* is the problem.

REFERENCES

1. Harrison, P. J., and Stevens, C. F., 'A Bayesian Approach to Short-term Forecasting', *Operational Research Quarterly,* **22**, No.4, December 1971.
2. Harrison, P. J., and Stevens, C. F., 'Bayesian Forecasting', *Journal of the Royal Statistical Society, Series B (Methodological),* **38**, No.3, 1976.

The evolution of a management cybernetics process

In October 1973 I became associated with a large mutual life insurance company. It began with interviews, jointly and severally, with the senior officers of the company, with the exception of the President. The President and I met at a later time. That first meeting was not a success, but he and I were to get over our barriers in the years to come, as this case history will explain.

At that time the company launched a concerted effort to improve their planning processes. It subsequently came to a notable fruition. But it is not relevant to this Note to talk in detail about that work. This Note concerns only my own cybernetic interventions, over a period of years, in the management process of the company.

In Note One, I spoke of the meaning of 'success'. The story that will now be told is, I think, a success story. It robs cybernetics of any claim to miraculous cure, and so it should. But the cybernetics is not irrelevant: if it were, I should not have the permission of those managers to publish the whole story. The real cure is dragged forth from the internal strength of the enterprise. It is implemented by the personal strength of dedicated managers. The cybernetician stands in the role of GPF. This title was awarded to me by the Chairman of a British company, whose name is Nigel Foulkes. It stands for 'Guide, Philosopher, and Friend'. It is a much better title, surely than 'Technocrat'.

It is wholly appropriate to start our story of the evolution of a *cybernetic process* with the organizational dynamics of the company before anyone there had even heard of cybernetics. We go back to *before* 1973.

BC: BEFORE CYBERNETICS

This tale has been told in a company report. It explained that a task force had been set up to develop an approach to reorganization, which was perceived to be necessary, and that this task force identified 'three major areas of weakness'.

In the words of the report:

- 'The old company had been organized essentially along functional lines. The style of management was what might be called 'paternally autocratic', a style quite common in our industry at the time.'

- 'Not only was our functional approach constraining us in the marketplace, but the orientation towards specialists was not producing the generalist kind of management talent necessary for running a complex organization.'

- 'And finally, we lacked a capability for systematically sensing and reacting to the changes that were building up in the environment.'

Following these conclusions, the report continues, 'a series of major changes was set in motion'. Three phases were identified by the same company report:

'In Phase I, marketing divisions were created, integrating some of the major functions on a territorial basis, rather than the total company level, in order to place responsibility closer to the scene of action.'

At the same time a version of accountability management, or management by objectives, was introduced and a conscientious attempt was made to move towards a more participative style of management.

Phase II quickly followed. The decentralization of authority unleashed a remarkable enthusiasm. Activity blossomed and expenses rocketed, highlighting the fact that we were operating with an inadequate control system. Plans had been laid to develop a broad new information system; but these had to be accelerated, with initial emphasis on expense budgeting and monitoring.

Phase III. During the whole period of reorganization, there had been a marked increase in human stress and strain. The change in management style placed heavy demands on both the new management and on personnel. There was a shift of emphasis from specialists to managers; there were changes in career pattens; there was a new emphasis on productivity, and pay was geared to performance.

Again, developments that had been planned in the human resource field had to be accelerated. Management made unusual efforts to communicate with the staff and each other. Special meetings were held. The house organ was changed from a glossy monthly magazine to a bi-weekly news sheet providing a running commentary on the train of events; letters to the editor provided an avenue through which personnel could draw attention to problems; a confidential channel was created in which people in distress had access to professional help; major efforts were made to help the managers learn their new jobs, and to help people learn to work in groups.

In a somewhat different aspect of Phase III, the internal audit was rejuvenated, with new authority and new vigour, to provide another means of ensuring that the new delegation of responsibility did not turn into abdication.

And finally, senior management created a semi-formal management committee to help co-ordinate the operations of the company.'

It was at this point that a company officer was introduced to the cybernetics of the viable system. He made an exhaustive study of *Brain of the Firm,* in which the nomenclature of the viable system is identical with that used in this book. He mapped the experience recounted above onto the model, and came up with the following identifications (in his words again):

- 'The attempt to create responsible marketing divisions matched the postulation of viable components in System One.'

- 'The introduction of accountability management granted at least a degree of autonomy to these quasi-viable units.'

- 'Phase II emphasized the need for a mechanism beyond the command and accountability channel which could foster self-regulation through feedback.'

- 'Phase III dramatized the importance of rich intercommunication and the absolute necessity of providing parasympathetic channels to relieve stress and strain.'

- 'Taken together, these points support the proposition that internal stability is to be achieved by a clever managerial use of these three channels.'

- 'The formation of the management committee was an attempt to use the collegiate form of authority as a means of obtaining reliable results from fallible human components.'

- 'The search for a satisfactory approach to corporate planning acknowledged a concern that we were close to being a 'decerebrate cat' — that is, that we were virtually cut off at the neck in lacking a coherent mechanism for creating a future in a rapidly changing world.'

All this being so, the cybernetic process was already clearly in action. But now it was recognized for what it was. It was not until this point that I myself was called in.

FIRST CYBERNETIC INTERVENTION

It was October 1973. And it was exciting to find that so much of the cybernetic reality of this viable system was already understood. I also found it commendable and humanly satisfying that a top management group should be so open in their first interaction. For, when all the cybernetic criteria had been listed and examined, the question posed was this:

> Can you tell us how it is that this team,
> which is working with all honesty and frankness,
> and which devotes unlimited hours to free-ranging discussion,
> finds it almost impossible
> to reach consensus about anything at all?

By the time this question became explicit, I had already concluded that System One of the first level of recursion was in reality divided into two viable systems on the horizontal axis. The management team was not working on this basis. They thought of territorial markets as one possible model of System One, which would therefore have many components — as many as their marketing areas across the world. They also thought of functional activities (such as marketing itself, accounting, actuarial acitivity) as possible components of System One, without realizing that no *functional* activity can itself be a viable system. In short: you cannot hive-off a function to an independent existence, because it cannot carry its substantive content with it. The content belongs to the corporation as a whole.

The two components of System One that were immediately recognizable at the first level of recursion were quite straightforwardly: insurance and investment.

Now those men who had arrived in the top management group via the *insurance* component of System One gave this kind of account of the company (I caricature for brevity):

'We are an aggressive, market-oriented firm.
It is our job to get out into the field, and to *sell*.

PS: This produces a lot of income. That had better
be competently invested, because policies will
eventually mature.'

On the other hand, those top management men who had arrived via the investment and functional component of System One gave a rather different account of the company (still caricaturing):

'We are an extremely knowledgeable actuarial and investment
firm. It is our job to use our expertise in the markets, in order to
maximize return for our policyholders.

PS: We need a lot of money to provide our stock-in trade.
Will someone sell a lot of insurance, please, to provide the cash.'

Well, I did say 'caricature'. Actuarial specialists most certainly worked across the board; and both groups were wholly aware of each other. The point was however, that there was *no formal mechanism* directed to their linkage (the squiggly vertical lines between the circles of System One). The linkage was achieved in practice by powerful effort at the level of System Five. Thereby was the company successful. But in cybernetic terms, there was a diagnosis here. It was also the answer to the question as posed.

The top management team were in difficulties about their concensus, not because of issues relating to market areas nor yet to functional responsibilities, but because their perceptions of the total system were at total variance. A sketch entitled: 'Descriptive and Diagnostic Model of the Existing Organization' was prepared and demonstrated with slides. This was Year One of the intervention (November 1973).

516

A cybernetic assault of this sort is hard to accommodate. And naturally the usual processes of an interpersonal kind within the top management team were continuing. Soon one member was to leave the company; soon, a differentation of status between remaining members would become apparent. Another member would leave and be replaced. But the cybernetic evaluation of affairs was now part of the whole picture. And I felt very much party to the whole affair.

SECOND CYBERNETIC INTERVENTION

A year passed. During this time much happened. The company tried to apply the model of the viable system, in some detail, to the whole corporation. As a result, questions were formally addressed to me — all relating to the measurement of variety and the handling of information. But these questions were related to the model that they had created. I was very uneasy about this. It did not seem to obey the axioms of viability; therefore the questions could not be directly answered.

A memorandum was submitted criticizing this particular application of the model, because of what I considered to be confusions about the five subsystems and the viable systems involved in System One. I also felt that different levels of recursion were being confused. But it certainly seemed that the questions could not be answered until the issue of the nature of the corporation had been resolved. The memorandum called this the Joint Normative Decision. It would be Joint, because 'both sides' (investment and insurance) would be in agreement. It would be Normative, because it would exercise a *governing intention* for the firm. It would be a Decision, because the top group would have made a firm commitment as to the nature of the corporation.

These contentions were of course derived from the original model, which diagnosed the fundamental weakness of the insurance-investment components of System One: namely that they did not have any machinery to implement the four principles of organization as between themselves — requisite variety, channel capacity, transduction, and dynamism.

The memorandum went on to talk over the issues raised about managerial information in the light of this criticism; and it drew up a Plan of Actions intended to get to grips with a proper use of the viable system model that would then (but only then) be available to answer questions about information. A week-long meeting was planned to discuss the Plan of Actions. It aborted; too much else was happening. A major shift of power in the top echelon was occurring. And it is worth noting that many good efforts to improve matters in any organization are often withdrawn for completely adventitious reasons. It also seemed at this time that much activity was being promoted without a secure foundation. Therefore the memorandum included this statement:

> 'a great appearance of competence and expected victory in a forthcoming battle might be created by marching soldiers around the battlefield in complicated manoeuvres, digging trenches, shouting commands, and blowing bugles. But if the generals have not yet agreed upon the reason for the war, nor identified the enemy, nor formulated their campaign, all of this activity is nugatory.'

The plea was addressed to facing up to the Joint Normative Decision, to building the model properly in all its recursions, and to educing the consequences. It was another assault, again hard for the enterprise to accommodate. This abstract is included here to demonstrate something about consultant-client relationships. It is necessary to speak thus directly; it is necessary to be heard to be speaking thus directly. People do not want to waste their time and money on soft-soap.

On the face of things, nothing much happened. But consultations continued; and so we came to the next instalment.

THIRD CYBERNETIC INTERVENTION

It was now Year Three (July 1975). A company officer and I were enabled to spend two weeks together. We determined to analyse in full detail the insurance component of the organization — since that was his background. We made recordings of many of our conversations, which were subsequently edited. These had a considerable impact on the President. In fact we 'covered the waterfront'. But the detailed model of insurance proved to be a turning-point with an insurance-side man, who was soon to become Executive Vice President of the Company.

The work resulted in a hugely elaborate insurance model. But the *corporate* model was still not in evidence. Therefore the fundamental issues pinpointed in the first year could not be addressed; and (as was seen later with hindsight) the detailed model of insurance activity managed to confuse three different levels of recursion. This experience underlined, in cybernetic terms, the absolute need to determine the total recursive system before engaging in such detailed work. Well: never mind hindsight. The fact was known to me as a cybernetician in advance as a methodological principle. But the cybernetician qua *consultant* knew very well that he could work only on those aspects of the total system that were transparently available. The black boxes always have to wait.

Was this exercise, hardly achieved, therefore a waste of time? Far from it. The global cybernetics were a mess. But the sheer force of the analytic capability of variety engineering made its point. In particular it made its point with that member of the top management team who was, as has been mentioned, soon to emerge as Executive Vice President. And he was not even supposed to be present at the meeting called to discuss this somewhat recondite work. Why did he come? The answer to that question has everything to do with the effective management of any institution. We perforce rely on the human genius to know how, precisely, to apply itself. This is in reality, all cybernetics apart, *the heart of enterprise.*

Even so: by working in such detail on a major component of the business, the seriousness of the approach was established. The cybernetic process was continuing. And so was the inter-personal process of command...

As a result, there was a slight hiatus. Although I was in sporadic contact with the corporation, many threads of enquiry were now floating free. And still no-one would underwrite the basic necessity — to get agreement on the global model of the company, considered as a multiple recursion of the viable system.

FOURTH CYBERNETIC INTERVENTION

Year Four arrived. It was early in 1976.

The hope that a multi-recursion model could be made was still thwarted. There were doubts about its value, and disagreements about the proposed arrangement of the recursions involved. It is difficult for people without training in epistemology to understand the nature of such a model; they tend to think that it has to be either 'right' or 'wrong'. But these words are inappropriate, because the model is not an organization chart, but an *account* of the firm's activity in terms of the criteria of viable systems — and this account is either useful or not. The top management group eventually took this point on trust, but were not yet ready to do so.

Meanwhile, we had set out to make a variety analysis of the insurance activity. We had the structural model (including information flows) that we had together constructed the previous year; we had access to all the relevant data. We proceeded, by many iterations, towards a quantification. The discoveries we made led to a new initiative.

It has frequently been emphasized that the measurement of variety is not an exact science. We are seeking an understanding of the variety amplifiers and attenuators whereby the firm meets the requirements of Ashby's Law. I set out to measure the variety of the system whereby the company's insurance model of itself was conducted. This self-model, reflected in the total information system (and in its computer classification system, and therefore in the cost of its computers) was contained in a set of heavy paper manuals — the 'bibles' of the business. It took a whole day's work to understand the system as thereby exemplified.

The company identified itself as operating in nine lines of business, for which eight different funding arrangements were available; it operated in four distinct areas: life insurance, deferred annuities, equities, and vested annuities. In each of these areas, there was identified a variety of *type of plan,* and within these *sub-types,* together with a demarcation of both paying periods and of benefit periods.

Then the ostensible variety of the insurance operation, as revealed by the 'bibles', and reflected in the information coding structure, looked like this:

	Field	*No. of Possible States*
	Fund	8
	Line of Business	9
Insurance	Plan Type	6
	Sub-type	71
	Pay period	49
	Benefit period	49
Deferred Annuities	Plan Type	2
	Sub-type	56
	Pay period	49
	Benefit period	49
Equities	Plan Type	1
	Sub-type	8
	Pay period	49
	Benefit period	49
Vested Annuities	Plan Type	9
	Sub-type	51
	Pay period	49
	Benefit period	49

This ostensible variety is multiplicative, and works out to something more than thirty million million possible states of the system. Thus in order to identify a particular item — a business transaction with one client — we need to select *one* out of that total variety. I call it the 'ostensible' variety because the informational structure of the codes shows this generating capacity.

> **Technical note:** This measure determines the *selection entropy* of the system. This is given by the equation:
>
> $$H = -\Sigma\, p_i \log_2 p_i$$
>
> where the probabilities within any one selection (for instance each one of the 56 plan sub-types) are disbalanced. In this context, however, these probabilities are not heavily biased, and the equation collapses to:
>
> $$H = -\Sigma \log_2 V$$
>
> where V is the variety of each component in the selection.
>
> Thus all that is necessary is to determine the number of *bits* (that is, $\log_2$) represented by each selection. These are then additive instead of multiplicative, which makes 'ball-park' computation very easy. It is also a direct measure of the number of yes-no decisions required to focus on a final selection, which is helpful in the managerial as well as the computer context.

Well, the system as so far investigated (in its self-model of the 'bibles') has requisite variety to lay roughly eight thousand insurance contracts on every person alive in the world: it postulates some 2^{80} variety. This seems an excessive provision, even given the notorious population explosion. But it is not surprising, nor at all unusual, that reductionist categorization leads to implicit proliferations of variety which large computers are required to handle — ranging largely, of course, over empty space. My driving licence, for instance, registers me under nineteen alphanumeric characters, and in another square under twelve others (this second trivially encoding my date of birth, which I am permitted to chop off the licence where it appears 'in clear': so much for privacy).

Such proliferation of variety is clearly nonsensical, and no management could handle it. The 'real' system, however inefficient, must be far less grandiose. Then why is it not systematically identified, instead of being presented as a lexicon? It is because people do not think in terms of *regulatory* systems but of *classification* systems. This confusion leads to vast and escalating expense in libraries, hospitals, universities... and every other social system, including insurance companies.

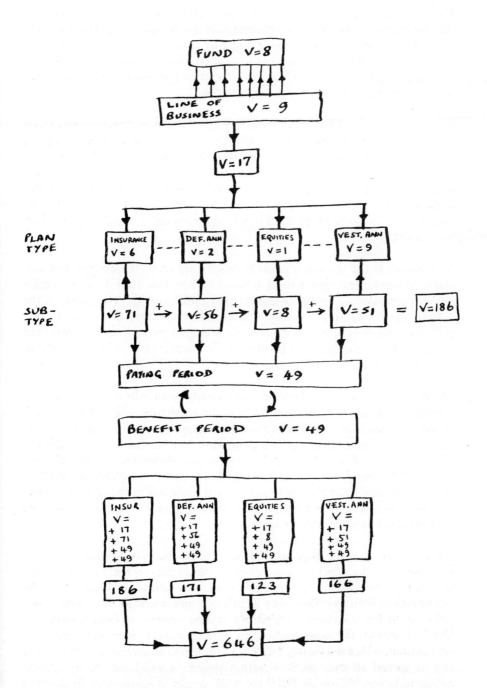

Figure 95.   The system of attenuation which actually procures requisite variety
(the arrows here *specify*)

The new version of the insurance system depicted in Figure 95 replaces the classificatory account with the beginnings of a regulatory one. The arrows in this diagram are meant to show determining routes. It seems that to select a line of business determines the fund to be used: thus the variety of $8 + 9 = 17$ is a purely additive function, and this variety of seventeen feeds the entire system — without combinatorial implications.

Next, it seems clear that the sub-plan determines the plan. This notion is surely counter-intuitive to the reductionist mind, which says: first determine the plan, and then discriminate its sub-type. But the realities are otherwise. The insurance agent is attempting to match his available products to the client's needs. It seemed to me that Ashby's Law demands that he must be doing this at the sub-plan level, whereupon the plan concerned would simply be a name in large type for the name in small type of the sub-plan — since it is *that* which matters to the client.

Assuming that the insurance agent is dealing across-the-board with the sub-plans, he embraces a variety of $71 + 56 + 8 + 51 = 186$. That is less than eight bits: a professional can easily handle that much variety. The 'plan' is the heading for the sub-plan, and the funding is no concern of his. The paying period and the benefit period interact, according to the nature of the plan; but we certainly do not need to invoke multiplicatory varieties between them, because each helps to determine the other.

At the end of the line, therefore, the variety with which the managerial regulatory system needs to cope is 646 at the maximum — less than ten bits. Whereas the classificatory-cum-reductionist approach implies eighty bits. My submission to the company at this point said: 'the variety we are handling is *very much less* than many people have obfuscated themselves to believe', for I had heard the story. It went on to mention the 'vast redundancy of variety in the classification system', and to say: 'this is irrelevant to the control system; but the control system is bemused into thinking that it *is* relevant'. We need redundancy, but not nearly so much.

What the new systemic diagram (Figure 95) really shows is that attention must be directed to the contract: the sub-plan that relates to the individual. But obviously, everyone in insurance knows this already! Then, says the cybernetician with curiosity, why is this not mentioned in the 'bibles', nor reflected in the company's regulatory system (except at local levels), nor matched within the huge computing arrangements? Somehow, that key relationship, which the variety analysis so far shows as *determining* everything else, is spread all over an information system in which all variety sources appear to be combinatorial. But if the 'real' system of attenuation (80 down to 10 bits) is how regulation is actually made possible, then Figure 95 ought to be reformulated according to the best variety engineering that can be accorded to the basic facts. This was attempted in a diagram of which Figure 96 is an improved version, which cut the requisite regulatory variety once again — this time by nearly half (646 to 386).

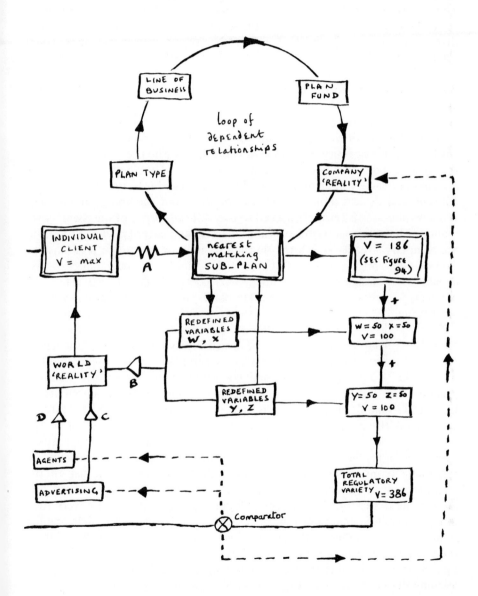

Figure 96.   A redesign for Figure 95, offering a cybernetic model of the regulatory process that minimizes control variety

The argument was that the crucial item in controlling selection entropy is the sub-plan. This is what actually absorbs the variety of the individual client. This variety ($v = 186$) is augmented by the redefined variables (here called w, x, y, z) which were intended to assimilate the variety contained in the interactions of the paying period and the benefit period in the original system of 'forty-nines'. The estimated varieties of $v = 50$ for each of the four non-combinatorial variables were, I reckoned, overestimates; with proper actuarial attention, then, it seemed that a target of eight rather than ten regulatory bits would achieve control. . . .

But before moving to the possible consequences of that, we should further assess the meaning of Figure 96. The systems analysis points to the attenuator marked A as the crux of the insurance business. This is the point at which the very high variety of the individual, which we might measure by the selection entropy of 'one of four billion human beings', and who needs to be treated as if s/he were indeed a unique state of the system called humanity, is handled by a regulatory variety of eight bits ($= 256$). Of course this is done by a range of conventional devices (not *your* precise age, but your age *group,* and so on). But a comparator is certainly needed to contrast the variety of the client's own reality with the variety of the insurance offered, and to feed back the results to the company's reality — which, through its loop of dependent relationships (top of diagram) is capable of changing the sub-plan format: that is to say, capable of redesigning the product. This comparator will also affect the company's behaviour in the market-place, through its agents and its advertising.

An ill-designed attenuator A could be disastrous to the company, if the client felt too ill at ease with his description by the sub-plan. ('I don't agree that I'm overweight, I am big-boned; I shall not accept a loading on the standard premium' — and so much more.) But the company is using amplifiers B, C, and D to mollify these reactions. The terms of the policy itself, insurance advertizing (in which other companies are collaborators in defining the appropriate degree of variety reduction), and the training of agents, are all contributors to the world 'reality' that the client accepts as normal. In cybernetic terms, then, there is a balancing loop between the use of the attenuator and the amplifiers aimed at maintaining requisite variety and answerable to the four Principles of Organization (see text) that govern such loops. This is a System Four job, par excellence. It is at least plausible that the first company to redesign this loop (which includes all three feedbacks from the comparator) would rapidly gain a reputation for meeting clients' needs more sensitively — since the variety matching of attenuator A would now be a learning device.

The aim of designing a regulatory system based on eight bits of information relates to the existing range of products, since these currently *define* what sort of person the client is allowed to be. Now this is not a static definition, at least in the company concerned. New products are constantly being designed and marketed; and the system sees itself as adaptive to its market in terms of social as well as actuarial trends. The fact remains however that when an agent interviews a prospective client, he must encourage him to climb onto one of the Procustean beds manufactured as the company's 'current range'. The question poses itself: whether it would be possible to use the learning loop analysed above to make the company responsive to the individual prospective client in real time, without reducing this variety by categorization in advance. For, however adaptive the existing system tries to be, it is certainly committed to this principle at present.

In probing this question, I set out to model the process whereby the existing system (common to all life insurance companies) arose in the first place, in order to understand how it might be cybernetically redesigned. Here is the argument:

At time t_1

Start an insurance company. The variety of insurable states of insurable people tends to infinity. It is not possible to offer an infinite number of plans.

Then divide 'risk' arbitrarily into x specific risks.

Divide 'people' into y arbitrary categories.

Work out the actuarial consequences of xy plans.

This is a first statement of attenuator A: it has $V = xy$ variety, conceived as a *constraint* on $V \to \infty$, with which we started.
It would be possible to fund this insurance in a very large number of ways. Constrain this number to z ways.

So the business plan has variety $V^* = xyz$.

We have done much attenuating, but we have invented a variety generator *within the business*.

At time t_2

Observe that the xyz mix is losing market opportunities. Enrich the range of risks covered from x to X. Make more dicriminations among people: y goes to Y. Make more ingenious funding arrangements to exploit the investment market, forcing z up to Z.

$$V^*t_2 = XYZ \gg xyz$$

We are now amplifying, by relaxing constraints. The business is becoming more complicated by virtue of its *internal* variety generation.

At time t_3

The authorities (government) observe the variety proliferation

$$V^*t_1 \ll V^*t_3 \quad \textbf{and predict} \ll V^*t_{n+1}$$

They decide to 'constrain' V^*t_{n+1} **in advance**, in order to protect people from possible exploitation.

Thus regulations are introduced at time t_3 which would *attenuate* V^*t_{n+1}, but effectively *amplify* V^*t_3 when they are introduced, because they have to be met at that point.

Then at any time t_n — which is **now** — we are dealing with an existing system that has

(a) grown by accretion in response to commercial opportunities, whereby it has equipped itself with huge variety generators (enshrined in clanking computers and creaking software) which are capable of proliferating ludicrous amounts of variety, and

(b) has had its variety hugely increased by government actions that amplify variety **now** in response to a *feed-forward attenuator*.

I had been well-schooled by the company to acknowledge that it necessarily lived in two different realities which much increased the complexity of its managerial process. One is the business reality in which the company must remain a viable system in the sense of this book; the other is the legal reality in which it acknowledges the law and obeys it. Usually in business, the second is merely a constraint on the first. But in insurance, the two realities are complete and different accounts of the business — so that the enterprise can survive only in the intersect between them. The above analysis, which is reflected in Figure 97, stumbled, (I thought) on the reason why; and this had consequences later, as shall be seen.

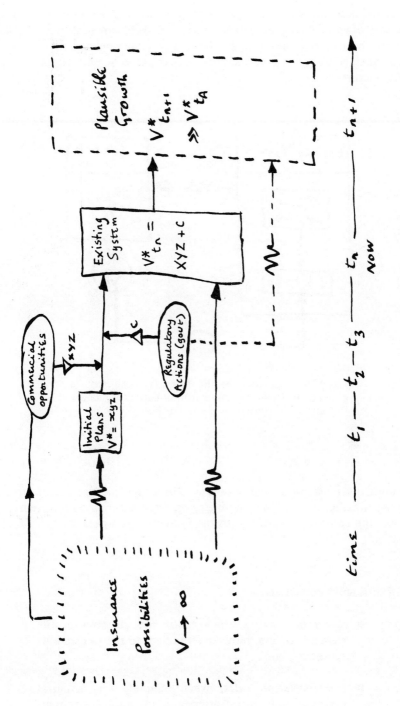

Figure 97. Accretion of variety, much of it illusory, in existing system. Note the effect of amplifier C (see text)

528

Now if the company has the capacity to proliferate variety adequate to the expression of two different activities, which — in their sum — raise a necessary eight bits of information to eighty bits, then somewhere in all of this is embedded an eight-bit variety generator. This ought to be isolated, and Figure 98 is its picture.

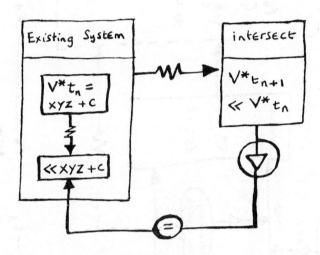

Figure 98. Isolation of the Intersect, competent to generate the *legitimate* component of current regulatory variety in the enterprise

In making this isolation, I tried to take account of the question that led to this analysis: 'whether it would be possible to use the learning loop (of Figure 96) to make the company responsive to the individual prospective client in real time ... '

Thus I distinguished between

- *description rules,* which relate the personal profile elements of the individual's variety to the elements of sub-plans, and

- *transformation rules,* which embody the actuarial expertise that turns attenuator A into a contract-producing machine.

To illustrate these terms, and how the two sets of rules interact, I gave these examples:

To find the area of a rectangle:

Method 1 (compare our 'existing system'):

Construct a matrix showing numbers 1 to 1000 on each axis. Calculate 1,000,000 answers; enter these answers in the elements of the matrix.
Look up answers in this Lexicon as required.
(Note: if only three rectangles (equals individuals of *this* type) are ever encountered, we have somewhat over-invested in this methodology.)

Method 2 (the variety generator):

Store the transformation rule:

multiply x by y,
output.

Accept by description rule a value for x and for y.
Apply transformation rule.

Secondly, consider the case of a circle:

The transformation rule is:

multiply x by x
multiply by π
output

The description rule measures the radius of a particular circle. Note: π is invariant.

These simple expedients introduced the design for an insurance variety generator which would use descriptive rules for the prospective client, transformation rules for the actuarial expertise to be applied to the descriptions, pick out the statutory invariants that apply in the 'second reality', and cement all of this into a box of microprocessing chips. This box could then be handed to the agent, at very low cost (much lower than his use of a terminal in the branch office to speak to the mighty but somnolent dinosaur computer at head office). It points the way to highly sensitive selling (because it handles Ashby's Law by design rather than by historical inadvertance), and to a vast reduction in cost. I do not give any further details here; partly because they were preliminary, and partly because this company is still my client . . .

It has to be acknowledged that the ideas of this fourth intervention appeared and remain recondite to the company's officials. The company's account of the investigation says: 'the investigation may have within it, when the time is ripe, the seeds of an improved method of generating control variety for the company'. With affection I can say to my friends that I have heard this talk before; and maybe I shall have carved on my tombstone: 'his time was finally ripe'. But see Note One (On Success), and await the Tenth Intervention.

In any case, the acquisition of these insights had two important consequences for me. Firstly, the variety analysis suggested a completely new way of designing the attenuation system. Secondly, the variety analysis raised very grave doubts in my own mind about the effective handling of variety reduction *between recursions,* in terms of the Law of Cohesion. But the recursive model through which to examine the issue did not yet exist. Both these results will be referred to again in this case study. At any rate, and at that time, it was clear to us all that the company could not handle my cybernetic initiatives in this regard. And this fact gave special prominence to the long-standing criticism that there was something radically wrong with System Four activity at the corporate level of recursion. It is not that the ideas were rejected (that would have been legitimate) but that there was no machinery for investigating them.

Besides, while all this was going on, further significant changes were taking place in the top management structure of the company: there were many preoccupations. The cybernetician was, for a time, lost in the consultant. But it was clear to me that the next intervention had to result in the multi-recursive model — or no more specifically cybernetic work could be accomplished.

FIFTH CYBERNETIC INTERVENTION

In year Five (1977) that very breakthrough occurred. If the 'GPF' after five years of GPF-ing cannot (as was said earlier) have some advice accepted on trust, it would be a pity. The advice was, of course, to invest at last in the creation of the total model of the company as a viable system. It was finally accepted; despite all the reservations that had been made in the past, and which were not withdrawn. Such a moment ought to be regarded as a real triumph for the manager-scientist relationship. It well demonstrates how that collaboration really works.

This is the moment to remark that the collaboration spanned the physical distance of the Atlantic Ocean. Meetings were frequently held, on both sides of 'the pond', but much work had been conducted through the medium of audio tape. All concerned were practised in its use. Even so, it was overwhelming (in both senses of the word) to find such warm-hearted effort in helping to make the model. Tapes arrived in Britain from all eight members of the senior management group. All were expansive and candid. All were long, ranging from three-quarters of an hour to two hours.

What follows is an account of the modelling and diagnostic processes, which the company officer and I jointly undertook in Wales. Of course, I accepted full responsibility for the cybernetics and the conclusions; but it cannot be over-emphasized that work of this kind requires the full-scale involvement of the client organization, and that this normally has to be channelled (as it has been in this case) through a committed officer of the company who enjoys the total confidence of his colleagues at home.

It is also of interest to record that the following account was first communicated to the senior management by means of the diagrams and several hours of audio-tape. This medium offers something approaching requisite variety between human beings who already know each other, and the nuances of each other's voices, that printed reports often lack. The words used here are an amended version of the written report made at the Eighth intervention; of course, a great deal had been done about the criticisms made in between, and what follows should therefore be taken as an 'historical document'.

The recursive mappings

It was said earlier that a recursion of viable systems is not properly based if it merely forces the organization chart onto the Procrustean bed of the viable system model. We have instead to look at the criteria of viability, and detect within the actual organization a recursive sequence that meets those criteria at each level.

It is usually best to begin with the basic operations of the enterprise, calling these the System One of the lowest level of recursion. Higher levels of organization certainly exist; at first sight it may look as if these *must* be viable systems themselves. But higher levels of organization are in fact abstractions: they are arbitrary groupings of the basic operations, working with aggregated data. For example, the territorial divisions of the company and the functional divisions of the company both look as if they might be viable systems; but neither set responds to the cybernetic criteria. In fact, the first set turns out to be a discrimination of environments; while the second turns out to be the professional embodiment of activities that occur on the connexions between sub-systems of viable systems, and indeed between whole recursions of viable systems (in accordance with the Law of Cohesion).

This is in itself an important conclusion. For the supposition that these two sets both constitute viable systems, whereas in practice they manifestly *interlace* (rather than *nest*), causes confusion. The standard resolution of the confusion is the so-called 'matrix organization' approach. If two aspects of the enterprise are running orthogonally to each other across the managerial space, then why not create a matrix to represent that space... Each element of the matrix then represents the interaction between one territory and one functional specialism. Well, this may be a useful conceptual model of a practical problem; but if it leads to a committee for each matrix element, the practical problem will certainly be exacerbated. The confusion is better resolved by understanding the recursion of viable systems that underlies the organizational conventions.

Now the basic operations of the company consist of insuring and investing: these are the operations that create wealth. Therefore they were chosen as representing the fundamental level of recursion — as distinct viable systems. For (referring here to the First Intervention) each activity could in principle exist independently. Insurance could place the proceeds of its activity with an investment group; investment could obtain its operating funds elsewhere.

Looking first at insurance, we find that the basic operation is the management (in every sense) of a product. This surely constitutes a viable system: *any* product can be designed, made, sold, and so forth, if it is a good product, on its own strengths. But there are a great many products within the company. Then we may look for a next level of recursion, wherein the viable system comprises a *set* of products, jointly managed. Immediately, we find the obvious example: group insurance. It follows that the next level of recursion will constitute insurance as a whole, and as distinct from investment (although, since investment has *not* been hived off, there will be insurance-investment interactions at every level of recursion). Then we have three insurance recursions, embedded in the enterprise itself. It follows that the fundamental product recursion is the fourth recursion.

Turning to investment, the picture is totally different. The effort of modelling the investment activity as a viable system made the obvious distinctions between types of investment; and this produced the discrimination of the elements of System One. But variety analysis of this basic level of recursion, conceived as a viable system, indicated a mode of management that permits variety to be absorbed to the full at this fundamental level. This was a remarkable discovery for me: I had not met a similar situation before. That is to say, the company needs to discriminate four levels of recursion in order to conceive of itself as an insurance company, and to disciminate two levels of recursion to conceive of itself as an investment company. There seem to be three reasons for this asymmetry.

In the first place, the environments of investment (although covering very similar geographic zones to those of insurance marketing) are quite differently divided. There are few countries within which funds will be moved; and the exchanges within these countries are closely integrated between themselves — because of international fiscal policy. In the second place, *and therefore,* the management of investment (which might appear to be divisible over several levels of recursion) is in fact impacted. That is to say, there exists a nest of portfolio managements at the fundamental level of recursion which necessarily reflects the integration of the exchanges in the environment. Thirdly, there is so powerful an interaction between the operations (circles) that the 'squiggly lines' concept of their connectivity has to be altogether replaced by the potent 'looping' concepts to which the Four Principles of Organization directly apply.

Variety analysis underwrites this compression of the viable system called investment. Remarkably, the necessary variety generation can be, and is, handled — because variety is continuously absorbed in all three domains of the vertical plane (namely, environments, operations, central command) that are given in objective reality. How is it suddenly possible to invoke such a notion as 'objective reality' in this context, whereas the basic cybernetic teaching calls all systems subjective? The answer is clear: such a process as investment-under-constraint (where the constraints are both professional caveats and governmental edicts) creates a special universe of discourse. The 'objective reality' is, as a consequence, a function of the conventions which are accepted by the financial confraternity: it is virtually the invention of a shared subjectivity from which no-one entitled to do this business can escape. Whether this is fair comment or not, there can be no doubt of the variety attenuation involved.

The mapping process therefore yielded a recursive system which is cursorily represented in Figure 99. In fact, it would be very possible to model one element of *Recursion Two Investment* at the third level of recursion, namely the management of physical assets. The Real Estate operation is certainly a viable system. However this was not investigated as the managerial problem in its own right that it undoubtedly is, because its role in Recursion Two is so well understood. This is not true of the insurance recursions, as shall be seen shortly.

The diagnoses

A serious and thrustful company such as this is constantly gnawing at issues which are perceived as based somehow in unresolved problems. That is to say, symptoms of difficulty are noticed at various places and levels in the enterprise, and become a syndrome that presents itself to the corporate

534

consciousness. When a thoroughgoing model is employed diagnostically, we would expect these issues to be pinpointed. It is unusual (though not unknown) for totally exotic issues to be raised: indeed, the familiarity of the issues themselves is part of the validation of the mapping of the model. So the diagnoses do not hit the enterprise altogether traumatically. On the other hand, the diagnoses present a *coherent account* of conditions already recognized as pathological. Thus the cybernetic contribution is to relate the issues (which would normally be debated separately, and almost in a vacuum) within the context of the recursive model of viable systems.

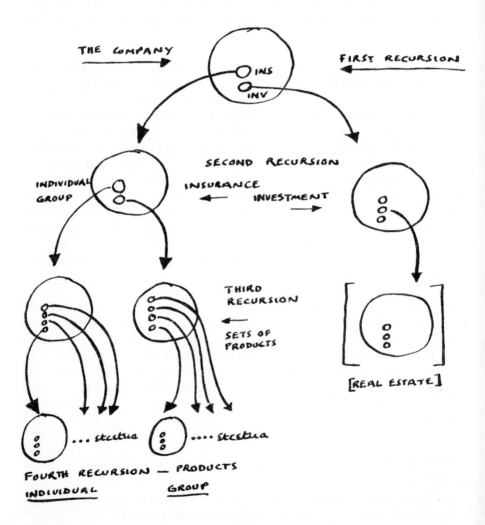

Figure 99.   The General Scheme of Recursions of the Viable System for this company

● In recursion Four, the insurance product:

the company was already debating the issue of product management. The diagnosis says that System One (see Figure 100) is exceptionally strongly connected operationally (see the strong arrows between the operational circles), and is powerfully administered by System Three. Moreover, it has a legitimate System Four, concerned with the enhancement of the product, and of the field operations relating to it. All of this provides the illusion that the product level of recursion is already a thoroughly viable system. But the diagnosis declares that System Five itself is void.

Where then resides accountability for the product? Tracing through the nest of four recursions, the quite surprising answer is that product accountability resides with the President of the corporation himself. This must be a pathological condition — that the President is operating as a surrogate System Five in the *fourth* level of recursion, whereas his post obviously belongs to the *first* level.

Can the model explain this vast anomaly; and in particular can it explain why System Five 'at Recurison Two (Insurance) cannot offer a surrogate System Five for the fourth recursion? Indeed it can. The product has, in its very inception, an investment *doppelganger*. Each premium raised on each policy is earning — must earn — an appropriate return. Its capacity to do so is underwritten by actuarial expertise, which is an anti-oscillatory System Two function at this fourth level of recursion, wherein (see diagram) the investment potential of the product is part of the environmental scene. It cannot be other; because the investment recursion is not product-oriented. The investment recursion is oriented wholly towards financial markets. The crossover-point between insurance and investment is not reached until Recursion One, where actuarial activity is far from being a System Two damping function (as shall be seen) but is the major *regulator* of the company's whole activity. The Chief Actuary is directly responsible to the President, and THAT is why the President operates as a surrogate System Five at the fourth level of recursion.

Obviously it is a matter for management to decide what to do about this situation. There are many possible solutions. The role of the cybernetician is to monitor the discussion of incipient organizational changes to see if they are themselves answerable to the criteria of viability. But the diagnosis itself points to a key issue (and perhaps this was *not* recognized). If there *were* a concept of product management, then its System Five would want to know all about the investment potential of the product. Hence, if the President were to relinquish the role of surrogate System Five in Recursion Four, there would have to be totally new linkages between the investment nest of recursions and the insurance nest. Probably, then, there would be four investment recursions as well; because the same issue arises at each level. If so, the strangeness of the

536

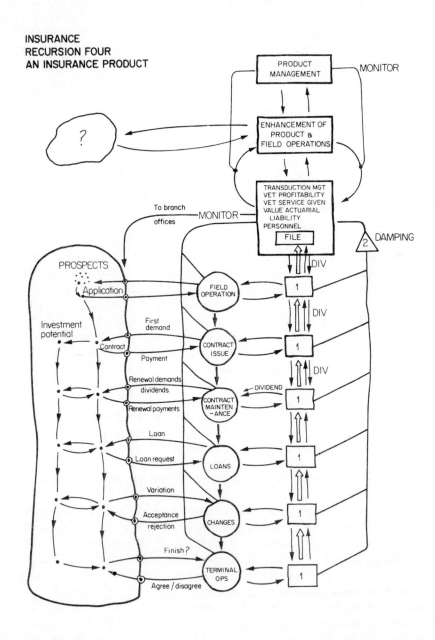

Figure 100.   Insurance, Recursion Four — an Insurance Product

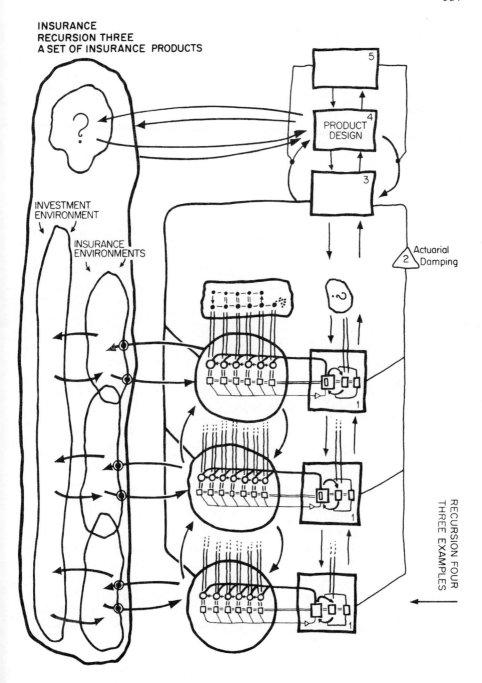

Figure 101. Product Insurance, Recursion Three — a *set* of Insurance Products (Note: three examples of Recursion Four may be seen embedded, by turning the page through 90°)

four-insurance/two-investment recursions would be seen to be not merely an aesthetic disbalance...

There are three more diagnostic remarks to be made at the product level of recursion.

(i) There is a very unusual intervention, coming apparently from System Three, in the *transduction* capabilities of System One with its environment.

It is, according to the cybernetic criteria, the responsibility of System One to attend to the transduction of its operations (circles) with the environment. In this case, branch offices are the primary transducers.

But the product has no unique representation in this transduction. And this is undoubtedly because the product (witness the absence of System Five) is not yet a viable system.

(ii) If the First Axiom of Management is to be met by design, rather than by accident, there has in the past been a weakness in the monitoring function between System Three and the operations (circles) within Recursion Four. It seems that the recent emergence of activity indices will go a long way to meet this inadequacy.

(iii) The existence of a System Four is very special, because it is missing in the three higher levels of recursion.

It seems probable that product enhancement, and the consideration of the future of the field operations relative to it, (which certainly do exist) are being administered from the *second* level of recursion in a surrogate fashion. This is almost inevitable, if Recursion Four (Insurance) is not itself a viable system.

The success of these two activities probably accounts for most of the success of the Company as a whole. Then the question of a two-recursion displacement in the viable systems context requires urgent attention.

● In Recursion Three, the set of insurance products (see Figure 101):

Group Insurance, as has already been remarked, has pride of place. It *is* a set of products, and it has its own management structure. The remarkable diagnosis is that there are no more 'businesses' of this type.

As with the issue of product management, the issue of separate 'businesses' has become a major preoccupation of the corporate consciousness. It is of no consequence whether this development has been conditioned by the continuing cybernetic analysis over the years. But, by the diagnostic stage, the cybernetic analysis has much to say on the point.

How is the variety of the whole range of products attenuated, so that it is possible to regulate the activity of insurance (Recursion Two) as a whole?

At the end of the present account of the fourth cybernetic intervention, 'grave doubts were noted about the effective handling of variety reduction between insurance recursions. The variety analysis at that time indicated very clearly that an attenuation from the *product* level directly to the *whole-of-insurance* level was not strictly within the compass of the managerial mind: the variety was so high that no normal management system could expect to supply requisite variety.

For this reason, the Third Recursion arrived in the nest of mappings: the *set* of insurance products. That the postulate of this recursive level had some validity was evidence by the existence of Group Insurance as a managerial entity. But the diagnosis was that (this entity apart) the Third Recursion **did not exist.** Therefore, it was also likely that the piece of it that was already in place, namely Group Insurance, would probably be misconceived to some degree. And so indeed it is contended: because there is a wholly predictable confusion at the marketing transducers about the status of such a managerial entity as Group Insurance. To the branch offices, this insurance is merely one kind of *product*.

For the rest, the diagnosis declared that many conventions existed within the enterprise for grouping sets of products in terms of description (by territories again, by par and non-par, by endowments, and so forth), but there were no agreed *managerial* units which could be countenanced as viable systems. There are no Fives or Threes, then, at Recursion Three (apart from Group). So how is this level of recursion in practice held together?

Once again, the answer is by System Four. It is the actuarial prowess whereby products — and now sets of products — are conceived, enhanced, made economically stable in terms of investment, and indeed offered as marketable propositions, that accounts for the validity of a system that lacks explicit Five, Three, AND ONE activity. It has a System Two, once again; but this derives from System Four reflections, rather than from the non-existent System Three synergies.

Two further diagnostic points were made:

(i) the insurance-investment linkages are still in question, because they are still (see the argument regarding Recursion Four) relegated to the *environment* of the viable system. They are not components of managerial effectiveness until Recursion One is reached.

(ii) insofar as managerial effectiveness for Recursion Three and Four is pushed upward to Recursion Two (which is the case), instead of being delegated downwards *from* Recursion Two (which is hardly possible, in the absence of the metasystemic components of these quasi-viable systems), control of expenses must be very difficult to accomplish.

In effect, this kind of regulation — which is a System Two function — is working out of Recursion Two, and attempts to span two more recursions as well as its own. Then it would be very surprising indeed if symptoms of instability at the two levels of recursion were not in evidence.

● In Recursion Two, the whole of the *insurance* activity:

we are confronted with a viable system that is largely complete. It answers to the criteria of viability in general. The diagnoses now are more minute; but because of the higher level of recursion, they are by no means unimportant.

Firstly, as far as Figure 102 is concerned, the convention whereby the operational circles are drawn to be roughly proportional to their 'value' is surely helpful. And we notice a System One 'investment only' operation within Group, which is very small — but could in principle become very large. Diagnostically speaking this is of great interest. It refers to cover provided for other insurers; from the viewpoint of this enterprise, then, it is an insurance activity (because it belongs here) that does not happen to be insurable ... Diagnostically, then, perhaps it is a cancerous growth? Consideration should be given to moving this to the investment side of the house.

Secondly, a close enquiry into the articulation of System Two is called for. Four species of regulatory damping are indicated on the diagram. They refer to: housekeeping (e.g. computer manuals); accounting practice (i.e. the conventions whereby the books of the company are made consistent with each other, and are made to conform to legislation); actuarial damping (i.e. the *highly* professional rules whereby this business may be conducted at all); house style (e.g. the letter-heads, the newsletters, and so on, that help to give the company an identity in the minds of all its publics).

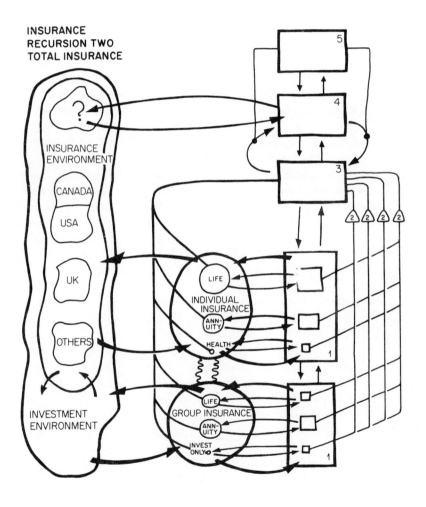

541

Figure 102.   Insurance, Recursior Two — Total Insurance

These diverse activities are not perceived (this is a diagnosis) as mutually interactive, in the role of oscillatory regulation. If they were, and if the performance of System Two were deliberately studied as a component of the viable system at this level of recursion, there would (this is a prediction) be changes in all four modes. Moreover, other modes of System Two activity would be identified that have not so far been identified. What, for example, is the System Two role (*not* the System Four role) of Sales Conferences at Recursion Two?

Thirdly, we are *yet again* faced with the interaction of insurance and investment, which is *yet* again, relegated to an environmental interaction — except insofar as actuarial expertise brings them together. Certainly, this works. But such functional activity on the part of Recursion One is **not** a significant aspect of the *management* of insurance (Recursion Two). Therein lies the diagnostic judgment.

Fourthly, we reach a very strange diagnosis indeed. There is no System Four at this level of recursion. The diagnosis is strange because it was *only* a System Four that was discovered to represent the Five-Four-Three metasystems at Recursion Three and Four. Now, suddenly, we have a manifest System Five and System Three; but there is **no** System Four. The reason is obvious: the Four function for total insurance, Recursion Two, is already dissipated in the third and fourth levels of recursion. The System Four problems of Recursion Two as such are not addressed. That is because they are viewed as the sum of the problems that relate to the lower levels; but this is not true.

Many new things could be done with the concept of insurance. It may well be that a mutual life company has already and firmly decided not to enter the fields of motor-car, ship, aeroplane, or house insurance. If so, that is fair enough. But the System Four activity in this Company, if there were one, would ask itself other questions than these. 'We insure Life, What is Life?' It surely turns out that Life is more than the guarantee of material worth to one's dependents. Life includes the capacity to earn, the opportunity to indulge in leisure pursuits, the security of intellectual capital, and so on. Which insurance companies anywhere are considering these insurance possibilities? The answer in terms of this account is probably none. And that is because none of them commands a System Four at Recursion Two. Only this company, of course, among insurance companies, knows what that last sentence even means. Herein lies the strength of the model as a diagnostic tool: it points especially to voids.

In short, System Four of Recursion Two is not 'all about marketing existing products' — or even extensions of these. Therefore this putative System Four, which people imagine to be in place, is all about Recursions Three and Four in their own eyes; but they are mistaken.

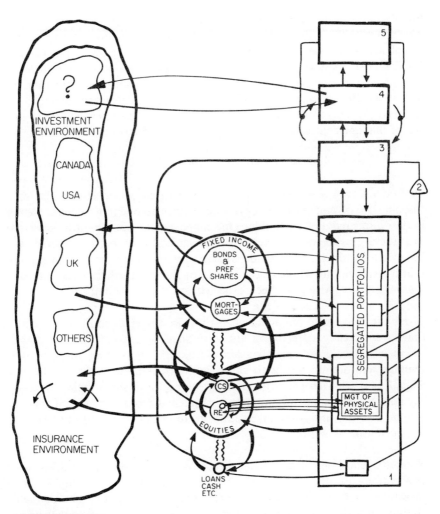

INVESTMENT
RECURSION TWO
TOTAL INVESTMENT

Figure 103. Investment, Recursion Two — Total Investment

Fifthly, it is only in the light of such considerations that anyone can talk about new methods of marketing *at this level of recursion*. It may well be that new methods of marketing have nothing to do with Recursion Three and Four. They may have everything to do with insurances that have not yet been invented.

Sixthly, it has to be noted that when great attention is paid to such issues (if it is), such activity is in itself potentially destabilizing to the existing business. People will surely say, to be brief: 'What the hell is going on?' This, in its turn, is a diagnostic remark. For it ought to be accepted, but is not, that such things are indeed going on. If they are not going on, the enterprise in the long run is not viable. But of course any such going-on-ness is threatening to everyone on the payroll. Therefore there is, here as in any other enterprise, an onus on senior management to explain why it supports a System Four at all.

- In Recursion Two, the whole of the investment activity:

we find a very strange version of the viable system model. Here is the massive 'looping' involvement of the operational circles between themselves. Here also is the 'impacted' set of System One management boxes which reflects that operational involvement. These features have already been explained, as has the extent to which they provide a variety attenuating system of such potency that it soaks up the whole of the variety of the two further levels of recursion that might otherwise have been expected to exist. See Figure 103.

These are diagnostic remarks, when they are taken in conjunction with the diagnoses already offered on the insurance recursion. But the diagnosis uniquely relevant to *this* diagram is that the impacting of System One management activity seems to *subsume* the roles of both System Three and Five. For if all synergistic functions are cared for at the System One level (by the impacting) there is nothing left for System Three to do. And if there is no System Four, then System Five cannot be discriminated, and must be part of the impacting as well.

Well: System Four does appear to be void. We remarked earlier on the conventions (professional and governmental) that are applied to the investment activity. These are so severe that it seems likely that any genuine System Four developments would lead to proposals that were either unethical or illegal, or both!

*** The alarm that this situation generates in the cybernetician, because he is concerned with viability criteria, is matched by concern within the industry: although the industry does not understand cybernetics, nor use its language, it knows very well that it is hidebound by regulatory processes that could easily stifle evolution. This is a classic case, from the societary standpoint, of

545

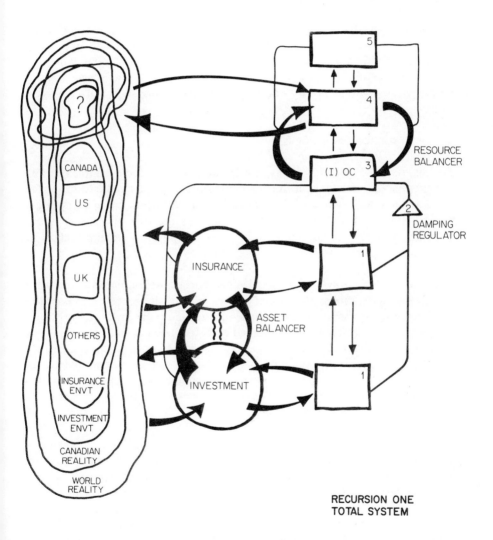

Figure 104.   The Company, Recursion One — Total System

counterproductive regulation. In order to protect the citizen, professional and governmental rules are in force which restrict insurance companies in their marketing, in their investment, and above all in the financial cover that they must provide against the liabilities that policies yet to mature constitute, to the point of unrealism. What is an *enterprise* to do, if it is not allowed to be enterprising?

*** The answer to this question, cybernetically, is that it is System Four's job to tackle the problem. Yet, at Recursion Two, there is no System Four in either insurance (since that kind of activity has been soaked up in recursion Three and Four) or investment (since it is impacted within System One). In the final diagnosis, we shall ask if there is a System Four in Recursion One, the corporation itself. But the answer is already entailed. If there were such an entity, the two Systems Four at Recursion Two could not conceivably be void ...

● Recursion One is the corporation entire:

The diagram at Figure 104 looks, but is not, simple. It looks simple, because System One (as was stated at the beginning of this story) is reduced to the two operational components of insurance and investment. It is complicated because the 'squiggly line' connexion between the two operations is best described as a huge dynamo that in fact 'runs the business'. The model calls it 'the asset balancer'.

In all the years of applying this model, I had not seen so *intimate* a relationship within the operations of System One. There are often *commanding* relationships: as when iron ore is first mined, then reduced to pig iron, then converted to steel, then rolled or forged and so on. Recursion Four insurance exhibits this kind of relationship. Very often, at Recursion One, the interactions between the components of System One are restricted to the competition for capital — as happens in a conglomerate corporation. But in this insurance company: *intimacy* is the only word, and the story of the first cybernetic intervention explains why.

Textbooks say that in this situation management needs a whole collection of committees. Variety analysis says that their sporadic, variety-attenuating activities cannot possibly succour the dynamic interaction required. Now: if the corporation had not solved this problem, somehow, the firm would not exist. They had solved it in human terms. And humans, having roughly equivalent variety (ten-to-the-ten neurons, a need for sleep and so on) can usually cope — if the institution provides for their requisite interaction. The firm, it seemed, had achieved this, but at an astonishingly informal level.

In Year One of this story, there had been an executive committee and an investment committee which between them seemed to be dealing with all managerial matters of major importance. Examining these processes, I came to the conclusion that they constituted a System Three masquerading as a System Five. This was a very early diagnosis. Over the years of the cybernetic interventions, the character of the key committee of internal management was radically changed. If it really was a Three Committee, it should be so constituted: for example, the President should not be a member. His role should be reserved for presiding over some kind of policy group in System Five.

Five years later, at the time of the diagnosis, the key managerial committee had become the *Insurance* Operations Committee, matching the *Investment* Committee, and therefore, in terms of this model, each had the appearance of a System Five at Recursion Two — which ostensibly made a great deal of sense. But by careful study of the activities of the two bodies via the structural model, a different picture emerged.

The Insurance Operations Committee was not fulfilling the function of System Five at Recursion Two Insurance, but the function of System Three in Recursion One. The Investment Committee, on the other hand, was fulfilling the function of System One in Recursion Two Investment — because of the impacted nature of the management — and also some part of the System Five function in Recursion One. That in turn was because the President, who had indeed left membership of the Operations Committee, was still very much in the chair of the Investment Committee.

The diagnosis of Recursion One therefore argued that the prefix 'Insurance' in front of 'Operations Committee' was no longer appropriate, and should be dropped. This was agreed (but the old name withstood the decision!). This was not a fussy terminological issue. Reference has been made to 'the asset balancer', and to the apparent informality of its operation. We would expect, via the model, to find a synergistic management activity in System Three that would reify the concept of dynamic interaction between the two System One operations of Recursion One. This activity had at last emerged in the Operations Committee; and the overt sign that System Three was properly constituted for this recursion level was the fact that the presence of the most senior *investment* officer of the company had at last its impact. This had been brought about in various ways, but it was real. Hence the advocacy for the change of name.

If this could be formally recognized, that would be a big advance in making clear what the metasystem (Three-Four-Five) was, and how it actually worked. Hitherto, the metasystem had simply been seen as that group of human beings who clearly wielded authority within the Company. But now, since System Three was pinpointed, and if System Five (though not yet pin-pointed) *fairly* clearly involved a small but influential group gathered round the President, this also served to point to the void that should be System Four. The diagnosis about this void had always been firm — that is, before the total model was constructed. No person, no committee, had any accountability for the Four function; no task force, no specialist group, existed to work in this area. It follows that the Four function must have been spread across the minds and discussions of the senior management. But this is never an adequate response to the challenge of the future in a rapidly changing society.

In fact, said the diagnosis, there had to be an investment (perhaps in money, but certainly in time, talent, care and attention) in System Four activity at Recursion One; and the sum of Four activity at *lower* levels of recursion in no sense took the place of this activity. A cultural myth existed that, somehow or another, new ideas 'bubble up' through the organization. No doubt they do. But in the nature of things such ideas will relate to the existing paradigm as to the nature of the business, and therefore they will stop bubbling up at the level of recursion to which they relate. And if, alternatively, such an idea were directed to fracturing the paradigm, how could it be received, properly heard, in the void of System Four? It would result only in an echo. Not only was this (diagnostically) predictable: it had already happened to the conclusions of the fourth cybernetic intervention ...

The diagram went on to emphasize the role of what the diagram calls 'the resource balancer'. This is supposed to monitor the investment (as above defined) between Three and Four activity, and is cybernetically speaking a crucial role in the maintenance of viability. But it is difficult to organize the reification of this concept in the absence of a System Four. Finally, the diagnosis discussed weakness in System Two, but declared that these could not be attended to until the logic of viability in the lower levels of recursion had been improved.

SIXTH CYBERNETIC INTERVENTION

This intervention was marked by a diversity of affairs.

In the first place, there had to be long and detailed discussions about the model and its diagnoses. As was said at the outset, it is not right to expect that drastic actions should instantly be taken in response to such inputs; for as was said later, it would be destabilizing to the enterprise if they were. I have often noticed, in the past and other contexts, that when consultancy is used in that way it is often merely an excuse for deliberate destabilization: that is, the management is in deadlock, and seeks to blame necessarily vicious action on an outsider. That is no way to evolve a viable system.

Instead, key implications of the cybernetic process to this date were carefully worked out in several fields. Many developments within the company, particularly its planning processes which were rapidly evolving, were examined through the insight provided by the cybernetic model. Surely this is the main value of such work: to provide a framework for viability, and to inject the language of viability into discussions which otherwise revolve mainly on the conflict of personalities and the apportioning of personal power.

In practice, there was no repudiation of the model, of the diagnoses, nor of consequential advice, by anyone in the senior management team. If there had been, there would have ensued great difficulties. But, as has been argued throughout, this is not a claim by the consultant to total acceptance, and not a commitment by the company to gross reform. It is all part of a cybernetic *process;* and the greek word $\kappa\upsilon\beta\epsilon\varrho\nu\eta\tau\eta\varsigma$ simply means steersman.

It will be no surprise that, out of the whole diagnostic application of the model, two issues were in the limelight. One was the notion of a missing Recursion Three Insurance; and this was being paralleled institutionally by the notion that the company in fact consisted of a number of 'businesses' — a notion to which the cybernetic analysis leant much support. The other was the set of problems in Recursion One: the role of the Operations Committee as constituting System Three, the absence of System Four, the consequent failure to notice an institutional embodiment of 'the resource balancer', and the imprecise constitution of System Five in the corporate perspective.

At this stage, therefore, I wrote a two-page note entitled: *Articulation of the Metasystem*. This was a very direct paper, involving personalities. Its main cybernetic points were to emphasize that System Three now existed (and should be recognized as such, dropping the prefix 'Insurance'); that System Four did not exist, and should be created in some form; that the resource balancer was finding an embodiment, even in the absence of System Four (which meant that Four was being created almost incidentally); and that the System Five policy group stood in need of definition. Obviously, from the cybernetic standpoint, this group consisted necessarily, but not necessarily exclusively, of the President himself, qua Five, of the Chairman of the now-accepted Three, of the missing Four, and of the heads of the two components of System One: investment and insurance. Equally obviously, the group could be formally constituted only as the result of the continuing negotiation between the personalities involved. This negotiation was impeded by the total obscurity surrounding the Four role.

Therefore, in an effort to clarify the realities of the metasystem, I now asked the protagonists to undertake a small experiment. Clearly, each senior official saw himself (correctly) as having a role in *each* of Systems Three, Four, and Five. If each would roughly allocate his time (of 100 per cent) between the three roles, and if each would estimate the time allocated to the three roles by his colleagues, then it would be possible to see how the metasystem saw *itself*. The hope was that this exercise would dramatically reveal inattention to System Four. It did not. It did give the impression that the System Four function at the corporate level was not yet understood.

SEVENTH CYBERNETIC INTERVENTION

It was now the Sixth Year (1978), by which time I confess that I felt myself an integral part of the senior management team. I had no authority at all, but was very conscious of a responsibility. (That is obvious from the story; it is noteworthy that some glib management slogans maintain its impossibility.)

Every conceivable issue was alive and well, and mostly they were being handled in due time and with managerial aplomb. The void at System Four in Recursion One, however, matched by similar voids in both components of Recursion Two, had become a major focus of attention. What should be done?

The first requirement was to exemplify System Four issues at the corporate level — since the allegation had been that they were misconceived to be the kinds of issue extant at lower levels of recursion, but writ large. Three points were made.

(i) Just suppose that it is implicit in the state of society, its legislation, its economy, its technology, and so forth, that the corporation has no long-term future. It is a possibility. (For example, a government could virtually nationalize life insurance.) What sort of future does the company, consisting of all its personnel and all their knowledge and expertise, do then? Does it liquidate itself? Does it negotiate its assimilation by something else (such as a government scheme)? Does it use its powers to undertake new enterprise altogether? And what is the status of its policy-holders in such a scenario? This is extreme thinking, but it is a good place to start for just that reason. Original thinking is difficult to extract from the existing paradigm. Therefore it is a useful device to change the paradigm. One such notional change is (as above) to envisage the potential destruction of the enterprise as it is.

Another, which was devised and has been widely employed by Professor Russell L Ackoff of the Wharton School at Pennsylvania University, is to envisage the enterprise as *idealized*. In short: what would we ideally like the enterprise to be and to do, if it were not shackled by all the constraints under which it currently operates? Ackoff has been known to contend that if this study is done, it often turns out that people say: 'But this is terrific! Let us drop the constraints'.

In either event, System Four is in action. It is loosening-up the enterprise thinking. It is asking the company to breathe.

(ii)   Working down to a more realistic version of point (i), System Four must be in a position to wrestle with the admitted constraints, rather than merely to accept them.

What exactly are the external regulatory systems that, as was mentioned earlier, inhibit the enterprise's activity? It is not the regulat*ors* that ought to be considered. They are sitting impassively, static; they defy abolition. But they are simply monuments to a dynamic regulatory *system,* which continuously behaves, and can therefore be influenced in one direction or another at all times — if the mode of behaviour is understood. It is a System Four job to acquire that understanding, even under a System Five umbrella that contents itself with deploring the regulat*ors* that the regulatory system imposes.

Once the understanding is there, strategies influencing the external regulatory system can be cogently debated . . .

(iii)   A totally different example of a realistic version of point (i) concerns technological development.

Enterprises for which *information* is the stock-in-trade are in a very special case where electronic technology is concerned. They have all been transformed, within twenty-five years, by the computer revolution. But, despite all warnings in advance, they have allowed the main-frame manufacturers to dictate the mode of automative developments. Therefore the company houses a museum of computer dinosaurs. And if a nice new dinosaur is carefully hatched from the carefully nurtured eggs of this so-recent past, it would be a dereliction of archaeological duty not to add the newcomer to the museum . . .

Meanwhile: micro-processing. I had long been urging the opinion that within only a few years there will be a data-handling revolution that will make the original computer revolution of the fifties seem trivial.

There *could* be an entirely new method of selling insurance, whereby the high variety of the individual at risk could be matched by requisite actuarial variety carried in a small box of integrated circuits. It was to this possibility that the variety analysis of the Fourth Intervention referred. The idea may be vacuous: who can say? What can be said is that only System Four can handle it, and that System Four is void.

These three points were advanced as exemplars of Four activity. They were accepted as 'making sense'. And of course the management came to see what they were up against in embodying a System Four. The diagnosis had said:

- to what degree ought a response to such matters be institutionalized?

- it should not be institutionalized beyond the degree to which it can integrate with the dynamic whole of the viable system that is already in place;

- you can always raise capital, but you cannot easily raise managerial resource at the top level of the company.

This was indeed the rub. Everyone was very busy. The idea of bringing in a Director of Development from outside had no verisimilitude. And it was just for these reasons that System Four did not exist.

Then everything pointed to a *continuing negotiation* of the articulation of the metasystem, which had been going on for years and in all aspects of the viable system; but focussed with deliberation and care, for a short while, on the whole 'Four' issue.

****

The diagram at Figure 105 shows how the missing System Fours at Recursions One and Two are dynamically related, and how surrogates for them might be generated by the existing managerial subsystems (Fives and Threes).

Therefore the proposal: the Policy Group itself, however constituted, meets in a System Four capacity. It identifies a set of Four activities, based on the previous discussion and this diagram, and thereby creates a NORMATIVE PLAN for future development. It decides how each activity should be staffed, organized, steered and monitored. It decides how this set of activities should be integrated. This would be tantamount to nominating a Director of Development from within. If no obvious *individual* 'emerges' from this process, maybe the policy group decides to continue in existence for some time — to fulfil that role collegiately.

The diagram points to the three void Systems Four, at Recursion One and Two, and connects them with a heavily marked dynamic circle — for of course they **must** be so strongly connected.

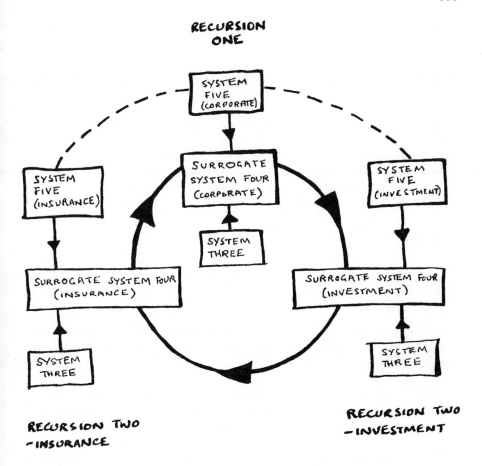

Figure 105.   Proposed System for the creation of a surrogate System Four at
the corporate level of recursion

Here are the terms of reference for the first meeting of the Surrogate System
Four:

In preparation

all nominated members, having reconsidered the cybernetic process in the
company, and having considered especially the processes of the Sixth and
Seventh cybernetic interventions in which they were all implicated, should
prepare a list of issues which ought to be addressed under the heading of
System Four;

each member should ask himself how best the necessary work could be initiated. In particular:

● who are the people to join which activities, and who should be in charge of each?

● is any external consultant required to each activity?

● to whom should each development team report?

● if more than one sponsor is nominated, how should the sponsors themselves be integrated?

● what is the time-scale of the initial reviews?

The Agenda

for this meeting ought to take care of themselves. This Surrogate System Four must be, before anything else, a *self-organizing system* in the cybernetic sense.

That is to say: if there is an 'order of business' indicating priorities, we can be sure that the order is pre-emptive. Nobody will know what the priorities are until AFTER the meeting — if then.

The first person to speak is the person who, because of his preparation (see above) demands to speak first.

The meeting should grow organically out of such demands, which calls for an insightful chairmanship.

While all of this activity was being incubated, the company realized that the time had certainly come to talk openly about its own cybernetic process. Thus it was part of the Seventh Intervention that preparations were made to disseminate information 'down the line'. Work was commissioned whereby the story would be introduced to all employees through the in-house journal; and a preliminary conversation was recorded on video-tape, so that everyone could obtain a feel for the entire exercise. Neither of these efforts was successful, although neither was in any sense damaging. Communications *across* levels of recursion are extremely hard to facilitate, in short; and we need to understand better the transaction process whereby messages are encoded and recoded to these ends. (Most talk about communications assumes a single level of recursion.)

An Intervention in these Interventions

This meta-intervention will prove slightly complicated, but it is necessary to make completely clear what is happening in this story.

*In March 1978 I was making the Seventh Intervention **up to but not including** the proposal with which that intervention ends. The break-point was marked by a row of asterisks.*

Discussion with the President and his chief officers had centred almost entirely on the System Four Issue. Nevertheless I was concerned that they had not yet perceived the 'cybernetic drift'. They might jump to conclusions about Systems Four.

*Therefore, in order to establish that 'cybernetic drift', I wrote this case study, and submitted it **including** the proposal (with its diagram), in early May. Up to this point, what has been written here (following the title BC: BEFORE CYBERNETICS) was that submission, with minor changes, and the addition of the detailed variety analysis — which had been circulating separately. The present introduction was obviously unnecessary; the original introduction was the initial version of Note One. Attention is drawn to the 'three points' of Intervention Seven, and to the remarks about all Systems Four in the diagnoses. Two paragraphs there are now marked like this: ***. Although they reflected much discussion, they were not so marked in the original text.*

EIGHTH CYBERNETIC INTERVENTION (ABORTED)

This occurred in July 1978. The intent had been to discuss this very report — which is to say, its account of the first seven interventions, and in particular the proposal made in the last diagram.

After all, despite any difficulties there might be in the *staffing* of the corporate System Four, it seemed that it was at last becoming clear what the notion meant to the corporation. Moreover, we now had the viable system model in four recursions, and there are two strong points about this:

- Chapter Nine says 'the elaborated model provides exactly the 'screen' on which to focus System Four activity';

- it argues in detail the cybernetic requirement for System Four to contain a model of itself (see Figures 40 and 41).

Finally, there was the very practical matter of generating some *action,* to which the proposal for discussion was addressed. We had been talking about System Four for long enough; and so my notes contained a third point. It was a remark that had been made a long time previously by a member of the senior management team; and it was to be (I thought) the text for a sermon at this point. He had said:

- 'It's time to stop reading the driving manual, and get out in the traffic'.

In the event, I found myself severely up-staged. The phrase 'no System Four, eh?' became tiresome. The firm was in the throes of absorbing a large block of business from another company. Thereby it would add significantly to the stability of its home base, and improve the service it could offer in the market.

The press and television as usual handled this naively. They over-simplified the issues. In the host country, this was to be 'a merger'. In the country of the taken-over company, it had 'formulated an intention to withdraw'. But it was by no means a simple matter of the taking-over company's 'moving in'. What I observed was an example of how a System Four mobilizes itself for action, despite massive legal, fiscal, and even political constraints, and despite the non-existence of an *articulated* System Four itself! Therein lies a problem. If System Four is disseminated, and has no *focus,* there is bound to be trouble later ...

But when we discuss (see Note 1) what counts as 'implementation' in management science, and what is to be called 'success', it is surely enough to perceive that the cybernetics played a certain role in such an event as this. It is a bonus (other managers of other management scientists who may well need this incentive: please note) to be told as much by the company president.

NINTH CYBERNETIC INTERVENTION

This was made in writing, in the following terms:

There were, in cybernetic terms, many loose threads floating about as the result of the foregoing diagnoses.

One of them concerned the whole question of stochastic filtration (see Note Four) of managerial information.

A second concerned the impact of microprocessing on the future of the insurance business (see this report).

A third concerned the consolidation of a system Four that had so effectively sprung into being to handle the merger affair.

All issues of this kind still needed to be advanced.

But — in straight managerial terms — *how were any such matters to be compared with the immediate task of creating the new company?* The management had no choice but to get on with that task, as from Day One. All sorts of urgent decisions had to be taken day by day.

Thus I wrote, in part:

- what will happen about the amalgamation of the two companies cannot be predicted.

However: it is predictable (in terms of the model of the viable system) that either:

- the other company will be assimilated, piece by piece — and dissolve; or

- unresolvable problems will be generated by the other company's will to retain its own identity.

there is no point in *predicting* which will happen.
There *is* point in asking which is *intended.*

Does anyone REALLY KNOW?

For the moment, it is unarguable that two large enterprises are trying to get together.

Therefore, at least in the short run, we are considering

Recursion Zero

This constitutes an amalgam — of whatever sort — of two companies who wish to be, and jointly remain, *a viable system.*

> Recursion Zero has a bipartite System One. It consists of two components, which are exactly the two companies.

Then all conceivable problems fall neatly into place.

As to System One:

Where are the 'squiggly-line' connexions?

As to System Three:

This (and forgive me, only this) is what you are successfully embodying right now.

As to System Five:

JUST EXACTLY WHAT IS THIS INTENDED TO BE?

That is a diagnostic remark.

Surely (since this is an amalgamation of *Mutual* Life Companies), System Five includes the policyholders of both concerns. Hitherto, they have not known each other.

This matters.

As to System Two, Recursion Zero:

Create it fast.

As to System Four, Recursion Zero:

There absolutely **must** be (even yet) a new resurgence of the notion of your System Four (which upstaged me), to become Recursion Zero's System Four. *It is yet another level of recursion to consider.*

Here, at this very moment, is all my concern.

Exactly what constitutes the new company?

Think of ambivalent intentions; think of unpredictable events . . .

In conclusion:

● *please do not forget —*

　　the model of any viable system —

　　especially,

　　not now.

Well, that is it.

TENTH CYBERNETIC INTERVENTION

There was uneasiness expressed in that report. Extreme and dedicated effort was being expended in attending to necessary issues as they arose: that was clear. But viable systems are highly resistant to change; and if they are to be changed then they have to be viewed in the context of viability at a higher level of recursion ...

The merger deal in fact fell through. Obviously, the next intervention began with a post mortem about that. But the president and his senior officers all took a positive attitude to the affair: they wanted to learn from the experience, which was not necessarily over.

We had reached the seventh year of this work, and the tenth intervention: but the problems referred to in the paper *Articulation of the Metasystem* (sixth intervention) had yet to be resolved. The President himself was by now keenly aware that the matter was urgent.

Intense conversations were therefore held, and (as of this writing) appeared successful. There was agreement about the shape of the metasystem, and about the roles of the key people concerned. The problem of 'distancing' was much discussed: that is to say — how could the metasystem be prevented once again from collapsing into System Three? Obviously, came the agreed answer, by the creation of an appropriate System Four. It had always existed (it *has* to exist), but it should be 'pointed to' — made more apparent; *focussed.* Moreover, there would have to be a definite and senior accountability this time.

Suddenly this idea became plausible in the context of the actual people, departments, and information systems involved. Action is now intended. But if the articulation of the metasystem, and its proper internal 'distancing', are to become effective through the pinpointing of System Three (completed) and of System Four (imminent), where stands System Five? It was the discussion of this problem with the President and the Executive Vice President which might turn out to be the most productive outcome of the tenth intervention.

The other major topic of this intervention concerned the missing third recursion. The notion that insurance products should be grouped was beginning to gain acceptance. There was much discussion of the requisite varieties involved in linking the fourth to the second level of recursion. And here was the practical snag: under such groupings, the 'new businesses' thereby created might easily become dangerous competitors of each other in the company's own branch offices. Considerable time was spent in trying to elucidate which sorts of groupings would and would not be safe. It was my in-house cybernetic confrère, the 'company officer' referred to so often in this note, who had provided the key to that ...

That makes a good note on which to end. The heart of the enterprise is embodied in its own people. Consultants cannot catalyse interactions that do not exist, or are persistently and perversely held at bay.

This end is still a beginning.

'Call this a case study?'

(I hear an HBS graduate say)

'there is no proven outcome.'

Yes: I call it a case study — and just because of that.

Life is a process, not a justification.

APPENDICES

562

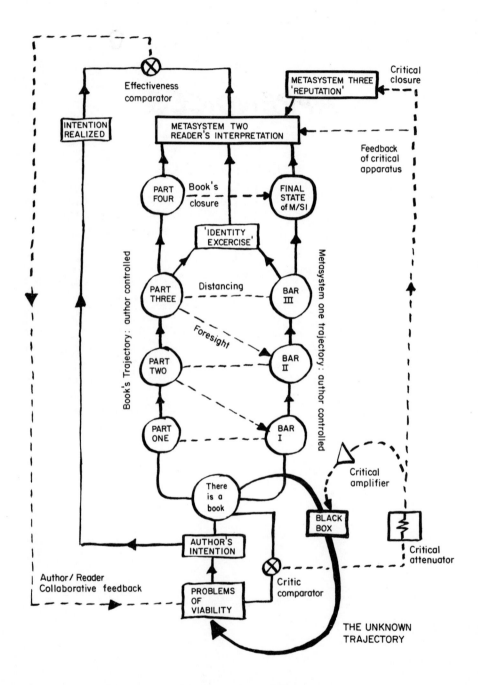

Figure 106. The cybernetics of *The Heart of Enterprise*

Summary of appendices

Appendix One consists of a glossary of the rules of the viable system that have been educed in this book.

Appendix Two makes an unusual approach to the vexed problem of bibliographical support for the student of the viable system.

Appendix Three offers a very condensed summary of some major points: every viable system belongs to a multiple *set of recursions; there are always cross-overs between these recursions, of which the subjective perception by the viable system of itself may not be aware (and may never understand) and which other observers may glimpse but not be able to understand either; the critical apparatus applied to any piece of work introduces attenuation of the work's variety, and also amplifies the critical selectivity into the unknown trajectory that affects the consequences; the notion of closure is central to the mathematics of viability — thus the last page of the book closes the book into itself.*

Here is a final diagram, Figure 106, to aid the understanding of the book. It is especially for the convenience of those who do not recognize the cybernetic machinery of the scenes in the bar and or Appendix Three. They are invited to list the ten cybernetic points continually exemplified in the bar, as the author has summarized above the purposes of Appendix Three (both with reference to Figure 106). Here is a tip: don't criticize, recognize.

APPENDIX ONE

GLOSSARY OF RULES FOR THE VIABLE SYSTEM

APHORISMS:

The First Regulatory Aphorism

>It is not necessary to enter the black box
>to understand the nature
>of the function it performs.

(page 40)

The Second Regulatory Aphorism

>It is not necessary to enter the black box
>to calculate the variety
>that it potentially may generate.

(page 47)

PRINCIPLÆS:

The First Principle of Organization

>Managerial, operational and environmental varieties, diffusing
>through an institutional system, tend to equate;
>they should be **designed** to do so with minimum damage to
>people and to cost.

(page 97)

The Second Principle of Organization

>The four directional channels carrying information between
>the management unit, the operation, and the environment
>must each have a higher capacity to transmit a given
>amount of information relevant to variety selection in a
>given time than the originating subsystem has to generate it
>in that time.

(page 99)

The Third Principle of Organization

> Wherever the information carried on a channel capable of distinguishing a given variety crosses a boundary, it undergoes transduction; the variety of the transducer must be at least equivalent to the variety of the channel.

(page 101)

The Fourth Principle of Organization

> The operation of the first three principles must be cyclically maintained through time without hiatus or lags.

(page 258)

THEOREM:

Recursive System Theorem

> In a recursive organizational structure, any viable system contains, and is contained in,
> a viable system.

(page 118)

AXIOMS:

The First Axiom of Management

> The sum of horizontal variety disposed by
> *n* operational elements
>   equals
> the sum of vertical variety disposed on the six
> vertical components of corporate cohesion.

(page 217)

The Second Axiom of Management

> The variety disposed by System Three resulting from
> the operation of the First Axiom
>   equals
> the variety disposed by System Four.

(page 298)

The Third Axiom of Management

> The variety disposed by System Five
> equals
> the residual variety generated by the
> operation of the Second Axiom.

(page 298)

LAW:

The Law of Cohesion for Multiple Recursions of the Viable System

> The System One variety accessible to
> System Three of Recursion x
> equals
> the variety disposed by the sum of the metasystems of
> Recursion y for every recursive pair.

(page 355)

APPENDIX TWO

SELECT BIBLIOGRAPHY FOR THE VIABLE SYSTEM

It is not at all surprising that people demand a supportive reading list for a book of this kind. It is not surprising either that it cannot be provided: at least, not in a form for which a consensus of cyberneticians could be found. The fact is that 'the viable system' is not an acknowledged entity; references are a librarian's nightmare. And since earlier of my books than this one have been reported as having been listed under both Anthropology and Zoology, and all steps of the alphabet in between, including History, it is altogether clear that there is a mammoth problem in dealing with this matter at all.

Let the reader share in this problem, and I shall explain the difficulty. During my life I have read many books. I have kept those that mattered to me, and given the remainder to others. This residue amounts to roughly two thousand volumes. All of them, naturally enough, seem to be relevant to this book. But I do not have the time to list them, and you do not have the time to read them. 'Well then', you might very well say, 'pick out the best and the most relevant'.

The task is beyond my capability. If I take down one volume — a 'must' — from the shelves, I at once observe that the book on either side of it is also a 'must'. The dilemma has confronted me for thirty years. Therefore I tried to make a cybernetic analysis of all that variety, and the argument went like this.

We list books according to the alphabetic name of each author. This has nothing to do with the content. Therefore we split up the list under subject headings, and then revert once again to the alphabetic listing. But the 'subjects' belong to the historic categorization of science: the viable system does not belong to that list. It seems, therefore, that we are trying to express a multi-dimensional issue in the linear mode.

Therefore the notion arose that maybe two dimensions would at least be better than one. In Figure 107 appears a map; it is a *model* of a reading list. Of course, it has still been necessary to make the selections. It has to be said that they are quite arbitrary. But at least this map breaks down the linear convention.

It is obvious that the unusual layout is meant to convey something. Please try to interpret that meaning, in which both segmentation and concentricity are used in a rather casual way. That means: I have put points onto a two-space; but do not use a theodolite to comprehend them, because the topology will certainly prove to be inconsistent. The map is more of an artistic than a scientific statement.

The viable system is in the centre of this map. Move the dots around as you will, or ignore them. Add other dots. This Select Bibliography is intended to have the makings of a learning machine.

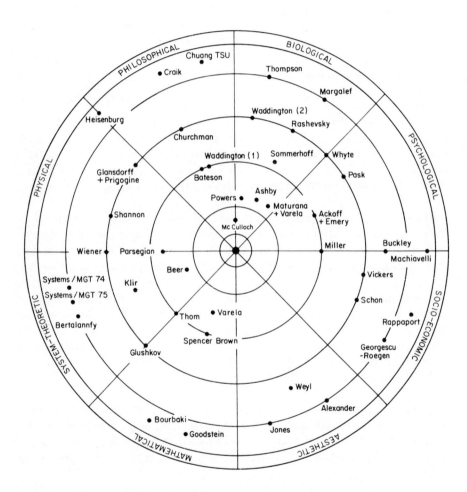

Figure 107. Model of a Reading List. Names on this map refer only to the particular books listed in the Select Bibliography

Select bibliography — Refer to diagram 'Model of a Reading List'

Alexander, Christopher, *Notes on the Synthesis of Form,* Harvard UP, 1966.

Ackoff, R.L., and Emery, F.E., *On Purposeful Systems,* Aldin-Atherton. N.Y. 1972.

Ashby, W. Ross, *An Introduction to Cybernetics,* Chapman and Hall, 1956.

Bateson, Gregory, *Steps to an Ecology of Mind,* Ballantine Books, N.Y. 1972.

Beer, Stafford, *Brain of the Firm,* Allen Lane, 1972.

Bertalannfy, Ludwig von, *General Systems Theory,* George Braziller, N.Y., 1968.

Bourbaki, N., *Eléments de Mathématique, Theorie des Ensembles,* Fascicule de Résultats, Herman, Paris, 1958.

Buckley, Walter, *Modern Systems Research for the Behavioural Scientist,* Aldine, Chicago, 1968.

Chuang Tsu, *Inner Chapters,* Wildwood House, London 1974.

Churchman, C. West, *The Systems Approach,* Delacote Press, N.Y. 1968.

Craik, K.J.W., *The Nature of Explanation,* CUP, 1952.

Georgescu-Roegen, Nicholas, *The Entropy Law and the Economic Process,* Harvard UP, 1971.

Glansdorff, P and Prigogine, I, *Thermodynamics, Theory of Structure, Stability and Fluctuations,* Wiley Inter 1978.

Glushkov, Viktor M., *Introduction to Cybernetics,* Academic Press, 1966.

Goodstein, R.L., *Recursive Number Theory,* North-Holland, Amsterdam, 1957.

Heisenburg, Werner, *Physics and Philosophy,* George Allen & Unwin, 1959.

Jones, J. Christopher, *Design Methods,* Wiley, 1970.

Klir, George J., *An Approach to General Systems Theory,* Van Nostrand, 1969.

McCulloch, W.S., *Embodiments of Mind,* MIT Press, 1965.

Machiavelli, *The Prince,* Penguin edition, 1970

Margalef, Ramon, *Perspectives in Ecological Theory,* University of Chicago, 1968.

Maturana, Humberto, and Varela, Francisco, *Autopoietic Systems,* Harvard monograph Pending publication.

Miller, J.G., *Living Systems,* McGraw-Hill, 1978.

Parsegian, V.L., *This Cybernetic World,* Doubleday, 1972.

Pask, Gordon, *The Cybernetics of Human Learning and Performance,* Hutchinson Education, 1975.

Powers, William T., *Behaviour: The Control of Perception,* Aldine, Chicago, 1973.

Rappaport, Roy A., *Pigs for the Ancestors,* Yale U.P., 1967.

Rashevsky, Nicolas, *Mathematical Principles in Biology,* Charles C Thomas, Illinois, 1961

Schon, Donald A., *Beyond the Stable State,* Random House, N.Y. 1971.

Shannon, Claude E., and Weaver, Warren, *The Mathematical Theory of Communication,* University of Illinois Press, 1962.

Sommerhoff, G., *Analytical Biology,* OUP, 1950.

Spencer-Brown, G., *Laws of Form,* Allen & Unwin, 1969.

Systems and Management Annual 1974, Russell L Ackoff (Ed), Petrocelli Books, N.Y., 1974.

Systems and Management Annual 1975, C. West Churchman (Ed).

Thom, Réné, *Stabilité Structurelle et Morphogénèse,* W A Benjamin, 1972.

Thompson, D'Arcy, *On Growth and Form,* C.U.P., 1942.

Varela, Francise J., *A Calculus for Self-Reference,* Int. J. General Systems, 1975, Vol.2, pp.5-24, Gordon and Breach

Vickers, Geoffrey, *Freedom in a Rocking Boat,* Allen Lane, The Penguin Press, 1970.

Waddington, C.H., *Tools for Thought,* Paladin, 1977. (Ref.1 on map)

Waddington, C.H., *The Strategy of the Genes,* Allen & Unwin, 1957 (Ref.2 on map)

Weyl, Hermann, *Symmetry,* Princeton U.P., 1952.

Whyte, Lancelot Law, *Internal Factors in Evolution,* Tavistock Publications, 1965.

Wiener, Norbert, *Cybernetics,* 2nd Edition, M.I.T. and John Wiley, 1961.

APPENDIX THREE

A REVIEW OF THIS BOOK

from: *The Putative International Journal of Pure and Applied Recursivity*
BEER, STAFFORD, *The Heart of the Enterprise,* John Wiley, 1979.

Readers of his earlier books will know that Stafford Beer has employed a variety of expository, not to say arresting — some have called them annoying; and elucidatory, not to say possibly pedagogic (which is not necessarily a pejorative word) — some would say confusing; but perhaps not: we can be sure that opinions differ, and this book is no exception to the rule (although, if it were, it is well known, indeed it can be shown, that the exception proves the rule), and the reader must make his own judgment about it.

Outstandingly, then, readers of this Journal will wish to note that when, for example, a group of people is assembled in a bar, and provided that all of them are not intoxicated at the time, which is often the case (although that should not be taken to be an imputation against the brewing industry, or against publicans, or even against their customers), some of them will be **women,** or ought to be, on a statistical basis, unless the sample is unrepresentative of the population as a whole, which it usually is — for good enough reasons, especially in this managerial case, and frankly it ought to be stopped and there should be a law. However, it comes to your reviewer's attention that there *is* a law; and this is of course a severe criticism of the author's excluding women from bars — unexcused by what he says concerning the past, which *was actually over* before the book was published, and concerning the future, which *had not actually happened* when he was writing about what he might very likely (note the positivist fallacy) call 'now', despite all the epistemological difficulties implicit in whatever is important.

In the light of this, attention must be drawn to everything that goes on in bars (according to this example), because this has enormous relevance to understanding whatever is metasystemic to whatever does *not* go on in bars, if anything of serious import does not go in bars, which is open to considerable doubt, as our applied recursionists (as opposed to — or rather as distinct from — our pure recursionists) know very well, or if they do not ought meta-metasystemically to recognize, sooner or later, when the relevance of my example has come to its fruition — or not, as may prove to be the case.

The whole question is **'when?'** — and the author does not address this question; nor does he list any bars; nor is the vital importance of recursivity (which is after all the topic of this Journal) brough home completely until the very last page of the final Appendix — which is much too late to satisfy discerning readers, of whom I am the outstanding example; and that is just not good enough for a book that purports to be, after all, a book devoted to those very matters to which it is devoted — and the author does not at any point deny it.

These major criticisms, however, do not imply that the book should not be read — indeed, absolutely to the contrary — especially as the author is an authority on issues on which [(although it is not at all clear to someone who has not yet read the book, which is another of its shortcomings), there exists this whole book concerning them (which I know about, although I have not had the time in this all-too-busy age to read much of it)] he is an authority — which must be perfectly obvious to the discerning readers of this Journal, since I am after all undertaking this review in the first place (an event not without its own importance), and even though Stafford Beer's sentences, like his inadequate list of references (does he not have access to a computer?), if they were to be credible in academic circles, are much too short.

C.W.R.W.
Dyfed, Wales.

Index

580

582